Suzanne Haneef

A HISTORY OF THE PROPHETS OF ISLAM

Derived from the Quran,
Ahadith and Commentaries

Volume Two

Library of Islam

Library of Congress Cataloging in Publication Data

Bibliographical references.
1. Prophets, Pre-Islamic. I. Author. II. Title.
BP137.T331997 297'.1228 77-25941
ISBN: 1-930637-19-5

Published by
Library of Islam

Distributed by
KAZI Publications, Inc.
3023 W. Belmont Avenue
Chicago, IL 60618
(T) 773-267-7001; (F) 773-267-7002
email: info@kazi.org online catalog: www.kazi.org

Dedication

To the one at whose hands I learned Islam,
with deepest respect, gratitude and love.

VOLUME TWO

MOSES THROUGH JESUS

A HISTORY OF THE PROPHETS OF ISLAM

Derived from the Qur'an,
Ahadith and Commentaries

ACKNOWLEDGEMENTS

With deep gratitude, I acknowledge the following authors' and publishers' permissions to cite material from the works listed below:

Abul-Qasim Publishing House, Jeddah, Saudi Arabia, publisher of *The Qur'an, Arabic Text with Corresponding English Meanings*, English revised and edited by Saheeh International (1997).

Shaykh Muhammad al-Akili, translator and editor of *The Beauty of the Righteous and Ranks of the Elite* (1996).

Dar al-Taqwa, Ltd., publisher of Ibn Kathir's *Signs Before the Day of Judgement*, Second Edition, translated by Huda Khattab (1992).

Fons Vitae, publisher of *Mary the Blessed Virgin of Islam*, by Aliah Schleifer (1997).

Hakim Investment Holdings (M. E.) Limited, U.K., publisher of *The Commentary on the Qur'an*, by Abu Ja'far Muhammad b. Jarir al-Tabari, translated by J. Cooper, published by Oxford University Press (1987).

Yahya Hendi, author of *The Descent of Jesus son of Mary at the End of Time (A Translation of al-Suyuti's Nuzul 'Isa ibn Maryam Akhir al-Zaman) with Explanatory Notes* (1993).

Material quoted from *The History of al-Tabari, Volume I: General Introduction and From the Creation to the Flood*, translated by Franz Rosenthal, is reprinted by permission of the State University of New York Press © 1989, State University of New York. All rights reserved.

Material quoted from *The History of al-Tabari, Volume II, Prophets and Patriarchs*, translated and annotated by William M. Brinner, is reprinted by permission of the State University of New York Press © 1986, State University of New York. All rights reserved.

Material quoted from *The History of al-Tabari, Volume III, The Children of Israel*, translated by William M. Brinner, is reprinted by permission of the State University of New York Press © 1991, State University of New York. All rights reserved.

Material quoted from *The History of al-Tabari, Volume IV, The Ancient Kingdoms*, translated by Moshe Perlmann, is reprinted by permission of the State University of New York Press © 1987, State University of New York. All rights reserved.

Material quoted from *The Qur'an and Its Interpreters, Volume One*, by Mahmoud M. Ayoub, is reprinted by permission of the State

Maps were created by Yusuf Siddiqui using data from the USGS and ESRI, Inc.

My warmest thanks go to my friend, Salma al-Houry, translator of *Selection of Prophetic Hadiths & Muhammadan Wisdoms*, by as-Sayed Ahmad al-Hashimi, published by Dar al-Kutub al-Ilmiyah, Beirut (1993), for her invaluable help in translating *ahadith*.

Table of Contents

LIST OF MAPS

Sources

THE QUR'AN AND COMMENTARIES

Abdullah Yusuf Ali. *The Holy Qur'an: Text, Translation and Commentary*

A. J. Arberry. *The Koran Interpreted*

Muhammad Asad. *The Message of the Qur'an*

Mahmoud Ayoub. *The Qur'an and Its Interpreters, Volumes One and Two*

Abdalhaqq and Aisha Bewley. *The Noble Qur'an, A New Rendering of its Meaning in English*

Muhammad Taqi-ud-Din al-Hilali and Muhammad Muhsin Khan. *Interpretation of the Meaning of the Noble Qur'an in the English Language*

Ibn Kathir. *Al-Tafsir Ibn Kathir (The Commentary of Ibn Kathir)* (Urdu)

Ibn Kathir. *Tafseer Ibn Katheer: Juz' 'Amma (Part 30 of the Qur'an)*, translated by Sameh Strauch

S. Abul A'la Maududi. *The Meaning of the Qur'an*

Marmaduke Pickthall. *The Meaning of the Glorious Qu'ran*

Saheeh International. *The Qur'an, Arabic Text with Corresponding English Meanings*

Abu Ja'far Muhammad b. Jarir al-Tabari. *Commentary on the Qur'an, Volume One*, translated by J. Cooper

HADITH

Sahih al-Bukhari, translated by Dr. Muhammad Muhsin Khan, 1974

Sahih Muslim, translated by Abdul Hamid Siddiqi, undated

Sunan Abu Dawud, translated by Ahmad Hasan, 1990

Mishkat al-Masabih, translated by James Robson, 1963

Al-Muwatta, translated by 'A'isha 'Abdarrahman at-Tarjumana and Ya'qub Johnson, 1982

COMMENTARIES ON STORIES OF THE PROPHETS

Ibn Kathir. *Qasas al-Anbiya' (Stories of the Prophets)* (Arabic)

Al-Tabari. *Qasas al-Anbiya' (Stories of the Prophets)* (Arabic)

Al-Tabari. *The History of al-Tabari, Volume I: General Introduction and From the Creation to the Flood*, translated and annotated by Franz Rosenthal

Al-Tabari. *The History of al-Tabari, Volume II: Prophets and Patriarchs*, translated and annotated by William M. Brinner

Al-Tabari. *The History of al-Tabari, Volume III: The Children of Israel*, translated and annotated by William M. Brinner

Al-Tabari. *The Ancient Kingdoms, Volume IV: The Ancient Kingdoms*, translated and annotated by Moshe Perlmann

REFERENCE WORKS

Shaykh Muhammad al-Akili. *The Beauty of the Righteous and Ranks of the Elite*

The Holy Bible, New International Version

Cyril Glasse. *The Concise Encyclopedia of Islam*

Ibn Ishaq. *The Life of Muhammad*, translated by A. Guillame

Qadi 'Iyad. *Muhammad, Messenger of Allah (Ash-Shifa of Qadi 'Iyad)*, translated by Aisha Abdurrahman Bewley

Edward William Lane. *An Arabic-English Lexicon*

Martin Lings. *Muhammad: His Life Based on the Earliest Sources*

Ahmad ibn Naqib al-Misri. *The Reliance of the Traveller*, translated by Noah Ha Mim Keller

Abdullah Abbas Nadwi. *Vocabulary of the Holy Qur'an*

John Penrice. *A Dictionary and Glossary of the Qur'an*

Hans Wehr. *Arabic-English Dictionary: The Hans Wehr Dictionary of Modern Written Arabic*, edited by J. M. Cowan, Third Edition

SPECIAL SOURCES FOR THIS VOLUME

Muhammad 'Ata ur-Rahim. *Jesus, A Prophet of Islam*

Eli Barnavi. *A Historical Atlas of the Jewish People from the Time of the Patriarchs to the Present*

Edwin Bernbaum. *Sacred Mountains of the World*

James Henry Breasted, Ph.D. *A History of Egypt from the Earliest Times to the Persian Conquest*

Joy Collier. *The Heretic Pharaoh*

David Daiches, *Moses, the Man and His Vision.*

Emel Esin, *Mecca the Blessed, Madinah the Radiant*

Al-Ghazali. *Al-Ghazali, On Disciplining the Soul*, translated by T. J. Winter

Al-Ghazzali. *The Book of Knowledge, being a translation with notes of the Kitab al-'Ilm of al-Ghazzali's Ihya' 'Ulum al-Din*, translated by Nabih Amin Faris

Al-Ghazali. *The Jewels of the Qur'an*, translated by Muhammad Abul Quasem

Al-Ghazali. *The Mysteries of Almsgiving*, translated by Nabih Amin Faris

Al-Ghazali. *The Remembrance of Death and the Afterlife (Kitab dhikr al-mawt wa-ma ba'dahu). Book XL of The Revival of the Religious Sciences (Ihya 'ulum al-din)*, translated with an introduction and notes by T. J. Winter

Louis Golding. *In the Steps of Moses*

Michael Grant. *The History of Ancient Israel*

James E. Harris and Kent R. Weeks. *X-raying the Pharaohs*

Yahya Hendi. *The Descent of Jesus son of Mary at the End of Time (A translation of al-Suyuti's Nuzul 'Isa ibn Maryam Akhir al-Zaman) with Explanatory Notes*

Jenny Jobbins. *The Red Sea Coasts of Egypt, Sinai and the Mainland, a Practical Guide*

Ibn al-'Arabi. *The Bezels of Wisdom*, translated by R. W. J. Austin

Ibn Kathir. *The Signs Before the Day of Judgement*, translated by Huda Khattab

Ibn Qayyim al-Jawziyah, *Zad al-Ma'ad*

Robert W. Mond. *The New Testament in Question*

Pierre Montet. *Lives of the Pharaohs*

P. H. Newby. *Warrior Pharaohs, The Rise and Fall of the Egyptian Empire*

Donald Redford. *Egypt,Canaan, and Israel in Ancient Times*

Aliah Schleifer. *Mary the Blessed Virgin of Islam*

Ayman Taher. *Sinai, Guide of the Peninsula and the Red Sea*

KEY TO ABBREVIATIONS OF SOURCES FOR THIS VOLUME

THE QUR'AN AND COMMENTARIES

The Holy Qur'an: *Q*

Abdullah Yusuf Ali translation: Ali/*Q*, footnote

Muhammad Asad translation: Asad/*Q*, chapter:footnote

Mahmoud Ayoub, *The Qur'an and Its Interpreters*: Ayoub/*Q*, volume:page

S. Abul A'la Maududi translation: Maududi/*Q*, chapter:footnote

Ibn Kathir, *Tafsir (Commentary)*: Ibn Kathir/*T*, chapter:verse

Ibn Kathir, *Tafseer Ibn Katheer, Juz' 'Amma:* Ibn Kathir/*Juz' 'Amma*

Al-Tabari, *Commentary*: Tabari/*C*, I:page

HADITH

Sahih al-Bukhari: *Bukhari*, volume:*hadith* number

Sahih Muslim: *Muslim*, *hadith* number

Sunan Abu Dawud: Abu Dawud, *hadith* number

Mishkat al-Masabih: Mishkat, hadith number

Al-Muwatta: Muwatta, hadith number

COMMENTARIES ON STORIES OF THE PROPHETS

Ibn Kathir, *Qasas al-Anbiya'*: Ibn Kathir/*Q*, prophet's name

Al-Tabari, *Qasas al-Anbiya'*: Tabari/*Q*, prophet's name

Al-Tabari, *History of al-Tabari*: Tabari/*H*, volume:page number

ALL OTHER WORKS

Al-Akili, *Beauty of the Righteous and Ranks of the Elite*: Akili/*Beauty*

Ata ur-Rahim, *Jesus, A Prophet of Islam*: 'Ata ur-Rahim/*Jesus*

Barnavi, *A Historical Atlas of the Jewish People from the Time of the Patriarchs to the Present*: Barnavi/*Atlas*

Bernbaum, *Sacred Mountains of the World*: Bernbaum/*Mountains*

Breasted, *A History of Egypt from the Earliest Times to the Persian Conquest*: Breasted/*History*

Collier, *The Heretic Pharaoh*: Collier/*Pharaoh*

Daiches, *Moses, the Man and His Vision*: Daiches/*Moses*

Glasse, *Concise Encyclopedia of Islam*: Glasse/*Encyclopedia*

Golding, *In the Steps of Moses*: Golding/*Moses*

Grant, *The History of Ancient Israel*: Grant/*Israel*

Harris and Weeks, *X-raying the Pharaohs*: Harris and Weeks/*Pharaohs*

Hendi, *The Descent of Jesus son of Mary at the End of Time*: Hendi/*Jesus*

Ibn Ishaq, *The Life of Muhammad*: Ibn Ishaq/*Muhammad*

Ibn Kathir, *The Signs Before the Day of Judgement*: Ibn Kathir/*Signs*

Keller, *Reliance of the Traveller*: Keller/*Reliance*

Lings, *Muhammad, his life based on the earliest sources:* Lings/*Muhammad*

Montet, *Lives of the Pharaohs*: Montet/*Pharaohs*

Newby, *Warrior Pharaohs, The Rise and Fall of the Egyptian Empire:* Newby/*Pharaohs*

Qadi 'Iyad, *Muhammad, Messenger of Allah (ash-Shifa of Qadi 'Iyad):* Qadi 'Iyad/*Ash-Shifa*

Schleifer, *Mary, the Blessed Virgin of Islam*: Schliefer/*Mary*

Taher, *Sinai, Guide of the Peninsula and the Red Sea:* Taher/*Sinai*

THE STORY OF MOSES (MUSA) AND AARON (HARUN)

peace be upon them

These are the verses of the clear Book. We relate to you [Muhammad] something of the tidings of Moses and Pharaoh in truth for a people who believe. (28:2-3)

Then after them [Noah and the prophets who followed him], We sent Moses to Pharaoh and his chiefs, but they behaved wrongfully with them. Then see what was the end of the corrupters! (7:103)

In the name of God, the Merciful, the Compassionate

PART ONE: THE BEGINNING OF MOSES' LIFE

1. BY WAY OF INTRODUCTION

All We relate to you [Muhammad] of the tidings of the [earlier] messengers is that by which We make your heart firm. And there has come to you, in this, the truth and an instruction and a reminder for the believers. (Holy Qur'an 11:120)

The Qur'anic account of the life of Moses, God's peace and blessings be upon him, is a powerful epic, so complex that it requires to be broken up into segments corresponding to the major phases of this great prophet's life. Consequently, the story is here presented in seven parts: The Birth of Moses and Subsequent Events; Moses' Young Manhood; The Call to Prophethood; Moses and Pharaoh; After the Exodus; *Ahadith* Concerning Moses; and The Story of Moses and Khidr.

From the fact that Moses (A) is mentioned in no less than thirty-five different chapters or *surahs* of the Qur'an, it can be understood that putting together all the parts of his history into one continuous narrative presents a major challenge, especially because the sequence of events is not always clear. Indeed, the Qur'anic 'ordering' of the events of this highly complex chronicle often appears to be interchangeable, for rather than being a historical account, the narrative focuses on Moses' relationship with his Lord, his noble character and inspired actions. And when one goes to the interpretation of the Qur'anic material, the matter is further complicated by the fact that the classical commentators often give several interpretations or even versions of the same event.

Here, as in other stories, we have given precedence to reports attributed to 'Abdullah ibn 'Abbas (R), known as Ibn 'Abbas, the cousin of the Holy Prophet (S), who is generally acknowledged as the foremost of the Qur'anic commentators. Central to our narrative is Ibn 'Abbas' account known as "*Al-Hadith al-Futun*, the Report of the Trials [of Moses]," which perhaps goes all the way back to the Prophet (S) himself — or, if not, at least back to Ibn 'Abbas (R).[1]

---

[1]This *hadith* is reported in segments in al-Tabari's *History*, Volume Three, and in Ibn Kathir's *Tafsir (Commentary on the Qur'an)* in connection with verses 20:36-40. It is also reported in entirety in Ibn Kathir's *Qasas al-Anbiya' (Stories of the Prophets)*, where it follows the story of

The story behind this *hadith* is that one evening the Prophet's Companion,[2] Sa'id ibn Jubayr (R), came to Ibn 'Abbas (R) and asked him to explain to him God's saying to Moses, **"We tried you with a [difficult] trial"** (20:40). Ibn 'Abbas (R) responded to this request by saying that if Ibn Jubayr would return the following day, he would tell him the story in full detail, which he did. In our narrative, Ibn 'Abbas' account is reported in segments related to the relevant portions of the story, comprising our second source of information about Moses (A) after the Qur'an.

In our accounts of Moses (A) and the prophets who succeeded him, the commentaries and interpretations of early classical scholars, primarily al-Tabari and Ibn Kathir, have been supplemented, where useful, with material taken from contemporary Qur'anic translators and commentators. Occasionally we have also referred to material from the Old and New Testaments, either in support of the Qur'anic text or to point out its contrast to it.

Moses under the title, "Mention of the *hadith* which is called *al-Futun* [the Trials], which includes the story of Moses from the beginning to the end." In concluding his report of this *hadith*, Ibn Kathir states:

> Ibn 'Abbas attributed this *hadith* to the Prophet (S). This is how it appears in [the *hadith* collection of] al-Nisa'i and is reported by Ibn Jarir [al-Tabari] and Ibn Abi Hatim in their commentaries, with the narrator being Yazid bin Harun. However, God alone knows whether this *hadith* may perhaps stop at Ibn 'Abbas, who most probably took it from Judaic sources. Some also say that it may be from K'ab al-Ahbar [an early Muslim convert from Judaism], and I heard from my teacher that it is from K'ab al-Ahbar, but God knows best. (Ibn Kathir/*Q*, "Musa")

[2]The designation "Companion of the Prophet" (*sahabi*, plural, *sahabah*) refers to the Muslims of the time of Prophet Muhammad (S).who saw, knew or interacted with him.

2. THE IMPORTANCE OF MOSES

And mention Moses in the Book. Indeed, he was chosen, and he was a messenger and a prophet. (19:51)

And he was distinguished in God's sight. (33:69)

Among the prophets of Islam, Moses, God's peace and blessings be upon him, occupies a position of central importance. As mentioned in Volume One, he ranks among the five greatest prophets of all time — those with whom God Most High made a covenant in the spiritual world to convey His Message and guidance to mankind, as indicated in the verse,

> **And [mention, O Muhammad,] when We took from the prophets their covenant, and from you, and from Noah and Abraham and Moses and Jesus son of Mary — and We took from them a solemn covenant.** (33:7)

After reading about Moses' rescue from death in infancy, his escape after the killing of the Egyptian, his call to prophethood and the miraculous signs with which he was invested, his lengthy dealings with the tyrannical Pharaoh and the arrogant ruler's eventual destruction, and his difficult and troubled role as the leader of his nation (***ummah***), we may easily understand the reasons for his exalted rank among the prophets.

Indeed, from the beginning of his life, Moses (A) was granted powerful miracles and signs, which we will detail in their place, and was supported by divine power. Moses (A) was also honored by God's speaking to him directly without any intermediary, as is mentioned in the verses, **God spoke to Moses with [direct] speech** (4:164), and, **"O Moses, indeed, I have chosen you over all mankind for My messages and with My speech"** (7:144). Moses (A) was, moreover, the first prophet to have been granted a divinely-revealed law (***shari'ah***) for governing the lives of his people.

Throughout the centuries since their revelation in the Qur'an during the period 610 to 632 after Christ, the stories of the prophets have fired the imagination and interest of Muslims, young and old. But as we pointed out in Volume One, God the All-Knowing did not narrate them in the Qur'an as a historical narrative or for the purpose of entertainment. Nothing in the Qur'an is random; each word, each letter proceeds from divine wisdom. Therefore, every detail reported in the Qur'an concerning any prophet contains a spiritual truth, a lesson, a warning or an inspiration, both for Muhammad (S) himself, for the first community of Muslims of his time, and for all who have believed in him and will follow him up to the Last Day, according to God's words,

> **All We relate to you [Muhammad] of news of the messengers is that by which We make your heart firm. And there has come to you, in this [Qur'an], the truth and an instruction and a reminder for the believers.** (11:120)

Moses' name is mentioned in the Qur'an more often than that of any other prophet — 136 times, while his brother Aaron (A) is mentioned twenty-one times. After Muhammad (S), to whom the Qur'an is firstly addressed and who is alluded to on virtually every page, the story of Moses (A) is reported in the greater detail than that of any other prophet, portions of it being repeated again and again, with variations. And we may well wonder about the reason for this.

Obvious and significant parallels exist between the prophets Moses and Muhammad, God's peace and blessings be upon them. These may be summarized as follows:

First, both prophets were harrassed and persecuted by the non-believers to whom they brought God's Message, and both were faithful and steadfast in proclaiming that Message in the face of the immense challenges and difficulties that confronted them. Moses' story therefore contained extremely valuable lessons for the Prophet (S) and his community concerning the critical importance of patience and steadfastness under afflictions, trials and persecutions.

Second, both prophets were granted a revealed law, Moses (A) for his people and Muhammad (S) for all mankind, by means of which they established God-centered faith communities based on divine guidance. As God says,

> **Indeed, We sent down the *Taurat*,[3] wherein was guidance and light. By it, the prophets, who surrendered [to God], gave judgment for the Jews, as did the rabbis and scholars, by that with which they were entrusted of God's scripture, and they were witnesses to that.** (5:44/47)

> **Before it [the Qur'an], the scripture of Moses was a guide and a mercy.** (11:17)

---

[3]The original scripture revealed to Moses by God, of which some unidentified portions may remain in the existing Torah.

Third, through the Qur'anic account of Moses' life, God Most High conveyed many important lessons to His Last Prophet (S) for dealing with various kinds of people, especially unbelievers. And fourth, by means of this account, a strong warning was also conveyed to the Muslim community against the sort of faithless behavior that had been typical of the rebellious, deviant segment Moses' people. And indeed, these lessons sank in and were heeded.

Fifth, the narrating of Moses' story in such detail bore an integral relationship to the Jewish tribes living in Medina during the Prophet's time. Despite the commitment they had made to follow and support the Prophet (S) after he settled among them, they behaved in a deeply hostile and treacherous manner toward him and their Muslim fellow-citizens. Numerous verses of Moses' story were therefore addressed to them as a reminder of their ancestors' past dealings with their own chief prophet and law-giver, that they might thereby be moved to accept and follow the guidance revealed through his final successor in prophethood, concerning whom God Most High revealed,

> **He has sent down to you [Muhammad] the Scripture with truth, confirming what was before it. And He revealed the *Taurat* and the *Injil*[4] previously as guidance for people.** (3:3-4)

Finally, the lessons contained in Moses' story were by no means intended solely for these early communities. Indeed, his history contains numerous, extremely important examples, admonitions and wisdoms for the generality of mankind, which will be mentioned in their place in our narrative as we proceed.

---

[4]The *Injil* (Evangel or Gospel) is the Arabic name of the scripture revealed by God to Jesus, not to be confused with the four Gospels of the New Testament.

3. HISTORICAL BACKGROUND

Say, [O Muhammad:] "Travel though the earth and observe what was the end of those before [you]. Most of them were *mushrikin*."[5] (30:42)

As we saw previously, the king who ruled Egypt during the time of the prophet Joseph (A) was one of the Hyksos dynasty — that is, the Amalekite conquerors of Egypt. Since the Hyksos, who had conquered Egypt in about 1790 B.C., were themselves foreigners in the land, a Semitic people closely related by race and lifestyle to the Israelites, their regime's tolerance of their own kind of people may have eased the settling of Jacob's large family in Egypt.

It is reported that by permission of the Hyksos king, the Israelites established themselves in a place called Goshen, mentioned in Gen. 45:10; 46:28-29, 34; 47:1-6, 27. Goshen is said to have been a barren desert region in northwestern Egypt suitable for the life of these nomadic people and their herds, where they lived apart from the Egyptians as a distinct ethnic and religious group, keeping to what their prophet ancestors, Abraham, Isaac, Jacob and Joseph (A), had enjoined upon them of God's religion.

However, in about 1550 B.C., when the Egyptians revolted against the Hyksos kings and overthrew them, the Israelites' situation changed dramatically. At that time, a pharaoh came to power who had nothing but contempt for the foreign descendants of the Hebrew patriarch Jacob, regarding them as a despised race, fit to be subjugated and harrassed. Consequently, the Israelites were enslaved, persecuted and abused by their Egyptian masters until such time as God Most High raised among the descendants of Abraham two great brother prophets whose importance in the history of religion has hardly been equaled.

REFERENCES: Commentaries: Tabari/*H*, III:32; Ali/*Q*, Appen. IV. Other works: Barnavi/*Atlas*, p. 3; Breasted/*History*, pp. 214, 220; Daiches/*Moses*, pp. 23-24; Golding/*Moses*, p. 68; Montet/*Pharaohs*, p. 171.

---

[5]Polytheists, those who worship or attribute divinity to anyone or anything other than God.

4. THE PHARAOH OF MOSES' TIME

Indeed, Pharaoh exalted himself in the land and he was surely of the transgressors. (10:83)

By the will of God, the All-Knowing, All-Aware, the lives of Moses (A) and the ruler of Egypt of his time were inseparably connected.

The proper name of this monarch is never mentioned in the Qur'an. Rather, he is simply known by the generic title of the rulers of Egypt, ***Fir'aun*** or Pharaoh. And because of the manner of this pharaoh's dealings with his subjects, the Arabic word "***fir'aun***" has come to denote a cruel tyrant or oppressor.

A great deal is known by present-day scholars about the pharaohs of Egypt. However, historians, without exception, have had great difficulty in positively identifying the pharaoh of Moses. Several theories have been put forward as to his identity, but all must be rejected on one ground or the other. Hence, in spite of what anyone may claim, and tremendous amounts of both scientific detective work and speculation, up to this time, his true identity remains uncertain, a historical mystery.[6]

The Qur'anic text informs us that this pharaoh was married to a lady whom the classical commentators identify as Asiyah daughter of Muzahim. According to some, she was an Israelite, while others say that she was an Amalekite — that is, of the people of Canaan. Whatever the case may have been, Asiyah was a most extraordinary woman, a believer of such tremendous faith that God mentions her in the Qur'an together with the blessed virgin Mary (A) as **an example for those who believe** (60:11).

Asiyah's outstanding rank and faith are also mentioned in a number of ***ahadith***. The Holy Prophet (S) said concerning her:

> Many among men reached perfection, but none among women reached perfection except Asiyah wife of Pharaoh and Mary daughter of 'Imran[7] (***Bukhari***, 4.623)
>
> Among the women of mankind, Mary daughter of 'Imran, Khadijah daughter of Khuwaylid, Fatimah daughter of Muhammad, and Asiyah wife of Pharaoh are sufficient for you. (***Mishkat***, 6181)

---

[6]For more details concerning the identity of Moses' pharaoh, please see Appendix A, "The Identity of the Pharaoh of the Exodus," page 173.

[7]In another, identical ***hadith*** (***Bukhari***, 5:113) which is cited on page 330, Mary is named first.

The best of the women of the people of Paradise are Khadijah daughter of Khuwaylid, Fatimah daughter of Muhammad, Mary daughter of 'Imran, and Asiyah daughter of Muzahim, the wife of Pharaoh. (Nisa'i)

Sufficient for you are the four mistresses [*sayyidat*] of the women of mankind: Fatimah daughter of Muhammad, Khadijah daughter of Khuwaylid, Asiyah daughter of Muzahim, and Mary daughter of 'Imran. (Ibn 'Asakir)

The best women among mankind are four: Mary daughter of 'Imran, Asiyah wife of Pharaoh, Khadijah daughter of Khuwaylid, and Fatimah daughter of Muhammad, the Messenger of God. (Tirmidhi)

REFERENCES: Commentaries: Tabari/*Q*, "Musa"; Tabari/*H*, III:31-32; Ibn Kathir/*Q*, "The Story of Jesus Son of Mary"; Ayoub/*Q*, II:97, 123-124, 126-127; Schleifer/ *Mary*, pp. 64, 69, 80, 128, fn. 23.

5. The Oppression of the Israelites

Indeed, Pharaoh exalted himself in the land and made its people into factions, oppressing a sector among them, slaughtering their sons and letting their women live. Indeed, he was among the corrupters. (28:4)

The Qur'anic story of Moses, God's peace and blessings be upon him, opens with the chronicle of the sufferings of the Israelites in Egypt under Pharaoh. This also constitutes the first theme of "The *Hadith* of the Trials [of Moses],"[8] in which a major portion of Moses' story is reported by Ibn 'Abbas (R).

This account begins as follows:

> One day among Pharaoh's courtiers there was mention of the promise that God had made to His Friend, Abraham (A) — namely, that among his descendants there would be prophets and kings.[9] Some of them remarked that the Children of Israel were still waiting for this to occur, not doubting it. Previously they [the Israelites] had had the idea that this prophecy would be fulfilled through Joseph son of Jacob, but when he died, they said, "God would not have promised Abraham that [which was not fulfilled]."[10]
>
> Pharaoh then said, "Then what do you advise?"
>
> The chiefs then established an advisory council to take care of this matter. This council came to the conclusion that they should establish a new department of police. The task of this force would be to patrol the streets, and as soon as they heard of the birth of a male child among the Israelities, he was at once to be seized and slaughtered. (*Hadith* of the Trials)

---

[8]This *hadith* will subsequently be referred to as the "*Hadith* of the Trials." All references to it are from the same source — namely, the section entitled "Musa" in Ibn Kathir's *Qasas al-Anbyia' (Stories of the Prophets).*

[9]A reference to God's promise to Abraham, **"I will surely make you a leader of mankind"** (2:124).

[10]It is also reported that Pharaoh had a dream in which he saw a fire coming out of Jerusalem, spreading until it engulfed the houses of Egypt, burning the Egyptians and destroying their dwellings, while the Israelites remained. Troubled by what he had seen, Pharaoh called together his astrologers, soothsayers and magicians to enquire about the meaning of his dream. They replied, "A man will come from the land of the Israelites" — meaning Jerusalem — "for whose sake Egypt will be destroyed" (Ibn Kathir/*Q*, "Musa"; Tabari/*H*, III:33-34).

Accordingly, there was now initated a period of oppression of the Israelites under this pharaoh, the unrivaled ruler of Egypt. Since, like other Egyptian pharaohs, he regarded himself as a god to be worshipped by his subjects, he accepted no authority over himself and did whatever he pleased without accountability to any higher power, as is clear from the words,

> **Pharaoh said, "O chiefs, I have not known you to have a god other than me."** (28:38)

> **But he denied and disobeyed. Then he turned his back, striving, and he gathered [his people] and called [to them] and said, "I am your most exalted Lord."** (79:21-24)

Concerning this tyrant, al-Tabari says, "Among the pharaohs there was none more insolent than he toward God, or haughtier in speech, or longer-lived in his rule." There was, moreover, "no pharaoh more ruthless, harder-hearted, or of more evil character toward the Israelites than he" (Tabari/*H*, III:32).

Enslaving their males, Pharaoh divided the Israelites into separate groups for such tasks as building, raising crops and the like. He also ordered the masters of slaves to bring their non-Israelite outdoor slaves inside to do domestic work, while, in exchange, the Israelites were sent outside to do the hardest, most disagreeable tasks.

Then, as his counselors had suggested, he ordered the killing of every male infant born among them but commanded that the females be spared. Consequently, when a girl baby was born, Pharaoh's soldiers would let it live, but in the case of a male, they would call the executioners, who would cut it into pieces in front of its parents.

But it was soon realized that this policy was self-defeating, for if the slave population continued to be thus drastically reduced, the Egyptians themselves would be burdened with all the difficult tasks that the Israelite males had assumed up to that point. Consequently, Pharaoh ordered that the newborn males be killed each alternate year, allowing the males of the following year to live.

Thus did the progeny of Abraham, Isaac and Jacob (A) endure dreadful hardships and torments under this tyrannical ruler. Many centuries later, in His final revelation to mankind through Muhammad (S), God Most High was to remind their descendants of the awful trials their people had faced under Pharaoh and his officials, saying:

> **And [recall, O Children of Israel,] when We saved you from the people of Pharaoh, who afflicted you with the worst torment,**

slaughtering your sons and letting your women live. And in that was a tremendous trial from your Lord. (2:49, 7:141, also 14:6)

REFERENCES: Qur'an: 20:40; 2:49; 28:3-4. Commentaries: Ibn Kathir/*Q*, "Musa"; Ibn Kathir/*T*, 28:3-6; Tabari/*Q*, "Musa"; Tabari/*C*, I:297-303; Tabari/*H*, III:32-34, 37-38; Maududi/ *Q*, 7:fn. 93.

6. Moses' Birth and Rescue from Death

Pharaoh's family took him up, that he might become an enemy to them and a [source of] grief. (28:8)

Among the families of the Israelites, 'Imran son of Izhar and his wife, known in Arabic as Umm Musa (the mother of Moses), were both descendants of Levi, one of the twelve sons of Jacob or Israel (A).[11]

This couple had a daughter named Miriam (Maryam), who is said to have been about ten or twelve when the events reported in this story took place, as well as a son named Aaron (Harun). Says Ibn 'Abbas (R):

> Aaron was born during the year the boys were spared, and his mother gave birth to him openly. But the following year, when she was pregnant with Moses, her heart was full of anxiety and sorrow. (Here Ibn 'Abbas added parenthetically to Sa'id ibn Jubayr, to whom he was narrating the story, "And this was one of the trials that befell Moses, O Ibn Jubayr — that God placed him in the womb of his mother by His Will [at such a time].")
>
> But God inspired to her, **"Do not fear nor grieve. Indeed, We will restore him to you and will make him among the messengers"** [28:7]. And He commanded that when he was born, she should make a chest for him, put him in it, and place it in the river. (*Hadith* of the Trials)

After the baby's birth, a further inspiration came to Umm Musa:

"Nurse him," she was instructed. **"Then, when you fear for him, drop him in the chest and drop it into the river, and the river will cast it onto the bank."**[12]

---

[11]'Imran (Amram, mentioned in Ex. 6:18, 20; Num. 3:19; I Chr. 6:2-3, 18) is an important name in the history of Judaism, Christianity and Islam. For not only was 'Imran the father of the prophets Moses and Aaron, but he was also the ancestor, through Aaron, of the priests of the Jews. The father of the virgin Mary, the 'Imran for whom the third *surah* of the Qur'an is named, was among his descendants. As for Moses' mother, her name is given as Jochebed in Ex. 6:20 (in which she is referred to as both Amram's wife and his father's sister) and in Num. 26:59.

[12]Here and in the above account of Ibn 'Abbas, the following two verses are combined:

> **"Nurse him. Then, when you fear for him, put him into the river, and do not fear nor grieve. Indeed, We will restore him to you and will make him among the messengers."** (28:7)
>
> **"Drop him in the chest and drop it into the river, and the river will cast it onto the bank; there will take him up an enemy to Me and an enemy to him."** (20:39)

Accordingly, Umm Musa had a carpenter make a water-tight chest for her baby. She then moored the little chest to reeds at the bank of the great, wide Nile. Whenever the Egyptian soldiers came around, checking, she would put the baby into the chest, and when they left she would take him out.

The anxious mother now spent all her time at the river bank, watching and listening keenly, and tending to her child. She was his only source of nourishment, as he nursed from no breast other than hers.

This continued for some time. Then one day, without Umm Musa's noticing, an Egyptian informer suddenly appeared. There was not a second in which to think about what it was best to do. Instinctively, to save her baby from death, she dropped him into the chest and set it afloat in the river.

> When the chest floated away out of her sight, [continues Ibn 'Abbas,] Satan started putting doubts in her mind and she began to think, "Alas, it would have been better if I had kept him with me, even if he were killed in front of my eyes! At least I would have the satisfaction of shrouding and burying him with my own hands. But now I have thrown him to the creatures of the river and its fishes!"
>
> The chest floated to a dock at Pharaoh's palace. Maid servants were present there and they picked up the chest, but when they decided to open it, they became afraid, thinking that someone would accuse them of stealing. So they took the closed chest to the queen. (*Hadith* of the Trials)

Now, it is traditional knowledge in Islam that the prophets were the most lovely and endearing of mankind, created thus by God so that people might be drawn to them like spiritual magnets and desire to follow their ways. And it is said that the baby Moses was so beautiful that anyone who saw him immediately loved him. Therefore, reports Ibn 'Abbas (R),

> When the chest was opened in front of her [Asiyah], it contained a child, and God put such love for him in her heart that she loved him as she had never loved anyone before. (*Hadith* of the Trials)

At the same time, she immediately understood why this exquisite baby had been put into such a terrifyingly dangerous situation. And her tender heart was moved with compassion for the child and his mother.

Thus it was that, by the decree of the Best of Planners, **Pharaoh's family took him up, that he might become an enemy to them and a** source of **grief** — the means by which the arrogant Pharaoh and his supporters, including his chief lackey Haman, would eventually reap what they had sown, for **indeed, Pharaoh and Haman and their troops were transgressors** (28:8).

Ibn 'Abbas' describes what happened next, saying:

> When the executioners heard about this matter, they approached Pharaoh's wife with their knives in order to slaughter him. ("So, O Ibn Jubayr," Ibn 'Abbas said to his listener, "that was among the trials.")
>
> The queen replied, "Let him be until I come to Pharaoh and ask him to give him to me, for this single one will not increase the number of the Israelites. If he gives him to me, all will be well. Otherwise, you have the authority to kill him."
>
> She then came to Pharaoh and told him that this child would be **"a comfort of the eye for me and for you"** [28:9].
>
> Pharaoh replied, "He may be that for you, but as for me, I have no need of him." (Here Ibn 'Abbas commented: "The Prophet, God's peace and blessings be upon him, said, 'If he had said that he would be a comfort for my eyes, as his wife had said, God would have guided him as He guided her, but God prohibited that to him.'") (*Hadith* of the Trials)

Nonetheless, Asiyah continued to plead with her hard-hearted husband for the lovely Israelite baby.

"Do not kill him!" she begged. **"Perhaps he may benefit us or we may adopt him as a son"**[13] (28:9). And, by the Will of the Decreer of all things, Pharaoh agreed to her request. Quite naturally, **they did not perceive** (28:9) the future consequences of their action on their own lives. Nor could they possibly have imagined the impact that the helpless infant whom the queen held in her hands was to have on the future course of human civilization.

Now, obviously the very first thing a baby needs is milk. And once she had secured his life from Pharaoh and his executioners, the queen set about looking for a wet nurse for the child.

> So taking Pharaoh's permission, [Ibn 'Abbas continues,] she came back to her apartments and called all the women of her household to see whether he would accept any of them as a wet nurse. But he refused the breast of each woman who tried to nurse him. The queen was therefore extremely anxious, thinking that this beautiful baby would die of starvation. Then, after reflecting a little, she ordered that he be taken outside into the street and among the people, hoping to find a wet nurse for him. However, he would not accept any. (*Hadith* of the Trials)

---

[13]Note that these words are identical to what was said by Potiphar to his wife when he brought Joseph home after purchasing him as a slave (12:21).

But what was happening meanwhile to the mother of the exquisite baby? At this point in his account, Ibn 'Abbas (R) cites God's words:

> **And Umm Musa's heart became empty of everything [but her son]. She would almost have disclosed [the truth] about him if We had not fortified her heart, that she might be among the believers. (28:10)**

Indeed, it was an ordeal to shake the stoutest heart. Too well aware that at any instant the frail little chest might be swamped by a wave on that huge river and her darling drowned, devoured by a fish, or ground up in the ferocious jaws of a hungry crocodile, the anguished mother could hardly restrain herself from blurting out the truth about him. At that point, she all but lost sight of God's inspiration to her, **"Do not fear nor grieve. We will surely restore him to you and will make him among the messengers"** (28:7),[14] and would have revealed her secret if God **had not fortified her heart** (28:10). And even as she was torn between hope and fear, the divine plan for both the present and the future was at work, as the baby was taken from the river and brought to Asiyah.

> Then when Umm Musa became too apprehensive, she told his sister to find out what had happened to him, [saying, **"Follow him!"** (28:11) as he floated downstream along the shore,] and to see if she would be able to hear any mention of Moses, [asking], "Is my son alive or has he been eaten by wild creatures?" And she forgot what God had promised her [concerning her child]. (*Hadith* of the Trials)

Accordingly, his sister **watched him from a distance while they did not notice** [28:11]. Upon hearing that a woman was being sought to nurse him, she came forward joyfully and said, **"Shall I direct you to a household that will feed him for you, while they are sincere to him?"**[15] [28:11-12].

> As soon as she had said that, the people suspected that this girl knew this child, and that she also knew where he had been born. ("Therefore, O Ibn Jubayr," said Ibn 'Abbas, "this was another of the trials.") But God gave the girl enough sense to say, "Who would not like to have this baby, who is so loved by our queen, and who would not like to acquire

---

[14]Note the similarity between this and what was revealed to Joseph, both during his childhood vision and his ordeal in the well. In this manner does the Most Merciful sometimes open a glimpse of the future to His servants who are being tested so they may find the courage to go on, even under the most trying circumstances.

[15]In 20:40, it is, **"When your sister went and said, 'Shall I direct you to someone who will feed him?'"**

all the rewards and favors for her household [that will come with being his nurse]?" So they accepted this reasoning and let her go, asking her, "Where is this wet nurse you are talking about?"

She said, "Wait a bit. I will bring her." Then she ran home and told the mother this good news. And the mother came running with great eagerness, and she took her son in her lap and gave her breast to him, and the child drank and drank until he was satisfied.

The news was taken to the palace. The queen ordered that the wet nurse and the child be brought to her, and when she saw the mother feeding the baby and that he was satisfied and nursing properly, she became very glad and said, "O dear nurse, I love this child more than anything else in the world! Stay with me in the palace and feed him."

Umm Musa replied, "This is impossible. How can I leave my other children at home and stay with you? But if you wish, give this child to me. I will take him home and will not spare anything in providing for him."

The queen had no other option, and so the mother brought Moses to her house. Because of this child, that particular locality [of Israelites] was spared Pharaoh's oppression. (*Hadith* of the Trials)

Thus does God the All-Knowing, say, **And We had previously withheld him from** all **wet nurses** (28:12), making it clear that the refusal of the infant Moses to accept any breast but his mother's was an integral part of His incredibly subtle, all-embracing plan. In this manner was Moses (A), by yet another miracle, returned to his mother after having been miraculously saved from death in the river, and twice from the executioner's knife.

"And I bestowed love upon you from Myself, that you might be reared under My eye," the beneficent Lord was to say to Moses (A) many years later. **"Then We restored you to your mother, that she might be content and not grieve, and that she might know that God's promise is true"** (20:39-40; 28:13).

In these deeply compassionate words, we see the tender concern of the Most Merciful for Umm Musa's natural feelings for her newborn son. But as this child was vital to the well-being of his mother, so also was this mother vital to the well-being of her child. As if to confirm the high respect and honor that God assigns to motherhood, He placed the foundation of His prophet-to-be with his believing mother, who had already been informed by divine inspiration that her son would be among His messengers, so that he might take both his bodily nourishment and his spiritual foundation from her among his own people.

Thus was Umm Musa's implicit following of the divine command, despite the unsurmountable difficulties it presented, rewarded by God's saving her son from death. And so the beautiful Israelite baby lived and thrived. It is said that because in the Egyptian language "water" was "*mu*" and "tree" was "*sha*," the child was named Musa because he had been found in the water among trees.

REFERENCES: Qur'an: 20:37-40; 28:7-13. Commentaries: Ibn Kathir/*T*, 28:7-13; Ibn Kathir/*Q*, "Musa"; Tabari/*C*, I:309; Tabari/*H*, III:30-31, 34-36, 38-40; Maududi/*Q*, 28:fns. 9, 12-13, 15.

7. MOSES' INTRODUCTION TO PHARAOH

Indeed, he [Pharaoh] was a haughty one among the transgressors!
(44:31)

After these initial trials, the period of Moses' nursing was passed in his parents' house, in the company of his siblings, Miriam, Aaron and whatever other children there may have been. It is said that because of Moses' standing with Pharaoh's wife, the Israelites were saved from the forced labor and other injustices that Pharaoh had inflicted upon them.

> After some time, [Ibn 'Abbas continues,] Pharaoh's wife ordered that the child be brought to her, and so a day was fixed. All the courtiers and government officials were ordered to escort the child from his house to the palace with full pomp and ceremony. And when he came out of his house, everyone brought him gifts, and with great honor and in procession he was brought before the queen, who also showered him with gifts. And she said, "I will take him to Pharaoh, who will also give him gifts and honors."
>
> When she came to him, she put him in Pharaoh's lap, and he caught hold of his beard and tugged at it vigorously. At that, Pharaoh became suspicious, and one of his courtiers said, "Do you not see that this is what God promised His prophet Abraham? He thinks that he will inherit you and rise high above you and overthrow you. Therefore, send for the executioners to kill him!" ("So, Ibn Jubayr," Ibn 'Abbas commented, "this was another trial among all the trials by which he was tried.")
>
> Pharaoh's wife came forward, pleading with Pharaoh, and she said to him, "O Pharaoh, what are you thinking about this child whom you have given to me?"
>
> Pharaoh replied, "Do you not see that he wants to overthrow me and rise above me?" (*Hadith* of the Trials)

Thus, the matter took a serious turn. But doubtless Asiyah had managed to live with her cruelly egotistical husband through the use of her wits, surviving, with God's help, by strategems when needed. And now, as God inspired her, she quickly proposed a scheme by which she hoped to save the child.

> She then said, "Let us settle this affair between you and me, and ascertain the truth. Bring two burning coals and two pearls, and put them in front of him. If he picks up the pearls and avoids the coals, we will know that he understands what he is doing, but if he picks up the coals and does not look at the pearls, we will know that he does not distinguish between coals and pearls, and has no understanding."

> So they brought two burning coals and two pearls, and he reached for them but they removed them from him for fear that they would burn his hands. And the queen said, "Do you not see?" Thus God turned him [Pharaoh] from him after what he had intended concerning him, and **God accomplished His purpose** through him [65:3]. (*Hadith* of the Trials)

According to another account from Ibn 'Abbas (R), the queen put a sapphire ornament and a burning coal in front of Moses (A).[16]

> She said, "If he picks up the sapphire, he is able to reason, so kill him, but if he picks up the coals, he is just a child." Then Gabriel (A) came and put the coal in his hand, and Moses (A) put it in his mouth, burning his tongue, and that is mentioned in God's saying, [through the mouth of Moses, when he received the call to prophethood at Mount Sinai,] **"Loosen the knot from my tongue, that they may understand my speech"** [20:27-28]. (Tabari/*Q*, "Musa")

The arrogant Pharaoh would likewise later refer to Moses' difficulty in speaking, demanding of his people, **"Am I not better than this one who is insignificant and hardly makes himself clear?"** (43:52).

And here ends the extraordinary account of the birth of Moses, God's peace and blessings be upon him, and his miraculous rescue from death in infancy and early childhood.

REFERENCES: Qur'an: 20:27-28; 43:52. Commentaries: Ibn Kathir/*Q*, "Musa"; Ibn Kathir/*T*, 20:27; Tabari/*H*, III:36, 40-41; Tabari/*Q*.

---

[16]In yet another account of this story reported from Ibn 'Abbas, a date is mentioned instead of the pearls or the sapphire ornament.

PART TWO: MOSES' YOUNG MANHOOD

8. THE ACCIDENT

"Then you killed a person but We saved you from the affliction, and We tried you with a [difficult] trial." (20:40)

After Umm Musa brought Moses (A) to the queen, he remained in the royal palace and grew to maturity, blest with a strong, well-built body. It is said that he was known and regarded as Pharaoh's son, living as Pharaoh lived, wearing what he wore, traveling as he traveled, and sailing with him in boats on the Nile.

Did Moses (A) grow up believing in and worshipping the Egyptian gods — including his foster father, Pharaoh? The answer to this question must be a most emphatic "No," for God says of him,

> **When he reached his full strength and was mature, We granted him judgment and knowledge. And thus do We reward the doers of good** (28:14).

These words indicate that Moses (A) was granted **judgment and knowledge** as a reward for being among the **doers of good**, something that could never be said of one who worshipped false gods. It is, moreover, an Islamic tradition that no one who was granted prophethood ever worshipped anyone but his Creator. Indeed, everything that follows from this point in the story speaks of the depth of Moses' faith and the fact that he was among the chosen and elect of his Lord (19:51, 20:41), which would be inconceivable if he had been, prior to that time, an idolater.

Had Moses (A) then been in contact with his family and people after the end of his period of nursing? It is clear that he had, for years later, when prophethood was bestowed upon him and he was commanded to go to Pharaoh, he asked God to **"appoint an assistant for me from my family — Aaron, my brother"** (20:29-30), who is **"more clear in speech than I"** (28:34), an obvious indication that he knew his family members and their characteristics. The Qur'anic account of this segment of the story also makes it clear that Moses' loyalty and sympathy were with his own people rather than with the Egyptians, as is further suggested by the saying of Ibn 'Abbas (R):

> When he grew up and became a man, none of the people of Pharaoh could oppress or treat the Children of Israel with harshness, to the extent that they were secure from all such things. (*Hadith* of the Trials)

Although Moses' Israelite origin had been kept secret from his people, it is evident from what follows that he has grown up with the worldview of a believer, having clear knowledge of his descent from his prophet-ancestors and their teachings and practices. It is also likely that, through his mother, a woman of tremendously strong faith, he would have grown up fully aware of his miraculous rescue from death in infancy. And unquestionably his foster-mother, Asiyah, would also have imparted to him something of her vibrant faith.

At the same time, he would have been thoroughly familiar with the mentality and belief of the Egyptians among whom he lived, and keenly conscious of his people's sufferings and trials under his adopted father's rule. It is therefore probable that Moses (A) grew up knowing equally well the way of faith and truth, and the way of unbelief and falsehood — the way of the arrogant, oppressive Pharaoh, who imagined himself to be the supreme lord on earth. And, as we shall see, the knowledge of both was to be of vital importance to him in time to come.

Then, abruptly, by the plan of the All-Wise, the All-Aware, an incident occurred which was to change the entire course of Moses' life.

According to a report from Ibn 'Abbas (R), one day Pharaoh sailed in a boat without Moses. When Moses (A) heard of this, he set sail after him and disembarked at Memphis. **And he entered the city at a time of inattention by its people** (28:15) — that is, during the afternoon siesta, when the market-places were closed and the streets were empty.

And he found therein two men fighting, one from his faction, an Israelite, **and one from his enemy,** an Egyptian. **Then the one from his faction called to him for help against the one from his enemy** (28:15). Ibn 'Abbas (R) supplies further details:

> When Moses (A) was walking in the direction of the city, he came upon two men fighting, one of them a pharaonite and the other an Israelite. And the Israelite asked him for help against the pharaonite.
>
> Then Moses became very angry because he [the Israelite] had reached out to him, knowing his position among the Israelites and his protection of them; for apart from Umm Musa, people did not know [concerning his connection with them] but that it was due to nursing

[among them], unless God [Himself] had informed Moses of that about which He did not inform anyone else.[17]

Then Moses struck the pharaonite and killed him, and no one saw the two of them except God, the Almighty and Glorious, and the Israelite. And when Moses had killed the man, **he said, "This is of Satan's doing. Indeed, he is a clear, misleading enemy!"** [28:15].

Then **he said, "My Lord, indeed I have wronged myself, so forgive me!" and He forgave him. Indeed, He is the Forgiving, the Merciful. He said, "My Lord, because of the favor You have bestowed upon me, never will I be a supporter of criminals!"**[18] **And he became, within the city, fearful and anticipating** the spread of the news [28:16-18].

Then they came to Pharaoh and said to him, "The Israelites have killed a man from among Pharaoh's people. So secure our rights for us and do not be lenient to them."

He said, "Search for his murderer and whoever is a witness against him, for indeed it is not proper for the king or the chiefs of his people to execute anyone without evidence or proof. Therefore, pursue the knowledge of that for me so that I may secure your rights for you." (*Hadith* of the Trials)

REFERENCES: Qur'an: 20:40; 28:14-17. Commentaries: Ibn Kathir/*Q*, "Musa"; Tabari/*Q*, "Musa"; Tabari/*H*, III:36-37, 41-43; Maududi/*Q*, 28:fns. 19, 26.

---

[17]That is, while the Israelite was aware of Moses' standing with his people and his protection of them, he ascribed it to Moses' having been nursed by an Israelite woman under the patronage of the queen. For aside from what God Himself might have revealed to Moses concerning his origin, no one but Umm Musa and probably his immediate family knew that he was her son and an Israelite.

[18]This **"favor"** is said to refer to the power, prestige and the worldly benefits Moses had been granted as Pharaoh's adopted son. Some classical commentators understood the last sentence to mean that Moses thereby committed himself to sever his relations with Pharaoh and his tyrannical regime, which had established a corrupt system in the land, dividing Egyptian society into opposing factions and oppressing Moses' people.

9. The Escape

So he departed therefrom, fearful and anticipating. He said, "My Lord, save me from the wrong-doing people!" And when he directed himself toward Midian, he said, "Perhaps my Lord will guide me to the sound way." (28:21-22)

Ibn 'Abbas (R) details the complex events that followed, saying:

Then the following day, while they were searching and not finding any evidence, Moses passed by the same Israelite, fighting with another pharaonite. He [again] asked for his help against the pharaonite; it was by chance that he countered Moses when he did. But he [Moses] was regretful about what had occurred and appalled by what he had seen; consequently, he became very angry [with the Israelite]. And while he was approaching to seize the pharaonite, he said to the Israelite, because of what he had done the previous day and this day, **"Indeed, you are an obvious mischief-maker!"** [28:18].

When the Israelite looked at Moses after what he had [just] said to him and observed that he was angry as he had been the previous day when he killed the pharaonite, he feared for his life, for he had called him **"an obvious mischief-maker."** He supposed that it was whom he [Moses] meant to seize, although it was not; rather, he intended to seize the pharaonite. But in his fear, the Israelite blurted out, **"O Moses, do you intend to kill me as you killed a person yesterday? You only want to be an oppressor in the land and do not want to be of the amenders"** [28:19], saying this out of fear that Moses intended to kill him.

The event of the previous day had had no witnesses except that Israelite. But when the Israelite accused Moses of intending to kill him as he had killed a person the previous day, the Egyptian with whom the Israelite was fighting had all the evidence he needed against him.

The two stopped fighting, and the pharaonite went to report what he had heard from the Israelite, [namely, his saying to Moses,] **"Do you intend to kill me as you killed a person yesterday?"** Then Pharaoh dispatched his executioners to kill Moses.

Pharaoh's men took the main road in search of him, certain that he would not escape them. Then a man from Moses' faction came from the farthest part of the city, taking a short cut. He reached him ahead of them and informed him of this, [saying,] **"O Moses, indeed the chiefs are deliberating concerning you, to kill you, so leave; indeed, I am**

> **among the sincere advisors to you"** [28:20]. ("So, O Ibn Jubayr," Ibn 'Abbas added, "this was one of the trials.") (*Hadith* of the Trials)

Moses (A) needed no further urging. His worst fears had materialized. After having grown up as a prince in Pharaoh's household, he was now, without having intended any harm, a wanted murderer, an outlaw, a fugitive from justice.

So he departed therefrom, fearful and anticipating. "My Lord," he prayed, **"save me from the wrong-doing people!"**[19] (28:21).

But where was he to go? Perhaps there was no clear thought in his head. He knew only that he must flee for his life, and thus his feet went in the direction chosen for him by his Lord. Says Ibn 'Abbas (R):

> Moses set out toward Midian. He had not previously experienced any hardship and he did not know the route. But, depending on his Lord, the Mighty, the Glorious, he prayed, **"Perhaps my Lord will guide me to the sound way"** [28:22]. (*Hadith* of the Trials)

REFERENCES: Qur'an: 28:18-22. Commentaries: Ibn Kathir/*Q*, "Musa"; Tabari/*H*, III:37, 42-43.

---

[19]Moses' referring to Pharaoh and his advisors as **"wrong-doing people"** is understood as being general in meaning, relating to the error of their beliefs and dealings, perhaps especially with regard to his people, not to their present action against him.

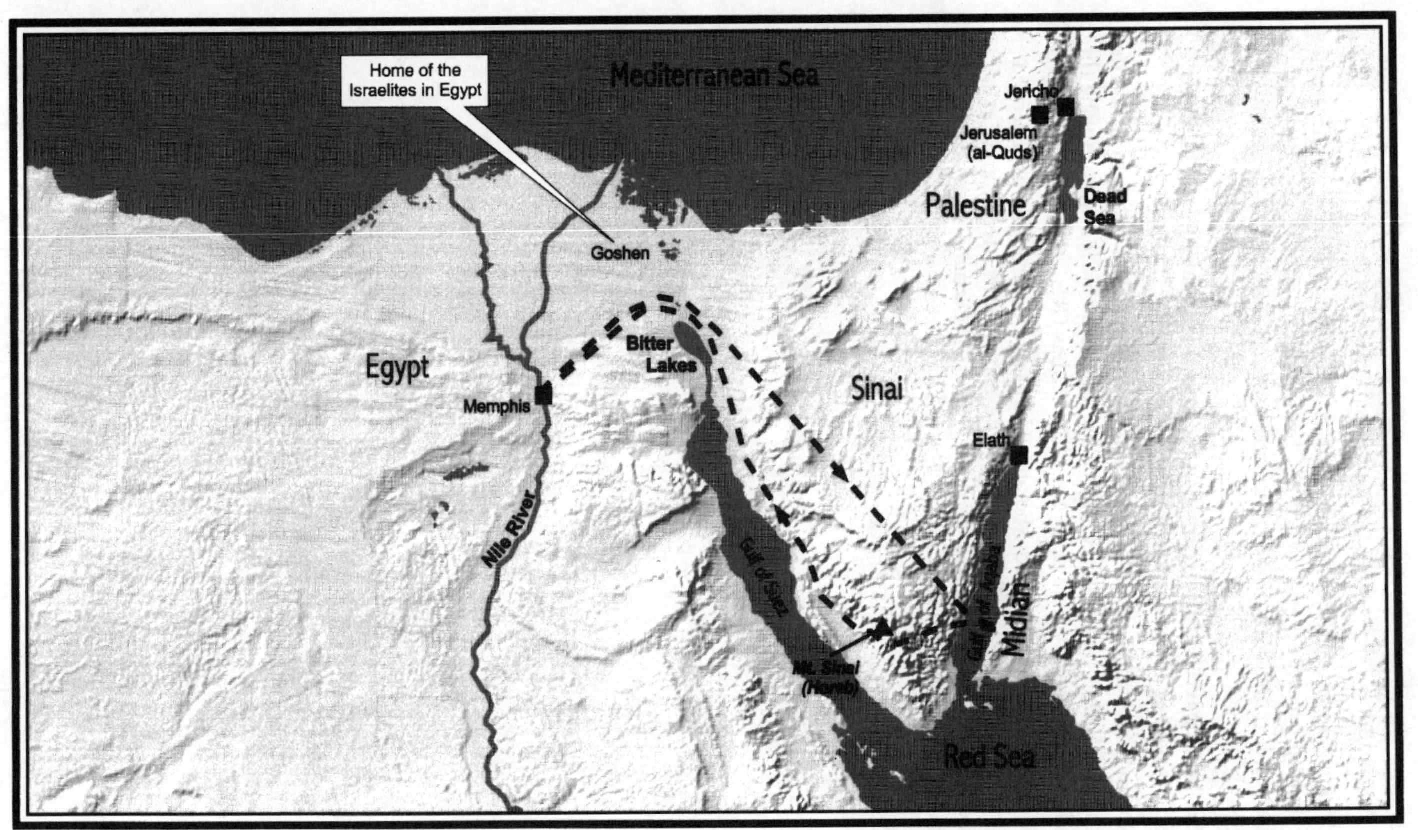

Map 10. Moses' travels to Midian

10. MOSES IN MIDIAN

So he watered for them; then he withdrew into the shade and said, "My Lord, indeed, I am in need of any good You may grant to me." (28:24)

Moses (A) pressed on toward Midian, a land of bedouins like his own people, where the law of Pharaoh did not reach.[20] No doubt he was keenly alert throughout his journey, apprehensively watching and listening for any sign that he was being followed.

We are already familiar with the name of Midian (Madyan) from the story of the prophet Shu'ayb (A), whose time period is uncertain. If indeed Shu'ayb (A) lived before the time of Moses, as some commentators suppose, the territory inhabited by his people would earlier have been devastated by volcanic eruptions and earthquakes.[21] In that case, it is likely that Moses (A) now went to a different part of Midian, a vast region comprising the eastern and western coasts of the Gulf of 'Aqabah. And because the inhabitants of Midian were Arabs of Amorite stock who were descended from Abraham (A) and were therefore ethnically, linguistically and religiously related to the Israelites, they could be depended on for assistance.

Without any resources, Moses (A) foraged for whatever meager food he could find.[22] Sa'id ibn Jubayr (R) says that by the time he reached Midian eight days and nights later, he was at the point of starvation, for he had had nothing to eat except the leaves of trees, and because he had fled barefoot, the soles of his feet were worn out.

> When he arrived at the watering-place of Midian, he saw a group of shepherds **watering** [their flocks], **and he found, apart from them, two women, keeping back** [their flocks].
>
> He asked them, **"What is your situation?"** [28:23] — that is, "Why are you standing back from the people?"

---

[20]Another report attributed to Ibn 'Abbas states that an angel came to Moses as he was leaving Egypt by its side roads and guided him to Midian (Tabari/H, III:37).

[21]Please see Volume One, "Shu'ayb," pages 492-493, for details.

[22]Local tradition has preserved the site of this well a few miles north of Maqna on the western coast of the Gulf of 'Aqabah (see MaududiQ, 28:footnote 33).. It is not to be confused with the supposed well of Moses inside Saint Catherine's Monastery, whose location on the slopes of Mount Sinai, where Moses later received the call to prophethood while he was traveling ***away*** from Midian, seems to clearly invalidate the claim that this is where he watered the women's flocks.

The two said, "We have no power to contend with so many people. We are waiting for whatever is left of the water." (*Hadith* of the Trials)

"We cannot water our flocks **until the shepherds drive away** their flocks from the water," they explained, for as modest, believing women, it was out of question for them to mingle and jostle with the rough, unchivalrous shepherds at the watering place. Then, as if to clarify the reason for their being in such an uncongenial situation, they added: **"And our father is an old man"**[23] (28:23).

Then he watered for them and drew up large quantities of water with the bucket, so that their flock was the first to be watered,[24] and then they left with their sheep and went to their father. And he sat down under a tree and prayed to God, saying, **"My Lord, indeed I am in need of any good You may grant to me"**[25] [28:24].

When the women returned to their father, he asked them how it was that they had come back so early this day, and the sheep also seemed to be satisfied and well-watered. The women informed him what Moses had done, so the father told one of them to go back and bring the stranger to him. So she came and requested Moses to come with her to her father. (*Hadith* of the Trials)

When she **came to him, walking with shyness,** she said, **"Indeed, my father invites you, that he may compensate you for having watered for us"** (28:25).

Accepting the invitation, Moses (A) stood up in order to follow the woman home. But watchful of himself and wary of letting any unacceptable thought come to his heart, he asked her to walk behind him so that he would not look at her, and to guide his steps by giving directions. And as they pro-

---

[23]That is, since their father was too old or weak to water the flocks that constituted their livelihood and since there were no reliable men available, the women had no choice except to do the watering themselves, although such work was obviously unsuitable for them.

[24]According to another report, they all waited. When the shepherds had finished watering, without any concern for the needs of the two women, they covered the mouth of the well with a large rock. Although the rock was so large that it required ten men to move it, Moses was able to move it by himself. He then drew up bucketfuls of water for the women's flocks, and then they quickly set out for home.

[25]Ibn 'Abbas reports that these words referred to Moses' desperate need for food after his long journey (Ibn Kathir/*Q*, "Musa"; Tabari/*H*, III:44). It is also reported that one of the two women heard him say this.

ceeded onward, whenever necessary the woman threw a stone to indicate the way to him rather than letting him hear the sound of her voice.

The father of the two women was a believer. Ibn 'Abbas (R) states that his name was Jethro (Yathra), as mentioned in the Book of Exodus, and that he was the ruler or priest of Midian.[26]

Then when Moses (A) **came to him and related the story to him** (28:25),

> **He said, "Do not fear. You have escaped from the wrong-doing people** [28:25]. Neither Pharaoh nor any of his people have any authority over us. We are not in his domain."
>
> One of the two [women] then said, **"O my father, hire him. Surely the best one you can hire is the strong and the trustworthy"** [28:26].
>
> Then the father's vigilance was aroused and he asked her, "How do you know about his strength and his trustworthiness?"
>
> The daughter said, "His strength was known when he watered our goats by hauling up the big bucket with strength and power, and I have not seen any other man stronger than he in this watering. And as for his trustworthiness, he looked toward me when I approached him and made myself known to him. Then, when he saw that I was a woman, he lowered his head and did not raise it until I had conveyed your message to him. Then he said to me, 'Walk behind me and show me the way,' and no one does this except one who is trustworthy."
>
> The father then became at ease, and he affirmed her truthfulness and his heart cleared of any doubt concerning his daughter. Then he said to him, **"Indeed, I desire that one of these, my two daughters, marry you on the condition that you hire yourself to me for eight years. If then you complete ten, that will be from your side, but I do not want to put you into difficulty. You will find me, God willing, among the righteous"** [28:28]. (*Hadith* of the Trials)

---

[26]Some classical commentators were of the opinion that, because of his association with Midian, Jethro was the prophet Shu'ayb. However, the Qur'an contains no mention of the father's being a prophet or of his people, their sins or their punishment.

"That is agreed between me and you," Moses (A) replied. **"Whichever of the two terms I complete, let there be no ill feeling toward me. And God is Witness over what we say"** (28:28).

REFERENCES: Qur'an: 28:24-28. Commentaries: Ibn Kathir/*Q*, "Musa"; Tabari/*Q*, "Musa"; Tabari/*H*, III:37, 43-45, 47; Maududi/*Q*, 28:fns. 32-34; Asad/*Q*, 7:fn.67. Other works: Golding/*Moses*, p. 203; Taher/*Sinai*, p. 46.

11. THE STAFF OF MOSES

"It is my staff. I lean on it and bring down leaves for my sheep with it, and I have other uses for it." (20:18)

This segment of Moses' history would not be complete without the mention of his staff, which is said to have come into his possession in the following manner:

After Moses (A) had come to an agreement with his host about his term of service and marriage, the old man told one of his daughters to bring him a staff so he might give it to Moses (A) for herding his flocks. However, the staff she brought was one that had been given to him by an angel in the guise of a man and consequently he did not want to part with it.[28] Hence, when she brought it to him, he told her to take it back and bring another.

The woman put it down and tried to take another, but try as she might, no staff would come to her hand except that one. Although her father kept sending her back, each time she would return with the same staff in her hand.

Seeing this, Moses (A) picked up the staff, took it out and used it to herd the flocks. The old man felt regret over this, saying, "This was entrusted to me." And he went out to meet Moses (A), saying, "Give me the staff."

"It is my staff," Moses (A) replied, refusing to give it up. Thus, they argued over it, and at length they agreed to appoint the first man whom they met as an arbitrator.

An angel then came walking along and he decided between them, saying, "Put the staff on the ground. It will belong to whomever can lift it." When the old man tried to lift it he was unable to, but Moses (A) took it in hand and lifted it. Consequently, the old man left it to Moses.

What was this staff? Outwardly it was probably like any staff that shepherds of that time used to herd sheep or goats and beat down leaves from trees for them to eat, having two prongs at the top and a hook at its end that were used for these purposes. But that was only its external appearance, for in truth, it was a powerful spiritual weapon possessing extraordinary miraculous properties, about which we will speak in the next section.

REFERENCES: Tabari/*Q*, "Musa"; Tabari/*H*, III:45.

---

[28]It is also said that this staff had come from Paradise with Adam and had been passed down from prophet to prophet until it came to Moses.

12. THE COMPLETION OF MOSES' TERM IN MIDIAN

"Then you stayed for years among the people of Midian." (20:40)

It is reported that Moses (A) married the woman who had invited him to her home, whose name is given in Ex. 2:21 as Zipporah.

As for the length of Moses' term of service to her father, once Prophet Muhammad (S) was reciting *Surah Ta Ha*, the twentieth *surah*, in which verses 9 through 99 relate to Moses. When he came to Moses' story, he said, "Moses hired himself for eight or ten years in return for preserving his chastity and receiving his food" (*Mishkat*, 2989). Ibn 'Abbas (R), however, was absolutely definite about the period of Moses' service, saying, "He completed the longer and better of the two. Indeed," he added, "a prophet of God, peace and blessings be upon him, always does what he says" (*Bukhari*, 3.849), meaning that a prophet always choses what God likes and never accepts the easier alternative for his own personal satisfaction. Ibn 'Abbas (R) further said,

> Eight [years of service] were obligatory on Moses, and he added two [more] years, thus fulfilling ten. God had decided the period for him, so he completed ten years." (*Hadith* of the Trials)

The period Moses (A) spent in Midian was perhaps one of deep, intensive spiritual training. It may be that, in the solitude of its vast, empty spaces, while he herded his flocks, his heart was opening more and more to his Lord in preparation for the high destiny He had ordained for him. For when his years of service were complete, he was ready for the most awesome of all spiritual experiences: the encounter with God, the Praised and Exalted, and the call to prophethood.

REFERENCES: Tabari/*Q*, "Musa"; Tabari/*H*, III:46; Maududi/*Q*, 28:fn. 40.

Part Three: The Call to Prophethood

13. Moses' Journey to Mount Sinai

Has the story of Moses reached you [Muhammad]? — when he saw a fire and said to his family, "Stay here. Indeed, I have seen a fire. Perhaps I may bring you a burning branch or find guidance at the fire."
(20:9-10)

When Moses had completed the term of service to his father-in-law (28:29), he decided to return to Egypt to visit his people. His arrival, however, would have to be kept secret, for he remained a wanted man on account of the murder he had committed.[28]

During the ten years of Moses' absence from Egypt, Pharaoh had reverted to the persecution of the Israelites, **slaughtering their sons but keeping their females alive** (28:4).[29] Once again their lives had become unbearable due to his cruel and inhumane policies.

Now, it is stated both in Ex. 2:23 and in the Talmud that the pharaoh of Moses' childhood had died during his stay in Midian and another pharaoh had become the ruler of Egypt. However, the words of Pharaoh when he and Moses (A) met after Moses' return to Egypt from Midian, **"Did we not raise you among ourselves as a child, and you remained among us for years of your life? And then you did your deed that you did and you were among the ungrateful"** (26:18-19), indicate that the speaker was none other than the pharaoh in whose palace he had grown up. Consequently, it seems evident that the same pharaoh was responsible for the persecution of the Israelites during the period of Moses' birth as well as during his manhood.

By the Will of the Best of Planners, it happened that one rainy winter's night, as Moses (A) was traveling toward Egypt with his family, he reached the

---

[28]The fact that this still remained an issue is clear from Moses' subsequent words, **"My Lord, indeed, I killed a person from among them, so I fear that they will kill me"** (28:33), and, **"They have a crime against me, so I fear that they will kill me"** (26:14), as well as from Pharaoh's reminding Moses in 26:19, quoted above, of **"your deed that you did."**

[29]It is also possible that there were two or more different periods of oppression of the Israelites, one before and at the time of Moses' birth and another during the current period.

vicinity of Mount Sinai.[30] However, he had lost the way and did not know which direction to take.

While Moses (A) was trying unsuccessfully to kindle a fire, all at once **he noticed a fire from the direction of the mountain** (28:29).

He said to his family, "Stay here. Indeed, I have seen a fire." And since a fire obviously involves people, he added, **"Perhaps I may bring you information from it or find guidance at the fire"** for the journey, **"or a burning firebrand, that you may warm yourselves."**[31]

Then, leaving his family behind, Moses (A) set out toward the mountain, never imagining that his life was about to be transformed in the most extraordinary manner possible.

REFERENCES: Qur'an: 20:9-10; 27:7; 28:29. Commentaries: Ibn Kathir/*T*, 28:29-32; Ibn Kathir/*Q*, "Musa"; Tabari/*H*, III:48-50. Other works: Taher/*Sinai*, p. 4.

---

[30]This mountain is known in Arabic by several names: Al-Tur or Jebel al-Tur (the Mountain), Tur Sina (Mount Sinai), and Jebel Musa (the Mountain of Moses). Part of a volcanic massif, Mount Sinai is a barren, jagged peak rising to a height of more than 2355 meters/7300 feet.

[31]Here, three passages are combined:

> **And has the story of Moses reached you [Muhammad], when he saw a fire and said to his family, "Stay here. Indeed, I have seen a fire. Perhaps I may bring you a burning branch or find guidance at the fire." (20:9-10)**
>
> **[Mention, O Muhammad,] when Moses said to his family, "Indeed, I have seen a fire. I will bring you information from it or bring you a burning brand, that you may warm yourselves." (27:7)**
>
> **Then, when Moses had completed the term [of service] and was traveling with his family, he noticed a fire from the direction of the mountain. He said to his family, "Stay here. Indeed, I have seen a fire. Perhaps I may bring you information from it, or a burning firebrand, that you may warm yourselves." (28:29)**

14. GOD MOST HIGH SPEAKS TO MOSES

And mention Moses in the Book. Indeed, he was chosen, and he was a messenger and a prophet. And We called him from the right side of the mountain and brought him near, confiding.[32] (19:51-52)

Has there reached you [Muhammad] the story of Moses, when his Lord called to him in the sacred valley of Tuwa? (79:16)

Here begins the account of one of the most awesome events ever to take place on this planet — the direct encounter of the Lord of creation, may His glory be exalted, with one of His human servants without any intermediary.[33] The report is narrated by the only possible eyewitness, God Almighty Himself, speaking, in the following verses addressed to Muhammad (S), of an event about which no human being could possibly have known except through divine revelation:

> **You were not at the western side [of Mount Sinai] when We decreed the command to Moses, nor were you among the witnesses [of what occurred];**[34] **but We brought forth [many] generations, and long was their span. And you were not a dweller among the people of Midian, reciting to them Our verses, but rather We were senders [of them]. And you were not at the side of the mountain when We called [Moses], but [you were sent as] a mercy from your Lord, to warn a people to whom no warner had come before you, that they might be reminded.**[35] (28:44-46)

---

[32]Thus, the Prophet (S) was to refer to Moses as *Naji-Ullah*, God's confidant (*Mishkat*, 5762).

[33]This is evident from the words, **God spoke to Moses with [direct] speech** (4:164), and, **"O Moses, indeed, I have chosen you above all people for My Messages and for My speech"** (7:144). However, the fact that Moses was also visited by the Angel of Revelation, Gabriel, is clear from the ***hadith*** concerning Waraqah bin Naufal, cited on pages 491-494.

[34]The meaning here is that since thousands of years had elapsed since the time of Moses, Muhammad (S) could not possibly have known anything of Moses' experience except as informed by God.

[35]In a similar vein, comments Ibn Kathir, God Most High also says concerning the virgin Mary, **That is of the tidings of the Unseen which We reveal to you [Muhammad]. And you were not with them when they cast their pens as to which of them should be responsible for Mary, nor were you with them when they disputed [concerning it]** (3:44), and, at the end of the story of Joseph, **This is of the tidings of the Unseen which We reveal to you [Muhammad]. And you were not with them when they put together their plan, while they** conspired

Moses (A) followed the light of the distant fire until he reached a valley called Tuwa at the flank of Mount Sinai.[36] No one was in sight, but in front of him was a green tree, surrounded by a fire whose flames mounted upward, while the greenness of the tree increased. When he looked up, he saw that its light reached the sky, and that it was not indeed a fire but a light — the Light of God, the One, the Unique.[37]

Then when he came to it, he was called to from the right side of the valley in a blessed spot, from the tree, "O Moses, indeed I am Allah,[38] Lord of the worlds!" (28:30).

We can imagine Moses (A), standing in stunned silence, his heart almost stopping within his chest, or falling upon his face, totally overwhelmed by awe, or perhaps on the verge of losing consciousness from the ineffable majesty of the encounter with God Most High. And the divine Voice spoke to him further, saying:

"Blessed are those who are in the fire and whoever is around it.[39] And glory be to Allah, Lord of the worlds!" And, as if to remove any lingering doubt from the heart of the trembling servant, It repeated: **"O Moses, indeed, it is I — Allah, the Almighty, the Wise** (27:8-9).

(12:102), attesting to the prophethood and veracity of Muhammad (S), and his knowledge of what could not possibly be known except by revelation from on high.

[36]Local tradition points to the foot of Mount Sinai as the site of the burning bush. In the fourth century, Christians found refuge from persecution at this spot. In around 365 CE, the emperor Constantine had a church constructed here, which in the sixth century was enclosed within the Monastery of St. Catherine, built by the emperor Justinian. These two structures remain standing to this day, under the control of Greek Orthodox monks. A tree or bush, said to be the burning bush of Moses, grows within the monastery compound. In 1106, the Chapel of St. Basil inside the monastery was converted into a mosque, and at around the same time, a mosque was also built at the summit of Mount Sinai

[37]Al-Tabari says that here "fire" (***nar***) is synonymous with "light" (***nur***) — that is, the spiritual illumination that God grants to His prophets. The Holy Prophet (S) said, "God's veil is light [or, in another version of the ***hadith***, "fire"]. If this veil were removed, the glory of His Countenance would burn His creation up to the limit of His sight" (***Muslim***, 343-344). When asked if he had seen his Lord, the Prophet (S) said, "I saw light" (***Muslim***, 342). And speaking on behalf of his Lord by divine inspiration, he said, "Between Me and My slave are seventy thousand veils of light" (***Mishkat***, I, ***Bab al-Masajid***).

[38]Because these are the words of God concerning Himself, we have here replaced the generic name "God" with "Allah," the proper Name by which He has been known in Arabic since the beginning of time and by which He refers to Himself throughout the Qur'an.

[39]Ibn Kathir gives the meaning of this as, "Blessed is the Pure and Holy One who is in this fire, and blessed are the angels who are around Him" (Ibn Kathir/*T*, 27:8).

"O Moses," he was told, **"indeed, I am your Lord, so take off your sandals.**[40] **Indeed, you are in the sacred valley of Tuwa. And I have chosen you, so listen to what is revealed** (20:11-13).

"Indeed, I am Allah," the divine Voice repeated. **"There is no deity except Me, so worship Me and establish *salat* for My remembrance"**[41] (20:11-14).

God Most High then spoke to Moses (A) of His eternal divine plan, and the testing of each soul and its requital in the Hereafter, saying, **"Indeed, the Hour** of Judgment **is coming. I virtually conceal it, that each soul may be recompensed according to what it strives for.**[42] **Therefore, do not let that one deviate you from it"** — that is, from losing sight of the Hereafter as the final destination — **"who does not believe in it but follows his own desires, lest you perish"**[43] (20:15-16).

Thus, through this unparalleled encounter with God, the Holy and Exalted, and the opening of the divine revelation to his heart, was prophethood bestowed upon Moses, God's peace and blessings be upon him. The search for an earthly fire had led the awe-stricken Israelite to the divine light of his Lord.

We may find ourselves wondering how a mere man, a weak, finite, utterly insignificant mortal, could carry the tremendousness of being thus addressed

---

[40]The command to Moses to take off his sandals is mentioned in Ex. 3:5. In keeping with this command, pilgrims remove their shoes inside the Chapel of the Burning Bush in the Monastery of St. Catherine. This reflects the Islamic rule that places of worship are not to be polluted by the dirt of the outdoors; hence, shoes are removed before entering mosques. In fact, in many places in the Muslim world and elsewhere, shoes are taken off and left at the door of the house for the sake of cleanliness.

[41]*Salat* is the worship prescribed by God through His prophets throughout the ages and practiced by Muslims.

[42]That is, so that the testing of human beings may continue and so that they will not cease striving for God's pleasure, the time of the Last Hour has been concealed from their knowledge.

[43]These sentences have an obvious connection to Moses' future mission to the god-king, Pharaoh, whom he was to remind of the inevitability of the Day of Judgment, whose time is known only to God but for which all human beings are advised to prepare throughout their lives. At the same time, Moses was also warned against letting his faith and understanding be affected by the one in whose palace he had been raised, for while Pharaoh might be the supreme ruler in Egypt, he was so misguided as to deny and defy the Lord of Majesty and Honor, imagining himself to be free of accountability, following his own false notions and desires.

by the Lord of the heavens and the earth. Perhaps one has to be a Moses to know the answer to this question. But one thing seems certain.

During the years of his childhood and youth, his young manhood with its difficult trial and his long exile in Midian, Moses (A) had been in training for this momentous hour and all that was to follow from it. Prophethood and messengership were not suddenly thrust upon an unprepared, incapable, unwilling mortal. Rather, all that had occurred up to this time, each event of Moses' life, had played its part in preparing him for it, for without such preparation he would not have been able to bear such an overwhelmingly awesome experience. By the mere fact of its occurrence, we can understand that Moses (A) must have been ready for it. Otherwise, he would doubtless have collapsed and expired on that very spot.

REFERENCES: Qur'an: 19:51-52; 20:11-16; 27:8-9; 28:30, 44-46. Commentaries: Tabari/*H*, III:48, 50-51; Ibn Kathir/*T*, 27:8-9, 28:30, 20:11-12; Ibn Ishaq/***Muhammad***, p. 107; Maududi/*Q*, 19:fn. 31, 27:fns. 8-11, 28:fns. 62-64, 20:fn. 10; Asad/*Q*, 27:fn. 7; Lings/***Muhammad***, p. 44. Other works: Taher/***Sinai***, pp. 20, 35, 42, 44, 46.

15. The Miracles of the Staff and the White Hand

"Those are two proofs from your Lord to Pharaoh and his chiefs."
(28:32)

The divine speech now took a completely different turn. Questions and commands were addressed to Moses (A) one after another in rapid succession.

"And what is that in your right hand, O Moses?" (20:17), the divine Voice enquired.

Perhaps this astonished Moses (A) still further. The Creator, the exalted, indescribably majestic Lord of the universes, was speaking to him — ***and He was asking him about his shepherd's staff!*** And dumbfounded, he answered the question with utter simplicity, based on his ordinary human perception of the wooden stick in his hand.

"It is my staff," he replied, almost as if conversing with a person. **"I lean on it and bring down leaves for my sheep with it, and I have other uses for it"** (20:18).

"Throw it down, O Moses!" (20:19; also 27:10, 28:31).

Dumbly, Moses (A) obeyed. **So he threw it down, whereupon**, to his utter amazement, **it was a snake, moving swiftly** (20:20). It is said that the two prongs at the top of the staff became the snake's mouth and fangs, and its hook became a quivering crest on its back.

Then when he saw it writhing as if it were a snake, he turned in flight and did not return[44] (27:10, 28:31).

"O Moses," the Voice commanded, **"approach and do not be afraid. Indeed, you are among the secure"** (28:31). These words were followed by a further reassurance:

"O Moses, do not fear. Indeed, the messengers need not fear in My Presence; neither need he who does wrong and then substitutes good after evil, for indeed I am Forgiving and Merciful[45] (27:10-11).

---

[44]Living in that region, Moses was obviously accustomed to snakes. But this was no ordinary snake. Ibn Kathir says that it was a huge python, which immediately swallowed a big tree and then a large rock, inspiring Moses' terror (Ibn Kathir/*T*, 20:17-21, 28:29-32). This snake is referred to variously as ***hayyatun tas'aa*, a snake, moving swiftly** (20:20); ***jaan*, a [small] snake** (27:10, 28:31); and ***thu'baanun mubin*, an obvious python** (7:107).

Then came yet another command. **"Grasp it"** — the snake — **and do not be afraid,"** he was told. **"We shall restore it to its previous state"** (20:21).

Obeying blindly, Moses (A) retraced his steps, advancing toward the fast-moving snake. And when he reached out his hand and seized it, it again became his familiar staff.

Then came another, seemingly unrelated order: **"And put your hand into your bosom. It will come forth white, without blemish — another sign, that We may show you some of Our greater signs."**[46]

Wonderstruck, Moses (A) did as he had been ordered. His hand instantly became shining white — not with a whiteness like that of leprosy, but, it is said, luminous like the moon.

Then came yet another command: **"And draw your arm close to yourself** as protection **against fear"** (28:32).

By these words, two distinct commands having two different purposes were conveyed to Moses (A). By the first, he was instructed to put his hand into the front opening of his garment, whereupon it would come out shining white — the second of the two miracles or signs bestowed upon him as proof of his messengership. And by the second command, he was instructed to draw his arm close to himself whenever he felt afraid, a personal means of reassurance granted to him by his compassionate Lord for overcoming his natural human fear under the severe trials which, unbeknownst to him, lay ahead.

REFERENCES: Qur'an: 20:17-23; 27:10-12; 28:31-32. Commentaries: Ibn Kathir/*T*, 27:10-11, 28:29-32; Tabari/*H*, III:51; Maududi/*Q*, 27:fns. 12-15, 28:fn. 45; Asad/*Q*, 27:fn. 11, 7:fn. 85; Ali/*Q*, fns. 2549, 3248.

---

[45]While these words apply generally to all people who do wrong and afterwards repent, at the same time they are also applicable specifically to Moses' accidental killing of the Egyptian, his immediate repentance, and God's forgiveness of his sin. Moses' luminously white hand may have been another assurance.

[46]Here the following verses are combined:

> **"And put/insert your hand into bosom; it will come forth white, without blemish."** (27:12, 28:32)
>
> **"And draw your hand to your side; it will come forth white, without blemish — another sign, that We may show you some of Our greater signs."** (20:22-23)

16. THE COMMAND TO GO TO PHARAOH

And We certainly gave Moses the scripture and appointed his brother Aaron with him as an assistant. (25:35)

Then, suddenly, came the first startling reference to Moses' mission and the purpose of his having been granted these miraculous signs.

"Those are two proofs, among nine signs, from your Lord to Pharaoh and his chiefs,"[47] the divine Voice declared. **"Indeed, they are a transgressing people!** (28:32; 27:12).

"Go to Pharaoh," came the order. **"Indeed, he has transgressed. And say to him, 'Would you purify yourself and let me guide you to your Lord, that you may fear?'"** (20:24; 79:18-19). That is, do you, O Pharaoh, desire to respond positively to your Lord's call and grow in grace so that you may become submissive, obedient and humble after having previously been cruel, tyrannical and arrogant? **"Go to the wrong-doing people, the people of Pharaoh,"** the divine Voice repeated. **"Will they not be mindful of God?"** (26:10-11).

Thus did God Most High convey to Moses (A) the command to return to the insolent, oppressive ruler of Egypt who regarded himself as a god, armed with no weapon other than the miraculous signs he had been granted. His mission was to invite Pharaoh and his chiefs and supporters to acknowledge their Creator as Lord, accept His guidance, and come to Him in humility and submission.

Then, as Moses (A) began to grasp the significance of his Lord's order and the tremendousness of the task for which he had been chosen, he became deeply troubled with doubts and questions about his ability to carry it out, as two grave obstacles immediately presented themselves to his mind.

One was that, while such a mission required fluency and eloquence in speaking, he had a speech impediment that would seriously hamper his ability to communicate with those to whom he was sent.

"My Lord," he said, voicing this concern, **"expand my breast for me and ease my task for me, and loosen the knot from my tongue, that they**

[47]That is, the changing of the staff to a snake and the luminous white hand were the first of nine signs granted to Moses to convince Pharaoh and his notables of the truth of his mission. The other seven signs are detailed on pages 81-84.

may understand my speech"[48] (20:25-28). **"Indeed, I fear that they will deny me and that my chest will tighten and my tongue will not be fluent"** (26:12-13).

Then, as if in answer to his own thought, an idea suddenly occurred to him.

"And my brother Aaron is more clear in speech than I, so send him with me as a support, confirming me. Indeed, I fear that they will deny me" (28:34), he said. And he restated his request, saying:

"Appoint for me an assistant from my family — Aaron, my brother. Increase my strength through him and let him share my task, that we may glorify You much and remember You much. Indeed, You are ever seeing of us" (20:29-34).

"We shall strengthen your arm through your brother and grant you both authority so they will not reach you," God Most High replied. **"With Our signs, you and those who follow you will be the victors"** (28:35). Thus did God not only grant Moses' request for an assistant from his own family, but He also granted that assistant the authority of prophethood, as suggested by the words, **And We granted him, out of Our mercy, his brother Aaron as a prophet** (19:53).[49]

Relieved of this concern, Moses (A) then mentioned the other matter that he was certain would render the carrying out of his mission impossible:

"And they have a crime against me. My Lord, indeed, I killed a person from among them, so I fear that they will kill me" (26:14, 28:33).

"By no means!" the All-Knowing Lord assured him. **"Go, both of you, with Our signs. Indeed, We are with you, listening"** (26:15). That is, We

---

[48]Concerning this supplication, Ibn Kathir comments that, because prophets are very modest in making personal requests of their Lord, Moses merely asked to be able to speak plainly enough to be understood by those whom he was going to address (Ibn Kathir/T, 20:27-28). However, by the granting of his request, he was both enabled to speak plainly enough to be understood and given Aaron as an assistant.

[49]In this context, it is reported that once when the Prophet's wife 'A'ishah stayed with some bedouins on the way to '*Umrah*, she heard someone asking which brother had benefitted his brother most. No one was able to answer this question until one of the bedouins said that he knew the answer. 'A'ishah looked at the man, thinking how bold he was to state that he knew something without prefacing it with "*Insha'Allah*, God willing." When the people asked the bedouin to tell them who it was, he replied, "It is Moses, who, through his supplication, had his brother made a prophet." 'A'ishah then commented that although she was surprised by his answer, she realized that he was speaking the truth (Ibn Kathir/*T*, 20:29-30).

are aware of every plot they may frame and every action they may intend, and We are completely, absolutely, in control. **"Go to Pharaoh and say, 'Indeed, we are messengers of the Lord of the worlds'"** (26:16), meaning, "We are emissaries of God Almighty, who is calling you, through us, to surrender to Him."

Then came a further command, one that presented even greater difficulties: that after calling Pharaoh to acknowledge and submit to his Creator, Moses and Aaron were to say to him, **"Send the Children of Israel forth with us"** (26:16-17). That is, as authorized representatives of God Almighty, on whose behalf we are speaking, we are requesting you to permit our people to leave Egypt and put an end to the degrading bondage in which you have held them.

These were tremendously heavy and troubling orders. But then, to give Moses (A) courage and reassurance concerning what lay ahead, his Lord spoke to him about how lovingly and miraculously He had safeguarded him in the past, mentioning the three dangerous and deadly trials through which He had earlier protected His chosen servant, saying:

"And We already conferred favor upon you another time, when We inspired to your mother what We inspired: 'Drop him in the chest and drop it into the river, and the river will cast it onto the bank. There will take him up an enemy to Me and an enemy to him' (20:37-39).

"And I bestowed love upon you from Myself, that you might be reared under My Eye," the Most Gracious Lord continued, **"when your sister went and said, 'Shall I direct you to someone who will feed him?' Then We restored you to your mother, that she might be content and not grieve** (20:39-40).

"Then you killed a person but We saved you from the affliction, and We tried you with a trial. And you stayed for years among the people of Midian. Then you came here at the decreed time, O Moses. And I chose you for Myself" (20:41).

By these tender words did the merciful Lord assure His startled, anxious bondsman he was a very special, beloved servant of His who would always be under His divine protection and guidance, and that he was destined never to stand alone but to be always supported by heavenly power. He further made Moses (A) aware that all that had happened to him up to this moment, including the heavy trials to which he had been subjected, had been by His divine ordaining, that Moses might reach the high station and exalted destiny decreed for him.

Summarizing these events, Ibn 'Abbas (R) says:

After that, Moses traveled with his family, and there is the matter of the fire and the staff and the hand which God has described in the Qur'an. And Moses complained to God Most High that he feared the people of Pharaoh because of the killing and about his having a speech impediment, for he had a defect in his tongue which prevented him from speaking much, and he asked his Lord to support him with his brother Aaron so that he might say for him much of what he was unable to say clearly with his own tongue. So God the Exalted and Glorious granted him what he asked and unloosed the defect in his tongue. And God sent a revelation to Aaron, commanding him to meet him. (*Hadith* of the Trials)

Nothing is known of the details of this meeting between Moses (A) and his elder brother. But during or after it, further instructions were addressed to the two prophets by their Lord.

"Go, you and your brother, with My signs, and do not slacken in My remembrance. Go, both of you, to Pharaoh. Indeed, he has transgressed. And speak to him with gentle speech, that perhaps he may be reminded or fear" (20:42-44).

"Our Lord," they said, **"indeed, we are afraid that he may act hastily against us or that he may transgress all bounds"**[50] (20:45).

"Do not fear," God Most High reassured them. **"Indeed, I am with you both. I hear and see"** (20:42-46).

Despite these extremely strong divine assurances, however, the situation was fraught with the gravest dangers and dilemmas for Moses (A). Had he not been raised as Pharaoh's son, living with him in his palace and accepting all sorts of favors and bounties from his royal hand? And had he not killed a man, although purely by accident, and fled from Pharaoh's punishment like a common criminal? How then was he now, several years later, to appear before the god-king, not as his adopted son but as one claiming to be a prophet, appointed by the Lord of the heavens and earth — and, if that were not enough, to order him to release the enslaved, oppressed Israelites and permit them to depart from Egypt with him?

---

[50]Meaning that Pharaoh might act impulsively and without reflection, committing whatever transgressions he pleased in order to prevent the two prophets from carrying out their appointed mission.

Nonetheless, Moses (A), whose understanding had been completely transformed during this unprecedented encounter with the Lord of Glory and Majesty, surrendered his will and prepared himself to obey the divine command. Whereas but a short while earlier he had been a raw, simple shepherd who naively said to God Almighty that his staff was a tool he used for herding his flocks,[51] he had now been raised to the rank of the messenger of the Most High, who had witnessed something of his Lord's miraculous signs and tasted something of spiritual realities.

What he had taken to be a fire was in truth the light of God. His old familiar staff was, on another plane of existence, a writhing serpent, and on a still deeper level, an agent of truth that devoured falsehood. The hand that held the staff was, in the realm of spiritual realities, a radiant, shining entity, totally different from his ordinary physical limb, and a manifestation of divine power.

From all this, it had become clear that underlying all physical appearances are deeper realities known only to God Most High, which He reveals to such of His servants as He chooses. By the light of this new spiritual insight, Moses (A) would be able to discern the true nature of the actors whom he was now to encounter in his life-drama. While on the earthly plane Pharaoh might seem to be an all-powerful god-king, ruling unchallenged over the land of Egypt, in reality he was nothing but a finite mortal, the helpless slave of his All-Powerful Creator, whom He could destroy at the instant of His willing it. On yet another level of reality, he was the archenemy of God and of truth, at war with Him, His chosen messengers and His believing servants, the personification of all Godless, anti-religious systems and regimes up to the end of the world. The magicians Moses (A) was later to encounter, who on an earthly plane were sorcerers manipulating people's perceptions and senses by their craft, were potential believers in their Lord, destined to be among His chosen and beloved servants. Al-Samiri, the clever fabricator of the Golden Calf, was, at one level, a man endowed with spiritual insight, and on another, a misguided evil genius, doing Satan's work among the Israelites.

Through this unveiling, the new prophet was given the assurance that he need not depend, as people ordinarily do, upon physical means and resources, but solely upon his Lord, the Dominant and Powerful, the Protector of the believers. He had thus passed from the stage of reliance upon material causes

---

[51]This raises an interesting paradox: While God Most High is the Unique, the Self-Sufficient, free of all needs, independent of all His creation, the Glorious, Majestic and Exalted, He may nonetheless condescend to reach His servants at their own level, even to the extent that the preceding conversation could take place with Moses concerning his common shepherd's staff.

and means to total reliance upon the Trustworthy Guardian, who is able to do whatsoever He wills. And through this dawning of understanding of the realities underlying appearances and his Lord's wisdom and power at work in all things, did God Most High prepare His chosen servant for the immensely daunting task before him.

REFERENCES: Qur'an: 19:53; 20:24-46; 25:35; 26:10-17; 27:12; 28:32-35; 79:18-19. Commentaries: Ibn Kathir/*T*, 20:27-41, 28:32-35; Ibn Kathir/*Juz' 'Amma*, p. 31; Tabari/*H*, III:51-52; Asad/*Q*, 20:fn. 29; Ali/*Q*, fns. 3244, 3246-3247.

PART FOUR: MOSES AND PHARAOH

17. THE DIALOGUES

These are the verses of the clear Book. We relate to you [Muhammad] something of the tidings of Moses and Pharaoh in truth for a people who believe. (28:2-3)

Then after them [the earlier prophets], We sent Moses to Pharaoh and his chiefs, but they behaved wrongfully with them. Then see what was the end of the corrupters! (7:103)

Guided and directed by their Lord, Moses and Aaron (A) proceeded as they had been commanded.

It is reported that when they went to Pharaoh's palace and were given permission to enter, they did not waste words or stand on formality. Instead, they proclaimed their mission forthrightly, calling on Pharaoh to acknowledge his Creator and accept the authority that He had vested in them as His emissaries.[52]

Numerous Qur'anic passages speak of the meetings between Pharaoh, surrounded by his chief officials and advisors, and the two brother prophets. These passages contain virtually no mention of time, place or circumstance. Indeed, there is so little emphasis on such matters in the Qur'anic narratives in general that the prophets, their people and their adversaries often seem almost depersonalized, representing prototypes and models of character and conduct rather than specific personalities or groups of people related to a specific time and place.

---

[52]Ibn 'Abbas says that when God commissioned Moses and Aaron, He advised them not to be deceived by the garment in which He had clothed Pharaoh, who could not utter a single word or blink his eye without His leave, nor to be deceived by the comforts and pleasures of this world, which comprise the lot of the ornate and the luxury of the opulent. If He willed, their Lord said, He could clothe the two of them in greater finery than any that Pharaoh could produce. His withholding it from them was therefore not because they were unworthy of it but because He had clothed them with such honor and exaltedness that beside it the world was insignificant, for He protects His deputies from this world and its pleasures and finery as a shepherd protects his flock from eating poisonous grass in order to illumine their stations and purify their hearts. And anyone who persecutes or causes fear to His deputies has declared war on God Himself and will meet with His severe wrath on the Last Day (Akili/*B*, p. 10).

This is clearly no accident but is rather the product of the deepest divine wisdom, for these stories are meant to serve as examples and lessons in which personal and historical details have little relevance. As such, they generally represent prototypes of commitment to truth, righteousness and submission to the divine Will and command, or to evil, injustice and obedience to the commands of Satan and the lower self.

At the same time, we humans are curious creatures. It is therefore again by divine wisdom that Muslims assiduously sought details related to the Qur'anic narratives, eager for anything that might have bearing on what God, the All-Wise and All-Knowing, had deemed of sufficient importance to mention in His Last Testament.

Three dialogues are reported between Moses (A) and Pharaoh which inform mankind of what could never have been known except through divine revelation — namely, the manner in which Moses' mission to Pharaoh was carried out. We cite these below without regard to their sequence in time, which is unknown. In each, Moses' earnest attempt to appeal to Pharaoh's intelligence and reason is evident. Then, when the arrogant ruler failed to respond to truth and reason came the next step: to convince him by miraculous proofs of his Creator's limitless power.

From these dialogues, it will be seen that Pharaoh showed no serious interest in reflecting on what Moses (A) was saying to him. Rather, certain of his power over the killer-turned-prophet, he amused himself at Moses' expense in front of the high officials, advisors, priests and other notables who always surrounded and supported him. And when Moses (A) showed him God's signs, despite the fact that these signs presented unrefutable evidence of a power at work unlike that of any earthly source, the proud ruler and his chiefs turned away and made light of them, ascribing them to mere magic.

REFERENCES: Tabari/*Q*, "Musa"; Tabari/*H*, III:52, 54.

26:16-33

"Indeed, we are messengers of the Lord of the worlds,"[53] Moses (A) announced boldly to Pharaoh, **"commanded to say to you, 'Send the Children of Israel forth with us.'"**

[53] In 7:104 and 43:46, it is, **"I am a messenger from/of the Lord of the worlds."**

Recognizing Moses immediately, Pharaoh reacted with both surprise and fury at seeing this outlaw, his former adopted son, standing before him and challenging his power and authority in the name of the Supreme Deity — and not only that, but giving him orders in His name, as well. But from the fact that he did not attempt to argue with the command that had been conveyed to him concerning the Israelites, it is clear that he understood Moses' meaning well enough.

His initial defense was to heap reproaches on Moses (A) related to the past.

"Did we not bring you up among ourselves as a child, and you stayed among us for years of your life?" he demanded. **"And then you did your deed that you did and you were among the ungrateful."**

Perhaps this was precisely what Moses (A) had expected. But since his innocence in the inadvertent killing of the Egyptian had been accepted by his Lord, he was able to reply to Pharaoh's charges without either fear or guilt.

"I did it, then, while I was among the erring," he replied, referring to the fact that the killing had been accidental, not deliberate murder. **"Then I fled from you when I feared you, but my Lord granted me wisdom and made me among the messengers."**

He then delivered a stinging rebuke to Pharaoh's reproach of ingratitude:

"And this is the favor of which you remind me: that you have enslaved the Children of Israel!"[54]

Doubtless, Pharaoh had not expected such a direct and bold confrontation. Yet, for reasons that we cannot know — perhaps because such a length of time had elapsed, or possibly because Moses' reproach evoked some trace of guilt within his heart — he did not refer further to the matter of the killing. Instead, he changed the subject abruptly, thereby evading the issue of his treatment of the Israelites.

"And what is the 'Lord of the worlds'?" he asked lightly, referring to Moses' earlier words.

"Lord of the heavens and the earth and whatever is between them, if you were but to be convinced," Moses (A) proclaimed, appealing to Pharaoh's understanding.

---

[54]That is, "If you had not oppressed and enslaved my people, there would have been no need for my mother to have taken the drastic action that resulted in my being brought up in your palace."

"Do you not hear?" Pharaoh demanded sarcastically of those around him.

"Your Lord and Lord of your earlier ancestors," Moses (A) continued, disregarding the interruption.

"Indeed, your 'messenger' who has been sent to you is mad!" Pharaoh exclaimed to his courtiers.

"Lord of the East and the West and whatever is between them, if you were but to use reason," Moses (A) went on, speaking as one inspired.

"If you take a god other than me," Pharaoh exploded, **"I will surely have you imprisoned!"**[55]

"Even if I brought you something obvious?" Moses (A) asked.

"Then bring it, if you are of the truthful!" Pharaoh retorted contemptuously.

Then he threw down his staff, whereupon it was an obvious snake,[56] **and he drew forth his hand, whereupon it was** shining **white to the onlookers.**[57]

REFERENCES: Tabari/*H*, III:52-55; Maududi/*Q*, 26:fns. 18, 20, 24, 27-29; Ali/*Q*, fns. 3147-3151, 3154, 1075-1076.

---

[55]Literally, **"I will surely place you among the imprisoned."** In light of the fact that the Egyptians worshipped a multitude of gods, Pharaoh's saying **"If you take a god other than me"** is to be understood in the sense of the supreme authority in the land. Says Muhammad Asad, "In the religion of ancient Egypt, the king (or 'Pharaoh', as each of the rulers was styled) represented an incarnation of the divine principle, and was considered a god in his own right. Hence, a challenge to his divinity implied a challenge to the prevalent religious system as a whole" (Asad/*Q*, 26:fn. 17). Such a challenge may therefore have been an offense punishable by imprisonment — or worse.

[56]Yusuf Ali points out that the snake was given considerable importance in Egyptian mythology, for it was believed that the powerful sun-god Ra had defeated the serpent Apophis, symbolizing the victory of light over darkness. In addition, many of the Egyptian gods and goddesses were believed to take the form of snakes to impress their enemies. Thus, the changing of Moses' staff into a snake turned the contempt of Pharaoh and his courtiers into terror, as God defeated them according to their own understanding and logic (Ali/*Q*, fn. 1075).

[57]Yusuf Ali suggests that this miracle may have been the more impressive of the two, for Moses' white hand shone with a pure, heavenly radiance, as if to offset the evil of the serpent that he had brought forth only moments earlier. In the purity of the white hand, the Egyptians may have recognized a sacred light that no magician's artifice could produce (Ali/*Q*, fn. 1076).

20:47-56

"Indeed, we are two messengers of your Lord, so send the Children of Israel forth with us and do not torment them," the brother prophets proclaimed to Pharaoh, as God had commanded them. **"We have come to you with a sign from your Lord. And peace be upon him who follows the guidance. Indeed, it has been revealed to us that the punishment will be upon him who denies and turns away."**

"Then who is the Lord of you two, O Moses?"[58] Pharaoh asked with the same idle curiosity.

"Our Lord is He who gave each thing its nature and then guided it," Moses (A) replied. His task was simply to deliver the Message: that God Most High is the One who creates all things, grants His creations their natures, forms and characteristics, and then guides them to the destinies He has decreed for them.

"Then what is the case of the former generations?" Pharaoh demanded, setting a trap for Moses. Perhaps he imagined that the returned criminal would be so naive as to denounce the earlier generations of idol-worshipping Egyptians, thereby losing any sympathy he might otherwise have gained among the people.

But the All-Wise Lord had instructed Moses (A) to speak to Pharaoh **with gentle speech** (20:44) that might move his heart, not to engage him in philosophical debates. **"The knowledge of it is with God in a record,"** Moses (A) replied simply. **"My Lord neither errs nor forgets."**[59]

---

[58]It is noteworthy that while Moses had spoken to Pharaoh of **"your Lord,"** Pharaoh, to show his utter disdain for the two prophets and their God, responded by asking about **"the Lord of you two."**

[59]After the words, **"My Lord neither errs nor forgets,"** God Most High adds:

> — **He who has made the earth as a bed for you and inserted roadways for you upon it, and has sent down water from the sky and brought forth therewith species of diverse plants. Eat [of them] and pasture your cattle! Surely in that are signs for those of intelligence. From it [the earth] We created you, and into it We shall return you, and from it We shall bring you forth another time.** (20:53-55)

The commentators differ as to whether these verses form part of Moses' speech to Pharaoh or are a parenthetical comment by the divine Author of the Qur'an to mankind generally, as is suggested by the three-fold use of the pronoun **"We"** in the last sentence. We have followed the latter view, which is held by al-Tabari, Ibn Kathir and al-Razi, among the classical commentators, and is reflected in the Maududi, Asad, Hilali-Khan and Saheeh translations.

And We certainly showed him Our signs, all of them, God Most High continues, **but he denied and rejected.** That is, out of sheer arrogance, Pharaoh denied the obvious fact that these signs had come from the Creator of the heavens and the earth, refusing to be sufficiently humble to declare his submission to Him and accept His guidance.

REFERENCES: Tabari/*H*, III:52-55; Maududi/*Q*, 20:fns. 21-26; Asad/*Q*, 20:fns. 31, 34; Ali/*Q*, fns. 1075-1076, 2572-2575.

7:104-108

"O Pharaoh," Moses (A) declared to the proud ruler, **"indeed, I am a messenger from the Lord of the worlds, obliged not to say other than the truth about God. I have come to you with clear evidence from your Lord, so send the Children of Israel forth with me."**

"If you have come with a sign, then produce it, if you are among the truthful," Pharaoh commanded.

Then he threw down his staff, whereupon it was an obvious snake, and he drew forth his hand, whereupon it was shining **white to the onlookers.**

Summarizing this segment of the story, Ibn 'Abbas (R) says:

> The two [prophets] went together to Pharaoh, and they stood at his gate but he would not admit them. Finally, after a long wait, he admitted them and they said, **"Indeed, we are messengers of your Lord"** [20:47; 26:16]. And he responded, **"So who is the Lord of you two, O Moses?"** [20:49], and they informed him as is reported to you in the Qur'an. And Pharaoh asked, "What do you desire?" and mentioned the killing, and Moses gave the excuse which you have heard, and then Moses said, "I desire that you believe in God and send the Children of Israel forth with me," but he rejected them and said, **"If you have come with a sign, then produce it, if you are among the truthful"** [7:106].
>
> Then he threw down his staff and it became a huge snake, which rushed toward Pharaoh with open jaws. When Pharaoh saw it coming toward him, he leaped from his throne in terror and appealed to Moses to keep it from him, which he did. And he took his hand out of his bosom and it became white — that is, without leprosy. Then he put his hand back into it and it reverted to its former hue. (*Hadith* of the Trials)

REFERENCES: Tabari/*H*, III:53; Ibn Kathir/*Q*, "Musa"; Asad/*Q*, 7:fn. 85; Ali/*Q*, fns. 1071-1076.

18. The Summoning of the Magicians

Then after them [Noah and his successors], We sent Moses and Aaron to Pharaoh and his chiefs with Our signs, but they behaved arrogantly and were a sinful people. And when the truth came to them from Us, they said, "Indeed, this is obvious magic." (10:75-76)

Then, when Our visible signs came to them, they said, "This is obvious magic." (27:13)

Pharaoh was both astounded and awed by the two tremendous miracles Moses (A) had shown him.[60] But as the ruler of a land in which all kinds of magic, sorcery and occult arts were practiced at his command and with his approval, he had an immediate explanation for these signs, an explanation whereby he was able to avoid considering the source of power behind such unprecedented occurrences.[61]

Insulating himself against any questioning concerning what had occurred, **he said to the chiefs around him, "Indeed, this is a skilled magician who wants to drive you out of your land by his magic"** (26:34-35; also 7:110).

"Indeed, this is obvious magic!" (10:76; 27:13), his courtiers and advisors echoed.

"Do you speak thus **about the truth when it has come to you?"** Moses (A) retorted. **"Is *this* magic?"** meaning, "How can you be so mindless as to confuse miracles with magic, for miracles pertain to truth and reality, while magic is a falsification of reality, and truth cannot be mistaken for falsehood by people of understanding. **"But never will the magicians prosper!"** (10:77), for indeed those who engage in occult practices — prohibited in every true religion — can never hope to attain any good.

---

[60]Various commentators report that before seeing Moses' signs, Pharaoh had been so constipated that his bowels had moved only once in forty days, and his not producing excrement was taken by his people as an indication of his superhuman power. But afterwards, because of the effect of Moses' huge, fearsome snake, he was constantly occupied in the toilet.

[61]The prevalence of magical practices and the importance of magicians in ancient Egypt is well-documented by historians. For example, P. H. Newby mentions that during this period of Egyptian history there was a great reliance on magic, its practitioners and their trappings, even by "the centralized, autocratic state," which used such means to coerce its citizens into conformity (Newby/*Warrior Pharaohs*, page 172; also pages 123, 249, 369-370, 498). Donald B. Redford's book, *Egypt, Canaan, and Israel in Ancient Times*, also contains several references to magic and magicians (pages 89, 383, 385, 427-428, 410, 411, fn. 88).

But the courtiers had a ready defense.

"Have you come to us to turn us away from what we found our fathers doing, and that you two may have glory in the land?" they demanded. **"But we are not believers in you!"** (10:78). And reducing the matter to an issue of rank and power, they added: **"Shall we believe in two mortals like ourselves, while their people are in bondage to us?"** (23:47).

"My Lord is most knowing of who has come with guidance from Him and whose will be the final Home," Moses (A) declared. That is, God knows that He has sent me with the true guidance, and He knows that only those who are guided will attain the Home of the Hereafter. **"Indeed, the wrong-doers will not prosper!"** (28:37).

Pharaoh and his chiefs then took counsel together. **"So what do you advise?"** (7:110; 26:35), they asked one another.

"Defer him and his brother, and send gatherers into the cities, who will bring you every skilled magician" (7:111-112; 26:36-37), they decided by common consent.[62]

"Have you come to us to drive us out of our land by your magic, O Moses?" Pharaoh then demanded of his former adopted son. **"Then we will surely provide you with magic like it, so fix an appointment between ourselves and you which neither we nor you will fail to keep, in an assigned place"** (20:57-58).

Perhaps this was precisely what Moses (A) had hoped for. Trusting totally in his Lord's power, he expected such an encounter to make truth distinct from falsehood to the onlookers — perhaps especially to Pharaoh himself. He therefore unhesitatingly proposed for the magic contest a time that would ensure the greatest attendance, saying, **"Your appointment is the day of the festival, when the people assemble at mid-morning"** (20:59-60).

Pharaoh's command, **"Bring me every skilled magician"** (10:79), then went forth, summoning his cadre of well-trained sorcerers from the various parts of his realm. Even though the proud ruler had been deeply awed and shaken by the signs Moses had shown him, he managed to brush the matter aside, certain that his most talented, famous magicians would be able to over-

---

[62]Concerning the reaching of this decision by mutual consultation between Pharaoh and his advisors, please see footnote 63.

come the magic of this upstart Israelite. Soon Moses would taste his invincible power!

Then Pharaoh departed, and he assembled his plan and then came (20:60).

REFERENCES: Qur'an: 7:109-112; 10:75-79; 20:56-60; 23:45-47; 26:34-37; 27:13; 28:36-37; 51:38-39. Commentaries: Tabari/*H*, III:53, 55-57, 61; Ibn Kathir/*T*, 20:56-60.

19. The Magic Contest

And [as for God's signs,] they rejected them, although their souls were convinced of them, out of injustice and self-exaltation. Then see what was the end of the corrupters! (27:14)

And Moses was denied. (22:44)

Then the magicians were assembled for the rendezvous of a well-known day, and it was said to the people, "Will you gather, that we may follow the magicians if they are the victors?" (26:38-40).

And when the magicians came to the place of the contest, **they said to Pharaoh, "Will there indeed be a reward for us if we are the victors?"** (26:41, 7:113).

"Yes," he replied, **"and indeed you will then be among those near** to me" (26:42, 7:114).

Thus did Pharaoh bribe the magicians with promises of future glory if they defeated his enemy, representing not themselves but ***him***. The summons to his people to **follow the magicians if they are the victors** actually meant, "We will reaffirm our confidence in Pharaoh through the triumph of his sorcerers, and then, by following them, we will follow him."

It is probable that a huge crowd of people answered the summons and gathered to watch the competition between the throng of Pharaoh's mightiest magicians and the two solitary Israelites. Undoubtedly the magicians were all outfitted in attire suggestive of their awesome power, which dazzled the eye and produced fear in the heart. They brought with them their magical accoutrements, evidently consisting of cords or ropes and staffs, and perhaps many other tools of their trade. Moses and Aaron (A) certainly stood out in sharp contrast — two plain, simple men clad in the most ordinary clothing, one of whom carried nothing more awe-inspiring than a wooden shepherd's staff.

According to the account of Ibn Kathir, Pharaoh set up his throne at the field of the contest. All his courtiers and ministers took their seats, and the people assembled. The magicians stood row upon row in front of his throne, and Pharaoh encouraged them, saying, "Show your skill to the utmost so that its remembrance may remain on earth."

Then from the other side, *Kalim-Ullah*, the Speaker-with-God, Moses, God's peace and blessings be upon him, began to admonish the assembled magicians.

"Woe to you!" he exclaimed. **"Do not fabricate a lie against God, lest He destroy you with a punishment, and whoever fabricates** falsehood **will be defeated"** (20:61).

Hearing these words, the magicians **disputed their affair among themselves and concealed their private conversation** (20:62) from the two prophets.

Some of them, realizing that this was not the speech of a magician, concluded that these two men were probably messengers of God. But others had a different view.

"Indeed, these are two magicians who want to drive you out of your land by their magic and do away with your ideal religion" (20:63), they decided among themselves. "These two brothers are nothing but high-calibre sorcerers. You have now found favor in the sight of the king, and are wealthy and enjoying life. But if these two are victorious today, they will take over the land, driving you out of it and destroying your religion, and you will become poor and debased. Therefore, let us all be united and show the best of our skills and defeat them — and you have already heard that the king will make you his special courtiers. **So,"** they advised one another, **"resolve upon your plan and then approach in ranks. And he who is victorious today will prosper!"** (20:64).

Ibn 'Abbas (R) reports the preceding events as follows:

> Then he [Pharaoh] consulted with his chiefs around him and asked their opinion, and they said to him, **"Indeed, these are two magicians who want to drive you out of your land by their magic and do away with your ideal religion"**[63] [20:63]. They told him to deny Moses'

---

[63]Similar words occur in three passages: (1) 20:63, cited above, following the words, **So they [the magicians] disputed their affair among themselves and concealed their private conversation;** (2) **"Indeed, this is a skilled magician who wants to drive you out of your land"** (7:109-110), spoken by Pharaoh's chiefs; and, (3) **"Indeed, this is a skilled magician who wants to drive you out of your land by his magic"** (26:34-35), spoken by Pharaoh. The second and third passages are followed by the words, **"Defer him and his brother, and send gatherers into the cities, who will bring you every skilled magician"** (7:111-112, 26:36-37). Although, in the account of Ibn 'Abbas above, the words, **"Indeed, these are two magicians who want to drive you out of your land by their magic and do away with your ideal religion"** (20:63), are attributed to Pharaoh's chiefs, al-Tabari, Ibn Kathir and other early commentators state that they were spoken by the magicians (Ibn Kathir/*Q*, "Musa"; Tabari/*H*, III:57, 61). But regardless of whether the actual words were uttered by Pharaoh, his chiefs or the magicians, it is evident that all of them spoke with the same voice concerning Moses and his "signs," and no doubt made similar comments many times over.

demands and advised him to summon his magicians, who would defeat him.

He then called for all the magicians from across the land and they all gathered. They asked, "What kind of magic does Moses do?"

Pharaoh's people told them that he changed a staff into a snake. They said, "Is that all? We can change our staffs and cords into snakes, and no one on this earth can compete with them. But first, a reward should be set for us."

Pharaoh promised to bestow great rewards upon them, make them his favorite courtiers, and give to them abundantly. Then they announced that on the day of the festival, at about mid-day, they would hold a competition at such-and-such field. It is reported that this festival was on the tenth of Muharram.[65]

The people gathered at that field to see who would be victorious, saying to one other, **"Will you assemble, that we may follow the magicians if they are the victors?"** [26:40]. (*Hadith* of the Trials)

Before beginning the contest, the magicians did Moses (A) the courtesy of asking him who was to begin, perhaps because they secretly realized that the power behind this plain, simple, solitary man must be from a source greater than theirs.

"O Moses," they said to him, **"either you throw, or** otherwise **we will be the first to throw"** (20:65).

"Rather, you throw"[66] (20:66), Moses (A) replied.

So they threw their cords and staffs,[67] **exclaiming, "By Pharaoh's might, indeed, it is we who are the victors!"** (26:43-44). **And when they threw, they spellbound the eyes of the people and struck terror into them, and they produced stupendous magic** (7:116).

---

[65]That is, the first month of the Arabic lunar calendar, which pre-dates Islam by perhaps thousands of years.

[66]This is mentioned in three other passages as well: **They said, "O Moses, either you throw or we will be the [first] ones to throw." He said, "Throw!"** (7:115-116); and, **Then, when the magicians arrived, Moses said to them, "Throw whatever you will throw!"** (10:80, 26:43).

[67]Ropes and cords have long been used in foretelling the future and other occult practices, as mentioned in Qur'an 113:4.

As Moses (A) watched, **their cords and their staffs seemed to him, due to their magic, as though they were moving. And Moses felt fear within himself**[67] (20:66-67).

Then the divine inspiration came to his heart: **"Do not fear. Indeed, you will be the uppermost. And throw what is in your right hand"**[68] — the staff. **"It will swallow up whatever they have fabricated"** (20:68-69). This was followed by the further reassurance: **"What they have fabricated is only a magician's trick, but never will the magician prosper, whatever he may aim at"**[69] (20:68-69).

The fear then left Moses' heart. He quickly grasped the reality underlying these appearances: that the "magic" wrought by the sorcerers was simply an illusion, so much mental and visual trickery without substance, meant to fool the unwary. But what he held in his hand was invested with the power and authority of the Lord of the worlds.

"What you have produced is mere magic," he proclaimed boldly. **"God will surely bring it to nought. Indeed, God does not amend the work of the corrupters, and God will establish the truth by His word, even if the sinners detest it!"** (10:81-82).

Then Moses threw his staff, and it became a gigantic serpent. And facing all the illusory snakes simulated by the sorcerers' magic, **at once it swallowed up whatever they were falsifying** (7:117; 26:45).

Then Moses (A) seized the serpent and again it became his familiar staff in his hand. **Thus was the truth confirmed and what they** — Pharaoh and his supporters — **did was nullified, and were overcome on the spot and overturned, debased** (7:117-119).

---

[67]Muhammad Asad suggests that the spellbinding of the eyes of the people indicates that the magicians produced an effect based on mass hallucination, which affected even Moses temporarily (Asad/Q, 20:fn. 48).

[68]In 7:117, it is, **"Throw your staff!"** These verses provide an important insight into the world of appearances and illusions. By a feat of magic, the magicians' staffs and ropes turned into swiftly-moving snakes. Then, by an act of God — a miracle, not magic — the simple shepherd's staff in Moses' hand, an implement externally similar to the magicians' staffs, became the destroyer of these illusions.

[69]Literally, **"wherever he may come,"** meaning regardless of whether he aims at a good or an evil end. That is, if someone's intention is to invoke occult forces to influence the course of events or to create illusions that delude people, it does not matter whether his intention is "good" or "bad" because the act itself is sinful and strictly prohibited.

Says Ibn 'Abbas (R):

Then after they had cast a spell on the eyes of the people, they said to Moses, **"O Moses, either you throw, or we will be the ones to throw first."** So **he said, "Throw!"** [7:115-116], whereupon **they threw their cords and staffs, and said "By Pharaoh's might, indeed, it is we who are the victors!"** [26:43-44].

When Moses saw this magic of theirs, he felt fear in his heart, and then God revealed to him, **"Throw your staff!"** [7:117].

When he threw it, it became a huge python, which rushed toward all these staffs and cords, and all of them went into its mouth until there was not a single staff or cord that was not swallowed by it. (*Hadith* of the Trials)

REFERENCES: Qur'an: 7:113-119; 10:80-82; 20:61-69; 26:38-45; 27:14. Commentaries: Ibn Kathir/*Q*, "Musa"; Ibn Kathir/*T*, 20:60-64, 7:115-119; Tabari/*H*, III:56-58, fn. 329, 61-62; Maududi/*Q*, 20:fns. 41-42; Asad/*Q*, 20:fn. 48-49.

20. THE END OF THE MAGICIANS

Then the magicians fell down in prostration. (7:120, 20:70, 26:46)

Pharaoh's magicians had been defeated, but not Pharaoh himself. Even though Moses (A) had shown him **the greatest sign**, the turning of the staff into a huge and terrifying serpent, still he **denied and disobeyed. Then he turned his back, striving** (79:20-22) against God and against truth. Thus, God says,

> **He fooled his people and they obeyed him. Indeed, they were a transgressing people.** (43:54)

But although Pharaoh was able to fool most of his people, he could not fool them all. Seeing the tremendous power which the solitary Israelite had unleashed with his simple shepherd's staff, the company of magicians at once recognized that it bore no resemblance to the conjured-up illusions they were accustomed to producing.

Then the magicians fell down in prostration, exclaiming, **"We believe in the Lord of the worlds, the Lord of Moses and Aaron!"** (7:120-122, 26:46-48, 20:70). And it is reported that while they were in prostration, God Most High showed them their places in Paradise. Says Ibn 'Abbas (R):

> When the magicians saw this, they understood that this was no magic but was rather a true miracle or sign from God, and that magic cannot produce such a thing. They said, "If it had been magic, it would not have reached the level of our magic, so it must be from God. Therefore, we believe in God and in what Moses has brought, and we all turn to God, repentant." Thus did God break the back of Pharaoh and his partisans at this place. And the truth became apparent and **what they did was nullified, and they were overcome on the spot and overturned, debased** [7:118-119].
>
> While this was taking place, Pharaoh's wife was praying fervently to God the Glorious to make Moses victorious over Pharaoh and his followers. Pharaoh's people saw her praying but they thought that she was praying for her husband's victory, whereas her concern and prayers were all for Moses. (*Hadith* of the Trials)

Now, as commonly understood, the meaning of a contest is that whoever wins is declared the victor and the other side accepts its defeat. But according to the warped logic by which Pharaoh operated, no one was allowed to win but *his* side, regardless of the actual facts of the case. Hence, his instinctive reaction to the defeat of his magicians was to declare that they were all traitors and co-conspirators with his enemy, and that they must be annihilated for having given their allegiance to the contender against him.

Consequently, he now began to angrily accuse the magicians and malign them in the eyes of the people.

"You believed in him before I gave you permission!" (7:123, 20:71, 26:49), he raged. **"Indeed, he is your leader who has taught you magic"** (20:71, 26:49), he added, thereby indirectly admitting Moses' superiority over them. Then he reversed himself, saying, **"Indeed, this is a conspiracy which you plotted in the city, to drive its people out of it"**[70] (7:123).

Regarding it as critical that he assert his authority and impose upon the magicians such a punishment as would deter all future rebellion, the cruel tyrant now uttered a blood-chilling threat against his previously respected and admired sorcerers:

"But you are going to know! (26:49; 7:123). **Therefore, I will surely cut off your hands and feet on opposite sides, and I will crucify you upon the trunks of palm trees, and indeed you will know which of us is more severe and more lasting in punishment!"** (20:71; also 7:124, 26:49).

But after witnessing the unmistakable miracle that Moses had wrought, the magicians, whose main preoccupation earlier had been the excellent rewards they would receive at Pharaoh's hand if they were victorious, were not to be intimidated by any threat. Among the most astute of Pharaoh's subjects, they knew beyond any doubt that no one could do what the solitary Israelite had done by any human means or power, and that the Lord of the universes must therefore be his source of power, helper and supporter.

Unlike Pharaoh and his courtiers, they were too honest to deny the truth once it had become obvious to them, and at the same time too intelligent. Being alert to the signs of the spiritual realm, they immediately grasped that if they denied the truth after it had become clear to them, their final destiny would be far worse than anything Pharaoh could contrive for them in this world — and continuing their lives on Pharaoh's terms was unthinkable. At

---

[70]Al-Suddi reports that prior to the contest, Moses and the chief of the magicians met. "Do you agree that if I overcome you, you will believe in me and will testify that I have come with the truth?" Moses asked him. "Yes," the magician replied, adding, "Tomorrow I will bring such magic as no other magic can defeat, so, by God, if you defeat me, then indeed I will believe in you and will bear witness that you are on the truth." Now, Pharaoh had been observing the two of them during this conversation, and because of this he said, **"Indeed, this is a conspiracy which you have plotted in the city, to drive its people out of it"** (Tabari/*Q*, "Musa"; Tabari/*H*, III:61).

that point, nothing could shake their faith or their determination to remain steadfast in it — not even Pharaoh and his gruesome threats, which they knew well enough he would certainly carry out against them.

"No matter" (26:50), their spokesman then replied to Pharaoh. **"Indeed, we will return to our Lord** (26:50, 7:125).

"Never will we prefer you over what has come to us of clear proofs and over Him who created us," he continued fearlessly. **"Therefore, decree whatever you will decree. You can decree only concerning this worldly life. Indeed, we have believed in our Lord, that He may forgive us our sins and that which you compelled us to of magic.**[71] **And God is best and most enduring!** (20:72-73).

"Indeed," he went on, **"we only hope that our Lord will forgive us our sins, because we were the foremost of the believers"** (26:50-51) — that is, the first to proclaim our faith after seeing the clear evidence of the truth. And addressing Pharaoh, he said, **"And you are taking revenge upon us only because we believed in our Lord's signs when they came to us. Our Lord,"** he prayed fervently, **"pour out upon us patience and let us die as *muslims*"** (7:126).

The Qur'an is silent about their fate. But Ibn 'Abbas (R) reports that when they said, **"Our Lord, pour out upon us patience and let us die as *muslims*"** (7:126), Pharaoh carried out his threat, killing them and cutting them up. Thus, it is said, in the morning they were magicians, but by the day's end they were martyrs in the cause of God (Ibn Kathir/*T*, 20:70; Tabari/*H*, III:62).

REFERENCES: Qur'an: 7:120-126; 20:70-73; 26:46-51. Commentaries: Ibn Kathir/*T*, 20:70-73, 7:118-119; Ibn Kathir/*Q*, "Musa"; Tabari/*H*, III:57-58, 61-62; Tabari/*Q*, "Musa"; Maududi/*Q*, 7:fns. 91-92, 20:fns. 43-45, 26:fn. 40; Asad/*Q*, 7:fn. 92, 26:fn. 26; Ali/*Q*, fn. 2596; Saheeh Translation, fn. 1713.

---

[71] Ibn 'Abbas reports that Pharaoh had earlier taken forty children from the Israelites and given them to his magicians to be trained in their craft. These forty, now men, were among the magicians present at this gathering (Ibn Kathir/*T*, 20:70-73). However, in a more general sense, the magic practiced in ancient Egypt was part of the state system of deception based upon its false religion, which was forced upon both its practitioners and upon the people. As head of this religion, Pharaoh was ultimately to blame for his magicians' role in this widespread process of deception, for during this period of history people followed the religion of their ruler. This explains why the magicians' accepting the faith of Pharaoh's enemies, Moses and Aaron, constituted a major act of rebellion against Pharaoh's well-established order, warranting, in the eyes of Pharaoh, the most horrendous of punishments.

21. THE FURTHER OPPRESSION OF THE ISRAELITES

And [recall, O Children of Israel,] when We saved you from the people of Pharaoh, who afflicted you with the worst torment, slaughtering your sons and letting your women live. And in that was a tremendous trial from your Lord. (2:49; 7:141)

After the initial burst of fear that Moses (A) had evoked in Pharaoh, the tyrannical king became even more stubborn, proud and oppressive. As for the **visible signs** that had been shown to him and his chiefs, **they denied them, although their souls were convinced of them, due to unrighteousness and self-exaltation** (27:13-14).

The words, **"although their souls were convinced of them,"** make it clear that Pharaoh and his nobles, advisors and priests knew quite well that the signs which Moses (A) had brought were of a completely different order than their customary magical practices and that Moses' power could only come from a divine source. Indeed, this was so clear and evident that the dealers in magic themselves had been willing to die the most horrible death for the sake of their newly-found conviction.

But still Pharaoh **denied and disobeyed. Then he turned his back, striving** against God, **and he gathered** his people **and called out and said, "I am your most exalted Lord!"** (79:21-24). For although the tremendous miracle he had just witnessed had made clear to him beyond all doubt that Moses was empowered by God Almighty, nonetheless, in his immense arrogance and pride, he denied the truth, competing with the Creator of the heavens and the earth for lordship over His servants.

But while Pharaoh had now recovered from the loss of face brought about by the defeat of his magicians, Moses' challenge to his authority still remained.

"Will you leave Moses and his people to make corruption in the land and abandon you and your gods?" (7:127), his chiefs asked him, perhaps eager to have him solve the problem once and for all.

"We will kill their sons and let their women live, and indeed we are dominant over them" (7:127), Pharaoh replied, reinforcing the torments he had instated earlier. His magicians might have been defeated and eradicated, but his power over his Israelite slaves remained unchallenged. And he now took the matter a step further, intending to eliminate the self-proclaimed 'prophet' altogether.

"Leave me to kill Moses, and let him call upon his Lord!" he mocked. **"Indeed, I fear that he will change your religion or that he will cause corruption in the land"** (40:26), he added, using the possibility of Moses' subverting his people's religion or changing the prevailing system, of which he was the central figure, as a pretext for killing him.

"Indeed, I have taken refuge in my Lord and your Lord from every arrogant one who does not believe in the Day of Accounting" (40:27), Moses (A) responded when he heard of this threat, as if to say, "My Lord is as much your Lord as my Lord, O Pharaoh, and it is His support I seek against the evil plots of those who deny the meeting with Him." And he boldly repeated the order that God Almighty had conveyed to Pharaoh through him:

"Turn over to me God's servants." Then, to assure Pharaoh and his elite that he spoke by divine authority, he added, **"I am surely a trustworthy messenger to you. And do not be haughty toward God. Indeed, I have come to you with clear authority, and indeed, I have taken refuge with my Lord and your Lord lest you stone me.[72] And if you do not believe in me, then leave me alone"** (44:18-21), meaning, "At least do not interfere with my carrying out the mission with which my Lord has entrusted me."

REFERENCES: Qur'an: 2:49; 7:127; 27:13-14; 40:25-27; 44:17-21; 79:21-24. Commentaries: Ibn Kathir/*Juz' 'Amma*, pp. 31-32; Tabari/*H*, III:62; Maududi/*Q*, 40:fn. 43; 79:fn. 11; Asad/*Q*, 28:fn. 36, 44:fn. 10-11.

[72]Perhaps referring to Pharaoh's threat to kill him, mentioned in 40:26. An alternative meaning is **"lest you revile me."**

22. THE SECRET BELIEVER AND HAMAN

And We certainly sent Moses with Our signs and clear authority to Pharaoh and Haman and Qarun, but they said, "A magician and a liar!" And when he brought them the truth from Us, they said, "Kill the sons of those who believe with him and let their women live." And the plot of the unbelievers is not but in error. (40:23-25)

And We desired to confer favor upon those who had been made weak in the land, and to make them leaders[73] **and make them inheritors, and to establish them in the land, and to show Pharaoh and Haman and their troops, through them, that which they had feared.** (28:5-6)

Among the courtiers, ministers, priests and other highly-placed officials who propped up Pharaoh's ego and false pride, enabling and supporting him to persist in arrogance and oppression, two specific individuals are mentioned: Haman, who is said to have been Pharaoh's chief official and supporter, and Qarun, a proud, corrupt, enormously wealthy Israelite who was somehow in league with Pharaoh.

At the same time, Ibn 'Abbas (R) reports, there were three believers among the Egyptians: Pharaoh's wife Asiyah; the man who had warned Moses years earlier after his killing of the Egyptian; and a certain secret believer from among Pharaoh's people, whose words have been memorialized in *Surah Ghafir* (The Forgiving), also known as *Surah al-Mu'min* (The Believer) (40:28-44). If there were other Egyptians who accepted the truth, they were afraid to admit it openly, for

> **No one believed in Moses except [some] offspring of his people, out of fear of Pharaoh and his supporters, that they would persecute them. And indeed Pharaoh exalted himself in the land, and indeed he was of the transgressors.** (10:83)

---

[73]These words, Muhammad Asad notes, are "an allusion to the historical fact that the Hebrews were the first to accept a monotheistic creed in a clear, unequivocal formulation, and thus became the forerunners of both Christianity and Islam" (Asad/*Q*, 28:fn. 5). The reference to the **"leaders"** among the Children of Israel may also be related to Abraham's supplication that his descendants would be leaders of mankind (2:124; see Volume One, page 336). At the same time, God's response to Abraham's prayer, **"My covenant does not include the wrong-doers"** (2:124), makes it clear that spiritual leadership is not assigned on the basis of lineage or kinship but rather of sincerity of heart, mindfulness of God, and deeds done for the love of Him.

As for Asiyah, it is reported by the eminent Companion of the Prophet, Salman al-Farisi (R), that after Pharaoh became aware of her faith, he tortured her in various ways. But when he forced her to stand in the burning sun during the heat of summer, God sent angels to shade her and showed her her place in Paradise so that her faith became stronger.

She would always enquire about whether Moses (A) was victorious in his struggle against Pharaoh and would pray for his success. When Pharaoh came to know of this, he said, "Bring a big rock and make her lie down. If she repents, free her, as she is my wife, and bring her back with honor. Otherwise, throw that rock on her and kill her."[74]

Accordingly, a large rock was brought and she was made to lie down. When the people were about to throw the rock on her, she lifted her eyes toward Heaven. Then God removed the veils from her eyes and showed her her palace in Paradise. At that moment, her soul left her body, and when the rock was thrown on her she was already dead.[75]

One of the best women who ever lived, God Most High memorialized Asiyah's deep nobility of character, certainty of faith and greatness of heart in the words,

> **God sets forth an example of those who believed: the wife of Pharaoh, when she said, "My Lord, build for me, near You, a House in Paradise, and save me from Pharaoh and his doings, and save me from the wrong-doing people."**[76] (66:11)

---

[74]In two verses, 38:12 and 89:10, Pharaoh is referred to as the **possessor of *al-awtad***, meaning pegs, poles or stakes. According to Ibn 'Abbas and other classic commentators, ***awtad*** refers to Pharaoh's armies, who obeyed his commands. Qatadah interpreted ***awtad*** as referring to a marquee supported by ropes and stakes, in which Pharaoh's entertainers would amuse him. Yet another interpretation is that Pharaoh ordered four stakes to be put in place, to which he had his wife bound, putting heavy stones upon her back until she died (Ibn Kathir/*T*, 66:11). The tyrannical peoples named in 89:6-10, including Pharaoh, are described as

> **Those who committed oppression in the lands and increased the corruption therein. Then your Lord poured upon them the scourge of punishment. Indeed, your Lord is in observation!** (89:11-14)

[75]Another report from Salman al-Farisi mentions that although Asiyah died of torture in the dungeon of Pharaoh's palace because of her faith and her belief in the prophethood of Moses, God supported and strengthened her throughout her awesome ordeal, alleviated her suffering, and showed her her place in Paradise (Akili/*B*, pp. 203-204).

[76]This verse, in which Asiyah is mentioned in together with the blessed virgin Mary, is cited in full on page 326.

May God's peace and blessings be upon that saintly, noble woman, whose generosity, compassion, keen intelligence and wisdom God made the means of preserving Moses (A) from destruction, to become a source of light and guidance for mankind!

Concerning the second believer, the man who had warned Moses (A) to flee, we have no information. We do, however, know something about the third, the Secret Believer, who emerges in the verses of the Qur'an not as an identifiable individual but as a means by whom God Most High conveyed His guidance to Pharaoh and the people of Egypt, and, in a general sense, to all mankind.

Who was this man? God refers to him simply as **a believing man from Pharaoh's family who concealed his faith** (40:28). Some commentators say that he was a cousin of Pharaoh's who had kept his belief hidden, which is in keeping with al-Tabari's statement that Pharaoh would not have tolerated the Secret Believer's words if he had not been related to him (Ibn Kathir/*T*, 40:28).

The Secret Believer somehow became aware of Pharaoh's threat to kill Moses (A). And with extraordinary courage, he confronted the oppressive ruler and his establishment.

"Would you kill a man merely **because he says 'My Lord is God,' while he has brought you clear proofs from your Lord?"** he asked, reminding them that there was a Creator above the self-styled 'god,' Pharaoh. **"And if he should be lying, then his lie is upon him,"** meaning that if Moses were lying, they would be free of blame for his lie, **"while if he should be truthful, there will befall you something of that** punishment **which he promises you. Indeed, God does not guide one who is a transgressor and a liar"** (40:28). The subtle meaning here is that since Moses is a truthful, rightly-guided believer, bringing clear proofs from his Lord, Pharaoh's claim that he is a transgressor and a liar is obviously false.

We note in this speech the repeated references to God. Since the concept of a Supreme Being was an integral part of the Egyptian belief-system, what Moses (A) brought was obviously not strange or new. This again makes it clear that, like the unbelievers before them, Pharaoh and his chiefs did not reject his message due to any difficulty in believing in the truth of what he was saying, but rather out of fear of losing their power and privileged way of life.

"O my people," the Secret Believer continued earnestly, **"today sovereignty is yours, as dominant in the land. But who would protect us from God's punishment if it came to us?"** (40:29). That is, at the present time you have been granted such power and authority in your domain that you appear to be its invincible masters. But since God alone is the Arranger and Controller of the affairs of His creation, this applies only to the present moment. If then He should decide to punish you for your denial of Him and your misdeeds, especially for the killing of His prophet that your ruler is now contemplating, no one would be able to protect you from Him.

In response to this, Pharaoh posed as the champion of the right, while controlling his people through subtle deceit which continued to fool them.

"I do not show you but what I perceive," he proclaimed, **"nor do I guide you but to the way of right conduct"** (40:29). Thus, as is common among oppressors, by arguing that he was merely acting according to his best insight and trying to do what was good for his people, he justified his denial of his Creator and his intention of eliminating His messenger. **And Pharaoh led his people astray and did not guide them** aright (20:79), God Most High says of him. And further:

> **We certainly sent Moses with Our signs and clear authority to Pharaoh and his chiefs, but they followed Pharaoh's command, and Pharaoh's command was not rightly-guided. He will be at the head of his people on the Day of Resurrection and take them to the Fire, and wretched is the place to which they will be led! And they were followed by a curse in this [life] and on the Day of Resurrection. And wretched is the gift that will be given [to them]!** (11:96-99)

The divine Author of the Qur'an then adds, in confirmation of this account:

> **That is of the tidings of the cities which We relate to you [Muhammad]; of them, some are [still] standing and some are [like] a reaped harvest.** (11:100)

But the Secret Believer had not yet finished what he had to say.

"O my people," he continued, **"indeed, I fear for you the like of the Day of the Confederates,"** referring to the earlier communities of disbelievers who had allied themselves against God and His prophet-representatives; **"— like the case of Noah's people and 'Aad and Thamud and those after them,"** whose histories were obviously, on the evidence of this statement, quite familiar to the Egyptians. **"And God desires no injustice for** His **servants** (40:30-31).

"And, O my people," he continued, **"indeed, I fear for you the Day of Calling."** That is, the Day when the universe will be shattered, the earth torn apart, and people devastated by terror, calling to one other in utter despair; "— **the Day when you will turn your backs, fleeing"** from the awfulness of God's judgment because you rejected faith and guidance, **"having no protector against God. And whomever God leaves astray, for him there is no guide"** (40:32-33).

The man now pressed home his point by referring to a matter related to the recent history of the Egyptians themselves, saying, **"And Joseph had already come to you previously with clear proofs"** (40:34). This is said to refer to the fact that long before Moses, God had sent Joseph (A) to the people of Egypt both as God's messenger and as *al-'Aziz*, a man of great worldly power and rank in the land. And although the Egyptians had not responded to him as a prophet when he called them to God, nonetheless, because of the authority he possessed, they had obeyed him in worldly matters.

"But you did not slip into doubt concerning that with which he came to you until, when he died, you said, 'Never will God send a messenger after him'" (40:34), the Secret Believer continued. By this, he reminded his people that although they had previously had doubted Joseph's prophethood, when he died they had become dejected, assuming that God would never send them another prophet. But now, when a new prophet had been sent among them, they had denied him as well.

"Thus does God leave astray one who is a transgressor and a skeptic"[77] (40:34), the Secret Believer went on, laying his life on the line by what his words implied concerning Pharaoh. And here God Most High adds parenthetically, referring to Pharaoh and all others who deny or challenge the signs He sends them without any warrant from Him:

> **Those who dispute about God's signs without any authority having come to them, great is the hatefulness [of that] in the sight of God and in the sight of those who believe. Thus does God seal over the heart of every arrogant oppressor! (40:35)**

But blind to every consideration except his own power and supremacy in the land, Pharaoh chose to ignore the advice and warnings of his kinsman.

---

[77]Through the words of this sincere, insightful man, God calls our attention to the hidden relationship between our inner state and His response: that straying originates with ourselves, and when we permit it to continue until it dominates our mindset, it is "confirmed" or "left" or "ordained" upon us. We may note that during the course of his speech, the Secret Believer refers to this very important question of straying and guidance three times, saying, **"Indeed, God does not guide one who is a transgressor and a liar"** (40:28); **"Whomever God leaves astray, for him there is no guide"** (40:33); and, **"Thus does God leave astray one who is a transgressor and a skeptic"** (40:34). This matter is referred to yet again in the following verse: **Thus does God seal over the heart of every arrogant oppressor!** (40:35).

"O chiefs," he proclaimed arrogantly, **"I have not known you to have any god other than me"**[78] (28:38).

Then he was struck by a novel idea, and turning to his chief advisor, he said, **"Therefore, kindle for me, O Haman, a fire upon clay** (28:38). **O Haman, build a tower for me, that I may reach the ways"** — and here the self-exalted ruler paused before uttering a monstrous challenge to God Almighty — **"the ways to the heavens, that I may mount up to the God of Moses. But indeed, I do consider him a liar!"** (40:37, 28:38).

In this wily manner did the arrogant king continue to play with the minds of his people, making a mockery of truth. **Thus was the evil of his deed made attractive to Pharaoh and he was diverted from the** right **way. And Pharaoh's plot** — that is, to kill Moses (A) and torment the Israelites — **was nothing but destruction** (40:37).

But still the Secret Believer had not concluded his urgent message to his people. At the risk of his life, he continued to call them to faith.

"O my people, follow me," he said. **"I shall guide you to the way of right conduct. O my people, this worldly life is but a** temporary **enjoyment, and indeed the Hereafter — that is the Eternal Home"** (40:38-39).

He then spoke to them about God's endless mercy and leniency in judgment.

"Whoever does an evil deed will not be recompensed but by the like of it," he assured his listeners. **"But whoever does a righteous deed, whether male or female, while being a believer — those will enter Paradise, provided for therein without count** (40:39-40).

"And, O my people," he went on with the utmost earnestness, **"how is it that I call you to salvation, while you call me to the Fire? You call me to disbelieve in God and associate with Him that about which I have no knowledge,"** meaning the false deities worshipped by the Egyptians, devoid

---

[78]Since the Egyptians worshipped a pantheon of gods, Pharaoh is not speaking of himself here as a god in the sense of the Creator or supreme deity, as is clear from the question addressed to him earlier by his chiefs, **"Will you leave Moses and his people to make corruption in the land, and abandon you and your gods?"** (7:127). Rather, as mentioned earlier, each pharaoh was regarded both by himself and his subjects as an incarnation of the divine principle, the manifestation of the qualities attributable to divinity, and hence as the undisputed supreme power and authority in the land of Egypt. This is discussed in Qur'anic commentaries of Maududi, 8:footnote 52, and Asad, 26:footnote 17 and 28:footnote 36.

of reality and power, **"while I call you to the Exalted, the Forgiving!"** (40:41-42) — that is, to the absolutely Real (*al-Haqq*).

He then tried to make them realize the total lack of sense and logic of their position.

"No doubt, that to which you call me has no claim to being invoked in the world or in the Hereafter, and indeed our return is to God, and indeed the transgressors," such as Pharaoh and his supporters, **"will be people of the Fire. Therefore, you will remember what I say to you"** when you face God's judgment. **"And I entrust my affair to God,"** he concluded. **"Indeed, God is ever seeing of His servants"** (40:41-44).

The Secret Believer's belief was secret no longer. He had made public his support for the enemies of Pharaoh and that he was, like them, a caller to the Lord of the heavens and the earth, whom Pharaoh regarded as his rival in power and sovereignty. Thus, the man was, by definition, a rebel and a threat to the prevailing system, and, like Moses and Aaron, in mortal danger of being eliminated. But the All-Powerful Lord is sufficient for His servants, and He saved the Believer from the dangers that surrounded him, while the most devastating retribution awaited Pharaoh and his supporters: —

> **So God protected him from the evils they plotted,[79] while Pharaoh's people were enveloped by the worst of punishment — the Fire; they are exposed to it morning and evening. And the day the [Last] Hour appears, [it will be said,] "Admit Pharaoh's people to the severest punishment."** (40:45-46)

REFERENCES: Qur'an: 10:83; 11:96-100; 28:5-6, 38; 40:23-46; 66:11; 89:10-14. Commentaries: Ibn Kathir/*T*, 66:11, 40:26-38; Ibn Kathir/*Q*, "Musa"; Tabari/*H*, III:56; Maududi/*Q*, 40:fns. 43-44, 47, 51, 61; Asad/*Q*, 28:fns. 5-6, 37; Ali/*Q*, 4406; Akili/*Beauty*, pp. 203-204.

---

[79]It is supposed that, because the Secret Believer was his relative and perhaps also a very important man in the kingdom, Pharaoh could not turn against him publicly and kill him on the spot. Consequently, he made secret plans to get rid of him, which God then brought to nought.

23. The Story of Qarun

Indeed, Qarun was of the people of Moses, but he was insolent toward them. And We granted him such treasures that their keys would burden a band of strong men. (28:76)

These verses introduce us to the third of the three prototypes of evil-doing, sinful deniers of God mentioned in the Qur'an in connection with Moses (A), Qarun.[80]

The early Qur'anic commentators report that Qarun was not only an Israelite but was also Moses' close relative, probably his paternal cousin. Despite this, however, he had allied himself with Pharaoh and his supporters as an oppressor of his own people, as is clear from the words,

> **We certainly sent Moses with Our signs and clear authority to Pharaoh and Haman and Qarun, but they said, "A magician and a liar!" And when he brought them the truth from Us, they said, "Kill the sons of those who believe with him and let their women live." And the plot of the unbelievers is not but in error.** (40:23-25)

We are not informed when or where the matters related to Qarun took place. But because, in Moses' own words, **"My Lord neither errs nor forgets"** (20:52), this again cannot be due to a divine 'oversight'. Rather, we must take it as an indication that time and place have no relevance to the lesson this story is meant to teach.

Due to this lack of information, the classical commentators differed as to whether the affair of Qarun took place while the Israelites were in Egypt or later, during their wanderings in Sinai, as is suggested by the story of Korah in the Old Testament. However, from the context of the passages concerning Qarun and the understanding of various classic commentators, we are led to infer that it took place in Egypt rather than after the Exodus.

---

[80]Qarun translates as Korah, a minor character in the Old Testament story of Moses (Num. 16:1-35, 26:8, 27:3). However, the Biblical account differs from that of the Qur'an in various respects. It takes place in Sinai after the Israelites' exodus from Egypt, when Korah challenges and rebels against the authority of Moses and Aaron, supported by 250 Israelites. Moses then calls Korah and his followers to gather for God's judgment concerning their claims. After God warns the Israelites to leave the vicinity, the ground splits open and Korah, his chief followers and all their properties are swallowed up, while the remainder of Korah's 250 followers are destroyed by fire.

This time-frame can be inferred, firstly, from the fact that God mentions Qarun in 40:23-25 quoted above together with Pharaoh and his second-in-command, Haman, and implicates Qarun in their wicked doings. Indeed, this coupling of Qarun's name with theirs suggests that he was a man of very high standing with Pharaoh — perhaps, it has been said, the third in rank in the kingdom because of his enormous wealth. The words, **Qarun was of the people of Moses, but he was insolent toward them** (28:76), further confirm that Qarun was in one camp with the enemies of his people and had joined forces with Pharaoh and his establishment against Moses and the Israelites.

The extent of Qarun's treasures, which were such **that their keys would burden a band of strong men** (28:76),[81] has been the subject of much speculation and comment among the early Qur'anic interpreters. It has been said that each treasure trove had a separate key which was as long as the span of a man's hand and that sixty mules were needed to carry all these keys. It is also claimed that, after the retinue of Pharaoh and Haman, Qarun's retinue was the most celebrated in Egypt for its pomp and splendor. But only God knows the truth.

Like all thankless, arrogant people, Qarun exulted and gloried in his wealth and luxury, imagining that it had come to him as the result of his own merit. And it is this aspect of his story that God presents as a lesson in the Qur'an.

Certain of Qarun's people who possessed understanding spoke to him about his attitude.

"Do not exult," they admonished. **"Indeed, God does not like the exulters. But seek, in what God has given you, the home of the Hereafter"** by doing deeds of charity and generosity with your wealth. **"Yet,"** at the same time, **"do not forget your share of the world,"** enjoying God's gifts within the limits of permissibility and what is pleasing to Him. **"And do good, as God has done good to you, and do not seek to make corruption in the land.**[82] **Indeed, God does not like the corrupters"** (28:76-77).

---

[81]The fact of Qarun's possessing such a huge amount of treasure in itself suggests that his affair took place in Egypt, for it is difficult to imagine that he could have left Egypt with it during the conditions of the Exodus, or that he would have been able to carry it about during the wanderings of the Israelites in Sinai.

[82]These words suggest that, because of his immense wealth, Qarun was up to some sort of mischief or corruption, which was well-known to his people.

"I was only given it because of knowledge I have" (28:78), Qarun boasted shamelessly, thereby opening himself to the divine anger. And God Most High says:

> **Did he not know that before him God had destroyed such generations as were stronger than he in power and greater in accumulation [of wealth]. (28:78)**

One day Qarun **came out to his people in his finery** (28:79). It is said that he wore luxurious saffron-colored garments and was mounted upon a white work horse with a purple saddle, showing off his enormous wealth.

Those who desired the life of this world (28:79) looked at him with envy. **"Oh, would that we had the like of what was given to Qarun!"** they said longingly. **"Indeed, he is the possessor of an immense fortune"** (28:79).

But those who had been given knowledge concerning the relative value of things understood otherwise. **"Woe to you!"** they reproached the others. **"God's reward is better for one who believes and does righteous deeds. And none is granted it except the patient"** (28:80). That is, the reward God has in store for believers who do good is infinitely better than anything that one can accumulate or even desire in this life. But this reward is to be earned by those who remain patient with the tests and trials that God sends — including the test of wealth, whether a surplus or a lack of it.

Now, Qarun had singled out Moses (A) as the special target of his enmity and wanted to destroy him.[83] Ibn 'Abbas (R) supplies the details:

> Qarun gave money to a prostitute to go to Moses while he was among the people and say, "You committed such-and-such an act with me." And she went and said this.
>
> Moses withdrew himself and prayed two *rak'ats*, and then he came to her and asked her to take an oath concerning what she had said and whether someone had set her up to say this. She then reported that Qarun had set her up to say that, and she asked God's forgiveness and repented of it.
>
> Then Moses fell down in prostration to God and prayed to Him against Qarun. And God revealed to him, "I have commanded the earth

[83]This may be at least in part what is implied by the words about Qarun's seeking **to make corruption in the land** (28:77).

to obey you," whereupon Moses commanded the earth to swallow him and his house.[84] (Ibn Kathir/*T*, 28:81)

And God says concerning him:

> **We caused the earth to swallow him and his house, and there was no group to help him apart from God, nor was he of those who could defend themselves. (28:8)**

Such was the frightful end of Qarun, whom God Most High named together with other arrogant enemies of faith, despite his being of Moses' people, saying:

> **And [We destroyed] Qarun and Pharaoh and Haman. And Moses had already come to them with clear evidences, and they behaved arrogantly in the land but they were not outrunners [of Our punishment]. So We seized each for his sin; and among them were those upon whom We sent stones, and among them were those who were overtaken by the clamor [*as-sayhah*], and among them were those whom We caused the earth to swallow, and among them were those whom We drowned. And it was not God who wronged them, but it was they who wronged themselves. (29:39-40)**

---

[84]In another version, it is said that one day Qarun came out in his finery with all his retinue, his mules and his slaves clad in silken garments, and he passed a place where Moses was addressing a group of Israelites. As he went by, everyone turned and looked at his procession. "What is all this pageantry?" Moses demanded. "The fact is that God gave you something above me and that is your prophethood," Qarun replied. "And He also gave me something above you and that is my wealth and glory. If you have any doubt that I am superior to you, let us go and pray to God against each other and see whose supplication is accepted." And Moses agreed (Ibn Kathir/*T*, 28:79).

In yet another version, it is reported that Qarun first prayed against Moses but his supplication was not accepted. Then Moses prayed, asking God to give him power over the earth so that it would obey him, and God accepted his supplication. Moses then commanded the earth, "O earth, seize him and his people!" whereupon they sank into the earth up to their ankles. He said, "Seize them further!" until they sank up to their knees. He said, "Seize them further!" until they sank up to their shoulders. Then he said, "Bring all the treasures and wealth here!" By a miracle, the treasures and wealth all appeared at that spot, and Qarun and his retinue saw it before their eyes. Moses then commanded the earth to swallow all the treasure, together with them, and immediately they all sank down and the earth became smooth over them. Afterwards, God revealed to Moses that despite Qarun's appealing to him for help and mercy, he had not helped him nor show him mercy, whereas if he had appealed to *Him*, He would have responded to him and helped him (Ibn Kathir/Q, "Musa").

Then, as the foolish ones who had envied Qarun's wealth and glory the previous day talked among themselves, the beginning of understanding dawned upon them.

"Ah, God expands provision for whomever He wills of His servants and restricts it!" they exclaimed. **"If God had not been gracious to us, He could have caused it to swallow us as well. Ah, never will the unbelievers prosper!"** (28:82).

Then, concluding the story of Qarun, God Most High summarizes its lesson by saying:

> **That home of the Hereafter — We appoint it for those who do not seek exaltedness upon the earth, nor corruption. And the [best] outcome is for the God-fearing.** (28:83)

REFERENCES: Qur'an: 28:76-82; 29:39-40; 40:23. Commentaries: Tabari/*H*, III:99-110; Ibn Kathir/*T*, 28:76-82, 29:39-40; Ibn Kathir/*Q*, "Musa"; Maududi/*Q*, 28:fn. 95; Asad/*Q*, 28:fn. 84; Ali/*Q*, fn. 3404.

24. THE NINE SIGNS

We certainly showed him [Pharaoh] Our signs, all of them, but he denied and rejected. (20:56)

We certainly granted Moses nine clear signs. (17:101)

During this period, the sufferings of the Israelites had continued unabated. Their newborn sons were slaughtered and their daughters spared for future servanthood, while their menfolk remained in their miserable, tortured bondage.

"Seek help with God and be patient," Moses (A) counseled them, assuring them of their Lord's unfailing care and support. **"Indeed, the earth belongs to God. He causes whomever He wills of His servants to inherit it, and the best outcome is for those who are mindful of Him"** (7:128).

But the pain of his people was too deep. **"We were harmed before you came to us and after you came to us"**[85] (7:129), they complained in their anguish, meaning that while they had suffered under Pharaoh in the past, Moses' coming to them as their prophet had brought them no relief.

But Moses (A) knew with unshakeable certainty what they did not know: that all things are governed by the infinite wisdom of the Lord of all creation. Their prophet knew, as they did not, that no matter how terrible things may sometimes seem, nothing escapes the knowledge of the All-Informed and All-Aware, nor is anything outside His all-inclusive divine plan. Although He sometimes puts His servants through tremendous trials, nothing that happens is without a reason and a purpose — and, to those who believe, some ultimate benefit and blessing.

Secure in this knowledge, Moses (A) encouraged the tormented Israelites to remain steadfast and wait for the working out of the divine Will. **"Perhaps your Lord will destroy your enemy and grant you succession in the land**

---

[85]There is no mention in the Qur'an of the incident related in Exodus 5, in which Moses asked Pharaoh to let the Israelites off work for three days so they could go to the desert and sacrifice to God. According to the Biblical narrative, not only did Pharaoh refuse this request, but he added immeasurably to the suffering of the Israelite slaves by ordering that they must now collect the straw for the bricks they produced, while maintaining the same production quota as previously, when they had been supplied with straw. At this, the Israelites complained bitterly to their two prophets about the trouble they had brought upon them.

and see how you will act" (7:129), he said, holding out to his people the hope that the All-Knowing Lord would eventually bring their affair to the best conclusion. At the same time, he reminded them that, as their past and present sufferings were a trial, so would the freedom and autonomy that God might grant them in the future likewise be a trial. How prophetic his words were to prove, indeed!

Not only did Pharaoh continue to torment the despised, enslaved Israelites, but he continued to defy the command of the Lord of the heavens and earth, delivered again and again through Moses, to permit them to leave Egypt.

> **And he and his forces behaved arrogantly in the land without right, and they supposed that they would not be brought back to Us. (28:39)**

God Most High had already sent them, through their chief prophet, undeniably miraculous signs — Moses' shining white hand and the changing of his staff into a gigantic snake, defeating the magic of the land's most powerful magicians. Yet Pharaoh, unwilling to admit his error or change his behavior, continued to deny and reject his Maker. **And he turned away with his supporters and said, "A magician or a madman!"** (51:39). Thus, God says:

> **We certainly sent Moses with Our signs to Pharaoh and his chiefs, and he said, "Indeed, I am a messenger of the Lord of the worlds." But when he came to them with Our signs, forthwith they laughed at them. (43:47-48)**

God then **chastised Pharaoh's people with years of famine and shortage of fruits, that perhaps they might be reminded** (7:130), afflicting them with a series of calamities or plagues, mentioned in the words,

> **Then We sent upon them the flood and locusts and lice and frogs and blood as distinct signs, but they were arrogant and were an evil-doing people. (7:133)**

The Qur'anic commentaries are full of stories about these plagues and their awfulness, which, one following the other, made life unbearable for the Egyptians. They are said to have consisted of the following:

As stated in God's words, uttered at the time of Moses' call to prophethood, **"[These are] among the nine signs to Pharaoh and his people"** (27:12), the first and second signs were the transforming of the staff into the gigantic serpent and Moses' shining white hand, while the third was the public defeat of the magicians. After these came the signs that affected the entire population: fourth, a severe famine; fifth, terrible rain and hail storms, accompanied by lightning, which destroyed the Egyptians' crops and homes by flooding; sixth, swarms of locusts, eating up the produce of the land; seventh, a severe infestation of small insects (lice and weevils), which tormented the people and attacked the granaries; and eighth, the appearance of hordes of frogs throughout the land, filling every place and causing great distress. The ninth and final sign was the turning of the water used by the Egyptians into blood, killing the fish and rendering the water so foul that the people could not drink from it for a week, although the Israelites' water remained unchanged (7:133). God says,

> **We did not show them any sign but that it was greater than its sister [sign], and We seized them with affliction, that they might perhaps turn back.** (43:48)

Recognizing that these calamities had come upon them for their sins, the Egyptians begged Moses to pray to his Lord to remove the punishment. **But when** he did so and **good came to them, they said, "This is our due."** Because of their intensely superstitious understanding of things, **if a calamity befell them, they ascribed an evil omen to Moses and those with him.**[86] **No matter what sign you bring us to bewitch us with,"** they would taunt, **"we will not be believers in you"**[87] (7:130-132).

Whenever a new plague befell them, Pharaoh and his chiefs would call Moses (A) and say, **"O magician, invoke your Lord for us by what He has promised you. Indeed, we will be guided!"** But when God, ever merciful, **removed the affliction from them, forthwith they broke their word** (43:49-50).

Another plague would then be sent. Again they would summon Moses (A) and repeat, **"O Moses, invoke your Lord for us by what He has promised you. If you remove the punishment from us, we will surely believe in you and will send the Children of Israel forth with you." But when God removed the punishment from them until a term which they were to reach, forthwith they broke their word** (7:134-135).

But still Pharaoh — who undoubtedly continued to enjoy the finest luxuries, notwithstanding the calamities that befell his people — did not cease to

---

[86]Here, the divine Author of the Qur'an adds parenthetically, as if to end forever the ascribing of evil omens to people or events, **Unquestionably, their 'evil omens' were only with God, but most of them do not know** (7:131).

[87]This statement shows how difficult it was for the Egyptians to use their reason under the influence of the prevailing false religious cults, with their emphasis on superstition and magic. The same notion is expressed in 27:13: **But when Our visible signs came to them, they said, "This is obvious magic."**

mock at Moses (A). **"Indeed,"** he declared insolently, **"I consider you, O Moses, to be under a spell"** (17:101).

But no one could put Moses (A) down. After the powerful miracles and signs he had been granted, and his lengthy dealings with the disbelievers and deniers of truth, he was now seasoned and mature, the confident representative of God Almighty, invested with divine authority.

"You certainly know that no one has sent down these signs except the Lord of the heavens and the earth as clear proofs," he retorted. Then, speaking to Pharaoh as he had just spoken to him, he added: **"And indeed I consider you, O Pharaoh, to be ruined!"** (17:102).

Still unmoved by the decisive proofs of the truth of Moses' mission, Pharaoh continued to call upon his people for support against the upstart prophet who did not cease to confront and challenge him.

"O my people," he exhorted, **"is not the kingdom of Egypt mine, and these rivers flowing beneath me? Then do you not see?"** And referring to Moses' insignificant status among the Egyptians, he added: **"Or am I not better than this one who is contemptible and can hardly speak clearly?**[88] **Then,"** if Moses is all he claims to be, **"why have not golden bracelets been placed upon him**[89] **or angels come in conjunction with him?"** (43:51-53).

Ibn 'Abbas (R) summarizes this segment of the story thus:

> After this defeat [of the magicians], Pharaoh became more rebellious. God then sent many calamities to warn him. Each time a sign appeared, he would become frightened and plead with Moses to pray that this calamity be lifted, whereupon he would release the Israelites. But when the calamity was removed, he would again become rebellious and would ask Moses whether his Lord was able to do anything in addition to these.
>
> Among the signs that came upon them were a storm, locusts, lice, frogs and blood in water, and there were many other very clear signs.

---

[88]The commentators offer two interpretations of these words. One is that they refer both to Moses' insignificance as a member of a despised, subject race and to the speech impediment which had afflicted him since early childhood. Another is that, since the impediment had been removed at Moses' request at Mount Sinai, and since, moreover, prophets are free of physical and mental imperfections, these words refer to Pharaoh's unwillingness to make sense out of what Moses was saying (see the commentaries of Maududi, 43:footnote 49; Asad, 43:footnote 43; and Yusuf Ali, footnote 4654).

[89]In ancient Egypt, golden armlets and necklaces were emblems of royalty and high rank.

> Whenever the calamity came, he ran and promised, but when it was lifted, he turned away and became arrogant. (*Hadith* of the Trials)

Nonetheless, in spite of Pharaoh's stubborn resistance, the deliverance of the Israelites' from their tortured, humiliating bondage was at hand. So, too, was the punishment of Pharaoh and his forces. For by defying the Lord of the universes and insisting that he was all-powerful and supreme in the land, Pharaoh had sealed his doom and that of his supporters:

> **Thus, he fooled his people and they obeyed him. Indeed, they were a transgressing people. And when they angered Us, We took retribution from them and drowned them all together, and We made them a precedent and an example for the later peoples. (43:54-56)**

REFERENCES: Qur'an: 7:128-135; 17:101-102; 28:39; 43:47-56. Commentaries: Ibn Kathir /*Q*, "Musa"; Tabari/*H*, III:59-60, 66-69; Maududi/*Q*, 17:fn. 113; 7:fns. 95-96; 43:fns. 43, 49; Asad/*Q*, 43:fns. 43-44; Ali/*Q*, fn. 4654.

25. THE EXODUS FROM EGYPT

And We inspired to Moses, "Travel by night with My servants. You will surely be pursued." (26:52)

Conveying God's guidance to Pharaoh and his people had been Moses' first mission, and we have seen the results of his efforts. But his second and equally important mission concerned his weary, suffering, broken-spirited people.

Moses (A) continued to reassure and encourage the Israelites, urging them not to give up hope. **"O my people,"** he said, **"if you believe in God, then rely upon Him, if you are** truly ***muslims***" (10:84).

"Upon God do we rely," they replied numbly, worn out by their trials. **"Our Lord, do not make us a** source of **temptation for the wrong-doing people, and save us, by Your mercy, from the disbelieving people"** (10:85-86).

And God Most High **inspired to Moses and his brother, "Make your people stay in houses in Egypt, and make your houses a *qiblah* and establish *salat*.**[90] **And give good tidings to the believers"** (10:87) of God's unfailing help and support for those who keep faith with Him.

Concerning this command, Ibn 'Abbas says that the Israelites complained to Moses (A) that they were unable to pray outdoors in front of others, so God ordered them to pray in their houses. The classical commentator Mujahid says that because the Israelites were afraid they would be killed if they prayed in their places of worship, they were instructed to pray privately in their homes, and to settle in houses close together (Ibn Kathir/*T*, 10:87). However, there is no indication of the time period covered by this command.

At length, after witnessing for so long the torment and anguish of his nation and realizing that no change could be expected from its oppressors, Moses (A) **called upon his Lord,** saying, **"These are a sinful people!** (44:22).

"Our Lord," he continued, **"indeed, you have granted Pharaoh and his chiefs splendor and wealth in the worldly life, our Lord, that they may lead people astray from Your path. Our Lord, obliterate their**

[90] *Qiblah* refers to the direction faced in *salat* (see Volume 1, pages 319-320).

wealth[91] **and harden their hearts so they will not believe until they see the painful punishment!"** (10:88).

"The supplication of the two of you has been answered,"[92] the All-Hearing, All-Knowing Lord responded. **"Therefore, both of you remain firm and do not follow the way of those who do not know"** (10:89). That is, do not follow the way of those who see only what is material and external but have no understanding of the secret divine wisdoms underlying all things, so that they falsely conclude from the worldly success of those who rebel against God that He will not help those who struggle for truth and that the struggle is therefore useless.

Thus did matters remain until the term decreed by God for the domination of Pharaoh and his supporters reached its limit. Then, dramatically, everything changed abruptly for both sides in the conflict between truth and falsehood.

The divine command then came to Moses (A): **"Travel by night with My servants and strike a dry path for them through the sea, not fearing to be overtaken nor afraid** of drowning. **You will surely be pursued. And leave the sea in stillness. Indeed, they are a troop to be drowned!"**[93] At last, for the two brother prophets, the time for action had come!

---

[91]It is said that God turned the property of the Egyptians into stone as a result of Moses' prayer against them. Indeed, some early Muslims reported seeing and handling remnants of petrified objects from Pharaoh's time (Tabari/H, III:68-69).

[92]These words are in the dual form. Although it often appears that only Moses is involved, throughout this story God Most High frequently addresses Moses and Aaron together. From this, we can understand that they operated as a single unit. It has been suggested that since both prophets are addressed here, Moses made the supplication, while Aaron said the "amens" (Arabic, ***amin***).

[93]Here, three passages are combined:

> **And We certainly inspired to Moses, "Travel by night with My servants and strike a dry path for them through the sea, not fearing to be overtaken nor afraid [of drowning]." (20:77)**
>
> **And We inspired to Moses, "Travel by night with My servants. You will surely be pursued." (26:52)**
>
> **"Then travel by night with My servants; you will surely be pursued. And leave the sea in stillness. Indeed, they are a troop to be drowned!" (44:23-24)**

The words, **"Leave the sea in stillness,"** in the third passage has been understood as an order to Moses to leave the sea as motionless and parted while Pharaoh and his troops crossed its dry bed as it had been during the Israelites' crossing, so that Pharaoh and his forces might unknowingly follow the path taken by the Israelites to their death.

Moses (A) now instructed the Israelites not to call out to one another, and to leave lamps lit inside their houses so it would appear that there were people inside. Then, as directed by his Lord, he set out with his people by night, ordering them to go in the direction of the sea. It is said that Aaron (A) was at the front of the band of escapees, leading them, while Moses (A) brought up the rear.

We may try to imagine the vast throng of people that accompanied the two prophets — men and women, young and old, children and babes in arms.[94] Fleeing from their masters, they took with them only whatever they were able to carry of their belongings. This included such gold and silver items they themselves possessed, as well as articles of value which the Egyptians had entrusted to them for safekeeping or which the Israelites had borrowed from them, and which, being now unable to return to their owners, they carried along on their journey.

Although they lived in a separate enclave in Goshen, the Israelites' escape was soon discovered. At that point, utterly vulnerable and defenseless, nothing stood between them and the certain death that awaited them when they were overtaken by Pharaoh's troops but intervention from Heaven. Except for those of the greatest faith, perhaps their legs and hearts were all but paralyzed with fear.

Enraged at having been outwitted, Pharaoh sent gatherers into the cities. **"Indeed, those are only a small band and indeed they are infuriating us,"** his officials proclaimed. **"But,"** they boasted, **"we are surely an alert society"** (26:53-56).

Then Pharaoh and his troops pursued them in tyranny and enmity at sunrise[95] (10:90, 26:60). Says Ibn 'Abbas (R):

> God then ordered Moses (A) to take the Israelites by night and set out from thence, so he took them all and started off in the night.
>
> In the morning, when Pharaoh's people saw that the Israelites had departed, Pharaoh summoned troops from various regions of his realm

---

[94] The number of Israelites leaving Egypt cannot be accurately estimated by scholars and historians. Some have said that two million left Egypt — an obvious impossibility — while others say 600,000. The lowest estimates put the figure at a few thousand.

[95] Al-Suddi states that the firstborn of the Egyptians died during the night and were buried at sunrise, preoccupying the Egyptians so completely that they did not set out in pursuit of the Israelites until early the next morning (Tabari/*C*, I:306-307; Tabari/*H*, III:63).

and ordered them to gather at one place. Then, with them, he started to pursue the Israelites. (*Hadith* of the Trials)

Meanwhile, Moses (A) and his people, journeyed onward as his Lord directed him until the sea faced him and he was unable to turn away from it.[96]

One of Moses' men, Joshua son of Nun (A), who later succeeded Moses (A) in prophethood, then asked, "Where did your Lord order you to go, O Moses?"

"Straight ahead of you," Moses (A) replied firmly.

At that, Joshua (A) urged his horse to enter the sea until it was submerged and carried away by the water. But he soon returned, saying, "Where did your Lord order you to go, O Moses? For, by God, you do not lie, nor are you deceived." This Joshua (A) did three times, impelled by the deep certainty of his trust in his Lord.

Then as **Pharaoh pursued them with his troops** (20:78), **when the two groups saw each other**, the terror-stricken Israelites cried out, **"We will surely be overtaken!"** (26:61).

"By no means!" Moses (A) reassured them. In spite of the apparent hopelessness of the situation, he possessed the absolute, unshakable certainty that God would protect and save his people. **"Indeed, My Lord is with me,"** he said firmly. **"He will guide me"** (26:62).

The divine inspiration then came to Moses (A): **"Strike the sea with your staff,"** and he did as he was ordered. At the touch of his staff — the conduit of the power of God Almighty — the sea, ever obedient to the command of its Lord and to those of His chosen servants whom He gives authority over it, **parted, and each part became like a towering mountain**. And God **brought the others there** (26:63-64).

---

[96]Many theories have been put forth as to the identity of the sea or body of water the Israelites crossed. Because the Red Sea separates Egypt and the Sinai peninsula, it was formerly supposed to have been the Red Sea. However, many researchers are now of the opinion that this sea was actually the Sea of Rushes or Reed Sea, Yam Suf, incorrectly translated as "Red Sea". Estimated to have been a smaller body of water than the Red Sea, the Reed Sea's location has been the subject of much speculation. Pierre Montet, author of Lives of the Pharaohs, identifies it as "almost certainly . . . the same as the Bitter Lakes" — lakes which, in ancient times, according to Maulana Maududi, were to the north of and connected to the Gulf of Suez separating Egypt from the Sinai Peninsula (see Maududi, *Qur'an*, 7:map 2). Further information concerning this body of water can be found in Collier, *The Heretic Pharaoh*, page 229; Daiches, *Moses, the Man and His Vision*, page 86; Golding, *In the Steps of Moses*, pages 104-106; Montet, *Lives of the Pharaohs*, page 200; and Newby, *Warrior Pharaohs*, page 167, among many other works.

REFERENCES: Qur'an: 10:84-90; 20:77-78; 26:52-56, 60-64; 44:22-24. Commentaries: Tabari/*C*, I:304-307; Tabari/*H*, III:62-64, 68-70; Ibn Kathir/*T*, 10:87, 26:63; Ibn Kathir/*Q*, "Musa"; Maududi/*Q*, 10:fns. 87, 90, 44:fn. 23; 7:map 2; Ali/*Q*, fn. 4708. Other works: Golding/*Moses*, p. 94.

26. THE END OF PHARAOH

Has there reached you [Muhammad] the story of the troops of Pharaoh and Thamud? (85:17-18)

And there certainly came warning to the people of Pharaoh. They denied Our signs, all of them, so We seized them with a seizure of one Almighty and Omnipotent. (54:41-42)

It is reported by Ibn 'Abbas (R) and other classical commentators that when the Israelites had entered the dry sea bed, not a single one of them remaining behind, Pharaoh and his troops approached the sea.

Pharaoh was mounted on a black stallion with a full tail, and when he reached the edge of sea, which remained fixed in its divided state, the stallion was afraid to advance. Then all at once the angel Gabriel (A) appeared in front of him, mounted on a mare in heat. And when Pharaoh's stallion saw her and caught her scent, he rushed after her into the dry sea bed.

Seeing this, Pharaoh's troops followed, with Gabriel (A) at their head. They were urged on by the angel Michael (A), mounted on a mare at their rear, saying, "Keep up with your companions!"

Now, there was among the Israelites a man called al-Samiri (meaning "the Samaritan"). Ibn 'Abbas (R) gives his proper name as Musa bin Zafar. Although this man had originated among a people who worshipped cows, he lived in Egypt and had joined himself with the Israelites. And while al-Samiri had professed *islam* among them, the love of cow-worship was still in his soul.

Ibn 'Abbas (R) says that al-Samiri had been hidden in a cave by his mother at birth due to fear of his being killed, and the cave had closed up on him. Then Gabriel (A) had come to him and fed him with his fingers, in one of which there was milk, in another honey, and in another ghee. Gabriel's feeding of the boy continued until he grew up.[97]

---

[97]Looking ahead to al-Samiri's role in corrupting the Israelites' faith (see pages 114-115), we may again marvel at the subtle and mysterious workings of God's Will. For just as Moses was saved from death in infancy to become a source of light and guidance for his people, so was al-Samiri saved in childhood to become a trial and a source of calamity to the same people. We may also recall Abraham's being hidden in a cave — to this day a place of pilgrimage in Urfa, Turkey — during his childhood, that he might live to become one of the greatest spiritual leaders of mankind.

When al-Samiri now saw Gabriel (A) by the sea, he recognized him and scooped up a handful of dust from under the hoof of his mare. It was put into his mind, "You will not throw this onto anything, saying, 'Be such-and-such,' without its being according to your words."

This handful of dust remained in al-Samiri's hand until he had crossed to the other shore. We shall soon see what use he made of it.

As Pharaoh and his troops were crossing the dry sea bed in pursuit of the Israelites, God's command went forth to the sea to seize them. The two divided, piled-up mountains of waves then came crashing down upon them all, **and there covered them, of the sea, that which covered them** (20:78).

Ibn 'Abbas (R) reports that the angel Gabriel (A) stuffed Pharaoh's mouth with mud or pebbles so that he would be unable to say any word for which God might show him mercy (Tabari/*H*, III:65, 71). No longer a mighty king who could command his world but a fragile, solitary, unaided mortal whose life was ebbing away, he now came face to face with the ultimate reality of human existence. Denying the inevitability of meeting with his Creator until this, his final moment of truth, now, **when drowning overtook him** and he could do nothing but surrender his soul, **he said, "I believe that there is no God except the One in whom the Children of Israel believe, and I am of the *muslims*"** (10:90).

"*Now*, while previously you had rebelled and were of the corrupters!" came the divine response. **"But today We shall save you in body, that you may be a sign for those who succeed you. And indeed, many among mankind are heedless of Our signs"** (10:91-92). And God **drowned him and those with him, all together** (17:103), while the Israelites **were looking on** (2:50): —

> **Then We brought the others there, and We saved Moses and those with him, all together. Then We drowned the others. Indeed, in that is a sign, yet most of them are not believers. And indeed, your Lord — He is the Almighty, the Merciful. (26:64-68)**

Ibn 'Abbas (R) provides further details of the preceding events, saying:

> God sent an inspiration to the sea:[98] "When Moses strikes you with his staff, you are to divide yourself into twelve passages so that each tribe

[98]This should not surprise us, for every atom of creation belongs to God and is under His command, direction and control. Although many researchers and scientists have attempted to give scientific and rational explanations for the parting of the sea, no theory has as yet succeeded in

of the Israelites can pass through the passages, and after they have crossed them and Pharaoh's people try to cross through you, you are to close in on Pharaoh and his followers."

But Moses had neglected to strike the sea with his staff, and it was roaring, fearful that Moses might strike it with his staff and it might be unaware of it, and thus become disobedient to God, the Mighty and Glorious. Meanwhile, Pharaoh's army approached them, and Moses' people became frightened and said to Moses, **"We will surely be overtaken!** [26:61]. Therefore, do what God has commanded you to do! We do not believe that either God or you are liars."[99]

He said, "I was told that when I reached the sea, it would give way to twelve passages," and while he was saying this, he recalled that he had been commanded to strike it with his staff. So he struck the water with his staff, and when Pharaoh's army was very close to the last of the Israelites, the water dried and the passages appeared, and Moses went through these passages, and his nation with him. And when Moses and his people had crossed, Pharaoh and his people entered those passages and the sea closed in upon them as it had been commanded.

Then Moses' people said to him, "We are afraid that perhaps Pharaoh did not drown and we will not believe in his death." So Moses called upon his Lord and He brought the body of Pharaoh [before their eyes] until they were certain that he was dead. (*Hadith* of the Trials)

Thus did Pharaoh, who regarded himself as a divine being accountable to no one, come to a terrible and painful end, together with his troops — an end that is mentioned again and again in Qur'anic verses such as the following:

> **Thus, he intended to frighten them out of the land, but We drowned him and those with him all together.** (17:103)
>
> **In Moses [was a sign], when We sent him to Pharaoh with clear authority. But he turned away with his supporters and said, "A magician or a madman!" So We seized him and his troops and flung them into the sea, and he was blameworthy.** (51:38-40)

---

giving a clear or valid explanation of what had to be, regardless of the means by which it happened, a miraculous divine intervention, not a coincidence.

[99]This refers to Moses' promise on God's behalf, **"By no means [will we be overtaken and slaughtered]! Indeed, my Lord is with me; He will guide me"** (26:62).

When they angered Us, We took retribution from them and drowned them all together, and We made them a precedent and an example for the later peoples. (43:55-56)

And We certainly gave Moses the scripture and appointed his brother Aaron with him as assistant. And We said, "Go, both of you, to the people who have denied Our signs." Then We destroyed them with [complete] destruction. (25:35-36)

Indeed, We have sent to you [the unbelievers of Muhammad's time] a messenger as a witness over you, as We sent a messenger to Pharaoh. But Pharaoh disobeyed the messenger, whereupon We seized him with a disastrous seizure. (73:15-16)

Then God seized him, an exemplary punishment for the latter and the former.[100] **Indeed, in that is a lesson for one who fears God.** (79:25-26)

All that Pharaoh and his supporters had acquired and treasured of the life of this world had been stripped away from them, as if it had never been in their possession: —

Then We took retribution from them and drowned them in the sea because they denied Our signs and were heedless of them. . . . And We destroyed what Pharaoh and his people had produced and what they had built. (7:136, 137)

So We ousted them from gardens and springs, and treasures and distinguished sites. Thus [it was]! And We caused the Children of Israel to inherit them. (26:57-59)

How many gardens and springs did they leave behind, and crops and distinguished sites, and comforts in which they rejoiced! Thus [it was]! And We caused another people to inherit them, and the heavens and the earth did not weep for them, nor were they reprieved. (44:25-30)

But far worse than this would be the terrible destiny awaiting Pharaoh and his supporters when they met their Lord: —

He [Pharaoh] was arrogant, he and his troops, in the land without right, and they supposed that they would not be returned to Us. Thereupon We seized him and his troops, and flung them

---

[100]This has been understood as referring to Pharaoh's punishment in the Hereafter as well as in this world's life, or to the punishment for his latter and former transgressions — namely, his setting himself up as a god, his denial of God's prophets, and his oppression of the Israelites.

into the sea. Then see what was the end of the wrong-doers! And We made them leaders, inviting to the Fire, and on the Day of Resurrection they will not be helped. And We caused a curse to overtake them in this world, and on the Day of Resurrection they will be among the despised. (28:40)

Tradition has preserved the memory of the place where the destruction of Pharaoh and his forces occurred: a spot on the northwestern coast of the Sinai peninsula beside a mountain called Jebel Hamam Fira'un al-Mal'un (the Mountain of the Accursed Pharaoh's Bath), which rises to a height of 494 meters (1656 feet) above sea level. Nearby, at a sulphurous spring known as Hamam Fira'un (Pharaoh's Bath), very hot water gushes out and flows toward the sea. The bedouins of this area say it was here that Pharaoh and his army drowned while pursuing Moses (A) and his people. Indeed, it is believed that Pharaoh's spirit still haunts the area.

Many hundreds of years later, God Most High was to address the descendants of the Israelites though the tongue of His Last Prophet, Muhammad (S), and remind them of these awesome trials through which their people had passed, saying:

And [recall] when We saved you from the people of Pharaoh, who afflicted you with the worst torment, slaughtering your sons and letting your women live. And in that was a tremendous trial from your Lord. And [recall, O Children of Israel,] when We parted the sea for you, and We saved you and drowned Pharaoh's people while you were looking on. (2:49-50)

This detailed Qur'anic account of the interaction between Moses (A) and one of the greatest tyrants in history, followed by the story of his ignominous end, is intended to serve as a lesson and warning to all those who are rebellious, arrogant and tyrannical, striving, like Pharaoh, against God Almighty and oppressing His servants, that their transgressions are not unheeded. And God Most High links the name of Pharaoh with that of the oppressive peoples of earlier prophets who were destroyed by divine punishment, saying:

Before them, the people of Noah and 'Aad and Pharaoh, possessor of the stakes, denied, and Thamud and the people of Lot and the dwellers in the thorn bush. Those were the factions; each denied the messengers, wherefore My punishment was justified. (38:12-14; also 50:12-14)

[Theirs is] like the case of the people of Pharaoh and those before them: they disbelieved in God's signs, so God seized them for their sins. Indeed, God is Powerful and Severe in punishment. . . .

Like the case of the people of Pharaoh and those before them. They denied their Lord's signs, so We destroyed them for their sins, and the people of Pharaoh We drowned. And all were wrong-doers. (8:52, 54; also 3:11)

And Pharaoh and those before him and the Overturned Cities committed sin, and they disobeyed the messenger of their Lord, so He seized them with a severe seizure. (69:9-10)

Have you [Muhammad] not considered how your Lord dealt with 'Aad, Iram of the lofty columns, the like of which had never been created in the lands, and [with] Thamud, who hewed out the rocks in the valley; and [with] Pharaoh, possessor of the stakes — those who committed oppression in the lands and increased the corruption therein? Then your Lord poured upon them the scourge of punishment. Indeed, your Lord is in observation! (89:6-14)

This story also contains a vital lesson for people living under harsh and oppressive conditions which they are powerless to change of the necessity of patience and steadfastness until God's help comes: —

Or do you think that you will enter Paradise while there has not come to you the like of that which came to those who passed on before you. They were touched by suffering and adversity, and were so shaken that the messenger and those who believed with him said, "When will God's help come?" Unquestionably, God's help is near! (2:214)

O you who believe, seek help through steadfastness and *salat*. Indeed, God is with the patient. . . . And We will surely test you with something of fear and hunger and loss of wealth and lives and fruits; but give good tidings to the steadfast, who, when calamity afflicts them, say, "Indeed, we belong to God and indeed to Him we will return." Those are the ones upon whom are blessings from their Lord and mercy. And it is those who are the rightly-guided. (2:153, 155-157)

Moses (A) is thus the prototype of steadfastness and perseverance under trials, and his community, during the period of their bondage in Egypt, the example of patient bearing of suffering and oppression.

On the day of the Israelites' deliverance from Pharaoh — known in Islam as 'Ashura Day, the tenth day of the lunar month of Muharram — Moses (A) fasted in thankfulness to God, as mentioned in the following *ahadith*:

> This is a great day, the day on which God saved Moses and drowned the people of Pharaoh, so Moses fasted in thankfulness to God. (*Bukhari*, 4:609)
>
> This is the day on which God rescued the Children of Israel from their enemy, so Moses fasted on it. (*Bukhari*, 3.222)

When Prophet Muhammad (S) emigrated from Mecca, the city of his birth, to Yathrib (Medina) in response to the invitation of its Muslim population, he found the Yathribite Jews fasting on the day of 'Ashura. When he enquired about it, they replied, "This is the day on which Moses was victorious over Pharaoh." The Prophet (S) then said, "We [Muslims] are closer to Moses than they. Therefore, fast on it" (*Bukhari*, 6:261; also 4:609, 3:222). That is, since the ***ummah*** of Muhammad (S) has the strongest commitment to following the ***sunnah*** (practice) of previous prophets, it is incumbent on its people to follow Moses' ***sunnah*** in this regard. Concerning this, Ibn 'Abbas (R) said,

> I did not see the Prophet, God's peace and blessings be upon him, more intent on fasting on any day, preferring it over others, than this day, the day of 'Ashura, and this month — that is, the month of Ramadan. (*Bukhari*, 3:224)

Accordingly, the tenth of Muharram is widely observed as an voluntary fast day by Muslims throughout the world.

REFERENCES: Qur'an: 2:49-50; 3:11; 7:103, 136-137; 8:52, 54; 10:90-92; 17:103; 25:35-36; 26:57-59; 28:40; 43:55-56; 44:25-31; 51:38-40; 54:41-42; 73:15-16; 79:25-26. Commentaries: Tabari/*C*, I:304-306, 311-312, 317; Tabari/*H*, III:65, 70-72, 75-76; Ibn Kathir/*Q*, "Musa"; Maududi/*Q*, 10:fn. 92; Ayoub/*Q*, I:98-100; Keller/*Reliance*, 12.1(2). Other works: Taher/*Sinai*, p. 14.

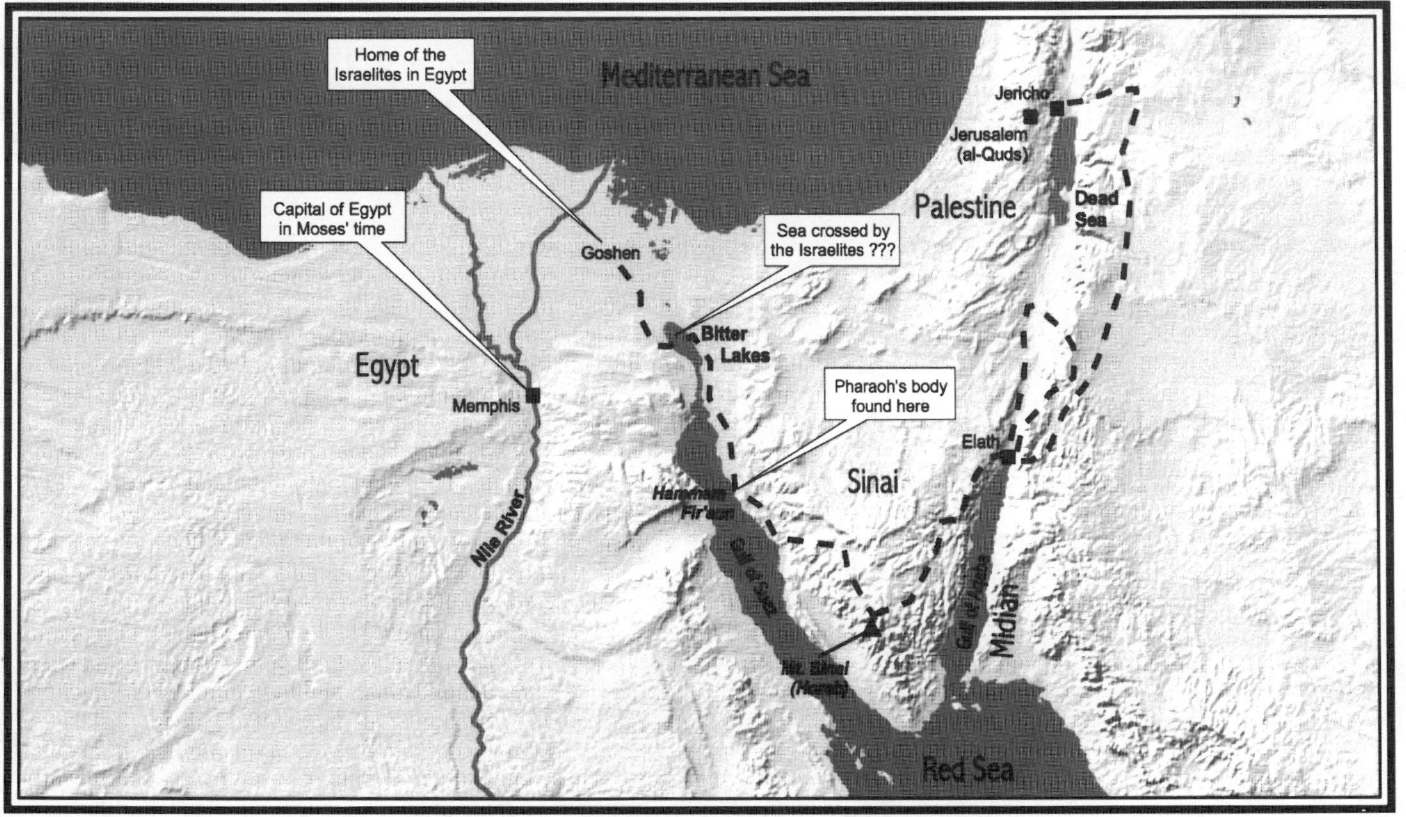

Map 11. The route of the Israelites to the holy land

PART FIVE: AFTER THE EXODUS

27. THE BEGINNING OF THE ISRAELITES' WANDERINGS IN SINAI

We certainly saved the Children of Israel from the humiliating torment — from Pharaoh. Indeed, he was a haughty one among the transgressors! And We certainly chose them, knowingly, above mankind, and We granted them such signs wherein was a clear trial. (44:30-33)

Ask the Children of Israel how many a clear sign We granted them. (2:211)

Having crossed the dry sea bed and witnessed the annihilation of their enemies, the Israelites were now safe in the desert of Sinai, which lay between them and their destination — Palestine, the sacred land of their forefathers.[101]

The Sinai peninsula is a vast, triangular-shaped body of land lying between Egypt and the Arabian peninsula. Apart from its sea coasts and scattered oases, Sinai is a harsh, bleak desert broken by rock outcroppings and ancient volcanic tracts and peaks, some of which may possibly have been active at the time of Moses (A). In the center of the lower part of the peninsula, one among a range of wild, jagged peaks, stands Mount Sinai, the holy mountain at which Moses (A) had earlier received the call to prophethood.

Outwardly, the Israelites were an undistinguished group of fleeing ex-slaves, worn out by a long collective history of suffering. Apart from the few meager goods and valuables they had been able to carry with them on their flight from Egypt, they possessed nothing whatsoever of this world. But God Most High, the Knower of all things, looks beyond the external and the temporal. And in His divine wisdom, He had chosen these descendants of His Friend, Abraham (A), for a unique mission: to be the witnesses to His Oneness and the recipients of His guidance in the midst of an otherwise pagan world, according to His words:

We certainly granted the Children of Israel the scripture and judgment and prophethood, and provided them with good things

---

[101]Palestine was then, as it is now, comprised of the area between the Jordan River and the Mediterranean Sea.

and preferred them above mankind,[102] **and granted them clear proofs of the matter [of religion].** (45:16-17)

O Children of Israel, recall My favor that I bestowed upon you and that I preferred you above mankind. (2:47, 122)

God's choosing or preferring the Israelites above the rest of mankind is clarified in Moses' later words: **"O my people, remember God's favor to you when He appointed prophets among you,"** meaning that He favored you above all the peoples of the earth by sending His deputies among you to convey to you His guidance. "And He **made you sovereigns,"** free, independent people, in charge of your own destiny, **"and granted you what He had not granted anyone among mankind"** (5:20/22) — that is, the pure, pristine faith that He prescribed for the children of Adam, known as *islam*, and the trust of conveying it to humanity.

At the same time, that God's choosing and preferment of the Israelites refers specifically to this period of their history is made clear by other Qur'anic verses.[103] One of these is God's informing Moses (A), in a passage which we

---

[102] ***"Faddalnakum 'ala-l-'alamin"*** — literally, **"We preferred them above the worlds."** For the meaning of ***"al-'alamin,"*** please see Volume One, page 25, footnote 13.

[103] In keeping with this understanding, al-Tabari states that the meaning of 2:47 above is that God Most High preferred the ancestors of the Jews, to whom these words were addressed, "above the world of those among whom, and in whose era" the Israelites had lived. Qatadah states, "He preferred them above the world of that time." Abu-l-'Aliya emphasizes that God preferred them by virtue of the kingdom, the messengers and the scriptures He granted them "above the world of those who existed at that time; for there is a world for each era" (Tabari/C, I:290). And Ibn Kathir states:

> God mentions that He preferred the Children of Israel over all the people of that time. Each time is called an ***'alam.*** It does not mean that they are preferred over the previous or the future people. It is similar to a verse which says, **"O Moses, I have chosen you above mankind [*'ala-n-nas*]"** [7:144], meaning of his own time; and similarly, concerning Mary, **"O Mary, indeed,** I have **preferred you above the women of mankind [*'ala nisa'ai-l-'alamin*]"** [3:42], meaning [the women] of that time, because the Mother of the Believers, Khadijah, is preferred over her or at least equal to her, and so is Asiyah bint Muzahim, the wife of Pharaoh, and also the mother of the believers, 'A'ishah [as is discussed on pages 327-329 of this volume]. (Ibn Kathir/T, 44:32)

Thus, the meaning of ***al-'alamin*** varies according to usage, embracing as wide a range of meanings as "all the worlds" down to "everyone" or "anyone," as is evident from yet another verse: Lot's people saying to their prophet, **"And have we not prohibited you from [protecting or showing hospitality to] everyone [*'ani-l-'alamin*]."**

will cite shortly, that His special mercy was reserved for the followers of **the Unlettered Prophet,** and that it is **those who believe in him and honor him and support him and follow the light which was sent down with him . . . who will be the successful** (7:157).

A second indication is contained in God's saying to the nation of Muhammad (S) some two thousand years after Moses (A),

> **You are the best *ummah* brought forth for mankind. You enjoin what is right and forbid what is wrong, and you believe in God.** (3:110)

These words make it clear that the community of the Last Prophet (S), whose message and example are intended for all mankind up to the end of this world, is the best of all the faith communities that ever existed, as is only natural and to be expected because it *is* the last and final one. This point is further clarified in the Prophet's saying that his ***ummah*** is the completion of seventy nations, the last of them, the best of them, and the dearest to God (Ahmed, Ibn Majah).

However, this is not to be understood as unalterable choice or unconditional promise with respect to the individuals or groups who comprise this ***ummah***, for God Most High instructs Muhammad (S) to say to the Muslims, past, present and future,

> **Then if you turn away, He will replace you with another people; then they will not be like yourselves.** (47:38)
>
> **If He wills, He can do away with you, O people, and bring others [in your place]. And God is ever able to do that.** (4:133)
>
> **Your Lord is Free of Need, the Possessor of Mercy. If He wills, He can do away with you and grant succession after you to whomever He wills, just as He produced you from the descendants of another people.** (6:133)
>
> **Have you not observed that God created the heavens and the earth in truth? If He wills, He can do away with you and produce a new creation, and that is not difficult for God.** (14:19-20; also 35:16-17)

Thus, over the centuries, new groups of people have entered into Islam and become its most earnest, committed carriers, while earlier groups have become decadent, misguided or passive, leaving the torch to be borne by others. It is thus evident that, rather than being a fixed, unchangeable and unqualified choice for all time to come, God's choosing or preferrment of people is related both to His Will and to their response to His Will.

As the Israelites had earlier been bound together not only by common ancestry but also by a common legacy of shared suffering, they were now to be connected by their commitment to keeping to the guidance their Lord would reveal for them. Moses (A) was God's representative and spokesman, his people's link with their Creator. And now that terrible, long years of affliction in Egypt were behind them, his task was to forge the descendants of Israel into a nation obedient God's commands, assisted by his brother Aaron.

"Bring your people out of darknesses into light and remind them of the days of God,"[104] God Most High commanded him. **"Indeed, in that are signs for every patient and thankful one"** (14:5).

Moses (A) therefore encouraged his broken-spirited, dejected, dispossessed people, journeying across a barren desert to an unknown destination, by reminding them of their Lord's divine support and aid. **"Remember God's favor to you when He saved you from Pharaoh's people, who were afflicting you with the worst torment and were slaughtering your sons and letting your women live,"** he exhorted. **"And in that was a tremendous trial from your Lord"** (14:6; also 2:49, 7:141).

"If you are thankful," their Lord proclaimed to them through Moses' tongue, **"indeed, I will grant you increase. But,"** He warned, giving a hint of things to come, **"if you are ungrateful,"** denying Me and the favors I have granted you, **"indeed, My punishment is severe"** (14:7).

Moses (A) then emphasized to his people that their gratitude or lack of it could neither benefit nor harm their Creator in the least. **"If you are ungrateful, you and everyone who is on the earth,"** he said, **"yet God is Free of** all **need and worthy of** all **praise"**[105] (14:8) — that is, independent of all

---

[104]Ibn Kathir interprets "days of God" as referring to God's having released the Israelites from Pharaoh, parting the sea for them, shading them with the cloud cover, granting them manna and quails as food during their wanderings in Sinai, and many other divine favors (Ibn Kathir/*T*, 14:5).

[105]Elsewhere, God says, **O mankind, you are the ones in need of God, while God is free of [all] need, worthy of [all] praise** (35:15). This is also expressed in part of a ***hadith qudsi***, in which God Most High says, through the mouth of Muhammad (S):

> O My slaves, you can never attain to harm of Me so that you would harm Me, nor attain to benefit of Me so that you would benefit Me. O My slaves, if the first of you and the last of you, and your humans and your jinn, were to be as God-fearing as the most God-fearing heart of any one man among you, that would not increase My dominion in the least. O My slaves, if the first of you and the last of you, and your humans and your jinn, were to be as wicked as the most wicked heart of any one man among you, that would not decrease My dominion in the least. O My slaves, if the first of you and the last of you, and your humans and your jinn, were to rise up in one place and make a request

created things and in need of nothing from any of His servants. Rather, it was they who, utterly weak and lacking all resources, were in need of God's mercy and grace at every moment of their lives.

In Egypt, the Israelites had been tried by slavery and suffering. That chapter of their collective life behind them, their next challenge was to evolve, through the leadership of their prophets, into a righteous community living by the guidance that God was shortly to reveal through Moses (A). Sinai was to be the backdrop of their next tests, the second forge of their faith, in which their commitment to the mission for which they had been chosen was to be challenged.

During the long years they were destined to wander in it, they would commit sin after sin, mistake after mistake, repeatedly proving unfaithful to the covenant taken of them by their Lord, who had rescued them from one kind of slavery, only to become slaves to their own weakness of will, indifference and lack of faith. Therefore, while physically the vast Sinai desert now lay between the Israelites and their destination, on another level, a far graver barrier was their own weak and uncommitted internal state.

With this introduction, we now enter the second phase of Moses' prophetic career — that of his mission to his own people. The events reported in this part of his story are found in numerous passages of the Qur'an, often so closely interwoven that it is difficult to determine their historical sequence. Therefore, while the ordering of events we have followed here is based on the interpretation of various classical commentators, it should be borne in mind that this ordering is not clearly stated and there may be more than one understanding of it. However, since the divine Author of the Qur'an did not see fit to specify it, we may again conclude that the historical sequence of events has little relevance, and that what is important is rather the lessons imparted by the events themselves.

REFERENCES: Qur'an: 2:47, 57, 122; 7:137, 160; 14:5-8; 37:114-118; 44:30-33; 45:16-17. Commentaries: Tabari/*C*, I:270-271, 290-291; Ibn Kathir/*T*, 44:32; Maududi/*Q*, 44:fn. 28; Ali/*Q*, fn. 4712; Asad/*Q*, 4:fn. 15.

---

of Me and I were to grant each one what he requested, that would not decrease what I have any more than a needle decreases the ocean if put into it. (*Muslim*, 6246; *Mishkat*, 2344)

28. THE DIVINE PROVISION

We divided them into twelve tribes, nations. And We inspired to Moses, when his people asked him for water, "Strike the rock with your staff." Then there gushed forth from it twelve springs. Each [tribe of] people knew its drinking place. And We shaded them with the overcast and sent down to them manna and quails, [saying,] "Eat of the good things that We have provided you." And they did not wrong Us, but [rather] they wronged themselves. (7:160)

As the Israelites journeyed across bleak, inhospitable Sinai without any means to provide for themselves, the Most Merciful Lord showed His love and care for them by meeting all their needs without their having to make the slightest effort.

At God's order, Moses (A) **divided them into twelve tribes** or **nations** (7:160). Then, **when his people asked him for water** (7:160), **Moses prayed for water** for them (2:60). God then directed him to a certain rock and revealed to him, **"Strike the rock with your staff." Then there flowed from it twelve springs. Each** tribe of **people knew its drinking place** (2:60, 7:160), thereby averting any disputes over the water.

God Most High also **shaded them with the overcast**[106] (2:57, 7:160) — that is, with something like a continuous canopy shielding them from the blazing sun. Further, without having to plow, sow or harvest, hunt or trap, the wandering Israelites were fed, for their Provider sent to them, in that barren desert, two staple foods: ***mann*** and ***salwa*** (2:57, 7:160, 20:80),[107] the manna and quails mentioned in Ex. 16:4-5, 14 ff., 31-36, and Num. 11:4-9.

---

[106]Arabic, "***ghamam***". While this is commonly translated as "clouds," al-Tabari says, "*Ghamam* is that which overcasts (*ghamma*) the sky and covers it with clouds and dark dust and other things which veil it from the eyes of gazers. . . . It has been said that the *ghamam* which God spread as shade for the Children of Israel was not cloud. . . . What God described as *ghamam* is no more likely to have been a cloud than [it is to have been] something else which covered the face of the sky" (Tabari/C, I:327-328). Ibn 'Abbas comments that the canopy shading the Israelites was cooler and more wholesome than an ordinary cloud, being the cloud in which God will descend on the Day of Resurrection (according to His saying, **In canopies of clouds** [2:210]), and the cloud in which the angels came down during the Battle of Badr (Ayoub/Q, I:105). And while the Biblical account suggests the possibility that this canopy may have been the smoke of one or more volcanoes, perhaps of Mount Sinai itself, this in no way diminishes the miraculousness of an occurrence that was so fortuitously arranged by divine providence at such a time.

[107]*Mann* is a sweet, sticky substance secreted by certain trees that grow in Sinai, Iraq and other areas of the Middle East. To this day, *mann* is available in the region in processed form as a

These two foods came to them regularly, day after day, without fail. **"Eat of the good things that We have provided you"** (2:57, 7:160, 20:81), their Sustainer instructed them through the tongue of Moses (A). Says Ibn 'Abbas (R):

> This was in the desert. [God] had spread the overcast to shade them, had sent down manna and quails upon them, and had given them clothes which did not wear out or become dirty. A cubic rock was set among them, and Moses was commanded to strike the rock with his staff.[108] Twelve springs gushed forth from it, three from every side, one for every tribe. And every time they left a halting-place they would find this rock with them in the place in which it had been with them where it had been in the first place.[109] (Tabari/*C*, I:344)

But while the people were told to **eat and drink of God's provision** (2:60), a solemn warning and intimation of things to come was also conveyed to them.

"Do not act wrongfully in the land, causing corruption" (2:60), they were told. And again: **"And do not transgress regarding them"** — the manna and quails[110] — **"lest My anger descend upon you, and the one upon whom My anger descends has certainly fallen. But indeed,"** came the divine reassurance, **"I am the Forgiver of the one who repents and believes and does righteous deeds and then continues in guidance"** (20:81-82).

---

popular sweet. Ibn 'Abbas says that this ***mann*** fell from the sky onto trees and the Israelites fed on it as they wished (Tabari/*C*, I:327-333).

[108]This confirms Ex. 17:6-7, in which "the rock at Horeb {Sinai]" is mentioned and Moses is told, "Strike the rock, and water will come out of it for the people to drink." Maulana Maududi reports that this rock can be seen to this day near Mount Sinai, with its twelve openings for each of the twelve tribes of Israel (Maududi/*Q*, 2:fn. 76).

[109]According to another opinion which holds that the prophet Shu'ayb was Moses' father-in-law, this rock was brought by Adam from Paradise and passed on from generation to generation until it came to Shu'ayb, who gave it to Moses, together with the staff. Some commentators also say this was the rock on which Moses later put his clothes while bathing, mentioned on page 145.

[110]This warning is said to have been related to the Israelites' hoarding of these two staples (as mentioned in Ex. 16:19-20), rather than trusting that they would unfailingly come to them on a daily basis according to their needs.

REFERENCES: Qur'an: 2:57, 60; 7:160; 20:80-82. Commentaries: Tabari/*C*, I:327-332, 343-346; Tabari/*H*, III:76, 82-83; Ibn Kathir/*T*, 2:60, 20:81; Ibn Kathir/*Q*, "Musa"; Ayoub/*Q*, I:105; Maududi/*Q*, 2:fn. 76; Asad/*Q*, 44:fn. 16; Ali/*Q*, fn. 71.

29. The Israelites' First Tests

Do people suppose that they will be left at [merely] saying "We believe," and they will not be tested? (29:2)

After the awesome miracle that the Israelites had recently witnessed in the parting of the sea and the drowning of Pharaoh and his troops, it might be supposed that they would have been filled with faith and the certainty of God's mercy and protection. True, they had suffered terribly in Egypt, but that had been their test during that particular phase of their community's collective life. It was now behind them, and the forging of their nation's future lay in their hands.

Often, when people go through the fire of intense suffering, they come out stronger, purer, deeper and more faithful than before. And while this was true of a handful of steadfast believers among Moses' people, it was not the case with the majority. Rather than strengthening their trust and commitment to their beneficent Creator, their suffering had rendered them defeated and dispirited. Moreover, instead of being the inspired carriers of the message of their Creator's Oneness and sovereignty, most of them had become confused by their exposure to Egyptian values, religion and culture. Uncertain of the truth of their own beliefs, they were incapable of grasping the greatness and uniqueness of their mission as the carriers of the true, pristine, God-centered faith in the midst of the prevailing paganism of the time.

The constant sameness of their daily diet proved to be one of the Israelites' first tests in Sinai. Instead of remaining grateful and satisfied with what they were granted with unfailing regularity and without any effort on their part, together with the ever-present water supply from the rock and the overcast shading them from the sun, they quickly became fed-up with the monotony of their diet of manna and quails.

Not understanding the fact that in God's all-wise plan everything has its time and place, and that they would have to prove themselves by patience and steadfastness in walking toward their goal, they began to grumble and ask for easy solutions and gratifications.

"O Moses," they complained, **"we can never endure one kind of food. So call upon your Lord for us to bring forth for us, from what the earth produces, some of its herbs and its cucumbers and its garlic and its lentils and its onions"** (2:61).

Thus began the trivialization of the Israelites' faith and the weakening of their relationship with their beneficent Lord through ill manners and petty demands. **"Would you exchange that which is inferior for that which is better?"** Moses (A) reproached them. **"Go to** any **town,**[111] **and indeed you will have what you have asked!"** (2:61).

Another test soon awaited them, for **they came upon a people devoted to idols of theirs.** Accustomed to the idol-worship of the Egyptians and finding it attractive, the people whom the Most Merciful Lord had but recently miraculously rescued from bondage and certain death felt a desire for a similar idol of their own. **"O Moses,"** they demanded, **"appoint a god for us, just as they have gods"**[112] (7:138).

"Indeed, you are a people behaving ignorantly!" Moses (A) retorted. **"Surely those"** — the idol-worshippers whom they wished to imitate — **"what they are engaged in is destroyed and what they are doing is in vain. Shall I seek for you a deity other than God, while He has preferred you above mankind?"** (7:138-140) That is, how can you possibly be so foolish and faithless as to imagine worshipping some false deity when the Lord your God has shown His love and preference for you by sending you guidance through His prophets, thereby making you the testifiers to His Oneness and Omnipotence to the peoples of the earth, and has but recently saved you from enslavement and annihilation? Says Ibn 'Abbas (R):

> Then they went on and they came upon a people who were worshipping some idols. When the Israelites said to him, "O messenger of God, make some idols for us like theirs," Moses said angrily, **"Indeed, you are a people behaving ignorantly!** You have seen so many signs and witnessed so many events but it did not teach you anything. You have neither learned a lesson nor do you have any shame!" (*Hadith* of the Trials)

---

[111] This is the most widely accepted interpretation of the words ***"ahbitu misran."*** An alternative, less preferred interpretation is, **"Go to Egypt."**

[112] It is reported that when Prophet Muhammad (S) went forth to the Battle of Hunayn, he passed by a tree called Dhat Anwat belonging to the local idol-worshippers, on which they hung their weapons. The people then asked him to appoint for them a Dhat Anwat like that which those people had. At that, the Prophet said, "May God be glorified! This is like what the people of Moses said when they asked him to appoint a god for them, just as other people had gods. By Him in whose hand is my soul, you will certainly follow the practices of your predecessors!" (*Mishkat*, 5408).

Then, in the verse that follows this dialogue between the Israelites and Moses (A), addressed to the descendants of Moses' people, the Jews living in Medina during the Prophet's time, the divine Author of the Qur'an evokes poignant memories of the Israelites' degrading bondage in Egypt, from which God had miraculously rescued them, saying:

> **And [recall, O Children of Israel,] when We saved you from the people of Pharaoh, who afflicted you with the worst torment, slaughtering your sons and letting your women live. And in that was a tremendous trial from your Lord.** (7:141, 2:49)

REFERENCES: Qur'an: 2:161; 7:138-140. Commentaries: Tabari/*C*, I:344-355; Tabari/*H*, III:72, 82-83; Ibn Kathir/*T*, 20:36-40; Ibn Kathir/*Q*, "Musa"; Ayoub/*Q*, I:105; Maududi/*Q*, 7:fn. 98; Asad/*Q*, 7:fn. 101.

30. Moses on Mount Sinai

O Children of Israel, We saved you from your enemy and made an appointment with you at the right side of the Mount,[113] **and sent down to you manna and quails.** (20:80)

Presently, God Most High **appointed for Moses thirty nights** (7:142) of seclusion in His Presence upon the holy mountain, Sinai.[114]

Before leaving for the meeting with his Lord, Moses (A) placed Aaron (A) in charge of the Israelites.

"Take my place among the people and do right, and do not follow the way of the corrupters"[115] (7:142), he instructed his brother, thereby indicating his awareness of the fact that there were already mischief-makers and corrupters among his people. And he promised to return after thirty nights. He did not yet know that it would be his destiny and most high privilege to complete the thirty nights by ten more.[116]

Then, leaving behind the heavy burdens of his community, Moses (A) secluded himself upon the rugged mountain.

---

[113]The plural form of the pronoun "you" in the phrase, **"made an appointment with you,"** suggests that God made an appointment with the Israelites collectively at the eastern side of Mount Sinai to receive the scripture through the tongue of Moses.

[114]A contemporary account describes Mount Sinai as follows:

> A perfect setting for inducing the visionary experiences of solitary contemplation, Jebel Musa rises to a height of 7455 feet above a haunting wilderness of shadowed ravines and twisting ridges. Rounded cliffs of reddish brown granite, sculpted and scoured by wind and water, blasted and burned by sand and sun, give the mountain the appearance of having gone through the hardening fires of a cosmic furnace. The eerie, primordial quality of the barren landscape, swept clean of all contaminating influences, evokes a sense of the pure and timeless place where Moses conversed with God. (Bernbaum, *Mountains*, p. 94)

The cave in which Moses spent his period of seclusion, a place of pilgrimage for Jews, Christians and Muslims alike, is at the summit of the mountain, as well as a church and a mosque.

[115]Aaron's deputyship is mentioned in a *hadith* reporting that when the Prophet (S) set out for the campaign of Tabuk, he appointed his cousin and son-in-law 'Ali ibn Abi Talib as his deputy in Medina. 'Ali, who was a renowned warrior, then asked him, "Are you going to leave me in charge of the children and women?" To this the Prophet (S) replied, "Are you not pleased to be to me in the rank of Aaron to Moses? — except that there will be no prophet after me" (*Bukhari*, 5:700).

[116]According to Arabic usage, a period of time referred to as "nights" comprises "days" as well.

"And what made you hasten away from your people, O Moses?" (20:83), God Most High asked the prophet whom He had so uniquely honored with His divine companionship and speech.

"They are close behind me, and I hastened to You, my Lord, that You might be well-pleased" (20:84), Moses (A) replied in utter humility.

According to several Companions of the Prophet (S), Moses (A) spent thirty days and nights in spiritual preparation, which included fasting. Further details are provided by Ibn 'Abbas (R), who states:

> They [the Israelites and their prophets] went a distance beyond that place [where they had asked Moses to make them a god and then camped]. Moses (A) then said to them, "Obey Aaron, for I am appointing him as my deputy and I am going to see my Lord. I will be gone thirty days."
>
> Then he went to the appointed place, and after completing thirty days and nights of fasting, he prepared himself to converse with God. But thinking that his mouth had a foul odor because of fasting, he took some grass and chewed on it. God then asked him — although He knew well the reason — why he had broken his fast. Moses (A) replied, "So that in conversing with You my mouth may smell sweet."
>
> God said, "Do you not know that the odor of the mouth of a fasting person is more pleasing to Me than musk?[117] Now you must fast an additional ten days, and then We shall converse."
>
> Moses then started fasting another ten days, and God says, **"[And We appointed for Moses thirty nights] and perfected them with ten [more], and thus his Lord's term was completed as forty nights"** [7:142]. (*Hadith* of the Trials)

God Most High alone knows what took place in that sacred meeting between Himself and His faithful, devoted prophet. But when God spoke to him, Moses (A), burning with intense love and yearning, longed with the deepest longing to see Him.

"My Lord," he begged, **"show me Yourself, that I may look at You"** (7:143).

---

[117]The Prophet (S) said, "By Him in whose hands is Muhammad's soul, the odor of the mouth of a fasting person is better in the sight of God than the scent of musk" (*Bukhari*, 3:128), for it is the sign of the faster's commitment to spiritual discipline and struggle (*jihad*) with his lower self (*nafs*) for the sake of his Lord.

"You will not see Me," his Maker replied. **"But look at the mountain, and if it remains in its place, then you will see Me"** (7:143).

Moses (A) did so. **Then when his Lord manifested Himself to the mountain, He caused it to crumble, and Moses**, a finite human being, unable to carry the magnificence of the Lord of all creation, **fell down unconscious**[118] (7:143). Says Ibn 'Abbas (R):

> [God] revealed of Himself no more than the equivalent of the tip of the little finger, and He sent the mountain crashing down, while Moses fell down in a faint. (Tabari/*H*, III:73)

When Moses (A) recovered, it was with the full awareness of the unseemliness of what he had asked of the God, the praised and exalted Lord of creation. **"May You be glorified!"** he exclaimed. **"I turn to You in repentance, and I am the foremost of the believers"** (7:143).

But God Most High knew that His prophet had asked to see Him only out of the deepest love and desire for Him, and hence He did not rebuke him for it. **"O Moses,"** came the gracious response, **"indeed I have chosen you above mankind for My messages and for My speech,**[119] **so keep to what I have given you and be among the grateful"** (7:144).

God Most High then **wrote for him, on the Tablets** of the Law, **admonition** to be drawn **from all things and explanation for all things** (7:145) regarding what is permissible and prohibited (***halal*** and ***haram***).[120] Some commentators say that what was inscribed on the Tablets was the *Taurat*, while others say that the Tablets preceded the *Taurat*.

---

[118]**Vision does not perceive Him** (6:103), God says concerning His exalted Self, the sight of whom no mortal except Prophet Muhammad (S) has ever been permitted to experience. Consequently, when Moses looked at the mountain and God sent down His divine manifestation upon it, it crumbled in front of Moses' eyes and he fainted from the awesomeness of the sight. The commentator al-Suddi said, "Angels surrounded the mountain, and the angels were surrounded by fire, and angels surrounded the fire, and those angels were surrounded by fire" (Tabari/*H*, III:73). These words suggest that, as indicated in Ex. 19:16-20, 20:18 and 24:15-18, the manifestation of God's Presence upon the mountain may have taken the material form of a volcanic eruption so awesome that even the most fearless and trusting of men could not remain conscious through it.

[119]In keeping with what is mentioned in footnote 104, God's choosing Moses **"above mankind"** refers to mankind of his own time, not of all times.

[120]According to Ex. 34:28 and Deut. 4:13, 10:4, the Tablets were inscribed with the "ten words" — the Ten Commandments mentioned in Ex. 20:3-17. For a discussion of the relationship of these commandments to Islam, please see Appendix B, "The Covenant, the *Taurat* and the Ten Commandments," on pages 183-187.

"Then keep to it with determination," the Lord God instructed His prophet, **"and order your people to keep to the best of it"** (7:145). That is, Moses himself was to practice what had been revealed with the utmost diligence, and he was to command his people to hold fast to the best of what they would find contained therein.

REFERENCES: Qur'an: 7:142-145; 20:83-84. Commentaries: Tabari/*H*, III:72-73; Ibn Kathir/*T*, 7:145; Ibn Kathir/*Q*, "Musa"; Maududi/*Q*, 7:fn. 100; Asad/*Q*, 7:fn. 104. Other works: Taher/*Sinai*, p. 44; Bernbaum/*Mountains*, p. 94.

31. THE GOLDEN CALF

And the people of Moses made ready, after him, out of their ornaments, the form of a calf that made a lowing sound. (7:148)

Then he [al-Samiri] brought forth for them the form of a calf that made a lowing sound, and they said, "This is your god and the god of Moses, but he has forgotten." (20:88)

During this period, Moses' absence had become a major test for the Israelites. Ibn 'Abbas (R) reports the details of the matter:

> Meanwhile, after thirty days, when Moses did not return according to promise, it was very troubling to them.
>
> Aaron then addressed them, saying, "When you came out of Egypt, you had with you the things borrowed from and entrusted to you by Pharaoh's people, and also things of your own similar to that.[121] In my view, you should now take an accounting of whatever is with you, for things borrowed and entrusted to you are not lawful [*halal*] for you, and we are not going to return any of these things to them, nor should we keep them with us for ourselves." Then he dug a pit and ordered all the people who had these possessions or ornaments with them to throw them into this pit, and then he lighted a fire over them so that they burned, saying, "Neither for us nor for them."
>
> [Among the Israelites] there was a person, al-Samiri, from among a people who worshipped the cow — a neighbor of the Israelites but not of the Israelites. He had gone with Moses and the Israelites when they departed, and it had occurred to him, when he saw the trace [of Gabriel's horse], to take a handful of it, and he had kept it with himself.
>
> On this occasion, when he passed by Aaron, Aaron said to him, "O Samiri, will you not throw what is in your hand?" although he had kept it for a long time but no one had seen it.
>
> He said, "This is a handful from the trace of the messenger [Gabriel] who was with you at the sea, and I will not throw it on any account unless you pray to God that when I throw it, it should become whatever I desire it to be."

---

[121]This is the meaning of the Israelites' subsequent declaration to Moses, **"We did not break the promise to you by our own will, but we were made to carry burdens of the people's ornaments, so we threw them, and thus did al-Samiri throw"** (20:87).

So he threw it, and Aaron prayed on his behalf. Then he [al-Samiri] said, "I desire that it become a calf," and then everything that was in that pit of [gold and silver] ornaments or copper or iron came together and became a hollow calf, neither having a spirit nor [the ability to] low. Ibn 'Abbas (R) said, "By God, it did not possess a sound of its own, but it was only that the wind passed through its backside and came out of its mouth, and that made the sound."

Then the Israelites were divided into divergent groups. One of the groups said, "O Samiri, what is this? You have the most knowledge of it."

He said, "This is your Lord, but Moses has lost his way."

Another group said, "We will not reject this until Moses returns to us. If it is our Lord, we will not have lost anything, and we can [always] return to it, but if it is not our Lord, we will follow whatever Moses says." And a third group said, "This is of Satan's handiwork. It cannot be our Lord, and we do not believe in it nor attest to it."

Aaron said, **"O my people, you are only being tested by it, and indeed, your Lord is the Most Merciful, so follow me and obey my command"**[122] [20:90].

They said, "What has happened to Moses that he promised thirty days and broke his promise? It is forty days since he left." And the foolish among them said, "His Lord has made a mistake and he is still searching for him." (*Hadith* of the Trials)

Thus, despite Aaron's warnings that they were merely being tested by the idol, his reminders that no other than the One, the Unique, could be their Lord, and his calling them to follow him and obey his orders, large numbers of Israelites were taken in by al-Samiri's deception. **"This is your god and the god of Moses, but he has forgotten"** (20:88), they declared. **"We will never stop being devoted to it until Moses returns to us"** (20:91).

They then became so zealously attached to the idol that **they absorbed the Calf into their hearts** (2:93). Ibn 'Abbas (R) states that their devotion to it went so far that they were obsessed by it and worshipped it, loving it with the deepest love (Tabari/*C*, I:312, 455; Tabari/*H*, III:76).

---

[122]In revealing the true story of the fabrication of the Calf, God exposes the falsity of the claim contained in Ex. 32:2-6, 24, 35, that it was God's prophet, Aaron, who fabricated this idol for his people to worship.

> **Did they not see that it could neither speak to them nor guide them to a way, and that it could not return a word to them, nor possess any power of harm or benefit for them?** (20:89),

asks the Creator of all things, as if marveling at their mindlessness.

Strong opposition to Aaron (A) then arose among the deviators, for they considered him weak and of no account, so much so that they nearly killed him (7:150). For his part, Aaron (A) was afraid that if he continued journeying onward with the believers who had remained with him, Moses might have cause to reproach him when he returned, supposing that he had caused division among the Israelites and had not heeded his word (20:94). He therefore stayed among the believing Israelites who were not seduced by the Calf, while its devotees continued with their perverted worship.

REFERENCES: Qur'an: 7:148; 20:88-91. Commentaries: Tabari/*C*, I:311-313, 453-455; Tabari/*H*, III:69-70, 72, 74-76; Ibn Kathir/*Q*, "Musa"; Ayoub/*Q*, I:99-101; Asad/*Q*, 7:fn. 113, 20:fn. 70.

32. THE JUDGMENT OF AL-SAMIRI

And [recall, O Children of Israel,] when We appointed for Moses forty nights. Then you adopted the Calf after him, while you were wrong-doers. (2:51)

Despite the fervent love of the misguided Israelites for their idol, at some point before Moses' return there arose among them the awareness of the enormous gravity of their sin against their Creator.[123] **And when regret overcame them and they saw that they had gone astray, they said, "If our Lord does not have mercy upon us and forgive us, we will surely be among the losers"** (7:149).

Meanwhile, as the period of Moses' seclusion on Mount Sinai drew to a close, God Most High gave His prophet a hint of what had occurred during his absence. **"Indeed, We have tested your people after you, and al-Samiri has led them astray"** (20:85), his Lord informed him. **"I shall soon show you the abode of the transgressors"** (7:145).

Thus forewarned, **Moses returned to his people, angry and grieved** (7:150, 20:86). In his hands he carried the Tablets, made of green chrysolite from Paradise, inscribed with God's sacred Law for the guidance of his people. Ibn 'Abbas (R) reports that after the meeting with his Lord, Moses' face was so radiant that no one could look at it, and thus it was veiled from sight (Tabari/*H*, III:73-74).

Reaching the Israelites' encampment, Moses (A) beheld with horror the idol that had been fabricated in his absence. After all the suffering the Israelites had endured in Egypt, after their miraculous escape from their enemies, after all his efforts to make them committed to their Maker, they had betrayed Him and substituted the statue of a cow for the Lord of creation!

"How evil is that which you have done in my place in my absence!" Moses (A) exclaimed. **"Would you hasten your Lord's command?"** (7:150), meaning "Were you in haste to bring down God's judgment upon yourselves?" And out anger for the sake of God the Exalted, whom his people had

[123] *Shirk* (ascribing lordship, divinity or its attributes to other than God) is the one sin that God does not forgive, as mentioned on page 409.

so gravely blasphemed, **he threw down the Tablets**[124] **and seized his brother by his head** and by his beard, **pulling him toward him** (7:150).

"O Aaron," Moses (A) demanded, **"what prevented you, when you saw them going astray, from following me? Have you then disobeyed my order?"**[125] (20:92-93).

"O son of my mother," Aaron (A) pleaded, **"do not take me by my beard or by my head! Indeed, I feared that you might say, 'You caused division among the Children of Israel and did not heed my word'"** (20:94). And appalled by his brother's supposing him to be in some way responsible for this unprecedented calamity, he added, **"Son of my mother, indeed, the people considered me weak and nearly killed me, so do not let the enemies gloat over me nor consider me among the wrong-doing people!"** (7:150).

When it became clear to Moses (A) that Aaron had had no part in the making of the idol, he immediately repented of having accused him unfairly. **"My Lord,"** he prayed, **"forgive me and my brother, and admit us into Your mercy, for you are the Most Merciful of the merciful!"** (7:151).

Then, as the prophet and judge of his people, he began to enquire into what had occurred in order to determine guilt and bring back the transgressors from their deviation.

"O my people," he said, **"did not your Lord make you a goodly promise?**[126] **Then was the time of its fulfillment too long for you, or did**

---

[124]Concerning this, Ibn 'Abbas reports the Prophet (S) as saying, "Being given information is not like seeing. God Most High gave Moses information about what his people had done regarding the Calf and he did not throw down the Tablets, but when he saw what they had done, he threw down the Tablets and they were broken" (*Mishkat*). Ibn 'Abbas also said, "The Messenger of God (S) was given seven long *surahs*, while Moses was given six. When he threw down the Tablets, two of them were withdrawn and four remained (Abu Dawud, 1454). Ibn 'Abbas also mentioned God's writing for Moses, **on the Tablets, concerning all things, admonition and explanation for all things** (7:145), as well as **guidance and mercy** (6:154, 28:43), saying that when Moses threw down the Tablets, God took away six-sevenths of what was inscribed but left one-seventh, in whose **inscription was guidance and mercy for those who are in awe of their Lord** (7:154) (Tabari/*H*, III:78).

[125]This refers to Moses' instructions to Aaron, before leaving for the holy mountain, to take his place among his people, do right, and not follow the way of the corrupters (7:142).

[126]What was this goodly promise that God had made to the Israelites? Maulana Maududi suggests that it refers to God's pledge to grant the Israelites His favors, which was fulfilled by His bringing them out of slavery in Egypt, destroying their enemy, and providing them freely with sustenance in the desert, or to His promise to grant them the Law and guidance (Maududi/*Q*,

you desire that wrath from your Lord descend upon you, that you broke your promise to me?" (20:86). That is, "God made you so many fair promises and granted you so many favors. But then you foolishly initiated this pagan practice and were unable to wait a little while for my return, doing that which made you deserving of God's wrath, and at the same time breaking your commitment to me to obey and worship Him alone."

"We did not break the promise to you by our own will," the guilty Israelites explained in an attempt to exonerate themselves. **"But we were made to carry burdens of the people's ornaments, so we threw them into the fire, and thus did al-Samiri throw"** (20:87). By this, they meant to say that they had not deliberately intended to assist in the fabrication of an idol but had merely followed Aaron's instructions for getting rid of the unlawful possessions in their hands. And thus the story of al-Samiri's role in the catastrophe came to light.

Moses (A) then turned his attention to the cunning fabricator of the Calf. **"And what is your case, O Samiri?"** (20:95), he asked, for in keeping with justice, every actor in this drama, both the evil and the good, must be heard before judgment was passed.

"I saw what they did not see," al-Samiri replied. **"So I picked up a handful of dust from the track of the messenger,"** Gabriel, **"and threw it, for thus did my lower self suggest to me"** (20:96).

Once the instigator of idolatry had openly admitted his guilt, Moses (A) did not waste words on reproaches or leave any room for excuses. Al-Samiri's offense, corrupting the pure religion of the holy Lord, who has no partner, equal or like, was unpardonable. And the prophet of God conveyed the divine sentence to the corrupter, saying:

"Then begone! And indeed, it will be your lot in this life to say, 'No contact,'[127] **and indeed you have an appointment"** on the inevitable Day of

---

30:fns. 64-65). Or perhaps it is contained in His saying, **"If you are thankful, I will surely grant you increase,"** (14:7), and, **"Indeed, I am with you. If you establish *salat* and give *zakat*, and believe in My messengers and support them, and lend God a goodly loan [by giving in charity], I will surely remove your sins from you and admit you to gardens [of Paradise] beneath which rivers flow"** (5:12/13). Or it may refer to God's assurance of His support and favor as long as the Israelites took no objects of worship other than Him, and were obedient to His commands and true to their unique, sacred mission of conveying His Message to other peoples.

[127]Ibn Kathir says that al-Samiri's punishment in this world was that no one would be able to touch him nor would he be able to touch anyone (Ibn Kathir/*T*, 20:97). This suggests a state of total isolation from human society — possibly, it has been said, due to leprosy.

Judgment "**which you will not fail to keep. And look at your 'god,' to which you remained devoted! We will certainly burn it and then scatter it widely in the sea. Your deity is only God, other than whom there is no deity! He encompasses all things in knowledge**" (20:97-98).

Then, in the verse that follows, the divine Author of the Qur'an confirms the absolute truthfulness and accuracy of the preceding account, saying,

> **Thus do We relate to you [Muhammad] something of tidings of what has preceded. And We have certainly given you, from Ourself, a message [the Qur'an]. (20:99)**

Summarizing this portion of the story, Ibn 'Abbas (R) reports:

> Then God spoke to Moses [on Mount Sinai] and conveyed to him whatever He desired to convey, and then He told him what had happened to his community in his absence.
>
> Moses then **returned to his people, angry and grieved**, and he said to them what you have heard of that which is in the Qur'an. **And he seized his brother by his head, pulling him toward him**, and **threw down the Tablets** [7:150] out of anger. And his brother gave his excuse and he asked for forgiveness for him.
>
> He then directed his attention to al-Samiri and said to him, "What induced you to do this?"
>
> Al-Samiri said, **"I picked up a handful of dust from the track of the messenger**, Gabriel, and I was aware of it, while it was concealed from you. **And thus did my lower self suggest to me"** [20:96].
>
> **He said, "Then begone! And it will surely be your lot in this life to say, 'No contact,' and you surely have an appointment which you will not fail to keep. And look at your 'god' to which you remain devoted! We will certainly burn it and then scatter it widely into the sea"** [20:97], although this did not free him [al-Samiri] from [attachment to] other gods. (*Hadith* of the Trials)

REFERENCES: Qur'an: 2:51; 7:145; 20:85-99. Tabari/*C*, I:454-455; Tabari/*H*, III:74, 77-78; Ibn Kathir/*T*, 7:150, 20:97; Ibn Kathir/*Q*, "Musa"; Ayoub/*Q*, I:126; Maududi/*Q*, 20:fns. 64-65, 74; Asad/*Q*, 7:fns. 14, 116, 20:fn. 83; Ali, fn. 2606.

33. The Seventy Israelites Meet with God

And [recall, O Children of Israel,] when you said, "O Moses, we will not believe in you until we see God openly." Then the blast seized you while you were looking on. Then We revived you up after your death, that you might perhaps be thankful. (2:55-56)

. . . **They said, "Show us God openly," whereupon the blast seized them for their wrong-doing.** (4:153)

Then, when the anger abated from Moses, he took up the Tablets, and in their inscription was guidance and mercy for those who are in awe of their Lord (7:154).

But although the material form of the idol had been now brought to an abrupt and disgraceful end, which demonstrated to its worshippers that it did not possess the slightest power, even to save itself, the impact it had had upon those who were devoted to it could not be so easily erased, for they had **absorbed the Calf into their hearts through their unbelief** (2:93), thereby opening themselves to the divine anger.

> **Indeed, those who adopted the Calf — wrath from their Lord and humiliation will encompass them in the life of this world, and thus do We recompense the fabricators of falsehood** (7:152),

God Most High says concerning the severe punishment awaiting those who had accepted this idol as a god in place of their Creator. But at the same time,

> **Those who did evil deeds and then repented after them and believed — indeed, your Lord is, after that, Forgiving and Merciful.** (7:153)

It was therefore critical that the Israelites now offer their repentance to God sincerely and atone for their sin as He would command. And Moses **chose seventy men of his people** (7:155) — the very best among them, according to the account of Ibn 'Abbas — to meet with God the Exalted.

It is reported that Moses (A) instructed the seventy to hasten to their Lord. They were to repent to Him for what they had done and implore His forgiveness for those whom they had left behind. And he ordered them to fast and purify themselves and their garments. Then he departed with them for Mount Sinai so that he might present them to his Lord at the time He had appointed for him, for he did not come to Him except with His permission and knowledge.

The seventy men did as they were ordered. And when they went with Moses (A) to the holy mountain to meet their Lord, they asked their prophet to request Him on their behalf to hear His divine speech. And Moses (A) agreed.

As Moses (A) neared the mountain, a column of cloud fell upon it so that the whole mountain was enveloped. The prophet of God entered into it, saying to his people, "Draw near!" And while Moses (A) was speaking to his Lord, such a radiant light appeared on his forehead that no one could look at him, and a veil was placed in front of him.

The people then drew near until, when they had entered the cloud, they fell down in prostration. Then they heard God Almighty speaking to Moses (A), commanding him to do this and prohibiting him from doing that.

This collection of commands and prohibitions constitutes the *Taurat* — that is, the original Torah, revealed word-by-word to Moses (A) by God, just as the Qur'an was later revealed word-by-word to Muhammad (S). We will speak about the *Taurat* in detail in Appendix B, pages 181-183.[128] For the present, we will merely note the importance of maintaining a clear distinction between the divine writ revealed to Moses (A) on Mount Sinai and the Pentateuch or first five books of the Old Testament, which are also known as the Torah.

Rather than being the direct words of God, the latter books are a history of mankind from the beginning of creation, focusing on the descendants of Abraham through his grandson Jacob or Israel, written by a number of different authors. In recent times Biblical scholars have identified several interwoven narratives of various writers in these books, often reporting variations on the same theme, thus making clear the existence of human interpolations into the original revelation to Moses, God's peace and blessings be upon him.

When God Most High had finished conveying His commands to Moses (A), the cloud was removed from him and he went to his people. But the Israelites' collective worship of the Calf and the weakness of faith that had preceded it had taken their toll. The effect of it was that, even after all they had seen of their Lord's signs, they were still uncertain in their belief. This they now expressed candidly, saying, **"O Moses, we will never believe in you until we see God openly"**[129] (2:55).

---

[128]Appendix II, On the *Taurat*, in Yusuf Ali's translation of the Qur'an also contains an interesting and useful commentary.

[129]Here, "believe in you" is said to mean that the Israelites would not accept Moses' truthfulness nor what he brought them without seeing God with their own eyes. In 4:153, the demand is

Then, because of the impertinence and presumptuousness of their demand, **the blast [*al-sa'iqah*] seized them for their wrong-doing** while they **were looking on** (4:153, 2:55). As a result, the seventy men were so profoundly startled and shocked that all of them died on the spot.

And when the quaking [*al-rajfah*] overtook them[130] (7:155), Moses (A) began humbly to plead with his Lord.

"My Lord, if You had willed, You could have destroyed them previously, and me as well," the much-tried prophet said. **"Would You destroy us for what the foolish among us have done? This is nothing but Your trial by which You permit to stray whomever You will and You guide whomever you will. You are our Protector, so forgive us and have mercy upon us, and You are the Best of Forgivers! And decree for us good in this world and in the Hereafter,"** he concluded. **"Indeed, we have turned to You"** (7:155-156).

Then, although Moses (A) had earnestly besought forgiveness for the seventy Israelites and for his people in general, God Most High unexpectedly `began to speak to him of another, as yet unheard-of people who would be the recipients of His special mercy, saying,

"My punishment — I strike with it whomever I will, but My mercy embraces all things. So I shall decree it for those who are mindful of Me and give *zakat*,[131] and those who believe in Our verses — those who follow the Messenger, the Unlettered Prophet whom they find inscribed in what they have of the *Taurat* and the *Injil*, who enjoins upon them the right and forbids them from the wrong, and makes permissible to them the good and prohibits to them the evil, and relieves them of their burden and the fetters which were upon them.[132]

"Show us God openly." The word **"*jahrah*"** in both these verses means plainly, publicly, openly and without the intervention of any veil or barrier.

[130]The meanings of **"*al-sa'iqah*"** and **"*al-rajfah*"** are explained in Volume One, pages 237-238. Conceivably what occurred was a volcanic eruption, accompanied, as such occurrences often are, by lightning and earthquake. In keeping with this interpretation, Maulana Maududi translates **"*rajfah*"** as "earthquake" (Maududi/*Q*, 7:155).

[131]That is, the poor-due (literally, "purification"), one of the five "pillars" or prescribed acts of worship in Islam, which consists of giving a small fraction of certain categories of wealth or property to the poor and needy, or for beneficial or charitable works. A number of Qur'anic verses, among them 2:83, 4:162, 5:12/13 and 21:73, make it clear that this obligation was prescribed by God for the communities of believers throughout history through their respective prophets.

[132]That is, the highest success would be attained by those who would follow the revealed guidance and example of the last of the messengers and prophets, Muhammad (S). His being **in-**

"Therefore," the divine speech concluded, **"those who believe in him and honor him and support him and follow the light which was sent down with him — it is those who will be the successful"** (7:157).

By these words was Moses (A) unexpectedly granted the high honor of receiving from his Lord tidings of the illustrious prophet who would follow him many centuries later, Muhammad, God's peace and blessings be upon him, the fulfillment and culmination of the prophetic line.

As for the seventy Israelites, Moses (A) continued to beg his Lord to restore the representatives of his people to life. He had chosen seventy men from among them, the very best, he said, but now he would have to return to the remainder of his people alone. After that, how would they possibly believe in him, with what would they trust him? And he poured out penitence to his Lord on behalf his community, beseeching and imploring Him until He restored the seventy men to life.

Summarizing this segment of the story, Ibn 'Abbas (S) states:

> The Children of Israel were greatly divided. Those who had been in agreement with Aaron were happy. Then they said to Moses, "O Moses, request your Lord from us to open the door of repentance on behalf of everyone and to remove from us our [evil] deeds."
>
> So Moses chose seventy men from among his people who were the best among the Children of Israel and who had [apparently] not associated anything with the truth. Then they went out to ask God for forgiveness, and the earth quaked with them [and they died].
>
> Then God's prophet was embarrassed on account of his people and on account of his delegation, and he said, **"My Lord, if You had willed, You could have destroyed them previously, and me** as well. **Would You destroy us for what the foolish among us have done?"** [7:155], for God knew that some of them still had the love of the Calf in their hearts and believed in it, and that is why the earth had quaked under them.

---

scribed in what they have of the *Taurat* and the *Injil* refers to the prophecies concerning him contained in the Old and New Testaments, which we will discuss in detail on pages 484-490. His making permissible the good and prohibiting the evil refers to the fact that he would permit lawful things that had previously been prohibited by custom or by human authority without divine sanction, as he would likewise prohibit unlawful things that had similarly been made lawful. His relieving believers of their burden and fetters refers to "the many severe rituals and obligations laid down in Mosaic Law, as well as to the tendency towards ascetcism [and monasticism] evident in the teachings of the Gospels" (Asad/Q, 7:fn. 125).

Then God said, **"My mercy embraces all things. So I shall decree it for those who are mindful of Me and give *zakat*, and those who believe in Our signs — those who follow the Messenger, the Unlettered Prophet"** [7:156-157].

Then Moses said, "O Lord, I was asking forgiveness for my people, but You are saying, 'My mercy is for another people.' If that is the case, why did you not delay my coming and bring me forth among the followers of this blessed man?" (*Hadith* of the Trials)

REFERENCES: Qur'an: 2:55-56; 7:149, 154-158. Commentaries: Tabari/*C*, I:320-326; Tabari/*H*, I:78-80; Ibn Kathir/*Q*, "Musa"; Maududi/Q, 7:fns. 112-117; Ali/Q, fn. 1127; Asad/Q, 7:125-127; Ayoub/*Q*, I:103-104.

34. THE REPENTANCE OF THE ISRAELITES

Furthermore, they adopted the Calf after clear evidences had come to them, but We pardoned that. (4:153)

After Moses (A) had pleaded with his Lord to restore the seventy men to life, according to the account of Ibn 'Abbas (R) and other commentators, he also begged Him to forgive his people for their worship of the Calf.

"No, not until they kill themselves,"[133] his Lord replied.

Moses (A) then conveyed his Lord's decree to his people, saying, **"O my people, indeed you have wronged yourselves by your adopting the Calf. So repent to your Maker and kill yourselves,"** meaning that the innocent among them were to kill those guilty of idol-worship. **"That will be best for you in front of your Maker"** (2:54), he added, for by expiating their sin during this life, they would be saved from the dreadful punishment of idolatry in the Hereafter.

Having forfeited their Lord's mercy and support due to the magnitude of their sin, the distraught Israelites were unable to offer any defense or excuse, nor were they able to disobey the explicit order of their Creator. Ibn 'Abbas (R) says that those who had worshipped the Calf then sat down with their cloaks drawn about them, while those who had not worshipped it rose up and took their weapons in their hands. Deep darkness covered them all, and they began to kill one another.

Moses (A) wept, surrounded by young boys and women who were pleading for forgiveness for their menfolk. And Moses (A) begged God to spare the remainder of his people before they were all annihilated.

Then God turned to the people in mercy and forgave them. Moses (A) ordered them to lay down their weapons, and when the darkness lifted, seventy thousand Israelites had been killed. Ibn 'Abbas (R) says that all those

---

[133]The seventy Israelites' meeting with God on Mount Sinai is reported in two passages, 2:54-55 and 7:155-157. The mutual killing of the Israelites is reported only in the first passage, where it is mentioned before the demand to see God openly.

A number of differing versions and sequences of these events are given by the classical commentators. However, in keeping with the requirements both of logic and of faithfulness to the account of Ibn 'Abbas in "The *Hadith* of the Trials [of Moses]," we have followed the sequence given here. An English translation of this interpretation can be found in al-Tabari's *History*, Volume III, pages 78-79.

who had been killed had done their penance, dying as martyrs, while those who survived had also done penance and were likewise forgiven, according to the words that follow,

> **Then He accepted your repentance; indeed, He is the Acceptor of Repentance, the Merciful** (2:54).

Says Ibn 'Abbas (R):

> God then told him that their repentance would consist of their killing one other, and even if a father encountered his son, he should slay him with his sword and not care about whom he slew.
>
> Then all those who had hidden their thoughts from Moses and Aaron repented, for they knew that God was aware of their sin. They acknowledged it and did what was commanded, and God forgave the slayer and the slain. (*Hadith* of the Trials)

REFERENCES: Qur'an: 2:54; 4:153. Commentaries: Tabari/*C*, I:316-319; Tabari/*H*, III:74-75, 79; Ibn Kathir/*Q*, "Musa"; Ayoub/*Q*, I:102-104.

35. THE COVENANT

And Moses certainly brought you clear proofs. Then you adopted the Calf after him, while you were wrong-doers. And [recall, O Children of Israel,] when We took your covenant and raised the Mount over you, [saying,] "Take what We have given you with determination and listen." They said, "We hear and we disobey," and they absorbed the Calf into their hearts through their unbelief. (2:92-93)

In a number of verses, God Most High speaks of the ***'ahd*** or ***mithaq*** — that is, the covenant, agreement or commitment that He took from the Children of Israel.

There is no authoritative report of when or where this covenant or commitment was made, nor whether it was made at one particular time and refers to a specific occurrence, or rather to a general understanding between God and the descendants of Abraham, Isaac and Jacob, peace be upon them. But once again, since God Most High **neither errs nor forgets** (20:52), we may conclude that these details are of no relevance. However, the verses cited above indicate that the covenant was made at some time after the affair of the Calf.

Now, this covenant with God Most High was not an optional matter; the Israelites were not asked whether they wished to accept it or given the choice of rejecting it. Rather, the covenant was what was imposed upon them by their Lord as the community He had chosen to carry His Message, and they were ordered to take what was given to them **with determination and listen** (2:93). That is, they were to accept the *Taurat* that had been revealed through Moses for their guidance, and to do what God had commanded them therein and refrain from what He had forbidden.

Concerning the covenant, God was to reveal many centuries later through His Last Prophet, peace and blessings be upon him,

> **O Children of Israel, recall My favor that I bestowed upon you, and fulfill My covenant [with you], that I may fulfill your covenant [with Me], and be in awe of Me.** (2:40)

It was as if God were saying to them, "You are the people I have appointed for this trust, so it is your responsibility, like it or not. And if you keep your part of the agreement I have made with you, I will also keep *My* part of the agreement."

Like it they did not. Indeed, the Israelites did not accept this covenant willingly or with any sense of the tremendous honor they had been granted as a people, for due to their long years of slavery in Egypt, coupled with the eroding of their beliefs due to their contact with paganism, they had become weak of faith, passive, indifferent and hard to motivate.

As a result, God Most High caused Mount Sinai to be raised above them for the taking of this covenant, as described in 2:92-93 cited at the beginning of this chapter and in the following verses:

> **And We granted Moses clear authority, and We raised the Mount over them for their covenant. . . . And we took from them a solemn covenant.** (4:153-154)
>
> **And [mention, O Muhammad,] when We raised the Mount over them as though it were a canopy and they thought that it would surely fall upon them, [and We said,] "Take what We have given you with determination and remember what is in it, that you may be mindful of God."**[134] (7:171; also 2:63)

The classical commentators understood these references to the "raising" of Mount Sinai over the Israelites as meaning that God caused the mountain to be suspended over them as if it were a canopy or roof, until they supposed that it would fall on them. It is said that when they expressed their unwillingness to accept their Lord's covenant, He caused His angels to lift up the mountain over them, telling them to accept the book of God, the *Taurat*, or it would be flung down upon them.

As long as the mountain towered over them, they agreed to observe the covenant, but when it was removed they turned back.[135] For although God Almighty had honored and favored them above all the peoples of the earth by

---

[134]According to Ibn Kathir, **"What We have given you"** in this verse refers to the *Taurat*; **"take it with determination"** means to act on it fully; and **"remember what is in it"** means to be constant in reading or reciting it (Ibn Kathir/T, 2:63-64).

[135]This interpretation is similar to that of the Talmud, in which it is stated, "The Holy One, blessed be He, inverted Mount Sinai over them like a huge vessel and declared, 'If you accept the Torah, well and good. If not, here shall be your sepulchre.'" The above understanding may be related to the fact that one of its reporters, Wahb bin Muhabbih, was a convert to Islam from Judaism among the second generation of Muslims.

Considering the possibility that Mount Sinai may have been an active volcano at the time of these events, the statement, "So the cloud of the Lord was over the tabernacle by day, and fire was in the cloud by night, in the sight of all the house of Israel during all their travels" (Ex. 40:38; also Num. 9:15-16), suggests that the Israelites may have remained within sight of the mountain's fire and smoke throughout much of their forty years of wandering, during which, it is said, they set out in the morning and returned to the same place in the evening.

entering into this solemn agreement with them, many of them still remained unwilling and uncommitted, hedging and looking for ways out; as God says:

> **Then you turned back after that [the acceptance of the covenant]. And if it had not been for the favor of God upon you and His mercy, you would surely have been among the losers.** (2:64)
>
> **Then you turned back, except a few of you, and you were resisting.** (2:83)

Says Ibn 'Abbas (R):

> Moses then turned toward the holy land, together with his people, and he took the Tablets, after his anger had subsided, and ordered them to put into practice the commandments therein.
>
> This was burdensome for them, and they balked and did not put them into practice. Then God raised the mountain above them like a canopy and they were afraid that it would fall upon them, so they held firmly to the scripture while they were looking at the mountain out of fear that it might fall upon them. (*Hadith* of the Trials)

REFERENCES: Qur'an: 2:40, 63-64, 83, 92-93; 4:153-154; 5:12/13; 7:171. Commentaries: Tabari/*C*, I:365-367, 422-429, 454-455; Ibn Kathir/*T*, 2:63-64, 2:93, 7:171, 20:36-40; Ibn Kathir/*Q*, "Musa"; Ayoub/*Q*, I:112-113; Maududi/*Q*, 2:fn. 81.

36. THE ISRAELITES' REFUSAL TO FIGHT

"O my people, enter the holy land that God has decreed for you, and do not turn back and become losers." (5:21/23)

Slowly and painfully, the Israelites continued their trek across the Sinai desert — *al-tih*, the "wilderness" of the Old Testament — toward the sacred land of their ancestors.

Throughout their long period of wandering, the beneficent Lord **shaded them with clouds and sent down to them manna and quails** (7:160, 2:57; also 20:80), and supplied them with garments that never wore out. Water was provided for them from the square rock which they carried about with them. Whenever Moses (A) struck it with his staff, **there gushed forth from it twelve springs**, three from each side, and **each** tribe **knew its drinking place** (7:160, 2:60).

At some point in the Israelites' journeying, God commanded Moses (A) to advance with them toward Jericho, a city close to Jerusalem in the land that was their destination. And God **delegated twelve leaders among them** (5:12/13).

"Indeed, I am with you," their Lord said to them through the tongue of Moses (A). **"If you establish *salat* and give *zakat*, and believe in My messengers and support them and lend God a goodly loan"** by spending for charity and good works, **"I will surely remove your sins from you and admit you to gardens** of Paradise **beneath which rivers flow. But whoever disbelieves among you after that has certainly strayed from the soundness of the way"** (5:12/13).

When his people neared Jericho, Moses (A) sent out the twelve leaders, each representing one of the tribes of Israel, as scouts. Their mission was to bring back information about the land and its people, who were reported to be giants.

The scouts found the place to be inhabited by very large, powerful, oppressive people. Well-aware that the Israelites would turn away from Moses if they knew what kind of adversaries they would have to contend with, the twelve men made a pact among themselves not to speak of this to anyone except their two prophets when they returned. However, when they reached home, ten of them immediately broke the pact, each one telling his near relatives about the fearsome people they had encountered. And as a result of this news, the Israelites became terrified of entering that territory.

Only two men among the twelve concealed what they knew from their people. Instead of talking about it to others, they went to Moses and Aaron (A), confiding the matter to them. But the harm had already been done by the ten who had talked. The Israelites were now too passive, fearful and lacking in trust in God to advance into the territory that they had been ordered to enter.

Moses (A) then reminded them of how wonderfully their Lord had guided and supported them up to this time.

"O my people," he exhorted, **"remember God's favor to you when He appointed prophets among you and made you sovereigns"** — that is, free, independent people, in charge of your own selves, your families and your possessions, after your miserable enslavement in Egypt — **"and granted you what He had not granted anyone among mankind.**[136] **O my people,"** he urged, **"enter the holy land that God has appointed for you, and do not turn back and become losers"** (5:20-21/22-23).

But the majority of Israelites had not learned any lessons from their previous experiences, either about reliance upon God or the need for initiative and courage. **"O Moses,"** they retorted, **"indeed, in it are a people of tyrannical strength,**[137] **and indeed, we will never enter it until they depart from it. But if they depart from it, then we will enter"** (5:22/24).

We can only imagine how that sorely-tried prophet must have felt at that point. After all his efforts with his people, the majority of them still remained so cowardly, weak-willed and lacking in trust in their Lord that they had no desire to help themselves.

Then two men from among those who feared, upon whom God had bestowed favor[138] (5:23/25), spoke up, saying, **"Enter upon them through**

---

[136]That is, the knowledge of God; the prophethood of their ancestors, Abraham, Isaac, Jacob and Joseph; the guidance conveyed through His chosen messengers; and the high honor of conveying His Message to mankind.

[137]"***Jabbarin***," meaning huge, gigantic or tyrannical people.

[138]Who these two were is not stated, but the prevailing opinion among commentators is that they were Joshua (Yusha) son of Nun and Caleb (Kilab) son of Jephunneh, Moses' brother-in-law. One report from Ibn 'Abbas states that they were the two scouts who had concealed the information about the inhabitants of Jericho (Tabari, *H*/III, 81). The "fear" mentioned in the first sentence may refer either to their fear of God or to the fear of the inhabitants of Jericho that gripped their people. However, Ibn 'Abbas suggests an alternative reading of this verse: **Then two men from among those whom they feared, upon whom God had bestowed favor** — that is, two men from among the feared inhabitants of Jericho who believed in Moses and had

the gate" — that is, by a direct, frontal attack — **"for when you have entered it, you will surely be victorious. And rely upon God, if you are believers!"** (5:23/25-26).

However, the Israelites were so lacking in resolve and steadfastness that they had no will to exert themselves, even on their own behalf.[139] **"O Moses,"** they responded reaching the utmost point of audacity toward God and their prophet, **"indeed, we will never enter it as long as they are in it. Then go, you and your Lord, and fight! We will surely stay here"**[140] (5:24/27).

With this ultimate piece of impertinence, it became clear to Moses (A) that his people were unwilling to be guided or helped. Incident after incident had demonstrated their weakness of purpose, faithlessness and deficiency of courage — and now *this!* No number of miracles, divine help, favors or mercies could move them to do what they should, for they were doomed by their ingrained inertia and lack of commitment. **"My Lord,"** he exclaimed, **"indeed, I do not have mastery except over myself and my brother. Then make a separation between us and the transgressing people [*fasiqin*]!"** (5:25/28).

And God Almighty accepted His prophet's prayer. **"Then indeed, it"** — the holy land of their forefathers — **"will be prohibited to them for forty years,"** He declared, during which **"they will wander across the land. So do not grieve over the transgressing people [*fasiqin*]!"** (5:26/29).

Thus it was that, because of the Israelites' disbelief, rebelliousness, passivity and lack of reliance upon their Lord, they were denied access to the land of their ancestors until many years later, when a new generation with a fresh

---

come over to him (Ibn Kathir/*Q*, "Musa"). This is clarified in the continuation of "The *Hadith* of the Trials" on page 134.

[139]This is also stated in such Old Testament verses as Num. 14:1-4, 10, 16:1-2, 41, 25:1-3; Deut. 1:26, 32, 35, 42-43; 9:6-14, 27; 31:16-21, 27-29 and many others.

[140]A moving *hadith* related to this verse is reported concerning the first battle in Islam, the Battle of Badr. The Prophet's Companion, 'Abdullah bin Mas'ud, said, "I witnessed al-Miqdad ibn al-Aswad [another Companion] in a scene that, if I had been the person involved in it, would have been dearer to me than anything corresponding to it." 'Abdullah continued: "He [Miqdad] came to the Prophet (S) while he was summoning [the Muslims to fight] against the idolaters. Then he [Miqdad] said, 'We will not say, as the people of Moses said, **"Then go, you and your Lord, and fight,"** but rather we will fight on your right and on your left and at the front of you and behind you.' Then I saw the face of the Prophet (S) beaming with happiness because of his words" (*Bukhari*, 5:288).

mentality would prove itself worthy of the divine trust that had been bestowed upon them. Because of this, it is reported, each day the people would set out, traveling across the land, carrying with them the rock that supplied them with water. Then at the end of the day's wandering, they would again find this rock at the place where it had been previously, where they would settle down for the night.

Summarizing these events, Ibn 'Abbas (R) says:

> Then they all went toward the holy land, and they found there a city inhabited by strong people of extraordinarily huge stature, and it is even said that their fruits were huge in size. Then they said, **"O Moses, indeed, in it are people of tyrannical strength.** We do not have power to fight them, **and indeed, we will never enter it until they depart from it. But if they depart from it, then we will enter"** [5:22/24].
>
> **Then two men from among those who feared said, "Enter upon them through the gate, for when you have entered it, you will surely be victorious"** [5:23/25]. An alternative reading of this is, **Then two men from among those whom they feared . . .** Yazid, a narrator of this ***hadith***, was asked, "Is that how you read it?" He said, "Yes, [they were] from among the giants. They had believed in Moses and had come to him, and they said, 'We know our people. If you are afraid because of what you observe of their stature and their numbers, in reality they are cowards and have no heart [for fighting].'" But other commentators have said that these two men were of the people of Moses.
>
> But the Israelites who were fearful said, **"O Moses, indeed we will never enter it as long as they are in it. Then go, you and your Lord, and fight! We will surely stay here"** [5:24/27].
>
> Then Moses (A) became extremely angry, and he prayed against them and called them **"*fasiqin*"**[141] [5:25/28], although he had not called them that previously, despite all their sins and rebelliousness. But this day God accepted what he called them, and He also termed them **"*fasiqin*"** [5:26/29] and prohibited this sacred land to them for forty years, so that they wandered across the land, each morning waking up and traveling without rest. (***Hadith*** of the Trials)

REFERENCES: Qur'an: 2:57, 60; 5:12/13, 20-26/22-29; 7:160; 20:80. Commentaries: Tabari/C, I:327-333, 343-346; Tabari/H, III:81-83; Ibn Kathir/Q, "Musa"; Ayoub/Q, I:105; Maududi/ Q, 5:fns. 42, 45-46; Asad/Q, 5:fn. 32.

---

[141] Meaning transgressing, rebellious, defiantly disobedient, iniquitous or sinful people.

37. THE INCIDENT OF THE SETTLEMENT

. . . And We granted Moses clear authority and raised the Mount over them for their covenant, and We said to them, "Enter the gate prostrating," and said to them, "Do not transgress concerning the Sabbath"; and We took from them a solemn covenant. (4:153-154)

The incident reported in this chapter is one of the matters mentioned in the Qur'an concerning the Israelites whose time frame is not clear. Hence, commentators differ as to whether it occurred during the time of Moses (A) or later, during the time of his successor, Joshua (A). However, the above verses suggest that it occurred during the time of Moses (A), as is confirmed in the account of the classical commentator Mujahid, which we will cite shortly.[142]

"Enter this town, dwell in this town,"[143] God commanded the Israelites through their prophet, **"and eat from it as you wish in abundance,"** (2:58, 7:161), meaning that they were to eat heartily, as they pleased, of the produce of a certain town which they were commanded to enter and settle. **"And enter the gate prostrating"** (2:58, 4:154, 7:161) in glorification of God and thanksgiving for His favors. **"And say, '*Hittah*[144] — relieve us of our burdens.' We will forgive your transgressions for you and will increase the doers of good"** in reward (2:58, 7:161). That is, they were to humbly beg God for forgiveness and release from the burden of their sins so that He might conceal and forgive their transgressions, while at the same time increasing the good deeds and rewards of those who did good among them.

---

[142]Three sets of verses speak of this incident. The first, 2:58-59, occurs just after the mention of the manna and quails, and before the mention of the water-giving rock. The second, 4:153-154, is given above. The third, 7:161-162, is preceded by verses concerning the water-giving rock and the supply of manna and quails. Please see the Qur'anic References at the end of "Moses," Part Six, for a complete citation of these and all other verses.

[143]"***Qaryah,***" meaning town, city, village or settlement. Ibn 'Abbas and other eminent commentators say that this town was Jerusalem, while others mention nearby Jericho, Damascus, Ramlah or other cities of the region (Tabari/C, I:334-335; Ayoub/Q, I:106).

[144]Most of the classical commentators were of the opinion that the word "***hittah***" means to remove a burden — in this context, the burden of sins. Some say that the people mentioned in this incident were told to say "*La ilaha illa-Llah,* there is no deity except God" because the proclamation of God's Oneness takes away the burden of sins. Others say that Hittah was the name of the eighth gate of Jerusalem, known as *Bab al-Hittah* (the Gate of Unburdening), or that it was the gate of the sanctuary in Jerusalem, which Moses and his people used to face while praying.

Thus, the object of what the Israelites were commanded to do was both to enjoy God's favors and seek His pardon for their sins in all humility. By this command, they were granted a new opening to His forgiveness and mercy through the unburdening of their previous misdeeds, and a chance to mend their ways. But instead of earnestly carrying out the order, **those of them who did wrong** made a game of the divine command and **substituted a saying other than that which had been said to them** (2:59, 7:162), replacing it with a nonsensical distortion of the word of repentance they had been ordered to say by their most generous Lord, as mentioned in the ***hadith***:

> It was said to the Children of Israel, **"Enter the gate prostrating and say '*Hittah.*' We will forgive your transgressions for you."** But they substituted [**a saying other than that which had been said to them**] and entered dragging themselves on their buttocks, and they said, "*Habbah fi sha'rah* [A grain in a hair]." (*Bukhari*, 6:165)

Mujahid said that Moses (A) ordered his people to enter by the gate, prostrating and saying **"*Hittah*,"** and the gate was lowered for them so that they would prostrate. But instead of prostrating, they scooted in on their buttocks, saying the word '*Hinta*' (meaning "wheat"). God then caused the mountain to shake over them; that is, He brought the root of the mountain out of the ground and raised it over them frighteningly, like a canopy. When they saw this, they entered prostrating in fear, with their eyes fixed on the holy mountain upon which God Most High had manifested Himself (Tabari/C, I:366, 339-340).

Then, because of their ridiculing of the divine command, God **sent down upon those who did wrong a torment [*rijz*] from the sky because they were transgressing** (2:59) and **because of the wrong they were doing** (7:162).

What was this **"torment"**? Various classical commentators have supposed that it was the plague because that is one meaning of the word **"*rijz*,"** which occurs in both 2:59 and 7:162, cited above. In support of this, they mentioned the saying of the Prophet (S), "The plague is *rijz*. It was sent upon a group of the Children of Israel, or upon those who were before you" (*Bukhari*, 4.679). However, there is no authoritative evidence that the calamity sent against the transgressors in this incident was the plague or that the Israelites or others afflicted by the plague mentioned by the Prophet (S) were those referred to in this incident. Consequently, God alone knows the nature of the punishment that befell those who defied and mocked His command.[145]

REFERENCES: Qur'an: 2:58-59; 4:153-154; 7:161-162. Commentaries: Tabari/*C*, I:334-342; Ibn Kathir/*T*, 2:58-59; Ayoub/*Q*, I:106-107; Asad/*Q*, 2:fn. 42.

[145]Another incident in which God's command was turned into a mockery concerns a group of Israelites who broke the strict rules concerning the sanctity of the Sabbath by using a trick to make it appear that they had not done so. Although a second group admonished them for this transgression, the first group did not desist and were severely punished by God. This incident is mentioned in three passages, 2:65-66, 4:154 and 7:163-166, each of which is preceded or followed by other matters related to the Israelites' wanderings in Sinai. It is also mentioned in 4:47, without connection to any other incidents. However, since Moses is not mentioned in any of the verses related to this incident, although it appears to relate to his time, and because Ibn 'Abbas is reported as having stated that it took place during the time of the prophet David (Ayoub/*Q*, I:113), we have not included it here.

38. The Incident of the Cow

And [recall, O Children of Israel,] when you killed a person and disputed about it, but God was to bring forth that which you were concealing. (2:72)

During the time of Moses (A), the Israelites were tried by yet another test, this time concerning an unsolved case of murder, mentioned in 2:67-73. And from the wording of the verse above, we must conclude that the incident involved was quite familiar to the Jews of Medina of the Prophet's time, to whom it was firstly addressed.

The report of this incident opens with the words,

And [recall] when Moses said to his people, "Indeed, God commands you to slaughter a cow."[146] (2:67)

This command was issued without any conditions or specifications: "Slaughter a cow, any cow you please."

The group of Israelites to whom the command was addressed reacted to it in disbelief, as if not understanding the reason for the command or how it ought to be carried out. **"Are you making a mockery of us?"** (2:67), they asked their prophet.

"I seek refuge with God from being among the ignorant!" (2:67), Moses (A) exclaimed, appalled at the suggestion that he would play with his Lord's commands.

However, instead of carrying out God's simple, unqualified order to sacrifice any cow that might be on hand, the people involved began to ask for details.

"Supplicate your Lord for us to make clear to us what she is" (2:68), they demanded.

---

[146]It is this cow for which the second *surah*, *Al-Baqarah* (The Cow), is named. The identity of the people to whom this order was given, and who subsequently demanded details, is not mentioned in the Qur'an. However, Ibn Kathir states that they were the people of the second town, who were being framed by the old man's nephews. Seeing no connection between the command to slaughter the cow and the identification of the murderer, they lacked sufficient trust in Moses to take his instructions at face value and questioned him in a manner that suggested that the order must be in error (Ibn Kathir/*T*, 2:67-73).

Moses (A) did as he was asked. **"He says, 'She is a cow neither old nor virgin but midway between that,'"** he informed them. **"So do as you are commanded"** (2:68), meaning that they were simply to carry out the order they had been given without asking further questions or making conditions.

But this did not stop their demand for specifications. **"Supplicate your Lord for us to make clear to us what her color is"** (2:69), they asked next.

To save his people from the sin of disobedience, Moses (A) again did as they asked.

"He says, 'She is a yellow cow, bright in color, pleasing to the beholders'" (2:69), he told them — that is, a cow of such pure, uniform yellow color that those who saw her would marvel at her beauty and perfection.

Not willing to accept even this quite specific answer, the people continued to demand further details. However, the wording of their next question suggests that they intended it to be the last.

"Supplicate your Lord for us to make clear to us what she is. Indeed, all **cows seem alike to us. And if God wills, we will surely be guided"**[147](2:70).

Still God Most High remained patient with them, and His prophet likewise. Moses (A) then conveyed his Lord's final answer to the people:

"He says, 'She is a cow neither broken-in to till the soil nor to water the fields, sound, with no blemish upon her'" (2:71) — that is, a heifer that has not yet not been trained to plow the ground or draw water for irrigation, that is healthy and free of physical defects, and whose hide is of a uniform and even color.

All the characteristics that had now been specified would be very difficult to find in combination in one animal, especially the hide of unmixed color. Concerning this, Ibn 'Abbas (R) comments that if the people had taken the first cow that came to hand and sacrificed her, it would have been sufficient for them. But because they pressed on relentlessly with their questions and annoyed Moses, God was hard on them (Tabari/C, I:384).

However, they had now received such clear, definitive replies to their questions that they had no choice except to obey. **"*Now* you have come**

---

[147]Concerning this, the Prophet (S) is reported to have said, "If the Children of Israel had not made this exception [of saying **'If God wills,'** indicating some willingness on their part to do what was commanded], they would not have been granted what they asked for" — namely, the description of the cow they were to sacrifice. However, Ibn Kathir reports that there is some doubt about the soundness of this ***hadith***. And God knows best (Ibn Kathir/*T*, 2:67-73).

with the truth!" (2:71), they said to Moses (A), as if implying that previously he had been lying.

It is reported that only one cow in the place met the specifications that had been given. Realizing that no other cow would serve their purpose, her owner asked an exorbitant price for her, which the people had no choice but to pay after all their questioning.

Moses (A) then ordered them to carry out the original command. **So they slaughtered her, although,** due to their extreme reluctance, **they almost did not** (2:71). This has been understood as meaning that they came very close to abandoning God's order because they simply did not want to obey it.

While the classical commentators differed concerning details, they all gave similar explanations of this passage. From among them, we cite here the interpretation of Ibn 'Abbas (R).

Among the Israelites during the time of Moses (A), there was an old man who was very wealthy. This man had no sons, and his two nephews, who were poor and propertyless, were his heirs. The man and his nephews all lived in a certain town which was close to another town.[148]

"If only our uncle would die and we could inherit his wealth!" the two nephews would think. Then, when he did not die as they hoped, Satan came to them, saying, "Why do you not kill your uncle, inherit his wealth, and claim blood-money from the people of the other town?" For whenever someone was murdered in that region, his body would be dumped between two towns. The distance between the dead man's body and the two towns would then be measured, and blood money would be claimed from the people of the town to which the body lay closest.[149]

---

[148]Note that although this incident is positively identified with Moses, the commentary indicates the people involved, like those in the incident of the Sabbath-breakers, were settled in a town, not wandering across the desert.

[149]The legislation concerning this is contained in Deut. 21:1-9. The following *hadith* sheds light on this practice:

> There was a man among the Children of Israel who had killed ninety-nine people. Then he went forth, asking [whether he might yet repent]. He came to an ascetic, asking that, and said to him, "[Is there] repentance [for me]?" He said, "No," so he killed him and then set out asking [further]. A man then said to him, "Go to such-and-such village," but death overtook him, and he turned himself in its direction. Then the angels of mercy and the angels of punishment disputed concerning him. And God inspired this [village] to come close and God inspired this [village] to keep distant, and He said,

When Satan had talked the nephews into doing this and their uncle's dying had taken too long for their liking, they murdered him.[150] Then they dumped his body at the gate of the town in which they did not live.

When the people of the second town awoke in the morning, the old man's nephews came to them. "Our uncle has been murdered at the gate of your town," they said. "By God, you will pay us the blood-money for him!"

"We swear by God that we did not kill him, nor do we know who did," the townspeople protested. "And we did not open the gate of our town after it had been bolted at night until we got up in the morning." And they went to Moses (A) concerning the matter.

But the old man's nephews had reached Moses (A) before them. "We found our uncle murdered at the gate of their town," they said.

"We swear by God that we did not kill him," the townspeople declared to their prophet. "And we did not open the gate of our town after it had been bolted at night until we got up in the morning."

The angel Gabriel (A) then brought Moses (A) a command from God, the All-Hearing, the All-Knowing:

"Tell them that God commands them to slaughter a cow and **strike him"** — the murdered man — **"with part of it"** (2:73) (Tabari/*C*, I:392-393; Ibn Kathir/*Q*, 2:67-73). And when they did so, God brought the dead man back to life so he could inform Moses (A) and those who had disputed concerning the matter about the identity of his murderer.

The dead man stood up. "Who killed you?" Moses (A) asked him.

"My nephew," came the reply, and the murdered man immediately returned to his state of death (Ibn Kathir/*T*, 2:67-73).

This incident, regardless of its precise details, is well-summarized by the classical commentator, Qatadah, who stated that a man was murdered among the Children of Israel, and each tribe among them accused another of the crime until the enmity among them had reached a dangerous pitch. They then took the matter to God's prophet, Moses (A), whereupon God revealed to him, **"Indeed, God commands you to slaughter a cow** [2:67] and **strike him with part of it"** [2:73]. Qatadah concluded his statement by saying, "It has been mentioned to us that his relative who was seeking to avenge his

---

said, "Measure what is between the two," and he was found to be closer by a span to this [village where he had intended to repent], so He forgave him. (*Bukhari*, 4:676)

[150]According to other interpretations, the murderer was one individual, not two.

blood was the one who had killed him on account of the inheritance between them" (Tabari/*C*, I:392). It is this that is meant by God's saying to the descendants of the Israelites through the mouth of His Last Prophet (S), just before the final verses of this narrative,

> **And [recall] when you killed a person and disputed about it, but God was to bring forth that which you were concealing. So We said, "Strike him with part of it.** (2:73)

Since this story has been narrated by its divine Author with virtually no background material, details or specifics, we must conclude that these are of no relevance. Rather, it is the lessons imparted by the story that are important. And they are as follows:

One lesson concerns God's ability to do all things, both precedented and unprecedented, including reviving the dead, whether on the Day of Judgment or, if He should so will, during this life.[151] Indeed, one of His divine Names or attributes is *al-Muhiy*, the Reviver or Giver of Life. In keeping with this meaning, after mentioning the revival of the murdered man, God says:

> **Thus does God bring the dead to life, and He shows you His signs, that you may understand** (2:73),

by granting mankind such evidences of His power to revive the dead on the Last Day as the unbelievers of the Prophet's time repeatedly denied.

This story also demonstrates that people may demand more and more details of a divine command simply as an excuse for not obeying it, and that, as a consequence of their unwillingness to obey, they may become more and more stubborn, rebellious and hard of heart. Thus it is that, in concluding the incident of the cow, God says:

> **Then your hearts became hardened after that, and they were like stones or even harder. For indeed there are stones from which streams gush forth, and indeed there are some of them**

[151]The following other instances of God's restoring people to life are mentioned in the Qur'an: (1) that of a group of people who left their homes **in many thousands, fearing death**, whereupon God commanded them to die and then **restored them to life** (2:243); (2) a man who was revived after having been dead for one hundred years, that he might know that **God is powerful over all things** (2:259), followed, significantly, by the verse concerning Abraham's asking God to show him how He gives life to the dead and the divine response of the hands-on parable of the four birds (2:260; see Volume One, pages 267-268); (3) the seventy Israelites who were restored to life on Mount Sinai after God had taken their souls (2:255); and (4) Jesus' raising the dead by God's leave (3:49, 5:110/113). There is also the well-known story of the People of the Cave (*Ashab al-Kahf*), mentioned in 18:9-26, who were revived after having being asleep for 309 years.

that split open and water flows out of them, and indeed there are some of them that fall down from fear of God. And God is not unaware of what you do. (2:74)

The second lesson of this story therefore concerns the necessity of unconditional obedience to God's orders *in the form in which they are given*, and the folly of demanding details of a command that have not been specified by the divine Law Giver, who never overlooks or forgets anything, thereby putting a whole community of believers, up to the end of time, into difficulties. The Prophet (S) emphasized the extreme seriousness of asking unnecessary questions by saying,

> Indeed, the worst sinner among Muslims is the one who asks about something which was not prohibited, and then it becomes prohibited on account of his asking. (*Bukhari*, 6:392)

This lesson was to be of vital importance to the first Muslim community during the twenty-three years in which the Qur'an was being revealed, curbing the natural human tendency to ask for details, referred to in the following verses:

> **Do you intend to question your messenger [Muhammad] as Moses was questioned previously?** (2:108)
>
> **O you who believe, do not ask about things which, if they are made clear to you, will distress you, for if you ask about them while the Qur'an is being revealed, they will be made clear to you. God has excused them,**[152] **and God is Forgiving and Forbearing.** (5:101/104)

---

[152]Meaning that God forgives what His servants do with regard to what He has left unspoken. The Prophet (S) said:

> Leave me as I leave you [that is, take what I say at face value without asking questions], for the only thing that destroyed those who were before you was their questioning and their disagreeing with their prophets. Therefore, when I prohibit you from something, avoid it, and when I order you to do something, do whatever you can of it. (*Bukhari*, 9:391)

Consequently, for Muslims, whatever the Prophet (S), as God's representative and spokesman, left unspoken, neither ordering nor forbidding it, is allowed (*mubah*). Whatever he forbade is unlawful (*haram*), and whatever he ordered is obligatory (*fard*) and binding to the extent of one's ability, in keeping with God's saying, **Whoever obeys the Messenger has obeyed God** (4:80); **Whoever obeys God and His Messenger has certainly achieved a great achievement** (33:71, also 24:52); **It is not for a believing man or woman, when God and His Messen-ger have decided a matter, that they should have any choice about their affair. And whoever disobeys God and His Messenger has certainly strayed into clear error** (33:36); and the

REFERENCES: Qur'an: 2:67-73, 108; 5:101/104. Commentaries: Tabari/*C*, I:376-396; Ibn Kathir/*T*, 2:67-73; Ayoub/*Q*, I:116-119; Maududi/*Q*, 2:fn. 84; Asad/*Q*, 5:fns. 120-121.

---

promise that whoever obeys God and His Messenger will be admitted to Paradise (4:13, 48:17) and attain God's favor (4:69).

39. THE SLANDERING OF MOSES

O you who believe, do not be like those who annoyed Moses; but God cleared him of what they said, and he was distinguished in God's sight.
(33:69)

As one incident followed another, the wandering Israelites continued to manifest disrespect, ingratitude and disobedience toward their Creator. Not only did the majority exhibit a half-hearted, contemptuous attitude toward their Lord by their repeatedly negative response to His commands,[153] but some of them also harmed their noble prophet by insolence, insults and even slander.

33:69 cited above refers to a specific instance in which Moses (A) was injured by the disrespectful and insulting behavior of his people. Concerning it, the Holy Prophet (S) said:

> Indeed, Moses was such a modest man that he used to cover his body completely, not exposing any of his skin. Then there injured him an injurer from among the Children of Israel, who said, "He covers himself in this manner because of a defect of his skin — either leprosy or a scrotal hernia or some other defect." And indeed, God desired to clear Moses of what they said about him.[154]
>
> One day he was alone, and he put his clothes on a rock and bathed. Then when he had finished, he went to take his clothes, but the rock ran off with his clothes. Moses then seized his staff and set out after the rock, saying, "My clothes, rock, my clothes!" until he came upon a crowd of the Children of Israel. Thus they saw him naked, the best of what God had created, and he was cleared of what they had said.
>
> Then the rock stopped, and he took his clothes, put them on, and began to hit the rock with his stick, and by God, the rock [still] bears scars from the effects of his hitting, three or four or five. And that is His saying, may He be exalted, **"O you who believe, do not be like those who annoyed Moses; but God cleared him of what they said, and he**

---

[153]This is mentioned again and again in such Old Testament verses as Ex. 14:11-12; 16:2-3; 17:2-4, and Num. 11:1, 4-15, 18-20; 14:1-4, 10, 26-27; 16:41-42; 20:2-5; 21:4-5.

[154]Moses was to be cleared of this allegation, first, because it was false and therefore constituted a slander against him. Moreover, since prophets are the most perfect among mankind, permitting such a slander to go unchallenged might have resulted in the undermining of his prophethood.

was distinguished in God's sight"[155] [33:69]. (*Bukhari*, 4.616; *Muslim*, 5849 -5850)

At some point — whether related to this incident or some other matter — this misbehavior of Moses' people toward him became so distressing that Moses (A) exclaimed, **"O my people, why do you injure me, while you certainly know that I am God's messenger to you?"**[156] (61:5). And in the continuation of this verse, the divine Author of the Book adds,

> **And when they deviated, God caused their hearts to deviate. And God does not guide a transgressing people.** (61:5)

Thus it was that, because of their rebellious attitude and indifferent response toward God's commands, their unwillingness to accept His covenant, and the annoyances, injuries and insults which Moses' people inflicted on him, they became more and more lost and astray. It was in this context that God Most High was to proclaim many hundreds of years later through the tongue of His Last Prophet (S) that the people of Moses (A) **did not wrong Us, but** rather, through their repeated transgressions, **they wronged themselves** (2:57; 7:160).

---

[155] A related version of this *hadith* begins, "The Children of Israel used to bathe naked, looking at one other, while Moses used to bathe alone, so they said, "By God, nothing prevents Moses from bathing with us except that he has a scrotal hernia" (*Bukhari*, 1:277). The remainder is very similar to what is cited above.

[156] It is reported that once, when Prophet Muhammad (S) was criticized for the manner in which he divided some war booty among the Muslims and the criticism was reported back to him, he said, "May God be merciful to Moses! He was injured more than this but he was patient" (*Bukhari*, 4:378, 4:617; also 8:122).

40. The Deaths of Aaron and Moses

And We certainly conferred favor upon Moses and Aaron, and We saved them and their people from the great affliction and supported them so they overcame, and We gave them the clarifying scripture and guided them to the straight path. (37:114-118)

As their Lord had decreed, the Israelites continued their fruitless wandering in Sinai for forty years.

Eventually all those over the age of twenty who had gone into the desert with Moses (A) died there, says Ibn 'Abbas (R), for none of those who had refused to enter the city of the giants with him lived to enter the holy land (Tabari/*H*, III:89). Nor did Moses (A) himself, for by the divine Will, he also died in the desert, preceded by Aaron (A).

Concerning the deaths of Aaron and Moses, God's peace and blessings be upon them, Ibn 'Abbas (R) and other Companions of the Prophet (S) report the following:

> God Most High revealed to Moses, "I am going to cause Aaron to die, so bring him to such-and-such a mountain."
>
> Then Moses and Aaron went to that mountain. When they reached it, there was a tree such as they had not seen before. When they went further, they saw a house. When they entered it, there was a bed upon which there was a cushion, and also a fresh, good smell.
>
> When Aaron saw this mountain, this house and what was in it, he was pleased and said, "O Moses, I would like to sleep on this bed."
>
> Moses said, "Then sleep on it!"
>
> He said, "Indeed, I am afraid that if the owner of this house returns he will be angry with me."
>
> Then Moses said, "Do not be afraid. I will deal with the owner of his house, so go ahead and sleep."
>
> Then Aaron said, "O Moses, sleep with me! Then if the owner of the house comes, he will be angry with both you and me."
>
> They both slept, and death came to Aaron. When he felt its touch, he said, "O Moses, you have deceived me!" And when he died, this house and the tree and the bed were all lifted up to the sky.
>
> Then when Moses returned to his people and Aaron was not with him, they said, "Moses has killed Aaron due to his jealousy because the Children of Israel loved him," for Aaron was much more lenient and pro-

tective of them than Moses, since there was a certain harshness toward them in Moses.

When this report reached him, he said to them, "Woe to you! Do you think I would kill my own brother?" Then when they insisted on this, he stood up and prayed two *rak'ats* and supplicated God, and the bed descended until they all saw it between the sky and the earth.

After that, when Moses was walking with his young man, Joshua, they encountered a black wind. When Joshua saw it, he thought it was the [Last] Hour, so he drew near to Moses and said, "The Hour has come while I am clinging to Moses, the prophet of God!"

But Moses slipped out of his shirt, leaving the shirt in Joshua's hands. Then when Joshua came to the Children of Israel with the shirt, they said, "You have killed the prophet of God!"

He said, "No, by God, I did not kill him, but he slipped away from me."

They did not believe him and wanted to kill him. He said, "If you do not believe me, give me three days' respite." Then he prayed to God, and a dream came to all those who were after him, informing them that Joshua had not killed Moses, but rather, "We have taken him up to Us," so they left him alone.

Not one of those who had refused to enter the settlement of the giants with Moses remained, for they all died without witnessing the conquest. (Ibn Kathir/*Q*, "Musa")

Concerning the death of Moses (A), Abu Hurayrah (R) reported that the Holy Prophet (S) said:

The Angel of Death was sent to Moses (A), and when he came to him, he hit him, [injuring his eye].[157] Then he returned to his Lord and said, "You sent me to a slave who does not want to die."

---

[157]In explanation of this *hadith*, the compiler of *ahadith*, Ibn Hibban, said:

When the Angel of Death said this to him, Moses did not recognize him, for he came to him in a form other than what he had known of him, just as Gabriel came [to Prophet Muhammad] in the form of a bedouin Arab [as reported in *Bukhari*, 6:30 and *Muslim*, 1], and just as the angels came to Abraham and Lot in the form of young men, due to which Abraham and Lot did not recognize them at first. Therefore, that is probably why Moses also did not recognize him, and that is why he gave him a blow and put out his eye; for he had entered his house without permission, and this contravenes our sacred Law [*Shari'ah*], since if someone peers into your house without permission you may put out his eye [as mentioned in the *hadith*, "If someone peers into your house

Then God restored his eye and said, "Go back and tell him to put his hand on the back of an ox, and for each hair his hand covers, he will have one year of life."

He [Moses] said, "O my Lord, *then* what will be?"

He said, "Then, *death!*"

He [Moses] said, "So, *now*!" And he asked God to bring him a distance of a stone's throw from the holy land.

Abu Hurayrah said, "The Messenger of God, God's peace and blessings be upon him, then said, 'If I were there, I would show you his grave by the road near the red sand-hill.'" (*Bukhari*, 2:423, 4.619; *Muslim*, 5851-5853)

May God's best blessings and eternal peace be upon Moses and Aaron, the two noble prophets who fulfilled their Lord's trust and labored so earnestly and faithfully in His service, about whom He says,

> **And We left [this invocation] for them among later generations: "Peace be upon Moses and Aaron!" Thus do We surely reward the doers of good. Indeed, they were among Our believing slaves.** (37:119-122)

REFERENCES: Ibn Kathir/*Q*, "Musa"; Tabari/*Q*, "Musa"; Tabari/*H*, III:85-91.

---

without permission and you hit him with a rock and injure his eye, there is no sin on you" (*Bukhari*, 9:26; Abu Dawud, 5153; *Mishkat*, 3526)]. (Tabari/*Q*, "Musa")

PART SIX: THE HOLY PROPHET SAID . . .

41. *AHADITH* CONCERNING MOSES

This is of the tidings of the Unseen which We reveal to you [Muhammad]. (3:44)

Among all humankind, past, present and future, no one was granted such knowledge of *al-Ghayb*, the unseen, spiritual realm, as the Seal of the Prophets, Muhammad (S), by means of which he possessed intimate, personal knowledge of earlier prophets and their communities. And out of this ocean of knowledge — which is still like a tiny drop in comparison to the limitless knowledge of the Creator — he often spoke about his brother prophet, Moses (A), further confirming Moses' exalted rank with his Lord.

In addition to the *ahadith* related to Moses (A) cited previously, the following have come down to us:

1. Once some of the Prophet's Companions were talking together. One said that God had taken Abraham as a friend; another said that He had spoken directly to Moses; another said that Jesus was God's word and spirit; and another said that God had chosen Adam. The Prophet (S) then came out to them and said, "I have heard what you said, and you are wondering that Abraham was God's friend, as indeed he was; and that Moses was God's confidant, as indeed he was; and that Jesus was His spirit and word, as indeed he was; and that Adam was chosen by God, as indeed he was." (*Mishkat,* 5762)

2. The Prophet (S) said, "Adam and Moses argued with one other. Moses said to Adam, 'O Adam, you are our father who failed us and caused our expulsion from Paradise.' Then Adam said to him, 'O Moses, God favored you with His speech and wrote [the Tablets] for you with His own Hand. Do you blame me for a matter that God decreed for me forty years before my creation?' So," the Prophet (S) added, "Adam prevailed over Moses [in argument]," repeating it three times. (*Bukhari,* 8:611, 6:620; *Muwatta,* 46.1.1)

3. Once when the Prophet (S) was passing through a valley called Azraq near Mecca, he said, "It is as if I see Moses," and he mentioned something about his coloring and his hair, "coming down from the mountain trail, and

he is putting his two fingers in his ears,[158] raising his voice in prayer to God, making *talbiyah* [the pilgrim's call]."[159] (*Muslim*, 319, also 318; *Mishkat*, 26.16.1)

He also said, "As for Abraham, you may look at your companion [meaning himself]. And as for Moses, he is a large, brown man on a red camel whose reins are made of palm fibre. It is as if I am looking at him while he is going into the valley, calling *talbiyah*." (*Muslim*, 320)

This indicates that Moses (A) made *Hajj* to the Sacred House, either physically during his lifetime or in the spiritual world.

4. The Holy Prophet's meeting with the earlier prophets during his Night Journey and Ascension (*al-Isra' wal-Me'raj*) at the site of Solomon's Temple in Jerusalem, known as *al-Masjid al-'Aqsa* (the Farthest Mosque), as well as in the seven heavens, is mentioned in the verse,

> **Exalted is He who took His slave by night from the Sacred Mosque [in Mecca] to Farthest Mosque, whose surroundings We have blest, to show him [something] of Our signs. Indeed, He is the Hearing, the Seeing.** (17:1)

And God Most High especially memorialized the Prophet's meeting with Moses (A) on that occasion in the words, **We certainly gave Moses the scripture, so do not be in doubt concerning his [Muhammad's] meeting [with him]** (32:23).

On the morning following this most sublime experience, when the Prophet (S) spoke about what had occurred during the night, he mentioned, among other things, that he had seen Moses, about whose stature, complexion, hair, and resemblance the people of his time he gave various descriptions.[160] Speaking from his spiritual vision, he also said:

> During my Night Journey, I passed by Moses near the red sand-hill, and he was standing in *salat* in his grave. (*Muslim*, 5858)
>
> The nations passed in review in front of me and I saw a great multitude of people covering the horizon. Then it was said, "This is Moses and his people." (*Bukhari*, 4.622)

---

[158]Probably for resonance, as in calling the *adhan* (call to prayer).

[159]The call, "Here I am, O our Lord!" which originated with Abraham (see Volume One, page 324). Ibn Kathir, in his *Qasas al-Anbiya' (Stories of the Prophets)*, has a section concerning the *Hajj* of Moses, the authenticity of which is based on the above *ahadith*.

[160]Mentioned in *Bukhari*, 4:462, 4:607-608, 4:647-648, and *Muslim*, 316-317, 320-322, 328.

5. In another *hadith*, the Prophet (S) spoke about his ascension to the seven heavens, in each of which he was welcomed and greeted, accompanied by his guide, the angel Gabriel (A).

After reporting his meeting with various prophets in the first, second, third, fourth and fifth heavens, the Messenger of God (S) gave a detailed account of his meeting with Moses (A), saying:

> Gabriel then ascended with me to the sixth heaven and asked that it be opened. It was asked, "Who is it?"
>
> He said, "Gabriel."
>
> It was asked, "Who is with you?"
>
> He said, "Muhammad."
>
> It was asked, "Has he been sent for?"
>
> He said, "Yes."
>
> Then it was said, "Welcome to him, and how excellent an arrival!"
>
> Then when I arrived, there was Moses. He [Gabriel] said, "This is Moses, so greet him."
>
> Then I greeted him and he returned it and said, "Welcome to the righteous brother and the righteous prophet!"
>
> Then when I left him, he wept. It was asked of him, "Why do you weep?"
>
> He said, "I weep because a young man will be sent after me, of whose *ummah* more will be admitted to Paradise than will be admitted from my *ummah*."[161] (*Bukhari*, 5:227)

The Holy Prophet (S) then related that Gabriel (A) ascended with him to the seventh heaven, where he was welcomed as before, and where he met and greeted Abraham (A). After that, he was admitted to the point of utmost nearness to his Lord, where there were shown to him certain ineffable spiritual realities beyond description. His narrative continues:

> Then *salat* was made obligatory on me, fifty prayers each day. Then I returned and passed by Moses, and he asked, "With what have you been charged?"
>
> I said, "I was charged with fifty prayers each day."

---

[161] Matter-of-factly and without boastfulness or pride, the Holy Prophet (S) said, "I will be the first among people to intercede in Paradise, and I will have the largest following among the messengers" (*Muslim*, 381).

He said, "Indeed, your ***ummah*** will not be capable of fifty prayers each day, and by God, indeed, I already tested the people before you and strove earnestly with the Children of Israel. Therefore, return to your Lord and ask for an alleviation for your ***ummah***."

Then I returned [to God] and He unburdened me of ten [prayers], and I returned to Moses and he said something similar to it. Then I returned [to God] and He unburdened me of ten [more], and I returned to Moses and he said something similar to it. Then I returned [to God] and He unburdened me of ten [more], and I returned to Moses and he said something similar to it. Then I returned [to God] and was ordered [to observe] ten prayers each day, and I returned [to Moses] and he said something similar to it. Then I returned [to God] and was ordered [to observe] five prayers each day.

Then I returned to Moses and he asked, "With what have you been charged?"

I said, "I have been charged with five prayers each day."

He said, "Indeed, your ***ummah*** will not be capable of five prayers each day, and indeed I already tested the people before you and strove earnestly with the Children of Israel. Therefore, go back to your Lord and ask for an alleviation for your ***ummah***."

I said, "I have asked my Lord until I am ashamed, so I am pleased and surrender [to His order]."

Then when I left, a Caller called to me, "I have concluded My ordinance and have alleviated My worshippers." (*Bukhari*, 5:227; also 9:608)

It is therefore God's honored prophet Moses (A) to whom Muslims owe the reduction of fifty prayers a day to five. Yet the Most Merciful, in His infinite generosity, has made those five prayers equivalent to the original fifty, for in another version of this ***hadith*** it is stated that the final time the Prophet (S) returned to his Lord to ask for a reduction in the number of prayers, God Most High said, "Those are five and those are fifty," meaning that the five prayers that He accepts were made equivalent to the fifty, adding, **"The word"** — that is, His original decree — **"will not be changed with Me"** [50:29] (*Bukhari*, 1:345; *Muslim*, 309, 313).

6. In earlier sections, we cited a number of ***ahadith*** that speak of the terrible distress of the believers on the Day of Judgment. Seeking respite, they will go first to Adam, then to Noah, and then to Abraham, asking them one after the other to intercede for them with their Lord.

To this, each of these great prophets will reply that this day God Most High is angry as He has never been before and will never be again, and that he is not the right person for this undertaking because of the mistakes he made during his lifetime, saying, "Myself, myself, myself!" The Prophet (S) then continued:

> The people will then go to Moses and say, "O Moses, you are God's messenger, and God favored you over the people with His Message and His speech.[162] Intercede for us with your Lord! Do you not see what a state we are in?"
>
> Moses will say, "Indeed, this day my Lord is angry with such anger as has never been before and will never be afterwards. I killed a person whom I had not been ordered to kill. Myself, myself, myself! Go to someone else. Go to Jesus!" (*Bukhari*, 6.236)

The believers will then go to Jesus, who will likewise refuse their request, but without mentioning any sin of his, and send them to Muhammad (S).

When they go to Muhammad, God Most High will give him permission to intercede for his ***ummah***[163] (*Bukhari*, 6:236; *Muslim*,, 378), or, in other versions, for anyone with the least bit of goodness or faith in his or her heart and who affirms that there is no deity except God (*Bukhari*, 9:507; *Muslim*, 375-377). Still other ***ahadith*** state that Muhammad (S) will be permitted to take people out of Hell without mentioning any condition (*Bukhari*, 9:532C, 2:553, 6:242; *Muslim*, 380, 373). And although Moses (A) will be too humble to consider himself fit to intercede, the fact that he be will among the prophets whose intercession is sought on the Last Day indicates his tremendous importance and rank.

7. Once while a Jew was showing an article for sale, he was offered a price for it that he disliked. He declined it, saying, "No, by Him who preferred Moses above mankind!" A man from among the ***Ansar*** [the Muslims of Medina] heard him, and he got up and hit him in the face and said, "Are you saying 'By Him who preferred Moses above mankind' while the Prophet (S) is in our midst?" The Jew then came to the Prophet and said, "Abu-l-Qasim,[164] indeed, I have a covenant of protection and a pledge [of security], so why did

---

[162] In *Bukhari* 9:532C, it is, "Go to Moses, a slave to whom God gave the *Taurat*, spoke directly, and brought near to Himself for conversation." Moses will say, "I am not fit for this undertaking," and will mention the mistake he made — that is, the killing of a person.

[163] In a number of ***ahadith*** (*Muslim* , 385-396), the Prophet (S) spoke of his desire and intention to use his special prophet's supplication (see Volume One, page 169) to intercede for his ***ummah*** on the Day of Resurrection.

[164] "Father of Qasim." According to a still-existing Arab custom, Muhammad (S) was referred to as the father of his first son, Qasim, who was born early in his marriage to his first wife, Khadijah, but died in infancy.

such-and-such hit my face?" The Prophet then asked the Muslim, "Why did you hit his face?" When he told him, the Prophet (S) became so angry that it could be discerned from his face, and he said,

> Do not make comparisons among God's prophets, for indeed the Trumpet will be blown and whoever is in the heavens and the earth will faint, except as God wills. Then it will be blown a second time and I will be the first to be resurrected, and there will be Moses holding onto the Throne. Then I will not know whether his fainting on the day of Mount Sinai sufficed for him or he was resurrected before me. And I do not say that there is anyone better than Jonah son of Matta. (*Bukhari*, 4:626, 9:52; *Muslim*, 5853-5856).

8. The Messenger of God (S) also said,

> Moses asked his Lord, "Who is the lowest in rank among the people of Paradise?"
>
> He [God] said, "He will be the person who will arrive after all the people of Paradise enter Paradise. It will then be said to him, 'Enter Paradise!' He will then say, 'O my Lord — *how*, when the people have already settled in their places and taken their shares?' It will then be said to him, 'Would you be pleased if you had a kingdom like that of one of the kings of the world?' He will then say, 'I would be pleased, my Lord!' Then He will say, 'That is for you, and the like of it, and the like of it, and the like of it.' At the fifth, he will say, 'I am well-pleased, my Lord!' Then He will say, 'It is for you and ten times its like, and you shall have whatever you desire and delights your eyes.' He will say, 'I am well-pleased, my Lord!'"
>
> He [Moses] asked, "Lord, and the highest of their ranks?"
>
> He [God] said, "They are those whom I desire. I establish their honor with My Hand and set a seal upon it, and the eye has not seen nor has the ear heard nor has it occurred to the heart of any human being [what I shall grant them]." And this is confirmed in the Book of God, the Mighty and Glorious, [in His saying,] **And no soul knows what has been kept secret for them of satisfaction for the eyes, as a recompense for what they used to do"** [32:17]. (*Muslim*, 363)

May endless honor, blessings and peace be upon Moses, one of the most excellent of God's servants! To him we say, as the angels will say to all those with whom He is well-pleased:

> **Peace be upon you for what you patiently endured. And excellent is the final Home!** (13:24)

PART SEVEN: THE STORY OF MOSES AND KHIDR

42. THE IDENTITY OF SAYYIDINA KHIDR (A)

We raise in degrees whomever We will, but over every possessor of knowledge is one [more] knowing. (12:76)

We now come to a story that is unique in the entire Qur'an, for it is actually a parable rather than a historical narrative. While Moses (A) is one of its two main characters, it is not related in any way to what we know of Moses' life-story, nor does it concern any major event in the life of the individual known and revered throughout the Muslim world as Sayyidina Khidr, peace be upon him, although he is the principal actor in the story.

Who was Khidr (A), or properly, *al-Khadir*, the Green One? This was in fact not his name but rather a title by which he was known, according to the saying of the Prophet (S),

> Al-Khadir was called so because he sat upon a white wasteland that became green after his sitting on it. (*Bukhari*, 4:614)

Scholars disagree as to whether Khidr (A) was a prophet, an angel or a friend of God (*wali* or saint). The majority consider him to be a prophet, and the mention of his name is always followed by the invocation reserved for prophets and angels, "Peace be upon him." And, as we have seen in previous stories, the holy people of Islam, its prophets and saints, are honored by their Lord with miracles and signs of divine empowerment, as was Sayyidina Khidr (A).

The story of the meeting of Moses and Khidr (A) is narrated in twenty-three verses of *Surah al-Kahf* (The Cave) (18:60-82); Sayyidina Khidr (A) is not mentioned anywhere else in the Qur'an. Further and fascinating details of this story have been supplied in a number of *ahadith* which give us the full picture of what transpired between one of the greatest of prophets, Moses (A), and the one whom his Lord had appointed to teach him that there is more to knowledge than what he had been granted.

In the *hadith* collection of al-Bukhari alone, we find six *ahadith* concerning Moses and Khidr, God's peace and blessings be upon them. All of these are reported by Ibn 'Abbas on the authority of Ubayy bin Ka'b (R). Of these, three (1:74, 1:78, 4:612), which are almost identical, summarize the story up to the meeting of the two and there they stop. However, in the others

(4:613, 6:249-6:251), the story is continued to the end of the Qur'anic account. In the *hadith* collection of Muslim, the story is also narrated in three lengthy *ahadith* (5864-5865, 5867), which are very similar to those of al-Bukhari. These accounts contain many minor but very interesting variations, and all are reported to go back to the Prophet (S) but with different chains of narrators.

We now proceed with the story, interweaving the Qur'anic narrative with *ahadith*.

REFERENCES: Glasse/*Encyclopedia*, pp. 224-225; Keller/*Reliance*, X219, p. 1067.

43. THE STORY

"May I follow you on the condition that you teach me from what you have been taught of right guidance?" (18:65-66)

Once Moses, the prophet of God, preached to the Children of Israel until their eyes shed tears and their hearts became tender, and thus he finished his address.[165]

A man then came to him and said, "O messenger of God, is there anyone on earth more knowing than you?"

"No," Moses (A) replied.[166]

God then rebuked Moses (A) for not having ascribed all knowledge to Him. And He revealed to him, "At the junction of the two seas,[167] there is a slave of Ours who is more knowing than you."

"O my Lord, how can I meet him?" Moses (A) asked. "Tell me of a sign by which I may recognize the place."

"Take a fish and put it in a basket, and you will find him at the place where you will lose the fish," came the divine reply. That is, "Take a dead fish and continue journeying until the spirit is breathed into it."

So Moses (A) took a fish and put it in a basket. He said to his young man, Joshua son of Nun, "I do not charge you with any responsibility but that you inform me where the fish parts from you."

"You have not asked for a great deal," the young man responded.

And Moses (A) expressed his determination to continue his journey until he found the one he was seeking, saying to the young man, **"I shall not cease** my quest **until I reach the junction of the two seas, or** otherwise **spend years** in searching" (18:60).

---

[165]In *Muslim*, 5865, it is stated that Moses was reminding his people of the days of God (14:5), with their blessings and trials.

[166]Other versions state that Moses was asked who was the most knowing person on earth, to which he replied, "I am" (*Bukhari*, 4.613, 6:249, 6:251). In yet another version, he replied, "I do not know of anyone on earth better or more knowing than myself" (*Muslim*, 5865).

[167]"***Al-bahrain,***" which can mean either to two seas or two rivers.

Moses (A) then set out, carrying the fish in the basket, and his attendant, Joshua son of Nun, accompanied him. And he went on, looking for the sign of the fish in the sea.

Eventually the two reached a rock, and Moses (A) put down his head and slept. And while Moses (A) was sleeping and Joshua was in the shade of the rock in a wet place, the fish moved about vigorously in the basket. However, the young man said to himself, "I will not arouse him until he wakes up,"[168] but then he forgot to tell him. And the fish slipped out of the basket and entered the sea, and God stopped the flowing of water on both sides of the path made by the fish so that it was like a tunnel or arch over it.[169]

When Moses (A) got up, his companion forgot to tell him about what had happened to the fish; as God says, **But when they reached the junction between them** — the two bodies of water — **they forgot their fish, and it took its course through the sea as in a tunnel** (18:61). And the two continued traveling throughout the day and night.

The following morning, Moses (A) said to his young man, **"Bring us our breakfast. We have certainly experienced fatigue in this, our journey"** (18:62), although he did not experience fatigue until he had passed the place concerning which God had instructed him.

Then, suddenly remembering, his young man said to him, **"Did you see, when we retired to the rock? Indeed, I forgot the fish, and none but Satan made me forget to mention it. And it took its course in the sea amazingly!"** (18:63).

"That is what we were seeking!" Moses (A) exclaimed. **So they returned, retracing their footsteps** (18:64), until they again reached the same rock.

There they found a man lying, covered with a garment,[170] whom God Most High describes as **a slave from among Our slaves to whom We had**

---

[168]According to other versions, Joshua also put down his head and slept (*Bukhari*, 6:249; *Muslim*, 5864). Here, one of the sub-narrators of this *hadith* adds that at this rock there was a spring called al-Hayat [Life], and no one came in contact with its water without becoming alive. Some of the water fell upon the [dead] fish, whereupon it moved, slipped out of the basket and entered the sea (*Bukhari*, 6:251).

[169]In *Bukhari*, 6:250, it is mentioned that the trace of the fish looked as if it were made on a rock.

[170]In other versions, it is stated that he was on a green carpet in the middle of the sea, covered with his garment (*Bukhari*, 6:249), one end of which was under his feet and the other under his head (*Bukhari*, 6:250).

granted mercy from Ourself and had taught him, from Ourself, knowledge (18:64-65). And Moses (A) greeted him with *salam* — that is, the traditional greeting of peace of believers.

Upon hearing this greeting, the man uncovered his face. "Is there such a greeting in my country?" he enquired in astonishment. He then asked, "Who are you?"

"I am Moses."

"Moses of the Children of Israel?"

"Yes."

"What then may your business be?"

"May I follow you on the condition that you teach me from what you have been taught of right guidance?"[171] (18:66).

"Indeed, you will never be able to have patience with me," the man replied. **"And how can you have patience concerning what you do not encompass in knowledge?** (18:67-68).

"O Moses," he went on, "indeed, I have certain knowledge from God's knowledge which He has taught me but you do not know it, and you have certain knowledge from God's knowledge which God has taught you but I do not know it. Is it not sufficient for you that the *Taurat* is in your hands and that the divine inspiration comes to you, O Moses? Indeed, I have such knowledge as is not suitable for you to learn, and indeed, you have such knowledge as is not suitable for me to learn."

"Nevertheless, I will follow you," Moses (A) responded. **"You will find me, God willing, patient, and I will not disobey you in any order"** (18:69).

"Then, if you follow me, do not ask me about anything until I make mention of it to you" (18:70).

So the two set out (18:71), walking on the seashore. Then a boat passed by them which carried the people of that shore to the people of the other, and they asked them to transport them. And the crew recognized Khidr (A), saying, "This is a righteous servant of God. We will not transport him for a fee."[172]

---

[171]Or, "I have come to you so that you teach me **from what you have been taught of right guidance"** (*Bukhari*, 4:613, 6:219, 6:250; *Muslim*, 5865).

[172]In *Bukhari*, 4:613, it is, "And they recognized Khidr and transported him without payment."

Then they **embarked in the boat** (18:71). A sparrow alighted upon its rim and dipped its beak into the sea once or twice. Khidr (A) then said to Moses (A), "By God, in comparison to God's knowledge, your knowledge and my knowledge and the knowledge of all creation is only like the amount that this bird has taken from the sea in its beak."[173]

Then all at once Khidr (A) took an adze and pulled out a plank,[174] but Moses (A) did not notice it until he had already torn out the plank with his adze.

"What have you done?" Moses (A) exclaimed, forgetting to whom he was speaking and the condition he had imposed on him. "The people are transporting us without any fare, but you have schemed against their boat. **Have you made a hole in it to drown its people? You have certainly done a grievous thing!"** (18:71).

"Did I not say that you would never be able to have patience with me?" (18:72), Khidr (A) replied.

This brought Moses (A) abruptly back to the commitment he had made and he was immediately sorry for his words. **"Do not take me to task for what I forgot nor be hard on me concerning my affair"** (18:73), he pleaded. And here the Prophet (S) added parenthetically, "The first was forgetting, the middle a stipulation, and the third an intention"[175]

So the two set out again, **until, when they encountered a boy, he killed him** (18:74). That is, Moses and Khidr (A) then left the boat, and while they were walking on the seashore, they came upon a group of boys, playing.

---

[173]In *Bukhari*, 4:613, Khidr's words are, "O Moses, my knowledge and your knowledge have not taken from God's knowledge except the like of what this sparrow has taken from the sea in its beak."

[174]Or an axe. An adze is an iron implement with a handle, having a wide, flat blade extending in one direction. The Arabic verb used here, ***"kharaq,"*** means to make a hole, break, bore or impair. A report from Ibn 'Abbas, however, states that, Khidr used a chisel and mallet that he carried with him to make a hole in the boat, which he then patched with a plank (Tabari/*H*, III:15).

[175]That is, Moses' first violation of the condition Khidr had made with him was due to forgetfulness. The middle violation bound him by a stipulation: **"If I should ask you about anything after this, then do not keep me as a companion. You will have received** a sufficient **excuse on my part"** (18:76), meaning that if I should violate my commitment another time, it will be with full awareness and acceptance of the consequences. The third violation was therefore deliberate and intentional.

Then, from among them, Khidr (A) caught hold of a spirited lad who was an unbeliever, and he laid him down and killed with a knife.[176]

"Have you killed a blameless person without his having killed **anyone?"** Moses (A) demanded in horror, again violating his agreement. **"You have certainly done a terrible thing!"** (18:74).

"Did I not say to you that you would never be able to have patience with me?" (18:75), Khidr (A) repeated.

"This is worse than the first," Moses (A) said, referring either to what Khidr (A) had just done or to his own questioning of him. Then he added: **"If I ask you about anything after this, then do not keep me as a companion. You will have received a** sufficient **excuse on my part"** (18:76), meaning, "If I ask you about anything further, you will have had justification enough from my side to part company with me."

So they set out until, when they came to the people of a town, they asked its people for food but they refused to offer them hospitality. And they found therein a wall about to collapse, whereupon he restored it (18:77). This is explained as meaning that the wall was falling over and Khidr (A) touched it with his hands or raised his hand above it, whereupon it became straight (*Bukhari*, 6:251).

"We came to these people and they did not feed us or show us hospitality, but yet you repaired their wall," Moses (A) protested. **"If you had wished, you could have taken payment for it"** (18:77).

"This is a parting between me and you," said Khidr (A). Then he added: **"I shall inform you of the interpretation of that about which you were unable to have patience** (18:78).

"As for the boat, it belonged to poor people working at sea, so I desired to render it defective, as there was a king after them who seized every boat by force" (18:79), he said. "I desired that if the boat passed by him, he would leave it alone because of its defect, and when they had passed [out of his territory], they would repair it and get benefit from it.

"As for the boy, his parents were believers but he was an unbeliever, **and we feared that he would overburden them by transgression and ununbelief,"** meaning that their love for him would induce them to follow him

---

[176]Other versions state that Khidr took hold of the boy's head, tore it out with his hands and killed him (*Bukhari*, 4:613, 6:249; *Muslim*, 5864), or that he took hold of him by the head and cut it off (*Bukhari*, 6:251).

in his false religion. **"So we intended that their Lord should substitute for them one better than he in purity and nearer to mercy** (18:80).[177]

"And as for the wall, it belonged to two orphan boys in the town and beneath it was a treasure belonging to them, and their father had been righteous. So your Lord intended that they reach maturity and extract their treasure, as a mercy from your Lord" (18:82). That is, for the sake of the righteous father, God had protected the treasure, inspiring His holy servant to fortify the collapsing wall under which it was buried so that the orphans' inheritance might remain concealed until the two boys had grown up and were entitled to claim it.

In conclusion, Khidr (A) then imparted the lesson of the entire experience to Moses:

> **"And I did not do it of my own accord. That is the interpretation of that about which you were unable to have patience"**[178] (18:82).

At the end of these various accounts, the Holy Prophet (S) added:

> May God have mercy upon Moses! If he had been patient, we would have been told something of the affair of the two of them. (*Bukhari*, 4:613; *Muslim*, 5864; also *Bukhari*, 6:249, 6:251)

> May God have mercy upon Moses! We wish that he had been patient until God had related to us [more] of the tidings of the two of them (or of the affair of the two of them). (*Muslim*, 5864; *Bukhari*, 6.249, 6.251, also 4.613)

> May God's mercy be upon us and upon Moses! If he had been patient, he would have seen marvels from his companion. But he said, **"If I should ask you about anything after this, then do not keep me as a companion. You will have received a [sufficient] excuse on my part."** [18:76] (Abu Dawud, 3973)

---

[178]The Prophet (S) said concerning this, "The boy whom Khidr killed was inherently an unbeliever, and if he had become established, he would have overburdened his parents with transgression and unbelief" (*Muslim*, 6434). It is said that **"better than he in purity"** was in response to Moses' referring to the boy as **"a blameless person"** (18:74), while **"nearer to mercy"** meant that the future child who would be substituted for their dead son would be closer to them in mercy and affection. The Prophet (S) also said that the parents were compensated for the loss of their son by a daughter (*Bukhari*, 6:250).

[178]It is noteworthy that Khidr used the word **"patience"** six times in speaking to Moses, while Moses himself used the word **"patient"** once.

REFERENCES: Qur'an: 18:60-82. *Ahadith: Bukhari*, 1:74, 1:78, 4:612-4:614, 6:249-6:251; *Muslim*, 5864-5865, 5867, 6434; Abu Dawud, 3973. Commentary: Tabari/*H*, III:1-18.

44. THE LESSONS OF THE STORY OF KHIDR

There is certainly a lesson in their stories for those of understanding. Never was it [the Qur'an] an invented narration, but rather a confirmation of what was before it and a detailed explanation of all things, and a guidance and mercy for people who believe. (12:111)

How are we to understand the subtle meaning of this story? Is it, as one might imagine at a casual glance, a message of indifference and callousness toward God's revealed Law, whereby Khidr (A) became a law unto himself, or is it rather an indication of knowledge that transcends what is obvious and apparent, even to so a great prophet as Moses (A)? In short, what is the purpose of God's relating this story in the Qur'an and what wisdoms can we derive from it?

To begin with, let us consider the meaning of **"the junction of the two seas"** or rivers which Moses (A) was seeking. While there have been many guesses as to the identity of these bodies of water, no one has any really authoritative information as to where they were. Nor indeed is this in any way relevant to the meaning of the story, for its message is beyond any externalist interpretation.

Rather, the scholars of inner, esoteric knowledge interpret these two seas as referring to the two kinds of divine knowledge that met in Moses and Khidr, peace be upon them — revealed knowledge relating to the concepts, values, laws and practices of true religion, and inner, secret knowledge conveyed directly to the hearts of certain honored slaves by their Lord. This is made clear by the description of Sayyidina Khidr as **a slave from among Our slaves to whom We had granted mercy from Ourself [*min ladunna*] and had taught him, from Ourself [*min ladunna*], knowledge** (18:65), **"*min ladunna*"** meaning that which is transmitted to the heart by God Himself.

Indeed, it was granted to Moses (A) to speak to God the Exalted directly and to receive from Him the divine Law for arranging the affairs of his people. But Khidr (A) was granted another kind of knowledge, knowledge which may at times lead its possessors to do things that seem strange, blameworthy or even evil to those who do not understand their significance. Khidr's explanation to Moses, **"I did not do it of my own accord"** (18:82), makes it clear that he was acting according to his Lord's direct orders rather than the dictates of law, morality, logic or even common sense.

Moses (A) had been commanded to practice and teach his people the knowledge that he had been granted of God's laws and commandments, serving as their example and guide. But the instructions that Khidr (A) had received from his Lord were secret commands for himself alone, not to be communicated or taught to anyone else. This explains his extreme reluctance to have even such an illustrious prophet as Moses (A) as a companion and observer, and why, well-aware that his actions would seem evil or misguided according to the knowledge that Moses (A) possessed, he said to him, **"Indeed, you will never be able to have patience with me. And how can you have patience with what you do not encompass in knowledge?"** (18:67-68).

But while the knowledge that Khidr (A) had been granted was in no way useful for Moses (A) and was also beyond his understanding, God Most High caused Moses (A) to catch a glimpse of it so that he would not be arrogant concerning his knowledge and imagine that it represented the limit of all possible knowledge. The words, **We raise in ranks whomever We will, but over every possessor of knowledge is one [more] knowing** (12:76), revealed in connection with the story of Joseph (A), make it clear that among God's servants there are differing ranks of knowledge, which is itself boundless, culminating in the absolutely limitless knowledge of the Creator, beside whose infinite and perfect knowledge all other knowledge is insignificant.[179]

Therefore, one important lesson of this story is that we must not be in a hurry to discard beneficial knowledge because it is different from the knowledge that we ourselves possess, or because it does not come from sources that our family, group or society acknowledge as valid or acceptable. Knowledge can be conveyed to us by any source that God Most High appoints: a man or a woman, a child, an old person, a rich or a poor one, an ill, handicapped or dying one, not merely by individuals who possess the outward marks of intellect and learning.

Therefore, those who are alert to their Lord's signs and messages make a determination of what constitutes beneficial knowledge, especially of faith and spiritual matters, continually asking for divine guidance and discernment. Then, surrendering their wills, they gladly accept whatever knowledge and wisdoms God the All-Knowing sees fit to send them by any means He may choose, rather than insisting that they must be with such-and-such scholar, in this university course or book, or at that specific time or place

---

[179]Thus, Imam al-Ghazali says that it is blameworthy to ask about matters that one is not competent to understand, and this was the reason why Khidr forbade Moses to ask any questions. "In other words, do not ask questions out of the proper time and season; the teacher is better informed than you are as to things you are capable of understanding and as to the appropriate time for making them known" (Al-Ghazzali, *The Book of Knowledge*, p. 131).

The story of Sayyidina Khidr (A) also underscores the fact that all things, regardless of appearances, are governed by the infinite wisdom of the Lord of the universes. Consequently, although the reason for some occurrence may often not be apparent to us and it may even seem terrible, ruthless and cruel, we must nevertheless know that, in the eternal plan of the All-Wise, All-Knowing, it has a reason, a purpose and a divine wisdom, related both to this world and to the Hereafter.

Thus, on an allegorical level Khidr (A) may be equated with any of the natural forces that affect our existence, such as wind, water or fire. When God commands them to be stable and benign for human life, they are; when He commands them to operate in ways that harm us, they do, as perfectly neutral agents of His Will. In either case, whether they bring us benefit or harm, they are, without exception, manifestations of God's infinite wisdom, knowledge and power. And we are asked to be patient with the circumstances and conditions of this life regardless of whether we understand their meaning and purpose or not, and to remain firm, steadfast and reliant upon God in every situation.

We note that in each of the three instances in which Sayyidina Khidr (A) did something that Moses (A), representing the normal perception of an individual with a sound mind and conscience, regarded as wrong, sinful or perhaps simply foolish, it had a beneficent purpose. The boat was damaged not, as it appeared, to drown its crew but, according to the secret knowledge imparted to Khidr (A) by his Lord, to save it from being seized, thereby putting an end to its crew's means of livelihood. The boy was killed not due to viciousness on the part of his killer, but, by divine command, to save his parents from misguidance and from the evil their child would have inflicted upon them if he had lived. The wall was set straight not because Khidr (A) did not think to ask for payment or to do a favor to the ungracious people of the town, but to safeguard the treasure that would in the future be claimed by the sons of the righteous father.

All this reinforces the eternal lesson that **God knows and you do not know** (2:232, 3:66, 24:19), which is perhaps the most important piece of information we possess for dealing with this complex and often confusing life we are in. For as good is an integral part of the divine plan, so is what we understand as evil, both being essential parts of the fabric of our lives, since we are constantly tested **with evil and with good as a trial** (21:35).

Sayyidina Khidr (A) may therefore be said to represent the multitudinous agents of God's Will, the causes and effects that we see operating in this life. Although he commits acts that seem barbarous and vicious, and which the mind and the heart are justified in rejecting based on such knowledge as we possess, nonetheless they are, in the absolute and unerring knowledge of the All-Wise Lord, that which is just and correct under the given circumstances. For this has to happen so ***that*** can happen, and so that all things may reach the destiny decreed for them by the Knower of all things.

We live in two planes of existence, the outer and the inner. From a simple, external point of view, we see that things operate according to obvious, material causes that we can to some extent recognize and understand, bringing about certain effects. But side-by-side with recognizable, physical causes, unseen causes are also constantly operating, according to the secret orders of the **Knower of the Unseen and the witnessed, . . . the Wise, the Informed** (6:74).

These unseen orders govern all things in our lives, arranging our relationship with everything that surrounds us. For we are not alone; we are bound, related, connected to everything and everyone in existence by invisible ties. Therefore, while on the external level we are ordered to obey God's rules and commands, conveyed by His prophets, at the same time, we are asked to understand that all things are governed by the infinite wisdom of the Creator, and to be patient with His secret commands, which surround us and tie us to everything in existence, as they operate in our lives, surrendering our wills to the divine Will.

45. THE TIMELESS ROLE OF SAYYIDINA KHIDR

. . . A slave from among Our slaves to whom We had granted mercy from Ourself and had taught him, from Ourself, knowledge.

(18:64-65)

According to Islamic tradition, Sayyidina Khidr (A) is a unique being, one of a kind, who has been granted life up to the end of this world.

It is a common belief among Muslims, including scholars and mystics, that because Khidr (A) drank from the Water of Life, he lives and will remain alive until the Day of Judgment.[180] Ibn al-'Arabi, *al-Shaykh al-Akbar* (the Greatest Shaykh), the thirteenth century Spanish Arab mystic whose monumental works on Sufism are known throughout the world, says that Sayyidina Khidr's name was Balya ibn Malikan, and he was in an army whose commander had sent him to look for water, which was lacking. Khidr (A) found the Water of Life and, not knowing that God granted longevity to anyone who would drink from it, drank (Wilson, "The Green Man," *Gnosis Magazine*, Spring 1991, p. 23). Thus, he is well-known throughout the Muslim world as a living human being endowed with miraculous powers, taking various forms and showing himself to people according to the divine command.[181]

Sayyidina Khidr (A) is the guide or shaykh of those solitary seekers of God who have no access to a living teacher. Besides this, he is also the patron and guide of many of the great saints (*awliya'*) of Islam. Ibn al-'Arabi himself was well-acquainted with him. He said, "I met him in Seville, where he taught me to submit to spirtual masters and not to contradict them" (ibid.). It is also reported that the great shaykh and compiler of *ahadith*, al-Nawawi, used to meet with Khidr (A) and converse with him, among many other unveilings.[182] And another great saint, Ibrahim ibn Adham, reported that he lived in a wil-

---

[180]A *hadith* concerning the end-time of this world, which is believed to refer to Sayyidina Khidr, is reported in the story of Jesus, page 464, footnote 129.

[181]An instance of this may be the following: Imam Bayhaqi reports a *hadith* stating that when Prophet Muhammad (S) passed away, those present heard a voice from the corner of the room giving them condolences. When they were asked if they knew who this was, they said that it was Sayyidina Khidr (*Mishkat*, Vol. 4, p. 1309). This is also mentioned in Qadi 'Iyad's famous work, *Ash-Shifa*, page 205.

[182]Reported in al-Sakhawi's work, *Biography of the Sheikh of Islam, the Pole of the Noble Saints and Jurists of Mankind, the Reviver of the Sunnah and Slayer of Innovation, Abu Zakariyya Muhyiddin al-Nawawi.*

derness for four years, during which God gave him his provision without any effort on his part. During that time, Khidr, the Green Ancient, was his companion, and he taught him the greatest Holy Name of God (Glasse/*Encyclopedia*, "Al-Khidr," p. 225).

May God's best blessings and peace be upon Sayyidina Khidr, the teacher of divine wisdoms to humanity and recipient of special divine favors from his Lord!

REFERENCES: Tabari/*H*, III:2-3; Glasse/*Encyclopedia*, "Al-Khidr," p. 225; Keller/*Reliance*, w9.10, p. 867, x219, p. 1067; Peter Lamborn Wilson, "The Green Man," *Gnosis Magazine*, Spring 1991, pp. 22-26.

APPENDIX A

THE IDENTITY OF THE PHARAOH OF THE EXODUS

The question of the identity of the pharaoh of the Exodus has puzzled and intrigued scholars and researchers over the centuries, especially in recent times. But despite much speculation and many claims concerning the man's identity, no definite conclusions have been reached concerning it.

Eli Barnavi, general editor of *A Historical Atlas of the Jewish People from the Time of the Patriarchs to the Present*, summarizes the problem as follows:

> [T]he reign of Ramses II (1279-1212 BC), known for its costly wars and vast building enterprises, may well have been the era of cruel oppression described in Exodus. But the only contemporary Egyptian source which actually mentions Israel is the stela (pillar with inscription) of King Merneptah from the fifth year of his reign (1207 BC), recording among his many victories: "carried off is Ashkelon, seized upon is Gezer. . . . Israel is laid waste, his seed is no more." This inscription implies that an entity named Israel indeed existed in Canaan at the time, yet it is difficult to determine precisely what it was. One thing, however, may be regarded as certain: if the Israelites indeed emerged out of Egypt, their migration took place before the end of the thirteenth century BC. (p. 4)

Consequently, after decades of highly complex investigation into the identity of the pharaoh of the Exodus, the most likely possibilities are Ramses II, his son Merneptah, and, finally, their predecessors, Akhenaten, Thutmose I or Thutmose II. We present below the pros and cons of each of these possibilities.

RAMSES II

Some Egyptologists believe the Pharaoh of Moses to have been Ramesses II, better known as Ramses the Great. This pharaoh reigned for sixty-seven years during roughly the first three-quarters of the thirteenth century B.C. Understanding, based on Pharaoh's words, **"Did we not bring you up among ourselves as a child, and you stayed among us for years of your life?"** (26:18), that the pharaoh of Moses' childhood and the Exodus are the one and the same, this period would have been amply covered by such a long reign.

Much of what is known of Ramses' character confirms the picture that is drawn of him in the Qur'an as **a self-exalter, of those who exceed the limits**

(44:31) — indeed, as one sufficiently arrogant to order the construction of a tower deemed high enough to **mount up to the God of Moses** (28:38; 40:37). It was Ramses II who constructed the gigantic monuments of Abu Simbel, other collosi at Thebes, Luxor and Karnak, and had built uncountable statues — "at Thebes alone, giants sixty feet high" (Montet/*Pharaohs*, pp. 184-185, 188). In the words of one scholar,

> Ramesses fathered over 150 children, was enormously proud of the fact, and lived so long that many of them died before he did. . . . He built more temples and had himself represented in more colossal statues than any other pharaoh. He usurped the monuments of his predecessors, even his own father's, and destroyed ancient temples for raw material to use in his own new buildings. He built a great new city. His inscribed utterances are so bombastic that he is sometimes dismissed as a self-glorifying megalomaniac, but this is a modern reaction and not how he was thought of in the ancient world. . . . His grandiloquence was in a wellworn tradition. The taste for the grandiose was nothing new. . . . Even so, Ramesses was a compulsive builder of the colossal and one wonders whether, deep down, it indicated a basic uncertainty about any values, even the central authority of pharaoh. (Newby/*Pharaohs*, p. 163)

At the same time, gentler aspects of Ramses' personality are documented that do not fit with the Qur'anic description. According to Pierre Montet,

> Throughout his life he was conscientous in the exercise of his kingship. His monstrous egoism was tempered by a kindness of heart which was appreciated by his soldiers, his artists, his family, and one may even say, by all his subjects. (Montet/*Pharaohs*, p. 194)
>
> For example, Ramses himself recorded "the way he looked after the interests of the quarrymen and stone carvers," giving them wheat, meat, clothes, and sandals with perfumes to anoint their heads on the day of rest. (Newby/*Pharaohs*, p. 164)

However, despite the similarities between Moses' pharaoh and Ramses II, the possibility of Ramses' being the Pharaoh of the Oppression and the Exodus is cancelled out by two insoluble contradictions. One is that although "Ramesses is the most likely candidate for the pharaoh of the Exodus . . . he would not in person have taken any part in the pursuit of the Israelites" (ibid., p. 175). The other is even more problematic: *the fact that Ramses II is known to have died in his bed in the year 1237 B.C.*

REFERENCES: Asad/*Q*, 10:fn. 112; Montet/*Pharaohs*, pp. 163-164, 184-185, 188, 194; Newby/*Pharaohs*, pp. 163-164, 175.

MERNEPTAH/MENEPTAH

The possibility that the Pharaoh of the Oppression and the Exodus might have been Merneptah (also written as Merenptah or Meneptah) is also widely held — and equally disputed.

In their book, *X-raying the Pharaohs*, James E. Harris and Kent R. Weeks write:

> The mummy of Merenptah, one of the many sons of Ramesses II, is of special interest because of the disoloration of the skin caused by salts. Early writers speculated that this occurred because the pharaoh drowned in the sea during the Exodus, but this is not true. The process of mummification at that time often produced such discoloration. (p. 44)
>
> Merenptah is believed to have been the pharaoh of the Exodus, and the heavy incrustation of salt on his skin has led some writers to claim that he was drowned in the Red Sea. Such a belief, of course, is entirely erroneous. The natron in which mummies were placed easily accounts for the salt on his body. (p. 157)

This is confirmed by P. H. Newby, who states:

> [I]n 1898, Meneptah's mummy was discovered. According to Exodus he had been lost in the Red Sea and the only comfort was that the mummy showed traces of salt. Salt is found on all mummies because natron, which is used in the process of mummification, consists not only of soda and a number of other things but common salt as well. (Newby/*Pharaohs*, p. 182)

Apart from this, two other matters seem to preclude the possibility that Merneptah was the Pharaoh of the Oppression. One is the fact that his reign lasted a mere thirteen years, making it impossible for him to have been the ruler both during Moses' infancy and adulthood.

The second is the famous "Israel stela," mentioned earlier, on which, in the year 1219 B.C., the exultant Merneptah reported the destruction of Israel and his seed. These words make it clear that "here he [Merneptah] is fighting Israel, already established as a people somewhere in Palestine. This is a state of affairs that could only have existed some considerable time after the Exodus" (ibid., p. 182).

This view is supported by David Daiches in *Moses, the Man and His Vision:*

> It is conceivable that this [inscription on the Israel stela] is a reference to the pursuit of the escaping Israelites, in which case the Pharaoh of the exodus would be Merneptah (*c.* 1224-1211), but this is unlikely. It is much more likely that this is a reference to Israelites settled in Pales-

> tine after the exodus (they were never called Israelites in Palestine before the exodus). This is consistent with a date of about 1270 BC for the exodus and with the biblical period of a generation in the wilderness before entry into Palestine. (p. 29)

Now, based on the Qur'anic statement that the land of Palestine was forbidden to the Israelites during the forty years of their wandering in Sinai (5:26/29), as well as the Biblical account (Ex. 16:35; Num. 14:33-34; Ps. 95:10-11), it seems evident that the settling of Palestine by the Israelites did not even begin until at least forty years after the Exodus. The time frame associated with the Israel stela mentioned above therefore virtually cancels out the possibility that either Merneptah or his father, Ramses II, could have been the pharaoh of the Exodus.

REFERENCES: Daiches/*Moses*, p. 29; Harris and Weeks, *X-raying the Pharaohs*, pp. 44, 157; Newby/*Pharaohs*, p. 182.

OTHER POSSIBILITIES

Consequently, in our search for the identity of Moses' pharaoh, we are thrown back to an earlier period — perhaps even to Hyksos times, according to a theory suggested by Joy Collier in her book, *The Heretic Pharaoh*. She writes:

> Expert opinion has placed the time of the Exodus in the reign of the nineteenth-dynasty king Seti I [who ruled from 1290-1279 B.C.]. Akhenaten had then been dead for over fifty years. But new and exciting evidence has come to light that makes it seem probable that Moses lived, not after, but before Akhenaten. This revelation brings a new dimension to the study of the heretic king, for if Moses lived before Akhenaten then there might have been a religious link between them. This thought opens up possibilities of a fascinating and credible historical reconstruction. (p. 91)

Further on, Collier states,

> Moses, revered in Egypt as well as by his own people, may have inspired the universalist ideas that had their apogee in the reign of Amenhotep III and that were brought to a tragic conclusion by Akhenaten. . . . The Egyptians also regarded him [Moses] as a great man and prophet. But, it seems, all mention of his early life and upbringing as a prince at the court of an Egyptian Hyksos king was suppressed. (p. 224; also p. 90)

Collier mentions still another possibility — that

> Moses was brought up at the Memphite court before the expulsion of the Hyksos. He returned from his exile in the reign of Thutmose I and led his people out of Egypt under Thutmose II. (p. 236)

It will be readily seen that the possibilities mentioned here are as fragmentary and inconclusive as the previous two. Thus, despite all the claims and counterclaims, the identity of Moses' pharaoh is perhaps one divine mystery whose solution the Arranger of all things has chosen to keep forever hidden from human knowledge.

But then, what of God's declaration to the drowning Pharaoh, **"This day We save you in body, that you may be a sign for those who succeed you"** (10:92)?

While some claim that this promise was fulfilled in the fact that the mummified bodies of Ramses II and Merneptah are housed to this day the Cairo Museum, according to the above analysis, this identification is false. We must therefore perhaps look again at the meaning of God's saying that he would save Pharaoh **"in body"** so that he would be a sign for those succeeding him.

The words inform us of only one fact: that the body of Pharaoh was saved as a sign for those who came after him. This could either mean that it was taken out of the water after drowning as a sign for the people of his time, as is confirmed by Ibn 'Abbas' previously-cited statement that the sea threw Pharaoh's drowned body on the shore in front of the eyes of the Israelites, or, alternatively, that it was preserved for ages to come.

Because of the conclusions reached above, it would seem that the former meaning may be the correct one. And even if this "body" should still exist somewhere on the planet, it remains, up to this time, at least, one of the Creator's well-guarded secrets.

REFERENCE: Collier/*Pharaoh*, pp. 90-91, 224, 236.

APPENDIX B

THE COVENANT, THE *TAURAT* AND THE TEN COMMANDMENTS

THE COVENANT

Much has been written by the classical commentators about the covenant between God and the Children of Israel. But, it may be asked, what did this often-mentioned covenant, compact, commitment or pledge consist of?

Based on the Qur'anic text, the first and most essential aspect of the covenant was the Israelites' commitment to take no one as Lord except their Creator, worshipping Him alone and obeying and keeping to His revealed law: —

> **And [recall] when We took a covenant from the Children of Israel, [commanding,] "Do not worship other than God."** (2:83)
>
> **And We gave Moses the scripture and made it guidance for the Children of Israel, [commanding] that you not take other than Me as Disposer of affairs, O descendants of those We carried in the Ark with Noah. Indeed, he was a thankful slave.** (17:2-3)

A second aspect of the covenant was the commitment to believe in and support God's messengers: —

> **And God certainly took a covenant from the Children of Israel, and We delegated twelve leaders among them. And God said, "Indeed, I am with you. If you establish *salat* and give *zakat*, and believe in My messengers and support them and lend God a goodly loan, I will surely remove your sins from you and admit you to gardens [of Paradise] beneath which rivers flow. But whoever among you disbelieves after that has certainly strayed from the soundness of the way."** (5:12/13)

We note that this command to the Israelites to believe in and support God's messengers, peace be upon them all, is general and does not mention any exceptions. Jesus (A) is therefore included in this command. So also is Muhammad (S), for God Most High says:

> **O Children of Israel, recall My favor that I bestowed upon you, and fulfill My covenant, that I may fulfill your covenant, and be in awe of Me. And believe in what I have sent down [to Muhammad], confirming that which is with you, and do not be the**

first to disbelieve in it. And do not sell My signs for a small price, and be mindful of Me. And do not cover the truth with falsehood or conceal the truth, while you know. (2:40-42)

These verses are very significant, for in them the covenant with the Israelites is directly linked to the divine command to believe in what God had revealed to His Last Messenger — that is, the Qur'an — confirming the earlier scripture that had been revealed to them through Moses (A). They were commanded not to be among those who rejected and disbelieved in God's final revelation, nor to barter the signs and evidences that had been sent with Muhammad (S) concerning his prophethood and the divine orgin of the Qur'an for some worldly benefit.

The Israelites were further commanded not to **cover the truth with falsehood or conceal the truth**, while knowing that it was the truth. But what was this **"truth"** that the Israelites and their descendants, the Jews, were ordered not to obscure or conceal?

It was, first, the *totality* of the divine Message that had been conveyed to them through Moses (A), which included not only belief in the Creator as the sole deity but also the essential accompaniment of it — belief in the Day of Resurrection and the Eternal Life, a basic element of the true, original faith that has been virtually suppressed in sections of Judaism.

This **"truth"** also included their foreknowledge of a prophet who would come among their brothers, the descendants of Abraham (A) through Ishmael (A), as is mentioned in the Biblical prophecies that we will cite later on pages 484-486 in connection with Jesus (A). Perhaps this may be, at least in part, what is meant by the words,

Those to whom We gave the scripture know him [Muhammad] as they known their own sons. But indeed, a party of them conceal the truth, while they know [it]. (2:146)

And this in turn relates to God's informing Moses (A), when he begged Him to restore the seventy elders to life, that His special mercy was decreed

for those who are mindful of Me and give *zakat*, and those who believe in Our signs [or verses] — those who follow the Messenger, the Unlettered Prophet [Muhammad] whom they find inscribed in what they have of the *Taurat* and the *Injil*, who enjoins upon them the right and forbids them from the wrong, and makes permissible to them the good and prohibits to them the evil, and relieves them of their burden and the fetters which were upon them. Therefore, those who believe in him and honor him and support him and follow the light which was sent down with him — it is those who will be the successful. (7:156-157)

Other aspects of the covenant are mentioned in 2:83, cited at the beginning of this appendix, which reads in full:

And [recall] when We took a covenant from the Children of Israel, [commanding,] "Do not worship other than God. And do good to parents and relatives and orphans and the poor, and speak good [words] to people, and establish *salat* and give *zakat*." Then you turned back, except a few among you, and you were resisting. And [recall] when We took your covenant, [commanding,] "Do not shed your blood nor drive one another out of your homes." Then you agreed, while you were witnessing. (2:83-84)

REFERENCES: Tabari/*C*, I:269-279, 365-367, 422-426, 454-455; Ayoub/*Q*, I:112-113, Ayoub/*Q*, II:238-240.

THE *TAURAT*

In the Qur'an, God Most High repeatedly mentions the scripture of Moses (A), the *Taurat*, speaking of it in the highest terms. It may therefore be asked, If the Qur'an is the complete and final revelation for all mankind up to the end of the world, why should a scripture that preceded it, revealed for the guidance of a small and limited population, be given such importance?

Perhaps the main reason is that, according to the Islamic understanding, the *Taurat* was an earlier statement of *islam*, the original, universal religion ordained by God and brought by all the prophets, and its sincere followers were among the *muslims* of the pre-Muhammadan era.[183]

---

[183]This is expressed in the following verses:

[Noah said,] "And if you turn away, I have asked no recompense from you. My recompense rests only upon God, and I have been commanded to be of the *muslims*." (10:72)

When his Lord said to him [Abraham], "Surrender!" [*aslim*] he said, "I have surrendered [*aslamtu*] to the Lord of the worlds." And this Abraham enjoined on his sons, and so did Jacob, [saying,] "O my sons, indeed, God has chosen the religion for you, so do not die except that you be *muslims*." Or were you witnesses when death approached Jacob, when he said to his sons, "What will you worship after me?" They said, "We will worship your God and the God of your fathers, Abraham and Ishmael and Isaac, one God, and we are surrendered [*muslimun*] to Him." (2:131-133; also see 2:127)

. . . Abraham was neither a Jew nor a Christian, but he was one inclining toward truth, a *muslim*, and he was not among the *mushrikin*. (3:67)

The following passages suggest that the original *Taurat* may have been, like the Qur'an, a comprehensive scripture containing material concerning God Most High, the spiritual realm, God's creation, His divine plan, and the histories of earlier prophets and their peoples, as well as divine legislation:

Then We gave Moses the scripture, completing [Our favor] upon the one who did good, and as a detailed explanation of all things and a guidance and mercy, that they might perhaps believe in the meeting with their Lord. (6:154)

Have you [Muhammad] not seen the one who turned away, and gave a little and begrudged? Does he have knowledge of the Unseen so that he beholds [the future]? Or has he not been informed of what was in the scriptures of Moses and Abraham, who fulfilled [his obligations]? — that no bearer of burdens shall bear the burden of another; and that man shall have nothing but what he strives for, and that his effort will be seen and then he will be

---

And strive for God with the striving due to Him. He has chosen you [Muslims] and has not placed upon you any difficulty in the religion: the faith of your father Abraham. He [God] named you "*muslims*" beforehand and in this [Qur'an]. (22:78)

Then We brought out whomever was in them of the believers [among Lot's people], but We did not find in them other than a single house of *muslims*. (51:35-36)

And Moses said, "O my people, if you believe in God, then rely upon Him, if you are [truly] *muslims*." (10:84)

[Solomon said,] "And we were given knowledge before her and we were *muslims*, and what she was worshipping apart from God diverted her. Indeed, she was of a disbelieving people." (27:42-43)

Then, when Jesus noticed disbelief among them, he said, "Who will be my supporters [in the cause] of God?" The apostles said, "We are supporters of God. We believe in God and bear witness that we are *muslims*." (3:52)

And [recall] when I inspired to the apostles, "Believe in Me and in My messenger [Jesus]," they said, "We have believed, so bear witness that indeed we are *muslims*.'" (5:111/114)

Say, [O Muhammad:] "We believe in God and what was revealed to us, and what was revealed to Abraham and Ishmael and Isaac and Jacob and the descendants [of Israel], and what was given to Moses and Jesus and the prophets by their Lord. We make no distinction between any of them, and we surrender [*muslimun*] to Him." And whoever desires other than Islam as a religion, never will it be accepted from him, and in the Hereafter he will be among the losers. (3:84-85)

recompensed for it with the fullest recompense; and that to your Lord is the final end, and it is He who causes to laugh and to weep, and that it is He who causes death and gives life, and that He creates the two mates, the male and the female, from a sperm-drop when it is emitted, and that upon Him [rests] the other bringing-forth, and that it is He who enriches and suffices. (53:38-48)

Another reason for the importance of the *Taurat* may be that it contained universal principles that would be restated by future prophets, including Jesus and Muhammad (S). It also contained all the specific rules necessary for the guidance of the first community on earth to be organized and governed by a true revealed law, as is suggested by the following verses:

We certainly gave Moses the scripture, that they might perhaps be guided. (23:49; also 2:253)

And [recall, O Children of Israel,] when We gave Moses the scripture and the criterion [of right and wrong], that perhaps you might be guided. (2:53)

We certainly granted Moses guidance and We caused the Children of Israel to inherit the scripture, as a guidance and a reminder for those of understanding. (40:53-54)

Before it [the Qur'an], the scripture of Moses was a guide and a mercy. (11:17)

Say, [O Muhammad:] "Who revealed the scripture that Moses brought as light and guidance to people?" Say: "God." (6:91)

The *Taurat* is also referred to as **guidance and light** (5:45/47); as **instruction and explanation of all things** (7:145); as **enlightenment for people and guidance and mercy, that they might be reminded** (28:43); and as **the criterion and a light and a reminder for those who are mindful of God, who fear their Lord unseen, while they are apprehensive of the [Last] Hour** (21:48-49). It was revealed complete God's favor **upon the one who did good** — that is, Moses (A) — **and as a detailed explanation of all things, and as guidance and mercy, that perhaps they might believe in the meeting with their Lord** (6:154).

However, again, it is important to bear in mind that the scripture referred to in these verses is the original *Taurat*, revealed word-for-word by God to Moses (A), not the existing Torah, which bears the imprint of the human authors who "edited" the divine speech. The following verses make it clear that not only did the original *Taurat* confirm what had preceded it of God's religion, but also that it was in turn confirmed by the scriptures that succeeded it

— that is, the *Injil* revealed to Jesus (A) and the Qur'an sent down to the Last Prophet (S):

> **He has sent down to you [Muhammad,] the Book with truth, confirming what was before it. And previously He revealed the *Taurat* and the *Injil* as guidance for people. And He revealed the criterion [of right and wrong].** (3:3-4)
>
> **And We have revealed the Book to you [Muhammad] in truth, confirming that which preceded it of the scripture and as a criterion over it.** (5:48/51)
>
> **That which We have revealed to you [Muhammad] of the scripture is the truth, confirming what was before it.** (35:31)
>
> **Before it [the Qur'an,] the scripture of Moses was a guide and a mercy. And this is a confirming scripture in the Arabic language to warn those who have done wrong and as good tidings to the doers of good.** (46:12)
>
> **Indeed, this is in the former scriptures, the scriptures of Abraham and Moses.** (87:18-19; also 53:36-37)

As for what was later added to the Law by the rabbis and scholars in their commentaries and commentaries on commentaries, all these were human additions for which God Most High did not reveal any authority. For He, the All-Knowing, the All-Wise, had included in the original *Taurat* all things necessary for the guidance of the Israelites and their descendants, the Jews, as indicated in the words,

> **Indeed, We sent down the *Taurat*, wherein was guidance and light. By it, the prophets, who surrendered [to God], gave judgment for the Jews, as did the rabbis and scholars, by that with which they were entrusted of God's scripture, and they were witnesses to that. Therefore, do not fear people but fear Me, and do not sell My revelations for a small price. And whoever does not judge by what God has revealed, then it is those who are unbelievers.** (5:44/47)

THE TEN COMMANDMENTS

It is generally supposed that what was written upon the Tablets of Moses (A) were the Ten Commandments, given in Ex. 20:3-17. But only God knows whether or not this was the case.

It is often asked whether Muslims believe in these commandments and whether there is an Islamic equivalent to them. The answer to this question is as follows:

While there is no single body of rules in Islam termed "the Ten Commandments," nine of the ten are also found in Islam. However, because the Old Testament was the work of many human authors, not the direct speech of the one divine Author, there is no way to know whether the laws given in Ex. 20:3-17 were the actual commandments revealed to Moses (A) by God — that is, whether some commandments may have been added or embellished, and conversely, whether there may have been additional commandments that were not included among the ten.[184] Indeed, the following *hadith* strongly suggests that this may have been the case.

It is reported that once the Prophet (S) was talking to two Jews who came to question him, and he mentioned nine commandments given to the Israelites:

> Do not ascribe partners to God. Do not steal. Do not engage in illicit sexual relations. Do not kill any person unjustly. Do not practice magic. Do not take usury. Do not accuse anyone unjustly and then take him to the judge to be executed. Do not slander chaste women [or, he said, do not run away from the battlefield]. And O Jews, it was commanded for you in particular to observe Saturday as the Sabbath. (Ibn Kathir/*T*, 17:101)

Some early Islamic scholars were of the opinion that the Ten Commandments are contained in the following Qur'anic verses, which prescribe a number of basic obligations for Muslims:

> **Say, [O Muhammad:] "Come, I will recite what your Lord has prohibited to you: Do not set up partners with Him, and goodness to parents, and do not kill your children due to poverty — We shall provide for you and them — and do not come near indecencies, what is apparent of them and what is hidden, nor kill a person whom God has prohibited [killing] except by [legal] right. This He has enjoined upon you, that you may use reason. And do not come near the orphan's property except by that which is best until he reaches maturity. And give full measure and weight in justice; We do not charge any soul except to its capacity. And when you speak, be just, even if a near relative [is concerned], and fulfill God's covenant. This has He instructed you, that you may remember. And this is My path, which is straight, so follow it, and**

[184]Ibn Kathir states that Moses was given nine "words of creation" — the nine signs to Pharaoh and his people — which relate to the physical world, and also ten "words of legislation" or commandments (Ibn Kathir/*Q*, "Musa").

do not follow other ways, for you will be separated from His way. This He has instructed you, that you may become mindful of God. **(6:151-153)**

In a point-by-point comparison of the Ten Commandments with the injunctions of Islam, the first commandment, to take no deity besides God, is nothing less than Islam's most fundamental principle. The Islamic creed or profession of faith (*Shahadah*), "***La ilaha illa-Allah*** — there is no deity except God,"[185] proclaims the renouncing of all other objects of worship besides the Creator, while at the same time acknowledging His Lordship and sovereignty, and one's own creaturehood.

The second commandment, not to make any idol, image or depiction of anything for the purpose of worshipping it, either as a representation of God or in addition to or in place of Him, is a corollary to the first and again is absolutely central to Islam. Indeed, the primary mission of all the prophets was to direct people away from the worship of idols and other false deities to the worship of the Incomparable, the Unique, who has no substance or form, nor any similarity to any created being. As a result, Islam absolutely prohibits making any sort of depiction of the Creator. This prohibition also extends to representations of prophets or others who may be given excessive respect, lest they be worshipped in the place of or in addition to God.[186]

The third commandment, not to take the name of God in vain, is also honored by Muslims. Although unfortunately this matter is often taken lightly in our time, it is considered detestable to swear by God's name for no serious purpose.

The fourth commandment concerns the Sabbath. This is the one commandment in which Islam differs from Judaism, for God ordained Friday (Jum'ah) as the special day of the week for the Muslim ***ummah*** — not as a day

---

[185]It is reported in a ***hadith*** that Moses asked his Lord to teach him something by which to make mention of Him or to supplicate Him. When God instructed him to say, "***La ilaha illa-Llah***," Moses replied that all His servants say this but he wanted something especially for himself. Then God Most High said, "O Moses, if the seven heavens and their inhabitants, apart from Me, and the seven earths were put on one side of a scale and '***La ilaha illa-Lah***' on the other, '***La ilaha illa-Llah***' would outweigh them [all]" (***Mishkat***, 2306).

[186]Although at one time miniatures depicting the Prophet (S) were common in some parts of the Muslim world, his face was never shown but was replaced with a featureless white veil surrounded by a white aura of flame. A similar practice was followed for angels, other prophets, Companions of the Prophet and saints.

of rest but of obligatory congregational prayer, observed at noon, as enjoined in 62:9.

The fifth commandment, honoring one's parents, is a very strongly stressed Islamic obligation, while dishonoring them is a grave sin, as is mentioned in several Qur'anic verses.[187]

The sixth commandment, the prohibition of killing, thereby honoring the sanctity of the life given by the Creator, is also critically important in Islam.[188]

---

[187]See 2:215; 4:1, 36; 6:151; 17:23-24; 29:8; 31:14-15; 46:15.

[188]God Most High says, **And do not kill the person whom God has prohibited [killing], except by [legal] right** (6:151, 17:33), thereby making it unlawful to kill anyone who has not incurred the death penalty for a capital crime, proven by a fair and impartial trial, except in warfare. Warfare, however, is permitted only for the purpose of repelling aggression or combating oppression, for God says, **Fight in the way of God those who fight you but do not commit aggression. Indeed, God does not like aggressors** (2:190). And He says,

> **Permission [to fight] has been given to those who are being fought, because they were wronged. And indeed, God is able to give them victory. [They are] those who have been evicted from their homes without right, only because they say, "Our Lord is God." And it were not that God checks some people by means of others, there would have been demolished monasteries, churches, synagogues and mosques in which the name of God is much mentioned. And God will surely support those who support Him. Indeed, God is All-Poerful and Almighty. (22:39-40)**

Warfare is to be waged between armies, and killing and harming civilians and non-combatants is clearly prohibited. In Islam, a single standard of justice applies equally to enemies and to friends, according to God's order, **O you who believe, stand firmly for God, witnesses in justice, and do not let hatred of a people prevent you from being just. Be just; that is closer to righteousness** (5:8/9).

The Prophet (S) gave the following instructions to Muslims concerning the conduct of war:

> Go in God's name, trusting in God and keeping to the religion of God's Messenger. Do not kill a weak old man, a young infant, a child or a woman. Do not be dishonest about booty but collect your spoils [as permitted]. Do right and act well, for God loves those who do well. (Abu Dawud, 2608)

Similar instructions were given by the first caliph of Islam, Abu Bakr as-Siddiq, to the Muslim army:

> Do not be deserters nor be guilty of disobedience. Do not kill an old person, a woman or a child. Do not injure date palms nor cut down fruit trees. Do not slaughter any sheep or cows or camels except for food. You will encounter persons who spend their lives in monastaries. Let them be and do not molest them.

And the following contract was made by the second caliph, 'Umar ibn al-Khattab, at the conquest of Eiliya (Jerusalem) with its Christians:

The seventh commandment, the prohibition of adultery or fornication, is also essential to Islam, which prescribes a number of measures to safeguard the the sanctity of the relationship between husband and wife, as well as the purity of society.[189]

The eighth commandment (the prohibition of stealing), the ninth (the prohibition of lying and bearing false witness), and the tenth (the prohibition of coveting and envying others), are all basic Islamic rules.

How can one explain the close correspondence between the divine Law prescribed for the Children of Israel and the *Shari'ah* of Islam? The reason should be obvious: that both originated from the same divine Source. Indeed, if they were not so similar, it would be impossible to believe in the continuity of God's Message, delivered through His prophets, throughout the course of mankind's life on earth. For as God Himself does not change, neither do His laws change, nor the distinction between good and evil, nor the basics of human nature. Consequently, what was brought by His true messengers, from the first to the last, must of necessity be the same, barring minor variations related to the specific conditions and needs of the communitie for whom they were revealed.

This is the protection which the slave of God, 'Umar, the commander of the believers, has granted to the people of Eiliya. The protection is for their lives and properties, their churches and crosses, their sick and healthy and for all their co-religionists. Their churches shall not be used as dwelling-places nor shall they be demolished, nor shall any injury be done to them or to their compounds or to their crosses, nor shall their properties be injured in any way. There shall be no compulsion for these people in the matter of religion, nor shall any of them suffer any injury on account of religion.

[189]For a discussion of this point, please see Volume One, pages 390-392.

QUR'ANIC REFERENCES — MOSES, AARON AND SAYYIDINA KHIDR

2:47-74

O Children of Israel, recall My favor that I bestowed upon you and that I preferred you above mankind. (47) And fear a Day when no soul will suffice for another soul in the least, nor will intercession be accepted from it, nor will compensation be taken from it nor will they be helped. (48)

And [recall] when We saved you from the people of Pharaoh, who afflicted you with the worst torment, slaughtering your sons and letting your women live. And in that was a tremendous trial from your Lord. (49) And [recall] when We parted the sea for you, and We saved you and drowned Pharaoh's people while you were looking on. (50)

And [recall] when We appointed for Moses forty nights. Then you adopted the Calf after him, while you were wrong-doers. (51) Then We forgave you after that, that perhaps you might be thankful. (52)

And [recall] when We gave Moses the scripture and the criterion, that perhaps you might be guided. (53) And [recall] when Moses said to his people, "O my people, indeed you have wronged yourselves by your adopting the Calf, so repent to your Maker and kill yourselves. That will be best for you in front of your Maker." Then He accepted your repentance; indeed, He is the Acceptor of Repentance, the Merciful. (54)

And [recall] when you said, "O Moses, we will never believe in you until we see God openly." Then the blast seized you while you were looking on. (55) Then We revived you after your death, that you might perhaps be thankful. (56) And We shaded you with the overcast and sent down to you manna and quails, [saying,] "Eat of the good things that We have provided you." And they did not wrong Us, but [rather] they wronged themselves. (57)

And [recall] when We said, "Enter this town and eat from it as you will in abundance, and enter the gate prostrating and say, '*Hittah* — relieve us of our burdens.' We will forgive your transgressions for you and will increase the doers of good [in reward]." (58) Then those who did wrong substituted a saying other than that which had been said to them, so We sent down upon those who did wrong a punishment from the sky because they were transgressing. (59)

And [recall] when Moses prayed for water for his people, so We said, "Strike the rock with your staff." Then there flowed from it twelve springs. Each people knew its drinking place. [It was said:] "Eat and drink of God's provision and do not act wrongfully in the land, causing corruption." (60)

And [recall] when you said, "O Moses, we can never endure one kind of food, so call upon your Lord for us to bring forth for us, from what the earth produces, some of its herbs and its cucumbers and its garlic and its lentils and its onions."

He said, "Would you exchange that which is inferior for that which is better? Go to any town, and then indeed you will have what you have asked!"

And humiliation and misery were settled upon them, and they drew upon themselves anger from God. That was because they disbelieved in the signs of God and killed the prophets without right. That was because they disobeyed and transgressed. (61)

Indeed, those who believe and those who are Jews and Christians and Sabeans — whoever believes in God and the Last Day and works righteousness will have their reward with their Lord, and no fear will be on them nor shall they grieve. (62)

And [recall, O Children of Israel,] when We took your covenant and raised the Mount over you, [saying,] "Take what We have given you with determination and remember what is in it, that you may be mindful of God." (63) Then you turned back after that. And if it had not been for the favor of God upon you and His mercy, you would surely have been among the losers. (64)

And you certainly knew about those among you who transgressed regarding the Sabbath, whereupon We said to them, "Be monkeys, banished!" (65) Thus We made it an exemplary punishment for those who were with them and those who followed, and a lesson for those who are mindful of God. (66)

And [recall] when Moses said to his people, "Indeed, God commands you to slaughter a cow."

They said, "Are you making a mockery of us?"

He said, "I seek refuge with God from being among the ignorant!" (67)

They said, "Supplicate your Lord for us to make clear to us what she is."

He said, "He says, 'She is a cow neither old nor virgin but midway between that,' so do as you are commanded." (68)

They said, "Supplicate your Lord for us to make clear to us what her color is."

He said, "He says, 'She is a yellow cow, bright in color, pleasing to the beholders.'" (69)

They said, "Supplicate your Lord for us to make clear to us what she is; indeed, [all] cows seem alike to us. And if God wills, we will surely be guided." (70)

He said, "He says, 'She is a cow neither broken-in to till the soil nor to water the fields, sound, with no blemish upon her.'"

They said "Now you have come with the truth!" So they slaughtered her, although they almost did not [do it]. (71)

And [recall] when you killed a person and disputed about it, but God was to bring forth that which you were concealing. (72) And We said, "Strike it with part of it." Thus does God bring the dead to life, and He shows you His signs, that you may understand. (73)

Then your hearts became hardened after that, and they were like stones or even harder. For indeed there are stones from which streams gush forth, and indeed there are some of them that split open and water flows out of them, and indeed there are some of them that fall down from fear of God. And God is not unaware of what you do. (74)

2:83-84

And [recall] when We took a covenant from the Children of Israel, [commanding,] "Do not worship other than God. And do good to parents and relatives and orphans and the poor, and speak good [words] to people, and establish *salat* and give *zakat*." Then you turned back, except a few among you, and you were resisting. (83) And [recall] when We took your covenant, [commanding,] "Do not shed your blood nor drive one another out of your homes." Then you agreed, while you were witnessing. (84)

2:87

And We certainly gave Moses the scripture and followed him by a succession of [other] messengers.

2:92-93

And Moses certainly brought you clear proofs. Then you adopted the Calf after him, while you were wrong-doers. (92) And [recall] when We took your covenant and raised the Mount over you, [saying,] "Take what We have given you with determination and listen."

They said, "We hear and we disobey," and they absorbed the Calf into their hearts through their unbelief. Say, [O Muhammad:] "How vile is that which your belief enjoins upon you, if you are believers!" (93)

2:108

Or do you intend to question your messenger [Muhammad] as Moses was questioned previously?

2:122

O Children of Israel, recall My favor which I bestowed upon you and that I preferred you above mankind.

2:136

Say, [O Muslims:] "We believe in God and what was revealed to us, and what was revealed to Abraham and Ishmael and Isaac and Jacob and the descendants [of Israel], and what was given to Moses and Jesus, and what was given to [all] the prophets by their Lord. We make no distinction between any of them, and we surrender to Him [in Islam]."

2:211

Ask the Children of Israel how many a clear sign We granted them.

2:253

Those messengers — We favored some of them over others. Among them were those to whom God spoke, and He exalted some of them in rank.

3:84

Say, [O Muhammad:] "We believe in God and what was revealed to us, and what was revealed to Abraham and Ishmael and Isaac and Jacob and the descendants [of Israel], and what was given to Moses and Jesus and the prophets by their Lord. We make no distinction between any of them, and we surrender to Him [in Islam]." (84)

4:153-154

The People of the Scripture ask you [Muhammad] to bring down to them a book from Heaven. But they had certainly asked a greater thing than that of Moses, for they said, "Show us God openly," whereupon the blast seized them for their wrong-doing. Furthermore, they adopted the Calf after clear evidences had come to them, but We pardoned that. And We granted Moses clear authority (153) and raised the Mount over them for their covenant, and We said to them, "Enter the gate prostrating," and said to them, "Do not transgress regarding the Sabbath," and We took from them a solemn covenant. (154)

4:163

And God spoke to Moses with [direct] speech. (164)

5:20-26/22-29

And [recall] when Moses said to his people, "O my people, remember God's favor to you when He appointed prophets among you and made you sovereigns, and granted you what He had not granted anyone among mankind. (20/22) O my people, enter the holy land that God has appointed for you, and do not turn back and become losers." (21/23)

They said, "O Moses, indeed, in it are a people of tyrannical strength, and indeed, we will never enter it until they depart from it. But if they depart from it, then we will enter." (22/24)

Two men among those who feared, upon whom God had bestowed favor, said, "Enter upon them through the gate, for when you have entered it, you will surely be victorious. And rely upon God, if you are believers!" (23/25-26)

They said, "O Moses, indeed we will never enter it as long as they are in it. Then go, you and your Lord, and fight! We will surely stay here." (24/27)

He [Moses] said, "My Lord, indeed I do not have mastery except over myself and my brother. Then make a separation between us and the transgressing people!" (25/28)

He [God] said, "Then indeed it will be prohibited to them for forty years, [during which] they will wander across the land. So do not grieve over the transgressing people!" (26/29)

6:84

And We granted him [Abraham] Isaac and Jacob; each [of them] We guided. And previously We guided Noah, and among his descendants, David and Solomon and Job and Joseph and Moses and Aaron. And thus do We reward the doers of good.

6:91

Say, [O Muhammad:] "Who revealed the scripture that Moses brought as light and guidance to people?" Say: "God [revealed it]."

6:154

Then We gave Moses the scripture, completing [Our favor] upon the one who did good, and as a detailed explanation of all things and guidance and mercy, that they might perhaps believe in the meeting with their Lord.

7:103-145, 148-162

Then after them, We sent Moses to Pharaoh and his chiefs, but they behaved wrongfully with them. Then see what was the end of the corrupters! (103)

And Moses said, "O Pharaoh, indeed, I am a messenger from the Lord of the worlds, (104) obliged not to say other than the truth about God. I have come to you with clear evidence from your Lord, so send the Children of Israel forth with me." (105)

He said, "If you have come with a sign, then produce it, if you are among the truthful." (106). Then he threw down his staff, whereupon it was an obvious snake, (107) and he drew forth his hand, whereupon it was white to the onlookers. (108)

The chiefs of Pharaoh's people said, "Indeed, this is a skilled magician (109) who wants to drive you out of your land, so what do you advise?" (110)

They said, "Defer him and his brother, and send gatherers into the cities (111), who will bring you every skilled magician." (112)

And the magicians came to Pharaoh. They said, "Ours will surely be a great reward if we are the victors." (113)

He said, "Yes, and indeed you will be among those near [to me]." (114)

They said, "O Moses, either you throw or we will be the ones to throw [first]." (115)

He said, "Throw!" and when they threw, they spellbound the eyes of the people and struck terror into them, and they produced stupendous magic. (116) And We inspired to Moses, "Throw your staff!" and at once it swallowed up whatever they were falsifying. (117) Thus was the truth confirmed and what they did was nullified, (118) and they were overcome on the spot and overturned, debased. (119)

And the magicians fell down in prostration. (120) They said, "We believe in the Lord of the worlds, (121) the Lord of Moses and Aaron!" (122)

He [Pharaoh] said, "You believed in him before I gave you permission! Indeed, this is a conspiracy which you plotted in the city, to drive its people out of it. But you are going to know! (123) I will surely cut off your hands and feet on opposite sides; then I will surely crucify you all." (124)

They said, "Indeed, we will return to our Lord. (125) And you are taking revenge upon us only because we believed in our Lord's signs when they came to us. Our Lord, pour out upon us patience and let us die as ***muslims***." (126)

And the chiefs of Pharaoh's people said, "Will you leave Moses and his people to make corruption in the land, and abandon you and your gods?"

He said, "We will kill their sons and let their women live, and indeed we are dominant over them." (127)

Moses said to his people, "Seek help with God and be patient. Indeed, the earth belongs to God. He causes whomever He wills of His servants to inherit it, and the best outcome is for those who are mindful of Him." (128)

They said, "We were harmed before you came to us and after you came to us."

He said, "Perhaps your Lord will destroy your enemy and grant you succession in the land, and see how you will act." (129)

And We certainly chastised Pharaoh's people with years of famine and shortage of fruits, that perhaps they might be reminded. (130) But when good came to them, they said, "This is our due." And if a calamity befell them, they ascribed an evil omen to Moses and those with him. Unquestionably, their 'evil omens' were only with God, but most of them do not know. (131) And they said, "No matter what sign you bring us to bewitch us with, we will not be believers in you." (132)

Then We sent upon them the flood and locusts and lice and frogs and blood as distinct signs, but they were arrogant and were an evil-doing people. (133) And whenever the punishment fell upon them, they said, "O Moses, invoke your Lord for us by what He has promised you. If you remove the punishment from us, we will surely believe in you and will send the Children of Israel forth with you." (134) But when We removed the punishment from them until a term which they were to reach, forthwith they broke their word. (135)

Then We took retribution from them and drowned them in the sea because they denied Our signs and were heedless of them, (136) and We caused the people who had been oppressed to inherit the east of the land and the west of it, which We had blest. And the fair word of your Lord was fulfilled for the Children of Israel because of what they had patiently endured. And We destroyed what Pharaoh and his people had produced and what they had built. (137)

And We took the Children of Israel across the sea and they came upon a people devoted to idols of theirs. They said, "O Moses, appoint a god for us, just as they have gods."

He said, "Indeed, you are a people behaving ignorantly! (138) Surely those — what they are engaged in is destroyed and what they are doing is in vain." (139) He said, "Shall I seek for you a deity other than God, while He has preferred you above mankind?" (140)

And [recall, O Children of Israel,] when We saved you from the people of Pharaoh, who afflicted you with the worst torment, slaughtering your sons and letting your women live. And in that was a tremendous trial from your Lord. (141)

And We appointed for Moses thirty nights and perfected them by ten [more], and thus his Lord's term was completed as forty. And Moses said to his brother Aaron, "Take my place among my people and do right, and do not follow the way of the corrupters." (142)

And when Moses came at Our appointed time and his Lord spoke to him, he said, "My Lord, show me [Yourself], that I may look at You."

He said, "You will not see Me, but look at the mountain, and if it remains in its place, then you will see Me."

Then when his Lord manifested Himself to the mountain, He caused it to crumble, and Moses fell down unconscious. And when he came to himself, he said, "May You be glorified! I turn to You in repentance, and I am the foremost of the believers." (143)

He said, "O Moses, indeed I have chosen you above mankind for My messages and for My speech, so keep to what I have given you and be among the grateful." (144) And We wrote for him, on the Tablets, concerning all things, admonition and explanation for all things, [saying,] "Then keep to it with determination, and order your people to keep to the best of it. I shall show you the abode of the transgressors." (145)

. . . And the people of Moses made ready, after him, out of their ornaments, the form of a calf that made a lowing sound. Did they not see that it could neither speak to them nor guide them to a way? They adopted it and were wrong-doers. (148) And when regret overcame them and they saw that they had gone astray, they said, "If our Lord does not have mercy upon us and forgive us, we will surely be among the losers." (149)

And when Moses returned to his people, angry and grieved, he said, "How evil is that which you have done in my place in my absence! Would you hasten your Lord's command?" And he threw down the Tablets and seized his brother by his head, pulling him toward him.

He [Aaron] said, "Son of my mother, indeed, the people considered me weak and nearly killed me, so do not let the enemies gloat over me nor consider me among the wrong-doing people!" (150)

He [Moses] said, "My Lord, forgive me and my brother, and admit us into Your mercy, for You are the Most Merciful of the merciful!" (151)

Indeed, those who adopted the Calf — wrath from their Lord and humiliation will encompass them in the life of this world, and thus do We recompense the fabricators of falsehood. (152) But those who did evil deeds and then repented after them and believed — indeed, your Lord is, after that, Forgiving and Merciful. (153)

And when the anger abated from Moses, he took up the Tablets, and in their inscription was guidance and mercy for those who are in awe of their Lord. (154)

And Moses chose seventy men of his people for Our appointment. And when the quaking overtook them, he said, "My Lord, if You had willed, You could have destroyed them previously, and me! Would You destroy us for what the foolish among us have done? This is nothing but Your trial by which You permit to stray whomever You will and You guide whomever You will. You are our Protector, so forgive us and have mercy upon us, and You are the Best of Forgivers. (155) And decree for us good in this world and in the Hereafter; indeed, we have turned to You."

He [God] said, "My punishment — I strike with it whomever I will, but My mercy embraces all things. So I shall decree it for those who are mindful of Me and give *zakat*, and those who believe in Our signs [or verses] (156) — those who follow the Messenger, the Unlettered Prophet whom they find inscribed in what they have of the *Taurat* and the *Injil*, who enjoins upon them the right and forbids them from the wrong, and makes permissible to them the good and prohibits to them the evil, and relieves them of their burden and the fetters which were upon them. Therefore, those who believe in him and honor him and support him and follow the light which was sent down with him — it is those who will be the successful." (157)

Say, [O Muhammad:] "O mankind, indeed I am the Messenger of God to you all, of Him to whom the dominion of the heavens and the earth belongs. There is no deity except Him; He gives life and causes death." So believe in God and His Messenger, the Unlettered Prophet, who believes in God and His words, and follow him, that you may be guided. (158)

And among the people of Moses is a community that guides by truth and establishes justice thereby. (159)

And We divided them into twelve tribes, nations. And We inspired to Moses, when his people asked him for water, "Strike the rock with your staff,." Then there gushed forth from it twelve springs. Each people knew its drinking place. And We shaded them with the overcast and sent down to them manna and quails, [saying,] "Eat of the good things that We have provided you." And they did not wrong Us, but [rather] they wronged themselves. (160)

And [mention] when it was said to them, "Dwell in this town and eat from it as you wish, and say '*Hittah* — relieve us of our burdens,' and enter the gate prostrating. We will forgive your transgressions for you; We will increase the doers of good [in reward]." (161)

Then those of them who did wrong substituted a saying other than that which had been said to them, whereupon We sent upon them a punishment from the sky because of the wrong they were doing. (162)

7:171

And [mention] when We raised the Mount over them as though it were a canopy and they thought that it would surely fall upon them, [and We said,] "Take what We have given you with determination and remember what is in it, that you may be mindful of God."

10:75-92

Then after them, We sent Moses and Aaron to Pharaoh and his chiefs with Our signs, but they behaved arrogantly and were a sinful people. (75) And when the truth came to them from Us, they said, "Indeed, this is obvious magic." (76)

Moses said, "Do you speak [thus] about the truth when it has come to you? Is this magic? But never will the magicians prosper!" (77)

They said, "Have you come to us to turn us away from what we found our fathers doing, and that you two may have glory in the land? But we are not believers in you!" (78)

And Pharaoh said, "Bring me every skilled magician." (79)

Then, when the magicians arrived, Moses said to them, "Throw whatever you will throw!" (80) And when they had thrown, Moses said, "What you have produced is [mere] magic. God will surely bring it to nought. Indeed, God does not amend the work of corrupters, (81) and God will establish the truth by His word, even if the sinners detest it!" (82) But no one believed in Moses except [some] offspring of his people, out of fear of Pharaoh and his supporters, that they would persecute them. And indeed Pharaoh exalted himself in the land and he was surely of the transgressors. (83)

And Moses said, "O my people, if you believe in God, then rely upon Him, if you are *muslims*." (84)

Then they said, "Upon God do we rely. Our Lord, do not make us a [source of] temptation for the wrong-doing people, (85) and save us, by Your mercy, from the disbelieving people." (86)

And We inspired to Moses and his brother, "Make your people stay in houses in Egypt, and make your houses a *qiblah* and establish *salat*, and give good tidings to the believers." (87)

And Moses said, "Our Lord, indeed, You have granted Pharaoh and his chiefs splendor and wealth in the worldly life, our Lord, that they may lead astray from Your path. Our Lord, obliterate their wealth and harden their hearts so they will not believe until they see the painful punishment!" (88)

He said, "The supplication of the two of you has been answered. Therefore, both of you remain firm and do not follow the way of those who do not know." (89)

And We took the Children of Israel across the sea, and Pharaoh and his troops pursued them in deviation and enmity until, when drowning overtook him, he said, "I believe that there is no God except the One in whom the Children of Israel believe, and I am of the *muslims*." (90)

"Now, while previously you had rebelled and were of the corrupters! (91) But today We shall save you in body, that you may be a sign for those who succeed you. And indeed, many among mankind are heedless of Our signs." (92)

11:17

And before it [the Qur'an], the scripture of Moses was a guide and a mercy.

11:96-100

And We certainly sent Moses with Our signs and clear authority (96) to Pharaoh and his chiefs, but they followed Pharaoh's command, and Pharaoh's command was not rightly-guided. (97) He will be at the head of his people on the Day of Resurrection and take them to the Fire, and wretched is the place to which they will be led! (98) And they were followed by a curse in this [life] and on the Day of Resurrection. And wretched is the gift that will be given [to them]! (99) That is of the news of the cities which we relate to you; of them, some are [still] standing and some are [like] a reaped harvest. (100)

11:110

And We certainly gave Moses the scripture, but there was disagreement concerning it.

14:5-8

And indeed, We sent Moses with Our signs, [saying,] "Bring your people out of darknesses into the light and remind them of the days of God." Indeed, in that are signs for every patient and thankful one. (5)

And [recall, O Children of Israel,] when Moses said to his people, "Remember God's favor to you when He saved you from Pharaoh's people, who were afflicting you with the worst torment, and were slaughtering your sons and letting your women live. And in that was a tremendous trial from your Lord." (6)

And [recall] when your Lord proclaimed, "If you are thankful, indeed, I will grant you increase, but if you are ungrateful, indeed, My punishment is severe." (7)

And Moses said, "If you are ungrateful, you and everyone who is on the earth, yet God is free of [all] need and worthy of [all] praise." (8)

17:2-3

We gave Moses the scripture and made it guidance for the Children of Israel, that you not take other than Me as Disposer of affairs, (2) O descendants of those We carried [in the ship] with Noah. Indeed, he was a thankful slave. (3)

17:101-103

And We certainly granted Moses nine clear signs, so ask the Children of Israel about when he came to them and Pharaoh said to him, "Indeed, I consider you, O Moses, to be under a spell." (101)

He said, "You certainly know that no one has sent down these except the Lord of the heavens and the earth as clear proofs. And indeed, I consider you, O Pharaoh, to be ruined!" (102) Thus, he intended to frighten them out of the land, but We drowned him and those with him, all together. (103)

18:60-82

And [mention] when Moses said to his young man, "I shall not cease [my quest] until I reach the junction of the two seas, or [otherwise] spend years [in searching]." (60) But when they reached the junction between them, they forgot their fish, and it took its course through the sea as in a tunnel. (61)

Then when they had passed beyond it, he said to his young man, "Bring us our breakfast. We have certainly experienced fatigue in this, our journey." (62)

He [the young man] said, "Did you see, when we retired to the rock? Indeed, I forgot the fish, and none but Satan made me forget to mention it. And it took its course into the sea amazingly!" (63)

He said, "That is what we were seeking!" So they returned, retracing their footsteps. (64)

Then they found a slave from among Our slaves to whom We had granted mercy from Ourself and had taught him, from Ourself, knowledge. (65) Moses said to him, "May I follow you on the condition that you teach me from what you have been taught of right guidance?" (66)

He said, "Indeed, you will never be able to have patience with me. (67) And how can you have patience with what you do not encompass in knowledge?" (68)

He [Moses] said, "You will find me, God willing, patient, and I will not disobey you in any order." (69)

He said, "Then, if you follow me, do not ask me about anything until I make mention of it to you." (70)

So the two set out until, when they had embarked in the boat, he made a hole in it. He [Moses] said, "Have you made a hole in it to drown its people? You have certainly done a grievous thing!" (71)

He said, "Did I not say that you would never be able to have patience with me?" (72)

He [Moses] said, "Do not take me to task for what I forgot nor be hard on me concerning my affair." (73)

So the two set out until, when they encountered a boy, he killed him. He [Moses] said, "Have you killed a blameless person without [his having killed] anyone? You have certainly done a terrible thing!" (74)

He said, "Did I not say to you that you would never be able to have patience with me?" (75)

He [Moses] said, "If I should ask you about anything after this, then do not keep me as a companion. You will have received a [sufficient] excuse on my part." (76)

So the two set out until, when they came to the people of a town, they asked its people for food but they refused to offer them hospitality. And they found therein a wall about to collapse, whereupon he restored it. He [Moses] said, "If you had wished, you could have taken payment for it." (77)

He said, "This is a parting between me and you. I shall inform you of the interpretation of that about which you were unable to have patience. (78)

"As for the boat, it belonged to poor people working at sea, so I intended to render it defective, as there was a king after them who seized every boat by force. (79) And as for the boy, his parents were believers, and we feared that he would overburden them by transgression and unbelief, (80) so we intended that their Lord should substitute for them one better than he in purity and nearer to mercy. (81) And as for the wall, it belonged to two orphan boys in the town and beneath it was a treasure belonging to them, and their father had been righteous. So your Lord intended that they reach maturity and extract their treasure as a mercy from your Lord. And I did not do it of my own accord. That is the interpretation of that about which you were unable to have patience." (82)

19:51-53

And mention Moses in the Book. Indeed, he was chosen, and he was a messenger and a prophet. (51) And We called him from the right side of the mountain and brought him near, confiding. (52) And We granted him, out of Our mercy, his brother Aaron as a prophet. (53)

20:9-99

And has the story of Moses reached you? — (9) when he saw a fire and said to his family, "Stay here. Indeed, I have seen a fire. Perhaps I may bring you a burning branch or find guidance at the fire." (10)

Then when he reached it, he was called, "O Moses, (11) indeed I am your Lord, so take off your sandals. Indeed, you are in the sacred valley of Tuwa. (12) And I have chosen you, so listen to what is revealed. (13)

"Indeed, I am Allah. There is no deity except Me, so worship Me and establish *salat* for My remembrance. (14) Indeed, the Hour [of Judgment] is coming. I virtually conceal it, that each soul may be recompensed according to what it strives for. (15) Therefore, do not let that one divert you from it who does not believe in it but follows his own desires, lest you perish. (16) And what is that in your right hand, O Moses? (17)

He said, "It is my staff; I lean on it and bring down leaves for my sheep with it, and I have other uses for it." (18)

He said, "Throw it down, O Moses!" (19)

So he threw it down, whereupon it was a snake, moving swiftly. (20) He said, "Take hold of it and do not be afraid. We shall revert it to its former state. (21) And draw your hand to your side; it will come forth white, without blemish — another sign, (22) that We may show you some of Our greater signs. (23) Go to Pharaoh. Indeed, he has transgressed." (24)

He [Moses] said, "My Lord, expand my breast for me (25) and ease my task for me, (26) and loosen the knot from my tongue, (27) that they may understand my speech. (28) And appoint an assistant for me from my family (29) — Aaron, my brother. (30) Increase my strength through him (31) and let him share my task, (32) that we may glorify You much (33) and remember You much. (34) Indeed, You are ever seeing of us." (35)

He said, "You have been granted your request, O Moses. (36) And We already conferred favor upon you another time, (37) when We inspired to your mother what We inspired: (38) 'Drop him in the chest and drop it into the river, and the river will cast it onto the bank; there will take him up an enemy to Me and an enemy to him.' And I bestowed love upon you from Myself, that you might be reared under My Eye, (39) when your sister went and said, 'Shall I direct you to someone who will feed him?' Then We restored you to your mother, that she might be content and not grieve.

"Then you killed a person but We saved you from the affliction, and We tried you with a trial. And you stayed for years among the people of Midian. Then you came here at the decreed time, O Moses. (40) And I chose you for Myself. (41)

"Go, you and your brother, with My signs, and do not slacken in My remembrance. (42) Go, both of you, to Pharaoh. Indeed, he has transgressed. (43) And speak to him with gentle speech, that perhaps he may be reminded or fear." (44)

They said, "Our Lord, indeed, we are afraid that he may act hastily against us or that he may transgress." (45)

He said, "Do not fear. Indeed, I am with you both; I hear and see. (46) Therefore, go to him and say, 'Indeed, we are two messengers of your Lord, so send the Children of Israel forth with us and do not torment them. We have come to you with a sign from your Lord. And peace be upon him who follows the guidance. (47) Indeed, it has been revealed to us that the punishment will be upon him who denies and turns away.'" (48)

He [Pharaoh] said, "Then who is the Lord of you two, O Moses?" (49)

He said, "Our Lord is He who gave each thing its nature and then guided [it]." (50)

He said, "Then what is the case of the former generations?" (51)

He said, "The knowledge of it is with my Lord in a record. My Lord neither errs nor forgets" — (52) He who has made the earth as a bed for you and inserted roadways for you upon it, and has sent down water from the sky and brought forth therewith species of diverse plants. (53) Eat [of them] and pasture your cattle! Surely in that are signs for those of intelligence. (54) From it We created you, and into it We shall return you, and from it We shall bring you forth another time. (55)

And We certainly showed him Our signs, all of them, but he denied and rejected. (56) He said, "Have you come to us to drive us out of our land by your magic, O Moses? (57) But we will surely provide you with magic like it, so fix an appointment between ourselves and you which neither we nor you will fail to keep, in an assigned place." (58)

He said, "Your appointment is the day of the festival, when the people assemble at mid-morning." (59) Then Pharaoh departed, and he assembled his plan and then came. (60)

Moses said to them, "Woe to you! Do not fabricate a lie against God, lest He destroy you with a punishment, and whoever fabricates will be defeated." (61)

Then they disputed their affair among themselves and concealed their private conversation. (62) They said, "Indeed, these are two magicians who want to drive you out of your land by their magic and do away with your ideal religion. (63) So resolve upon your plan and then approach in ranks. And he who is victorious today will prosper!" (64)

They said, "O Moses, either you throw or we will be the first to throw." (65)

He said, "Rather, you throw." Thereupon their cords and their staffs seemed to him, due to their magic, as though they were moving. (66) And Moses felt fear within himself. (67)

We said, "Do not fear. Indeed, you will be the uppermost. (68) And throw what is in your right hand; it will swallow up whatever they have fabricated. What they have fabricated is only a magician's trick, but never will the magician prosper, whatever he may aim at." (69)

Then the magicians fell down in prostration. They said, "We believe in the Lord of Aaron and Moses!" (70)

He [Pharaoh] said, "You believed him before I gave you permission! Indeed, he is your leader who has taught you magic. Therefore, I will surely cut off your hands and your feet on opposite sides, and I will crucify you upon the trunks of palm trees, and indeed you will know which of us is more severe and more lasting in punishment!" (71)

They said, "Never will we prefer you over what has come to us of clear proofs and [over] Him who created us. Therefore, decree whatever you will decree. You can decree only concerning this worldly life. (72) Indeed, we have believed in our Lord, that He may forgive us our sins and that which you compelled us to of magic. And God is best and most enduring." (73)

Indeed, whoever comes to his Lord as an evil-doer, for him will surely be Hell; he will neither die therein, nor live. (74) But whoever comes to Him as a believer, having done righteous deeds, for those will be the highest ranks — (75) gardens of perpetual abode beneath which rivers flow, wherein they will abide eternally. And that is the recompense of one who purifies himself. (76)

And We inspired to Moses, "Travel by night with My servants and strike a dry path for them through the sea, not fearing to be overtaken nor afraid [of drowning]." (77) Then Pharaoh pursued them with his troops, and there covered them, of the sea, that which covered them. (78) And Pharaoh led his people astray and did not guide [them aright]. (79)

O Children of Israel, We saved you from your enemy and made an appointment with you at the right side of the Mount, and sent down to you manna and quails, [saying,] (80) "Eat of the good things that We have provided you and do not transgress regarding them, lest My anger descend upon you, and the one upon whom My anger descends has certainly fallen. (81) But indeed, I am the Forgiver of the one who repents and believes and does righteous deeds and then continues in guidance." (82)

[God said,] "And what made you hasten away from your people, O Moses?" (83)

He said, "They are close behind me, and I hastened to You, my Lord, that You might be well-pleased." (84)

He said, "But indeed, We have tested your people after you, and al-Samiri has led them astray." (85)

Then Moses returned to his people, angry and grieved. He said, "O my people, did not your Lord make you a goodly promise? Then was the time too long for you or did you desire that wrath from your Lord descend upon you, that you broke your promise to me?" (86)

They said, "We did not break the promise to you by our will, but we were made to carry burdens of the people's ornaments, so we threw them, and thus did al-Samiri throw." (87)

Then he brought forth for them the form of a calf that made a lowing sound, and they said, "This is your god and the god of Moses, but he has forgotten." (88) Did they not then see that it could not return a word to them, nor possess any power of harm or benefit for them? (89) And Aaron had already said to them previously, "O my people, you are only being tested by it, and indeed your Lord is the Most Merciful, so follow me and obey my command." (90)

They said, "We will never stop being devoted to it until Moses returns to us." (91)

He [Moses] said, "O Aaron, what prevented you, when you saw them going astray, (92) from following me? Have you then disobeyed my order?" (93)

He said, "O son of my mother, do not take me by my beard or by my head! Indeed, I feared that you might say, 'You caused division among the Children of Israel and did not heed my word.'" (94)

He [Moses] said, "And what is your case, O Samiri?" (95)

He said, "I saw what they did not see, so I picked up a handful from the track of the messenger and threw it, and thus did my lower self suggest to me." (96)

He [Moses] said, "Then begone! And indeed, it will be your lot in this life to say, 'No contact,' and indeed you have an appointment which you will not fail to keep. And look at your 'god,' to which you remained devoted! We will certainly burn it and then scatter it widely in the sea. (97) Your deity is only God, other than whom there is no deity! He encompasses all things in knowledge." (98)

Thus do We relate to you [Muhammad] something of tidings of what has preceded. And We have certainly given you, from Ourself, a Message. (99)

21:48-49

And We certainly gave Moses and Aaron the criterion and a light and a reminder for those who are mindful of God, (48) who fear their Lord unseen, while they are apprehensive of the Hour [of Judgment]. (49)

22:44

And Moses was denied.

23:45-49

Then We sent Moses and his brother Aaron with Our signs and clear authority (45) to Pharaoh and his chiefs, but they behaved arrogantly and were a self-exalting people. (46) And they said, "Shall we believe in two mortals like ourselves, while their people are in bondage to us?" (47) So they denied the two of them and were among the destroyed. (48) And We certainly gave Moses the scripture, that they might perhaps be guided. (49)

25:35-36

And We certainly gave Moses the scripture and appointed his brother Aaron with him as an assistant. (35) And We said, "Go, both of you, to the people who have denied Our signs." Then We destroyed them with [complete] destruction. (36)

26:10-68

And [mention] when your Lord called Moses, [saying,] "Go to the wrong-doing people, the people of Pharaoh. (10) Will they not be mindful of God?" (11)

He [Moses] said, "My Lord, indeed I fear that they will deny me (12) and that my chest will tighten and my tongue will not be fluent, so send for Aaron. (13) And they have a crime against me, so I fear that they will kill me." (14)

He said, "By no means! Go, both of you, with Our signs. Indeed, We are with you, listening. (15) Go to Pharaoh and say, 'Indeed, we are messengers of the Lord of the worlds, (16) [commanded to say,] "Send the Children of Israel forth with us."'" (17)

He [Pharaoh] said, "Did we not bring you up among ourselves as a child, and you stayed among us for years of your life? (18) And then you did your deed that you did and you were among the ungrateful." (19)

He [Moses] said, "I did it, then, while I was among the erring. (20) Then I fled from you when I feared you, but my Lord granted me judgment and made me among the messengers. (21) And this is the favor of which you remind me: that you have enslaved the Children of Israel!" (22)

Pharaoh said, "And what is 'the Lord of the worlds'?" (23)

He [Moses] said, "Lord of the heavens and the earth and whatever is between them, if you were to be convinced." (24)

He said to those around him, "Do you not hear?" (25)

He [Moses] said, "Your Lord and Lord of your earlier ancestors." (26)

He said, "Indeed, your 'messenger' who has been sent to you is mad!" (27)

He [Moses] said, "Lord of the East and the West and whatever is between them, if you were to use reason." (28)

He said, "If you take a god other than me, I will surely have you imprisoned!" (29)

He [Moses] said, "Even if I brought you something obvious?" (30)

He said, "Then bring it, if you are of the truthful!" (31)

Then he threw down his staff, whereupon it was an obvious snake, (32) and he drew forth his hand, whereupon it was white to the onlookers. (33)

He said to the chiefs around him, "This is surely a skilled magician (34) who wants to drive you out of your land by his magic, so what do you advise?" (35)

They said, "Defer him and his brother, and send gatherers into the cities, (36) who will bring you every skilled magician." (37)

Then the magicians were assembled for the rendezvous of a well-known day, (38) and it was said to the people, "Will you gather, (39) that we may follow the magicians if they are the victors?" (40)

And when the magicians arrived, they said to Pharaoh, "Will there indeed be a reward for us if we are the victors?" (41)

He said, "Yes, and indeed you will then be among those near [to me]." (42)

Moses said to them, "Throw whatever you will throw." (43)

So they threw their cords and staffs, and they said, "By Pharaoh's might, indeed, it is we who are the victors!" (44)

Then Moses threw his staff, and at once it swallowed up whatever they were falsifying. (45) Then the magicians fell down in prostration. (46) They said, "We believe in the Lord of the worlds, (47) the Lord of Moses and Aaron." (48)

He [Pharaoh] said, "You believed him before I gave you permission! Indeed, he is your leader who has taught you magic, but you are going to know! I will surely cut off your hands and your feet on opposite sides, and I will surely crucify you all." (49)

They said, "No matter. Indeed, we will return to our Lord. (50) Indeed, we hope that our Lord will forgive us our sins, because we were the foremost of the believers." (51)

And We inspired to Moses, "Travel by night with My servants. You will surely be pursued." (52)

Then Pharaoh sent gatherers into the cities, (53) [saying,] "Indeed, those are only a small band (54) and indeed they are infuriating us. (55) But we are surely an alert society." (56) So We ousted them from gardens and springs (57), and treasures and distinguished sites. (58) Thus [it was]! And We caused the Children of Israel to inherit them. (59)

And they pursued them at sunrise. (60) Then, when the two groups saw each other, the companions of Moses said, "We will surely be overtaken!" (61)

He said, "By no means! Indeed, My Lord is with me; He will guide me." (62)

Then We inspired to Moses, "Strike the sea with your staff," whereupon it parted and each part became like a towering mountain. (63) Then We brought the others there, (64) and We saved Moses and those with him, all together. (65) Then We drowned the others. (66) Indeed, in that is a sign, yet most of them are not believers. (67) And indeed, your Lord — He is the Almighty, the Merciful. (68)

27:7-12

[Mention, O Muhammad,] when Moses said to his family, "Indeed, I have seen a fire. I will bring you information from it or bring you a burning brand, that you may warm yourselves." (7)

Then when he reached it, he was called, "Blessed are those who are in the fire and whoever is around it. And glorified be Allah, Lord of the worlds! (8) O Moses, indeed, it is I — Allah, the Almighty, the Wise. (9) And throw down your staff."

But when he saw it writhing as if it were a snake, he turned in flight and did not return. [God said,] "O Moses, do not be afraid. Indeed, the messengers need not fear in My Presence; (10) neither need he who does wrong and then substitutes good after evil, for indeed I am Forgiving and Merciful. (11) And put your hand into your bosom; it will come forth white, without blemish — among nine signs for Pharaoh and his people. Indeed, they are a transgressing people!" (12)

But when Our visible signs came to them, they said, "This is obvious magic." (13) And they rejected them, although their souls were convinced of them, out of injustice and exaltation. Then see what was the end of the corrupters! (14)

28:2-46, 48

These are the verses of the clear Book. We relate to you [Muhammad] something of the tidings of Moses and Pharaoh in truth for a people who believe. (3)

Indeed, Pharaoh exalted himself in the land and made its people into factions, rendering a group among them weak, slaughtering their sons but letting their females live. He was surely among the corrupters. (4) And We desired to confer favor upon those who had been made weak in the land, and to make them leaders and make them inheritors, (5) and to establish them in the land, and to show Pharaoh and Haman and their troops, through them, that which they had feared. (6)

And We inspired to Umm Musa, "Nurse him. Then, when you fear for him, put him into the river, and do not fear nor grieve. Indeed, We will restore him to you and will make him among the messengers." (7) And Pharaoh's family took him up, that he might become an enemy to them and a grief. Indeed, Pharaoh and Haman and their troops were transgressors. (8)

And Pharaoh's wife said, "A comfort of the eye for me and for you! Do not kill him. Perhaps he may benefit us or we may adopt him as a son," and they did not perceive. (9)

And Umm Musa's heart became empty. She would have disclosed [the truth] about him if We had not fortified her heart, that she might be among the believers. (10) And she said to Moses' sister, "Follow him!" so she watched him from a distance while they did not notice. (11) and We had previously withheld him from [all] wet nurses, so she said, "Shall I direct you to a household that will feed him for you, while they are sincere to him?" (12) Then We restored him to his mother, that she might be content and not grieve, and that she might know that God's promise is true. But most of them do not know. (13)

And when he reached his full strength and was mature, We granted him judgment and knowledge. And thus do We reward the doers of good. (14)

And he entered the city at a time of inattention by its people, and he found therein two men fighting, one from his faction and one from his enemy. Then the one from his faction called to him for help against the one from his enemy, whereupon Moses struck him and finished him. He said, "This is of Satan's doing. He is surely a clear, misleading enemy!" (15) He said, "My Lord, indeed I have wronged myself, so forgive me!" and He forgave him. Indeed, He is the Forgiving, the Merciful. (16) He said, "My Lord, because of the favor You have bestowed upon me, never will I be a supporter of criminals." (17)

And he became, within the city, fearful and anticipating, when suddenly the one who had sought his help the previous day called to him. Moses said to him, "Indeed, you are an obvious mischief-maker!" (18)

But when he intended to strike the one who was an enemy of both of them, he said, "O Moses, do you intend to kill me as you killed a person yesterday? You only want to be an oppressor in the land and do not want to be of the amenders." (19)

And a man came running from the farthest part of the city. He said, "O Moses, indeed the chiefs are deliberating concerning you, to kill you, so leave; indeed, I am among the sincere advisors to you." (20)

So he departed therefrom, fearful and anticipating. He said, "My Lord, save me from the wrong-doing people!" (21) And when he directed himself toward Midian, he said, "Perhaps my Lord will guide me to the sound way." (22)

And when he came to the water of Midian, he found there a crowd of people watering, and he found, apart from them, two women, keeping back [their flocks]. He said, "What is your situation?"

They said, "We cannot water until the shepherds drive away [their flocks], and our father is an old man." (23)

So he watered for them; then he withdrew into the shade and said, "My Lord, indeed I am in need of any good You may grant to me." (24)

Then one of the two women came to him, walking with shyness. She said, "Indeed, my father invites you, that he may compensate you for having watered for us."

Then when he came to him and related the story to him, he said, "Do not fear. You have escaped from the wrong-doing people." (25)

One of the two women said, "O my father, hire him. Surely the best one you can hire is the strong and the trustworthy." (26)

He said, "Indeed, I desire that one of these, my two daughters, marry you on the condition that you serve me for eight years. If then you complete ten, it will be from your side, but I do not want to put you into difficulty. You will find me, God willing, among the righteous." (27)

He [Moses] said, "That is [agreed] between me and you. Whichever of the two terms I complete, let there be no ill feeling toward me. And God is Witness over what we say." (28)

Then when Moses had completed the term and was traveling with his family, he noticed a fire from the direction of the mountain. He said to his family, "Stay here. Indeed, I have seen a fire. Perhaps I may bring you information from it, or a burning firebrand, that you may warm yourselves." (29)

Then when he came to it, he was called to from the right side of the valley in a blessed spot, from the tree: "O Moses, indeed I am Allah, Lord of the worlds! (30) And throw down your staff." But when he saw it writhing as if it were a snake, he turned in flight and did not return.

"O Moses, approach and do not be afraid. Indeed, you are among the secure. (31) Insert your hand into your bosom; it will come forth white, without blemish. And draw your arm close to yourself against fear, for those are two proofs from your Lord to Pharaoh and his chiefs. Indeed, they are a transgressing people!" (32)

He said, "My Lord, indeed, I killed a person from among them, so I fear that they will kill me. (33) And my brother Aaron is more clear in speech than I, so send him with me as a support, confirming me. Indeed, I fear that they will deny me." (34)

He said, "We shall strengthen your arm through your brother and grant you both authority so they will not reach you. With Our signs, you and those who follow you will be the victors." (35)

But when Moses came to them with Our signs as clear evidences, they said, "This is nothing but faked magic, and we have not heard of this among our forefathers." (36)

And Moses said, "My Lord is most knowing of who has come with guidance from Him and whose will be the final Home. Indeed, the wrong-doers will not prosper!" (37)

And Pharaoh said, "O chiefs, I have not known you to have a god other than me. Therefore, kindle for me, O Haman, a fire upon the clay and make a tower for me, that I may mount up to the God of Moses. But indeed, I do consider him among the liars!" (38)

And he was arrogant, he and his troops, in the land without right, and they supposed that they would not be returned to Us. (39) So We seized him and his troops, and flung them into the sea. Then see what was the end of the wrong-doers! (40) And We made them leaders, inviting to the Fire, and on the Day of Resurrection they will not be helped. (41) And We caused a curse to overtake them in this world, and on the Day of Resurrection they will be among the despised. (42)

And We certainly gave Moses the scripture, after We had destroyed the earlier generations, as enlightment for people and guidance and mercy, that they might be reminded. (43)

You [Muhammad] were not at the western side [of Mount Sinai] when We decreed the command to Moses, nor were you among the witnesses [of what occurred]; (44) but We brought forth generations [after Moses], and long was their span. And you were not a dweller among the people of Midian, reciting to them Our verses, but rather We were senders [of them]. (45) And you were not at the side of the mountain when We called [Moses], but [you were sent as] a mercy from your Lord, to warn a people to whom no warner had come before you, that they might be reminded. (46) . . . But when the truth came to them from Us, they [the pagan Quraysh] said, "Why is he [Muhammad] not given the like of what was given to Moses?" Did they not disbelieve in that which was given to Moses previously? They said, "[The Qur'an and the *Taurat* are but] two works of magic, supporting each other, and indeed we are disbelievers in both." (48)

28:76-82

Indeed, Qarun was of the people of Moses, but he was insolent toward them. And We granted him such treasures that their keys would burden a band of strong men, so his people said to him, "Do not exult. Indeed, God does not like the exulters. (76) But seek, through what God has given you, the home of the Hereafter, yet do not forget your share of the world, and do good, as God has done good to you, and do not seek to make corruption in the land. Indeed, God does not like the corrupters." (77)

He said, "I was only given it because of knowledge I have." Did he not know that before him God had destroyed such generations as were stronger than he in power and greater in accumulation [of wealth]? But the sinners will not be questioned about their sins. (78)

Then he came out before his people in his finery. Those who desired the life of this world said, "Oh, would that we had the like of what was given to Qarun! Indeed, he is the possessor of an immense fortune." (79)

But those who had been given knowledge said, "Woe to you! God's reward is better for one who believes and does righteous deeds. And none is granted it except the patient." (80)

Then We caused the earth to swallow him and his house, and there was no group to help him apart from God, nor was he of those who could defend themselves. (81) And those who had desired his situation the previous day said, "Ah, God expands provision for whomever He wills of His servants and restricts it! If God had not been gracious to us, He could have caused it to swallow us [as well]. Ah, never will the unbelievers succeed!" (82)

29:39-40

And [We destroyed] Qarun and Pharaoh and Haman. And Moses had already come to them with clear evidences, and they behaved arrogantly in the land but they were not outrunners [of Our punishment]. (39) So We seized each for his sin; and among them were those upon whom We sent stones, and among them were those who were overtaken by the clamor, and among them were those whom We caused the earth to swallow, and among them were those whom We drowned. And it was not God who wronged them, but it was they who wronged themselves. (40)

32:23-24

And We certainly gave Moses the scripture, so do not be in doubt concerning his [Muhammad's] meeting [with Moses]. And We made it [the *Taurat*] guidance for the Children of Israel. (23) And We appointed leaders from among them, guiding by Our command, when they were patient and were certain of Our signs. (24)

33:7

And [mention, O Muhammad,] when We took from the prophets their covenant, and from you, and from Noah and Abraham and Moses and Jesus son of Mary — and We took from them a solemn covenant.

33:69

O you who believe, do not be like those who annoyed Moses; but God cleared him of what they said, and he was distinguished in God's sight.

37:114-122

And We certainly conferred favor upon Moses and Aaron, (114) and We saved
them and their people from the great affliction (115) and supported them so they
overcame, (116) and We granted them the clarifying scripture (117) and guided
them on the straight path. (118) And We left [this invocation] for them among
later generations: (119) "Peace be upon Moses and Aaron!" (120) Thus do We
surely reward the doers of good. (121) Indeed, they were among Our believing
slaves. (122)

40:23-45

And We certainly sent Moses with Our signs and clear authority (23) to Pharaoh and Haman and Qarun, but they said, "A magician and a liar!" (24) And
when he brought them the truth from Us, they said, "Kill the sons of those who believe with him and let their women live." And the plot of the unbelievers is not but in error. (25)

And Pharaoh said, "Leave me to kill Moses, and let him call upon his Lord! Indeed, I fear that he will change your religion or that he will cause corruption in the land." (26)

But Moses said, "Indeed, I have taken refuge in my Lord and your Lord from every arrogant one who does not believe in the Day of Accounting." (27)

And a believing man from Pharaoh's family who concealed his faith said, "Would you kill a man because he says 'My Lord is God,' while he has brought you clear proofs from your Lord? And if he should be lying, then his lie is upon him, while if he should be truthful, there will befall you something of that which he promises you. Indeed, God does not guide one who is a transgressor and a liar.
(28) O my people, today sovereignty is yours, as dominant in the land. But who would protect us from God's punishment if it came to us?"

Pharaoh said, "I do not show you but what I perceive, nor do I guide you but to the way of right conduct." (29)

And he who believed said, "O my people, indeed, I fear for you the like of the Day of the Confederates — (30) like the case of Noah's people and 'Aad and Thamud and those after them. And God desires no injustice for [His] servants. (31) And, O my people, indeed, I fear for you the Day of Calling, (32) the Day when you will turn your backs, fleeing, having no protector against God. And whomever God leaves astray, for him there is no guide. (33)

"And Joseph had already come to you previously with clear proofs, but you did not cease to be in doubt concerning that with which he came to you until, when he died, you said, 'Never will God send a messenger after him.' Thus does God leave astray one who is a transgressor and a skeptic." (34)

Those who dispute about God's signs without any authority having come to them, great is the hatefulness [of that] in the sight of God and in the sight of those who believe. Thus does God set a seal upon the heart of every arrogant oppressor! (35)

And Pharaoh said, "O Haman, build a tower for me, that I may reach the ways (36) — the ways to the heavens, so I may mount up to the God of Moses; but indeed, I do consider him a liar!" And thus was the evil of his deed made attractive to Pharaoh and he was diverted from the way. And Pharaoh's plot was nothing but destruction. (37)

And he who believed said, "O my people, follow me; I shall guide you to the way of right conduct. (38) O my people, this worldly life is but a [temporary] enjoyment, and indeed, the Hereafter — that is the Eternal Home. (39) Whoever does an evil deed will not be recompensed but by the like of it; but whoever does a righteous deed, whether male or female, while being a believer — those will enter Paradise, provided for therein without count. (40)

"And, O my people, how is it that I call you to salvation, while you call me to the Fire? (41) You call me to disbelieve in God and associate with Him that about which I have no knowledge, while I call you to the Exalted, the Forgiving. (42) No doubt, that to which you call me has no claim [to being invoked] in this world or in the Hereafter, and indeed our return is to God, and indeed the transgressors will be people of the Fire. (43) Therefore, you will remember what I say to you, and I entrust my affair to God. Indeed, God is seeing of [His] servants." (44)

So God protected him from the evils they plotted, while Pharaoh's people were enveloped by the worst of punishment (45) — the Fire; they are exposed to it morning and evening. And the Day the Hour appears, [it will be said,] "Admit Pharaoh's people to the severest punishment." (46)

40:53-54

And We certainly granted Moses guidance, and We caused the Children of Israel to inherit the scripture, (53) as guidance and a reminder for those of understanding. (54)

41:45

And We certainly gave Moses the scripture, but there was disagreement concerning it.

42:13

He has ordained for you [mankind], as the religion, what He enjoined upon Noah and that which We have revealed to you [Muhammad], and what We enjoined upon Abraham and Moses and Jesus: to establish the [true] religion and not be divided concerning it.

43:46-56

And We certainly sent Moses with Our signs to Pharaoh and his chiefs, and he said, "Indeed, I am a messenger of the Lord of the worlds." (46) But when he came to them with Our signs, forthwith they laughed at them. (47)

And We did not show them any sign but that it was greater than its sister, and We seized them with affliction, that they might perhaps turn back. (48) And they said, "O magician, invoke your Lord for us by what He has promised you. Indeed, we will be guided." (49) But when We removed the affliction from them, at once they broke their word. (50)

And Pharaoh called out among his people; he said, "O my people, is not the kingdom of Egypt mine, and these rivers flowing beneath me? Then do you not see? (51) Or am I not better than this one who is insignificant and hardly makes himself clear? (52) Then why have not golden bracelets been placed upon him or angels come in conjunction with him?" (53)

Thus, he fooled his people and they obeyed him. Indeed, they were a transgressing people. (54) And when they angered Us, We took retribution from them and drowned them all together, (55) and We made them a precedent and an example for the later peoples. (56)

44:17-33

And before them, We had already tried Pharaoh's people, and there came to them a noble messenger, (17) [saying,] "Turn over to me God's servants. I am surely a trustworthy messenger to you," (18) and, "Do not be haughty toward God. Indeed, I have come to you with clear authority, (19) and indeed, I have taken refuge in my Lord and your Lord lest you kill me. (20) And if you do not believe in me, then leave me alone." (21)

Then he called upon his Lord, [saying,] "These are a sinful people!" (22)

[God said,] "Then travel by night with My servants. You will surely be pursued. (23) And leave the sea in stillness. Indeed, they are a troop to be drowned!" (24)

How many gardens and springs did they leave behind, (25) and crops and distinguished sites, (26) and comforts in which they rejoiced! (27) Thus [it was]! And

We caused another people to inherit them, (28) and the heavens and the earth did not weep for them, nor were they reprieved. (29) And We certainly saved the Children of Israel from the humiliating torment — (30) from Pharaoh. Indeed, he was a haughty one among the transgressors! (31) And We certainly chose them, knowingly, above mankind, (32) and We granted them such signs wherein was a clear trial. (33)

45:16-17

And We certainly granted the Children of Israel the scripture and judgment and prophethood, and provided them with good things and preferred them above mankind, (16) and granted them clear proofs of the matter. (17)

46:12

Before it [the Qur'an,] the scripture of Moses was a guide and a mercy. And this is a confirming scripture in the Arabic language, to warn those who have done wrong and as good tidings for the doers of good.

51:38-40

And in Moses [was a sign], when We sent him to Pharaoh with clear authority. (38) But he turned away with his supporters and said, "A magician or a madman!" (39) So We seized him and his troops and flung them into the sea, and he was blameworthy. (40)

53:36-37

Or has he not had been informed of what was in the scriptures of Moses (36) and Abraham, who fulfilled [his obligations]? (37)

61:5

And [mention, O Muhammad,] when Moses said to his people, "O my people, why do you injure me, while you certainly know that I am God's messenger to you?" And when they deviated, God caused their hearts to deviate. And God does not guide a transgressing people.

66:11

And God sets forth an example for those who believe: the wife of Pharaoh, when she said, "My Lord, build for me, in Your Presence, a home in Paradise, and save me from Pharaoh and his doings, and save me from the wrong-doing people."

79:15-26

Has there reached you [Muhammad] the story of Moses (15), when his Lord called to him in the sacred valley of Tuwa: (16) "Go to Pharaoh. Indeed, he has transgressed. (17) And say to him, 'Would you purify yourself (18) and let me guide you to your Lord, that you may fear?'" (19)

Then he [Moses] showed him the greatest sign, (20) but he denied and disobeyed. (21) Then he turned his back, striving [against God], (22) and he gathered [his people] and called out (23) and said, "I am your most exalted Lord!" (24) Then God seized him, an exemplary punishment for the latter and the former. (25) Indeed, in that is a lesson for one who fears God. (26)

87:18-19

Indeed, this is in the former scriptures, (18) the scriptures of Abraham and Moses.

The Stories of the Prophets of Israel

Joshua (Yusha)
Samuel (Shamu'il)
David (Dawud)
Solomon (Sulaiman)
Elijah (Ilyas)
Elisha (Alyasa')
Dhul-Kifl
Jonah (Yunus)

peace be upon them

And We granted him [Abraham] Isaac and Jacob; each [of them] We guided. And previously We guided Noah, and among his descendants, David and Solomon and Job and Joseph and Moses and Aaron. And thus do We reward the doers of good. And Zechariah and John and Jesus and Elijah — all were among the righteous; and Ishmael and Elisha and Jonah and Lot — and all [of them] We preferred above mankind, and some from among their fathers and descendants and brothers; and We chose them and guided them to a straight path. (6:84-87)

JOSHUA (A)

And We certainly gave Moses the scripture and followed him by a succession of [other] messengers. (2:87)

Although he is not mentioned by name in the Qur'an, Joshua (Yusha) son of Nun[1] is well-known in Islam as the prophet who succeeded Moses (A).

Earlier, Joshua was mentioned as the horseman who spurred his horse into the sea at the time of the Exodus. It is also said that Joshua was one of the two men who concealed the information about the giants from their people, as well as encouraging the Israelites to go and fight them. He was also the attendant or "young man" of Moses (A) in his journey of meeting with Sayyidina Khidr (18:60, 62-63).

It is said that after the Israelites had completed their forty years of wandering in the desert, God appointed Joshua (A) as a prophet and commanded him to journey toward Jericho and fight against the giants who lived there. Joshua (A) and those who were with him — the children of the previous generation of Israelites, who had by now all died — struggled against the city of the giants and eventually conquered it.[2] Says Ibn 'Abbas (R):

> None of those who had refused to enter the settlement of the giants and who had been with Moses remained to witness the conquest, for they all died before that. No one who was with Moses came out of the desert except Joshua son of Nun and Caleb son of Jephunneh, who was the husband of Miriam, the sister of Moses and Aaron, and they were the only two men [among all those who had accompanied Moses] who entered the holy land. (*Hadith* of the Trials)

It is not possible to say more than this concerning Joshua (A) with any degree of certainty, for while much has been said by the commentators about Joshua's fight against the giants and subsequent events, taken from the Old

---

[1]In keeping with I Chr. 7:27, al-Tabari gives the genealogy of Joshua as the son of Nun, son of Ephraim, son of Joseph, son of Jacob, son of Isaac, son of Abraham (Tabari/*H*, III:88). However, in view of the time that elapsed between Joseph and Joshua, some generations are obviously missing.

[2]Although there is disagreement among the Qur'anic commentators as to whether Jericho was conquered during the time of Moses or by Joshua after his death, the more correct opinion seems to be that it was after Moses' time.

Testament account, none of it is sufficiently authoritative to cite here. Perhaps he may be among those referred to in God's saying,

> **And [We sent revelations to] messengers about whom We have told you [Muhammad] and messengers about whom We have not told you.** (4:164; also 40:78)

REFERENCE: Tabari/*H*, III:81-82, 88-91, 94.

SAMUEL (A)

1. THE ARK OF THE COVENANT

And We said to the Children of Israel after him [Pharaoh], "Dwell in the land. . . ." (17:104)

By the divine Will, in due course of time the Israelites settled in Palestine. After their long, terrible years of oppression in Egypt and their lengthy wanderings in Sinai, they were finally permitted to put down roots in the sacred land of their ancestors: —

> **And We caused the people who had been oppressed to inherit the east of the land and the west of it, which We had blest. And the fair word of your Lord was fulfilled for the Children of Israel because of what they had patiently endured.** (7:137)
>
> **We certainly settled the Children of Israel in an agreeable abode and provided them with good things.** (10:93)

As we have seen, God Most High granted **Moses the scripture and made it a guidance for the Children of Israel.** As the first rule of their faith, He enjoined on them the strictest monotheism, commanding, **that you not take other than Me as Disposer of affairs, O descendants of those We carried in the Ark with Noah** (17:2-3). And He charged them to honor the sacred covenant He had taken from them and to guide their affairs by the divine laws revealed in the *Taurat*, saying, **"Take what We have given you with determination and remember what is in it, that you may be mindful of God"** (2:63, 7:171).

However, despite the fact that the difficult and rebellious generation that had left Egypt with Moses (A) had now passed away, the drift of the Israelites away from their faith continued. The trend toward idolatry that had begun with their demand, early in their desert wanderings, that Moses (A) make for them a god like the gods of other peoples, followed by the episode of the Golden Calf, had not ended in Sinai.

As they settled in Palestine, their descendants began to pollute their pure monotheistic faith with idol-worship and other pagan practices, in imitation of the habits of the local peoples.[1] Indeed, the books of the Old Testament are

[1]This trend is concisely summarized in the following passage:

full of references to the Israelites' backsliding, disobedience and faithlessness to their covenant with God, from the time of Moses (A) onward.

Despite these transgressions, there nevertheless remained among them a vivid reminder of their commitment to their Creator: the sacred Ark of the Covenant of God, a portable shrine containing what is known in Arabic as the *Sakinah* (Hebrew, *Shekhinah*), comprised of the **remains of what the family of Moses and the family of Aaron had left, carried by angels** (2:248).

The classical commentators spoke a good deal about the nature of the *Sakinah*. Among them, Ibn 'Abbas (R) and al-Suddi said that the *Sakinah* was a golden basin from Paradise in which the hearts of the prophets were washed.[2] 'Ata' said that it consisted of those signs that the Children of Israel recognized and at which their hearts grew calm. As for the **remains of what the family of Moses and the family of Aaron had left,** contained in the Ark, 'Ikrimah reported on the authority of Ibn 'Abbas (R) that these were the staff of Moses and fragments of the Tablets on which he had inscribed the *Taurat* on Mount Sinai. Others added to this the sandals of Moses, the turban and staff of Aaron, and a jar in which manna was stored (Ayoub/*Q*, I:240-241).

Al-Tabari says that the Ark was handed down as a sacred inheritance from one generation of Israelites to the other. As long as they advanced into battle with it, God Most High granted them victory over their enemies. But the time came when their misdeeds multiplied and they abandoned their covenant with God. Then, when they went out against their enemy, taking the Ark with them as was customary, they were defeated and the Ark was torn from their hands. They were then thrown into confusion and disorder, and were plundered and oppressed by their enemies.

Thus were the descendants of Abraham, Isaac and Jacob (A) caught up in cycles of deviation and error for which their Lord punished them, alternating with periods of repentance and reform during which He protected them from harm. During the periods of their sinfulness and wrong-doing, God permitted them to be dominated and oppressed by their enemies, while when they

---

The Israelites lived among the Canaanites, Hittites, Amorites, Perizzites, Hivites and Jebusites. They took their daughters in marriage and gave their own daughters to their sons, and served their gods. The Israelites did evil in the eyes of the Lord; they forgot the Lord their God and served the Baals and the Asherahs. (Judg. 3:5-7)

[2]Cf., ***Bukhari***, 9:608 and 5:227, in which it is reported that during the Holy Prophet's Night Journey and Ascension, angels removed his heart from his chest, washed it and filled it with faith (***iman***) and wisdom (***hikmah***) from a golden vessel.

repented, He saved them from the evil of those who intended evil toward them.

For 460 years after the death of Joshua (A), the Israelites were ruled by judges and leaders from among themselves, alternating with others who conquered and ruled over them. This continued until self-rule was instituted among them and prophethood was re-established through Samuel son of Bali, son of Alqamah.

REFERENCES: Qur'an: 2:248; 7:137, 168; 10:93; 17:104; 61:14. Commentaries: Tabari/*H*, III:125-127, 131; Ibn Kathir/*Q*, "Shamu'il"; Ayoub/*Q*, I:240-241; Maududi/*Q*, 2:fn. 270; Ali/*Q*, fn. 281.

2. SAMUEL'S APPOINTMENT TO PROPHETHOOD

And We certainly sent [messengers] before you [Muhammad] among the sects of the former peoples. (15:10)

Ibn 'Abbas (R), Ibn Mas'ud (R) and al-Suddi say that when the Amalekites became dominant over the Israelites in Gaza and Askelon, killing great numbers of them and humbling their menfolk, prophethood was cut off among the descendants of Levi. None of them remained except a single pregnant woman,[3] who prayed to God for a son. And when a boy was born to her, she named him Samuel (Arabic, Shamu'il or Ashmawil), the meaning of which in Hebrew corresponds to that of Ishmael — that is, "God heard my prayer."

When Samuel (A) was old enough, his mother sent him to the temple and turned him over to a pious elderly scholar, to remain with him and learn the *Taurat*.[4]

One night, when the boy had matured sufficiently to be granted prophethood, he heard a voice calling him while he was sleeping near his teacher. Frightened, he got up and asked his teacher if he had called him. Not wanting to alarm the boy, the old man merely told him to go back to sleep.

The boy slept again, but the voice called him a second time and again the same thing happened. At the third time, the angel Gabriel (A) appeared to him and said, "Go to your people and convey your Lord's Message to them, for God has sent you to them as a prophet."

Although Samuel's name is not mentioned in the Qur'an, he is referred to in three verses as **a prophet of theirs** (2:246) and **their prophet** (2:247, 2:248). It is believed that he was born some time after 1050 B.C.

REFERENCES: Qur'an: 2:246-248. Commentaries: Tabari/*H*, III:129-130, 133; Ibn Kathir/*Q*, "Shamu'il"; Ayoub/*Q*, I:237-239.

---

[3]She is identified in 1 Sam. 1 as Hannah, wife of Elkanah.

[4]This is Eli in 1 Sam. 2:11.

3. SAUL

And their prophet said to them, "Indeed, God has sent to you Saul as king." (2:246)

Some thirty years later, the Israelites faced many battles and their enemies oppressed them. **Then they said to a prophet of theirs,** and that was Samuel (A), **"Send to us a king and we will fight in the cause of God"** (2:246).

"Might it perhaps be that, if fighting were prescribed for you, you would not fight?" (2:246), Samuel (A) enquired shrewdly, knowing his people's mentality.

"And why should we not fight in the cause of God when we have been driven away from our homes and our children?" (2:246), they protested. Despite this claim of theirs, however, when fighting was prescribed for them, **they turned away, except a few of them** (2:246).

And their prophet said to them, "Indeed, God has sent to you Saul as king" (2:247).

Now, Saul (Arabic, Talut) son of Kish was from the tribe of Benjamin. He was a common man, having no wealth or other worldly attributes that would qualify him for kingship. The commentators 'Ikrimah (R) and al-Suddi say he was a water carrier, Wahb bin Munabbih (R) says he was a tanner, and others mention other occupations. And due to Saul's lack of rank among them, the people immediately began to protest his right to be their king.

"How can he have kingship over us while we are more worthy of kingship than he and he has not been given any measure of wealth?" (2:247), they demanded. They further argued that while prophethood belonged to the descendants of Levi and kingship to the descendants of Judah, Saul was from the tribe of Benjamin. As a result, they fell away from him, finding fault with his appointment.

Ibn Kathir and other commentators report that God then sent a revelation to Samuel (A), informing him of the sign of kingship: that it would belong to the man whose height was exactly equal to that of a certain staff. The men then came and measured themselves against the staff but none of them was equal to it except Saul.

"Indeed, God has chosen him above you and has increased him abundantly in knowledge and stature,"[5] Samuel (A) declared, attempting to make his people understand that Saul's appointment to kingship was by divine ordainment rather than by any human criterion of superiority. **"And God grants His sovereignty to whomever He wills, and God is All-Encompassing and Aware** (2:247).

"Indeed, a sign of his kingship is that the Ark will come to you, wherein is the *Sakinah* from your Lord and a remnant of what the family of Moses and the family of Aaron left behind, carried by angels," Samuel (A) continued. **"In that is surely a sign for you, if you are believers"** (2:248).

Samuel (A) then appointed Saul king over his people. Then, says Ibn 'Abbas (R), "The angels brought the Ark, carrying it between heaven and earth, while the people watched it, until they had placed it with Saul"[6] (Tabari/*H*, III:131).

REFERENCES: Qur'an: 2:246-247. Commentaries: Tabari/*H*, III:130-131, 135; Ibn Kathir/*Q*, "Shamu'il"; Ayoub/*Q*, I:239-241.

---

[5]Some commentators said this **"knowledge"** referred to matters related to warfare, while others said that it meant knowledge in general. As for **"stature,"** some said that it referred to Saul's strong stature and others to his beauty, as from the context it appears that he was the handsomest and most knowledgeable among his people after their prophet.

[6]According to one account, the Ark had been captured by idol-worshippers, among whom its presence wrought havoc and destruction. It was subsequently returned to the Israelites. However, according to the accounts of Qatadah and Rabi' ibn Anas, the Ark had been entrusted to Joshua by Moses, and it remained in the desert until angels brought it and placed it in Saul's house as a sign of his kingship, as mentioned above (Tabari/H, III:134, 131; Ayoub/Q, I:240-241).

4. THE TEST OF THE RIVER

Those who were certain that they would meet God said, "How many a small company has overcome a large company by God's leave! And God is with the patient." (2:249)

Led by King Saul, the army of the Israelites set out to fight their enemies, the Philistines, who were headed by their formidible king and strongman, Goliath.

And when Saul went forth with the troops, he said to them, "Indeed, God will test you by a river" — that is, the Jordan River, which lay between them and their enemy. **"Therefore,"** their king warned them, **"whoever drinks of it is not of me, and the one does not taste it, indeed he is of me, except him who** merely **takes** a sip **in the hollow of his hand"** (2:249). Thus did Saul indirectly convey to his men that only those who had sufficient firmness and self-control to be patient under severe tests could expect to be granted victory in the face of the overwhelming odds that awaited them that day.

Despite their king's warning, however, when the troops reached the river, **they drank from it, except a few of them** (2:249). As a result, only a small number of those who had set out with Saul crossed the river with him, while the remainder turned back. It is said that those who drank from the river became thirsty, while those who took only a sip from the palms of their hands had their thirst quenched.

Then, when Saul **had crossed it, he and those who believed with him**, and they beheld Goliath, many of his remaining men also turned back in flight, exclaiming, **"We have no power this day against Goliath and his troops!"** (2:249).

But, remaining firm and steadfast, **those who were certain that they would meet God** on the Last Day **said, "How many a small company has overcome a large company by God's leave. And God is with the patient"** (2:249).

It is said that after the majority of the Israelite troops had fled, Saul went to battle with 319 men. By the divine Will, this was the same number of men as would fight in the Battle of Badr, the first battle of the Muslims against the pagan Quraysh in the year 624 C.E. The Prophet's Companions who took part in this battle used to say that their number was that of the companions of Saul who crossed the river with him, who were more than 310 men, and none of them crossed the river with him but was a believer (*Bukhari*, 5:293-5:296).

And when they went forth to Goliath and his troops, they said, "Our Lord, pour out upon us patience and make our feet firm, and grant us victory over the disbelieving people" (2:250). And Saul promised to marry his daughter to the man who would kill Goliath.

REFERENCES: Qur'an: 2:249-250. Commentaries: Tabari/*H*, III:132-134, 136; Ibn Kathir/*Q*, "Shamu'il"; Ayoub/*Q*, I:240-242; Maududi/*Q*, 2:fn. 271.

David (A)

1. The Defeat of Goliath

Then they defeated them by God's leave and David killed Goliath, and God granted him kingship and wisdom and taught him of whatever He willed. And if God did not check some people by means of others, the earth would have been corrupted, but God is full of bounty to mankind. (2:251)

David son of Jesse (Arabic, Dawud bin Asa), who lived from 1006-965 B.C., was a descendant of Jacob's son Judah. Regarded in Islam as both a great prophet and king, David (A) is mentioned sixteen times in nine *surahs* of the Qur'an — eight times by himself, five times together with his son Solomon, and three times together with other prophets.

The youngest of Jesse's thirteen sons and a shepherd, David (A) was among the 319 steadfast Israelites who remained with Saul to fight against the Philistines.

The Philistine champion, Goliath, was an intimidating giant of a man. It is said that he came forward before the battle and demanded that a man from among the Israelites be sent to face him in single combat.

Now, David (A) was a mere youth who was unarmed except for a slingshot. Nevertheless, it was he who volunteered to go forth and fight the Philistine. And seeing him, Goliath said to him, "Go back, because I would hate to kill you."

"But I would love to kill *you*!" David (A) retorted. He took out three stones, and when he placed them together in the sling, they became as a single stone, which he hurled at Goliath. The missile struck him in the head, killing him, and his army fled. **Then they defeated them by God's leave and David killed Goliath** (2:251) with nothing more than three stones. And confirming the veracity of the Qur'anic account, the divine Author of the Book adds:

> **These are God's verses which We recite to you [Muhammad] in truth. And indeed, you are among the messengers.** (2:252)

And as if in response to the prayer for patience of those who fought against Goliath and his troops, God Most High says

> **And when they were patient and were certain of Our signs, We appointed leaders among them, guiding by Our command** (32:24),

perhaps referring to the illustrious prophet-kings, David and Solomon (A), and the righteous prophets of Israel who succeeded them.

REFERENCES: Qur'an: 2:251-252. Commentaries: Tabari/*H*, III:135-136, 141-143; Ibn Kathir/*Q*, "Dawud"; Ayoub/*Q*, I:243-244.

2. DAVID'S KINGDOM

And We strengthened his kingdom and granted him wisdom and discernment in speech. (38:18-20)

Saul then fulfilled his promise and married his daughter to David (A), proclaiming David's authority in his kingdom. Subsequently, David's prestige became very high among the Israelites, and they loved him and inclined toward him much more than toward Saul.

It is said that Saul's reign lasted forty years, at the end of which he was killed in battle, together with his sons. David (A) then became the ruler of all the tribes of Israel. **And God granted him kingship and wisdom, and taught him of what He willed** (2:251), bestowing upon him Samuel's prophethood and Saul's kingship, and endowing him with **judgment and knowledge** (21:79).

The commentators have given varied interpretations of the meaning of **"wisdom"** and what God **"taught"** David (A) in 2:251 above. The majority say that here wisdom refers to prophethood. Others say that what God taught him was the *Zabur* or Psalms, how to judge among people, and the language of birds and ants, while still others say that what he was taught was his beautiful voice and music

Yet others say, "Wisdom means that God taught him matters of religion and whatever He willed of worldly matters such as the making of armor, for iron became in his hands as malleable as wax" (Ayoub/*Q*, I:245). Thus, the words, **And We made iron malleable for him** (37:10), are understood as meaning that David (A) was inspired with the techniques of iron-working,[1] by means of which God **taught him the fabrication of coats of armor for you, that you might fortify yourselves against your [mutual] violence** (21:80).

---

[1]Speaking of the beginning of the Iron Age between 1200 and 1000, which was the period of David, Maulana Maududi says:

> This was the time when the secret of armour making, so closely guarded by the Hittites and the Philistines, became well known and even cheaper articles of daily use began to be made. The recent archaelogical excavations conducted in Edom, to the south of Palestine, which is rich in iron ore, have brought to light furnaces for melting and moulding iron. The furnace excavated near Ezion-geber, a port on the Gulf of 'Aqabah, in the time of Prophet Solomon, seems to have been built on the principles which are used in the modern blast furnaces. . . . (Maududi/*Q*, 21:fn. 72)

As for God's strengthening of his kingdom, mentioned in 38:18 above, in the words of one scholar, David (A) established "a well-organized kingdom which became the strongest empire in the Western region of the Fertile Crescent," extending the borders of the nation" and consolidating it around Jerusalem as its capital and religious center (Barnavi/*Atlas*, pp. 14-15).

REFERENCES: Qur'an: 2:251; 21:79-80; 34:10-11; 38:20. Commentaries: Tabari/*H*, III: 137-139, 143-144, 147; Ibn Kathir/*Q*, "Shamu'il"; Ayoub/*Q*, I:244-245; Maududi/*Q*, 21:fn. 72. Other works: Barnavi/*Atlas*, pp. 14-15.

3. DAVID'S PIETY

And remember Our slave, David, the possessor of strength; indeed, he repeatedly turned [to God]. (38:17)

It is reported that David (A) divided his time between worship, his wives (who are said to have numbered one hundred), and his people. And in spite of being a great and powerful king, David (A) also worked for his livelihood with his own hands.

Ibn Kathir says that the work by which David earned his provision was making coats of mail, one each day, for God had **made iron malleable for him** (Ibn Kathir/*T*, 34:10). **"Make full coats of mail and calculate the links,"** His Lord commanded him. **"And work righteousness. Indeed, I am Seeing of whatever you do"** (34:10-11). And the Holy Prophet (S) said:

> Never does anyone eat better food than what he eats from the work of his hands, and indeed the prophet of God, David, peace be upon him, used to eat from the work of his hands. (*Bukhari*, 3:286)
>
> Indeed, David, peace be upon him, used not to eat except from the work of his hands. (*Bukhari*, 3:287)
>
> The reciting [of the *Zabur*] was made easy for David, peace be upon him, for he used to order that his riding beasts be saddled and would complete the recitation before his riding beasts were saddled. And he did not eat except from the work of his hands. (*Bukhari*, 4:628; also 6:237)

Yet despite his power and rank, and all the obligations of kingship, livelihood and a huge family, David (A) remained a deeply devout, humble servant to his Lord, whose thankfulness, together with that of his son Solomon (A), is memorialized in God's saying,

> **We certainly granted David and Solomon knowledge, and they said, "Praise be to God, who favored us over many of His believing slaves."** (27:15)

Ibn Kathir reports that David (A) addressed his Lord, saying, "O Lord of the worlds, how can anyone thank you, because even to be able to thank You is Your favor?" And God replied, "O David, you have already thanked Me by recognizing that all favors are from Me" (Ibn Kathir/*T*, 34:12-13).

Indeed, David (A) occupied himself so diligently with his Lord's worship that God made it a lasting example for mankind. Concerning the acceptability and excellence of David's worship, the Holy Prophet (S) said:

> The fasting most dear to God was the fasting of David, who used to fast and not fast on alternate days. And the *salat* dearest to God was the

> *salat* of David. He used to sleep half the night, get up [to pray] for one-third of it, and sleep again for one sixth [of it]. (*Bukhari*, 4:631)
>
> David, peace be upon him, used to have an hour of the night in which he would arouse his family and say, "O family of David, awaken and pray, for indeed this is an hour in which God, the Almighty and Glorious, responds to the supplication, except for that of a magician or a tax-gatherer." (*Mishkat*, 1235)

David's worship is also mentioned in a number of *ahadith* narrated by the Prophet's Companion, 'Abdullah bin 'Amr bin al-'As (R), who said:

> The Messenger of God, God's peace and blessings be upon him, was told that I said, "By God, I will certainly fast by day and pray by night as long as I live." Then the Messenger of God, God's peace and blessings be upon him, said to me, "Are you the one who says I will fast by day and pray by night as long as I live?" I said, "I did say it." He said, "You surely cannot do that. So fast and eat, awaken and sleep, and fast three days of the month, for indeed the good deed is [rewarded] by ten like it, and that is like perpetual fasting." I said, "I can surely do better than that, O Messenger of God." He said, "Then fast a day and do not fast two days." I said, "I can surely do better than that." He said, "Then fast a day and do not fast a day. And that is the fasting of David, and that is the most balanced fasting." I said, "I can surely do better than that, O Messenger of God." He said, "There is nothing better than that." (*Bukhari*, 4:629)
>
> The Prophet, God's peace and blessings be upon him, said to me, "Have I not been told that you get up at night [to pray] and fast by day?" and I said, "Yes." Then he said, "If you do that, your eyes will be destroyed and you will torment yourself. Fast three days out of each month, and that is a perpetual fast or like a perpetual fast." I said, "Indeed, I am eager — that is, able — to do more." He said, "Then fast the fast of David, peace be upon him. He used to fast a day and not fast a day, and did not flee when he encountered [the enemy]."[2] (*Bukhari*, 4:630)

---

[2]The alternate-day fasting of David (A) is also mentioned in another *hadith*, which ends with the words, "[Fasting] three days out of each month" — meaning the three days of the full moon, known as the 'white days,' the thirteenth, fourteenth and fifteenth of each month — "and Ramadan each year is a perpetual fast. I am reckoning on God [to grant] that fasting on the day of 'Arafat" — the ninth day of the lunar month of Dhul-Hijjah, which is principal day of the *Hajj* — "may atone for the sins of the year that preceded it and the year that follows it, and I am reckoning on God [to grant] that fasting on the day of 'Ashura" — mentioned in Volume One, page 166, and this volume, pages 95-96 — "may atone for the sins of the year that preceded it and the year that follows it" (*Muslim*, 2602; *Abu Dawud*, 2419).

The Prophet (A) also spoke of David's moving supplications, saying:

"One of the supplications of David was, 'O God, I ask You for Your love and love of whomever You love and love of those who love You, and deeds which will cause me to attain Your love. O God, make Your love dearer to me than myself and my property and my family and cold water.'" The narrator [Abu Darda] said that when the Prophet (S) mentioned David and talked about him, he would say that he was the most pious of mankind. (*Mishkat*, 2485, 1495)

REFERENCE: Qu'ran: 27:15. Commentaries: Ibn Kathir/*T*, 34:10-13; Tabari/*H*, III:139, 143-147; Maududi/*Q*, 21:fn. 72.

---

of 'Arafat;" the ninth day of the lunar month of Dhul-Hijjah, which is principal day of the *Hajj*, "may atone for the sins of the year that preceded it and the year that follows it, and I am reckoning on God [to grant] that fasting on the day of 'Ashura," mentioned in Volume One, page 166, and this volume, page 96, "may atone for the sins of the year that preceded it and the year that follows it" (*Muslim*, 2602; *Abu Dawud*, 2419)

4. THE *ZABUR*

We certainly caused some prophets to excel others, and We granted David the *Zabur*. (17:55, 4:163)

David (A) was especially honored by being the recipient of a divinely-revealed scripture known as the *Zabur*, meaning "writing," "scripture" or "book". And since the Psalms are the sacred text ascribed to David (A), Muslims have equated the *Zabur* with the Psalms, although which psalms, if any, actually originated with David (A) is unknown.[3]

Earlier, we cited the Prophet's saying that the recitation of the *Zabur* was made easy for David (A) (*Bukhari*, 4:628, 6:237). And God Most High memorialized his recitation of it in the following verses, which indicate that the intensity and beauty of his praise and glorification was so powerful and moving that elements of the natural world, from the mountains to the birds, all glorified the Lord of the heavens and earth together with him:[4]

> **We subjected the mountains to glorify [Us] with David, and the birds, and We were doing [this].** (21:79)

---

[3]21:105 reads, **And We have already written in the *Zabur*, after the [previous] *dhikr* [mention, remembrance or scripture], that the land is inherited by My righteous servants.** It is therefore noteworthy that the words, "The righteous will inherit the land and dwell in it forever," are found among the Psalms (37:29).

[4]The Islamic belief that all the elements of the natural world are in a state of surrender to the One who created them, and that they praise and glorify Him in their own fashion, is mentioned in the following verses:

> **Whatever is in the heavens and the earth glorifes God, and He is the Almighty, the Wise.** (57:1, 59:24, 61:1, 62:1, 64:1)

> **Whatever is in the heavens and whatever is on the earth of creatures prostrates to God, and the angels, and they are not arrogant.** (16:49)

> **Do you not perceive that whomever is in the heavens and whomever is on earth and the sun and moon and stars and mountains and trees and moving creatures and many among mankind prostrate to God?** (22:18)

> **The seven heavens and the earth and whatever is in them glorify Him. And there is not a thing but that it glorifies [Him] with His praise, but you do not understand their glorification. Indeed, He is ever Forbearing and Forgiving.** (17:44)

> **Do you not see that God is glorified by whomever is in the heavens and the earth, and the birds with outspread wings? Each knows its prayer and glorification, and God is Knowing of what they do.** (24:41)

We certainly granted David favor from Ourselves. [We said,] "O mountains, repeat [Our praise] with him, and birds!" (34:10)

Indeed, We subjected the mountains [to praise God] with him, glorifying in the evening and after sunrise. And the birds were assembled, all repeating [God's praise] with him. (38:18-19)

Al-Tabari states that God did not grant anyone in creation a voice like David's. It is said that when he recited the *Zabur*, wild beasts would line up to look at him and listen to his voice (Tabari/*H*, III:143).

David's exquisite voice and recitation are mentioned in a ***hadith*** in which the Prophet (S) described a certain Companion who recited the Qur'an in an extremely beautiful voice as having been given "one of the wind instruments of the family of David" (***Bukhari***, 6:568; also ***Muslim***, 1734). On another occasion, the Prophet (S) said to one of his Companions who had recited the Qur'an, "If you had seen me while I was listening to your recitation last night! You have certainly been given a wind instrument from among the wind instruments of the family of David" (***Muslim***, 1735).

REFERENCES: Qur'an: 4:162; 17:55; 21:79; 34:10; 38:18-19, 24. Commentary: Tabari/ *H*, III:143.

5. THE TESTING OF DAVID

And David inferred that We had tried him, and he asked forgiveness of his Lord and fell down in prostration and turned [to Him] in repentance. (38:24)

We now come to the matter of the testing of David (A), mentioned in 38:21-25.

Because the nature of this test is not stated in the Qur'an, some of the classical commentators sought to provide an explanation of it from Judaic sources. However, since our intention here is to be as accurate and authoritative as possible, we will build our understanding of the subject solely on whatever is clear and unambiguous in the Qur'an, *ahadith* and the most reliable interpretations of the early commentators.

In attempting to understand this matter, the first thing that needs to be emphasized is David's exalted standing with his Lord, which is proclaimed in the following passage, addressed to Muhammad (S):

> **Be patient concerning what they say[5] and recall Our slave, David, the possessor of strength; indeed, he repeatedly turned [to God]. Indeed, We subjected the mountains [to praise God] with him, glorifying in the evening and after sunrise. And the birds were assembled, all repeatedly turning to Him. And We strengthened his kingdom, and granted him wisdom and discernment in speech. (38:18-20)**

Then, after this high commendation of David (A) coupled with the admonition to the Prophet (S) to remember him and emulate him, which in effect negates any charge of sin and wrong-doing, the divine Author of the Qur'an introduces the story of David's test, saying:

> **Has there come to you [Muhammad] the tidings of the disputants, when they climbed over the wall of the prayer chamber — when they went in to David and he was startled by them? (38:21-22)**

---

[5]That is, what was said by certain Meccan idol-worshippers and opponents of Islam — namely, **"Our Lord, hasten for us our share [of punishment] before the Day of Accounting"** (38:16). The Prophet (S) was asked to **be patient concerning what they say** by recalling the example of David, who **repeatedly turned to God.**

The wording of this passage suggests that the information contained therein is *the* correct and indisputable account of **the tidings of the disputants,** replacing all other accounts.

In their interpretation of these verses, the classical commentators stated that two men entered David's place of worship in his palace by climbing over the wall, startling him. **"Do not fear"** (38:22), they said, and proceeded to explain their errand.

"We are two disputants," they told him, **"one of whom has wronged the other. Therefore, judge between us with truth and do not exceed** it, **and guide us to the sound path"** (38:22).

One of the two then told the king his story.

"Indeed," he said, **"this, my brother, has ninety-nine ewes, while I have one ewe. And he said, 'Entrust her to me,' and he overpowered me in speech"** (38:23).

Since the case seemed simple and straightforward, David (A) did not hesitate to pronounce judgment.

"He has certainly wronged you in demanding your ewe in addition to his ewes," he declared. **"And indeed, many associates oppress one another, except those who believe and do righteous deeds, and they are few"** (38:24).

However, since those whose hearts are tuned in to their Lord are constantly alert to the subtle messages coming to them, often through the mouths or actions of His servants, it then occurred to David (A) that there was more to the matter than its obvious, outward meaning. **And David inferred that We had tried him, and he asked forgiveness of his Lord and fell down in prostration and turned** to Him **in repentance**[6] (38:24).

Concerning David's repentance, the Holy Prophet (S) said:

---

[6]Following the Prophet's practice (*sunnah*), Muslims customarily prostrate while reciting or reading certain Qur'anic verses in which prostration is mentioned. One such verse of prostration is 38:24 above. Concerning it, it is reported that Mujahid once asked Ibn 'Abbas, who used to prostrate at this verse, from where he knew to do so. Ibn 'Abbas replied, "Then do you not recite, **'And among his [Abraham's] descendants [were] David and Solomon** [6:84]. **Those are the ones whom God has guided, so emulate their guidance** [6:90]'? Now, David, peace be upon him, was among those whom your Prophet (S) was ordered to emulate. And as David, (A) prostrated at it [that is, at what is mentioned in 38:24], so the Messenger of God (S) prostrated at it" (*Bukhari*, 6:331, 6:330).

> He was never seen to laugh after his error nor to look directly at the sky because of his shyness before his Lord and he continued to weep for the rest of his life. It is said that he wept until the plants sprang up from his tears and until the tears formed ridges in his cheeks. It is said that he went out in disguise to learn what people thought of him and hearing himself praised only made him more humble.[7] (Qadi 'Iyad/*Ash-Shifa*, p. 79)

Now, God Most Gracious is *al-Sattar*, the Concealer or Veiler of the faults of His servants, and hence He did not reveal what David's "trial" consisted of. However, since the wording of 38:21-24 quoted above does not mention any wrong action on David's part, it is likely that it related to the realm of intention or desire. This understanding is confirmed by the verse that follows:

> **Then We forgave him that, and indeed, for him is nearness to Us and a goodly place of return.** (38:25)

It is quite unimaginable that God would bestow such high praise on a person, much less on a prophet, after he had followed his lust to commit the awful crime and sin that is reported of David (A) in the Old Testament, an explanation which was nevertheless accepted by some early Qur'anic commentators. God's saying,

> **We certainly caused some prophets to excel others, and We granted David the *Zabur*** (17:55),

further attests to David's high standing with his Lord, since he is mentioned in the same sentence as those prophets who excelled others.

Certainly the very next verse in the report of this incident, in which God says, addressing David,

> **"O David, indeed, We have made you a deputy [*khalifah*] on the earth, so judge between people with truth and do not follow desire, for it will cause you to stray from God's path. Indeed, those who stray from God's path will have a severe chastisement because they forgot the Day of Accounting"** (38:26),

confirms the former understanding, for instead of reproaching David (A) for a sin he had already committed, God Most High merely warned him against the disaster that would result if he followed his desire.

---

[7]This *hadith* begins with what is mentioned concerning David's praying and fasting in *Bukhari*, 4:631, quoted earlier on pages 233-234. The entire *hadith* is referenced by the author of *Ash-Shifa* to Muslim, Bukhari and a number of other compilers of *ahadith*.

Consequently, in keeping with the opinion of Ibn Kathir, we must seriously question the story that has come down to us in a ***hadith*** attributed to Anas bin Malik (R), reported by al-Tabari, as well as in the accounts of such classical commentators as al-Suddi and Hasan al-Basri, which connect the verses concerning the testing of David (A) with the Biblical story of David and Bathsheba, reported in 2 Sam. 11. What makes the authenticity of Anas' ***hadith*** all the more questionable, says Ibn Kathir, is that one of its transmitters is considered weak as a transmitter of ***ahadith***.

> Many commentators of the earlier and later generations have mentioned stories and reports, most of them taken from Judaic sources, and among them are, inevitably, false stories, [Ibn Kathir continues]. We have deliberately excluded these from our books and have confined ourselves to narrating the story as given in the Mighty Qur'an. And God guides whomever He wills to His straight path. (Ibn Kathir/*T*, 38:21-25)

This certainly seems the more correct view, for the story reported in the ***hadith*** of Anas (R) and in the much longer, detailed accounts of al-Suddi and Hasan al-Basri, reported by al-Tabari (Tabari/*H*, III:144-146), presents the following grave and insoluble problems:

First, it attributes a heinous crime to a prophet of God, thereby violating a cardinal tenet of Islam concerning prophethood: that prophets were free of deliberate sins, not to mention crimes. Indeed, the fourth caliph, 'Ali ibn Abi Talib (R), considered what had been ascribed to David (A) in the Biblical narrative so grave a slander as to declare that if anyone narrated the story of David in the manner in which it was told by the story-tellers, he would have him flogged with 160 stripes, that being a suitable punishment for slandering God's prophets (Asad/*Q*, 38:fn. 22).

Second, it raises the unanswerable question of why a deeply pious, God-fearing man, not to mention a prophet, who had ninety-nine wives would feel it necessary to plot to commit an extremely grave crime in order to possess the hundredth — the one ewe mentioned by the two disputants.

Third, one is led to wonder how a woman who was both virtuous and exquisitely beautiful would bathe in a place where she was visible to others, especially to a king to whom God had permitted an unlimited number of wives — and this in the absence of her husband.

Still another problem is the fairly close correspondence of Anas' ***hadith*** with the Biblical account, since in most instances there are major differences between the Qur'anic narratives and the Biblical texts. This in itself suggests that the commentators' accounts are taken directly from Judaic sources, which lack the authenticity requisite for the reporting of a matter of such gravity.

At the same time, Ibn Kathir, like al-Tabari, mentions that David had one hundred wives, among whom was the widow of Uriah, the mother of Solomon son of David (A), whom he married after a trial (Ibn Kathir/*Q*, "Dawud"). However, we emphasize that there is absolutely nothing in the Qur'anic verses reporting David's trial to suggest that he did what has been attributed to him, or indeed that he came near any major sin throughout his life. The words, **David inferred that We had tried him, and he asked forgiveness of his Lord. . . . Then We forgave him that** (38:24-25), neither state nor even imply that he committed a sinful act, but rather that his Lord tested him by something that may have been a matter of thought, desire or intention, and that he immediately repented and was forgiven.

"Therefore," in the words of Ibn Kathir, "it is best that we repeat only what is in the Qur'an, and it is the truth" (Ibn Kathir/*T*, 38:21-25). Hence we refrain from speculating further about the nature of David's trial, deferring to the magnificence of God's commendation of him,

> **Indeed, for him is nearness to Us and a goodly place of return (38:24-25),**

lest we commit the grave sin of slandering a righteous servant who was dearly loved by His Lord.

REFERENCES: Qur'an: 38:21-26. Commentaries: Ibn Kathir/*T*, 38:21-25; Ibn Kathir/*Q*, "Dawud"; Tabari/*H*, III:144-149; Maududi/*Q*, 33:fn. 89; Asad/*Q*, 38:fn. 22; Ali/*Q*, fn. 4178.

6. THE DEATH OF DAVID

Say, [O Muhammad:] "The Angel of Death, who has been entrusted with you, will take you; then you will be returned to your Lord." (32:11)

A *hadith* which we cited previously in the story of Adam (A) relates to David's term of life.[8]

This *hadith* begins with the creation of Adam (A), and then mentions that he sneezed, praised God, and exchanged greetings with the angels. God then showed Adam his closed Hands,[9] saying, "Choose whichever of them you wish."

"I choose my Lord's right Hand and both of my Lord's Hands are right and blessed," Adam said.

Then God opened His Hand, and it contained Adam and his descendants. "My Lord, what are these?" Adam asked.

"These are your descendants," God said.

Now, every person's term of life was written on his forehead, and among them there was a man who was the brightest of them (or, according to another wording, one with a bright gleam of light upon his forehead). "My Lord, who is this?" Adam asked.

"This is your descendant David, and I have written his period of life for him as forty years," God replied.

"My Lord, increase his life," Adam said.

"That is what I have written for him," God said.

"My Lord, I have given him sixty years of my life,"[10] Adam said.

"That is as you wish," God replied. (*Mishkat,* 4662)

In a report narrated by Abu Hurayrah (R), the Prophet (S) said that David (A) was a solicitous man, who would lock the doors whenever he left

---

[8]Volume One, pages 25 and 99. In view of this *hadith*, one is at a loss to explain both the life-span of David given by historians (1000 or 1006-965 B.C.) and in 2 Sam. 5:4, 10, which states that "David was thirty years old when he became king, and he reigned forty years."

[9]This must be interpreted in keeping with the Islamic understanding, which totally rejects all anthropormophic notions concerning God Most High. Please see Volume One, page 6, for the interpretation of such terms as God's "Hands," "Face," "Eyes" and "Throne".

[10]In the version of *Mishkat*, 118, Adam gives David forty years of his life.

his house. But one day, after he had locked them and gone out, his wife looked out and saw a man in the house.

"Who admitted this man?" she demanded. "He will certainly have cause for dismay when David returns!"

"Who are you?" David asked when he came and saw him.

"I am the one who fears no king, and who is not stopped by any chamberlain," the other replied.

"Then, by God, you are the Angel of Death," David (A) said. And he died upon the spot. (Al-Ghazali, *The Remembrance of Death*, pp. 43-44)

May God's peace, mercy and blessings be upon David, the dearly loved servant of his Lord!

SOLOMON (A)

1. THE HEIR OF DAVID

And to David We granted Solomon, an excellent slave. Indeed, he was one who repeatedly turned [to God]. (38:30)

Among the special favors that God Most High bestowed upon David (A) was his illustrious son Solomon (Sulaiman), who reigned from 965-928 B.C. **And Solomon inherited David** (27:16), not in the sense of becoming heir to his worldly wealth but rather the inheritor of his prophetood and the kingship of the Israelites. And he excelled both as a prophet and as a king.

Solomon (A) is mentioned seventeen times in seven *surahs* of the Qur'an — nine times by himself, five times together with David (A), and twice together with other prophets. The story of Solomon (A) is full of incidents, subtle metaphors and esoteric matters whose meanings have presented a challenge to Qur'anic interpreters. And as we shall see, certain aspects of his story were revealed by the Knower of all things in order to clear His honored prophet of the baseless charges that had been made against him, confirming both his prophethood and his uprightness, acceptability and high rank in His sight.

REFERENCE: Ibn Kathir/*T*, 27:16.

2. The Wisdom of Solomon

And We certainly granted David and Solomon knowledge, and they said, "Praise be to God, who favored us over many of His believing slaves." (27:15-16)

It is said that during David's reign, after Solomon (A) had reached mature manhood, his father would consult with him concerning his affairs.

Like David (A), to whom God Most High granted **wisdom and discernment in speech** (38:20, 2:251), Solomon (A) was blessed with extraordinary wisdom. His soundness of understanding and judgment are memorialized in the following Qur'anic verse,

> **And [mention] David and Solomon, when they gave judgment concerning the field, when people's sheep strayed into it, and We were witness to their judgment** (21:78),

whose interpretation is given by Ibn Mas'ud (R) as follows:

Once Solomon and David (A) were asked to give judgment concerning sheep that had strayed into the field of certain people by night. This field was a vineyard whose clusters had sprouted and were destroyed by the sheep.

When David (A) passed judgment in favor of the owner of the vineyard, Solomon (A) suggested a more equitable settlement: that the vineyard should be turned over to the owner of the sheep, to be tended until it was restored to its former state, while the sheep should be turned over to the owner of the vineyard so that he might make a profit from them until the vineyard was restored (Tabari/*H*, III:152-153). Thus, in the continuation of the passage above, God Most High says,

> **And We caused Solomon to understand it. And to each We granted judgment and knowledge.** (21:79)

Another example of Solomon's depth of wisdom and judgment is mentioned in the following ***hadith***:

> There were two women with their two sons. A wolf came and went off with the son of one of them, and she said to her companion, "He has gone off with your son." The other said, "He has gone off with *your* son!" The two of them then sought the judgment of David, peace be upon him, and he passed judgment concerning it in favor of the elder one. Both of them then went to Solomon son of David, peace be upon him, and told him [about the matter], and he said, "Give me a knife. I will divide him [the remaining son] between the two of them." The younger one said, "Do not, may God have mercy upon you! He is *her*

son." He then passed judgment concerning it in favor of the younger one.[1] (*Bukhari*, 8:760; 4:637)

According to a report by Ibn Abi Hatim, David (A) once tested Solomon (A) with several questions. Then, when Solomon (A) gave wise and understanding replies, David (A) informed him that he was a prophet.

"What is the best thing?" David (A) asked him

"Trust in God and belief in Him," Solomon (A) replied.

"What is worst thing?"

"Unbelief after belief."

"What is the sweetest thing?"

"God's mercy."

"What is the coolest thing?"

"God's forgiveness and people's forgiving one another." (Ibn Kathir/*T*, 38:30-33)

REFERENCES: Qur'an: 27:15-16; 21:78-79. Commentaries: Ibn Kathir/*T*, 38:30-33; Tabari/*H*, III:152-153.

[1]Cf., 1 Kings 3:16-28.

3. Solomon and the Horses

[Mention] when there were presented before him in the afternoon the swift, excellent, highly-trained horses. And he said, "Indeed, I have preferred the love of the good because of the remembrance of my Lord," until they disappeared into the veil. He said, "Return them to me," and began to stroke [their] legs and necks. (38:31-33)

Solomon's dominion, power, and wives are legendary. It is said (perhaps in imitation of 1 Kings 11:3) that he had seven hundred wives and three hundred concubines, while others reverse this figure.

Regardless of the accuracy of these numbers, we can infer from them that Solomon's manly power was far beyond the ordinary. This is confirmed by a number of related ***ahadith*** in which it is stated that once Solomon (A) declared, "Tonight I will make the rounds of one hundred women, or ninety-nine.[2] Each of them will bring forth a horseman [*faris*] who will fight in the path of God." Then his companion said to him, "Say, '***Insha'Allah*** — God willing!'" But he did not say "***Insha'Allah***" and none of them gave birth except a woman who brought forth a partial male. The Prophet (S) added: "By Him in whose hand is Muhammad's soul, if he had said '***Insha'Allah***,' they would all have been horsemen, striving in the path of God" (***Bukhari***, 4:74A, 4:635, 7:169, 8:711).

In this connection, Solomon (A) was also renowned for his horses, which were used in his military campaigns.[3] He evidently possessed great numbers of steeds, for 1 Kings, 4:26, reports that he owned "four thousand stalls for chariot horses, and twelve thousand horses."

According to Ibn Kathir, during his reign, Solomon (A) was presented with some horses that stood on three legs, while raising the fourth (Ibn Kathir/Q, "Sulaiman"). Various claims have made about these horses — for example, that they were twenty in number, or, according to another report, twenty thousand, and even that they had wings. But God knows the truth.

---

[2]In ***Bukhari***, 7:169, it is one hundred women; in ***Bukhari***, 8:711, ninety; and in ***Bukhari***, 4:635, seventy.

[3]The Prophet (S) spoke affectionately of horses, saying, "Good is interlinked with the forelocks of horses until the Day of Judgment" (***Bukhari***, 4:102, 104, 4:836; ***Muslim***, 4614), and "There is blessing in the forelocks of horses" (***Bukhari***, 4:103; ***Muwatta***, 21.19.44).

Solomon's horses are memorialized in the verses cited at the beginning of this chapter. This passage is understood as meaning that one afternoon Solomon's finest steeds of war were marshalled before him. In consideration of the horses' role in his battles in the cause of God, Solomon (A) reflected on how he **"preferred the love of the good"** — referring to the horses — **"because of [*'an*] the remembrance of my Lord"** — meaning fighting in God's cause — **until it**, the troop of horses, **disappeared into the veil** of distance. He then ordered that the horses be returned to him and began to **stroke** their **legs and necks** out of love for that which was useful for God's service.[4]

Now, these are verses whose context and significance may not be readily apparent. In order to understand them, we go to the verses that immediately precede them, which introduce a lengthy passage related to Solomon (A) in *Surah Sad* (38:30-40) — namely,

> **[This is] a blessed Book which We have revealed to you [Muhammad], that they might reflect on its verses and that those**

---

[4]Another, altogether different interpretation of this verse, based on the fact, mentioned elsewhere, that the observance of *salat* was prescribed for the prophets prior to Muhammad (S), is that Solomon became so absorbed in his excellent horses that he forgot to observe the late afternoon (*'Asr*) prayer. When he remembered it, **he said, "Indeed, I have preferred the love of the good** of this life **over [*'an*] the remembrance of my Lord," until it** — the sun — **disappeared into the veil** of night. After ordering that the horses be returned to him, he **began to stroke** their **legs and necks** with the sword, slaughtering them out of anger for the sake of God because his preoccupation with them had caused him to forget his prayer. And when he had done this in order to rid himself of that which distracted him from his Lord, He compensated him with something better than them in exchange — namely, the power to travel on the wind, which we shall mention shortly.

Although this interpretation has been accepted by a number of classical and modern commentators, certain matters have been added without any basis. The first is that Solomon missed his *salat*, although this is nowhere suggested by the Qur'anic wording. The second is that it was the sun that **disappeared into the veil** of night, an interpretation which is also not indicated by the wording; simple logic, moreover, suggests that it was the horses, mentioned in the previous sentence, that disappeared into the veil of distance, rather than the sun's disappearing into the veil of night, since neither the sun nor night are mentioned in the verse. The third unjustifiable assumption is that Solomon, rather than stroking the shins and necks of the horses, as the wording indicates, began to stroke them with his sword and slaughtered them.

Aside from these unwarranted interpolations, the notion that a prophet would slaughter innocent and useful animals because of his own error presents very serious problems. Ibn 'Abbas (R) confirms that Solomon (A) did not slaughter the horses but "started passing his hand on their necks and shanks with love" (Maududi/*Q*, 38:fn. 35). Al-Tabari also prefers the opinion that he did not punish an animal or destroy his property without a valid reason and without any sin on its part (Ibn Kathir/*Q*, 38:33).

of understanding might be reminded. And to David We granted Solomon, an excellent slave. Indeed, he was one who repeatedly turned [to God] (38:29-30),

In confirming the revelation of the Qur'an to Muhammad (S), the first verse of this passage makes clear that the subsequent account concerning Solomon (A) is of divine orgin. It also indirectly suggests that those who are aware of the incidents narrated concerning Solomon (A) in this account reflect on their true meaning and deeper significance, so that **those of understanding might be reminded**. A high commendation of Solomon (A) then follows in God's referring to him as **an excellent slave . . . who repeatedly turned** to Him (38:30). The verse of the horses then follows.

The incident of the horses demonstrates that, despite the kingship, power and miraculous gifts he had been granted, Solomon (A), like his father, remained ever deeply humble, thankful and devoted to God, in every instance valuing the divine favors he had been granted not for their own sake or for the satisfaction of his ego, but solely for the remembrance and glorification of his Lord.

Understood in this context, it is clear that the purpose of narrating the incident of the horses was to confirm how acceptable a slave Solomon was to God Most High, loving the good in his animals not because of attachment to a worldly object but purely for His sake, since these were the steeds used for fighting in His cause.

REFERENCES: Qur'an: 38:31-33. Commentaries: Ibn Kathir/*Q*, 38:33; Ibn Kathir/*Q*, "Sulaiman"; Maududi/*Q*, 38:fn. 35.

4. THE BODY ON THE THRONE

We certainly tried Solomon and placed a body on his throne; then he returned. He said, "My Lord, forgive me and grant me such a kingdom as will not belong to anyone after me. Indeed, You are the Bestower." (38:34-35)

The verses above follow immediately after those of the horses. Some very fanciful explanations of them have been suggested by certain classical commentators.[5] However, such respected interpreters of the Qur'an as Ibn Kathir and al-Razi considered these interpretations to be unauthenticated and unbacked by any *hadith* or sound chain of transmission, having originated in Judaic traditions. Writes Maulana Maududi:

> As a matter of fact, this is one of the most difficult places of the Qur'an, and we do not find any indisputable ground for giving a definite and absolute commentary of it. (Maududi/*Q*, 38:fn. 36)

All that is clear from these verses, which occur shortly after the mention of Solomon (A) as **an excellent slave** who **repeatedly turned** to God (38:30), is that God tried him in an unidentified manner by putting an unspecified **body on his throne**, after which **he returned**. This trial finished, Solomon (A) prayed, **"My Lord, forgive me"** — that is, for whatever faults I may have committed — **"and grant me such a kingdom as will not belong to anyone after me. Indeed, You are the Bestower."**

Concerning this prayer of Solomon's, the Holy Prophet (S) said:

> Solomon asked three things from God, two of which were granted to him, and I hope the third will be reserved for us [Muslims]: One, "Grant me judgment that agrees with Your judgment"; two, **"Grant me such a kingdom as will not belong to anyone after me"**; and three,

---

[5]The commentators Qatadah and al-Suddi tell two similar, lengthy, complicated stories concerning the matter of **a body on his throne.** In summary, it is said that a satan impersonated Solomon and, gaining control of his signet ring which was the source of his power, took over and ruled in his place for forty days. When the leaders of the Israelites recognized that this person was giving commands against the sacred law, they went to Solomon's wives and found that his private behavior was as improper as his public. When the wives read the *Taurat* in his presence, the satan ran off with Solomon's ring, which fell into the sea. Solomon, then leading a meager existence outside the palace, found his ring inside a fish, whereupon his power was restored and he returned to his former position. According to this interpretation, the **body on his throne** was that of the satan, and the words, **then he returned,** refer to Solomon's restoration to his former state after finding the ring (Ibn Kathir/*T*, 38:34; Tabari/*H*, III:169-172).

"That whoever comes out of his house to pray in this place of worship [Solomon's Temple] should be as sinless when he returns as if he had been born that day." (Ibn Kathir/*T*, 38:35-40)

Finding Solomon (A) deserving of such a grant, God Most High bestowed upon him extraordinary gifts: the ability to understand the speech of birds and animals; the power to control and travel on the wind; legions of soldiers, among whom were humans, jinn and birds; and troops of workers, including jinn and satans, who labored for him as he commanded.

Again, although Solomon's dominion and power surpsssed that of any other monarch of his time and indeed perhaps of all times, what emerges most clearly from the Qur'anic account and ***ahadith*** concerning him is his wisdom, piety, love of God, thankfulness and humility in the face of his Lord's tremendous favors.[6]

REFERENCES: Qur'an: 38:34-35. Commentaries: Ibn Kathir/*T*, 38:34-40; Tabari/*H*, III: 169-172; Maududi/*Q*, 38:fn. 36; Asad/*Q*, 38:fn. 32.

[6]As for the Biblical allegation that Solomon, under the influence of his non-Israelite wives, set up and worshipped idols (1 Kings 11:1-8), Muslims regard it as a blatant fabrication and slander against an illustrious prophet who was dear to his Lord, as is clear beyond any doubt from the verses in which God praises and commends him, all of which are cited in these pages.

5. SOLOMON'S INCOMPARABLE KINGDOM

"This is Our grant, so bestow or withhold without account." (38:39)

Historically speaking, one of the most important achievements of Solomon's reign was the establishment of a kingdom with a centralized, organized monarchy. And from a religious point of view, by far the most important of his works was the building of the Temple in Jerusalem, known in Arabic as *al-Masjid al-Aqsa,* the Farthest Mosque, enshrining the sacred Ark of the Covenant in a magnificent house of worship built on a sacred site appointed by God.[7]

We may well wonder how it would have been possible for the king of a small and insignificant country to build an edifice of such scale and magnificence as is described in 1 Kings 6 and 2 Chr. 3-4. The key to this question is found in the Qur'an, in which it is suggested (although the Temple is not referred to directly) that it was built, at least in part, by a non-human labor force, mentioned in God's saying,

> **Among the jinn were those who labored for him, by his Lord's leave**[8] (34:12).

God Most High granted Solomon (A) such control over these unseen beings that they did whatever he commanded them. Although they toiled for him against their will, as we shall soon see, perhaps like a modern-day chain gang, he made use of them for any purpose he wished, and those who disobeyed his commands were severely punished.

Some of the non-believing jinn or demons were divers who brought forth from the sea pearls and other valuables for their master: —

---

[7]The Companion Abu Dharr al-Ghifari asked the Prophet (S), "O Messenger of God, which *masjid* [place of worship] was built first?" He replied, "The Sacred Mosque [the K'abah, built by Abraham]." "Which next?" He replied, "The Farthest Mosque [Solomon's Temple]." "What was the period in between them?" He replied, "Forty [years]" (*Bukhari*, 4:636). The classical commentator al-Qurtubi suggests that this discrepancy between the time of Abraham and Solomon, who lived about one thousand years later, may mean that Abraham and Solomon only restored what had been built by those before them, just as the K'abah was built sucessively by Adam, angels and Abraham during their respective eras (Ayoub/*Q*, II:258-259).

[8]Concerning the nature and identity of jinn, please see Volume One, page 18. Appendix III at the end of Muhammad Asad's translation of the Qur'an contains some valuable material on the subject.

Among the satans were those who dived for him and did work other than that, and We were Guardian of them. (21:82)

As well as diving, they also built for him: —

[We subjected to him] the satans [among the jinn] — every [kind of] builder and diver, and others bound together in fetters. (38:37-38)

And God Most High caused **a spring of** molten **copper to flow for him** (34:12).[9] Perhaps it was partly from this material that his jinn laborers produced extraordinarily beautiful and magnificent structures and artefacts, and did many other things that were beyond human power: —

They made for him whatever he desired of elevated chambers [*maharib*], images [*tamathil*], basins like reservoirs [*jifanin kal-jawab*], and stationary cauldrons [*qudurin rasiyat*].[10] And whoever deviated from Our command among them, We will cause him to taste of the punishment of the blazing Fire![11] (34:12-13)

The objects mentioned in this passage may well have been part of the elaborate and precious furnishings of the Temple, one of the most magnificent structures of all times, constructed under Solomon's direction and command.

"Work, O family of David, in gratitude!" (34:13), God Most High commanded, addressing all those who were connected with the House of David, ordering them to do their best in thankfulness for His countless favors and to express it by words and deeds and in the heart. Yet, adds the Giver of all things and Knower of what is within the breasts, **Few of My servants are grateful** (34:13).

---

[9]Concerning this, Maulana Maududi writes:

> The great furnace which he [Solomon] had built at Ezion-geber for melting and moulding ores extracted from the copper and iron mines in the 'Arabah in Edom, has been confirmed by modern archaeological researches as well. This molten iron and copper was used in building ships besides being put to other uses. The Quran refers to this when it says: ". . . .and We made a fountain of molten copper to flow for him (Solomon). . . ." (XXXIV:12). (Maududi/*Q*, 21:fn. 74)

[10]Various commentators have said that ***"maharib"*** denotes beautiful buildings, the best part of a house, the place where the leader of a gathering sits, palaces, or places of worship. ***"Tamathil"*** are images or statues made of copper, clay or glass. ***"Jifanin kal-jawab"*** means basins or reservoirs in which water comes and goes, similar to a cistern or pond. ***"Qudurin rasiyat"*** refers to kettles of such size and weight that they could not be moved, in which Solomon had food prepared for his army (Ibn Kathir/*T*, 34:12-13).

[11]Since God had granted Solomon control over the jinn, they were constrained to do whatever he ordered them under the pain of divine punishment.

All this was from God's favor and bounty, which He bestows upon whomever He wills. And it was granted to Solomon (A) without accountability on the Day of Judgment for how he used it, according to God's declaration, **"This is Our grant, so bestow or withhold without account"** (38:39). The divine Author of the Book then adds concerning Solomon (A):

> **And indeed, for him is nearness to Us and a good place of return.** (38:39-40)

Says Ibn 'Abbas (R):

> Solomon son of David was asked to choose between knowledge, wealth or power, but he chose knowledge and was thereby blessed with wealth and power as well. (Al-Ghazzali, *The Book of Knowledge*, p. 15)

This is clarified by Ibn Kathir, who states that after the completion of the Temple, God Most High told Solomon (A) that because he had built it for Him, he could ask whatever he desired of Him. He then asked for the three things mentioned above. Ibn Kathir adds that after the death of David (A), God told Solomon (A) to ask whatever he wished. Solomon (A) then said, "O Lord, give me a heart that is always in awe of You, just as my father's heart was in awe of You, and fill my heart with Your love, as You filled my father's heart with Your love." And God was so pleased that His servant was asking for awe and love of Him that He granted him such a great kingdom as would not be granted to anyone else after that (Ibn Kathir/*T* 38:34-40).

REFERENCES: Qur'an: 21:82; 34:12-14; 38:37-39. Commentaries: Ibn Kathir/*T*, 34:12-13, 38:34-40; Ibn Kathir/*Q*, "Sulaiman"; Tabari/*H*, III:152-155, 157; al-Ghazzali, *The Book of Knowledge*, p. 15; Ayoub/*Q*, II:258-259; Maududi/*Q*, 21:fns. 74-75; Asad/*Q*, 34:fns. 15-17; Ali/*Q*, fns. 3804-3807.

6. SOLOMON'S CONTROL OF THE WIND

Then We subjected to him the wind, blowing by his command, gently, wheresoever he directed. (38:36)

And to Solomon [We subjected] the wind, blowing forcefully, proceeding by his command toward the land which We had blest [Palestine]. And We are ever Knowing of all things. (21:81)

Indeed, God Most High bestowed upon Solomon (A) favors and bounties beyond those granted to anyone before him or since, giving him control over humans, jinn, birds and the wind, and much territory and wealth.

These are among the miracles that God Most High grants to those whom He chooses among His deputies, the prophets, according to His saying, **We certainly caused some prophets to excel others** (17:55). The possession of such powers should not surprise us, for

> **He has subjected to you whatever is in the heavens and whatever in on the earth — all from Him. Indeed, in that are signs for a people who reflect.** (45:13)
>
> **Do you not see that God has subjected to you whatever is in the heavens and whatever is in the earth, and amply bestowed upon you His favors, [both] visible and hidden?** (31:20)

"Such things" as the special powers granted to Solomon (A) "occur not by our command but by God's," says the great Islamic scholar and mystic, Ibn al-'Arabi. However, Solomon's unique distinction was "that he could effect such things by personal command alone, without the need for spiritual concentration or the exertion of spiritual power. . . . [He] had only to utter the command to whatever he wished to subject, without the need for special [spiritual] states" (Ibn al-'Arabi, *The Bezels of Wisdom*, pp. 195-196).

Concerning the subservience of the wind to Solomon (A), it is said that it used to traverse a month's journey in an hour's time during the morning or evening, taking him wherever he wished to go, whether blowing gently or forcefully, as mentioned in the verses at the beginning of this chapter.

It is reported that Solomon (A) had a wooden platform. Whenever he went on a journey or wished to travel, says Ibn 'Abbas (R), he would take his seat upon his throne on this platform, with seats at his right and left. He would then give permission to the humans to take up their positions, with the jinn behind them and the demons behind the jinn. And he would send for the birds to shade to the whole entourage from above, and would order the wind — neither a heavy nor a light wind but one in between — to carry them all, **its morning [journey] a month and its afternoon [journey] a month** (34:12), **blowing, by his command, gently, wheresoever he directed** (38:36) (Tabari/*H*, III:157).

Ibn Kathir supplies further details, saying:

> He had a platform made of wood that would spread itself out to the extent he needed, and he would place on it all kinds of things, such as buildings, palaces, tents, furniture, horses, camels, baggage, personnel from among humans and jinn, and also some other animals and birds.
>
> Whenever he wanted to travel or do battle against a king or enemies in any country, he would place all these on his platform and would order the wind to lift it to a certain height between the earth and sky, and would then command the breeze to move it along.[12] If he wished to go faster than that, he would command the forceful wind, and it would carry it quickly to whatever place he wished to go and stop wherever he wished it to stop. Thus, he would set out in the early morning from Jerusalem and go to Istakhar [near Isfahan in Iran], which is a distance of one month, and would stay there up to the end of the day and then return to Jerusalem, [according to God's words,] **And to Solomon [We subjected] the wind, its morning [journey] a month and its afternoon [journey] a month** [34:12].
>
> Hasan al-Basri says: "In the morning he would start from Damascus and would alight in Istakhar and have his meal there, and from there go to Kabul to sleep. And between Damascus and Istakhar is a distance of one month's journey by fast horse, and between Istakhar and Kabul is a distance of one month's journey."[13] (Ibn Kathir/*Q*, "Sulaiman")

REFERENCES: Qur'an: 21:81; 34:12; 28:36. Commentaries: Ibn Kathir/*T*, 34:12, 38:36-40; Ibn Kathir/*Q*, "Sulaiman"; Tabari/*H*, III:153-155, 157; Ibn al-'Arabi, *The Bezels of Wisdom*, pp. 195-196; Keller/*Reliance*, x339, p. 1099.

---

[12]We may compare this to a huge aircraft or ship filled with people and cargo. The difference is that while our aircraft or vessels are powered by mechanical and electrical power, Solomon's platform was powered by the spiritual power granted to him, as God's *khalifah* (deputy) by the Creator of all things.

[13]Al-Tabari mentions an inscription in a dwelling near the Tigris River, written by a companion of Solomon's, whether a jinn or a human, which read, "We dwelt in it, but we did not build it; we found it already built. We came early in the morning from Istakhr and spent the midday rest in it. We will go from it in the evening, if God wills, and spend the night in Syria" (i.e., Palestine) (Tabari/*H*, III:154).

7. THE VALLEY OF THE ANTS

There is no creature on the earth or bird that flies with its wings but [that they are] communities like yourselves. (6:38)

As mentioned previously, one of the extraordinary gifts that had been granted to Solomon (A) was the ability to understand the speech of animals and birds in their own tongues.

"O people," Solomon (A) declared, proclaiming God's immense favors to him, **"we have been taught the language of birds and we have been given of all things. Indeed,"** he added, **"this is a manifest grace"** (27:16) from the Creator of the land and the earth and the sky.

The meaning of these words, says Ibn Kathir, is that God had granted Solomon (A) whatever he needed of equipment, armies, soldiers, personnel (both jinn and human), birds, animals and demons, and the knowledge, understanding and interpretation of the minds of creatures, and their speaking and keeping silent (Ibn Kathir/*T*, 27:16).

God Most High then mentions an incident concerning Solomon (A) which, although it relates to a seemingly very insignificant creature, is meant to teach mankind an important lesson — so much so that the *surah* in which it is mentioned (the twenty-seventh, in which verses 16-44 relate to Solomon) is named, after it, *Al-Naml* (The Ant).

One day Solomon rode forth with his army, consisting of **his troops of the jinn and humans and birds, and they were** marching with him **in measured order** (27:17), while the birds formed a canopy above them with their wings.

The armies of these three species went forward in formation, no one preceding or falling behind the other, **until, when they came to the valley of the ants, an ant said, "O ants, go into your dwellings, that you not be crushed by Solomon and his troops while they are unaware"** (27:17-18).

Understanding her words, the great king Solomon (A) **smiled, amused at her speech, and said, "My Lord, so dispose me that I may be thankful for Your favors which You have bestowed upon me and upon my parents, and that I may do righteous deeds which will please You. And admit me to Your mercy among Your righteous slaves"** (27:19).

In explanation of these verses, Ibn Kathir says:

> God Most High then says, **When they came to the valley of the ants, . . . "while they are unaware"** [27:17-18], and the ant warned her

companions that Solomon and his troops were not aware of their being there.

The object of narrating this is to show that Solomon understood what this ant told her nation [*ummah*], giving them a sound opinion and praiseworthy command, and a smile came to his lips because he was so happy and glad and elated that God had informed him of something that no one else understood. He therefore expressed deep gratitude to God Most High for this favor and supplicated Him that He would raise him among His righteous slaves, and God accepted his prayer.

His mother is included in his thankfulness for God's favors [by his mention of his parents], for she was a devout and righteous lady, as reported in a *hadith*:

> Solomon's mother said to him, "O my son, do not sleep too much at night because sleeping too much at night leaves a slave poor on the Day of Judgment"[14] [Ibn Majah]. (Ibn Kathir/*Q*, "Sulaiman")

Ibn Kathir also mentions a *hadith* related to ants, in which the Prophet (S) said:

> A prophet from among the prophets came out with people to supplicate God for rain, and they came upon an ant, raising its feet toward the sky [in supplication]. Then the prophet told his companions, "Go back, for it has already been accepted for you because of this ant." (Ibn Kathir/*Q*, "Sulaiman")

Perhaps Solomon (A) was that prophet, for al-Suddi said,

> During the time of Solomon, people were suffering from famine, so he ordered them to come out [to pray for rain]. Then there was this ant standing on her feet, raising her legs, and she was saying, "O our Lord, I

---

[14]Meaning that to awaken during night to pray is one of the best of deeds, heavy in the balance on the Day of Judgment. Night prayer, known as *tahajjud*; is mentioned in a number of Qur'anic verses, such as 3:17; 17:79; 39:9; 50:40; 51:16-18; 52:48-49; 73:6, 20; 76:26. Many *ahadith* also speak of the importance of waking up at night to pray, among them the following:

> Make use of *tahajjud*, for it was the practice of the righteous before you, and it is [the means of] nearness to your Lord and an expiation for evil deeds and the prevention of sins. (*Mishkat*, 1227)

> Each night, our Lord, the Blessed and Exalted, descends to the lowest heaven when the last third of the night remains, and He says, "Whoever calls Me, I shall respond to him. Whoever asks of Me, I shall give him. Whoever seeks My forgiveness, I shall forgive him." (*Bukhari*, 2:246; *Muwatta*, 5.8.30)

am one of Your creatures. Please do not deprive me of Your bounty!" Then God sent rain upon them. (Ibn Kathir/*Q*, "Sulaiman")

REFERENCES: Qur'an: 27:16-19. Commentaries: Ibn Kathir/*T*, 27:16-19, 34:12-13; Ibn Kathir/*Q*, "Sulaiman"; Maududi/*Q*, fn. 24.

8. THE QUEEN OF SHEBA

"I found a woman ruling them, and she has been given of everything and has a magnificent throne." (27:23)

The story of Solomon (A) and the Queen of Sheba follows immediately after the incident of the ants in *Surah al-Naml* (27:20-44). Among all the stories in the Qur'an, its meaning is one of the most subtle and difficult to grasp. It therefore requires strict adherence to the Qur'anic text and reliable commentaries rather than repeating various unauthenticated reports that have been propagated and accepted as true. Our main sources of information in the telling of this story are the Qur'anic *Commentary (Tafsir)* and *Stories of the Prophets (Qasas al-Anbiya')* of Ibn Kathir.

BILQUIS

Among Solomon's bird troops was a hoopoe, a brightly-colored bird with a long, curved bill and standing crest. It is reported by Ibn 'Abbas (R) and others that the hoopoe's task was to locate water when Solomon's entourage was traveling or camping in the desert, for God had endowed this bird with the ability to discern underground water, and when he guided them to it, they would dig and draw up water for their use.

As is customary for the troops of kings, all the varieties of birds in Solomon's army would stand before him, ready to do his bidding. Like the rest of his troops, they were kept under strict military discipline.

One day when Solomon (A) was traveling, **he reviewed the birds** (27:20) but did not find the hoopoe among them. Because those accompanying him were very thirsty and no one else knew how to find water, Solomon (A) was very angry.

"Why do I not see the hoopoe, or is he among the absentees?" he demanded. **"I will surely punish him with a severe punishment or slaughter him unless he brings me a clear authority"** (27:21). That is, "Because he is absolutely critical to the well-being of my troops, I will punish him severely or even impose the death sentence upon him unless he brings me a valid reason for his absence."[15]

---

[15]As in a human army, the punishment for desertion among Solomon's troops was evidently death.

But he — the hoopoe — **did not remain absent long. "I have encompassed in knowledge that which you have not encompassed,**[16] he announced to Solomon (A) upon his return, speaking with assurance and authority. **"And I have come to you from Sheba with sure information** (27:22).

"Indeed," the bird-officer continued, **"I found a woman ruling them, and she has been given of everything and has a magnificent throne. I found her and her people prostrating to the sun instead of God"**[17](27:23-24).

Thus did Solomon (A) come to have inside knowledge of the affairs of the Queen of Sheba (Saba'), to whom Islamic tradition gives the name Bilqis, a proud ruler descended from the common ancestor of the Arabs, Joktan (Qahtan). Some say that her father was a great king and her mother a jinn, but God alone knows. Her army, it is said, numbered hundreds of thousands, and she had 312 advisors and ministers. The name of her city was Ma'rib, which was located near Sana' in Yemen.

Every luxury was available to the queen. Ibn Kathir says that six hundred maids were always in attendance around her. The magnificent throne upon which she sat was eighty spans high and forty spans wide, covered with gold and studded with gems and pearls.

This throne stood in a grand palace having 360 windows on its eastern and western sides. These were constructed in such a way that each day the sun would rise at one of the eastern windows and set in the window opposite it in the west. And because the queen and her subjects were sun-worshippers, none of them worshipping the One who created them, they would all prostrate to the sun in the morning and evening.

> **And Satan has made their deeds pleasing to them and diverted them from the way so they are not guided — so they do not prostrate to God, who brings forth whatever is hidden in the the heavens and the earth, and knows what you conceal and what you dis-**

---

[16]These words do not mean that Solomon lacked prior knowledge of Sheba and its ruler, but rather that the hoopoe had brought him specific and detailed information that had not reached him previously.

[17]It is said that one of the ancestors of the people of Sheba was called 'Abd Shams (Slave of the Sun).

> **close. God — there is no deity except Him, Lord of the glorious Throne!**[18] (27:25-26)

"We shall see whether you are truthful or are of the liars," Solomon (A) replied to the hoopoe, expecting to determine by subsequent occurrences whether the bird was simply fabricating an excuse for his absence or was telling the truth. **"Take this letter of mine and deliver it to them,"** he ordered. **"Then withdraw from them and see what they will send back"** (27:27-28).

The hoopoe took the letter in his beak and flew to the queen's palace in Ma'rib. Finding her sitting in her private quarters, he respectfully put the letter in front of her and then stood deferentially aside.

The queen was extremely astonished by this, says Ibn Kathir, and also somewhat frightened. She picked up the letter and, breaking the seal, read it. She then summoned her ministers and chiefs for consultation.

"O nobles, there has surely been delivered to me a distinguished letter," she informed them, her words indicating that she had grasped the uniqueness and importance of the missive she had received[19] (27:29-31). **"Indeed, it is from Solomon, and indeed, it is,**

> **'In the name of God, the Merciful, the Compassionate. Do not be haughty toward me but come to me in submission.'"**

---

[18]Ibn Kathir and the majority of interpreters regard 27:25-26 as a continuation of the hopooe's speech. However, in the translations of Maududi and Hilaly-Khan, verses 23-24 are given as the bird's speech, while 25-26 are treated as a parenthetical comment by the divine Author of the Qur'an (see Maududi, 27:footnote 31). Because it is inconceivable that the words, **". . . [who] knows what you conceal and what you make known,"** could have been addressed by a subordinate to his king and commander-in-chief, we have understood it in the latter sense.

[19]The importance of Solomon's letter was obvious to the queen for a number of reasons, comments Ibn Kathir. First, instead of having reached her through a human envoy, the letter had been brought by a bird courier. Second, it was from Solomon, the great ruler of Palestine and Syria. Third, unlike the letters of any other ruler in the world, it began with the name of God. Fourth, it omitted mention of all other gods and goddesses. And fifth, it called upon the queen and her people not to be proud but to come to Solomon submitting. Solomon's words, **"Come to me in submission [*muslimin*],"** can be understood as meaning either "Come to me submitting to my superior strength and royal authority," or "Come to me submitting to God as *muslims*," the first meaning being compatible with Solomon's role as a king and the second with his role as prophet (Ibn Kathir/*T*, 27:36-37).

Then, puzzled as to what to make of the letter, with the explicit command it contained, she added, **"O nobles, advise me in my affair. I will not decide any matter unless you are present with me"**[20] (27:29-32).

But her advisors were likewise at a loss to understand. **"We are men of strength and great military might, but the command is yours,"** they replied. **"Therefore, consider what you will command"** (27:33). Thus did the queen's counselors return the decision concerning the matter to their ruler, indicating that they would accept whatever she saw fit to do.

The queen turned over the matter carefully in her keen mind. **"Surely, kings, when they enter a city, ruin it and render the most honored of its people the most debased,"** she mused. **"And thus do they do. But indeed,"** she announced, reaching a decision, **"I shall send them a gift and then see with what the envoys will return"** (27:34-35). That is, "If Solomon accepts my gift, he is just another king and perhaps there will be no harm in fighting him. But if he does not accept it, then this is something from God."[21]

The queen then dispatched her envoys to Solomon (A) with very valuable gifts, consisting of a great quantity of gold, pearls, jewels and perhaps other things. But when they came to Solomon, he said, **"Would you assist me with wealth? But what God has given me is better than what He has given you.**[22] **Rather, it is you who rejoice in your gift!"** (27:36). By this he meant to say, "Do you intend to bribe me into accepting your idolatry? That is impossible. My Lord has given me everything, and in this regard I am far better off than you, thanks be to God!"

---

[20]Or "unless you witness on my behalf." Maulana Maududi gives the meaning of this phrase as, "I regard your presence as necessary when I make a decision concerning important matters, and whatever decision I make, you should be present to testify that it is correct" (Maududi/*Q*, 27:fn. 38).

[21]Like the peoples of earlier prophets, the queen and her subjects did not deny or disbelieve in God's existence and power. Rather, due to ancestral traditions, lack of guidance and worldly considerations, they ascribed divinity to false gods, giving them the respect, obedience and worship that are due to the Creator alone.

[22]As God's prophet, Solomon did not speak these words out of pride or vanity, but simply to inform the envoys, and through them their queen, that he had no interest whatsoever in acquiring wealth. Rather, he was motivated solely by the desire that they acknowledge and worship the Creator of the heavens and the earth, or, if rejecting that, that they submit to a righteous system under his rule as God's prophet-king.

"Return to them," Solomon(A) instructed the queen's representatives. **"For indeed we will come to them with troops that they will be powerless to confront, and indeed we will drive them out of it debased, and they will be humbled"** (27:36-37). The meaning of these words, according to Ibn Kathir, is, "O messengers, take this gift back to those who sent you. They must come to us either as ***muslims***, accepting God's righteous law as the law of their land in the place of the false law originating from their false beliefs, or as our subjects, submitting to our royal authority."

REFERENCES: Qur'an: 27:21-37. Commentaries: Ibn Kathir/*T*, 27:41; Ibn Kathir/*Q*, "Sulaiman"; Tabari/*H*, III:157-159; Maududi/*Q*, 27:fns. 27, 29-31, 41-42; Ali/*Q*, fn. 3266; Keller/*Reliance*, x300, p. 1090.

THE ENLIGHTENMENT OF THE QUEEN

When the messengers returned to the queen, bringing back her gifts and conveying Solomon's message, she became convinced that he was indeed a true prophet and that no one could fight against him and be victorious. Accordingly, she dispatched a messenger to him, informing him that she was coming to him with all her chiefs in order to be convinced of the truth of his faith and acquire knowledge of it directly from him, thereby coming to terms with him rather than fighting him.

Leaving a deputy in her place to administer affairs, she locked up her immensely valuable throne behind seven doors. And giving instructions to her deputy to guard it carefully, she departed, it is said, together with a great number of chiefs, each of whom was accompanied by thousands of soldiers.

As the queen traveled toward Solomon's country, says Ibn Kathir, the jinn brought him minute-by-minute news of her progress.

"O chiefs," Solomon (A) said to his jinn officers when she approached, **"which of you will bring me her throne before they come to me in submission?"** (27:38).

A powerful one [*'ifrit*] from among the jinn immediately volunteered. **"I will bring it to you before you rise from your place,"** he announced — that is to say, before Solomon (A) had finished sitting in judgment to settle the affairs of his people, as he did from early morning until noontime. **"And indeed I am strong and trustworthy for this"** (27:39), the jinn continued, meaning that he was able to bring the queen's throne to Solomon intact, without any loss of its precious gemstones.

But Solomon (A) declared that he wanted the throne brought more speedily than that. At that, **one who had knowledge of the scripture said, "I will bring it to you before your glance returns to you"** (27:40).

Ibn 'Abbas (R) says that the speaker of these words was Asaf son of Barkhiya, a ***wali*** or holy man from among the Israelites who knew the greatest name of God.[23] Making ablution (***wudu'***) and telling Solomon (A) to raise his eyes and look as far as he could see, he began to call upon his Lord, beseeching Him to bring him the queen's throne.

Instantly the throne came out of the ground in front of the eyes of the entire assemblage. Now, the distance from Jerusalem to Ma'rib, the queen's capitol, is close to 1500 miles as the crow flies. To transport the massive throne which was locked up behind seven doors in a well-guarded palace, or indeed any other object, from such a distance in the blink of an eye is obviously something beyond any human capability. This was, therefore, one of the many miracles granted to Solomon (A), whose purpose in having the throne brought to him before the queen's arrival was to impress upon her the limitless power of God Almighty to do whatever He wills.

And when he saw it placed before him, Solomon (A), humble and devoid of all egotism, ascribed this miracle to the One who had granted it to him. **"This is from my Lord's favor,"** he said, **"to test me, whether I am grateful or ungrateful."** Then, to emphasize the blessings that come from being thankful, he added: **"And whoever is grateful, his gratitude is only for himself, and whoever is ungrateful, then indeed, my Lord is Free of Need and Generous"** (27:40). That is, God Most High has no need of anyone's gratitude. Totally independent of anything He has created, He is the Disposer of all affairs, the Bestower of all favors and grants upon His servants.

"Disguise her throne for her," Solomon (A) then commanded. **"We will see whether she will be guided or will be among those not guided"** (27:41).

---

[23]This is said to have been Asaph son of Berechiah, mentioned in I Chr. 6:39 and 15:17. Both the '*ifrit* who responded to Solomon's request and Asaph possessed the power to bring the queen's throne to Solomon, says Ibn Kathir. However, Asaph's power was more perfect than the jinn's because he was able to bring it with the speed of Solomon's glance, while the jinn, using the powers he possessed, was able bring it with the speed of movement — that is, before Solomon arose from his seat, for, using spiritual power and depending not upon himself but upon his Lord, Asaph was granted the miracle that he had promised, by virtue of his certainty, to Solomon (Ibn Kathir/*T*, 27:38-40).

It is said that Solomon (A) then ordered that some changes be made in the appearance of the throne to test whether or not the queen would have the discernment to recognize it. The impression one gets of the matter is that Solomon, aware of the queen's high intelligence and astuteness of judgment, intended to test her by a parable whose subtlety was suited both to his sagacity in propounding it and to her keen understanding in being able to grasp its meaning.

Then when she arrived, it was said to her, "Is your throne like this?" (27:42).

"It is as though it were it" (27:42), Bilquis replied, puzzled, meaning, "It is similar to it."

Ibn Kathir gives an elaborate analysis of this guarded, non-commital reply of the queen's, saying that she kept it deliberately vague because she did not want to admit outright, based on its appearance, that it *was* her throne. Due to her intelligence and acuteness of understanding, in a moment's time she considered both the possibility that it was her throne and that it was not, for while this throne resembled hers, it was nevertheless absolutely impossible according to human knowledge and experience that it could be it. Thus, because of the evident impossibility of its being her throne and her unawareness of the fact that anyone possessed the power to bring it, guarded as it was, from Yemen to Jerusalem, she answered in a manner that could be understood either way. And here Solomon (A) comments parenthetically, addressing all mankind,

> **"And we were given knowledge before her and we were *muslims*, and what she was worshipping apart from God diverted her. Indeed, she was of a disbelieving people."** (27:42-43)

Now, Solomon (A) had a palace made of glass, which his jinn had built for him. Underneath its glass floor was a cistern of water, in which, it is said, there were fish and other aquatic creatures. The glass of the floor was so smooth and transparent that one would see only the water underneath, unaware that something covered it.

It was then said to her, "Enter the palace." Then when she saw it, she supposed it to be deep water and uncovered her legs (27:44), lifting her skirt to keep it from trailing in the water, as women involuntarily do.

But Solomon (A) gently corrected her. **"Indeed,"** he said, **"it is a palace** whose floor is **made smooth with glass"** (27:44).

The purpose of inviting her into the palace was to impress upon her that there was someone greater than herself in his dominion, his court, his palaces and his wisdom, and that she ought therefore to abandon her

> vanity and pride [says Ibn Kathir]. She was then informed that she was mistaken in her understanding of what she saw: the floor was merely glass and she could proceed without wetting her feet. (Ibn Kathir/*T*, 27:41-44)

Then the queen understood. Keen and observant as she was, she had nonetheless been deceived by appearances. First, she had been unable to recognize and positively identify her familiar throne, whose presence in Solomon's domain was, to all intents and purposes, an impossibility. Then she had been deceived concerning the glass floor, even to the point of mistaking solid glass for water — and the great king Solomon had been witness to her confusion! Not only that, but she had lost her dignity in front of him by uncovering her legs, thereby showing how utterly mistaken she had been in her understanding. Thus, amid her shame and embarrassment, were her preconceptions turned upside-down.

Being so keenly intellgent, the queen immediately grasped the deeper implications of Solomon's subtle metaphor: that her worship of the sun was similarly related to mistaking appearances for reality. And being both wise and capable of humility, she did not hesitate to admit her mistake forthrightly.

"My Lord," she said, turning to her Maker in repentance, **"indeed, I have wronged myself, and I submit, with Solomon, to God, Lord of the worlds!"** (27:44).

According to the report of Ibn 'Abbas (R), Bilqis married Solomon (A). It is said that he returned her to the throne of Yemen, where his jinn constructed three palaces for her. Solomon (A) used to visit her on his platform, staying for three days and nights, and then return home (Ibn Kathir/*T*, 27:41-44).

Much as this story has been embellished over time, it was obviously not reported in the Book of God as a myth or for the purpose of entertainment. In the report of what actually took place between Solomon (A) and Bilquis, we discern a deep lesson about the nature of reality versus the limits of human perception and understanding.

The meaning conveyed by this story is that, regardless of what we may desire, imagine or suppose, reality is not to be confused with our wishes or conjectures, for it is entirely independent of our limited human notions and mental constructs. Rather, it is known only to the Creator, who is *al-Haqq*, the Truth, and who alone is able to inform us of it. Therefore, if we are to be rightly-guided and in conformity with reality or truth, we must conform our understanding to it, not try to make it conform to our own imperfect and often exceedingly incorrect ideas of how it is or should be. This means being willing to admit the incorrectness of our preconceptions, should that become clear to us, and to amend our understanding accordingly — in short, to surrender the partial and incomplete understanding of our minds for the endless knowledge and wisdoms of the Creator.

REFERENCES: Qur'an: 27:38-44. Commentaries: Ibn Kathir/*T*, 27:21-44; Ibn Kathir/*Q*, "Sulaiman"; Tabari/*H*, III:160-163, 167, fn. 845; Maududi/*Q*, 27:fns. 48-49, 55.

9. SOLOMON'S DEATH

And when We decreed death for him, nothing indicated to them his death except a creature of the earth, eating his staff. But when he fell, it became clear to the jinn that if they had had known the Unseen, they would not have remained in the humiliating punishment. (34:14)

The verse above refers to the death of Solomon (S). It is clarified in following *hadith*, in which Ibn 'Abbas (R) reports the Holy Prophet (S) as saying:

> Whenever Solomon, the prophet of God, peace be upon him, prayed, he would see a tree sprouting in front of him, and he would ask it, "What is your name?" and it would reply, "Such-and-such."
>
> Then he would say, "What are you for?" and if it was for planting, it would be planted, and if it was for medicine, it would be sprouted.
>
> One day, while he was praying, he suddenly saw a tree in front of him and he said to it, "What is your name?"
>
> It said, "Carob [*kharrub*]."
>
> He said, "What are you for?"
>
> It said, "For the destruction [*kharab*] of this house."
>
> [Understanding this as an indication of his approaching end,] Solomon said, "O my God, blind the jinn to my death so that people may know that the jinn do not know the Unseen."
>
> Then he cut it into a staff and supported himself upon it, and the jinn continued to labor until the termite [the **"creature of the earth"**] ate it and he fell down.
>
> It then became clear to the humans that if the jinn **had known the Unseen, they would not have remained in the humiliating punishment.** In explaining this verse, Ibn 'Abbas would add parenthetically, "They would not have remained for a year in the humiliating punishment [of forced labor for Solomon]. So the jinn thanked the termite and used to bring it water." (Ibn Kathir/*Q*, "Sulaiman")

The explanation of this verse and *hadith* is as follows:

As is clear from this and a number of other verses, the people of this period had extensive dealings with jinn. The reason for Solomon's prayer for the concealment of his death was that the jinn had deceived the humans into believing that they knew the Unseen, and hence into depending upon the false information the jinn gave them concerning it. When Solomon (A) became aware that his end was approaching, he hoped that when people realized that, despite the jinns' claims of knowledge of the Unseen, they were not even aware of the death of their own master, they would cease to believe in what the jinn communicated to them.

In answer to his prayer, when Solomon (A) died, his body was supported by the staff cut from the tree in such a life-like manner that the jinn did not realize he was dead.[24] Consequently, they continued in bondage to their master for an entire year after his death, until his staff collapsed after being eaten away by the termite and his body fell down. As a result of this, the people realized that if the jinn had really known the Unseen, they would not have continued toiling for Solomon against their will long after his demise.

May God's peace and best blessings be upon His noble prophet Solomon (A), whom He honored and entrusted with such an unparalleled gifts and greatness!

REFERENCES: Ibn Kathir/*Q*, "Sulaiman"; Tabari/*H*, III: 172-174; Maududi/*Q*, 34:fn. 23.

[24]This is also among the miracles that God granted to Solomon, even after his death, for it is obviously impossible for a dead body not to decay for a year, much less to resemble a living person so realistically that he is taken to be alive.

10. THE VINDICATION OF SOLOMON

It was not Solomon who disbelieved. (2:102)

In time, Solomon's prophetic role became obscured among the Jews and they began to ascribe the miraculous powers God had granted him to magic or sorcery, despite the fact that these are among the most heinous of all sins.[25]

Consequently, when the Holy Prophet (S) spoke of Solomon (A) as being among the messengers, the Jews of Medina said, "Are you not amazed at Muhammad? He claims that Solomon, the son of David, was a prophet! By God, he was only a sorcerer" (Tabari/*C*, p. 478), thus echoing what was ascribed to numerous other prophets by their people.

God Most High then revealed :

> **They followed what the satans had recited during the reign of Solomon. It was not Solomon who disbelieved but [rather] the satans disbelieved** (2:102).

These words are part of a lengthy, highly complex verse that has been the subject of much controversy among commentators, both as to its general meaning and the meanings of certain of its words. Since Solomon (A) is mentioned in it in the sentences quoted above only in order to absolve him of the false and baseless charge of unbelief and sorcery that had been leveled against him, we summarize briefly its interpretation, which is as follows:

It is said that, athough certain learned Jews **followed what the satans** or evil jinn **had recited** of magical formulas **during the reign of Solomon, it was not Solomon who disbelieved** by practicing magic and related arts, which, in the law of God, constitute nothing less than unbelief. Rather, it was the satans themselves who disbelieved and imparted such practices to people. And although these events occurred during Solomon's reign, God Most High

---

[25]Magic and other forms of occult practices are strictly prohibited in the Torah (Deut. 18:9-14). In Islam, such practices, which spread unbelief and confusion among people, are considered such grave sins that the Prophet (S) prescribed the death penalty for those who practice them (*Mishkat*, 3551). He named the practice of magic or sorcery as the second of seven "noxious things," the others being *shirk*; taking a life except in the cause of justice; dealing in usury; consuming the wealth of orphans; turning away from the enemy and fleeing from the battlefield; and accusing chaste women (*Bukhari*, 4:28). He also declared that three kinds of people would not enter Paradise: one who is addicted to alcohol, one who breaks the ties of kinship, and one who deals in magic (*Mishkat*, 3656). In his work, *The Major Sins*, the classical scholar al-Dhahabi ranks the practice of magic third (pages 16-17).

proclaims unequivocally that Solomon (A) was no way implicated in them, dissociating him forever from the imputation of sorcery and thus of unbelief (***kufr***). Perhaps this divine refutation of Solomon's unbelief and confirmation of his excellence and acceptability to his Lord may also have been intended to negate the Biblical allegation that "As Solomon grew old, his wives turned his heart after other gods, and his heart was not fully devoted to the Lord his God, as the heart of David his father had been," as well as to what is asserted in subsequent verses concerning the false gods that Solomon is said to have worshipped at the instigation of his foreign wives (1 Kings 11:4-8).

Says Ibn 'Abbas (R):

> The ordinary Jews believed that Solomon was not a prophet but a sorcerer. To clear the name of His true prophet, God Most High, through His Prophet [Muhammad], refuted this belief of the Jews. And since the Jews were averse to considering Solomon as a prophet, God gave some details of this event in this verse. (Ibn Kathir/*T*, 2:102)

And Ibn Kathir comments:

> The story [behind 2:102] in all its details goes back to the rabbis of the Children of Israel. There is no ***sahih*** [sound] ***hadith*** relating it with an unbroken chain of transmission going back to the truthful and infallible one [Muhammad], who does not speak out of caprice (see Q. 53:3). [. . .] We assent therefore to what is narrated in the Qur'an as God the Exalted had intended it, for He knows best the truth of all matters. (Ayoub/*Q*, I:133-134)

REFERENCES: Qur'an: 2:100-102. Commentaries: Tabari/C:I:475-481; Tabari/*H*, III:174; Ibn Kathir/*T*, 2:102; Ibn Ishaq/***Muhammad***, p. 255; Ayoub/*Q*, I:128-136.

11. THE LESSONS OF THE STORIES OF DAVID AND SOLOMON

For all are ranks according to what they have done. And your Lord is not unaware of what they do. (6:132)

From the stories of these two great prophet-kings, especially that of Solomon (A), with all its subtle nuances, important lessons emerge.

One of these is similar to the lesson of the story of Moses and Khidr (A): that God Most High bestows His gifts on whomever He wills, knowing best who is suitable to be the recipient of His grants for the carrying out of His eternal divine plan. And as God's power and dominion are endless and unimaginable, so too are the ranks and gifts that He is able to bestow upon His servants, either through what we perceive as ordinary means and causes, or by the granting of true spiritual powers, miracles or signs.

Now, in contrast to most of the earlier prophets with whose stories we are familiar, David and Solomon (A) were outstanding examples of worldly success and glory. Solomon (A) in particular was without peer among the sovereigns of the world, past or present. But despite the greatness of their ranks, accomplishments, and all the special favors that had been bestowed upon each of them, David and Solomon (A) remained deeply humble servants to their Lord, constantly acknowledging His gifts and blessings with praise and gratitude, as mentioned in Solomon's saying,

> **"My Lord, so dispose me that I may be thankful for Your favors that You have bestowed upon me and upon my parents, and that I may do righteous deeds that will please You. And admit me to Your mercy among Your righteous slaves"** (27:19).

Thus, while they ruled with the full authority of their station and powers, David and Solomon (A) never failed to recognize the Bestower of these grants, ascribing all greatness, glory and praise to Him, and never any trace of it to themselves.

Hence, their stories are a confirmation of God's words, **If you are thankful, indeed, I will grant you increase** (14:7). And this "increase" includes not only rank, power, wealth and other elements pertaining to this world's life, but also ranks of nearness to God Most High, which are the ultimate goal and most fervent desire of those whose hearts are fixed upon their Lord.

We hereby conclude the stories of these two noble prophets, beloved by God, about each of whom He said, in turn, **Indeed, for him is nearness to**

Us and a good place of return (38:25, 40). We hope that this account may have cleared up some of the misconceptions that have gained currency concerning them over the centuries. In the words of the All-Knowing, All-Aware,

> **We have not revealed the Book to you [Muhammad] but that you may make clear to them that wherein they have differed, and as guidance and mercy for a people who believe.** (16:64)

> **Indeed, this Qur'an relates to the Children of Israel most of that wherein they differ.** (27:76)

ELIJAH (A)

And Zechariah and John and Jesus and Elijah — all were among the righteous. (6:85)

And indeed, Elijah was among the messengers. (37:123)

As time passed, misdeeds continued to multiply among the Israelites. The gravest of these was that, forgetting their special relationship and covenant with their beneficent Creator, they adopted idols which they worshipped in His place, following the practices of the pagan peoples among whom they had settled.

This is mentioned in book after book, verse after verse of the Old Testament, as prophets such as Moses, David, Isaiah, Jeremiah and Ezekiel reproached their people for their faithlessness.[1] The books of the latter prophets contain numerous descriptions of the corruption of the Israelites of this period, as well as summaries of the calamities that God sent upon them for their transgressions, which went so far that **Those who disbelieved among the Children of Israel were cursed by the tongue of David and Jesus son of Mary**[2] (5:78/81).

As a result of their wrong-doing, God gave the Israelites into the hands of their enemies, who killed them and destroyed their homes and cities. Many were the invaders who hammered at them over the centuries: the surrounding tribes and nations, followed by the Assyrians, Persians, Greeks and Romans, despoiling their domains and causing untold sufferings to their people.

Nonetheless, despite their transgressions, God continued to call them back to Himself through messenger after messenger. But **whenever a messenger from God came to them, confirming that which was with them, a party of those who had been given the scripture cast God's scripture behind their backs as if they did not know** what it contained (2:101). Thus, the message of many of the Israelite warner-prophets was rejected, and the messengers themselves were denied and even killed,[3] as mentioned in God's saying,

---

[1]See, for example, Num. 25:1-3; Judg. 2:11-13, 3:7, 8:33, 18:30; 2 Ki. 17:7-17; Ps. 50:16-22, 78:7-64, 81:8-12; 106:6-43; Isa. 2:6-9, 3:16-26, 8:7-9, 30:9-17; Jer. 11:6-14 and numerous others.

[2]This verse will be discussed in detail in the story of Jesus, pages 411-413.

[3]The killing of prophets is mentioned in 2:61, 87, 91; 3:21, 112, 183; 4:155; 5:70/73.

We had certainly taken a covenant from the Children of Israel and sent messengers to them. Whenever there came to them a messenger with what their lower selves did not desire, they denied a group and killed another group. And they thought there would be no punishment, so they became blind and deaf. Then God turned to them in forgiveness; then [again] many of them became blind and deaf; and God is Seeing of whatever they do. (5:70/73)

The prophet Elijah or Elias (Arabic, Ilyas), a descendant of Aaron who lived in the northern kingdom of Israel between 875 and 850 B.C., is perhaps the prototype and representative of the Israelite prophets and warners after the time of Solomon (A). Elijah's name is mentioned four times in the Qur'an — twice in the verses cited at the beginning of this chapter and once in a third passage, which, although very brief, tells something of his story.

Elijah (A) was associated with the Israelite king Ahab, who ruled about one hundred years after Solomon (A), and he kept the king's affairs in order, says Ibn Kathir. For a time Ahab listened to Elijah (A) and believed in him, but later he began to worship the god Ba'al and commit other abominations.[4]

Elijah (A) tried to counter this greatest of all sins, calling his people back to their Maker. **"Will you not be mindful of God?"** he admonished. **"Do you call upon Ba'al and forsake the best of Creators — God, your Lord and the Lord of your earliest forefathers?"** (37:124-126).

But they denied him (37:127). And when the king and his people turned away from God's guidance, Elijah (A) prayed against them.

As a result of his prayer, there was no rain for three consecutive years. Consequently, the livestock, insects and trees were destroyed and the people were in misery. Then they came and pleaded with Elijah (A), saying that if he prayed for rain and rain came, they would believe in his prophethood.

Elijah (A) then prayed for rain and the rains came. But still the people turned away from him and refused to abandon their worship of idols. Finally, despairing of them, Elijah (A) prayed to God to relieve him of them and take him to Himself.

---

[4] Ba'al worship was prevalent from Babylon to Egypt, and among the polytheists of Palestine. When the Israelites settled in Palestine, they began to engage in social relations and intermarry with the idol-worshipping peoples around them, thus violating a major injunction of the Torah, and as a result idol-worship began to proliferate among them.

After this supplication, Elijah (A) was commanded to go to a certain place where he would find a steed, upon which he was to mount. Reaching the appointed place, he saw a steed of light and mounted it. Then he too became light and departed to the heavens.[5] As for his people, God says, **"Indeed they will be brought** to punishment, **except God's chosen slaves"** (37:127-128) — those among them who did not deny their prophet and who remained faithful to their Lord.

At the end of this account, which is reported with many more details by al-Tabari, Ibn Kathir says, "All this is reported by the People of the Scripture [Jews and Christians], and only God knows what is true" (Ibn Kathir/*T*, 37:123-132).

May God's blessings be upon Elijah, God's honored prophet, whom He memorialized by saying,

> **And We left [this invocation] for him among later generations: "Peace be upon Elijah!" Indeed, thus do We reward the doers of good. Indeed, he was among Our believing slaves.** (37:129-132)

REFERENCES: Qur'an: 6:85; 37:123-132. Commentaries: Ibn Kathir/*T*, 5:70-71/73-74, 37:123-132; Ibn Kathir/*Q*, "Ilyas"; Tabari/*H*, III:122-125; Maududi/*Q*, 17:fns. 6-7, 7:fns. 70-72, 37:fn. 71; Asad/*Q*, 37:fn. 48; Ali/*Q*, fn. 4112.

---

[5]Because of this, the Jews believed that Elijah would return to the earth, as prophesied in Mal. 4:5. Thus, it is reported that when John began to baptize people, he was asked if he was Elijah (John 1:21) (see page 487). The same was later supposed of Jesus (Mark 6:15).

ELISHA (A)

And Ishmael and Elisha and Jonah and Lot — and all [of them] We preferred above mankind. (6:86)

And remember Ishmael, Elisha and Dhul-Kifl — and all were among the excellent. (38:48)

When Elijah (A) was taken up, Elisha son of Shapat (Arabic, Alyasa' bin Akhtub) succeeded him as prophet and messenger to the Israelites. While Elisha (A) is mentioned in the Qur'an in the two verses cited above, nothing is reported concerning his life, and the classical commentators also report nothing authoritative concerning him.

Ibn Kathir states that Elisha (A) conveyed God's Message as long as He desired him to, calling his people to Him and asking them to follow the system of Elijah and his law until God took his soul. Then, after his time, the Israelites became oppressive and rebellious and killed their prophets.

May God's blessings be upon the prophet whom He mentions with such high commendation in the verses above!

REFERENCES: Commentaries: Ibn Kathir/*T*, 37:123-132; Ibn Kathir/*Q*, "Alyasa'"; Tabari/*H*, III:124-125; Ayoub/*Q*, I:238.

DHUL-KIFL (A)

And [mention] Ishmael and Idris and Dhul-Kifl; all were of the patient. And We admitted them into Our mercy; indeed, they were among the righteous. (21:86)

And remember Ishmael, Elisha and Dhul-Kifl — and all were among the excellent. (38:48)

Another prophet mentioned in the Qur'an who is believed to be among the prophets of Israel is Dhul-Kifl (A). But since nothing of his story is told either in the Qur'an or in *ahadith*, and he is mentioned only in the two verses above, his true identity is not known.

Some classical commentators, such as al-Tabari and Abu Musa al-Ash'ari, state that Dhul-Kifl (A) was not a prophet but a righteous man who prayed a hundred *rak'ats* each day. However, the majority of commentators consider him a prophet because of God's mentioning him together with prophets in the verses above.

Actually, "Dhul-Kifl" is not a name but rather a title, one meaning of which is "he who takes responsibility". It was given to him, it is said, because he took upon himself the observance of certain devotions, such as the lengthy prayers mentioned above. We note that 21:86 cited above mentions patience as a special quality of Dhul-Kifl's, and patience would certainly have been a quality of one undertaking such intensive worship, as well as of the other prophets with whom Dhul-Kifl has been identified, who are as follows:

1. Some commentators maintain that Dhul-Kifl (A) was Job's son Bishr. It is said that God commanded Bishr to call people to acknowledge His Oneness, and he remained in Syria all his life until his death at the age of seventy-five. The people of Damascus say that his grave is on Mount Qasiyun, the mountain of Damascus.

2. Other commentators say that Dhul-Kifl (A) was the third prophet to succeed Moses (A) after Joshua (A) and Caleb, identifying him with Hazqil, who in turn has been identified with the prophet Ezekiel.

3. Another possible meaning of "Dhul-Kifl" is "He of the guarantee." One interpretation connected with this meaning is that he was so named because he guaranteed to settle the affairs of people with justice. Another interpretation is that he was called Dhul-Kifl (A) because he told certain wicked Israelites that on a given day he would guarantee the appearance of seventy prophets whom they wanted to kill. Risking his life, he told the prophets to flee, for it was better that he be killed than all of them. Then, when the

would-be killers came to inquire about the prophets, Dhul-Kifl (A) informed them that they had gone and he did not know where. And God protected him from them.

4. Still other commentators have identified Dhul-Kifl (A) with Samuel (A), since both were said to have been born to aged, barren women. Others have identified him with Elijah (A).

5. Another opinion, held by Ibn 'Abbas (R), Mujahid and other commentators, is that Dhul-Kifl (A) was the successor of the prophet Elisha (A), whose name is mentioned together with his in 38:48 at the beginning of this chapter. These commentators tell the following story:

When Elisha (A) became old, he thought of appointing a successor while he was still alive to see how he would carry out his duties. He therefore assembled the people and said, "If anyone promises to do three things, I will appoint him as my successor: he should fast during the day, pray during the night, and never get angry."

"I will do it," said a man who was considered lowly among the people.

Elisha (A) postponed his decision until the following day, when he again repeated the same thing. Again the same person stood up, repeating, "I will do it." Elisha (A) then appointed him as his successor.

Then Satan ordered his helpers to go and distract the newly-appointed successor. When they were unable to do so, Satan himself took charge. Assuming the form of a poor old man, he went to the house of Elisha's successor in the afternoon — the only time he slept due to his praying throughout the night — and knocked at the door.

When the successor awoke and came to the door, the old man told him a long story in which he claimed to have been treated unjustly by his people, holding him in conversation until the successor's time of sleep had passed.

"Come to me in the evening and I will settle your affair," the successor said to the old man. But that evening, when the newly-appointed prophet went to his assembly and looked for him, he did not appear, nor he did come the following morning while the prophet was dispensing justice among the people. But at the time of his afternoon sleep, the old man reappeared and started knocking at his door.

A dialogue similar to that of the preceding day ensued, resulting in the prophet's again losing his sleep, and again the old man did not appear at the assembly in the evening. On the third day, however, the prophet posted a guard at his door.

The prophet then awoke, and seeing that the old man had gotten inside without permission, understood.

"Are you the enemy of God?" he asked.

"Yes," said Satan, "and I did all this to see whether you would get angry."

Consequently, because he had fulfilled the guarantee that he had given to Elisha (A), God called the prophet "Dhul-Kifl" (Ibn Kathir/*T*, 21:85-86; Ibn Kathir/*Q*, "Dhul-Kifl"). May God's best blessings be upon him!

REFERENCES: Qur'an: 21:86; 38:48. Tabari/*H*, II:143; Ibn Kathir/*T*, 21:85-86; Ibn Kathir/*Q*, "Dhul-Kifl"; Maududi/*Q*, 21:fn. 81; Ayoub/*Q*, I:233; Keller/*Reliance*, x115, p. 1045.

JONAH (A)

1. JONAH'S MISSION

. . . We revealed to Abraham and Ishmael and Isaac and Jacob and the descendants [of Israel], and Jesus and Job and Jonah . . . (4:163)

Indeed, Jonah was among the messengers. (37:139)

Jonah son of Amittai (Arabic, Yunus bin Matta) was a prophet whom God sent to the people of Nineveh, the capital of the kingdom of Assyria.

Nineveh was an ancient and famous city, so large that its circumference is said to have been about sixty miles. Among its remains, which are scattered on the left bank of the Tigris River opposite the city of Mosul in what is now Iraq, is a mound bearing the inscription, "*Nabi Yunus*" — that is, the prophet Jonah (A), who is believed to have dwelt there during the first half of the eighth century B.C.

Jonah (A) is mentioned in six *surahs* of the Qur'an — four times by his given name,[1] once as **the companion of the fish (*sahibi-l-hut*)** (68:48), and once as **he of the fish (*dha-n-nun*)** (21:87).

Jonah (A) was granted certain special honors and distinctions by his Lord. One of these is that the tenth *surah* of the Qur'an, *Yunus*, is named for him. Another is that he is the only prophet mentioned in the Qur'an whose sinful people repented and were thus spared divine punishment. And third, he was granted a very special supplication, which we will mention in its place.

Ibn 'Abbas (R) and other classical commentators report that when God ordered Jonah (A) to call the idol-worshipping people of Nineveh to Himself, they denied him and became arrogant in their unbelief and misdeeds.

When this state of affairs had continued for a long time, Jonah (A) informed his people that divine punishment would descend upon them after three days. Then he left them.

Subsequently, God Most High cast repentance and humility into the hearts of his people, and they regretted what they had done to their prophet. So they put on sackcloth and gathered in an open space outside the city,

---

[1]In two of these four verses (10:98, 37:13), Jonah is mentioned by himself, while in two others (4:163, 6:86) he is mentioned together with a number of other prophets.

where they separated the domesticated animals from their young so that they would bleat and moo, and they all supplicated God Most High for forgiveness, beseeching and crying to Him. Then the punishment, which had been made to hang over their heads like a dark cloud, was averted by the decree of the Most Merciful.

REFERENCES: Qur'an: 21:87; 37:139-140; 68:48. Commentaries: Tabari/*H*, IV:160-163, 165; Ibn Kathir/*Q*, "Yunus"; Maududi/Q, 37:fn. 85, 10:fn. 98.

2. THE FISH

And [mention] him of the fish, when he went away angry and he supposed that We would not decree [anything] for him. (21:87)

Indeed, Jonah was among the messengers, when he ran away to the laden ship. Then he cast lots and was of the losers. Then the fish swallowed him, while he was blameworthy. (37:139-142)

Upon learning that the punishment he had promised on a given day had been averted, Jonah (A) **went away angry** (21:87) with his Lord because he had been made to seem a liar, and thus he fell into Satan's trap. And supposing **that** God **would not decree for him** (21:87) anything out of the ordinary, **he ran away to the laden ship**[2] (37:140) — that is, a ship that was already heavily weighed down with its load.

Presently a storm struck. Understanding that it had occurred as divine retribution for the sins of someone on board, the crew cast lots to determine his identity.

Jonah (A) too cast lots with them, and he **was of the losers** (37:141). It is said that after the lot had fallen to him three times, he threw himself, by night, into the sea. Then, by the divine will, a whale or a huge **fish swallowed him, while he was blameworthy** (37:142).

A number of reasons have been suggested for Jonah's blameworthiness. According to some commentators, it was because of his haste in leaving his city before God commanded him to do so, contrary to the way of the prophets, due to his certainty of the inevitability of the punishment, thereby abandoning his divinely-appointed mission despite the possibility that the punishment might yet be averted. Others say that Jonah's fault was that he did not return to continue his mission with his people when he learned that the punishment had been averted. Still others suggest that Jonah (A) was blameworthy because he abandoned his people in anger due to their refusal to believe, or because he himself had fixed the day of the punishment, although God had not done so, and then he became angry because God had falsified his threat.

When Jonah (A) found himself in the belly of the fish, says Ibn Kathir, he supposed himself to be dead. Then, finding that his limbs worked when he moved them, he understood that he was still alive. And he fell down in pros-

---

[2]The verb here is "***abaqa***," which denotes the running away of a slave from his master.

tration to God the Exalted, saying, "O Lord, I have taken a place of prayer [*masjidan*] in a spot where no one has ever worshipped You before."

Then, Ibn Kathir continues, the fish dived into the ocean. And Jonah (A) heard the praise of the fishes, and even the praise of the pebbles, to the **Cleaver of the Grain and the Date Seed** (6:95), the Lord of the seven heavens and the seven earths and whatever is between them and whatever is under the earth, whether this praise is through their existence or through words, as God has informed us.

And **while he was distressed** (68:48), **he called out in the darknesses,**[3] **"There is no deity but You, glory be to You! Indeed, I have been among the wrong-doers"** (21:87), thus confessing his fault, expressing his repentance, and glorifying his Lord. And God Most High says,

> **And if he had not been of those who glorify [God], he would have remained in its belly until the Day they are resurrected. (37:142-144)**

The meaning of these words, according to Sa'id ibn Jubayr (R), is that if Jonah (A) had not glorified God there, had not worshipped Him with humility, repented to Him and implored His forgiveness, he would have remained in the fish's belly until the Day of Judgment and would have been resurrected from it. Other commentators, however, say that it means that he was **of those who glorify** — that is, a worshipper and an obedient servant who remembered God — before entering the fish (Ibn Kathir/*Q*, "Yunus").

We are not told how long Jonah (A) remained in the fish's belly. It has been said that it was for a morning or an evening, three days, seven days, or as long as forty days, but only God knows how much time passed over him in that terrible prison. Then, God says, **We** responded **to him and saved him** from the distress, adding: **And thus do We save the believers** (21:88).

Then God caused Jonah (A), to be cast, naked, onto **the bare shore while he was ill** (37:145) from the awful effects of his sojourn in the fish's stomach.[4] And He **caused a gourd vine to grow over him** (37:146) to shelter

---

[3]According to Ibn 'Abbas, Ibn Mas'ud and other commentators, the **"darknesses"** mentioned here refer to the darkness inside the fish, the darkness of the ocean, and the darkness of night (Ibn Kathir/*T*, 21:87).

[4]If a person's coming alive out of a fish's stomach sounds impossible, Maulana Maududi reports a similar occurrence off the coast of England in 1891, when a group of fishermen shipped out to sea to hunt whales. In front of their eyes, a fisherman named James Bartley was swallowed by a huge fish that had been injured. The following day the fish was found dead at sea. "The fisher-

and nourish him.[5] The distinguished Companion, Abu Hurayrah (R), said that God caused female antelopes and other animals that eat grass or soft sod to come to this plant and water it with their milk each morning and evening until it grew (Tabari/*H*, IV:166). It is also said God sent a wild she-goat to come and feed Jonah (A) milk because he was as weak as a new born baby or birdling, hardly able to breathe and without power to move.

Now, a subtle meaning is contained in God's words,

> **Then the fish swallowed him while he was blameworthy, and if he had not been of those who glorify, he would have remained in its belly until the Day they are resurrected.** (37:142-144)

That is, when Jonah (A) was swallowed by the fish, he was blameworthy for having abandoned his mission without God's order or permission, and possibly for the other reasons we have mentioned. This is alluded to in God's instructions to Muhammad (S), centuries later:

> **Be patient for the decision of your Lord and do not be like the Companion of the Fish, when he called out, while he was distressed** (68:48),

thereby advising the Holy Prophet to have patience with whatever his Lord might decree under all circumstances. This admonition was followed by the words,

> **If it had not been that a favor from his Lord reached him [Jonah], he would have been cast onto the bare shore while he was blameworthy, but his Lord chose him and made him among the righteous.** (68:49-50)

This indicates that after Jonah (A) had repented, confessed his fault and glorified his Lord inside the fish, when he was thrown up on the shore, he had

---

men hauled it up on board and when they cut open its belly, James Bartley came out alive. He had remained in the fish's belly for full 60 hours" (Maududi/*Q*, 37:fn. 82).

[5]In the Qur'an this plant is called ***"yaqtin"***. When asked what variety of plant Jonah's was, Abu Hurayrah stated that it was a vegetable of this kind (Tabari/H, IV:166) — that is, a species that does not stand on a stem but grows and spreads like a creeper, such as gourd, squash, pumpkin, cucumber, melon and the like. Ibn Kathir comments that the benefits of such a plant are that it grows very quickly, its leaves are broad and give good shade, flies do not come near it, and its produce can be eaten without peeling (Ibn Kathir/*T*, 37:146). The Holy Prophet (S) liked this kind of vegetable very much and would especially select it for eating from the serving dish (***Bukhari***, 7:344 7:346-348, 7:350, ***Muwatta***, 28.21.51).

been absolved of blame as **a favor from his Lord,** who **chose him and made him among the righteous** (68:49-50).

Jonah's ordeal is mentioned in a moving *hadith*. Abu Hurayrah (R) reported the Holy Prophet (S) as saying:

> When God desired to imprison Jonah in the fish's belly, He inspired to the fish, "Take him, but do not nip his flesh or break his bones." And when it moved with him to the bottom of the sea, Jonah heard a sound and said to himself, "What is this?"
>
> God then revealed to him while he was in the fish's belly, "This is the glorification of the creatures of the sea," and so he glorified God while he was in the fish's belly.
>
> The angels heard his glorification and they said, "O our Lord, we hear a weak voice from a strange place."
>
> He said, "That is My slave Jonah. He disobeyed Me, so I have imprisoned him in the belly of the fish at sea."
>
> They said, "The righteous slave, whose good deeds used to ascend to You day and night?"
>
> God said, "Yes."
>
> Then they interceded for him concerning it (saying, according to another version, "O our Lord, will You not show mercy to him who did what he did while he was in ease, in order to relieve him of this difficulty?"). So the fish was ordered to cast him onto the shore, as God said, **while he was ill** [37:145]. (Ibn Kathir/*Q*, "Yunus")

Eventually Jonah (A) returned to his people, or, according to another opinion, was sent to another people, for God says:

> **We sent him to a hundred thousand or more, and they believed, so We granted them enjoyment [of their lives] for a time (37:147-148),**

meaning that his people were permitted to continue their lives for their natural duration rather than being obliterated as a community by a sudden catastrophic punishment. Consequently, Jonah (A) occupies a unique position among all the prophets because, after hearing God's warnings from his lips, his people believed, repented and reformed. It is said that no decreed punishment was ever revoked except in the case of Jonah's people, according to God's words,

> **Has there not then been any city that believed so that its faith benefitted it except the people of Jonah? When they believed, We**

averted from them the punishment of disgrace in the life of this world and granted them enjoyment for a time. (10:98)

REFERENCES: Qur'an: 10:98; 21:87-88; 37:139-148; 68:48-50. Commentaries: Ibn Kathir/*Q*, "Yunus"; Ibn Kathir/*T*, 21:87, 37:139-148; Tabari/*H*, IV:160-166; Maududi/*Q*, 37:fns. 78, 80-83, 85, 21:fns. 84-85, 68:fn. 34, 10:fn. 100; Asad/*Q*, 37:fn. 54, 10:fn. 120; Ali/*Q*, fn. 4122.

3. JONAH'S SUPPLICATION

And he called out in the darknesses, "There is no deity except You, glory be to You! Indeed, I have been among the wrong-doers." Then We responded to him and saved him from the distress. And thus do We save the believers. (21:87-88)

Jonah's powerful supplication, uttered while in the belly of the fish, is one that is familiar and dear to Muslims, who use it frequently in times of crisis or need.

This supplication consists of three parts. The first, ***"La ilaha illa-Anta*** **— There is no deity except You,"** is a restatement of the Islamic testification to God's Oneness, "*La ilaha illa-Llah,* there is no deity except God." This constitutes the greatest of all words of praise, as stated in a *hadith* mentioning that God said to Moses,

> O Moses, if the seven heavens and their inhabitants, apart from Me, and the seven earths were put on one side of a scale and "*La ilaha illa-Llah*" on the other, "*La ilaha illa-Llah*" would outweigh them [all]. (*Mishkat*, 2306)

The Prophet (S) also said:

> Never does a slave [of God] say "*La ilaha illa-Llah*" sincerely without the doors of Heaven being opened for him, even reaching to the Throne [of God], as long as he avoids the major sins. (*Mishkat*, 2310)

The second part of this supplication, ***"Subhanaka*** **— glory be to You!"** is the acknowledgement of God's sovereignty, power and dominion, and the proclamation of His infinite glory and greatness. And the third, ***"Inni kuntu min adh-dhalimin*** **— indeed, I have been among the wrong-doers,"** is the sincere confession of sin and expression of repentance.

Concerning Jonah's supplication, the Holy Prophet (S) said,

> No Muslim supplicates with the supplication of Dha-n-Nun [He of th Fish] with which he supplicated his Lord while he was in the belly of the fish, ***"La ilaha illa Anta, subhanaka! Inni kuntu min adh-dhalimin,"*** without its being answered for him. (*Mishkat*, 2289)
>
> There is no worried person who supplicates with this supplication without its being answered for him. (Abu Dawud)

And the Prophet's Companion, S'ad bin Malik (R), reported,

> I heard the Prophet (S) say, "The appellation of God to which, if He is called by it, He responds and if He is asked by it, He gives, is that of the supplication of Jonah son of Matta." Then I said, "O Messenger of

> God, was that for Jonah specifically or for all the Muslims collectively?" He said, "It was for Jonah specifically and for the believers in general when they supplicate by it. Have you not heard the saying of God Most High, **"And he called out in the darknesses, 'There is no deity except You, glory be to You! Indeed, I have been among the wrong-doers.' Then We responded to him and saved him from the distress. And thus do We save the believers"** [21:88]. And that is a provision from God for whomever supplicates Him by it." (Ibn Kathir/*Q*, "Yunus")

Thus, the experience of Jonah (A) is both a lesson and a source of blessing and benefit for believers, for the powerful supplication that he uttered in the most distressful situation imaginable remains a source of mercy for all who call upon their Lord by means of it. May God's peace and blessings be on Jonah for all eternity!

REFERENCES: Ibn Kathir/*T*, 21:87; Ibn Kathir/*Q*, "Yunus".

FURTHER *AHADITH* CONCERNING JONAH

And Ishmael and Elisha and Jonah and Lot — and all [of them] We preferred above mankind. (6:86)

A number of other *ahadith* have come down to us concerning Jonah (A), as follows:

1. The Holy Prophet (S) strongly discouraged anyone's criticizing or passing judgment on Jonah (A), saying:

> I do not say that there is anyone better than Jonah son of Matta. (*Bukhari*, 4:626; *Muslim*, 5853).
>
> It is not befitting for anyone to be better than the son of Matta. (*Bukhari*, 6:328, 6:154-6:155)
>
> It is not befitting for a slave [of God] to say, "I am better than Jonah son of Matta." (*Bukhari*, 4:608, 4:624-4:625, 6:127, 9:630; *Muslim*, 5859-5861)
>
> Whoever says, "I am better than Jonah son of Matta," has lied. (*Bukhari*, 6:128, 6:329)

2. Previously we mentioned the Prophet's saying, while passing through the valley of Azraq near Mecca, that it was as if he were seeing Moses coming down the mountain trail, putting his fingers in his ears and making *talbiyah*, the pilgrims' call.

In the continuation of this *hadith*, it is reported that when the Prophet (S) came to another mountain track, he asked its name, and on being told that it was Harsha, he said, "It is as if I see Jonah son of Matta on his red camel with a woollen coat around him. The halter of his camel is of palm fibre. He is passing through that valley, making *talbiyah*" (*Muslim*, 318, 319; *Mishkat*, 26.16.1). This indicates that, like Moses, Jonah (A) made *Hajj* to the Sacred House of God in Mecca, either spiritually or during his lifetime in this world.

3. The prophet Jonah (A) also figures in a moving incident in the life of the Holy Prophet (S), which is as follows:

After years of rejection of God's Message by the idolaters of Mecca, Muhammad (S) went to the nearby city of Ta'if in an attempt to call its people to Islam.

There, he met with three of its leading men, but they spoke insultingly to him and stirred up their slaves and louts to insult and shout at him until a crowd had gathered against him, forcing him to take refuge in an orchard.

Once he had entered it, the crowd began to disperse. And tethering his camel to a palm tree, he made for the shelter of a vine and sat in its shade.

Now, Ta'if is a green and fertile place, where the Meccans liked to own property. The orchard in which the Prophet (S) had taken refuge belonged to two prominent Meccan brothers, 'Utbah and Shaybah bin Rabi'ah, and the two happened to be sitting in a corner of their garden when Muhammad (S) entered it. They had witnessed what the rabble had done to him and were indignant about the way they had treated a man of their tribe, the Quraysh, especially one having the same ancestor as theirs, 'Abdu Manaf.

When the Prophet (S) reached a place of safety in the orchard, he spoke to his Lord, saying, "O God, to You do I complain about the weakness of my power, the feebleness of my resources, and my insignificance before the people. O Most Merciful of the Merciful, You are the Lord of the oppressed and You are my Lord! To whom will You entrust me: to some distant stranger who will be displeased with me or to an enemy to whom You will give control over my affairs?

"If You are not angry with me, I do not care, but Your guarantee of protection is more spacious for me. I take refuge in the light of Your Face, by which darknesses are illuminated and the affairs of this world and the Hereafter are rightly-ordered, lest Your anger descend on me or your displeasure fall on me. It is for You to censure me until You are well-pleased with me. There is no power and no might except with You!"

Although they were idolaters, 'Utbah and Shaybah felt compassion for Muhammad (S). So they called a young Christian slave of theirs named 'Addas, instructing him to put a bunch of grapes on a platter and give them to Muhammad (S) to eat.

'Addas did as he had been told. And as the Prophet (S) put his hand to the grapes, he said, "In the name of God," before eating.

'Addas looked keenly at his face. "By God," he exclaimed, "those words are not what the people of this country say!"

"Then what country are you from," the Prophet (S) enquired, "and what is your religion?"

"I am a Christian of the people of Nineveh," 'Addas replied.

"From the town of the righteous man, Jonah son of Matta!" the Prophet (S) exclaimed.

"How do you know about Jonah son of Matta?" 'Addas asked in surprise.

"He is my brother," the Prophet (S) replied. "He was a prophet and I am a prophet." Then 'Addas bent over him, kissing his head and his hands and feet.

When 'Utbah and Shaybah saw this, they exclaimed to one another, as if with one voice, "So much for your slave! He has already been corrupted." And when 'Addas returned to them, leaving the Prophet (S) to eat the grapes, they said, "Shame on you, 'Addas! What made you kiss that man's head and his hands and his feet?"

"Master, there is nothing on earth better than this man," 'Addas replied confidently. "He has told me about things that only a prophet could know."

"Shame on you!" they exclaimed, their compassion now turning to anger. "Do not let him seduce you from your religion, for your religion is better than his."

REFERENCES: Ibn Ishaq/*Muhammad*, pp. 192-193; Martin Lings/*Muhammad*, pp. 98-99.

QUR'ANIC REFERENCES — THE PROPHETS OF ISRAEL

2:102

And they followed what the satans had recited during the reign of Solomon. It was not Solomon who disbelieved but [rather] the satans disbelieved.

2:246-252

Have you not considered the council of the Children of Israel after Moses, when they said to a prophet of theirs, "Send to us a king and we will fight in the cause of God."

He said, "Might it perhaps be that, if fighting were prescribed for you, you would not fight?

They said, "And why should we not fight in the cause of God when we have been driven away from our homes and our children?" But when fighting was prescribed for them, they turned away, except a few of them. And God is Knowing of the wrong-doers. (246)

And their prophet said to them, "Indeed, God has sent to you Saul as king."

They said, "How can he have kingship over us while we are more worthy of kingship than he and he has not been given any measure of wealth?"

He said, "Indeed, God has chosen him above you and has increased him abundantly in knowledge and stature. And God grants His sovereignty to whomever He wills. And God is All-Encompassing and Aware." (247)

And their prophet said to them, "Indeed, a sign of his kingship is that the Ark will come to you, wherein is the *Sakinah* from your Lord and a remnant of what the family of Moses and the family of Aaron left behind, carried by angels. In that is surely a sign for you, if you are believers." (248)

And when Saul went forth with the troops, he said, "Indeed, God will test you by a river. Therefore, whoever drinks of it is not of me, and whoever does not taste it, indeed he is of me, except him who [merely] takes [a sip] in the hollow of his hand." But they drank from it, except a few of them.

Then, when he had crossed it, he and those who believed with him, they said, "We have no power this day against Goliath and his troops."

But those who were certain that they would meet God said, "How many a small company has overcome a large company by God's leave! And God is with the patient." (249) And when they went forth to Goliath and his troops, they said, "Our Lord, pour out upon us patience and make our feet firm, and grant us victory over the disbelieving people." (250)

Then they defeated them by God's leave and David killed Goliath, and God granted him kingship and wisdom, and taught him of whatever He willed. And if God did not check some people by means of others, the earth would have been corrupted, but God is full of bounty to mankind. (251)

These are God's verses which We recite to you [Muhammad] in truth. And indeed, you are among the messengers. (252)

4:163

Indeed, We have revealed to you [Muhammad] as We revealed to Noah and the prophets after him; and We revealed to Abraham and Ishmael and Isaac and Jacob and the descendants [of Israel], and Jesus and Job and Jonah and Aaron and Solomon, and We granted David the *Zabur*.

5:78/81

Those who disbelieved among the Children of Israel were cursed by the tongue of David and Jesus son of Mary. That was because they disobeyed and transgressed the limits.

6:84-87

And We granted him [Abraham] Isaac and Jacob; each [of them] We guided. And previously We guided Noah, and among his descendants, David and Solomon and Job and Joseph and Moses and Aaron. And thus do We reward the doers of good. (84) And Zechariah and John and Jesus and Elijah — all were among the righteous; (85) and Ishmael and Elisha and Jonah and Lot — and all [of them] We preferred above mankind, (86) and some from among their fathers and descendants and brothers, and We chose them and guided them to a straight path. (87)

10:98

Has there not then been any city that believed so that its faith benefitted it except the people of Jonah? When they believed, We averted from them the punishment of disgrace in the life of this world and granted them enjoyment for a time.

17:55

And We certainly caused some prophets to excel others, and We granted David the *Zabur*.

21:78-82, 85-88

And [mention] David and Solomon, when they gave judgment concerning the field, when people's sheep strayed into it, and We were witness to their judgment. (78) And We caused Solomon to understand it, and to each We granted judgment and knowledge.

And We subjected the mountains to glorify with David, and the birds, and We were doing [this]. (79) And We taught him the fabrication of coats of armor for you, that you might fortify yourselves against your [mutual] violence. So will you then be thankful? (80)

And to Solomon [We subjected] the wind, blowing forcefully, proceeding by his command toward the land which We had blest. And We are ever Knowing of all things. (81) And among the satans were those who dived for him and did work other than that, and We were Guardian of them. (82)

. . . And Ishmael, Idris and Dhul-Kifl — all were among the patient. (85) And We admitted them to Our mercy. Indeed, they were among the righteous. (86)

And [mention] him of the fish, when he went away angry and he supposed that We would not decree [anything] for him. And he called out in the darknesses, "There is no deity except You, glory be to You! Indeed, I have been among the wrong-doers." (87) Then We responded to him and saved him from the distress. And thus do We save the believers. (88)

27:15-44

And We certainly granted David and Solomon knowledge, and they said, "Praise be to God, who favored us over many of His believing slaves." (15)

And Solomon inherited David. And he said, "O people, we have been taught the language of birds and we have been given of all things. Indeed, this is a manifest grace." (16)

And his troops of jinn and human and birds were gathered for Solomon, and they were [marching] in measured order, (17) until, when they came to the valley of the ants, an ant said, "O ants, go into your dwellings, that you not be crushed by Solomon and his troops while they are unaware." (18)

Then he smiled, amused at her speech, and said, "My Lord, so dispose me that I may be thankful for Your favors which You have bestowed upon me and upon my parents, and that I may do righteous deeds which will please You. And admit me to Your mercy among Your righteous slaves." (19)

And he reviewed the birds and said, "Why do I not see the hoopoe, or is he among the absentees? (20) I will surely punish him with a severe punishment or slaughter him unless he brings me a clear authority. (21)

But he did not remain [absent] long, and he said, "I have encompassed [in knowledge] that which you have not encompassed, and I have come to you from Sheba with sure information. (22)

"Indeed, I found a woman ruling them, and she has been given of everything and has a magnificent throne. (23) I found her and her people prostrating to the sun instead of God, and Satan has made their deeds pleasing to them and diverted them from the way so they are not guided" — (24) so they do not prostrate to

God, who brings forth whatever is hidden in the heavens and the earth, and knows what you conceal and what you disclose. (25) God — there is no deity except Him, Lord of the glorious Throne! (26)

He [Solomon] said, "We shall see whether you are truthful or are of the liars. (27) Take this letter of mine and deliver it to them. Then withdraw from them and see what they will send back." (28)

She said, "O nobles, there has surely been delivered to me a distinguished letter. (29) Indeed, it is from Solomon and indeed, it is, 'In the name of God, the Merciful, the Compassionate. (30) Do not be haughty toward me but come to me in submission.'" (31)

She said, "O nobles, advise me in my affair. I will not decide any matter unless you are present with me." (32)

They said, "We are men of strength and great military might, but the command is yours; therefore, consider what you will command." (33)

She said, "Surely, kings, when they enter a city, ruin it and render its most honored people the most abased, and thus do they do. (34) But indeed, I shall send them a gift and then see with what the envoys will return." (35)

Then when they came to Solomon, he said, "Would you assist me with wealth? But what God has given me is better than what He has given you. Rather, it is you who rejoice in your gift! (36) Return to them, for indeed we will come to them with troops that they will be powerless to confront, and indeed we will drive them out of it abased, and they will be humbled." (37)

He said, "O chiefs, which of you will bring me her throne before they come to me in submission?" (38)

A powerful one from among the jinn said, "I will bring it to you before you rise from your place, and indeed I am strong and trustworthy for this." (39)

One who had knowledge of the scripture said, "I will bring it to you before your glance returns to you."

And when he saw it placed before him, he said, "This is from my Lord's favor, to test me, whether I am grateful or ungrateful. And whoever is grateful, his gratitude is only for himself, and whoever is ungrateful, then indeed, my Lord is Free of Need and Generous." (40)

He said, "Disguise her throne for her; we shall see whether she will be guided or will be among those not guided." (41)

Then, when she arrived, it was said, "Is your throne like this?"

She said, "It is as though it were it."

[Solomon said,] "And we were given knowledge before her and we were *muslims*, (42) and what she was worshipping apart from God diverted her. Indeed, she was of a disbelieving people." (43)

It was said to her, "Enter the palace." Then when she saw it, she supposed it to be deep water and uncovered her legs.

He said, "Indeed, it is a palace [whose floor is] made smooth with glass."

She said, "My Lord, indeed I have wronged myself, and I submit, with Solomon, to God, Lord of the worlds!" (44)

34:10-14

And We certainly granted David favor from Ourselves. [We said,] "O mountains, repeat [Our praise] with him, and birds!" And We made iron malleable for him, [saying,] (10) "Make full coats of mail and calculate the links, and work righteousness. Indeed, I am Seeing of whatever you do." (11)

And to Solomon [We subjected] the wind, its morning [journey] a month and its afternoon [journey] a month; and We caused a spring of copper to flow for him. And among the jinn were those who labored for him, by his Lord's leave. And whoever deviated from Our command among them, We will cause him to taste of the punishment of the blazing Fire! (12)

They made for him whatever he desired of elevated chambers, images, basins like reservoirs, and stationary cauldrons. "Work, O family of David, in gratitude!" But few of My servants are grateful. (13)

And when We decreed death for him, nothing indicated to them his death except a creature of the earth, eating his staff. But when he fell, it became clear to the jinn that if they had had known the Unseen, they would not have remained in the humiliating punishment. (14)

37:123-132

And indeed, Elijah was among the messengers, (123) when he said to his people, "Will you not be mindful of God? (124) Do you call upon Ba'al and forsake the Best of Creators — (125) God, your Lord and the Lord of your earliest forefathers?" (126) But they denied him, so indeed they will be brought [to punishment], (127) except God's chosen slaves. (128) And We left [this invocation] for him among later generations: (129) "Peace be upon Elijah!" (130) Indeed, thus do We reward the doers of good. (131) Indeed, he was among Our believing slaves. (132)

37:139-148

Indeed, Jonah was among the messengers, (139) when he ran away to the laden ship. (140) Then he cast lots and was of the losers. (141) Then the fish swallowed him, while he was blameworthy, (142) and if he had not been of those who glorify, (143) he would have remained in its belly until the Day they are resurrected. (144) Then We cast him onto the bare shore while he was ill; (145) and We caused a gourd vine to grow over him; (146) and We sent him to a hundred thousand or more, (147) and they believed, so We granted them enjoyment for a time. (148)

38:17-26

Be patient concerning what they say and recall Our slave, David, the possessor of strength; indeed, he repeatedly turned [to God]. (17) Indeed, We subjected the mountains [to praise God] with him, glorifying in the evening and after sunrise. (18) And the birds were assembled, all repeating [God's praise] with Him. (19) And We strengthened his kingdom, and granted him wisdom and discernment in speech. (20)

And has there come to you the tidings of the disputants, when they climbed over the wall of the prayer chamber — (21) when they went in to David and he was startled by them?

They said, "Do not fear. [We are] two disputants, one of whom has wronged the other. Therefore, judge between us with truth and do not exceed [it], and guide us to the sound path. (22)

"Indeed, this, my brother, has ninety-nine ewes, while I have one ewe. And he said, 'Entrust her to me,' and he overpowered me in speech." (23)

David said, "He has certainly wronged you in demanding your ewe in addition to his ewes. And indeed, many associates oppress one another, except those who believe and do righteous deeds, and they are few." And David inferred that We had tried him, and he asked forgiveness of his Lord and fell down in prostration and turned [to God] in repentance. (24)

Then We forgave him that, and indeed, for him is nearness to Us and a goodly place of return. (25) "O David, indeed, We have made you a deputy on the earth, so judge between people with truth and do not follow desire, for it will cause you to stray from God's path. Indeed, those who stray from God's path will have a severe chastisement because they forgot the Day of Accounting." (26)

38:30-40

And to David We granted Solomon, an excellent slave. Indeed, he was one who repeatedly turned [to God]. (30)

[Mention] when there were presented before him in the afternoon the poised, swift horses. (31) And he said, "Indeed, I have preferred the love of the good because of the remembrance of my Lord," until they disappeared into the veil. (32) [He said,] "Return them to me," and began to stroke [their] legs and necks. (33)

And We certainly tried Solomon and placed a body on his throne; then he returned. (34) He said, "My Lord, forgive me and grant me such a kingdom as will not belong to anyone after me. Indeed, You are the Bestower." (35) Then We subjected to him the wind, blowing by his command, gently, wheresoever he directed, (36) and the satans — every [kind of] builder and diver, (37) and others bound together in fetters. (38) "This is Our grant, so bestow or withhold without account." (39) And indeed, for him is nearness to Us and a good place of return. (40)

38:48

And remember Ishmael, Elisha and Dhul-Kifl — and all were among the excellent.

68:48-50

Then be patient for the decision of your Lord and do not be like the Companion of the Fish, when he called out, while he was distressed. (48) Had it not been that a favor from his Lord reached him, he would have been cast onto the bare shore while he was blameworthy, (49) but his Lord chose him and made him among the righteous. (50)

The Family of 'Imran

Zechariah (Zakariyah)
John (Yahya)
Mary (Maryam)
Jesus ('Isa)

peace be upon them

And We granted him [Abraham] Isaac and Jacob; each [of them] We guided. And previously We guided Noah, and among his descendants, David and Solomon and Job and Joseph and Moses and Aaron. And thus do We reward the doers of good. And Zechariah and John and Jesus and Elijah — all were among the righteous; and Ishmael and Elisha and Jonah and Lot — and all [of them] We preferred above mankind, and some from among their fathers and descendants and brothers; and We chose them and guided them to a straight path. (6:84-87)

PART ONE: ZECHARIAH, JOHN AND MARY

1. BY WAY OF INTRODUCTION

Indeed, God chose Adam and Noah and the family of Abraham and the family of 'Imran above mankind, descendants of one another. And God is Hearing and Knowing. (3:33-34)

As we have seen in the preceding narratives, **God chooses as His messengers whomever He wills** (3:179). But at the same time, as the above verses indicate, there is the kinship among the messengers.

In this passage — after the mention of Adam (A), the ancestor of the human race, followed by Noah (A), from whose three believing sons all mankind is descended,[1] and Abraham (A), the father of all the known prophets after his time — we are introduced to the last link in the chain of Israelite prophets: the family of 'Imran, which includes the prophet Zechariah, his son John, the Virgin Mary, and Jesus Christ, peace be upon them all.

As mentioned previously, Jesus (A) is revered as the fourth among the five most illustrious prophets of Islam (*'ulu-l-'azm*), the others being Noah, Abraham, Moses and Muhammad, God's peace and blessings be upon them. Accordingly, no one can claim to be a Muslim without believing in Jesus (A) as a great and honored messenger of God.

The Qur'an contains twenty-two passages, ranging in length from between one to thirty-one verses, related to Jesus (A), who is known in Islam as 'Isa ibn Maryam (Jesus son of Mary) or 'Isa Masih (Jesus Christ). In these passages, Jesus (A) is mentioned thirty-four times by name or by one of his titles: nine times simply as **"Jesus"**[2]; twice as **"the son of Mary"** (23:50, 43:57); thirteen times as **"Jesus son of Mary"**;[3] twice as **"the Messiah"** (4:172, 9:30); five times as **"the Messiah, son of Mary"** (5:17/19 [twice], 72/75, 75/78; 9:31); and three times as **"the Messiah, Jesus son of Mary"** (4:157, 171; 3:45).

Much of this material is quite complex and is repeated more than once. Our approach to it has been to divide it into into seven parts. Part One con-

---

[1]Please see Volume One, page 167.

[2]In 3:52, 55, 59 and 43:63 the name "Jesus" is mentioned by itself, while in 2:136, 3:84, 4:163, 6:85 and 42:13 it is mentioned together with the names of other prophets.

[3]In 2:87, 253; 5:46/49, 78/81 (together with David), 110/113, 112/115, 114/117, 116/119; 19:34; 33:7 (together with the four other greatest prophets); 57:27; and 61:6, 14.

sists of the interconnected stories of Zechariah, John and Mary, peace be upon them, with special emphasis on the place of Mary (A) in Islam. Part Two concerns the life and mission of Jesus (A), derived from the Qur'anic text, while Part Three focuses on the nature, identity and role of Jesus (A), again based on relevant verses of the Qur'an.

Part Four is a commentary on the numerous Qur'anic passages related to the divinity or sonship of Jesus (A), the doctrine of the Trinity and objects of worship other than God. This section is necessarily lengthy and involves considerable repetition, for in order to be as thorough and complete as possible, we have included in our text every Qur'anic verse directly or indirectly related to these themes. The reader is encouraged to take from this material whatever is of particular interest and pass over the remainder, if desired, in order to complete the reading of the book to the end.

Part Five is devoted to citing further *ahadith* concerning Jesus (A). Part Six concerns matters related to the second coming of Jesus (A), which is an article of faith in Islam, while Part Seven concerns prophecies, including that of Jesus (A), related to the Last Prophet, Muhammad (S). Finally, in the Qur'anic References section, we cite in full all the Qur'anic verses related to each of the above topics, followed by a glossary of the terms found in this volume and an exhaustive index.

While we have not gone deeply into theological issues related to Jesus, God's peace and blessings be upon him, they are nonetheless present as a constant background to the material and interpretations presented here. However, our objective in this work is not to enter into discussions of doctrine, but simply to present the Islamic perspective, as derived from the Qur'an, *ahadith* and relevant commentaries.

The interpretations used in this work concerning the family of 'Imran are taken from a number of classical and modern sources. Three works by the renowned eighth century commentator, Ibn Kathir — his *Tafsir (Commentary on the Qur'an)*, *Qasas al-Anbiya' (Stories of the Prophets)*, and *The Signs Before the Day of Judgment* (an extract from his historical work, *Al-Bidayah wal-Nihayah, The Beginning and the End*) — are our main classical sources. The works of three contemporary scholars, Mahmoud Ayoub, Aliah Schleifer (may God rest her soul) and Yahya Hendi, have provided us with other valuable material, supplemented as useful by the commentaries of the recent Qur'anic translators and commentators, Abul A'la Maududi, Muhammad Asad and Yusuf Ali.

We present this material in the hope that it may clear up some of the confusion and misunderstandings about the nature and role of Jesus, God's peace and blessings be upon him, bringing us back to the pristine understanding of him that characterized the first generation of his followers: that he was God's blest and honored prophet, following in the line of the prophets who had preceded him, which is the understanding of Muslims, past, present and yet to come.

2. THE DEDICATION AND BIRTH OF MARY

[Mention, O Muhammad,] when the wife of 'Imran said, "My Lord, indeed, I pledge to You what is in my womb, consecrated [to You], so accept this from me. Indeed, You are the Hearing, the Knowing." (3:35)

'Imran son of Mathan was in charge of prayers and sacrifices at the Temple in Jerusalem. He was a descendant of Levi son of Jacob through both David and Aaron (A), from whose line came all the priests of the Jews.

'Imran's wife was named Hannah. She was also a descendant of Aaron (A) and a devoted worshipper of her Lord. But while Hannah was pregnant, her husband passed away.[4]

In keeping with the family calling of priesthood, Hannah dedicated to God the child in her womb, whom she anticipated would be a boy, saying, **"My Lord, indeed I pledge to You what is in my womb, consecrated** to You, **so accept this from me. Indeed, You are the Hearing, the Knowing"** (3:35).

But **when she gave birth to her** — a girl-child — Hannah became confused and uncertain about the commitment she had made. **"My Lord,"** she said, **"I have given birth to a female," whereas God was aware what she had given birth to. "And the male is not like the female"**[5] (3:36).

According to Ibn Kathir, the words, **"Whereas God was aware what she had given birth to,"** are generally understood as a parenthetical statement by God Himself. By these words, out of His knowledge of the tremendous matters that were in store for this newborn female, God exalted both the mother and her daughter, whom He would make, together with her holy son, **a sign for mankind** (21:91).

---

[4]'Imran is mentioned three times in the Qur'an, not as a living person but in relation to his family (3:33), his wife (3:35) and his daughter, Mary (66:12). The third *surah*, *Ale 'Imran* (The Family of 'Imran), which contains much of the material concerning Zechariah, John, Mary and Jesus, is named for him.

[5]The classical commentator al-Razi states that no female had ever been consecrated to the Temple before Mary, and hence God's accepting her consecration was in itself an indication of her exalted rank. Hasan al-Basri states that Hannah's vow to dedicate her child to God was the result of divine inspiration, "just as Abraham beheld the sacrifice of his son in a dream and knew that it was a divine commandment, although it was not a revelation; just as the mother of Moses was inspired, and she cast him afloat, and it was not revelation" (Schleifer/*Mary*, p. 86).

As for the the words that follow, **"And the male is not like the female,"** some commentators are of the opinion that they constitute a continuation of this divine parenthesis, while others say they are the continuation of Hannah's speech.

Understood in the latter sense, these words have been interpreted as an expression of sorrow on Hannah's part that she had not been granted the son she desired purely for the service of her Lord, or because a female cannot be a prophet. They have also been understood as meaning that the male is better suited to the hardships of Temple service than the female, particularly because women are bound by restrictions of worship related to their reproductive cycle.[6] Still another meaning may be that no male could do what this very special female was going to do, for the destiny that was reserved for this newborn girl-child was beyond anything her mother could ever have dreamed of. Taken all together, the meaning is that God was obviously infinitely more aware than Hannah herself that she had given birth to a female, for it was through this female that He would grant Hannah what she desired of Him (Ibn Kathir/*T*, 3:33-37).

"And I have named her Maryam," Hannah continued, addressing her Lord. It has been said that because in Hebrew the name Maryam or Mary means "handmaiden" or "female worshipper," Hannah meant by these words to ask God's protection for her daughter from all error so that her actions might be in keeping with her name. **"And I seek refuge in You for her and her descendants from Satan the accursed"** (3:36).

And God Most High accepted this supplication, for, as reported by Abu Hurayrah (R), the Holy Prophet (S) said,

> Satan jabs each human being in the sides while his mother delivers him, except Mary and her son. (*Muslim*, 6429, also 5838)
>
> No child is born but that Satan touches it when it is born, whereupon it starts crying because of Satan's touch, except Mary and her son. Abu Hurayrah (R) then said, "Recite, if you wish, **'And I seek refuge in**

---

[6]The classical commentators evidently based this interpretation on Islamic rather than Judaic rules, which differ markedly. According to Jewish law, the menstruating woman (***niddah***) is regarded as impure and is therefore bound by a set of complex regulations regarding what she may or may not touch, do or use, especially in relation to her husband. In Islam, there are no such restrictions. However, because menstruation and postpartum bleeding invalidate the state of purity prescribed for worship, Muslim women are exempt from praying, fasting, reading the Qur'an and engaging marital relations during these occasions.

You for her and her offspring from Satan the accursed.'" (*Bukhari*, 6:71; *Muslim*, 5837)

Thus did Mary, God's peace and blessings be upon her, begin her life exempt from the touch of the Evil One, which is the common lot of mankind, and consecrated to her Lord. Yet even with this, no one could possibly have dreamed of the exalted destiny that awaited her.

REFERENCES: Ibn Kathir/*T*, 3:33-37; Ibn Kathir/*Q*, "Zakariyah"; Tabari/*H*, IV:102-103; Ayoub/*Q*, II:93-99; Schleifer/*Mary*, 24-25, 78-79, 86; Hendi/*Jesus*, pp. 57-59; Asad/*Q*, 3:fn. 25.

3. THE PROPHET ZECHARIAH (A)

And Zechariah and John and Jesus and Elijah — and all were among the righteous. (6:85)

Zechariah (Zakariyah), son of Ladun, a descendant of Levi, Aaron and Solomon, was the prophet of his time and a priest. His name is mentioned seven times in the Qur'an.[7]

Zechariah (A) was married to Mary's close relative, who was likewise a descendant of Aaron (A).[8] And while his wife is not named in the Qur'an, according to the first chapter of Luke, she was named Elizabeth (Arabic, 'Ashya).

Like Abraham (A) and Sarah before them, Zechariah and Elizabeth were childless. Not only was Elizabeth barren, but by the time of Mary's birth she and Zechariah (A) had reached advanced old age.

At some point in her young life, Mary (A) was turned over to the priests of the Temple in Jerusalem, her kinsmen, for rearing. Some commentators say that this took place after her mother's death. However, Ibn Kathir states that her mother took her to the Temple and left her there in the care of its servants, the priests, who were the descendants of Aaron (A), saying, "I have dedicated my daughter to the service of God, and now it is your task to take care of her."

Since Mary's father 'Imran had been an important figure in the Temple, the priests were all eager to take charge of his daughter. But Zechariah said, "I have the most right to her because I am her aunt's husband, so I shall bring her up."

The other priests disputed this, demanding to draw lots to determine the guardianship of the child. Consequently, **they cast their pens** — the quills which they used to write the Torah — to decide **which of them should be responsible for Mary** (3:44). It is said that the priests, twenty-seven in number, went to the Jordan River and cast their pens into it to settle the matter. And all the pens sank or were carried away by the current except Zechariah's.

---

[7]In 3:37-38; 6:85; 19:2, 7, 11; 21:89.

[8]Despite some disagreement among the classical commentators concerning the kinship between Mary and Elizabeth, because the Prophet (S) referred to John and Jesus as maternal cousins (*Bukhari*, 5:227), it is likely that Elizabeth was Hannah's sister — that is, Mary's aunt.

REFERENCES: Ibn Kathir/*T*, 3:37-44; Ibn Kathir/*Q*, "Zakariyah"; Ayoub/*Q*, II:99-100; Schleifer/*Mary*, pp. 25-26, 108, fn. 19; Maududi/*Q*, 19:fn. 2; Asad/*Q*, 3:fns. 26, 31.

4. Mary's Young Years

So her Lord accepted her with gracious acceptance and caused her to grow in a goodly manner and placed her in the care of Zechariah. (3:37)

Thus, by the Will of the All-Wise, the All-Knowing, Mary (A) grew up under the guardianship of her aged kinsman and his wife, her aunt, who were such godly people that their Lord said of them,

> **Indeed, they used to hasten to good deeds and supplicate Us in hope and fear, and they were humbly submissive to Us.** (21:90)

In this manner, says Ibn Kathir, did God Most High accept Hannah's dedication of her child, granting Mary (A) the best of outer and inner beauty and goodness, and causing her to be brought up among His righteous servants, that she might acquire from them righteousness and knowledge of the religion (Ibn Kathir/T, 3:37).

During Mary's growing years, the classical commentators report, Zechariah (A) made ready for his ward a secluded prayer room (*mihrab*) in the vicinity of the Temple. When needed, she would be occupied in Temple service. Otherwise, apart from the duration of her menses, when she would leave her sanctuary and go to stay with her aunt, she would remain in this room, engaged in worship.

The accounts of several commentators suggest that the young Mary (A), trained by her prophet-kinsman Zechariah (A) in detachment from the world, total surrender, deep reverence and humility before her Lord, remained in solitude in her sanctuary, occupied with devout worship by day and night.[9] Knowing no other habits or ways of life, the earnest, holy child was committed body and soul to this path — so much so, it is said, that her piety became renowned among the Jews.

---

[9]Writes Aliah Schleifer in her book, *Mary the Blessed Virgin of Islam*:

> Indeed, Mary's piety continues to be a symbol for Muslims of all times, partly due to the existence of her sanctuary (*mihrab*), which is located underground in the eastern part of the *haram ash-sharif* (the Noble Sanctuary) in Jerusalem, and is known as 'the cradle of 'Isa'. It is said that supplication (*du'a'*) there is *mustahabb* (highly recommended), and that it is desirable to recite the Qur'anic Chapter of Mary [*Surah* 19] there and perform the *sajda*, i.e. to perform a formal, but voluntary prayer. In fact, when Muslims attempt to express the esteem they have for Mary's outstanding capacity for obedience, they often become quite passionate. (p. 61)

Since contemporary society largely overlooks or ignores the tremendous spiritual inclinations and potential of children, largely occupying them with trivia and meaningless, spiritually-deadening pursuits, such commitment on the part of a child may sound to us unnatural or forced. However, Mary is certainly not alone among those mentioned in the Qur'an as possessing high spirituality as a child, for a similar aptitude is evident in the early years of Abraham, Ishmael, Joseph, Samuel, John, Jesus and Muhammad, peace be upon them all. Indeed, this is likely to have been a characteristic of all prophets and holy people. It is therefore not so astonishing that a pure-hearted child, brought up in an atmosphere of wholehearted devotion to God and having no purpose or activity except worship and service, should be able and willing to dedicate herself to it with such single-minded devotion.

The signs of divine election then began to be manifested upon Mary (A), as the veil between the material and spiritual worlds dissolved within her being, and she was opened more and more to the heavenly realm.

The first sign about which we are told was that **each time Zechariah went in to her in the sanctuary, he found provision with her** (3:37), meaning, according to the most common interpretation, summer fruit in winter and winter fruit in summer. And the aged prophet voiced his astonishment, saying, **"O Mary, whence does this come to you?"** (3:37).

"It is from God," Mary (A) replied simply, speaking with the certitude of direct experience. **"Indeed, God provides for whomever He wills without reckoning"**[10] (3:37).

---

[10]A similar incident is reported concerning Fatimah, the daughter of the Holy Prophet. Once, when the Prophet (S) had gone without food for several days because there was none to be had, he went to houses of his wives, looking for something to eat. Finding that they too had nothing, he went to the home of Fatimah, who likewise had nothing. A neighbor then sent Fatimah two loaves of bread and a bit of meat. Preferring the Prophet (S) to herself and her family, she sent her sons, Hasan and Husain, to him to ask him to come and eat. When she brought the dish to him, she found it full of bread and meat. Although astonished, she understood that this was by God's favor. When the Prophet (S) saw the food, he thanked God and said, "Whence does this come to you, O daughter?" She replied, as Mary had replied to Zechariah, "O my father, **it is from God. Indeed, God provides for whomever He wills without reckoning."** The Prophet (S) then said, "Praise be to God who made you, O daughter, like the mistress of the Children of Israel, for whenever God provided her with some sustenance and she was asked about it, she would say, **'It is from God. Indeed, God provides for whomever He wills without reckoning.'"** The Prophet (S) and his entire family — Fatimah, her husband 'Ali, their sons Hasan and Husain, and the Prophet's wives — then ate until they were full. Even then, the contents of the dish had not diminished, and Fatimah fed all the neighbors from it (Ibn Kathir/*T*, 3:37).

The second sign of God's election, perhaps at around the same period, was that Mary (A), now nearing or having reached the age of maturity, was visited by angels.

"O Mary," they said, **"indeed, God has chosen you and purified you, and has preferred you above the women of mankind. O Mary, be devoutly obedient [*qanut*] to your Lord, and prostrate and bow like those who bow** to Him in prayer"[11] (3:42-43). That is, in gratitude for these divine favors and, doubtless, in preparation for the extraordinary circumstances that were soon to come upon her, Mary (A) was to continue steadfastly in devout obedience and unflagging worship of her Lord (3:43).

Following the above verses, God the All-Knowing addresses the one to whom they were revealed, His Last Prophet (S), saying,

> **That is of the tidings of the Unseen which We reveal to you. And you were not with them when they cast their pens as to which of them should be responsible for Mary, nor were you with them when they disputed [concerning it]. (3:44)**

By these words, God once again confirms Muhammad's prophethood, proclaiming to mankind his having been informed, through divine revelation, of the details of unknowable events that had taken place hundreds of years prior to his time — events that, as part of the history of Jesus Christ (A), have ever since been surrounded by mystery, confusion and controversy.

REFERENCES: Ibn Kathir/*T*, 3:37-43; Ibn Kathir/*Q*, "'Isa son of Mary," "Zakariyah"; Ayoub/*Q*, II:99-105; Schleifer/*Mary*, pp. 26-28, 56-57, 61, 108, fns. 24-25; Maududi/*Q*, 3:fn. 36.

---

[11]The word **"*qanut*"** means obedience with humility and presence of mind, as in God's saying, **To Him belongs whatever is in the heavens and the earth. All are devoutly obedient [*qanitun*] to Him** (2:116, 30:26). It is said that Mary used to stand so long in *salat* that her ankles would swell, and that ***qanut*** means engaging in such lengthy prayers.

5. ZECHARIAH'S SUPPLICATION

[This is] a mention of the mercy of your Lord to His slave Zechariah, when he called to his Lord a secret call. (19:3)

Seeing in the heavenly provision granted to Mary the tangible evidence that God the All-Powerful does whatever He wills, it occurred to Zechariah (A) to hope that he might somehow be granted, by a similar miracle, a son, despite his advanced age and his wife's barrenness.

Then **he called his Lord in secret** (19:3; also 3:38, 21:89). This means, according to Ibn 'Abbas (R) and other commentators, that he went into the sanctuary, closed the doors, and earnestly prayed.

"My Lord," Zechariah (A) said, pouring out his feebleness and need, **"indeed, my bones have weakened and my head has turned white, but never have I been unblest in my supplication to You, my Lord.**

"And indeed," he continued, **"I fear the successors after me,"** meaning his relatives who would inherit his religious authority, **"and my wife is barren. So grant me, from Yourself, an heir who will inherit me and inherit from the family of Jacob. And make him, my Lord, well-pleasing"** (19:4-5).

In asking for an heir, says Ibn Kathir, Zechariah (A) was not referring to an inheritor of his property, for, as a simple man, he had no wealth to inherit.[12] Moreover, according to a *hadith*, prophets are not to be inherited; whatever they leave behind is charity (*Bukhari*, 5:367). Rather, Zechariah (A) meant a son who would succeed him and the descendants of Jacob in carrying on the prophetic line and mission (as it is said, **Solomon inherited David** [27:16], referring to David's prophethood, not his wealth), for he did not see anyone among his relatives who was capable of carrying on his prophetic work among the Jews. And he asked that this successor might be well-pleasing, meaning beloved because of his high moral character and piety (Ibn Kathir/*T*, 19:1-6).

"My Lord," Zechariah (A) implored, **"do not leave me solitary"** — that is, without an heir whom I can trust — **"while You are the Best of Inheritors**[13] (21:89). **My Lord, grant me, from Yourself, a goodly off-**

---

[12]According to a *hadith*, Zechariah was a carpenter (*Muslim*, 5863).

[13]Meaning the One who remains after all else has passed away.

spring," meaning, it has been said, one with the goodness of Mary. **"Indeed, you are Hearer of supplication"**[14] (3:38).

And the angels called him while he was standing in prayer in the sanctuary (3:39). **"O Zechariah,"** they said, **"indeed, We give you good tidings of a boy whose name will be Yahya"** — that is, John. **"We have not appointed this for anyone previously"**[15] (19:7).

This son, the angels continued, would confirm **a word from God** — his cousin, Jesus (A), who would come into the world soon after him. And he would be **honorable and abstinent, and a prophet from among the righteous** (3:39).

Zechariah (A) reacted to the angels' announcement with natural astonishment. **"My Lord,"** he exclaimed, **"how will I have a boy when my wife has been barren and I have reached extreme old age?"**[16] (19:8). But, it is said, since this was the same prophet who had just begged his Lord to grant him a son, here **"How?"** does not mean "*How can* such an impossible thing happen?" but, rather, "*In what way* is it going to happen?"[17]

---

[14]Ibn Kathir says that Zechariah prayed, "O You who feed Mary fruit out of season, grant me a son out of my season." An early Qur'anic commentator says, "He stood in the night and quietly prayed, fearing lest anyone who might be present might hear him, and said, 'O Lord, O Lord, O Lord!' And God Most High replied, '*Labbayk, labbayk, labbayk!* — Here I am, here I am, here I am!'" (Ibn Kathir/*T*, 3:38-41; Ibn Kathir/*Q*, "Zakariyah").

[15]This is understood as meaning that no one had been given the name Yahya previously and that no one would be similar to him. The word "Yahya" literally means "He lives." And while Ibn 'Abbas relates this name to God's revivifying his mother's barrenness through him (Ayoub/*Q*, II:109), it has also been related to his revivifying people's faith.

[16]In 3:40, it is, **"My Lord, how will I have a son when I have reached old age and my wife is barren?"** Some commentators say that these words were addressed to the angel, while others say they were addressed to God Himself.

[17]Ibn Kathir comments that Zechariah's surprise at the tidings of John, even though he had just besought God to grant him a son, was primarily due to his wife's barrenness, for she had not borne a child thoughout her life. He compares Zechariah's reaction to that of Abraham and Sarah when they were given the news of Isaac, stating that the latter's reaction was related more to their advanced age than to Sarah's barrenness, since Abraham had fathered his son Ishmael by Hagar some years earlier. This is suggested by Abraham's saying to the angels, **"Do you give me [this] good tidings although old age has come upon me?"** (15:54), and Sarah's question, **"Am I to bear a child when I am an old woman and this, my husband, is an old man?"** (11:72) (Ibn Kathir/*T*, 19:1-11). Al-Qurtubi suggests that Zechariah sought to understand, first, how he could father a child under the conditions affecting him and his wife or whether they would both be reverted to an age at which this would be possible; second, whether he would have this child from his present wife or from some other woman; and third, why he should merit such a favor in view of his and Elizabeth's condition (Ayoub/*Q*, II:113).

"Thus!" was the angel's reply. **"Your Lord says, 'It is easy for Me, for I created you previously while you were nothing'** (19:9). **Such is God,"** he continued. **"He does whatever He wills"** (3:40).

The meaning of this, says Ibn Kathir, is, "What you have requested is not difficult for God. Indeed, you have seen much more wondrous things from Him, such as your own existence, for you were not present before He created you, according to His words, **'Has there [not] come upon man a period of time when he was not a thing [even] mentioned?'"** [76:1] (Ibn Kathir/*T*, 3:40).

"My Lord, appoint a sign for me" (3:41, 19:10), Zechariah (A) begged.

"Your sign is that you will not be able to **speak to people for three days and three nights except by gesture,** although being **sound"**[18] (3:41, 19:10), he was told. **"And remember your Lord much, and glorify Him in the evening and the morning"** (3:41).

Then, the Qur'anic narrative continues, **he came out to his people from the *mihrab* and signaled to them to glorify [God] morning and evening** (19:10-11).

Some commentators have interpreted Zechariah's not being able to speak for three days as a punishment for questioning what he had been told by the angels. However, nothing in the above verses suggests God's displeasure with Zechariah (A) or any reason for punishment. Another interpretation, which seems more correct, is that he was deprived of the power to speak so that, during his three days of silence, he might devote himself exclusively to the remembrance of his Lord, the Praised and Exalted, not occupying his tongue with anything other than praising and thanking Him for the divine favor that he had been promised.

Concerning verses 3:38-41 above, Ibn Kathir comments

> While he was in his place of worship, the angels called out, [saying] that you will have a son and you are to name him Yahya, and they told him that these tidings were not from themselves but from God.[19]

---

[18]Two speeches of the angel are combined here: **"Your sign is that you will not [be able to] speak to people for three days except by gesture"** (3:41), and, **"Your sign is that you will not speak to the people for three nights, [although being] sound"** (19:10). Ibn Kathir says that **"sound"** means that Zechariah's inability to speak would not be the result of any illness or defect in his tongue, for although he was prevented from speaking to people, he was nevertheless able to recite and glorify his Lord (Ibn Kathir/*Q*, "Zakariyah").

[19]Referring to the angel's words, **"Indeed, God gives you good tidings of Yahya"** (3:39).

The name Yahya, which is derived from "*hayy*," meaning "living," signified that he would be endowed with a life of faith and would be the first to believe in Jesus and confirm his prophethood. Qatadah says that John followed the path of Jesus exactly. Ibn 'Abbas says, "These two were maternal cousins. John's mother would tell Mary, 'I feel as though the child in my womb is bowing to the child in your womb,' and this was his confirmation [of the **word from God**, as mentioned in 3:39]."

"Honorable" [***sayyid***] means forbearing, devoted to knowledge and worship, learned in religion, and not overpowered by anger. **"Abstinent"** [***hasur***] means one who does not come to women or have children, and is not subject to sexual desire.

Zechariah was then given the good tidings, "Your son will also be a prophet" [3:39], which was a greater favor than the previous tidings [that he would have a son]. When he heard these tidings he was surprised, for from all appearances this thing seemed impossible, and he said, **"How will I have a son? . . ."** [3:40], whereupon the angels said, "Nothing is impossible for God. He is not subject to any causes. He has willed it and He will do this" [3:40].

He then asked for a sign from God Most High and was told, "You will not [be able to] speak to people for three consecutive days, and although you will remain sound of body, you will be able to communicate with people only by gestures [3:41, 19:10]. And during these days you are to engage yourself in remembering God and mentioning His Name" [3:41]. (Ibn Kathir/*T*, 3:38-41)

REFERENCES: Qur'an: 3:38-41, 19:3-11, 21:89. Commentaries: Ibn Kathir/*T*, 3:37-41, 19:1-11; Ibn Kathir/*Q*, "Zakariyah"; Ayoub/*Q*, II:105-122; Asad/*Q*, 15:fn. 22, 21:fn. 85, 19:fns. 5, 7-8; Ali/*Q*, fns. 2461, 2465.

6. JOHN (A)

So We responded to him and granted to him John and rectified his wife for him. (21:90)

Thus was the barrier of Zechariah's old age and Elizabeth's barrenness miraculously set aside so that God's prophet, John (A), might come into the world. Ibn 'Abbas (R) says that Zechariah was 120 and his wife ninety-eight at the time of John's annunciation (Ayoub/Q, II: 113).

Like Mary (A), John (A) was a deeply spiritual child, immersed in devotion to his Lord and possessing every good characteristic from an early age, as is clear from the words,

> **[God said,] "O John, adhere to the scripture with determination." And We granted him judgment as a boy, and affection from Us and purity, and he was mindful of God and dutiful to his parents, and was not arrogant or disobedient. And peace be upon him the day he was born and the day he dies and the day he will be raised alive!** (19:12-15)

Ibn Kathir's interpretation of this passage is as follows:

> According to the good tidings from God, Zechariah had a son and named him John. While he was a child, God taught this son the knowledge of the Torah and all the commandments contained therein. Thus, He mentions here His favors: that He not only granted him a son, but granted him a son who had knowledge of the scripture during his childhood. And He commanded John to adhere to the teachings of the Torah with determination, and to study it and strive to understand and interpret it.
>
> During his childhood, he was also given understanding, knowledge, discerment, determination, wisdom and forbearance. From the beginning, he was greatly devoted to good deeds and spent his time worshipping God and serving people. When children of his age would ask him to play, he would reply, "I was not created for play."
>
> **"Affection from Us and purity"** means that God endowed him with love, kindness and purity, and **"he was mindful of God"** means that he feared God. In short, he was free of all sin and abounded in good deeds throughout his life. He was also submissive to his parents and treated them with great kindness. He never disobeyed his father or his mother. If they told him not to do something, he did not do it, and rebelliousness and disobedience were not in his nature.

Because of his purity and lovely characteristics, God granted him peace at the three occasions that are critical for a human being, the first when he is born, the second when he dies, and the third when he is resurrected. These three occasions are when a human being enters from one world to a different world, the first being from the mother's womb into this magnificent universe. Then, at death, he encounters creatures that he has neither encountered nor seen during his life, and likewise, on the Day of Judgment, he will be amidst a huge crowd under different circumstances. So God granted him peace and security for those three occasions. (Ibn Kathir/*T*, 19:12-15)

REFERENCES: Ibn Kathir/*T*, 19:12-15; Ayoub/*Q*, II:107-113; Ali/*Q*, fn. 2747.

AHADITH AND TRADITIONS CONCERNING JOHN

John (A), known to Christians as John the Baptist, is mentioned five times in the Qur'an by name.[20] He is also mentioned in a number of ***ahadith***, which speak of his asceticism, purity, piety and nearness to his Lord.

The Prophet (S) is reported to have said that on the Day of Judgment everyone will come with some sins except John (A).[21] Qatadah said, "Let alone sin, he never even ***intended*** a sin" (Ibn Kathir/*Q*, "Zakariyah").

The Holy Prophet (S) reported meeting both John and Jesus, God's peace and blessings be upon them, during his miraculous ascension to the heavens (***Me'raj***), saying that when he arrived in the second heaven, accompanied by the angel Gabriel (A),

> There were John and Jesus, who were maternal cousins. He [Gabriel] said, "These are John and Jesus, so greet them." Then I greeted them and they responded and said, "Welcome to the righteous brother and righteous prophet!" (***Bukhari***, 5:227)

In another ***hadith***, it is reported that once when John and Jesus were together, Jesus said to John, "Please ask forgiveness for me because you are better than I." John replied, "You ask forgiveness for me because you are better than I." Jesus (A) then said to him, "You are better than I because I said, 'Peace be upon ***me***' [19:33], while God says, 'Peace be upon ***him***'" [that is,

---

[20]In 3:39; 6:85; 19:7, 12; 21:90.

[21]Ibn Kathir says that this ***hadith*** is ***mursal***, meaning that its chain of transmission does not go all the way back to the Prophet (S). The same ***hadith*** is also reported with two complete chains but both chains are weak. And God knows best (Ibn Kathir/*Q*, "***Zakariyah***").

upon John][22] [19:15]. Indeed, God has raised both of them to a high station (Ibn Kathir/*Q*, "Zakariyah").

It is also reported that the Prophet (S) said:

> God gave John son of Zechariah five commands, to act on them and order the Children of Israel to act on them. When he was slow in doing so, Jesus (A) said to him, "You have been given five commands, to act on them and to tell them to the Children of Israel to act on them. So either you convey them or I shall convey them."
>
> John said, "O my brother, I am afraid that if you precede me in this, I will be punished or swallowed up because of it," and he assembled the Children of Israel in the Temple in Jerusalem until the Temple was filled. Then he sat in a place of honor and praised and glorified God and said, "God the Mighty and Glorious has commanded me five things, to act on them and order you to act upon them.
>
> "The first of them is that you should worship God without ascribing any partner to Him, and the likeness of that is that of a slave whose master bought him with his own wealth of silver or gold, but the slave gave his earnings to someone other than his master. Would any of you then like to be like that slave? Indeed, God created you and provides for you, so worship Him alone and do not ascribe any partner to Him.
>
> "And God Most High has commanded you to observe *salat*. When you are in *salat*, do not turn your faces. Indeed, God [Himself] faces the person in *salat* who does not turn this way or that.
>
> "And He has commanded you to observe fasting. The likeness of one who fasts is that of a man who has with him a bottle of musk, sitting among his people while he himself and all others are enjoying the scent of that musk, and indeed, the odor of the mouth of one who is fasting is better with God than the scent of musk.[23]
>
> "And He has commanded you to give charity. The example of one who gives charity is like that of a man who is captured by his enemies and they have tied his hands to his neck and are taking him to strike his neck, and he tells them, 'Would it be acceptable to you if I gave you ransom

---

[22]This refers to Jesus' words concerning himself, **"And peace be upon me the day I was born and the day I die and the day I will be raised alive!"** (19:33), and God's saying about John, **And peace be upon him the day he was born and the day he dies and the day he will be raised alive!** (19:15).

[23]See the *hadith* cited in footnote 117, page 111.

money?' and he gives them whatever money, little or much, he has to save himself.

"And He commands you to remember God the Mighty and Glorious much. The example of that is like a man who is pursued by his enemies, and he runs into a strong fortress and saves himself from them, and it is best for the slave [of God] to protect himself from his enemy, Satan, through the remembrance of God [*dhikr-Allah*], the Mighty and Glorious." (Ibn Kathir/*Q*, "*Zakariyah*")

Ibn Kathir also reports numerous incidents concerning John, peace be upon him. While these may not represent actual occurrences, we cite some of them here because they reflect the purity of heart, piety and asceticism which are the chief characteristics ascribed to this noble prophet in Islam.

It is said that John (A) used to keep away from people, spending much of his time in the desert, and that his food was the leaves of trees and sometimes locusts, and his drink was the water of springs. And he would say to himself, "Who is more favored than you, O John? Who is in greater luxury?"

It is also said that Jesus son of Mary (A) and John son of Zechariah (A) were walking together when John (A) bumped into a woman. Afterwards Jesus (A) said to him, "O my cousin, today you committed an error which I think cannot be forgiven you." John asked, "What happened, my cousin?" Jesus replied, "You bumped into a woman." John replied, "By God, I was not aware of it." Jesus said, "Glory be to God! Your body is with me, but where is your soul?" John said, "It is suspended at the Throne, and indeed, if my heart had been content with [the company of] Gabriel, I would have supposed that I did not know God at all." Ibn Kathir, however, says that there is some strangeness in this report.

It is reported that once John's father went out in search of him and found him near the Jordan River. When the two met, they wept copiously out of fear of God and intense devotion to Him. The commentator Mujahid said, "The food of John son of Zechariah was from trees, and he used to weep so much out of fear of God that there were marks on his face from the flow of his tears."

It is said that once when Zechariah (A) did not see his son John (A) for three days, he went out to the desert to search for him. Then he found that John (A) had dug a grave and was standing in it, weeping. Zechariah (A) said, "O my son, I have been searching for you for three days, while you are standing in this grave that you have dug, weeping and weeping!" John (A) replied, "O my father, did you not tell me that between Paradise and Hell there is a plain that cannot be crossed except by much weeping?" Then Zechariah (A) said, "I weep, too, O my son." And the two wept together (Ibn Kathir/Q, "Zakariyah").

Perhaps this blessed prophet-father and son are among those included in God's saying, after the report of Zechariah's prayer for a son, his visitation by angels, the annunciation and birth of Jesus (A), and the mention of other prophets in *Surah Maryam:*

> **Those were the ones upon whom God bestowed favor of the prophets from among the descendants of Adam, and among those whom We carred [in the ark] with Noah, and among the descendants of Abraham and Israel, and among those whom We guided and chose. When the signs of the Most Merciful were recited to them, they fell down prostrating and weeping.** (19:58)

REFERENCE: Ibn Kathir/Q, "Zakariyah".

7. The Deaths of Zechariah and John

Each soul will taste death. And We test you with the evil and the good as a trial, and to Us you will be returned. (21:35)

A number of stories are told by the classical commentators concerning the martyrdom of Zechariah and John, God's peace and blessings be upon them. However, since these do not seem sufficiently authoritative, we will not report them here. At the same time, the following ***hadith*** confirms that not only did John (A) meet with a martyr's death, as reported in the Gospels,[24] but his father as well:

One day the Prophet (S) came to the Companions while they were mentioning the excellence of the prophets. One of them said, "Moses, the one who spoke to God." Another said, "Jesus, the spirit of God and His word," and another said, "Abraham, the Friend of God." While they were speaking thus, the Prophet (S) said, "What about the martyr, son of the martyr, who wore camel's hair and ate from trees out of fear of sin?" Ibn Wahhab, the last of the chain of reporters of this ***hadith***, said, "The Prophet, God's peace and blessings be upon him, meant John son of Zechariah" (Ibn Kathir/*Q*, "Zakariyah").

John the Baptist — the prophet Yahya, may God's peace and blessings be upon him and his noble father — is buried in the famed Omayyad Mosque in Damascus, Syria. Muslims from every part of the world visit his grave, paying their respects and invoking God's peace upon him, as if echoing the blessing which his Lord invoked upon him for all time to come:

Peace be upon him the day he was born and the day he dies and the day he will be raised alive! (19:15)

REFERENCES: Ibn Kathir/*Q*, "Zakariyah," "The Killing of John"; Tabari/*H*, IV:120; Schleifer/*Mary*, pp. 35-36.

---

[24]Matt. 14:10, Mark 6:27-28, and Luke 9:9.

8. The Blessed Virgin Mary (A)

God sets forth an example for those who believe: the wife of Pharaoh, when she said, "My Lord, build for me, with You, a house in Paradise, and save me from Pharaoh and his doings, and save me from the wrongdoing people." And Mary daughter of 'Imran, who preserved her chastity, and We breathed into her of Our Spirit, and she believed in the words of her Lord and His scriptures, and was of the devoutly obedient. (66:11-12)

The Greatness of Mary's Rank

Mary, God's peace and blessings be upon her, occupies a very special and unique place in Islam. And the reasons for this are numerous.

First of all, she was honored and memorialized in the nineteenth *surah* of the Qur'an, *Maryam*; her story and that of her illustrious son is narrated in its first thirty-seven verses. Mary (A) is mentioned in the Qur'an thirty-six times — eleven times by her given name,[25] once as the **"sister of Aaron"** (19:28), once as **"the one who preserved her chastity"** (21:91), and twenty-three times in reference to Jesus (A) in the phrase, **"son of Mary"**.

Mary (A) is the only woman mentioned in the Qur'an by name, for in accordance with Arab custom which does not familiarize women by calling them by their given names, all other women mentioned in the Qur'an are referred to as the wife, mother, sister or daughter of such-and-such (e.g., the mother of Moses, wife of Pharaoh, etc.). Mary (A) is also known among Muslims by the titles of *al-'Adhra'*, the Virgin, and *al-Batul*, denoting a woman who withdraws from worldly affairs and withholds herself from men, having no desire for them, in order to devote herself entirely to worship.[26]

Two Qur'anic passages attest to Mary's exalted rank: 66:12 above and the angels' saying, **"O Mary, indeed, God has chosen you and purified you, and preferred you above the women of mankind"** (3:42), mentioned earlier.

---

[25]These verses are 3:36-37, 42-45; 4:156, 171; 19:16, 27; 66:12.

[26]Whether Mary's viriginity was perpetual or ended with her marriage to Joseph is not known. The words, . . . **who preserved her chastity** (21:91, 66:12), do not imply that she never married, as marriage is itself a means of preserving chastity, but rather that she fortified herself through her pure faith and devout worship against anything that could detract from her inner and outer purity and sanctity. We will speak more about the matter of Mary's marriage to Joseph shortly.

The early commentators discussed the wording of 3:42 in detail. Their conclusions may be summarized as follows:

God's "choosing" of Mary (A) is evident from the special divine gifts that were bestowed upon her: God's accepting her consecration to Him, a favor never granted to any other female; His saving her at birth from the touch of Satan, which is the common lot of all mankind; His making her exclusively occupied with His obedience and worship, guiding and protecting her from error, and granting her lovely attributes and characteristics; His providing her with heavenly sustenance; and His granting her to hear the speech of angels.

God's "purification" of her consisted of His purifying her of everything that could harm her or detract from her exalted state, from being touched by men, from unbecoming deeds and habits, and from the immorality with which she would later be charged.

The indications that God had "preferred" Mary (A) **above the women of mankind** were that she would be visited by the angel Gabriel (A), who would convey to her the divine revelation; that she would assent to what God had decreed for her without questioning or asking for a sign; that she would become, among all the women on earth, the mother of a child without the agency of a man through the act of God; that as a newborn, her son would speak and testify to her innocence of the immorality of which she was accused; and that she would be, together with her holy son, **a sign for mankind** (21:91, also 23:50).

As we saw earlier in connection with Asiyah, number of *ahadith* also confirm Mary's exalted rank. Among them are the following:

> The best among women [of earlier times] is Mary daughter of 'Imran, and the best among women [of later times] is Khadijah.[27] (*Bukhari*, 4:642)
>
> Sufficient for you are the four mistresses [*sayyidat*] of the women of mankind: Fatimah daughter of Muhammad, Khadijah daughter of Khuwaylid, Asiyah daughter Muzahim, and Mary daughter of 'Imran. (Ibn 'Asakir)
>
> The best women among mankind are four: Mary daughter of 'Imran, Asiyah wife of Pharaoh, Khadijah daughter of Khuwaylid, and Fatimah daughter of Muhammad, the Messenger of God. (Tirmidhi)

---

[27]The words in brackets are later interpolations to the Prophet's words whose validity cannot be confirmed.

The Holy Prophet (S) once drew four lines on the ground and asked, “Do you know what these are?” Those present said, “God and His Messenger know best.” The Prophet (S) then said, “The best of the women of the people of Paradise are Khadijah daughter of Khuwaylid, Fatimah daughter of Muhammad, Mary daughter of ‘Imran, and Asiyah daughter of Muzahim, the wife of Pharaoh. (Al-Nisai)

Abu Hurayrah (R) reported the Holy Prophet (S) as saying, “The women of the Quraysh are the best among camel-riding women, most tender toward children and most careful of their husbands’ possessions.” Abu Hurayrah (R) then added: “But Mary never rode a camel” (*Bukhari*, 4:643), meaning that although she never rode a camel like the women of the Quraysh whom the Prophet (S) praised, Mary (A) was nonetheless among the best of women.

The following *hadith* also speaks of the greatness of Mary’s rank, placing her among the handful of luminous souls who excelled even the best of the Prophet’s Companions, who were like stars in the firmament of godliness:

> If I were to swear, I would swear an oath that no one will enter Paradise before the early members of my *ummah* [i.e., the first Muslims] . . . except a few [*bida‘t ‘ashar*, i.e., from eleven to nineteen people], among whom are Abraham, Ishmael, Isaac, Jacob, the founders [of the tribes of Israel], Moses, Jesus, and Mary daughter of ‘Imran. (Al-Qurtubi, *Jami‘*)

Among the Best of Women or the Best Among Women

In the light of 66:12 and 3:42 cited above and the numerous *ahadith* proclaiming her excellence, the classical commentators unanimously acclaimed Mary (A) as being one of the best of womenkind. However, as is evident from the interpretation of *Bukhari*, 4:642 above, they disagreed as to whether she was the best of women of her own time or of all times.

Considering yet another *hadith*—

> Among the women of mankind, Mary daughter of ‘Imran, Khadijah daughter of Khuwaylid, Fatimah daughter of Muhammad, and Asiyah wife of Pharaoh are sufficient for you. (*Mishkat*, 6181)

— al-Razi concludes that, while these four noble women were chosen above other women, the angels’ saying that God preferred Mary (A) **above the women of mankind** (3:42) indicates that she was chosen and preferred above *all* other women. He adds that the “statements of those who limit this preference for her to her own time have missed the obvious meaning” of this passage (Schleifer/*Mary*, 71). And indeed, because God declares *twice* in 3:42 (using the same verb, "*istafaki*") that He chose and preferred her, this would seem to be a warranted conclusion.

Al-Qurtubi argues similarly, saying that the self-evident meaning of the Qur'an and *hadith* "demands the conclusion that Mary is the most preferred woman of all the world, from Eve to the last woman on earth at the Final Hour"[28] (Schleifer/*Mary*, p. 72; Ayoub/*Q*, II:124). And he mentions a *hadith* reported by Ibn 'Abbas (R), stating that

> The mistresses [*sayyidat*] of the women of humankind are Mary, then Fatimah, then Khadijah, and then Asiyah (Ayoub/*Q*, II:124).

The Prophet's saying,

> Khadijah was preferred above the women of my *ummah* as Mary was preferred above the women of all nations" (Tabarani),

is also cited in support of this understanding. So is the following *hadith:*

> During the year of the opening of Mecca, the Prophet (S) called his daughter Fatimah and spoke to her privately, and she wept. He then spoke to her again and she laughed. When the Prophet (S) died, she was asked about her weeping and her laughing, and she replied, "The Messenger of God (S) informed me that he was going to die and I wept. He then informed me that, with the exception of Mary daughter of 'Imran, I would be the chief lady among the inhabitants of Paradise, so I laughed."[29] (*Mishkat*, 6184)

Prophet or Saint

What rank, then, does Islam ascribe to Mary, God's peace and blessings be upon her?

We have already mentioned God's speaking of her as **a truthful, righteous woman [*siddiqah*]** (5:75/78), meaning a holy woman or saint (*waliyyah*). But was she, in addition, also a prophet, who was granted miracles (*mu'jizat*) in keeping with the miracles of other prophets?

---

[28]Al-Qurtubi relates the first mention of God's choosing Mary — **"Indeed, God has chosen you"** — to her devoutness, and the second — **"and has preferred you above the women of mankind"** — to her bearing of Jesus (Ayoub/*Q*, II:124).

[29]In another version, the Prophet (S) asks Fatimah if she would not like to be the chief of the women of Paradise or of the women believers (*Bukhari*, 4:819).

Neither the Qur'an nor *ahadith* provide a definitive answer to this question. However, it was thoroughly pondered by the early commentators, who addressed it from every possible direction.[30]

While Mary (A) meets all the criteria for prophethood (but not of messengership, since she was not sent to any community), the question of whether or not a woman can be a prophet remained, for many commentators, an unresolved issue. Based on the words, **And We did not send before you [Muhammad], as messengers, except men [*rijalan*] to whom We revealed** (12:109, 16:43, 21:7), some argued that a prophet could not be other than a male.[31] Consequently, in keeping with God's saying, **His mother was a truthful, righteous woman [*siddiqah*]** (5:75/78), most classifed Mary (A) as a *siddiqah* or holy woman, which is mentioned in the following verse as the highest of all ranks in Paradise after that of prophet:

> **Whoever obeys God and the Messenger — those will be with the ones upon whom God has bestowed favor among the prophets and the affirmers of truth [*siddiqin*] and the martyrs and the righteous [*salehin*]. And excellent are those as companions! (4:69)**

Ibn Kathir's position is that if Mary (A) had been a prophet, 5:75/78, cited above, would have been the place to mention it. He therefore concluded that she was not a prophet but a ***siddiqah*** (Ibn Kathir/*T*, 5:75/78).

Others were of the opinion that because of all her prophet-like qualities and miracles, Mary (A) was indeed a prophet. Various arguments were put forward in support of this interpretation. These included the fact that, in response to Hannah's prayer, among all humankind, only Mary and Jesus, God's peace and blessings be upon them, were protected from the touch of Satan — and for whom would this be suitable if not for a prophet?

Also cited as proof of Mary's prophethood was the *hadith*,

> Many among men were reached perfection, but none among women reached perfection [***kamala***] except Mary daughter of 'Imran and Asiyah wife of Pharaoh.[32] (*Bukhari*, 5:113, 4:643)

---

[30]This is discussed in detail in Volume II of Mahmoud Ayoub's work, *The Qur'an and Its Interpreters*, pages 122-130, and in the fourth and fifth chapters of Aliah Schleifer's book, *Mary the Blessed Virgin of Islam*.

[31]However, Schleifer points out that the masculine noun "*rijal*" in 12:109, 16:43 and 21:7 may include both genders (Schleifer/*Mary*, p. 74).

[32]In another version, the words, "And the excellence of 'A'ishah over women is like the excellence of *tharid* [crumbled bread moistened with broth] over the rest of foods" are added at the end (*Bukhari*, 5:113). In yet another, this statement about 'A'ishah occurs at the beginning, fol-

In the light of this, al-Qurtubi argued that because prophets constitute the most perfect types of human beings, the perfection mentioned in this *hadith* refers to prophethood, indicating that Mary and Asiyah were prophets. He cited two verses which, in his view, confirm Mary's prophethood: 3:45, in which Gabriel (A) conveys to her the revelation, as he did to other prophets, and 21:91, in which God states that He made her **a sign for mankind**, attesting to His limitless power. Al-Qurtubi also suggested the possibility that Mary (A) may have been both a righteous woman (*siddiqah*) — that is, a saint — as well as a prophet (*nabiyyah*), as in the case of the prophet Idris, whom God mentions in 19:56 as being **a truthful one and a prophet (*siddiqan nabiyya*)** (Schleifer/*Mary*, p. 81).

Similarly, Ibn Hazm had no hesitation about classifying Mary (A) as a prophet, stating that God sent Gabriel (A) to her with a message that constituted true prophethood and that He granted her miracles, such as sending her heavenly sustenance in her *mihrab*. He commented that Mary's being mentioned among a number of prophets in *Surah Maryam*, prefaced by the words, **Those were some of the prophets upon whom God bestowed favor** (19:58), makes it impossible to exclude her from among them. Nor does the Qur'anic statement, **His mother was a woman of truth** [***siddiqah***, 5:75/78], preclude Mary (A) from also being a prophet, for in 12:46 the prophet Joseph (A) is referred to as a **truthful one** [***siddiq***] (Schleifer/*Mary*, p. 85).

In support of Mary's being a prophet, it may further be argued that Mary (A) is mentioned at the end of a long series of prophets — Abraham, Isaac, Jacob, Lot, Noah, David, Solomon, Job, Ishmael, Idris, Dhul-Kifl, Jonah, Zechariah and John — in *Surah al-Anbiya'* (The Prophets), in the verse,

> **And [mention] the one who preserved her chastity, and We breathed into her of Our Spirit, and made her and her son a sign for mankind. (21:91)**

And Muslims throughout the world follow the mention of her name with the invocation reserved for prophets and angels, "'*Alayha-s-salam* — peace be upon her."

However, all these factors notwithstanding, since there is no scriptural proof of Mary's prophethood, the matter remains inconclusive. Although Mary (A) received revelation through the angel Gabriel (A), as did the prophets, and her many miracles — the provision of heavenly food in her sanctuary;

---

lowed by what is cited above, followed by the statement cited earlier that the women of the Quraysh were the best among camel-riding women (*Bukhari*, 4:643).

the first visitation by angels; the angelic annunciation of her son and his miraculous conception; the voice speaking beneath her; and her newborn son's defending her honor — are the miracles of a prophet, Mary (A) was not granted a message of guidance for a community. Rather — like Abraham's wife Sarah, to whom the angels also spoke (51:30, 11:73); Hagar in her encounter with the angel (Vol. One, pp. 295); and Moses' mother, who was directed by divine inspiration to the extraordinary means by which her son was saved from death (20:39, 28:7) — she was miraculously granted a messenger-son.[33]

Hence, whether or not Mary (A) was a prophet perhaps remains immaterial in the face of her eminence among womenkind and her high honor with her Lord. In the words of Ibn al-'Arabi, who, without entering into the controversy, focuses upon her special spiritual gifts, she was "for God [*li' Llah*], by God [*bi' Llah*], and on the authority of God [*'ani' Llah*]" (Schleifer/*Mary*, p. 91). Writes Aliah Schleifer,

> Mary in traditional Sunni Islam is an important figure in herself. Her position is not just that of the most exalted category of women, but she is ranked in the highest category of all human beings. In fact, from the perspective of those scholars who consider Mary to be a prophetess, she is considered equal to this aspect of her son Jesus (A). And to those who focus on Mary's outstanding spiritual achievements, she is seen to have been blessed with stages of spiritual development that approach those of Prophet Muhammad (A). In no case is Mary seen solely as the mother of Jesus. Rather, a reverse attitude seems to prevail.[34]
>
> . . . According to the classical Sunni scholars, Mary is, thus, by virtue of God's will, a spiritual luminary who in her primary role as woman slave of God became an ideal of sincerity, faith, devoutness, submission and purity, and who by virtue of these characteristics was opened to God's eternal word and then granted the secondary role of mother. Mary is, therefore, a sign for all Muslim believers, male or female. (Schleifer/*Mary*, pp. 95-96)

REFERENCES: Ibn Kathir/*T*, 3:42-33; Schleifer/*Mary*, pp. 43, 62-63, 65-67, 70-96; Asad, Q, 21:87; Ayoub/*Q*, II: 122-130; Hendi/*Jesus*, pp. 59, 62.

---

[33]We note that in the case of Sarah, Hagar, Umm Musa, and, in part, Mary, the divine inspiration or addressing by angels was related to the lives of their prophet-sons, while Asiyah too played a vital maternal role in relation to Moses. At the same time, Asiyah and Mary (A) are mentioned in 66:12 cited at the beginning of this chapter as prototypes of holy women in their own right, without reference to the prophets in their lives.

[34]That is, through the repeated references to Jesus as **the son of Mary.**

9. THE ANNUNCIATION

And [mention] the one who preserved her chastity, and We breathed into her of Our Spirit, and made her and her son a sign for mankind.
(21:91)

We now come to an event unparalleled in the entire history of mankind — the conception of a child without the agency of a man.[35]

The divine Author of the Qur'an introduces the subject in the following words, addressed to Muhammad (S):

> **And mention Mary in the Book, when she withdrew from her family to a place toward the East and kept seclusion apart from them.** (19:16-17)

This **place toward the East** — said to be the spiritually preferred, most luminous direction — is reported to have been in the eastern part of Jerusalem, perhaps just outside the Temple precincts, or possibly Mary's sanctuary inside it. Al-Suddi reports, on the authority of Ibn 'Abbas, Ibn Mas'ud (R) and others, that the seclusion mentioned in this verse occurred when Mary left her *mihrab* during one of her menstrual periods and separated herself from her family members by a screen of walls. The annunciation occurred afterwards, when she had bathed and was again in a state of purity for worship (Tabari/*H*, IV:118-119; Schleifer/*Mary*, p. 30).

Then, God Most High says, **We sent to her Our spirit** — the angel Gabriel[36] — **and he appeared to her as a well-proportioned man** (19:17).

"Indeed, I seek refuge in the Most Merciful from you, if you are God-fearing!" (19:18), the terrified Virgin exclaimed.

"I am but the messenger of your Lord," the angel replied, **"to bestow upon you a pure boy"** (19:19).

"How can I have a boy while no man has touched me and I have not been unchaste?" (19:20), Mary (A) asked in utter bewilderment, meaning, "I

---

[35]The annunciation is reported in two Qur'anic passages: *Surah Ale 'Imran*, 3:45-51, and *Surah Maryam*, 19:16-21, in which it is followed by the description of the birth of Jesus in verses 23-33. Our account is drawn from both *surahs*, interspersed with the commentary of Ibn Kathir.

[36]The holy spirit, Gabriel, is mentioned in connection with Jesus in three other verses: **And We granted Jesus son of Mary clear proofs and supported him with the holy spirit** (2:87, 253), and, **O Jesus son of Mary, recall My favor upon you and upon your mother when I supported you with the holy spirit** (5:110/113).

am neither married nor have any intention of marrying, nor am I a loose woman."

"Thus!" the angel said. "Your Lord says, 'It is easy for Me, and that We may make him a sign for mankind and a mercy from Us. And it is a matter decreed'" (19:21).

In his commentary on this verse, Ibn Kathir states that the words, **"That We may make him a sign for mankind,"**[37] refer to God's power to create all kinds of creatures by various modes of creation. For indeed He created Adam (A) without either a father or a mother, Eve from a male without a female, Jesus (A) from a female without a male, and the rest of humankind from both a male and a female.

God refers to Jesus (A) in the above verse as **"a mercy from Us"** because he summoned people to Him both during his childhood and maturity, calling them to worship their Lord without ascribing any partner to Him who transcends the taking of a wife or children or partners or opposites or equals, Ibn Kathir continues. His saying, **"And it is a matter decreed"** means that this matter, about which there was no question, was an unalterable reality of God's divine ordaining. These words have also been interpreted as a euphemism for Gabiel's breathing the soul of Jesus (A) into the opening of Mary's garment, whereupon she immediately conceived (Ibn Kathir/*T*, 19:16-21).

"O Mary," the angel continued,[38] clarifying the matter further to the holy Virgin, **"indeed, God gives you good tidings of a word from Him, whose name will be the Messiah, Jesus son of Mary, distinguished in this world and the Hereafter, and among those brought near** to Him. **He will speak to people in the cradle and in maturity, and will be among the righteous"** (3:45-46).

"My Lord," said Mary (A), addressing herself humbly to her Creator, **"how will I have a child when no man has touched me?"** (3:47).

---

[37]Jesus' being a sign or coming with a sign from God is mentioned three times in the angel's annunciation speech, in the words that Jesus himself would later speak: **"Indeed, I have come to you with a sign from your Lord"** (3:49); **"Indeed, that is a sign for you, if you are believers"** (3:49); and **"And I have come with a sign from your Lord"** (3:50). God also says, **That We may make him a sign for mankind** (19:21); **We made her and her son a sign for mankind** (21:91); and, **And We made the son of Mary and his mother a sign** (23:50).

[38]Although 3:45 begins, **When the angels said. . .**, the speaker to Mary here was evidently but one angel, Gabriel.

"Such is God," the angel replied. **"He creates what He wills.**[39] **When He decrees a matter, He but says to it 'Be!'" and it is"** (3:47).

By these words, it was made clear to Mary (A) that the son she was to bear would come into being by the direct command of his Lord, setting aside the natural processes by which human beings invariably arrive in this world. Indeed, says Ibn Kathir in his commentary on these verses, this not a great thing for God, for since all possibilities are in His hands, He is free to create whatever He wills, as and how He pleases. Moreover, when He says 'Be!' there is no delay in that thing's coming into being (Ibn Kathir/*T*, 3:47).

Jesus (A) would be known as **"a word from God."** According to the interpretation of al-Tabari, this was because he came into being through the divine word of command, "Be!" However, Ibn 'Abbas (R) and others state that Jesus himself was the word from God (Ayoub/*Q*, II:131).

The name and title by which every believer would recognize Mary's son would be **the Messiah,**[40] **Jesus son of Mary,** referring him to his mother because he had no father, while at the same time negating his being the Son of God. And he and his mother would be **distinguished** in the sight of God **in this world and the Hereafter**.

---

[39]Here, Ibn Kathir makes a subtle point: that when Zechariah asked a similar question during the annunciation of John — **"My Lord, how will I have a boy when I have reached old age and my wife is barren?"** [3:40] — the angel replied, **"Such is God; He *does* whatever He wills"** (3:40). But in response to Mary's question, she was told, **"Such is God; He *creates* whatever He wills"** (3:47), in order to show those who worship false deities that Jesus was a being created by God (Ibn Kathir/*T*, 3:45-47).

[40]The classical commentators have given differing interpretations of the word *al-Masih* — that is, the Messiah or Christ. Ibn Kathir and others stated that Jesus was called so because of his continuous journeying (***siyahah***) without having any fixed residence. Others said that he was called ***al-masih*** because he used to pass his hand (***masaha***) over the infirm or blind, healing them by God's leave, or that Gabriel touched him (***masahahu***) with his wing when he was born as a protection against Satan. Al-Qurtubi explained the word as meaning one who is anointed (***mamsuh***) with the holy oil with which the prophets were anointed (Ayoub/*Q*, II:131-132). Zamakshari said that "the word ***al-masih*** is an honorific title derived from the Hebrew ***mashiha*** which means the blessed one" (ibid., p. 132). Nisaburi stated, "He was called al-Masih because when God touched (***masaha***) Adam's back and brought out of it all his descendants [see Q. 7:172], He did not return Jesus to his place. A prophetic ***hadith*** relates that 'God allowed all the atoms to return to Adam's loins, but retained the atom of Jesus and his spirit with Him until He cast them into Mary. Jesus was thus called al-Masih, that is, one who was touched (***mamsuh***) by God" (ibid., p. 133) (for the previous mention of this event in the spiritual world, known as "The Day of Promises," please see Volume One, pages 80-81).

God Most High would reveal His scripture to Mary's son and bestow upon him many blessings in this world and in the Life-to-Come, and he would be among **those brought near** to Him — that is, among the greatest of all prophets. The fact that he would speak to people **in the cradle**, calling them to the worship of their Lord even in his infancy, would be one of his miracles, while **in maturity** God would grant him revelation,[41] making him a guide both in word and deed, and **among the righteous** (Ibn Kathir/*T*, 3:45-51).

"And He will teach him the book and wisdom, and the *Taurat* and the *Injil*," the angel continued, describing to Mary (A) the characteristics of the holy son whom she was to bear, **"and make him a messenger to the Children of Israel, saying, 'Indeed, I have come to you with a sign from your Lord, in that I mold for you from clay, as it were, the form of a bird; then I breathe into it and it becomes a bird by God's leave. And I cure the blind and the leper and revive the dead by God's leave.[42] And I inform you about what you eat and what you store in your houses. Indeed, in that is a sign for you, if you are indeed believers.**

"'And I have come confirming what was before me of the *Taurat* and to make permissible for you some of what was previously prohibited to you. And I have come to you with a sign from your Lord, so fear

---

[41]Jesus' speaking in infancy is mentioned again in 5:110/113, which we will discuss on page 357. Al-Tabari says that God mentioned Jesus both as an infant and a mature man to show that he was born and passed through infancy and youth to adulthood like all other human beings. The miracle of speaking in the cradle was granted to him as a sign of his prophethood and of God's omnipotence.

While it has been said that Jesus spoke with the same prophetic authority in infancy and maturity, some commentators hold that he spoke only on one occasion in infancy: to assert his mother's innocence of the sin of which she was accused, for otherwise such an extraordinary event would have been known, preserved in historical accounts, and passed down by Jesus' followers. On the other hand, it has also been suggested that the fact of his speaking in infancy may have been suppressed (although it was mentioned in a scripture called "The Gospel of the Infancy," which was discarded by the early church fathers, together with a number of other books) because the words he spoke as a newborn, **"I am the slave of God"** (19:30), contradict Christian doctrine. As for Jesus' speaking **in maturity [*kahlan*]**, the commentators have given a number of differing interpretations. Among them is the understanding that, because Jesus did not reach middle age, he will speak to people when he returns to the earth during its end-time up to his death, when he will be of mature and advanced age (see Part Five, "The Second Coming of Jesus"). This is discussed in detail in Ayoub, ***The Qur'an and Its Interpreters, Volume II,*** pages 135-139.

[42]These miracles are discussed further on pages 357-358 in connection with 5:110/113.

God and obey me. Indeed, God is my Lord and your Lord, so worship Him. This is a straight path'" (3:48-51).

Thus, by the proclamation of God's holy messenger, Gabriel (A), were the tidings of Jesus ('Isa) (A) conveyed to the blessed Virgin. Prepared as she was for this moment by her years of self-surrender and unflagging worship, Mary (A) accepted the angel's announcement so completely that she did not even ask for a sign, as Zechariah (A) had done under similar circumstances. There is not the slightest hint that, after asking the obvious question, **"How will I have a child when no man has touched me?"** (3:47), and receiving the angel's assurance that the matter would be accomplished by an act of God, she did anything but surrender her will to what her Lord had decreed for her, for **she believed in the words of her Lord and His scriptures, and was of the devoutly obedient.** (66:12)

And God Most High says, **We breathed into her of Our Spirit**[43] (21:91, 66:12), and she conceived.

REFERENCES: Qur'an: 3:45-50, 5:110/113, 19:16-21, 21:91. Commentaries: Ibn Kathir/*T*, 19:16-21, 3:45-51; Ibn Kathir/*Q*, "Mention of the Birth of the Slave and Messenger, Jesus, son of Mary, the Virgin"; Tabari/*H*, IV:118-119; Asad/*Q*, 19:fns. 15-16, 3:fn. 36; Ayoub/*Q*, II:131-154; Schleifer/*Mary*, pp. 30-31.

[43]Since these words can also be read as **We breathed into her through Our spirit [Gabriel],** some commentators, including al-Tabari and Ibn Kathir, state that Gabriel breathed or blew into Mary's bosom or her garment and thereby she conceived (Ibn Kathir/*T*, 4:171, 66:12; Tabari/*H*, IV:113). However, other commentators, such as al-Razi and Zamakhshari, holding to the reading given in the text above, state that the breathing of God's Spirit into the body signifies endowing it with life, as in God's saying concerning the creation of Adam, **"Then, when I have formed him and breathed into him of My Spirit, fall down in prostration to him"** (15:29, 38:71-72). Similar words — **Then He proportioned him and breathed into him of His Spirit** (32:9) — are also used to describe the creation of each human being.

PART TWO: THE LIFE AND MISSION OF JESUS

10. "SO SHE CONCEIVED HIM AND WITHDREW WITH HIM TO A REMOTE PLACE": THE BEGINNING OF JESUS' LIFE

So she conceived him and withdrew with him to a remote place. Then the pains of childbirth drove her to the trunk of a palm tree. She said, "Oh, if only I had died before this and had been forgotten, utterly forgotten!" (19:23)

Although the Qur'an contains numerous verses related to Jesus' role and identity, apart from the narrative of his birth, it contains very little information about his actual life. And this is equally true of the collections of *ahadith.*

While emphasizing the unreliability and lack of authenticity of the Biblical account, many Muslim scholars have not hesitated to borrow from it extensively concerning the life of Jesus (A), repeating many stories found in the Gospels, with variations. However, since these are based on sources for which we find no reliable Islamic validation, we will not repeat them here. Instead, our approach will be to connect the threads of the numerous Qur'anic verses concerning Jesus (A) and derive from them whatever can be understood concerning his life-story and mission.

THE BIRTH OF JESUS (A)

Nothing is mentioned in the Qur'an or *ahadith* about the course of Mary's pregnancy. But, as is clear from what follows, as time passed and her condition began to be obvious, she was tortured by fear and anxiety, for it was absolutely inconceivable that a Jewish woman of good family, especially one such as hers, could be pregnant out of wedlock. Indeed, the punishment prescribed for such an offense in Jewish law was nothing less than stoning to death (Deut. 22:21).

Joseph the carpenter is mentioned in connection with Mary (A) by some Qur'anic commentators. However, the connection is inconclusive and without confirmation from any authoritative Islamic source — an evident borrowing from Christian sources, accepted on faith rather than on reliable evidence. Such accounts are guardedly preceded by expressions such as "it is said," "they say," or "Christian sources say," or followed by the phrase, "And God knows best."

According to one such account, Joseph was Mary's companion in Temple service. When he became aware of her condition, knowing well the excellence of her family and her character, the depth of her piety and sanctity, he realized that the matter was beyond his understanding. Hence, he indirectly and delicately asked her to explain it to him.

Mary (A) replied in like manner, indirectly making Joseph understand that she was pregnant by the act of God. A number of commentators then repeat something like the Biblical story of the nativity and the flight from Egypt. Writes Aliah Schleifer:

> In fact, in traditional Muslim sources Joseph's relationship with Mary is frequently not clarified, or he is mentioned as her companion and relation only, because there is no revealed basis for anything more specific, such as the statement that he was her fiance and later became her husband, both of which are generally attributed to the Gospels, if mentioned at all. Ibn al-Qayyim [al-Jawziyah] further claims that Mary and Joseph were from different tribes and thus could not have been married to each other as this was against Jewish law. (Schleifer/*Mary*, p. 29)

Finally, the possibility of Mary's having been married to Joseph, at least at the time of Jesus' birth, is clearly nullified by the Qur'anic references to the accusations of immorality leveled against her following the birth of Jesus (A) (9:28, 4:156).

We are therefore left to ponder, on our own, the state of a holy woman, immersed since early childhood in pure worship and devout service to God, who now became horrifyingly aware that she would soon be the butt of vile accusations, evil slanders and lewd suppositions, or even subject to the prescribed punishment. Yet despite the fear and anxiety which certainly filled her heart throughout the months before the birth, there surely would have remained within her, like a bright beacon of hope, the assurances conveyed by the angel, sustaining and supporting her as she carried the physical and emotional burden of her pregnancy within the solitude of her inner being, perhaps unsupported by anyone except her Lord.

At some time before the birth of her son, Mary (A) **withdrew with him to a remote place** (19:22). The event itself is described in a lengthy, deeply moving passage (19:22-26) which reflects the Most Merciful Lord's tender compassion for the agony of Mary's overwhelmingly difficult situation.

Then the pains of childbirth drove her to the trunk of a palm tree,[44] the account begins. Tortured in mind and body, Mary (A) cried out, **"Oh, if only I had died before this and had been forgotten, utterly forgotten!"**[45] (19:23).

But he called her from beneath her, saying, **"Do not grieve. Your Lord has provided a stream beneath you. And shake the trunk of the palm tree toward you; it will drop ripe, fresh dates upon you.**[46] **So eat and drink and be consoled. And if you see any human being, say, 'Indeed, I have vowed a fast to the Most Merciful, so I will not speak to any mortal today'"**[47] (19:24-26).

Who was **"he,"** the caller? While many commentators say that it was the newborn Jesus (A), others are of the opinion that Jesus (A) did not speak until his mother brought him in front of her people, and that the voice was that of Gabriel (A). Whatever the case may have been, it was a proof to the helpless, suffering Virgin of her Lord's loving concern for her desperately needy state and a reassurance that she would not be left to deal with such unsurmountable difficulties on her own.

Then she brought him to her people, carrying him (19:27). And the storm descended, as she had known it would, upon her head.

---

[44]Some commentators say she went eight miles away from Jerusalem to Bethlehem, for in a *hadith* concerning the Prophet's Ascension (*Me'raj*), Bethlehem is mentioned as the birthplace of Jesus (Schleifer/*Mary*, p. 32). Others, however, say that he was born in Nazareth, thus originating the Arabic word for "Christian," "*Nasara*" (Ibn Kathir/*T*, 19:22; Schleifer/*Mary*, 33-34).

[45]This, states Ibn Kathir, is an argument for the permissiblity of wishing for death under persecution, for when Mary was slandered and no one believed what she was saying, despite the fact that she was a pure and devout worshipper who remained most of the time in the Temple, she asked for death by wishing that she had never been born and were totally forgotten (Ibn Kathir/*T*, 19:23).

[46]It is obviously impossible for a woman, much less one in Mary's condition, to shake a mature palm tree. But when Mary shook the tree, making the effort she had been commanded to make, God miraculously caused it to drop its ripe, fresh dates beside her. From this, it has been argued that there uis no better food for a woman following delivery than dates, whether fresh or dry. The Holy Prophet (S) used to put some softened date pulp into the mouth of newborn infants (*Bukhari*, 7:376, 7:378, 7:379, 7:714), a custom called *tahnik* which many Muslims observe to this day. And he said, "Respect your uncle, the date palm, because it was created from the same soil from which Adam was created. There is no other tree having both male and female parts that is self-pollinated" (Ibn Kathir/*T*, 19:23).

[47]This is commonly understood as meaning a fast from speaking, not from eating or drinking, for as is clear from 19:24-25, Mary had already eaten and drunk that day.

"O Mary," her relatives exclaimed, **"you have certainly done an unheard-of thing! O sister of Aaron,**[48] **your father was not an evil man, nor was your mother a loose woman"** (19:28) — that is, "None of your family is of ill-repute or evil behavior, and this is absolutely unimaginable for someone of your background and character." It is said that they accused her of committing fornication with her guardian Zechariah (A)[49] or with her cousin, Joseph the carpenter.

When Mary (A) found herself in this critical situation, she did not attempt to defend herself or to reply, for she was in the state of one fasting. Instead, depending upon her Lord, **she pointed to him** (19:29), her newborn son, signifying that her accusers should address themselves to him.[50]

"How can we speak to one who is a child in the cradle?" (19:29), her kinfolk demanded, meaning, "You are merely making an excuse and a mockery of us by pointing to the child, as if a nursing infant could speak and explain!"[51]

But the infant Jesus (A) did in truth begin to speak.

"Indeed," he said, **"I am the slave of God. He has ganted me the scripture and made me a prophet, and has made me blest wherever I am, and He has charged me with *salat* and *zakat* as long as I live, and goodness to my mother, and has not made me harsh and difficult.**[52]

---

[48]**"Sister of Aaron"** may either mean that Mary had a brother named Aaron or it may refer to her descent from the prophet Aaron. It is reported that when the Prophet (S) sent Mughirah bin Shu'bah to the Christians of Najran, they said, "You read 'O sister of Aaron' [in this verse,] whereas Moses was before Jesus by this much." When Mughirah returned and asked the Prophet (S) about it, he replied, "They used to give names after their prophets and the righteous people before them" (*Muslim*, 5326).

[49]Some commentators say that the reason the Jews wanted to kill Zechariah was because of this charge against him.

[50]Perhaps this may be taken as an evidence that the one who had **called her from beneath her** was Jesus, for having seen that her newborn son had miraculously been granted the power of speech, Mary left her defense from this horrendous slander to him.

[51]Once two people came to the Prophet's Companion, 'Abdullah bin Mas'ud. When one greeted him while the other did not, Ibn Mas'ud asked the latter, "Why did you not greet me?" He explained that he had vowed that he would not speak to anyone that day. Ibn Mas'ud then said, "Break your vow and greet people and talk with them, for this was only for Mary. God permitted her to do so as an excuse" (Ibn Kathir/*T*, 19:26).

[52]This declaration of the All-Knowing Lord concerning Jesus should serve to clear him of the callous words that he is reported to have spoken to his mother in John 2:4, "Dear woman, why do you involve me?" (New International Version), or in the far harsher wording of the King James

And peace be upon me the day I was born and the day I die and the day I shall be raised alive!" (19:30-33).

Concerning this passage, Ibn Kathir says:

> This is the first speech of Jesus son of Mary. The first thing he asserted was that he was a **slave of God** [19:30], acknowledging his servanthood to his Lord Most High and declaring that God, his Lord, is highly exalted above what wicked people ascribe to him in being God's Son, while he is but a slave and His messenger and the son of His handmaiden.
>
> Next, he cleared his mother of that which ignorant people were accusing her by saying, **"He has granted me the scripture and made me a prophet"** [19:30], for God does not grant prophethood to one born of what they alleged.
>
> Elsewhere, God speaks of **their uttering a great slander against Mary** [4:156]. This refers to the fact that there was a party among the Jews at that time who said that she had become pregnant through fornication, so God cleared her of this vicious slander, saying of her that she was a truthful, righteous woman [***siddiqah***] [5:75/78] and that He had appointed her son as a prophet. That is why Jesus said, **"He has made me blest wherever I am"** [19:31], for wherever he was, he called people to the worship of the one God who has no partner, transcending the imperfection and shortcoming of taking a son or a wife — holy is He and highly exalted above this!
>
> And he said, **"He has charged me with *salat* and *zakat* as long as I live"** [19:31], for it is the duty of each of God's slaves to stand before Him in *salat* and to do good to His creatures through charity or *zakat*. . . . Then he said, **"And [He has charged me with] goodness to my mother"** [19:32], emphasizing his mother's right on him, and also indicating that he had no parent other than her. **"He has not made me harsh or difficult"** [19:32] means, "I am not rough, harsh or uncouth, and none of my words or deeds is against God's commands and obedience to Him." As for **"Peace be upon me the day I was born and the day I die and the day I shall be raised alive"** [19:33], these are the three most important days of a human being's life, as we explained previously in the story of John (A). (Ibn Kathir/*Q*, "Mention of the Birth . . .")

Version, "Woman, what have I to do with thee?" Another example of Jesus' alleged lack of feeling for his mother is found in two almost identical passages, Matt. 12:48-50 and Mark 3:33-35.

Thus was born, by the act of the Most High, a child who was forever to change the face of both history and religion — Jesus Christ, God's **word which He conveyed to Mary and a spirit from Him** (4:171), the illustrious descendant of Abraham, Isaac, Jacob, Aaron and David (A), concerning whom He says:

> **Such was Jesus son of Mary — a declaration of the truth about which they are in dispute. It is not for God to take a son, may He be glorified! When He decrees a matter, He but says to it "Be!" and it is.** (19:34-35)

REFERENCES: Qur'an: 19:22-34. Commentaries: Ibn Kathir/*T*, 19:16-37; Ibn Kathir/*Q*, "Mention of the Birth of the Slave and Messenger, Jesus, son of Mary, the Virgin"; Tabari/*H*, IV:113-114, 119-120; Ayoub/*Q*, II:123, 125, 168; Schleifer/***Mary***, pp. 28-38, 111, fn. 44; Hendi/*Jesus*, pp. 60-61; Asad/ *Q*, 19:fns. 20, 22-24; Ali/*Q*, fn. 2479.

11. "We Sheltered Them on a Height": The Emigration of Mary and Jesus

We made the son of Mary and his mother a sign, and sheltered them on a height, a place of repose and flowing springs. (23:50)

As the above verse informs us, God made Jesus (A) and his mother **a sign.**

This **"sign"** relates to Mary's conceiving Jesus (A) without a father, says Ibn Kathir in his commentary on this verse. Because of it, some people went to the extreme of accusing Mary (A) of immorality because of her unmarried state, as is evident from the reference to **their uttering a great slander against Mary** (4:156). At the same time, others went to the opposite extreme and elevated Jesus (A) to the status of a god, in marked contrast to the fate of many earlier messengers, who were rejected and despised because of their prophethood (Ibn Kathir/*T*, 23:50).

As for the remainder of 23:50 above, most commentators believe it refers to Mary's flight from King Herod during his murderous rampage against the male infants of the Jews mentioned in Matt. 2:13-18 — some say together with her husband, Joseph the carpenter. However, God alone knows the truth of this matter. Whatever the circumstances may have been, the wording suggests that Mary (A) left home with her son and sheltered or took refuge on the **"height"** — Arabic, **"*rabwah*,"** meaning a high, fertile ground with water, grass and green vegetation.

Where this was is not known. However, it has been speculated that it may have somewhere in Egypt or Syria (i.e., Palestine), either near Jerusalem, Ramlah or Damascus.

Evidence seems to point to the last possibility, for the classical scholar al-Suyuti reports a ***hadith*** in which a man once asked the Prophet (S) about Mount Qasiyun outside Damascus, to which the Prophet (S) replied, "On it, Jesus son of Mary and his mother were given refuge." Al-Suyuti adds that whoever goes there must not shorten his *salat* and his *du'a'* (supplications), for it is the place where supplications are answered. Therefore, adds al-Suyuti, whoever wants to visit the site of the *rabwah*, "[L]et him go to the highest peak between the two rivers, and climb up to the cave upon Mount Qasiyun, and pray there, as it is the house of Jesus and his mother when they took refuge from the Jews" (Schleifer/*Mary*, pp. 38-39).

This is the final mention of Mary (A) in the Qur'anic chronicle of Jesus' life. As for the remainder of her life, according to one tradition, during her later years she dwelt at a place called Meryemana near Ephesus in Turkey, which is marked by a small stone chapel on a wooded hillside. Al-Suyuti reports that she is buried in the Church of Gethsemane in Jerusalem, while Ibn 'Asakir says that she and the apostles are buried in the cemetery of al-Faradis (al-Dahdah) in Damascus (Schleifer/*Mary*, p. 43).

May God's peace and highest blessings be upon that holy, surrendered servant, the example to all womankind, throughout eternity!

REFERENCES: Ibn Kathir/*T*, 23:50; Schleifer/*Mary*, pp. 38-43; Maududi/*Q*, 23:fns. 43-44; Asad/*Q*, 23:fn. 26.

12. "WE GRANTED HIM THE *INJIL*": THE DIVINE REVELATION TO JESUS

And We certainly sent Noah and Abraham, and established prophethood and scripture among their descendants. . . . Then We sent, following in their footsteps, Our messengers, and We followed them with Jesus son of Mary and granted him the *Injil.* (57:26-27)

He has sent down to you [Muhammad] the Book [the Qur'an] with truth, confirming what was before it. And previously He revealed the *Taurat* and the *Injil* as guidance for people. (3:3-4)

One of the special honors and divine favors that God Most High bestowed upon Jesus (A) was the revelation of a scripture known as the *Injil* or "Evangel," meaning "Gospel" or "Good Tidings".

The *Injil* is mentioned in twelve verses of the Qur'an.[53] Of these, ten relate to Jesus' role and identity; we will discuss them shortly. The two that relate to our present topic, Jesus' life-story, are the following:

> **"He will teach him the book [*al-kitab*] and wisdom, and the *Taurat* and the *Injil.*"** (3:48)
>
> **"[O Jesus, recall] when I taught you the book [*al-kitab*] and wisdom, and the *Taurat* and the *Injil.*"**[54] (5:110/113)

Some commentators interpret the word "***al-kitab***" in these two verses as referring to the art of writing, which Jesus (A) knew. Others say that it refers to divinely-revealed books or scriptures in general, or to those revealed scriptures other than the *Taurat* and *Injil* (since the *Taurat* and *Injil* are mentioned in these two verses as being other than the **"the book"**), such as the *Zabur*.

As for **"wisdom,"** al-Tabari states that it refers to the practice of earlier prophets which God revealed to Jesus (A) (Ayoub/*Q*, II:139). Ibn Kathir says that it refers to the understanding of religion — that is, purifying one's inner self in order to attain submission and sincerity to God, doing good deeds and avoiding evil, and seeking God's pleasure through obedience to Him, while

---

[53]These are 3:3, 48, 65; 5:46-47/49-50, 66/69, 68/71, 110/113; 7:157; 9:111; 48:29; 57:2.

[54]As mentioned in Chapter 9, 3:48 comprises part of Gabriel's annunciation speech to Mary, while 5:110/113 is mentioned in the context of what God will say to Jesus on the Day of Judgment, reminding him of the divine favors granted to him as His messenger (5:109-110/112-113).

shunning His displeasure by avoiding disobedience (Ibn Kathir/*T*, 2:127-129). Perhaps we may also suggest that it refers to that inner understanding that is granted to sincere servants by their Lord whereby the sacred Law is applied and matters or events are perceived and interpreted by the light of the heart, and a grasp of the deeper realities and subtle interconnections that are hidden from those who see only what is apparent and obvious.

It is said that after Jesus (A) had acquired such essential knowledge of the art of writing and of religion as is meant by **"the book and wisdom,"** God Most High taught him the knowledge of the *Taurat*.[55] All this prepared him to receive the *Injil*, a new, original revelation from his Lord.

Concerning the actual contents of the *Injil*, no information is given either in the Qur'an or in *hadith*. Although it may have contained some of the teachings attributed to Jesus (A) in the four Gospels, it is impossible to confirm this, much less to identify which particular teachings. And that is itself by the decree of the All-Knowing, the All-Wise, for reasons that He alone knows.

But while the *Injil* was a new revelation specifically granted to Jesus (A), its message certainly was not new. Rather, it was a confirmation of the true, pristine religion ordained for mankind by the Creator, *islam*, and a validation and confirmation of what remained of the original *Taurat*, for God Most High says:

> **And We sent, following in their footsteps, Jesus son of Mary, confiming that which preceded him of the *Taurat*, and We granted him the *Injil*, wherein was guidance and light, and confirming that which preceded it of the *Taurat*, as guidance and instruction for the righteous.** (5:46/49)

> **[Jesus said,] "O Children of Israel, indeed I am the messenger of God to you, confirming what preceded me of the *Taurat*."** (61:6)

The words, **following in their footsteps** in 5:46/49, make it clear that Jesus (A) adhered to the path and traditions of the Israelite prophets who preceded him. This informs us that one vital aspect of his mission was to confirm to the Jews **that which preceded him/it of the *Taurat*** (significantly, mentioned *twice* in this verse), for he had not been commanded to abolish the

---

[55]God's "teaching" of Jesus mentioned in 3:48 and 5:110/113 may be understood as meaning either that God taught him from Himself or that He caused him to be taught.

sacred Law but rather to verify and uphold what had remained unchanged of it up to his time.[56]

At the same time, Jesus (A) also declared,

> **"And [I have come] confirming what preceded me of the *Taurat* and to make permissible for you some of what was [previously] prohibited to you."** (3:50)

These words have led some commentators to suppose that the *Injil* abrogated certain commands of the *Taurat*. Others, however, say that it did not abrogate any of its laws but rather demonstrated that various matters that had been added or subtracted by Jewish scholars were not actually divine injunctions.[57]

The conclusion of most interpreters is, therefore, that Jesus (A) both confirmed the laws of the *Taurat* and at the same time made lawful certain things that had been prohibited — prohibited not by God but through rules imposed by the Jews upon themselves for which He had not revealed any authority. This is in keeping with the words of Jesus (A),

> **"I have come to you with wisdom and to make clear to you some of that wherein you differ"** (43:63).

In summary, then, Jesus (A) clearly proclaimed that adherence to the *Taurat* was the basis of his mission, but freed from the unwarranted man-made additions and interpolations that had become attached to it over time.

REFERENCES: Qur'an: 3:3-4, 48, 50; 4:160; 5:46/49, 110/113; 27:76; 43:63; 57:26-27; 61:6. Commentaries: Ibn Kathir/*T*, 2:127-129, 5:47/50, 5:111/114; Ayoub/*Q*, II:139-140, 149-154; Hendi/*Jesus*, p. 78.

---

[56]Cf., Matt. 5:17, in which Jesus is reported as saying, "Do not think that I have come to abolish the Law or the Prophets; I have not come to abolish them but to fulfill them."

[57]The understanding that Jesus (A) abolished certain laws which the Jewish rabbis and scholars had incorrectly attributed to Moses, Jacob (Israel) or other prophets is also suggested by the verse, **Then, for wrong-doing on the part of the Jews, We made unlawful for them,** by the tongues of their men of religion, certain **good foods which had been lawful to them** (4:160). Another, related verse, **All food was lawful to the Children of Israel except what Israel [Jacob] had prohibited to himself before the *Taurat* was revealed. Say, [O Muhammad:] "Then bring the *Taurat* and recite it, if you are truthful. And whoever invents a falsehood about God after that, then those are the wrong-doers"** (3:93-94), is discussed in Volume One, pages 329-330.

13. "I Have Come to You with Wisdom": The Teachings of Jesus

And when Jesus came with clear proofs, he said, "I have come to you with wisdom and to make clear to you some of that about which you differ, so be mindful of God and obey me. Indeed, God is my Lord and your Lord, so worship Him. This is a straight path." (43:63-64)

The Qur'anic account contains very little information concerning Jesus' actual teachings — and, like many other matters about which its divine Author is silent, this again is no 'accident'.

Virtually the only clearly-defined teaching of Jesus (A) mentioned in the Qur'an is his proclamation of his own humanity and servanthood. Indeed, in the very first words to come from his lips, he stated that he was **the slave of God**, who had been granted the scripture and made a prophet (19:30). Moreover, he repeatedly declared that **"God is my Lord and your Lord, so worship Him,"** and that this and nothing else was the straight path (3:51; also 5:72/75, 117:120; 19:36; 46:64).

As for Jesus' overall mission, the Qur'anic text informs us that God made him **a messenger to the Children of Israel** (3:49). In his prophetic role, as we have seen, he clarified aspects of their faith about which they differed (43:63), **confirming what** had been revealed **before him of the *Taurat*** (3:50, 5:56/59, 61:6), while at the same time making permissible for them **some of what was** previously **prohibited** to them (3:50). Like the prophets who preceded him, he was charged with two basic acts of worship, ***salat* and *zakat***, the prescribed prayer and charity, throughout his life (19:31), but whether he enjoined this on his followers or they practiced it already, as observant Jews, is not known.

This in essence summarizes what is stated in the Qur'an concerning Jesus' mission and teachings. As for *ahadith*, although the Holy Prophet (S) spoke of Jesus (A) often, it was primarily in the context of his spiritual knowledge of him, discussed in Chapters 21 and 24, and of Jesus' second coming, which is the subject of Chapters 22 and 28–30. Consequently, *ahadith* concerning Jesus' actual teachings are rare. Among them are the Prophet's saying,

> Jesus saw a man stealing and asked him, "Did you steal?" He said, "No, by God, other than whom there is no deity!" so Jesus said, "I believe 'By God' and disbelieve my eyes." (*Bukhari*, 4:653; *Muslim*, 5840)

'A'ishah (R) reported that her father, Abu Bakr as-Siddiq (R), once came to her and asked if she had heard the supplication that the Messenger of God

(S) had taught, mentioning that Jesus son of Mary (A) taught it to his apostles and that he used to say that even if one of them were burdened with a debt the size of a mountain, God the Mighty and Glorious would settle it for him. She said,

> He used to say: "O God, Dispeller of care, Remover of grief, Responder to the plea of the needy, Most Merciful of this world, Most Compassionate of the Hereafter, I ask You that you bestow upon me mercy from Yourself by which You will leave me in need of mercy from none but You." ('Abd al-Qadir al-Gilani, *Sufficient Provision for Seekers of the Path of Truth*, Vol. Four, p. 353)

Ibn Kathir mentions the following ***hadith***, about which he says, "This a strange ***hadith***, but since it is full of good advice, we have reported it":

> Jesus (A) passed by a ruined city, and he was astonished and said, "O Lord, command this city to respond to me."
>
> Then God inspired to the city, "O ruined city, answer Jesus!"
>
> The city then called out, "O my beloved Jesus, what do you want of me?"
>
> Jesus said, "What has happened to your trees? What has happened to your rivers? What has happened to your palaces? Where are your inhabitants?"
>
> The city replied, "O beloved, the promise of your Lord came to pass, so my trees dried, my rivers were absorbed, my palaces became ruined, and my inhabitants died."
>
> Jesus asked, "Where is their wealth?"
>
> The city replied, "They gathered it from permissible and prohibited sources, but it is all in my belly. And to God belongs the inheritance of the heavens and the earth!"
>
> Jesus (A) then called out, "I am surprised at three kinds of people: the one who seeks the world while death is seeking him; the one who builds palaces while the grave is his destination; and the one who engages in hearty laughter in it [the world] while Hell-fire is in front of him."
>
> "O son of man, you are not satisfied with much nor content with little. You collect your wealth for him who does not thank you,[58] and you are proceeding toward your Lord while you have no excuse [for your faults]. And indeed, you are a slave of your belly and your sexual desire.

[58]Although this refers to one's inheritors, it may also mean one's ***nafs*** or lower self, which never appreciates anything but always demands more and more without limit.

Indeed, you fill your belly until you enter your grave, and you, O son of man, see your gathered wealth in someone else's scale." (Ibn Kathir/*Q*, "*Fasl – 'Isa*")

THE WISDOM TRADITIONS

If the accounts in the Gospels are in any way reflective of reality, we can understand that out of his inspired wisdom, Jesus (A) taught his people by means of lessons, parables and examples that would speak to their hearts, emphasizing inner piety and purity rather than outward observance. Hence, in addition to what is reported in the Qur'an and the few ***ahadith*** that have come to us concerning his teachings, many apocryphal reports of Jesus' actions and sayings, which fall under the heading of "wisdoms," have come down to us from various sources.

These reports, according to Muhammad 'Ata ur-Rahim, "were originally gathered together by the earlier followers of Jesus, especially those who spread to Arabia and North Africa" ('Ata ur-Rahim/*Jesus*, p. 222). And since many of the followers of these followers who accepted Islam during the time of the Prophet (S) brought with them reports that they had retained concerning Jesus (A), these traditions were passed down from one generation of Muslims to the next.

While the authenticity of these traditions is by no means established, we cite a number of them here as examples of the understanding of the personality and teachings of Jesus Christ (A) that is prevalent among Muslims, reflecting the deep piety and devout abstinence, profound humility, purity of heart and compassion that are regarded as his chief characteristics.

Sufyan al-Thawri reported Jesus (A) as saying,

> The love of the world and the love of the Hereafter cannot be together in the heart of the believer, just as water and fire cannot be in the same vessel. (Ibn Kathir/*Q*, "*Fasl – 'Isa*")

Imam Malik, one of the great compilers of ***hadith***, reported that Jesus (A) said,

> Do not speak much without the mention of God, for you will harden your hearts. A hard heart is far from God, but you do not know. Do not look at the wrong actions of people as if you were lords; look at your [own] wrong actions as if you were slaves. Some people are afflicted by wrong action and some people are protected from it, so be merciful to the people of affliction and praise God for His protection. (*Muwatta*, 56.3.8)

Ibn Kathir reported that Jesus (A) used to wear [coarse] wool, that he ate of the leaves of trees, that he did not have a house, a family or any wealth, and that he never kept anything for the morrow. He also reported its being said that Jesus (A) will be at the head of the ascetics on the Day of Judgment. Among the sayings Ibn Kathir attributed to Jesus (A) are the following:

> The love of this world is the root cause of every error, and sight excites desires in the heart.
>
> O weak son of man, fear God as much as you are able, remain in the world as a guest, and adopt places of worship in your houses. Teach your eyes to weep, your body to be patient and your heart to reflect, and do not prepare for tomorrow's provision, for it is an error.
>
> The lover of the world is like one who drinks from the ocean: the more he drinks, the more his thirst increases, until he is killed.
>
> Satan is with the world, and his deception is with wealth and his abode is with desires.
>
> Just as kings have left wisdom for you, leave the world for kings.
>
> Be happy with the least of the world, keeping your religion intact, as the people of the world are happy with the least of the religion and the intactness of the world. (Ibn Kathir/*Q*, "*Fasl* – 'Isa")

In a similar vein, it is also reported that Jesus (A) said:

> In the last days there will be learned men who teach abstinence in the world but will not be abstinent themselves, who will teach men to take delight in the next world but will not take delight in it themselves, and who will warn men against coming before rulers [to ask for favors] but will not refrain themselves. They will draw near to the rich and keep far from the poor; they will be pleasant to great men but will shrink from humble men. Those are the brethren of the devils and the enemies of the Merciful. ('Ata ur-Rahim/*Jesus*, p. 224)
>
> The world consists of three days: yesterday which has passed, from which you have nothing in your hand; tomorrow, of which you do not know whether you will reach it or not; and today in which you are, so avail yourself of it. (ibid., p. 223)
>
> The world is both seeking and sought. He who seeks the next world, this world seeks him until his provision in it is complete; and he who seeks the present world, the next world seeks him until death comes and seizes him by the neck. (ibid., p. 223)
>
> My seasoning is hunger, my undergarment is fear of God, my outergarment is wool, my fire in winter is the rays of the sun, my lamp is the moon, my riding beast is my feet, and my food and fruit are what the

earth brings forth (i.e. without cultivation). At night I have nothing and in the morning I have nothing, yet there is no one on earth richer than I. (ibid., p. 223)

The following incidents and sayings are also attributed to Jesus, God's peace and blessings be upon him

The apostles asked Jesus (A), "How is it that you can walk on water and we cannot?" Then he said to them, "What do you think of the dinar and the dirham?" They replied, "They are good." He said, "But they and mud are alike to me." (ibid., p. 223)

One day Jesus (A) struck his hands on the earth, then closed them and then opened them. In one of his hands was gold and in the other stones. He said to his companions, "Which of the two has more value in your heart?" They said, "This gold." He said, "To me, both are the same." (Ibn Kathir/Q, "*Fasl – 'Isa*")

John and Jesus (A) met. Jesus was laughing, so John said, "O my cousin, why are you laughing, as if you are in safety?" Jesus said, "Why do I see you gloomy, as if you have given up hope?" God then revealed to both of them, "The one who meets his friend with cheerfulness is dearer to Me." (ibid.)

Jesus (A) passed by a dead creature and people said, "What a terrible smell!" He responded, "What beautiful teeth!" teaching them not to backbite. (ibid.)

Someone asked Jesus (A) about the gravest trial for people. He said, "The fall of a scholar, because when the scholar falls he takes with him a great part of mankind." He is also reported to have said, "O evil scholars, you sat at the gates of Paradise but did not enter it, and you did not invite the poor, who entered it. Indeed, the worst of people in the sight of God is the scholar who seeks the world through his knowledge." (ibid.)

Jesus (A) met a pig and greeted him, saying, "Go in peace." He was asked about it and said, "I do not like to make my tongue move with evil speech." (Qadi 'Iyad/*Ash-Shifa*, p. 79)

Jesus (A) was asked, "Why do you not ride a donkey?" He replied, "I exalt God too much to be occupied with looking after a donkey." He used to wear hair and eat from trees. He did not even have a house. He slept wherever sleep overtook him. The name he most liked to be called by was "the very poor." (ibid., p. 7)

Jesus said to the apostles, "Eating barley bread and drinking pure water today in this world is plenty for him who wishes to enter Paradise tomorrow." (Murata, *The Tao of Islam*, p. 262)

The following sayings were attributed to Jesus (A) by Imam al-Ghazali, may God bless his sacred soul, one of the greatest Islamic scholars and mystics of all time:

> The angels will not enter the house of him who turns the beggar empty away. (*The Mysteries of Almsgiving*, p. 76)
>
> How could he who persists in the paths of this world while his destination is the hereafter, or he who seeks knowledge to show off and not for the sake of following its precepts, be counted among the learned? (*The Book of Knowledge*, p. 161)
>
> Blessed is he who renounces a present desire for the sake of something which he has not beheld. (*On Disciplining the Soul*, p. 56)
>
> O assembly of disciples! Make your bellies hungry, that haply your hearts may behold your Lord! (ibid., p. 89)
>
> Beware of glances, for they sow desire in the heart, which is temptation enough. (ibid., p. 173)
>
> Pay no attention to your provisions for tomorrow, for if tomorrow is to be part of your lifetime then your provisions will come with it, whereas if it is not to be, then you should pay no attention to the lifetimes of others. (*The Remembrance of Death and the Afterlife*, p. 29)

In a lengthy narrative, the Prophet's Companion, Wahb bin Munabbih (R), said that the apostles once said to Jesus (A), "It is said that God's deputies are not subject to fear nor shall they grieve,"[59] and they asked him to tell them who these were. Then, out of the perfection of his own inner state, he described to them that which perhaps cannot be so described except by one who has reached that state.

They are those who look deep into the earth while others look at the surface, Jesus (A) said, who observe what is hidden while others are attracted to passing pleasures, and who focus on the consequences of this world's life, while others seek its immediate profits. They let die in themselves whatever might shame them and renounce what will ultimately leave them. They are satisfied with little of this world and do not waste their time in discussing what is ephemeral.

> What they receive from this world becomes a burden and a cause of their sorrow, and they are adamant in refusing to look at other attractions therein. What comes to them as lawful they renounce, and the success

[59]A reference God's saying, **Unquestionably, the friends of God [*awliya'-Allah*, holy ones, saints] — no fear shall be on them nor shall they grieve** (10:62).

> that may cross their path they turn down. When their dwellings fall apart, they do not rebuild them, and when their desire for this world dies in their hearts, they do not renew it.

Instead, they employ their determination and will to secure their true comfort in the home of the Hereafter, having bartered the pleasure and comfort of this world in exchange for comfort in the Eternal Life. Consequently, because they have sold what is passing and for such a small price purchased what is everlasting, they are the really happy ones.

> They look at the people who love this world and see them as dead and toiling in-between one calamity after another. They recall death and renounce the idea of occupying themselves with this life.

They truly love God Most High, loving to speak of Him and constantly invoking His remembrance. They walk by His light and invite others to do so as well. God's glorious Book is proclaimed through them. They establish it and live by it; it speaks through them and with it they speak, and through them the glorious Book becomes known.

> They consider their trials as a vehicle for advancement despite the extreme sufferings they may endure. They find no peace except in what they seek, and they fear nothing except what should concern them most. (Akili/*Beauty*, pp. 9-10).

May God Most Gracious grant us the wisdom to benefit from these blessed words and let them take root in our hearts!

REFERENCES: Ibn Kathir/Q, "*Fasl – 'Isa*"; al-Ghazali, *The Mysteries of Almsgiving*, p. 76; al-Ghazzali, *The Book of Knowledge*, p. 161; al-Ghazali, *The Remembrance of Death and the Afterlife*, p. 29; al-Ghazali, *On Disciplining the Soul*, pp. 56, 89, 173; Qadi 'Iyad/*Ash-Shifa*, p. 79; Akili/*Beauty*, pp. 9-10; Murata, *The Tao of Islam*, p. 262; 'Ata ur-Rahim, *Jesus*, pp. 221-227.

14. "Indeed, I Have Come to You with a Sign from Your Lord": The Miracles of Jesus

And We granted Jesus son of Mary clear proofs. (2:87, 253; 5:110./113)

"O Jesus son of Mary, recall My favor to you and to your mother when I supported you with the holy spirit [Gabriel,] and you spoke to people in the cradle and in maturity; and when I taught you the book and wisdom, and the *Taurat* and the *Injil*; and when you molded from clay, as it were, the form of a bird by My leave, then you breathed into it and it became a bird by My leave, and you cured the blind and the leper by My leave; and when you brought forth the dead by My leave; and when I restrained the Children of Israel from you when you came to them with clear proofs, and those who disbelieved among them said, 'This is nothing but obvious magic.'" (5:110/113)

Jesus, God's peace and blessings be upon him, was the prophet of miracles. Indeed, his very life began with one of the greatest miracles of all times. And God miraculously supported this special creation of His **with the holy spirit,** the angel Gabriel (2:87, 253; 5:110/113).

Jesus' first miracle after his birth was his understanding human speech and speaking **to people in the cradle** (3:46, 5:110/113). According to the interpretation of Ibn Kathir, the words that he uttered as a newborn infant —

> **"Indeed, I am the slave of God. He has granted me the scripture and made me a prophet, and He has made me blest wherever I am, and has charged me with *salat* and *zakat* as long as I live, and goodness to my mother, and has not made harsh and difficult. And peace be upon me the day I was born and the day I will die and the day I will be raised alive"** (19:30-33)

— made clear to his mother's accusers that one granted such a miracle and special divine favors could not be the product of what they imagined, but rather was an extraordinary being with a very special destiny.

A further miracle, described as **"a sign from your Lord"** in the annunciation verse 3:49 and mentioned in 5:110/113 above, was Jesus' molding **"from clay, as it were, the form of a bird"** and then breathing into it, whereupon it became a living bird and flew away, for God had granted him the power to breathe life into dead matter — indeed, into dead flesh. However, Jesus (A) repeatedly stressed to his people that such miracles were **by God's leave** (3:49, 5:110/113), not by his own power. Indeed, this fact is mentioned seven times in these two verses. For while molding the clay and breathing into it was Jesus' act, says Ibn Kathir, the act of creating it as a live bird was God's, just as, in the matter of his conception, the act of breathing into Mary (A) was Gabriel's, but the act of creating was God's.

Jesus (A) also **cured the blind** from birth **and the leper**, great miracles because these were two chronic, incurable infirmities, and he **revived** or **brought forth the dead** — all of these, again, **by God's leave** (3:49, 5:110/113).

In this context, Ibn Kathir comments that the prophets were given miracles appropriate to the people of their time. Since during the time of Moses (A) magic predominated and magicians were greatly revered, God Most High granted Moses (A) such a powerful miracle that the magicians immediately understood that it could not be produced by magic but was rather a true grant from God; consequently, they hastened to prostrate and enter into Islam, and they became near to God. But since Jesus (A) was sent during a time of great doctors and scholars, he was granted such miracles as were suited to the mentality of his people. Not only is curing leprosy and the congenital blindness outside of anyone's power, but all the more is breathing life into lifeless clay and raising the dead, since such things can only occur by God's leave.

Jesus (A) was also miraculously able to inform people about what they ate and what they stored in their houses (3:49),[60] as if to say, "These are proofs of my truthfulness and that what I am teaching you is from God, so why do you not believe? **Indeed, in that is a sign for you, if you are believers"** (3:49). A further miracle, God's granting the apostles a heavenly repast due to Jesus' supplication (5:112-115/115-118) is detailed in the next chapter.

A final miracle was God's restraining **those who disbelieved** among the Jews from killing Jesus (A) when he **came to them with clear proofs**[61] — that is, his miracles, the divine evidences of his claim to prophethood — which

---

[60]The early commentators gave a number of interpretations of the words, **"I inform you about what you eat and what you store in your houses"** (3:49). Perhaps the most convincing of these is that Jesus informed his people about what they ate and stored up of the heavenly food that God sent down at the request of his apostles (see pages 362-364), although they had been commanded not to conceal or keep any of this food for the following day. However, since the nature of this miracle is not explained by the divine Author of the Book, what is important is to accept it as stated without concern for its details, which are known with certainty only to God.

[61]The **clear proofs** that Jesus brought are mentioned in 2:87, 253; 5:110/113; 61:6.

those who disbelieved among them regarded as **"nothing but obvious magic"** (5:110/113). This subject will be the theme of Chapter 16.

REFERENCES: Qur'an: 2:87; 3:47-51, 59; 5:110/113; 19:30, 35; 21:91; 23:50; 61:6. Commentaries: Ibn Kathir/*T*, 3:45-51, 5:109-110/112-113; Ibn Kathir/*Q*, "Mention of the Birth of the Slave and Messenger, Jesus, son of Mary, the Virgin"; Ayoub/*Q*, II:131-154.

15. "We Are God's Helpers": The Apostles

O you who believe, be supporters of God, even as Jesus son of Mary said to the apostles, "Who will be my supporters for God?" The apostles said, "We are supporters of God." And a faction of the Children of Israel believed and a faction disbelieved. Then We strengthened those who believed against their enemy and they became dominant. (61:14)

Then, when Jesus became aware of disbelief among them, he said, "Who will be my supporters for God?" The apostles said, "We are supporters of God. We believe in God and bear witness that we are *muslims.* Our Lord, we believe in what you have revealed and follow the messenger, so inscribe us among the witnesses." (3:52-53)

Among the matters reported concerning Jesus (A) in the Qur'an is the fact that he had an unspecified number of apostles.

These apostles or disciples, whose number is not known, are referred to in the Qur'an as "***hawariyun,***" singular, "*hawari*". Since one meaning of this word is "white," various commentators relate the term *hawari* to the apostles' wearing white garments, to their being tanners, or to the purity of their hearts. More to the point, however, *hawari* also means a counselor, advisor; one who acts sincerely, honestly or faithfully; a true, sincere friend or assistant; or, in this context, a particular and select assistant of a prophet.[62]

In 61:14 above, we are informed that while **a faction of the Children of Israel believed** in Jesus' prophethood and the guidance he brought from God, another **faction disbelieved.**

Then, when Jesus became aware of disbelief among them, he said, "Who will be my supporters for God?" (3:52), meaning, "Who will be my

---

[62]Referring to the following *hadith*, Ibn Kathir notes that the word *hawari* actually means "helper" or "assistant":

On the Day of the Confederates (that is, the Battle of the Trench in the fifth year after the Prophet's emigration to Medina in 627 A.C.), when the Prophet (S) called for volunteers, Zubayr bin al-Awwam came forward. When the Prophet (S) called again and still only Zubayr came forward, the Prophet (S) said, "Each prophet has a *hawari*, and my *hawari* is Zubayr" (*Bukhari*, 4:100).

helpers in calling people to God and supporting me in my work?" or "Who will follow me to reach God?"

The apostles said, "We are supporters of God (3:52, 61:14). **We believe in God and bear witness that we are *muslims*. Our Lord, we believe in what You have revealed and follow the messenger,** Jesus, **so inscribe us among the witnesses"** (3:52-53).

The words, **"We believe in God and bear witness that we are *muslims*,"** may be understood as meaning either, "We believe in God and bear witness [concerning ourselves] that we are *muslims*," or, "We believe in God, and [you, O Jesus,] bear witness that we are *muslims*." Al-Tabari interprets this verse as being

> an assertion by God that *islam* is His faith with which He sent Jesus and all the prophets before him. It is neither Christianity nor Judaism. This verse is, therefore, a dissociation of Jesus by God from all those who accept Christianity as a religion, as He dissociated Abraham from any faith other than *islam*.[63] (Ayoub/Q, II:158-159).

The words of the apostles that follow, **"Inscribe us among the witnesses,"** have been variously interpreted as meaning, "Record us as being among those who witness to Your Oneness," "As those who witness to the truthfulness of Your prophets," or "As being among the *ummah* of Muhammad, God's peace and blessings be upon him."

Yet another interpretation is, "Record us as being in the company of those who witness." And since God declares that on the Last Day **We will surely question those to whom a message was sent, and We will surely question the messengers** (7:6), that company consists of the prophets, of those who testify to God's Oneness and the truthfulness of His messengers, and of the *ummah* of Muhammad (S). Perhaps the meaning is best summarized by al-Tabari, who interprets **"Inscribe us among the witnesses"** as meaning, "Record our names with the names of those who witness to the truth, affirm Your [O]neness, believe in Your messengers, and abide by Your commands and prohibitions" (Ayoub/Q, II:162-163).

REFERENCES: Qur'an: 3:52-53; 61:14. Commentaries: Ibn Kathir/T, 3:52-53; Ayoub/Q, II:158-165; Asad/Q, 3:fn. 42, 61:fn. 15.

---

[63]That is, in God's saying that **Abraham was neither a Jew nor a Christian, but he was one inclining toward truth [*hanifa*], a *muslim*, and he was not among the *mushrikin*** (3:67).

THE SPREAD TABLE

The apostles are mentioned again in the following verse, a continuation of the passage quoted at the beginning of Chapter 14, in which God Most High addresses Jesus (A) on the Day of Resurrection and reminds him of the divine favors granted him during his lifetime:

> **"And [recall] when I inspired to the apostles, 'Believe in Me and in My messenger.' They said, 'We believe, so bear witness that indeed we are *muslims*.'" (5:111/114)**

This verse informs us that when the apostles were ordered by divine inspiration to believe both in their Lord and in his holy messenger, Jesus, they responded in words similar to 3:52-53, quoted on page 360, saying, **"We believe, so bear witness that indeed we are *muslims*."** That is, they testified to their own belief, and at the same time they called upon Jesus (A) to testify that they had surrendered to God in the pure, original faith conveyed through all the prophets, *islam*.

In the next verse of this passage — the continuation of what God Most High will say to Jesus (A) on the Day of Resurrection — Jesus (A) will be asked to recall the event for which the fifth *surah*, *Al-Ma'idah* (The Spread Table), is named; that is,

> **When the apostles said, "O Jesus son of Mary, could your Lord send down to us a table from Heaven?"[64] (5:112/115).**

Taken aback by the boldness of their request, Jesus (A) replied, **"Fear God, if you are believers!"** (5:112/115).

But the apostles insisted, saying, **"We desire to eat from it and let our hearts be reassured and know that you have been truthful to us and be among the witnesses of it"** (5:113/116).

Deferring to their plea, Jesus (A) then prayed, **"O God, our Lord, send down to us a table from Heaven, to be a festival for us, for the first of us and the last of us, and a sign from You. And provide for us, and You are the Best of Providers"** (5:114/117).

---

[64]The meaning of the question, **"Could your Lord send down to us a table from Heaven?"** was given by the Prophet (S) as, "Could you prevail upon your Lord to send? . . ." suggesting uncertainty, not of God's ability to do what was asked, which would imply doubt and disbelief among the apostles, but of Jesus' ability or willingness to make such a request. In accordance with this understanding, the Prophet's wife 'A'ishah reportedly stated that Jesus' disciples knew better than to ask whether God is able to *do* something. Rather, they were asking whether Jesus was able to make this request of his Lord (Asad/Q, 5:fn. 137).

"Indeed, I will send it down to you," came the divine response. **"But"** — because it was a request verging on audacity and unbelief — **"whoever among you disbelieves afterwards, I will surely punish him with a punishment by which I have not punished anyone among mankind!"** (5:115/118).

Commenting on these verses, Ibn 'Abbas (R), al-Tabari and other respected Qur'anic interpreters said that Jesus (A) ordered his apostles to fast for thirty days. When they had completed this period, they asked Jesus (A) to request that a table be sent down from Heaven.

Jesus' response, **"Fear God if you are believers!"** was an admonition to them to be satisfied and thankful and not make conditions with God. But the apostles replied that they desired **to eat from it and let** their **hearts be reassured** that God had accepted their fasting and responded to their desire for heavenly food, so that it might be a feast day for them, and so that they might, moreover, be **among the witnesses** of it to others (5:113/116). It is said that they argued that they had fasted for thirty days as Jesus had instructed them, and that if anyone serves someone for thirty days, he should be compensated with either food or wages.

In response to Jesus' supplication, a table, laden with seven fishes and seven loaves of bread — or, it has been said, with fruits of Paradise — came down from Heaven and settled in front of them. And all of them ate from it.

According to the commentator Qatadah (R), the heavenly table sent down to Jesus (A) and his apostles also constituted a test from God, for Jesus (A) ordered the people not to conceal any of the food that had come down to them or keep any of it for the following day. But they disobeyed his order. He then told them what they had done, saying, **"I inform you about what you eat and what you store in your houses. Indeed, in that is a sign for you, if you are believers"** (3:49). Then, in keeping with God's warning that **"whoever among you disbelieves afterwards"** by disobeying the divine command not to store up any of the heavenly food, **"I will surely punish him with a punishment by which I have not punished anyone among mankind"** (5:115/118), they were metamorphosed into pigs (Ayoub/*Q*, II:143).

This is confirmed in a ***hadith*** narrated by 'Ammar bin Yasir (R), which reports the Prophet (S) as saying,

> The Spread Table was sent down from Heaven with bread and meat, and they were commanded not to be unfaithful nor store up for the morrow. But they were unfaithful and stored up and laid by for the morrow, so they were transformed into monkeys and pigs. (*Mishkat*, 5150)

'Ammar (R) also said that people used to come and eat of this food without its finishing. They were told that if they did not save it, it would continue perpetually, but if they tried to save it they would be punished as no other people had been punished previously. But they cheated from the very first day (Ibn Kathir/*T*, 5:112-115/115-118).

REFERENCES: Qur'an: 3:49, 5:111-115/114-118. Commentaries: Ibn Kathir/*T*, 5:112-115/115-118; Ayoub/*Q*, II:143; Asad/*Q*, 5:fn. 137.

16. "THEY DID NOT KILL HIM NOR CRUCIFY HIM": HOW JESUS LEFT THIS WORLD

They did not kill him nor crucify him, but it was made to appear so to them. . . . Of a certainty they did not kill him. Rather, God raised him to Himself, and God is Almighty and Wise. (4:157-158)

In His Last Testament, the Qur'an, God Most High addresses one of the most fundamental points of Christian doctrine, the crucifixion of Jesus (A). And He does so in a very clear, direct manner, for in three brief passages which we will shortly discuss in detail, He, the All-Knowing, informs us of what no human being could possibly have known except through divine revelation — namely, how Jesus Christ (A) left this world.

While the belief that Jesus (A) was put to death on the cross is central to Christian theology, at the same time the doctrine of the crucifixion raises a number of extremely difficult, unanswered and unanswerable questions, which indeed call into question the very nature and attributes of God Himself, as commonly agreed upon by all revealed religions. Among these questions are the following:

Since God is eternal and does not die, how could Jesus be God or God be Jesus if he died, even for an instant? What was happening to God while Jesus was being put to death, and how did the universe continue during the period of His death? Moreover, if God is All-Powerful and is the sole giver of life and death, what power or force is there that could take away *His* life? Again, if Jesus (A) is God, why did he cry out while on the cross, as stated in Matt. 27:46 and Mark, 15:34, "My God, my God, why have you forsaken me?" echoing Psalm 22? And finally, if it is actually to be supposed that God, the Almighty, All-Powerful Creator whose divine Will guides and directs all things, suffered the horrendous disgrace and torment of being beaten, exposed almost naked in public, and left to die in unspeakable agony in the manner of a common criminal, what kind of a God is that?

If, on the other hand, Jesus (A) is God's Son, why did the All-Merciful Lord need to sacrifice him in order to forgive and save mankind from eternal damnation? Could He not have exercised His attributes of perfect mercy and justice without torturing His only son in a manner that makes one shudder to contemplate — and all because He was somehow unable or unwilling to forgive the genetically-transmitted sin of the ancestor of the human race? If He deemed such a tremendous sacrifice to be necessary, how is it possible to believe in His divine justice, or in His love and compassion for mankind when He had none for His own son?

Perhaps the occurrence of Jesus' crucifixion has never been seriously challenged since Christian doctrine took its final form — except by One. And that One is God Himself, who states unequivocally and emphatically in the verses cited above *that it simply did not take place.* Jesus, God's peace and blessings be upon him, was neither crucified nor killed. Rather, according to Islamic belief, God Most High raised him up to Himself. He remains alive with his Lord and will return to the earth during its final period prior to the Day of Judgment to complete his mission and die, like every other created being.[65]

The thought that Jesus, God's peace and blessings be upon him, may not have been crucified is so radical, in the Christian frame of reference, that it almost boggles the mind, since his crucifixion is one of the "givens" of history as we know it. But if in fact he was not crucified, then what actually took place?

In answer to this question, the divine Author of the Qur'an throws out some intriguing hints for us to ponder. These will be the subject of the remainder of this chapter.

"THE FACTIONS AMONG THEM DIFFERED"

A clue to the circumstances preceding Jesus' departure from this world is contained in two related passages:

> **[Jesus said,] "And indeed, God is my Lord and your Lord, so worship Him. This is a straight path." But the factions from among them differed. Then woe to those who disbelieved from the scene of a tremendous Day!** (19:36-37)
>
> **And when Jesus came with clear proofs, he said, "I have come to you with wisdom and to make clear to you some of that about which you differ, so be mindful of God and obey me. Indeed, God — He is my Lord and your Lord, so worship Him. This is a straight path." But the factions from among them differed. Then woe to those who have done wrong from the punishment of a painful Day!** (43:63-65)

---

[65]Jesus' second coming will be discussed in detail in Chapters 22 and 28-30.

The words, **"the factions among them differed,"** which occur in both of these passages, have a double application. On the one hand, they refer to the differences that arose concerning Jesus (A) after his time, evoking stern warnings of the awesome scenes and punishments of the Day of Judgment for **those who disbelieved** (19:37) in his prophethood, as well as for **those who have done wrong** (43:65) by ascribing divinity to him. At the same time, they also refer to the differences that arose among the Jews when Jesus (A) dwelt among them.

While the specific nature of these differences is not mentioned in the Qur'anic account, history attests to the fact that controversy arose as to whether Jesus (A) was more than human, a true prophet, or an imposter and destroyer of the faith. This understanding is confirmed by the previously-cited verses,

> **And a faction of the Children of Israel believed and a faction disbelieved. Then We strengthened those who believed against their enemy and they became dominant. (61:14)**

> **Then, when Jesus became aware of disbelief among them . . . (3:52)**

What all these passages confirm is the fact that (as stated in the four Gospels), during the brief period of Jesus' mission, disagreements concerning him arose among the Jews. The "disbelief" (***kufr***) mentioned in all these verses refers not to disbelief in God — an obvious impossibility, since those who "disbelieved" were Jews; indeed, the majority of those referred to may have been men of religion. Rather, this "disbelief" consisted of denial and rejection of Jesus' prophethood, which, in the Islamic frame of reference, is equivalent to denial of the One who appointed him as His prophet.

"Nothing But Obvious Magic"

As we have seen, some sincere, good-hearted Jews, perhaps including those perceived as lowly and sinful, accepted Jesus' prophethood and teachings, and followed his path. However, others, perhaps especially members of the religious elite — smug, self-righteous, and regarding religion as a matter of adherence to rituals and outward forms — rejected his prophethood, questioned his authority and challenged his understanding of the religion.

A clue to this is contained in the words, **Those who disbelieved among the Children of Israel were cursed by the tongue of David and Jesus son of Mary** (5:78/81), which we will discuss in more detail on pages 411-413. This verse suggests that, rather than trying to pacify or come to terms with the religious leaders, Jesus (A) condemned them for their falsity to what God had entrusted to them as the guardians of the faith, as is confirmed in such New Testament passages as Matt. 23:1-7, 13-34, Luke 11:42-52, 12:1 and others.

Thus, what seems likely is that Jesus (A), the holy, pure, pious ascetic prophet, whose heart was fixed upon his Lord, then became a center of controversy, which, perhaps in keeping with the divine command, he made no attempt to avoid. Perceiving him as trespassing on their preserve, threatening their authority and undermining their monopoly on religion, the Jewish religious elite reacted to him with the same bitter opposition and hostility as the chiefs of the unbelieving peoples of earlier prophets had done in the past, and as the unbelievers of Muhammad's time would do some five hundred years later.[66] Rather than accepting the miracles that Jesus (A) repeatedly wrought as divine confirmation of his prophethood, those who disbelieved in him fabricated charges of blasphemy and sorcery against him, as mentioned in God's saying, **When he came to them with clear proofs, they said, "This is obvious magic"** (61:6). The words,

> **[And recall, O Jesus,] when I restrained the Children of Israel from you when you came to them with clear proofs, and those who disbelieved among them said, "This is nothing but obvious magic" (5:110/113),**

suggest that this led to the demand for his death.

"RATHER, GOD RAISED HIM TO HIMSELF"

Three Qur'anic passages speak of the manner in which Jesus, God's peace and blessings be upon him, left this world. We will now examine these in detail, together with the interpretations of various classical commentators, in particular Ibn Kathir.

---

[66]This is a subtle point. Although those who accused Jesus of working magic may have been religious Jews, their denial of their prophets did not differ from that of the unbelieving peoples of Noah, Hud, Saleh, Abraham, Lot and Shu'ayb; from Pharaoh and his chiefs with respect to Moses; nor from the pagan Quraysh of Mecca who repeatedly ascribed the Prophet's Message and his Book to magic, as mentioned in 6:7, 10:2, 11:7, 21:3, 28:48, 34:43, 37:15, 38:4, 43:30, 46:7, 51:52, 54:2, 74:24. Thus, God says,

> **Similarly, there did not come to those before them any messenger but that they said, "A magician or a madman!" (51:52)**

> **They [the pagan Quraysh] say, "[The Qur'an and the *Taurat* are but] two works of magic, supporting each other, and indeed we are disbelievers in both." (28:48)**

3:54-55

And they schemed and God schemed, and God is the Best of Schemers. (54) **[Mention, O Muhammad,] when God said, "O Jesus, indeed, I will take you and raise you to Myself, and purify you of those who disbelieve and make those who follow you superior to those who disbelieve until the Day of Resurrection. Then to Me is your return, and I will judge between you concerning that about which you used to differ."** (55)

(54) According to the interpretation of commentators such as al-Tabari, Ibn Kathir and al-Qurtubi, **those who disbelieved** among the Jews plotted or schemed against Jesus (A) with the intention of killing him. But at the same time, God, the All-Informed and All-Aware, also "schemed".

A number of classical commentators note that while God Most High refers to Himself in this verse as **the Best of Schemers** (or Planners or Contrivers), it is obviously not possible to attribute deception to Him. However, al-Qurtubi mentions that some scholars have considered **Best of Schemers (*Khair al-Makirin*)**[67] to be one of God's Beautiful Names, so that it would be acceptable to pray, "O Best of Schemers, scheme for me!" Al-Qurtubi also reports that the Prophet (S) used to pray, "O God, scheme for me, and do not scheme against me" (Ayoub/Q, II:166). In the verse above, therefore, God's "scheming" refers to the manner in which He dealt with those who schemed against His chosen servant Jesus (A), thereby working out His divine plan for him in the face of their evil plot.

(55) God Most High then revealed to Jesus (A), **"Indeed, I will take you [*mutawaffika*] and raise you to Myself"** (3:55).

The word **"*mutawaffika*,"** which ordinarily means "I will receive you or cause you to die," has here been interpreted in a number of ways by the classical commentators. Some say that it means that God caused Jesus (A) to die temporarily, either for three hours of a day during which He raised him to Himself, or for three days, after which He restored him to life and raised him to Heaven. Another meaning given here to ***mutawwafika*** is that God caused

---

[67] These words also occur in 8:30, in God's saying to Muhammad (S), **And [recall] when those who disbelieved schemed against you to confine you or kill you or expel you [from Mecca]. But they scheme and God schemes. And God is the Best of Schemers.** A similar idea is expressed in 13:42: **And those before them schemed, but the scheme belongs entirely to God.** It is also echoed in 27:50 concerning the plotting of the nine evil ringleaders of Saleh's people: **And they schemed a scheme and We schemed, while they did not perceive.**

Jesus (A) to be like one who had died, for when God raised him to Heaven, he had no further relationship with this world. Yet another interpretation is that here ***mutawaffika*** means, "I will cause you to sleep, and will take you up in your sleep"; or, "I will receive you from the earth, in the same way as one would say, 'I have received in full what such-and-such owed me'"; or, "I will take you from this world, but not through death" (Ayoub/*Q*, II:169-170).

Al-Tabari states that although ***mutawaffika*** commonly means "I will cause you to die" (a meaning that would clearly be absurd here in light of God's decisive declaration in 4:157 that **they did not kill him**), it also means "I will receive, reclaim, or fully appropriate you." Citing a ***hadith*** reported by Hasan al-Basri mentioning the Prophet's saying to some Jews, "Jesus did not die, and he will return to you before the Day of Resurrection," al-Tabari interprets this passage as meaning that God received Jesus (A) from the earth and raised him to Himself, for this is in keeping with the many sound ***ahadith*** prophesying Jesus' return to the earth at its end-time and his eventual death during that period. Al-Tabari further supports this interpretation by saying that if God had already caused Jesus to die once (according to the common interpretation of ***mutawaffika*** mentioned above), He would not cause him to die a second time at the end of his second coming, as is mentioned in these ***ahadith*** (ibid., 169-171). Other classical commentators give related or similar interpretations of these words.

As for the interpretation of the latter part of 3:55,

> **"[I will] purify you of those who disbelieve and make those who follow you superior to those who disbelieve until the Day of Resurrection. Then to Me is your return, and I will judge between you concerning that about which you used to differ,"**

it may be summarized as follows:

"I will purify you . . ." means "I will cause you to be acquitted or cleansed of." **"Those who disbelieve"** refers to those who disbelieved in the prophethood of Jesus (A), or who corrupted his pure message by deifying him and accepting beliefs and practices that did not conform to his teachings. Consequently, the true believers who followed Jesus' faith and example (*sunnah*) up to the time of Muhammad (S) were granted superiority over those who rejected Jesus' prophethood or made exaggerated claims concerning him. Here, God Most High declares that these true believers will remain victorious over the others up to the Last Day, when He will judge among them all concerning their differences.

REFERENCE: Ayoub/*Q*, II:165-183.

4:155-159

The second passage related to the departure of Jesus (A) from this world is a sequel to 4:153-154, quoted previously, which refers to the Israelites' demand to see God openly; their worship of the Golden Calf; God's raising Mount Sinai over them due to their rejection of the covenant; and their being told to enter the gate humbly and not transgress the Sabbath.

This complex passage continues:

> **Then [punishment came upon them] because of their breaking of their covenant and their disbelief in God's signs, and their killing of the prophets without right and their saying, "Our hearts are wrapped" — no, rather, God has sealed them because of their unbelief, so they do not believe, except a few;** (155) **and [because of] their unbelief and their uttering a great slander against Mary,** (156) **and their saying, "Indeed, we killed the Messiah, Jesus son of Mary, God's messenger," while they did not kill him nor crucify him, but it was made to appear so to them. And indeed, those who differ concerning it are in doubt about it. They have no knowledge concerning it except the following of assumption, and of a certainty they did not kill him.** (157) **Rather, God raised him to Himself, and God is Almighty and Wise.** (158) **And there is no one among the People of the Scripture but will surely believe in him before his death, and on the Day of Resurrection he will be a witness against them.** (159)

(155-158) After the matters mentioned in 4:153-154,[68] God Most High here speaks of the Israelites' breaking of their covenant, their disbelief in God's signs, their killing the prophets without right,[69] and their assertion that their hearts were wrapped or covered from accepting guidance. God refutes the truth of this claim, stating that rather He caused their hearts to be sealed due to their own unbelief, **so they do not believe, except a few**.

Three sins of the Jews are then mentioned in 4:155-156, says Ibn Kathir. The first of these, **their unbelief,** refers to their denial of His prophets, together with their miracles and clear proofs. The second sin is the **great slander** which they uttered against the chaste virgin Mary (A), accusing her of fornication and alleging that Jesus (A) was the product of a prohibited act. And the third is their claim that they **killed the Messiah, Jesus son of Mary,**

---

[68]These verses are cited in "Qur'anic References — Moses," page 192.

[69]This is mentioned in such New Testament verses as Matt. 23:34-37 and Luke11:48-51.

God's messenger, whereas **they did not kill him nor crucify him, but** rather, by means of that which caused it to seem to Jesus' enemies that they had crucified and killed him, **it was made appear so to them,** or, according to another, equally valid reading, **But he** — another person who was taken to be Jesus and crucified in his place — **was made appear him to them**.

God Most High then declares that **those who differ concerning it** — Jesus' crucifixion and death — **are in doubt about it**. Instead of having certain knowledge, they are merely following assumptions, speculations, opinions or whatever they desire to believe. True knowledge about the matter can come only from the sole Witness and Knower of all things, God Himself. And He repeats a second time, with even stronger emphasis, that **of a certainty they did not kill him.**[70] **Rather, God raised him to Himself, and God is Almighty and Wise** (4:157-158).

Concerning the actual events surrounding Jesus' departure from this world, various classical commentators have given a number of differing accounts. From among these, we cite that of the most trusted guide to the Qur'an, 'Abdullah ibn 'Abbas (R), who stated the following:

When God intended to raise Jesus (A) to Heaven, he came to his companions from a spring of water in the house, where twelve of his apostles had gathered, and his head was dripping with water. He said, "Among you is one who will deny me twelve times after believing in me."

He then asked, "Which of you is willing to have my likeness cast upon him in order that he may be slain in my place and be with me in my station [in Paradise]?"

The youngest of them then stood up. Jesus (A) said to him, "Sit down!" But when Jesus (A) repeated what he had said previously, the same young man again stood up and said, "I will."

Then Jesus (A) said, "Then you be the one!" The likeness of Jesus (A) was then cast upon the young man and Jesus (A) was raised [bodily] to Heaven through an opening in the roof. The Jews then entered, seized the one who resembled him, and crucified and killed him. And one of them de-

---

[70]The fact that Jesus was not killed is also suggested, although not positively stated, in the previously-cited verse, **[And recall, O Jesus,] when I restrained the Children of Israel from you when you came to them with clear proofs, and those who disbelieved among them said, "This is nothing but obvious magic"** (5:110/113).

nied him twelve times after having believed in him (Ibn Kathir/*Q*, "Mention of the Raising of Jesus . . .").

As for the interpretations of other commentators, some are quite similar to that of Ibn 'Abbas (R), while others differ. However, since those that differ are derived from or related to the accounts in the four Gospels, they neither meet our criterion of authenticity nor offer conclusive evidence. At the same time, since God Most High never forgets or errs, the very absence of details in the Qur'anic account indicates that they have absolutely no relevance in the face of the one all-important, absolutely certain fact about which there can be no doubt or question because it is stated by the Knower of all things, both open and secret: that **they did not kill him nor crucify him but it was made to appear so to them** (or, in the other reading, **He [the other person] was made to seem him to them**). **. . . And of a certainty they did not kill him. Rather, God raised him to Himself** (4:157-158).

(159) As for the final verse of this complex passage, stating that there is **no one among the People of the Scripture but will surely believe in him before his death, and** that **on the Day of Resurrection he,** Jesus, **will be a witness against them,** we will discuss its interpretation in Chapter 22 in the context of the second coming of Jesus (A).

REFERENCES: Ibn Kathir/*T*, 4:155-159; Ibn Kathir/*Q*, "Mention of the Raising of Jesus (A) to Heaven and the Protection of the Lord"; Ayoub/*Q*, II:173-174; Hendi/*Jesus*, p. viii, 44.

5:117/120

The raising-up of Jesus (A) is mentioned in yet another verse. In it, speaking of the Last Judgment, Jesus (A) says to his Lord,

> **"I did not say to them except what You commanded me — to worship God, my Lord and your Lord. And I was a witness over them as long as I was among them; but when You took me up [*tawaffaytani*], You were the Observer over them, and You are Witness over all things." (5:117/120)**

The meaning here is that Jesus (A) was a witness of the deeds of his people as long as he was physically present among them. But when he was taken up (and the verb here is a form of the same verb used in 3:55), God alone remained as the Observer of what they did, as He is the Witness over all His creation. Taken together with the wording of 4:157 — **They did not kill him** — and of 3:55 — **Indeed, I will take you and raise you to Myself** — this verse constitutes further evidence of Jesus' not having been crucified and of his having being raised to God alive.

REFERENCES: Ibn Kathir/*T*, 3:54-55; 4:155-159; Ibn Kathir/*Q*, "Mention of the Raising of Jesus (A) to Heaven and the Protection of the Lord"; Ayoub/*Q*, II:165-183.

Part Three: The Nature, Identity and Role of Jesus

17. Tradition Versus Revelation

Those messengers — We favored some of them over others. Among them were those to whom God spoke, and He exalted some of them in rank. And We granted Jesus son of Mary clear proofs and supported him with the holy spirit [Gabriel]. If God had willed, those succeeding them would not have fought each other after the clear proofs came to them. But they differed, and some of them believed and some of them disbelieved. And if God had willed, they would not have fought each other, but God does whatever He intends. (2:253)

By around 75 to 85 A.C., three of the Christian Gospels — Matthew, Mark and Luke — had been finalized. The fourth, the Gospel of John, was finalized by about 90 A.C. A little more than two hundred years later, in 325, the Council of Nicea formalized the official doctrine of the Christian church, and by the close of the fourth century these four accounts of the life of Jesus (A) had ben adopted as the canonical gospels of the New Testament. Consequently, by the time the Qur'an was revealed to Muhammad (S) in the seventh century after Christ (during the twenty-two year period between the years 610 to 632 A.C., to be exact), these four Gospels had long since been accepted as the ultimate sources of Christian doctrine.

From the time of Jesus (A) up to the time of Muhammad (S), numerous Christian sects had come into being with differing understandings, not only of the nature of Jesus (A) but, as a corollary to it, of the nature of God, as **they divided their affair** of religion **among themselves** (21:93).

As a result, bitter controversies and conflicts arose, marked at times by bloodshed. Each sect emphasized a different aspect of Jesus' nature, life or mission, claiming truth and superiority over the others. By Muhammad's time, the earlier Christian sects that had revered Jesus (A) as a prophet were virtually extinct. Jesus Christ, God's peace and blessings be upon him, had by now been officially elevated to the status of the Son of God and one of the three Persons of the Trinity. Ibn Abbas (R) sums up the matter thus:

> His followers were divided into three sects. One sect said, "God was among us as long as He willed; then He rose up to Heaven," and these are the Jacobites. Another sect said, "The Son of God was among us as long as God desired him to be and then God raised him up to Himself,"

and these are the Nestorians. And the third sect said, "A slave of God and His messenger was among us as long as He wished, and then God raised him to Himself," and these are the ***muslims***.[71] The two disbelieving sects subsequently overpowered the ***muslims*** and killed them all, and ***islam*** remained absent until God sent Muhammad, God's peace and blessings be upon him. (Ibn Kathir/Q, "Mention of the Raising of Jesus . . .")

Similarly, al-Tabari summarizes these doctrinal differences among Christians by saying that they disagreed with one another concerning Jesus (A), some asserting that he was God, others that he was the Son of God, and yet others claiming that he was a **third of Three** (5:73) (Ayoub/Q, II:3).

It was against the backdrop of these varied assertions, in a land bordering Christian territories and having a very small Christian population, that the Qur'anic verses concerning Jesus (A) were revealed, by means of which God informed His Last Prophet (S) of the claims of the Christians and their validity or lack of it.

Now, Muhammad (S) was a portionless orphan who had been raised from an early age by his grandfather, 'Abd al-Muttalib, and afterwards by his uncle, Abu Talib, both leaders of a prominent family in Mecca, in which the prevailing religion was idolatry. Like most people in his community, Muhammad (S) did not know how to read or write, nor did he have any knowledge of the scriptures of earlier prophets, beyond, at most, such oral traditions as were a matter of public knowledge in the region.[72] Consequently, whatever

---

[71]Meaning that the true believers among Jesus' early followers who accepted his prophethood, followed the guidance revealed through him, and were faithful to the pristine faith ordained by God.

[72]One of the titles by which Muhammad (S) is known is **"the Unlettered Prophet (*al-Nabiyy al-Umiyy*)"**. His lack of literacy and unfamiliarity with previous scriptures is referred to in the following verses:

> **And before it [the revelation of the Qur'an], you [Muhammad] did not recite any scripture, nor did you write any with your right hand. In that case, indeed, the followers of falsehood would have doubted. (29:48)**
>
> **And thus have We revealed to you an inspiration from Our command [the Qur'an]. You did not know what is the scripture nor faith, but We have made it a light by which We guide whomever We will of Our servants. And indeed, you guide to a straight path. (42:52)**
>
> **"My mercy embraces all things. So I shall decree it for those who are mindful of Me and give *zakat*, and those who believe in Our signs [or verses] — those who follow the Messenger, the Unlettered Prophet whom they find inscribed in what they have of the *Taurat* and the *Injil*, who enjoins upon them what is right and**

was revealed to him by God came to an unbiased, uncritical individual who had neither ability nor interest in moulding the divine revelation into a given form.

Lacking knowledge of the other religions of his area, Judaism and Christianity, amidst the prevailing paganism, Muhammad (S) was therefore able to receive whatever God Most High sent down to him free of pre-existing notions that might have clouded his understanding. All that was conveyed to him by the holy spirit, Gabriel (A), including the numerous verses concerning Jesus (A), was therefore transmitted by him to the first Muslims, and, after them, to all mankind, exactly as it had come to him, without being filtered through a mind colored by preconceptions. As God says:

> **That is of the news of the Unseen which We reveal to you [Muhammad]. You did not know it, neither you nor your people, before this. Therefore, be patient; indeed, the [best] outcome is for the righteous.** (11:49)

At no time did Muhammad (S) claim to have originated the Qur'an. On the contrary, he repeatedly emphasized that it came, not from himself but, through Gabriel (A), from the Lord of the heavens and the earth,[73] who

---

forbids them from what is wrong, and makes permissible to them the good and prohibits to them the evil, and relieves them of their burden and the fetters which were upon them. . . . So believe in God and His Messenger, the Unlettered Prophet, who believes in God and His words, and follow him, that you may be guided." (7:157, 158)

It is He who sent among the unlettered a messenger from among themselves, reciting to them His verses and purifying them, and teaching them the scripture and wisdom, although previously they were in clear error. (62:2)

Indeed, We have revealed it as an Arabic Qur'an, that you may understand. We relate to you [Muhammad] the best of stories in what We have revealed to you of this Qur'an, although you were, before it, among the unaware. (12:2-3)

[73]This point is emphasized in numerous verses, among which are the following:

It was not for this Qur'an to be devised by any other than God, but rather [it is] a confirmation of what was before it and a detailed explanation of the [former] scripture, about which there is no doubt, from the Lord of the worlds. Or do they say, "He [Muhammad] fabricated it?" Say: "Then produce a *surah* like it and call upon whomever you can besides God, if you are truthful!" (10:37-38)

And indeed, it [the Qur'an] is the revelation of the Lord of the worlds. The trustworthy spirit [Gabriel] has brought it down upon your heart, that you [Muhammad] might be among the warners, in clear Arabic language. (26:192-196)

[This is] the revelation of the Book about which there is no doubt from the Lord of the worlds. Or do they say, "He fabricated it"? Rather, it is the truth

would obviously not speak other than the truth about Himself or His messengers, including Jesus (A). To those who believe in its divine origin, the Qur'an is therefore nothing less than the ultimate criterion for understanding all things, especially the otherwise unknowable nature of the Creator and His relationship with His creation, which is in turn critical to an understanding of the nature of Jesus (A). Thus, God says,

> **We have not revealed to you [Muhammad] the Book but that you might make clear to them that wherein they differ, and as guidance and mercy for a people who believe.** (16:64)

Christian belief, on the other hand, was arrived at, during the early centuries of Christianity, by a reverse process. During those formative years of the new faith, elements of monotheistic Judaism were blended with Graeco-Roman ideas and borrowings from the eastern mystery religions, with all their pagan elements. Because of the highly unusual things people heard about Jesus (A) — his miraculous conception and birth from a virgin mother; his speaking in infancy; his healing the sick and blind and raising the dead; his miraculous escape from crucifixion and ascension to God, which was misunderstood as rising from the dead — an identity and role was assigned to him that was cast in the mould of the confused, distorted beliefs about divinity current at the time, giving rise to a new hybrid religion that was part monotheistic and part pagan.

Consequently, while Islamic belief about Jesus (A) works *forward* from the revealed knowledge of who God is and who He is not, and the consequent limitations of everything other than God, the emerging Christian doctrine worked backwards from the supposed "knowledge" of who Jesus (A) was. Thus were traditions, legends and sayings crystallized into beliefs and dogmas which conformed to the prevailing pagan mindset, and which ended

---

from your Lord, that you [Muhammad] might warn a people to whom no warner has come before you, that perhaps they might be guided. (32:2-3)

Your companion [Muhammad] has not strayed nor has he erred, nor does he speak from fancy. It [the Qur'an] is nothing but a revealed revelation, taught to him by one mighty in power [Gabriel]. (53:2-5)

Indeed, it [the Qur'an] is the speech of a noble messenger [Gabriel] and it is not the speech of a poet — little do you believe; nor the word of a soothsayer — little do you remember. [Rather, it is] a revelation from the Lord of the worlds. And if he [Muhammad] had made up some sayings about Us, We would have seized him by the right hand; then We would have cut the aorta out of him, and there is none of you who could have withheld [Us] from him. (69:40-47)

by proposing a new identity for God Himself. The unique, partnerless Creator, who had proclaimed His Oneness through the tongue of every prophet since the appearance of mankind upon the earth, was now suddenly, without precedent, one of Three and the father of a son who shared in His divinity, or who even was, according to some interpretations, God Himself.

We have examined the Qur'anic verses that relate to the life story and mission of Jesus, God's peace and blessings be upon him. In this section, we will briefly summarize the Islamic understanding of his nature, identity and role. And since this understanding, derived from the Qur'anic text, stands out in sharp contrast to the teachings of mainstream Christianity concerning its founder, we hope that our discussion may shed some light on the question of who Jesus (A) really was and what his mission was intended to be, which has been a major issue among Christians themselves since virtually the earliest beginnings of Christianity.

18. The Islamic Understanding of Jesus

And We did not send before you [Muhammad] any messenger but that We revealed to him that there is no deity except Me, so worship Me. (21:25)

"A Word and a Spirit from God"

Because of the belief that Jesus (A) was a special, unique creation of God's who came into being by the direct command of his Lord, Jesus (A) is known among Muslims as "*Kalimat-Ullah*, God's word". This is also stated in the following verses:

"O Mary, indeed, God gives you good tidings of a word from Him, whose name will be the Messiah, Jesus son of Mary, distinguished in this world and the Hereafter, and among those brought near [to Him]." (3:45)

The Messiah, Jesus son of Mary, was but a messenger of God and His word which He bestowed upon Mary and a spirit from Him. (4:171)

This belief in Jesus' creation by the divine command in the womb of his virgin mother is such a central tenet of faith in Islam that the Holy Prophet (S) said,

> Whoever testifies that there is no deity except God, One, having no partner, and that Muhammad is His slave and His messenger, and that Jesus is God's slave and His messenger and His word which He bestowed upon Mary and a spirit from Him, and that Paradise is real and Hellfire is real, God will admit him into Paradise, no matter what deeds he may have done. (*Bukhari*, 4:644)

"Indeed, I Am the Slave of God"

As we noted in the story of Adam (A), every being — indeed, every atom of creation — is in a state of *'ubudiyat* or servanthood to its Creator, for **There is no one in the heavens and the earth but comes to the Most Merciful as a slave** (19:93). This includes even angels and prophets, the best of creation, about whom God says,

Glorified is He! Rather, they are [but] honored slaves. They do not precede Him in speech and they act by His command. He knows what is before them and what is after them, and they cannot intercede except for one whom He approves, and they are

apprehensive out of fear of Him. And whoever of them should say, "Indeed, I am a god besides Him," We would recompense that one with Hell. Thus do We recompense the wrongdoers! (21:26-29)

Whatever is in the heavens and whatever is on the earth of creatures prostrates to God, and the angels, and they are not arrogant. (16:49)

Thus, Jesus Christ, blest and honored though he was, was, like all other created beings, God's slave and servant, the son of His slave and servant, the blest and honored virgin Mary (A). God says,

He [Jesus] was nothing but a slave upon whom We bestowed favor, and We made him an example for the Children of Israel. (43:59)

Never would the Messiah disdain to be a slave to God, nor the angels, near [to Him]. (4:172)

Again, this was also the first attribute of Jesus (A) by which he identified himself, proclaiming, even as a newborn babe, **"I am the slave of God"** (19:30).

"My Lord and Your Lord"

As mentioned previously, the primary teaching of Jesus (A) reported in the Qur'anic account is God's being his Lord, as He is the Lord of all mankind. This is mentioned in the following five passages:

"And I have come to you with a sign from your Lord, so be mindful of God and obey me. Indeed, God is my Lord and your Lord, so worship Him. This is a straight path.'" (3:50-51)

They who say, "God is the Messiah, son of Mary," have certainly disbelieved, whereas the Messiah said, "O Children of Israel, worship God, my Lord and your Lord." (5:72/75)

"I did not say to them except what You commanded me: to worship God, my Lord and your Lord." (5:117/ 120)

"And indeed, God is my Lord and your Lord, so worship Him. This is a straight path." (19:36)

And when Jesus came with clear proofs, he said, "I have come to you with wisdom and to make clear to you some of that wherein you differ, so be mindful of God and obey me. Indeed, God — He is my Lord and your Lord, so worship Him. This is a straight path." (43:63-64)

Through these repeated statements, Jesus (A) emphatically proclaimed his humanity and creaturehood, refuting the assertions that he claimed to be divine or to be the Son of God. Thus did he make it clear that the **straight path** ordained by God can only be reached by firm adherence to believing in and and witnessing to His Oneness, uniqueness and sovereignty over all creation.

"THE SON OF MARY"

One of the first things likely to strike a reader of the Qur'anic passages concerning Jesus (A) is that God refers to him again and again as Mary's son. In fact, out of the thirty-four passages in which Jesus (A) is mentioned either by name or by one of his titles, he is referred to twenty-three times as the **son of Mary**. Perhaps this constitutes a subtle message from God the Exalted to mankind about who Jesus (A) was — that is, *the son of Mary because he had no other parent.*

Since many of the verses referring to Jesus (A) as the son of Mary contain other themes which we will discuss shortly, we will not quote all of them here. All of these verses are, however, quoted in our text, as well as in the Qur'anic References at the end of this story. Below, we quote the verses in which Jesus is mentioned in connection with his holy mother, God's peace and blessings be upon them both:

> **The Messiah, Jesus son of Mary, was but a messenger of God and His word which He bestowed upon Mary and a spirit from Him.** (4:171)
>
> **Say, [O Muhammad:] "Then who could prevail against God if He intended to destroy the Messiah, son of Mary, or his mother or everyone on the earth?"** (5:17/19)
>
> **The Messiah, son of Mary, was nothing but a messenger; messengers had passed on before him. And his mother was a woman of truth [*siddiqah*]. They both used to eat food. See how We make clear to them the signs; then see how they are deluded!** (5:75/78)
>
> **[The Day] when God will say, "O Jesus son of Mary, recall My favor to you and to your mother."** (5:110/113)
>
> **And [be mindful of the Day] when God will say, "O Jesus son of Mary, did you say to people, 'Take me and my mother as deities besides God?'"** (5:116/119)
>
> **Then she brought him to her people, carrying him. They said, "O Mary, you have certainly done an unheard-of thing! O**

sister of Aaron, your father was not an evil man, nor was your mother unchaste!" Then she pointed to him. They said, "How can we speak to one who is a child in the cradle?" He said, "Indeed, I am the slave of God. He has given me the scripture and made me a prophet, and He has made me blest wherever I am, and has charged me with *salat* and *zakat* as long as I live, and goodness to my mother, and has not made me harsh and difficult. And peace be upon me the day I was born and the day I die and the day I shall be raised alive!" (19:27-33)

And [mention] the one who preserved her chastity, and We breathed into her of Our Spirit, and made her and her son a sign for mankind. (21:91)

And We made the son of Mary and his mother a sign, and sheltered them on high ground, a place of repose and flowing springs. (23:50)

"Nothing But a Messenger"

In keeping with the understanding of the earliest followers of Jesus (A), who were, after all, observant Jews, God Most High proclaims again and again that Jesus (A) was a prophet-messenger like those who had preceded him.[74]

---

[74]The prophethood of Jesus is also mentioned in the following passages of the four Gospels:

When Jesus entered Jerusalem, the whole city was stirred and asked, "Who is this?" The crowds answered, "This is Jesus, the prophet from Nazareth in Galilee." (Matt. 21:10-11)

They looked for a way to arrest him, but they were afraid of the crowd because the people held that he was a prophet. (Matt. 21:46)

They were all filled with awe and praised God. "A great prophet has appeared among us," they said. (Luke 7:16)

"He was a prophet, powerful in word and deed before God and all the people." (Luke 24:19)

"Sir," the woman said, "I can see that you are a prophet." (John 4:19)

After the people saw the miraculous sign that Jesus did, they began to say, "Surely this is the Prophet who is to come into the world." (John 6:14)

Finally they turned again to the blind man, "What have you to say about him? It was your eyes he opened." The man replied, "He is a prophet." (John 9:17)

On hearing his words, some of the people said, "Surely this man is the Prophet." (John 7:40)

[Jesus said,] "Only in his hometown and in his own house is a prophet without honor." (Matt. 13:57; also Mark 6:4, Luke 4:43))

The following Qur'anic verses unmistakably link Jesus (A) to others in the prophetic line:

> **We certainly gave Moses the scripture and followed him by a succession of [other] messengers. And We granted Jesus son of Mary clear proofs and supported him with the holy spirit [Gabriel].** (2:87)
>
> **Say: "We believe in God and what was revealed to us, and what was revealed to Abraham and Ishmael and Isaac and Jacob and the descendants [of Israel], and what was given to Moses and Jesus, and what was given to [all] the prophets by their Lord. We make no distinction between any of them, and we surrender to Him [in Islam]."** (2:136, 3:84-85)
>
> **Those messengers — We favored some of them over others. Among them were those to whom God spoke, and He exalted some of them in rank. And We granted Jesus son of Mary clear proofs and supported him with the holy spirit [Gabriel].** (2:253)
>
> **Indeed, We have revealed to you [Muhammad] as We revealed to Noah and the prophets after him. And We revealed to Abraham and Ishmael and Isaac and Jacob and the descendants [of Israel], and Jesus and Job and Jonah and Aaron and Solomon, and We granted David the *Zabur*.** (4:163)
>
> **And We granted him [Abraham] Isaac and Jacob; each [of them] We guided. And previously We guided Noah, and among his descendants, David and Solomon and Job and Joseph and Moses and Aaron. And thus do We reward the doers of good. And Zechariah and John and Jesus and Elijah — all were among the righteous; and Ishmael and Elisha and Jonah and Lot — and all [of them] We preferred above mankind, and some from among their fathers and descendants and brothers, and We chose them and guided them to a straight path.** (6:84-87)
>
> **And [mention, O Muhammad,] when We took from the prophets their covenant, and from you, and from Noah and Abraham and Moses and Jesus son of Mary — and We took from them a solemn covenant.** (33:7)
>
> **He has ordained for you [mankind], as the religion, that which He enjoined upon Noah and which We have revealed to**

[Jesus said,] "In any case, I must keep going today and tomorrow and the next day — for surely no prophet can die outside Jerusalem!" (Luke, 13:33)

you [Muhammad], and which We enjoined upon Abraham and Moses and Jesus: to establish the religion and not be divided concerning it. (42:13)

And We certainly sent Noah and Abraham, and established prophethood and scripture among their descendants; and among them are the guided, but many of them are transgressors. Then We sent, following in their footsteps, Our messengers, and We followed [them] with Jesus son of Mary and granted him the *Injil.* (57:26-27)

In addition to these, the following passages, all of which we have quoted previously, unequivocally affirm Jesus' prophethood and messengership:

- Mary's being informed, during the annunciation, that God would make her son-to-be **a messenger to the Children of Israel** (3:48-49).
- The apostles' saying, **"We follow the messenger**, Jesus, and asking to be inscribed among the witnesses to the truth (3:52-53).
- God's mentioning His displeasure with the Jews because of their claim that they had **killed the Messiah, Jesus son of Mary, God's messenger** (4:157).
- God's proclaiming that **the Messiah, Jesus son of Mary, was but a messenger of God and His word which He bestowed upon Mary and a spirit from Him** (4:171).
- God's statement that **the Messiah, son of Mary, was nothing but a messenger; messengers had passed on before him** (5:75/78).
- Jesus' saying, **"Indeed, I am the slave of God. He has granted me the scripture and made me a prophet"** (19:30).
- Jesus' saying, **"O Children of Israel, indeed I am the messenger of God to you"** (61:6).
- God's mentioning Jesus (A) among the messengers in the context of **the Day God will assemble the messengers and say, "What was the response you received?"** (5:109/112).
- God's recalling, on the Day of Judgment, that He **inspired to the apostles, 'Believe in Me and in My messenger,'"** Jesus (5:111/114).

Part Four: Commentary on Verses Related to the Divinity of Jesus

19. The Nature of God

For that is God, your Lord, the Truth. And what is beyond truth but error. How then are you turned away? . . . And most them follow only assumption. Indeed, assumption does not avail against truth in the least. (10:32, 36)

As we saw in the preceding pages, God Most High affirms that Jesus (A) is a spirit and a word from Him, His slave, the son of his human mother, and His prophet and messenger. And as we will now see in the pages that follow, He also rejects, in the strongest language, the notion that He, the Praised and Exalted throughout eternity, could or would take a son for Himself, or any other partner in His divinity.

Indeed, the question of the identity of Jesus, God's peace and blessings be upon him, is nothing less than the question of the nature of God Himself. Is He a single, transcendent Being having a unique Essence and Nature that is not shared by anyone whomsoever, or are there others of the same "species" who are related to Him and share in His divinity? Does He have a spouse and beget children like those He creates, or is such a thing contrary to His exalted divine nature and majesty, and therefore in effect impossible? Can He perish or die, even for an instant of time, or is He unchanging and eternal? Is He able to do whatever He wills, or is He, like all created beings, subject to the laws of nature, destiny or change?

These and many other questions are central to the understanding of the identity and role of Jesus (A), for if we are clear about who God is (and also who He is *not*), then by extension we may be able to comprehend who and what Jesus (A) was without exceeding the limits of truth in either direction. Accordingly, we now cite, in sequential order, the Qur'anic verses related, directly or indirectly, to the divinity or Sonship of Jesus, the concept of the Trinity and objects of worship other than God, together with their interpretation, taken primarily from the *Tafsir* (*Commentary*) of Ibn Kathir.

20. Verses Concerning the Son of God, the Trinity and Related Matters

"They Say, 'God Has Taken a Son'"

2:116-117

They say, "God has taken a son." May He be glorified! Rather, to Him belongs whatever is in the heavens and the earth! All are devoutly obedient to Him. (116) **Originator of the heavens and the earth, when He decrees a matter, He but says to it "Be!" and it is.** (117)

Arguing against the fallacy of the claims of those who ascribe a son to the Most High, these verses stress God's transcendence and majesty, and the fact that all things, both animate and inanimate, originate with Him and are obedient to Him and His command.

As Causer of all things, the Creator is independent of all causes, and He uses any means, or even no means, to bring whatever He wills into being. Therefore, when He wills that a thing be manifested in existence, He has but to issue the divine command, "Be!" (and what that "Be!" consists of, He knows, while we do not) and it comes into being.

"Indeed, the Similie of Jesus with God Is Like That of Adam"

3:58-64

This is what We recite to you [Muhammad] of the verses and the wise Reminder. (58) **Indeed, the similie of Jesus with God is like that of Adam: He created him of dust, then He said to him "Be!" and he was.** (59)

The truth is from your Lord, so do not be among the doubters. (60) **Then whoever argues with you about it after the knowledge [of it] has come to you, say: "Come! Let us call our sons and your sons, and our women and your women, and ourselves and yourselves, and then earnestly supplicate and invoke God's curse upon the liars."** (61)

Indeed, this is the true narrative. And there is no deity except God, and indeed, God is the Almighty, the Wise. (62) **But if they turn away, then God is surely Knowing of the corrupters.** (63)

Say, [O Muhammad:] "O People of the Scripture, come to a word common between us and you: that we will not worship anyone but God, nor associate anyone with Him, nor take one another as lords besides God." But if they turn away, then say, "Bear witness that we are Muslims." (64)

(58-59) These verses follow the lengthy passage in *Surah Ale 'Imran* (3:33-57) which speaks of Mary's dedication and birth, Zechariah's supplication, the annunciations of John and Jesus (A), Jesus' miracles, mission and apostles, and God's raising him to Himself.

At the beginning of this passage, God Most High states that **this** — the preceding narrative concerning Jesus (A) — **is what We recite to you**, Muhammad, **of the verses and the wise Reminder,** the Qur'an. Then, focusing on Jesus' miraculous origin and birth, God declares that **the similie of Jesus with God is like that of Adam: He created him of dust, then He said to him "Be!" and he was**.

With repect to this comparison between Adam and Jesus (A), Ibn Kathir argues that God the Glorious and Exalted, who created Adam (A) and Eve without either a father or mother, is unquestionably able to create Jesus (A) without a father:

> Consequently, if it is possible to claim sonship for Jesus solely on the basis of his being created without a father, it is [even] more reasonable to claim this for Adam. . . . But rather it is that God, may His majesty be exalted, desired to manifest His power by creating Adam without either a male or female, Eve from a male without a female, Jesus from a female without a male, and the rest of mankind from a male and a female. Because of this, God said, **We shall make him [Jesus] a sign for mankind** [19:21], and, here, **The truth is from your Lord, so do not be among the doubters.** (Ibn Kathir/*T*, 3:59-64)

Al-Qurtubi mentions a subtle point concerning this verse: that while God created Adam out of dust but not Jesus, and He created Jesus out of the conditions of pregnancy in the womb but not Adam, the thing that Adam and Jesus have in common is that God created them both without a father. In a similar vein, al-Razi argues that while Adam had neither father nor mother, no one claims that he was God's Son. Consequently, if Sonship is not claimed for the one whom God created out of dust, there can be no justification for claiming it for the one who was created from the constituents of Mary's womb, although he likewise had no father (Ayoub/*Q*, II:185-186).

(60) At the conclusion of this passage, God Most High declares, **The truth is from your Lord, so do not be among the doubters**, thus pointing out that the truth cannot be from any source except Himself, the Knower of all things, especially the truth about events that have been distorted or obliterated with the passing of time. The meaning is, "Do not go to people for the truth but come to Me. And if what is presented by people as the truth contradicts what you have from Me, then have no doubt about where the truth actually lies."

(61) After this unequivocal statement concerning the truth of Jesus' origin and humanity, specific instructions are given to Muhammad (S): **Then whoever argues with you about it**[75] — the truth concerning Jesus (A) — **after the knowledge** contained in the preceding verses **has come to you**, you are to finally resolve the issue by saying to them, **"Come! Let us call our sons and your sons, and our women and your women, and ourselves and yourselves, and then earnestly supplicate and invoke God's curse upon the liars."**

This verse, known as *al-Ayah al-Mubahalah* (the Verse of Mutually Invoking God's Curse), was revealed in connection with a delegation of Christians from Najran, whose story we relate on pages 392-396.

(62-63) In these two verses, God Most High again attests to the truth of the preceding account concerning Jesus (A), proclaiming that **Indeed, this is the true narrative. And there is no deity except God, and indeed, God is the Almighty, the Wise,** as if to say, "This narrative and no other is the correct one, and any claim in any other narrative that there is a deity besides God, Almighty, All-Wise, is false." **But**, He concludes, **if they turn away** after this powerful proclamation of the truth, **then God is surely Knowing of the corrupters.**

(64) Further instructions to the Holy Prophet (S) then follow. He is to say, **"O People of the Scripture, come to a word common between us and you,"** meaning a statement of purpose that is mutually acceptable to both groups, as peoples whose faiths originated in divine revelation.

---

[75]An alternative reading is, **And whoever argues with you about him,** meaning Jesus.

The classical commentators ascribed both a general as well as a specific meaning to this verse. As for the general meaning, some scholars say that since **"People of the Scripture"** is a broad, inclusive term and there is nothing in this verse to suggest that one group of scriptuaries is meant to the exclusion of the other, God meant the people of both scriptures — that is, Jews *and* Christians.

The specific meaning of this verse, however, relates to the delegation of Christians from Najran, for when the Najranis refused to engage in the *mubahalah* or mutual invoking of God's curse, God commanded the Prophet (S) to do something that was easier for them — namely, to say to them, **"O People of the Scripture, come to a word common between us and you."**

This common **"word"** had three aspects about which the two groups were mutually to agree. These were, first, that they would not **worship anyone but God**; second, that they would not **associate anyone with Him,** meaning that they would not ascribe to anyone a share in God's divinity; and third, that they would not **take one another as lords besides God**.[76] If they then turned away, the Prophet (S) was to say to them, **"Bear witness that we are Muslims."**

The taking of others **as lords besides God** refers to the obedience that the People of the Scripture gave to their men of religion by obeying whatever they prescribed for them in place of God's laws, thereby rebelling against Him, says al-Tabari. In support of this interpretation, he cites the verse,

> **They have taken their scholars and monks as lords in place of God, and the Messiah, son of Mary, while they were not commanded except to worship one God** (9:31),

meaning that Jews and Christians had elevated their religious leaders to virtual divinity by accepting from them as permissible or prohibited that which God had neither made permissible nor prohibited. Al-Qurtubi and Ibn Kathir offer similar views (Ayoub/*Q*, II:203-204).

Al-Razi comments that the words, **We will not worship anyone except God, nor associate anyone with Him, nor take one another as lords besides God**, refer to the three common errors of Christians. The first of these is that they "worship someone other than God, that is Christ"; second, that

---

[76]This verse is also mentioned in an incident related to the response of the Byzantine emperor, Heraclius Caesar, to the Prophet's invitation to accept Islam, which we report in detail on pages 495-499.

"[t]hey associate others with Him . . . because they say that God is three: Father, Son and Holy Spirit," thereby affirming "three equal and eternal divine personalities"; and third, their "taking their rabbis and monks as lords instead of God." Moreover, says al-Razi, among Christians, when a person attains such a high spiritual state that God grants him miracles, "Even if they may not call such a person lord, they nonetheless invest him with the attributes of lordship" (ibid, II:206-207).

REFERENCES: Ibn Kathir/*T*, 3:59-64; Ayoub/*Q*, II:183-207.

The Story of the Christians of Najran

The revelation of the preceding passage is connected with the following incident related to the Holy Prophet, God's peace and blessings be upon him.

Toward the end of his life, after the Prophet (S) had won significant victories over the adversaries of Islam and had established it as the prevailing religion and law in Arabia, deputations came to him from neighboring lands.

During the ninth year after his emigration from Mecca (the *Hijrah*), a delegation of Christians came to him in Medina from Najran, a region in southwestern Arabia. This delegation was comprised of sixty horsemen.

Of these, fourteen were from among the Najrani nobles. Of these fourteen, three held positions of special authority among their people: al-'Aqib, called 'Abd al-Masih (Slave of the Messiah), the leader of his people, guardian of their affairs and chief advisor, whose opinion was never opposed; al-Ayham, known as al-Sayyid, the administrator who was in charge of transport and general arrangements; and Abu Harithah bin 'Alqamah, their bishop, scholar and religious leader, a man of great knowledge and zeal for their faith. Says the author of the well-known classical biography of the Holy Prophet (S), Ibn Ishaq (d. 219/824):

> They were Christians according to the Byzantine rite, though they differed among themselves in some points, saying [simultaneously] He is God; and He is the Son of God; and He is the third person of the Trinity, which is the doctrine of Christianity. (Ibn Ishaq/*Muhammad*, p. 271)

Hence, they would argue that because Jesus (A) used to raise the dead, heal the sick, proclaim the Unseen, and make clay birds into which he would breathe so that they flew away, he was God. They also argued that he was the Son of God because he had no known father and spoke in the cradle, as no one else had ever done. Further, they asserted that he was the third of Three because God says, "We have done, We have commanded, We have created and We have decreed," saying, "If He were one, He would have said, 'I have done, I have created,' and so on, but He is He and Jesus and Mary."

When the members of this delegation arrived in Medina, they went to the Prophet's mosque while he was praying the mid-afternoon prayer. They were clad in Yemeni garments, cloaks and mantles, and were so elegant and fine that the Prophet's Companions who saw them said that they never saw the like of them in any deputation that came afterwards.

When the time came for their prayers, they got up and prayed in the mosque, with the Prophet's permission, facing East. Afterwards, al-Sayyid and al-'Aqib spoke to the Prophet (S), and he invited them to accept Islam.

"We were Muslims long before you," they responded.

"You are lying," he said. "Your assertion that God has a son, your worship of the cross, and your eating of pork are keeping you from being Muslims."[77]

"Then who is his father, Muhammad ?"[78] they demanded.

---

[77]That is, since God had not revealed permission for these three things — rather, they had been prohibited or negated — the Najranis adherence to them invalidated their claim. In another account, their consumption of alcohol is mentioned as the third of the three obstacles to their being Muslims (Ayoub/*Q*, II:188).

[78]In addition to the account above, the following versions of this story have also been reported:

(1) The men of Najran accused the Prophet (S) of insulting their master, Jesus, by saying that he was a slave. The Prophet (S) replied that Jesus was indeed God's slave and His messenger and His word that He bestowed upon the pure virgin Mary. The Najranis then angrily demanded whether he had ever seen a man without a father, saying, "If you are telling the truth, then show us one like him." God then revealed to Muhammad (S), **Indeed, the similie of Jesus with God is like that of Adam: He created him of dust, then He said to him 'Be!' and he was** (3:59) (Ayoub/*Q*, II:183).

2) According to another report, four of the Najranis came to the Prophet (S), asking what he thought about Jesus. When Muhammad (S) replied that he was God's slave and His spirit and His word, they dissented, insisting that he was God Himself, who, having descended from His kingdom and entered into the body of Mary, was born from her in order to demonstrate His power and will. "Have you ever seen a man created without a father?" they demanded, whereupon this verse was revealed (ibid., p. 184).

(3) It is also reported that the two monks, al-'Aqib and al-Sayyid, issued an angry challenge to the Prophet (S), saying that if he were telling the truth he should show them a slave who performed miracles like those of Jesus mentioned in 3:49, concluding from the fact of these miracles that Jesus is God. The Prophet (S), with his usual deliberation, did not reply to them until Gabriel came to him, saying, "O Muhammad, **they who say, 'God is the Messiah son of Mary,' have certainly disbelieved"** (5:17/19, 72/75). The Prophet (S) then told Gabriel that the Najranis had asked him to inform them of another example like that of Jesus, whereupon

The Prophet (S) then became silent and did not reply to them. God Most High then revealed to him the first eighty-odd verses of the third ***surah***, *Ale 'Imran*, reporting the dedication and birth of Mary; Zechariah's guardianship of her and her heavenly provision; Zechariah's prayer for a son and the annunciation of John; the annunciation to Mary; Jesus' prophetic mission, miracles and apostles; God's raising of Jesus to Himself; and finally the verses,

> **This is what We recite to you [Muhammad] of the verses and the wise Reminder. Indeed, the similie of Jesus with God is like that of Adam: He created him of dust, then He said to him "Be!" and he was. The truth is from your Lord, so do not be among the doubters.** (3:58-60)

This was followed by the verse of ***mubahalah***:

> **Then whoever argues with you about it after the knowledge [of it] has come to you, say, "Come! Let us call our sons and your sons, and our women and your women, and ourselves and yourselves, and then earnestly supplicate and invoke God's curse upon the liars."** (3:61-63)

When the Prophet (S) challenged the two monks to hold the ***mubahalah***, they agreed that all of them would gather for that purpose the following morning. Accordingly, at the appointed time, the Prophet went out to meet them, accompanied by his son-in-law, 'Ali ibn Abi Talib (R), his daughter, Fatimah (R), and their two young sons, Hasan and Husain (R), his only surviving grandsons. He was wearing a voluminous cloak, which he spread out, enfolding himself and his family within it. Thus, **"our sons"** mentioned in 3:61 were the Prophet's two grandsons; **"our women"** was Fatimah (R), and **"ourselves"** were the Prophet (S) and 'Ali (R).

Seeing this, when the time came to invoke the mutual curse and the Prophet (S) called upon them to begin, the Najaranis hesitated. "O Abu-l-Qasim," they said, "allow us to consider our affair. Then we will come to you later with our decision."

They left him and consulted with their chief advisor, al-'Aqib (or, according to another account, a wise man among them). He said to them, "O Christians, you know very well that Muhammad is a prophet sent by God, and he has come with a decisive declaration about the nature of your master [Jesus]. You also know that no people has ever invoked a curse on a prophet and

---

Gabriel revealed, **Indeed, the similie of Jesus with God is like that of Adam: He created him of dust, then He said to him 'Be!' and he was** (3:59). (Ayoub/*Q*, 183).

seen its elders live and its youth grow up. If you do this, you will be exterminated. But if you decide to maintain your religion and stand by your belief about your master, then take your leave of the man and go home."[79]

They then returned to the Prophet (S), saying they had decided not to engage in the ***mubahalah*** with him, leaving him to his faith, as they would likewise continue in their faith. At the same time, they asked him to send with them one of his trusted Companions to adjudicate between them concerning certain financial disputes among them.[80]

The Prophet (S) then asked them to return to him in the evening, saying he would send with them a strong, trusted man. He deputed Abu 'Ubaydah bin al-Jarrah (R) for this task, saying, "Go with them and judge among them with the truth concerning the matters about which they differ." And the Prophet (S) said, "By Him who sent me with the truth, if they had accepted the ***mubahalah***, fire would have rained down over the valley [of Najran]."

The recognition of Muhammad's prophethood by the Najranis is clearly evident from the words of al-'Aqib reported above: "O Christians, you know very well that Muhammad is a true prophet and messenger, and he has come with a decisive declaration about the nature of your master," meaning, "Since Muhammad (S) is a prophet, he certainly knows the truth about Jesus Christ better than you do."

Moreover, if any lingering doubt still remained among the Najrani delegation either concerning Muhammad's prophethood or his knowledge of the true nature of Jesus (A), there remained one fact with which no one could argue: that Muhammad had staked not only his own life but the lives of his immediate family — his cherished daughter and her husband, who were among the closest of all people to him, and his two dearly loved grandsons who were his only male descendants — upon his conviction of the truth con-

---

[79]In another version, the Najrani wise man reproaches his companions, saying, "What have you done? If Muhammad is a prophet, and he invokes God against you, God would never anger him by not answering his prayers. If, on the other hand, he is a king, and he were to prevail over you, he would never spare you." He therefore advised his people, who had already agreed to meet with the Prophet, to say, "We seek refuge in God," if he asked them to keep their commitment to engage in the ***mubahalah***, and to repeat it again so that he would release them from it (Ayoub/Q, II:189).

[80]According to some accounts, they also agreed to pay ***jizyah***, the tax levied on the adult males of scriptuaries living under Muslim rule in lieu of military service, but this is not certain.

cerning Jesus (A) by his readiness to carry out the *mubahalah.*[81] And since no one would do such a thing except one who is either totally certain of the truth or completely insane, the only possibility left was what they already knew: that he was God's Messenger and what he had brought concerning Jesus (A) was from God.

REFERENCES: Ibn Kathir/*Q*, "Mention of the Birth of the Slave and Messenger, Jesus, son of Mary, the Virgin"; Ibn Ishaq/*Muhammad*, pp. 270-277; Lings/*Muhammad*, pp. 324; Ayoub/*Q*, II:1-5, 183-202.

"Nor Would He Order You to Take the Angels and the Prophets as Lords"

3:79-80

It is not for a mortal that God should grant him scripture and judgment and prophethood, and then he should say to people, "Be worshippers of me instead of God," but rather, "Be pious people of the Lord because of what you have taught of the scripture and because of what you have studied." (79) **Nor would he order you to take the angels and the prophets as lords. Would he order you to unbelief after you had been Muslims?** (80)

(79) Although these verses are quite general in meaning, their relationship to Jesus (A) is unmistakable. At the same time, it is reported on the authority of Ibn 'Abbas (R) that this verse was revealed when one of the chiefs of the Najrani Christians asked the Prophet (S) if he wished to be worshipped and taken as Lord. He replied:

> "God forbid that anyone be worshipped instead of God, or that we enjoin the worship of anyone but God. It is not with this that He sent me, or commanded me." (Ayoub/*Q*, II:234)

---

[81]The classical commentator Zamakhshari reports that after al-'Aqib had advised his fellow Christians against the *mubahalah*, he said, "O Christians, I see here faces," meaning those of 'Ali, Fatimah and their two sons, "for whose sake God would cause a mountain to move from its place, if He so wills. Therefore, do not engage in the *mubahalah* lest you perish and not one Christian would remain on the face of the earth till the Day of Resurrection." Zamakshari further reports that after the people of Najran chose to pay *jizyah* instead of engaging in the *mubahalah*, the Prophet (S) said, "By Him in whose hand is my soul, destruction hovered over the people of Najran, for had they held the trial of cursing, they would have been transformed into apes and pigs. Nor would the year have passed without all Christians being utterly annihilated" (Ayoub/*Q*, II:194).

He also said,

> "Do not praise me excessively as Jesus son of Mary was praised, but [rather] say, 'God's slave and His Messenger'" (*Bukhari*, 8:817),

considering servanthood to his Lord to be his highest honor and greatest source of honor and satisfaction.

The above passage constitutes God's unequivocal declaration that no one entrusted with divinely-inspired judgment, a revealed scripture and prophethood ever could or would ask people to worship or serve him instead of his Lord. Indeed, all the prophets called upon the believers in their communities to be sincere, **pious people of the Lord**[82] because they were the guardians and repositories of faith through their teaching of the scripture and their intensive study and recitation of it. It is further unimaginable that any prophet would order his people **to take the angels and the prophets** in general **as lords** in place of God, thereby enjoining unbelief after they had been Muslims, surrendering to God. The meaning of this passage is again closely related to that of

> **They have taken their scholars and monks as lords besides God, and the Messiah, son of Mary, while they were not commanded except to worship one God** (9:31),

which is discussed on pages 391 and 419.

What all these verses emphasize is that all the prophets, including Jesus and Muhammad (S), were emissaries of God the Praised and Exalted, and hence their mission was to call people to Him with absolute truthfulness and fidelity to the divine command. It is therefore inconceivable that any of them should ever have falsely claimed to be more than mortal or to deserve the worship and servanthood that are due to the Creator alone. Rather, as commanded by Him, they proclaimed that the way to approach God was through obedience to the divine guidance that had been revealed through them and the messengers who preceded and would follow them. This is also the theme of the next passage.

REFERENCES: Ibn Kathir/*Q*, 3:79-80; Ayoub/*Q*, pp. 233-238.

---

[82]"***Rabbaniyin***," meaning good, righteous men, worshippers, learned people, those firmly grounded in knowledge, science or religion, who practice what they know and instruct others.

"And Do Not Say 'Three'"

4:170-172

O mankind, the Messenger has come to you with the truth from your Lord, so believe in it; it is better for you. But if you disbelieve, then indeed, to God belongs whatever is in the heavens and the earth; and God is ever Knowing and Wise. (170)

O People of the Scripture, do not exceed the limits in your religion or say about God except the truth. The Messiah, Jesus son of Mary, was but a messenger of God and His word which He bestowed upon Mary and a spirit from Him. So believe in God and His messengers. And do not say "Three"; refrain — it is better for you. Indeed, God is but one God. Exalted is He above having a son! To Him belongs whatever is in the heavens and whatever is on the earth. And God is sufficient as Disposer of affairs. (171)

Never would the Messiah disdain to be a slave to God, nor the angels, near [to Him]. Whoever disdains His worship and is arrogant, He will gather them to Himself, all together. (172)

(170) As a preface to the subject of the Trinity, in the first verse of this passage God Most High issues a clear, decisive statement to all humanity that whatever was revealed to His Messenger Muhammad (S) in the Qur'an, whether concerning Jesus (A) or any other matter, is **the truth from your Lord**. Each one of mankind is urged to **believe in it** because to believe is **better for you** than adhering to beliefs or faiths that have been changed or distorted over time, thus becoming a confused mixture of fact and fable. **But**, God adds, **if you disbelieve** in this obvious truth after the knowledge of it has come to you, **whatever is in the heavens and the earth** belongs to God, and **God is ever Knowing and Wise** to decide your destiny and the destinies of all His creatures.

(171) In a strongly worded admonition, God Most High then exhorts the People of the Scripture, both Jews and Christians, neither to deny Jesus' prophethood nor to exceed the limits in their religion by ascribing divinity to him, nor to **say about God** anything **but the truth**. He then proclaims the true facts about Jesus Christ (A): that he was **but a messenger of God and His word which He bestowed upon Mary and a spirit from Him**. As mentioned previously, this is such a fundamental article of faith in Islam that the Holy Prophet (S) declared that anyone testifying that there is no deity except God, One, having no partner, and that Muhammad is His slave and His messenger, and that Jesus is God's slave and His messenger and His word that He bestowed upon Mary and a spirit from Him, and that Paradise is real and Hellfire is real, will be admitted to Paradise regardless of his deeds (*Bukhari*, 4:644).

After this introduction, God Most High introduces the subject of the Trinity, whether interpreted as God the Father, God the Son and God the Holy Ghost, or as God, Jesus and Mary. By advising the People of the Scripture to **believe in God and His messengers,** He makes it clear that sound belief has two aspects: first, belief in the Creator, and second, belief in His representatives, including Jesus (A), and, after Jesus, Muhammad (S). These words mean, by implication, "Believe in God as the only Lord and do not imply that His messengers were anything more than they actually were, based on what God Himself informs you."

Here the central principle of both Judaism and Islam is once again proclaimed: that God, the Praised and Exalted, Creator of all things, is but one, indivisible divine Being who is unique in His Essence and Nature, and is therefore far removed from having an offspring or a "Spirit" who comprise additional or separate parts of His Godhood, as well as from the attributes of created beings such as needing a partner or fathering a child. No one but God is God, for all things other than Him are, by definition, His creatures and slaves.

And do not say "Three," God then admonishes, adding, **Refrain — it is better for you.** Implicit in these words is the fact that this "Three" is something that they "say" rather than a thing having any basis in reality.

If there is any doubt about this, we have but to recall that throughout the history of revealed religion up to the time when Christianity was given doctrinal form, God was **but one God**, who is infinitely exalted **above having a son**, to whom **belongs whatever is in the heavens and whatever is on the earth**, and who is **sufficient as Disposer of affairs**. If God were indeed Three and He had intended His Son and the ambiguous Holy Spirit to be objects of worship, how then would He have concealed this all-important fact in His revelations to His messengers throughout the ages, only to spring it unexpectedly upon unsuspecting humanity after thousands of years of man's life on earth, suddenly requiring people to believe in it against all logic and historical precedent? Indeed,

> **We did not send any messenger before you [Muhammad] but that We revealed to him that there is no deity but Me, so worship Me.** (21:25)

This raises the question of the true identity of the third entity of the alleged Trinity, the Holy Ghost or Holy Spirit. Although according to Christian doctrine this Spirit is not identical with God the Father nor with God the Son but is yet another person of the triune Godhead, Islam corrects and dismisses this error simply and decisively. The repeated references in the Qur'an to **the spirit [*al-ruh*]** (70:4; 78:38; 97:4); **Our spirit [*ruhana*]** (19:17); **the holy spirit [*al-ruh al-qudus*]** (2:87, 253; 5:110/113; 16:102); and **the trustworthy spirit [*al-ruh al-amin*]** (26:193), make clear the existence of a misidentification of the bringer of Revelation, the angel Gabriel (A), with this strangely undefinable third person of the Trinity.

Now, despite the divine empowerment and authority with which he had been invested, Gabriel (A) was nonetheless a finite being, God's humble slave, a messenger from the heavenly realm who conveyed whatever his Lord directed him to convey to His earthly messengers, for **God chooses messengers from among angels and from among mankind** (22:75). Perhaps the following verses may be useful in understanding Gabriel's role in transmitting the divine revelation to Muhammad, God's peace and blessings be upon him:

> **Indeed, he [Gabriel] has brought it down to your heart by God's leave, confirming that which was before it, and as guidance and good tidings for the believers. (2:97)**
>
> **Say, [O Muhammad:] "The holy spirit has brought it down from your Lord with truth to make firm those who believe, and as guidance and good tidings for the Muslims." (16:102)**
>
> **And indeed, it [the Qur'an] is the revelation of the Lord of the worlds. The trustworthy spirit has brought it down upon your heart, that you might be among the warners, in clear Arabic language. (26:192-195)**
>
> **By the star when it descends, your companion [Muhammad] has not strayed nor has he erred, nor does he speak from whim. It [the Qur'an] is nothing but a revelation revealed, taught to him by one mighty in power [Gabriel], endowed with strength. And he [Gabriel] rose to [his] true form while he was in the higher horizon. Then he approached and descended, and was at a distance of two bow lengths or nearer, and he revealed to His slave [Muhammad] that which he revealed. The heart did not lie about what it saw. Will you then dispute with him [Muhammad] about what he saw? (53:1-12)**
>
> **Indeed, it [the Qur'an] is a word of a noble messenger [Gabriel], possessed of power and secure with the Owner of the Throne, obeyed and trustworthy. And your companion [Mu-**

hammad] is not mad. And he certainly saw him [Gabriel] in the clear horizon. (81:19:23)[83]

(172) Because his Lord is God, the Honored and Glorious, never would the Messiah **disdain to be a slave** to Him, **nor the angels,** who are so near to Him. This verse once again affirms the fact that the beings who are dearest to God — the prophets who are the noblest among His creation, including His honored Messiah, Jesus (A), and the angels who are constantly in His exalted Presence, glorifying Him and carrying out His orders — aspire to and desire no higher honor than His worship and service.[84] As for those who disdain to worship and serve Him, **He will gather them to Himself, all together,** on the Day of Resurrection to give an accounting of what they sent ahead for their souls.

Pride is suitable only for the Creator. As for created beings, who are utterly dependent upon Him for their very existence and for every need, for every heartbeat and every breath, pride does not befit them and is indeed a detestable characteristic, the one responsible for the fall of Iblis, a slave whose honors and ranks so went to his head that he imagined himself to be on the same level as God Almighty.

REFERENCES: Ibn Kathir/*T*, 4:170-172; Maududi/*Q*, 4:fns. 211, 215-216; Asad/*Q*, 4:fn. 181; Ali/*Q*, fn. 675-676.

The Story of the King of Abyssinia

The following incident from early Islamic history is related to the ***hadith*** cited on pages 380 and 398 in which the Prophet (S) referred to Jesus (A) as "God's slave and His messenger and His word which He bestowed upon Mary and a spirit from Him" (*Bukhari*, 4:644), and thus to one of the verses in the passage that is the subject of this section,

> **The Messiah, Jesus son of Mary, was but a messenger of God and His word which He bestowed upon Mary and a spirit from Him.** (4:171)

---

[83]The last two passages refers to Muhammad's initial encounter with Gabriel during the first revelation of the Qur'an in Hira' cave, which is described on pages 491-492.

[84]Involuntary servanthood is an unvarying condition of our existence and a given of our creaturehood. But if our servanthood to God becomes voluntary through the exercise of intention and will, it is that which enobles, distinguishes and gives us honor above all other creatures.

During the early years of Islam, when the Holy Prophet (S) saw how greatly the Muslims were suffering in Mecca under the persecution of the Quraysh, he encouraged them to emigrate to neighboring Abyssinia, whose king, known as the Negus (Arabic, Najashi), was a Christian. "The king will not tolerate injustice and it is a friendly country," the Prophet (S) said to the Muslims, "until such time as God relieves you of your distress."

Eighty-three people, not counting small children, left Mecca for Abyssinia. There they were received in a kindly manner by the Negus, who permitted them to settle and practice their religion, and they were not harmed by word or deed.

This alarmed the Quraysh, who sent two of their important men, 'Amr bin al-'As and 'Umarah bin Abi Mu'ayt, as envoys to the Negus, bearing precious gifts. The two envoys complained to the king, through his generals, that the Muslims had forsaken their former religion but had not adopted that of the Christians, having rather adopted a religion which they themselves had invented. And they asked the king to give up the Muslims and return them to themselves.

But instead of listening to their appeal, the Negus was angered by it. "No, by God," he said, "I will not give them up. No people who have sought my protection, settled in my country and chosen me rather than others shall be betrayed until I have summoned them and questioned them about what these two men allege. If they are as they say, I will give them up to them and send them back to their own people. But if what they say is false, I will protect them and see that they receive proper hospitality while under my protection."

When the Negus sent for the Muslims, they were troubled. "What will you say to the man when you come to him?" they asked one another.

"We will say what we know and what our Prophet commanded us, come what may," they resolved.

When they came into the presence of the Negus, they found that he had summoned his bishops, who had their sacred books opened around the throne. But in spite of this, the meeting between the Negus and the Muslims did not turn out favorably for the Qurayshite envoys.

Being people of faith, the Abyssinians were keenly sensitive to the difference between the sacred and profane. Thus, while they had commerical and political relations with the Meccan Arabs, they secretly despised them as heathens who had nothing in common with themselves. But when the group of Muslims, bearing the stamp of faith and piety, which was enhanced in many of them by great natural beauty, came before them, a murmur of astonishment arose from the bishops and others, for they saw that these Arabs were closer to themselves in spirit than any of the Quraysh whom they had previously encountered.

The Negus then began to question the Muslims, asking them what was the religion for which they had forsaken their people, without accepting his religion or any other. The reply was given by the Prophet's cousin, Ja'far ibn Abi Talib (R), on behalf of the entire group.

"O king," he said, "we were an uncivilized people, worshipping idols, eating dead flesh, committing abominations, breaking natural ties, ill-treating guests, and our strong devoured our weak. Thus we were until God sent us a messenger whose lineage, truthfulness, trustworthiness and purity we know.[85]

"He summoned us to acknowledge God's Oneness and to worship Him, and to renounce the stones and images that we and our fathers had formerly worshipped. He commanded us to speak the truth, fulfill our promises, be mindful of the ties of kinship and kindly hospitality, and refrain from crimes and bloodshed. He forbade us to commit abominations and to tell lies, to devour the property of orphans, and to slander chaste women. He commanded us to worship God alone and not to associate anything with Him, and he gave us orders about *salat*, *zakat* and fasting.

"We testified to his truth and believed in him," Ja'far (R) continued. "We followed him in what he had brought from God and worshipped God alone without associating anything with Him. We treated as prohibited what he prohibited and as permissible what he permitted. At that, our people attacked us, treated us harshly, and seduced us from our faith to try to make us revert to the worship of idols in place of the worship of God and to regard as permissible the evil deeds we once committed. Then, when they got the better of us, treated us unjustly, restricted our lives, and came between us and our religion, we came to your country, having chosen you above all others. Here we have been happy in your protection, and we hope that we will not be treated unjustly while we are with you, O king."

The Negus then asked if they had with them anything that had come from God. When Ja'far (R) said that they had, the Negus ordered him to recite it to him. Ja'far (R) then recited the following passage from *Surah*

---

[85]According to another version, Ja'far told the Negus that God had sent them the messenger who was foretold by Jesus when he spoke of **a messenger to come after me, whose name is Ahmad** (61:6). We will speak further about this prophecy in Chapter 31.

Maryam, which had been revealed to the Prophet (S) shortly before the departure of the Muslims to Abyssinia:

> **And mention Mary in the Book, when she withdrew from her family to a place toward the East and kept seclusion apart from them. Then We sent to her Our spirit, and he appeared to her as a well-proportioned man. She said, "Indeed, I seek refuge in the Most Merciful from you, if you are God-fearing!." He said, "I am only the messenger of your Lord, to bestow upon you a pure boy." She said, "How can I have a boy while no man has touched me and I have not been unchaste?" He said, "Thus! Your Lord says, 'It is easy for Me, and that We may make him a sign for people and a mercy from Ourself. And it is a matter decreed.'"** (19:16-21)

It is reported that when they heard what Ja'far (R) read to them, the Negus wept until his beard was wet and the bishops wept until their scrolls were wet. The Negus then said, "Of a truth, this and what Jesus brought have come from the same source." Then, addressing the Qurayshite envoys, he said, "You two may go, for, by God, I will never give them up to them and they shall not be betrayed."

However, even this did not end the plotting of the two envoys. "By God," one said to the other, "I will tell him that they claim that Jesus son of Mary is a slave."

Accordingly, in the morning he went to the king and told him that the Muslims said a dreadful thing about Jesus son of Mary, and that he should send for them and ask them about it.

At this, the Muslims conferred anxiously among themselves about what they should say concerning Jesus (A) when they were asked, and they resolved to say what God had said and what the Prophet (S) had brought, regardless of what might happen. So when they went into the royal presence and were asked, "What do you say about Jesus son of Mary?" Ja'far (R) replied, on behalf of their entire group:

"We say about him that which our Prophet brought, saying, 'He is the slave of God and His messenger and His spirit and His word, which He bestowed upon Mary [*Bukhari*, 4:644], the chaste virgin.'"

The Negus then picked up a piece of wood from the ground and said, "By God, Jesus son of Mary does not exceed what you have said by the length of this stick."

At this, the generals around him snorted, but he said, "Even though you snort, by God!" And to the Muslims he said, "Go, for you are safe in my country." He then repeated three times, "He who curses you shall be fined. Not for a mountain of gold would I allow a man of you to be hurt." And he dismissed the envoys, returning their gifts to them.

After this, however, the Abyssinians assembled and said to the Negus, "You have left our religion," and they revolted against him. He then made ready ships for Ja'far (R) and his companions, saying, "Embark in these and be ready. If I am defeated, go where you please. If I am victorious, then stay where you are."

He then took a paper and wrote on it, "He testifies that there is no deity except God and that Muhammad is His slave and Messenger, and he testifies that Jesus son of Mary is His slave and His messenger and His spirit and His word, which He bestowed upon Mary." Putting the paper into his robe near the right shoulder, he went out to the Abyssinians, who were drawn up in formation to meet him.

"O people," he said to them, "do I not have the best claim [to kingship] among you?" When they replied that he had, he said, "And what do you think of my life among you?" They replied that it was excellent. "Then what is troubling you?" he asked.

"You have left our religion and asserted that Jesus is a slave."

"Then what do *you* say about Jesus?"

"We say that he is the Son of God."

The Negus put his hand upon his breast over his robe, signifying, "He testifies that Jesus son of Mary was no more than *this*," referring to what he had written. Then his people were satisfied and went away, being happy under his rule and wanting only to be reassured.

The Negus then sent word to Ja'far (R) and his companions that they might disembark from the ships and return to their homes. And they continued to live in comfort and security in his country until such time as God opened the way for them to return home.

Some years later, when the Prophet (S) sent letters to the rulers of neighboring countries inviting them to Islam, one letter went to the Negus by the hand of his emissary. It read:

> From Muhammad, the Messenger of God, to the Negus, king of Abyssinia. Peace be upon him who follows true guidance. I praise God to you. There is no deity but Him, **the Sovereign, the Holy One, the [Source of] Peace, the Bestower of Faith, the Guardian** [59:23], and I bear witness that Jesus son of Mary is the spirit of God and His word

> which He bestowed upon Mary the Virgin, the good, the pure, so that she conceived Jesus. God created him from His Spirit and His Breath as He created Adam by His Hand and His Breath.
>
> I call you to God, the One without a partner, and to obedience to Him, and to follow me and believe in that which came to me, for I am the Messenger of God. I invite you and your people to God, the Glorious, the Almighty. I hereby bear witness that I have communicated my message and advice. I invite you to listen and accept my advice. Peace be upon him who follows true guidance.

To this, the Negus sent the following reply:

> From the Negus al-Asham bin Abjar to Muhammad, the Messenger of God. Peace be upon you, O Messenger of God, and mercy and blessing from God, besides whom there is no deity, who has guided me to Islam. I have received your letter in which you mention the matter of Jesus and, by the Lord of heaven and earth, he is no more than what you say.
>
> We fully acknowledge that with which you were sent to us and we have entertained your cousin and his companions. I bear witness that you are the Messenger of God, true and confirming [the prophets before you]. I have given my allegiance to you through your cousin and surrender myself, through him, to the Lord of the worlds. (*Zad al Ma 'ad*, 3/61; Ibn Ishaq/*Muhammad*, 657-658)

Toward the end of the Prophet's life, the Negus passed away. The Prophet (S) announced his death to the Muslims on the very day he died (*Bukhari*, 2:337; *Muwatta*, 16:14), saying, "Ask forgiveness for your brother" (*Bukhari*, 5:220). He further said, "Today a righteous man [or, in another wording, "a brother of yours"] has died, so stand and pray over your brother Ashamah" (*Bukhari*, 5:217, 2:406; *Muslim*, 2083), and he led them in the funeral prayer (*Bukhari*, 5:218, 5:219, 2:404).

"When the Negus died," reported the Prophet's wife 'A'ishah (R), "we were told that a light would be seen perpetually at his grave" (*Abu Dawud*, 2517).

REFERENCES: *Ahadith*: *Bukhari*, 4:644, 5:217, 5:220, 2:337, 2:404, 2:406; *Muslim*, 2083; Abu Dawud, 2517; *Muwatta*, 16:14; Ibn Qayyim al-Jawziyah, *Zad al-Ma'ad*, 3/60. Biographies: Ibn Ishaq/*Muhammad*, pp. 150-155, 657-658; Lings/*Muhammad*, pp. 81-84, 316. Other works: Akili/*Beauty*, pp. 97-102.

"They Who Say, 'God Is the Messiah, Son of Mary,' Have Certainly Disbelieved"

5:17/19

They who say, "God is the Messiah, son of Mary," have certainly disbelieved. Say, [O Muhammad:] "Then who could prevail against God if He intended to destroy the Messiah, son of Mary, and his mother and everyone on the earth?" And to God belongs the dominion of the heavens and the earth and whatever is between them. He creates whatever He wills, and God is Powerful over all things.

This is a very significant verse because in it the One who alone can define what constitutes belief in His sight proclaims that **they who say, "God is the Messiah, son of Mary," have certainly disbelieved**.

This disbelief rests on two grounds: first, because equating God Almighty, the exalted Creator, with a human being, born of a human mother, negates the most basic principle of all revealed faith, God's unique, exalted divine Essence, while at the same time ascribing to Jesus a false divinity that can never pertain to any created being whomsoever. Second, it denies the fact of Jesus' divinely-appointed prophethood.

Although among the noblest of mankind, Jesus and his mother (A) were nonetheless mortals. If God had willed to destroy them both, and everything in existence together with them, His is total control and command over all things. **He creates** — and likewise destroys — **whatever He wills, and God is Powerful over all things**. To put it another way, regardless of how marvellous some aspect of God's creation may be, it does not thereby cease to be a creation and become God.

As for the words, **God is the Messiah, son of Mary** (which are repeated in 5:72/75), there is no difference between saying "Jesus is God" and "God is Jesus," and indeed, as we saw in footnote 78 (2), some Christians of earlier times claimed that Jesus (A) was God Himself, who had descended from His kingdom, entered into the body of Mary and was born from her in order to demonstrate His power and will (Ayoub/*Q*, 184). Both wordings equally convey the enormity of supposing that the Creator, may He be glorified, could be born of a woman and experience all the normal needs and functions common to human beings, a notion that, in the Islamic frame of reference, is virtual blasphemy, as well as *shirk* — that is, ascribing divinity or its attributes to other than God — as is reiterated again in subsequent verses.

REFERENCES: Maududi/*Q*, 5:fns. 39-40; Ali/*Q*, 717.

"The Messiah, Son of Mary, Was Nothing but a Messenger"

5:72-79/75-83

They who say, "God is the Messiah, son of Mary," have certainly disbelieved, whereas the Messiah said, "O Children of Israel, worship God, my Lord and your Lord." Indeed, whoever ascribes partners to God, God has forbidden him Paradise and his abode is the Fire. And the wrong-doers will have no helpers. (72/75)

They who say, "God is a third of three," have certainly disbelieved, while there is no deity except one God. And if they do not desist from what they are saying, there will surely afflict the disbelievers among them a painful punishment. (73/76) **Will they not then repent to God and seek His forgiveness? And God is Forgiving and Merciful.** (74/75)

The Messiah, son of Mary, was nothing but a messenger; messengers had passed on before him. And his mother was a woman of truth. They both used to eat food. See how We make clear to them the signs; then see how they are deluded! (75/78)

Say, [O Muhammad:] "Do you worship, besides God, that which has no power of harm or benefit for you, while it is God who is the Hearing, the Knowing?" (76/79) **Say: "O People of the Scripture, do not exceed the limits in your religion beyond the truth, nor follow the fancies of a people who had previously gone astray and misled many, and have strayed from the soundness of the way."** (77/80)

Those who disbelieved among the Children of Israel were cursed by the tongue of David and Jesus son of Mary. That was because they disobeyed and transgressed. (78/81) **They used not to prohibit one another from wrong-doing that they did. Wretched indeed was that which they used to do!** (79/82)

(72/75) This lengthy passage deals once again with the whole complex of issues surrounding the attribution of divinity to Jesus, God's peace and blessings be upon him.

At the beginning, God Most High repeats the same hard-hitting words as occur at the beginning of 5:17/19: **They who say, "God is the Messiah [or Christ,] son of Mary," have certainly disbelieved,** adding, **whereas the Messiah himself said, "O Children of Israel, worship God, my Lord and your Lord."**

This verse again emphatically proclaims that equating God with Jesus, or Jesus with God, is tantamount to unbelief, for it is a denial of God's Oneness, uniqueness, transcendence, power, majesty and all the other attributes of divinity that distinguish Him from everything created — ***that make Him God***, so to speak. Such a notion is also a blatant falsification of the message with which Jesus (A) was sent and which he faithfully delivered to his people: that God was his Lord as well as their Lord, as He is the Lord of all things in existence, and that he himself was nothing but God's slave and messenger.

The last sentences of this verse — **Indeed, whoever ascribes partners to God, God has forbidden him Paradise and his abode is the Fire. And the wrong-doers will have no helpers** — are among the strongest warnings in the Qur'an against *shirk*, which God proclaims to be the worst of all sins, saying,

> **Indeed, God does not forgive *shirk*, but He forgives what is less than that to whomever He wills. And the one who commits *shirk* has certainly devised a tremendous sin.** (4:48, 116)

> **He who commits *shirk*, it is as though he had fallen from the sky and had been carried away by birds, or the wind had blown him down to a remote place.** (22:31)

(73-74/76-77) Again defining unbelief according to the divine criteria, God Most High then proclaims that **they who say, "God is a third of Three,"**[86] **have certainly disbelieved.** That is, although those who hold to such a notion may consider themselves to be believers, keeping diligently to the tenets of their faith, in God's sight they are unbelievers because they have violated truth and reality by ascribing divinity to a created being, **while there is no deity except one God.**

God then informs those who continue to deny His Oneness that **if they do not desist from what they are saying, there will surely afflict the disbelievers among them** — again meaning disbelievers according to *His* criteria — **a painful punishment**. At the same time, He urges them to **repent to God and seek His forgiveness,** assuring them that even after they have held, albeit with complete sincerity, such a false belief, **God is** ever **Forgiving and Merciful.**

(75/78) After having stated who Jesus (A) was *not*, God Most High then proceeds to state the truth of who he was.

---

[86]Meaning one of the three co-equal divine persons of the Trinity, without ranking them in any 'order.'

By the words, **The Messiah, son of Mary, was nothing but a messenger; messengers had passed on before him**, He, the All-Knowing, points out that Jesus (A) was one of the great company of mortal messenger-prophets who have dwelt upon the earth since the time of Adam (A). Then, by referring to Mary (A) as **a woman of truth [*siddiqah*]**, He clears her of two errors: both the slanders against her chastity and the exaggerations that would make her more than what He has said about her by calling her "the mother of God," "the Queen of Heaven," and the like.

The statement that Jesus and his mother (A) **both used to eat food**[87] drives home the point that because Mary and Jesus (A) required food and its subsequent digestion and elimination for survival, they could not have been divine. Yet although God makes **clear to them the signs,** most people are deluded concerning this matter, following the erroneous speculations and suppositions of religious figures, past and present, or their own personal fancies and imagination.

(76/79) As God's spokesman, Muhammad (S) is then told to say to those who attribute divinity to Jesus (A), **"Do you worship, besides God, that which has no power of harm or benefit for you, while it is God who is the Hearing, the Knowing?"** recalling Abraham's challenge to his idolatrous people when he said, **"Do you worship, besides God, that which neither benefits you in the least nor harms you?"** (21:66). In other words, "How can you be so unthinking as to give your worship to a finite being who is unable to do you either good or harm except as God permits, while it is God alone who hears and knows all things?" Indeed, it is a great irony that the one to whom divinity is ascribed is believed to have died the death of the worst of criminals, without power to save himself despite his ability to perform miracles, even crying out, "My God, my God, why have you forsaken me?" (Matt. 27:46, Mark 15:34).

(77/80) God then commands His Prophet (S) to caution the followers of the Jewish and Christian scriptures not to exceed the limits of truth in their religion nor to follow the false notions of their ancestors, who, by deviating from what God had revealed, became confused and in turn confused a great many others, and thus **strayed from the soundness of the way**.

(78-79/81-82) The next two verses refer to the general corruption of religion among the Israelites, which went so far that those who disbelieved

---

[87]Cf., **And We did not send before you [Muhammad] any of the messengers but that they ate food and walked in the markets** (25:20).

among them were **cursed**, first **by the tongue of David** (A) and, several centuries later, by **Jesus son of Mary** (A).

The reason for this cursing by these two prophets[88] was **because they disobeyed and transgressed the limits**, especially because **they used not to prohibit one another from wrong-doing that they did**, which is the duty of all believers, especially the men of religion among them.[89] And confirming the repeated condemnations of the persistent sins and transgressions of the deviant Israelites found in the Torah, the Psalms and the Gospels, God adds, **Wretched indeed was that which they used to do!**

A *hadith* sheds light on these two verses. The Holy Prophet (S) said, "In earlier times, when someone committed a sin among the Children of Israel, their scholars would rebuke them and attempt to restrain them. However, if they did not avoid the sins, they were not boycotted, and the same scholars continued social relations with them, and that is why God Most High cursed them through the tongues of David and Jesus, because they **disobeyed and transgressed the limits.**" The Prophet (S), who had been reclining against a cushion as he spoke, then sat upright and said, "No, no, by God! It is obligatory on you to prevent people from transgressing God's commands and to bring them back to obedience to the sacred Law [*Shari'ah*].[90] If you do not

---

[88]See Psalms 109 and 140, and Matt. 12:34, 23:1-33.

[89]Previous verses in the same *surah* allude to a similar theme: —

> **And you see many of them hastening to sin and aggression and devouring the prohibited. How wretched is what they have been doing! Why do not the rabbis and religious scholars forbid them from saying what is sinful and devouring the prohibited? How wretched is what they have been practicing! (5:62-63/65-66)**

[90]Enjoining the good and forbidding the evil (*'amr bil-ma'ruf wa nahy an al-munkar*) is a basic Islamic obligation, related to containing evil and wrong-doing by good advice and, if necessary, censure. It is stressed in several verses, such as the following:

> **Let there be among you a community inviting to the good and enjoining what is right and forbidding what is wrong. And those will be the successful. (3:104)**
>
> **You [Muslims] are the best community brought forth for mankind. You enjoin what is right and forbid what is wrong, and you believe in God. (3:110)**
>
> **They [the believers from among the People of the Scripture] believe in God and the Last Day, and they enjoin what is right and forbid what is wrong and hasten to good deeds. And those are among the righteous. (3:114)**
>
> **The believing men and believing women are supporters of one another. They enjoin what is right and forbid what is wrong, and establish *salat* and give *zakat*, and obey God and His Messenger. Those — God will have mercy upon them. Indeed, God is Almighty and Wise. (9:71, also 9:112, 22:14, 31:17)**

Concerning this important principle, the Prophet (S) said:

do so, God will also harden your hearts and His curse will be upon you as it was upon them" (Ahmad; also Abu Dawud, 4322-4323).

According to Ibn Kathir, Jesus' cursing of the Jews also relates to the excesses which a faction of them committed in relation to him, their prophet, in slandering his blessed mother, accusing him of sorcery, disbelieving in his prophethood, harboring enmity toward him, and attempting to kill him (Ibn Kathir/*T*, 5:72-79-75-81). This is reflected in the Prophet's saying to 'Ali ibn Abi Talib (R), who was to become the fourth caliph of Islam and endure martyrdom in the path of God, "You resemble Jesus, whom the Jews hated so much that they slandered his mother, and whom the Christians loved so much that they placed him in a position not rightly his"[91] (Tirmidhi, 6093).

Hence, among the three monotheistic faiths, Muslims constitute a unique community. For while the followers of the first deny the prophethood of both Jesus (A) and Muhammad (S), and those of the second deify Jesus (A) and deny Muhammad (S), accepting and honoring all of God's prophets and messengers, while affirming their humanity, is found among Muslims alone. Perhaps this is one of the meanings of God's saying,

> **And thus have We made you [Muslims] a middle community [*ummah*], that you might be witnesses for mankind and the Messenger [Muhammad] might be a witness for you. (2:143)**

REFERENCES: Ibn Kathir/*T*, 5:72-79/75-81; Asad/*Q*, 5:fn. 93; Ali/*Q*, fn. 787.

> God does not punish people because of the sins of a few, but when evil and sinfulness spread collectively, and in spite of their ability to prevent it they do not do so, then God Most High sends His punishment on all of them. (Ahmad)
>
> When people see something objectionable and do not change it, God will soon include them all in His punishment. (*Mishkat*, 5142; also Abu Dawud, 4324, 4325)
>
> When a sin is committed on earth, one who sees it and disapproves of it will be reckoned as one who was not present, while one who was not present and approves of it will be like one who sees [it committed]. (Abu Dawud, 4331)
>
> If a person sees people disobeying God while he is among them and he is displeased with them, it is as if he were not part of them, while if he is pleased with them, even though he is absent from them, it is as if he were one of them. (Abu Dawud)

[91]Afterwards, 'Ali himself was to say, "Two [kinds of] people will perish on my account: one who loves me so excessively that he praises me for what I do not possess, and one who hates me so much that he will be impelled by his hatred to slander me" (Tirmidhi, 6093).

"I Did Not Say to Them But What You Commanded Me: To Worship God, My Lord and Your Lord"

5:116-118/119-121

And [be mindful of the Day] when God will say, "O Jesus son of Mary, did you say to people, 'Take me and my mother as deities besides God'?"

He will say, "May You be glorified! It was not for me to say that to which I had no right. If I had said it, You would have known it. You know what is within my self but I do not know what is within Your Self; indeed, it is You who are Knower of the Unseen. (116/119)

"I did not say to them but what You commanded me: to worship God, my Lord and your Lord. And I was a witness over them as long as I was among them; but when You took me up, You were the Observer over them, and You are Witness over all things. (117/120) **If you should punish them, indeed, they are Your slaves; but if You forgive them, indeed, it is You who are the Almighty, the Wise."** (118/121)

This is the continuation of the passage in which God evokes scenes of the Day of Judgment —

the Day God will assemble the messengers and say, "What was the response you received?" They will say, "We have no knowledge. Indeed, it is You who are Knower of the Unseen."[92] **(109/113)**

God Most High will then say, **"O Jesus son of Mary, recall My favor to you and to your mother"** (110/113), and He will enumerate His special favors to Jesus and Mary (A) which we mentioned in our earlier discussion of these verses on pages 357-358. God will then recall His inspiring the apostles to believe in Him and His messenger, Jesus (111/114), followed by the report of the heavenly repast sent down to them (111-115/114-118).

---

[92]This reply of the messengers reflects, first, such utter humility before their Lord that when He, the Knower of all things, asks them for information about their own missions, they will not tell what they know but will refer all knowledge back to Him. Second, their reply indicates that they knew only as much as was given to them to know. As for what was in the hearts of those to whom they conveyed the Message, that was a secret between those servants and their Lord.

(116/119) This is followed by the first of the verses quoted above, which refers to God's asking Jesus (A) whether, while in this world, he had asked people to take him and his mother as deities besides Him.

Although nothing whatsoever is hidden from God Most High and He knows with perfect knowledge that this did not happen, says Ibn Kathir, He will question Jesus (A) concerning it both to give him honor and to affirm the truth to those who assert that Jesus (A) claimed to be the Son of God or divine. And with utmost humility, Jesus (A) will reply by glorifying his Lord and declaring that he did not say what he had no right to say — namely, that he was anything but God's slave and messenger. **"If I had said it,"** he will continue, **"You would have known it,"** for **"You know what is within my self and I do not know what is within Your Self; indeed, it is You who are Knower of the Unseen"** — that is, aware of the deepest and most subtle mysteries of Your creation, including what is in Your servants' hearts and minds.

(117/120) Jesus (A) will then clarify what he actually did say to his people while he was among them. **"I did not say to them except what You commanded me"** — namely, **"to worship God, my Lord and your Lord. And,"** he will continue, **"I was a witness over them as long as I was among them"** — that is, until You raised me to Yourself when they intended to crucify and kill me. **"But when You took me up** and I was no longer present to be a witness of their deeds, **You were the Observer over them, and You are Witness over all things."**

(118/121) "If you should punish them," Jesus (A) will continue, **"indeed, they are Your slaves."** That is, it is for You to judge your servants, and if You decree punishment for them it can only be because they have deserved it. **"But,"** he will add, **"if You forgive them, indeed, it is You who are the Almighty, the Wise,"** Knower for whom mercy is appropriate and for whom it is not.

Concerning these verses, the Holy Prophet, God's peace and blessings be upon him, said:

> You will be gathered [on the Day of Resurrection], and some people will be driven to the left side [that is, to Hell]. And I will say, as the righteous slave [Jesus] said, **"And I was a witness over them as long as I was among them. . . ,"** up to **"the Almighty, the Wise."** (*Bukhari*, 6:150)

The well-known Companion of the Prophet (S), Abu Dharr (R), reported that once the Prophet (S) stood in prayer the entire night up to morning, reciting the verse, **"If you should punish them, indeed, they are Your slaves,**

but if You forgive them, indeed, it is You who are the Almighty, the Wise." And the Prophet (S) said, "I have asked my Lord, the Mighty and Glorious, for intercession [*shafa'ah*] for my people, and He has granted it to me. And it will be granted, if God Most High so wills, for everyone who did not ascribe partners to Him" (Ibn Kathir/*T*, 5:116-118/119-121).

'Abdullah bin 'Amr bin al-'As (R) reported that the Prophet (S) once recited the saying of God Most High concerning Abraham, **"My Lord, indeed, they [the idols]] have led astray many among mankind. Therefore, whoever follows me, indeed, he is of me, and whoever disobeys me, indeed, you are Forgiving and Merciful"** (14:36); and Jesus, peace be upon him, said, **"If you should punish them, indeed, they are Your slaves, but if You forgive them, indeed, it is You who are the Almighty, the Wise"** [5:118./121]. And the Prophet (S) raised his hands [in supplication] and said, "O Lord, my ***ummah***, my ***ummah!***" and wept. Then God the Mighty and Glorious said, "O Gabriel, go to Muhammad and ask him — although your Lord knows well — why he is weeping," so Gabriel (A) came to him and asked him. The Prophet (S) then told Gabriel (A) what he had said, ["My ***ummah***, my ***ummah***!"], although God knew well. Then God said, "O Gabriel, go to Muhammad and say, 'Indeed, We will please you with regard to your ***ummah*** and will not displease you.'"[93] (*Muslim*, 397)

REFERENCE: Ibn Kathir/*T*, 5:116-118/119-121.

"How Could He Have a Son While He Does Not Have a Consort?"

6:100-102

But they have ascribed partners with God — the jinn, while He created them — and have falsely attributed to Him sons and daughters without knowledge. Exalted and high is He above what they attribute [to Him]! (100) Originator of the heavens and the earth — how could He have a son while He does not have a consort? And He created all things and He is Knowing of all things. (101) That is God, your Lord; there is no deity except

[93]This is similar to the verse addressed to Muhammad (S): **And your Lord is going to give to you, and you will be well-pleased** (93:5).

Him, the Creator of all things, so worship Him [alone]. And He is Disposer of all things. (102)

(100) In this passage, God Most High introduces the issue of some of the entities to whom the pagan Arabs attributed a share in His divinity — firstly, **the jinn,**[94] **whereas He created them**, and secondly, those **sons and daughters** whom they had falsely attributed to Him **without knowledge**.

As mentioned in Appendix B following the story of Abraham (A) in Volume One, the religion of pre-Islamic Arabia was a catch-all sort of polytheism, fed by many currents. Hence, the "sons" attributed to God by the pagan Arabs evidently included Jesus (A).[95] At the same time, the angels, who were believed to be female, were thought to be His "daughters," as mentioned in a number of verses.[96] All this was the work of Satan, who, from the time of his fall, had announced his intention to mislead and deviate mankind from God's straight path, excepting God's sincere servants among them, teaching them every kind of vile pagan belief, practice and superstition.[97]

(101) The passage then continues with very powerful arguments against the notion that God Most High could or would have an offspring (***walad***, meaning son or child).

The first of these is that God, the Praised and Glorious, is infinitely, unimaginably **exalted and high above what they attribute** to Him in similarity or resemblance to any of His creatures. Ibn Kathir comments on the meaning of this, saying that God the Exalted is complete in Himself, whereas an offspring is by definition the product of incompleteness, since, apart from the single, unique instance of Mary (A), one parent cannot produce offspring without another. Moreover, a child is derived from two parents and hence is of the same essence, substance and nature as they, whereas God Most High is the unique, self-sufficient **Originator of the heavens and the earth** and whatever is in them, whose divine Essence is not shared by any created being.

---

[94]The attribution of divinity to the jinn is mentioned in 6:100, 34:40-41 and 37:158.

[95]As evidence of this, it is recorded that pictures of Mary and Jesus and of Abraham had been placed inside the K'abah by the polytheist Arabs, together with depictions of angels and other beings whom they worshipped. According to some accounts, the Prophet (S) ordered that all these pictures be wiped out; according to others, he retained those of Mary, Jesus and Abraham (Ibn Ishaq/*Muhammad*, p. 552, 774; Lings/*Muhammad*, p. 300).

[96]These are 16:67, 17:40, 37:149-157, 43:15-16, 52:39, 53:21-22.

[97]This is mentioned in 4:118-119, 7:16-17, 15:39-40, 17:62 and 38:82-83. See also Volume One, pages 34-35.

How, then, He asks, **could He have a son** or a child, which is by definition the product of the union of two separate, incomplete partners, **while He does not have a consort**? Moreover, **He created all things**, and since a creation is not the same as or similar to the Creator, no creation can ever be imagined or said to be the Creator's "son" or "child".

(102) The words, **"That is God, your Lord,"** emphasize that God, the Almighty and Glorious, is who *He* proclaims Himself to be, not what any of His servants, out of their imaginations, desires or limited abilities to conceive of Him, may suppose Him to be. Indeed, any notions concerning Him not based on revealed knowledge will never be anything but guesswork, conjectures and illusions — in short, mind-products (***wahm***). God Most High then proclaims that **there is no deity except Him, the Creator of all things**, who alone is worthy of worship and who alone **is Disposer of all things**, known and unknown, both within the realm of human perception or outside it.

REFERENCES: Ibn Kathir/*T*, 6:100-102; Ibn Ishaq/*Muhammad*, pp. 552, 774, fn. 806; Lings/*Muhammad*, pp. 17, 300; Ali/*Q*, fn. 929; Asad/*Q*, 6:fns. 86-88.

"THE CHRISTIANS SAY, 'THE MESSIAH IS GOD'S SON'"

9:30-31

The Jews say, "Ezra is God's son," and the Christians say, "The Messiah is God's son." That is their saying with their mouths; they [but] imitate the saying of those who disbelieved [before them]. God will destroy them; how deluded they are! (30) **They have taken their scholars and monks as lords besides God, and the Messiah, son of Mary, while they were not commanded but to worship one God; there is no deity except Him. Far removed is He from what they associate with Him!** (31)

(30) In order to understand this reference to **"God's son"** in this verse, we must first examine the meaning and usage of the term, which occurs over and over in the Bible.

It was used of prophets and other godly men in both the Old and New Testaments. Thus, the genealogy of Joseph the carpenter is reported to go back to "Adam, the son of God" (Luke 3:38). God is said to have referred to Israel as "My firstborn son" (Ex. 4:22); to have said, "I am Israel's father, and Ephraim is my firstborn son" (Jer. 31:9); to have said about the writer of the Psalms, "You are my son; today I have become your father (Ps. 2:7); and to have said about Solomon (A), "He will be my son, and I will be his father" (1 Chr. 22:10; also 2 Sam. 7:14).

The use of the term, "sons (or children) of God," to express the human being's relationship to God is also common in both testaments. For example, in Gen. 6:2, we read, "The sons of God saw that the daughters of men were beautiful," while the writer of the Psalms said, "You are 'gods;' you are all sons of the Most High" (Ps. 82:6-7). To Moses (A) are attributed the words, "You are the children of the Lord your God" (Deut. 14:1). In the Book of Job it is stated, "One day the sons of God [in other translations, "angels"] came to present themselves before the Lord" (Job. 1:6, 2:1). Jesus (A) is reported to have said, "Blessed are the peacemakers, for they will be called sons of God" (Matt. 5:9). Likewise, in Romans 8:14, it is stated, "because those who are led by the Spirit of God are sons of God."

It is thus evident that the terms "son/sons/children of God" were used metaphorically in various different contexts, rather than meaning the literal offspring of God the Exalted. It is in keeping with this usage that God says, **But the Jews and the Christians say, "We are God's children [or sons] and His beloved"** (5:18/20).

However, when this expression was used of Jesus (A) after his departure from this world, it was taken out of its metaphorical context and, through the introduction of pagan elements that were absolutely alien to Judaism, transmuted into the sense of God's literal offspring.

Verse 30 informs us that two groups of people claimed sons for God: certain Jews who made this claim concerning Ezra, such an important reviver of the Torah that he has actually been considered as the founder of Judaism,[98]

---

[98]Ezra (or Esdras; Arabic, 'Uzayr), a descendant of Aaron, is mentioned only once in the Qur'an, in 9:30 above. Because of his being named here together with Jesus, many commentators concluded that he was a prophet. However, there is evidently no clear validation of this fact from the Prophet (S). Perhaps Ezra is among those referred to in his saying, "Among those who were before you of the Children of Israel, there were men who spoke [by divine inspiration] without being prophets, and if there is one of them among my ***ummah***, it is 'Umar" (***Bukhari***, 5:38). At the same time, Ezra's importance for Judaism cannot be underestimated. The following brief history may be useful.

Ezra, "a teacher well versed in the Law of Moses, which the Lord, the God of Israel, had given" (Ezra 7:6), was among the exiles in Babylon. In 458 or 428 B.C., when Babylon was conquered by Persia, the Persian king Ataxerxes sent Ezra back to Jerusalem to re-establish the religion of God and whatever pertained to it. Ibn Kathir says that although before his time the Torah had been virtually lost among the Children of Israel, God opened Ezra's breast, and he tied a pen to his finger and wrote the entire Torah. When the Israelites compared the manuscripts they had hidden away during the invasions with what Ezra had written, they found his writing to be in agreement with what they had. Seeing this, some ignorant people started saying that he must be God's son (Ibn Kathir/*T*, 9:30-31).

and the Christians concerning Jesus (A). However, God Himself strongly denounces these claims as nothing but a **saying with their mouths** in imitation of what unbelievers had said before them and as an evidence of their self-delusion.

(31) God Most High then declares that **they** — the People of the Scripture — **have taken their scholars and monks as lords besides God, and the Messiah, son of Mary, while they were not commanded but to worship one God.**[99] The Prophet (S) referred to this verse in his saying, "When scholars say something is prohibited, people take it as prohibited, and when they say something is permissible, they take it as permissible, and that is their worship of them." Ibn 'Abbas (R) says that these words refer to blindly following the judgment of religious scholars in matters of what is prohibited and permissible. Al-Suddi says that people started not referring to God's scripture

---

Muhammad Asad states that Ezra "restored and codified the Torah after it had been lost during the Babylonian Exile, and 'edited' it in more or less the form which it has today. . . . Ever since then he has been venerated to such a degree that his verdicts on the Law of Moses have come to be regarded by the Talmudists as being practically equivalent to the Law itself" (Asad/*Q*, 9:fn. 44). Indeed, the Jewish philosopher Spinoza went so far as to say that it was Ezra rather than Moses who composed the Pentateuch. It has also been said that it was from the time of Ezra that the Jewish faith, based on the then-accepted revison of the Torah, could legitimately be called Judaism and its followers, Jews. Further, it was Ezra who, more than anyone else, asserted that the mark of a Jew should not be race but observance of the Torah. From Ezra's time, the Torah became the Law and Jerusalem the only Jewish center officially committed to obeying it as its constitution. Ezra also renewed the priesthood of the Temple, and high priests replaced kings as heads of the Jewish nation.

The matter of the Jews' regarding Ezra as God's son is mentioned in two lengthy ***ahadith*** concerning the Day of Resurrection, in which it is stated that the Jews will be summoned for judgment and asked, "What did you use to worship?" to which they will reply, "We used to worship Ezra, God's son" (***Bukhari***, 6.105, 9:532B). The matter is also referred to in the classical biography of the Prophet by Ibn Ishaq, who states that Ibn 'Abbas once asked 'Abdullah ibn Salam, a Jewish rabbi who converted to Islam in the Prophet's time, why the Jews said that Ezra was the son of God. Ibn Salam replied that it was because Ezra wrote the Torah for the Children of Israel from his memory, whereupon they said, "Moses was not capable of bringing us the Torah except in written form, but Ezra came to us with it without its being written," and consequently some of them speculated that he must be God's son (Ibn Ishaq/***Muhammad***, p. 269). However, according to Muhammad Asad, most classical commentators agree that it was only the Jews of Arabia, rather than all Jews, who held this belief, which violates the most fundamental principle of Judaism. Asad cites a ***hadith*** quoted by al-Tabari in his commentary on the above verse, stating that once some Jews of Medina asked the Prophet (S), "How could we follow you when you have forsaken our ***qiblah*** and do not consider Ezra a son of God?" (Asad/Q, 9:fn. 44), whatever was meant by that.

[99]Other verses of related meaning are 3:64 and 3:79-80 (see pages 390-392 and 396-397).

but simply taking what came from their elders, and that is why God says that they were not commanded but to worship one God and to follow His law (Ibn Kathir/*T*, 9:30-31).

REFERENCES: Commentaries: Ibn Kathir/*T*, 9:30-31; Ibn Kathir/*Q*, "'Uzayr"; Tabari/*H*, IV:64-65; Ali/*Q*, Appen. 2; Asad/*Q*, 9:fn. 44; Ayoub/*Q*, II:205, 20. Biographies: Ibn Ishaq/*Muhammad*, p. 269; Lings/*Muhammad*, pp. 315-316. Other works: Mond/*The New Testament in Question*, pp. 40-41; Barnavi/*Atlas*, p. 33; Grant/*Israel*, pp. 190-191, 288.

"They Say, 'God Has Taken a Son'"

10:68-69

They say, "God has taken a son." May He be glorified; He is the Self-Sufficient! To Him belongs whatever is in the heavens and whatever is on the earth. No authority do you have for this [claim]. Do you say about God that which you do not know? (68) Say, [O Muhammad:] "Indeed, those who fabricate falsehood about God will not prosper." (69)

Here, as in several other passages, God Most High refutes the claims of those who ascribe to Him what is not befitting to His exalted divine nature, proclaiming that He is **the Self-Sufficient**, Independent of all He has created, far removed from any incompleteness, need or insufficiency, and absolutely free of any defect, blemish or flaw. He is also the Owner and Master of **whatever is in the heavens and whatever is on the earth,** and He requires nothing from any part of His creation to sustain Him or make Him complete.

The assertion that He **has taken a son** is made without any authority from Him. Rather, those who make it assert something that they do not know concerning Him, thereby perpetrating a grave falsehood that will prevent them from prospering either in this world or the Hereafter.

REFERENCES: Ibn Kathir/*T*, 10:68-69; Maududi/*Q*, 10:fn. 68.

"Do Not Take Two Deities"

16:51-52

And God said, "Do not take two deities. He is but one God; therefore, fear Me alone." (51) And to Him belongs whatever is in the heavens and the earth, and to Him is due perpetual obedience. Then is it other than God that you fear? (52)

In a similar vein, God Most High here refutes the notion of the existence of **two deities,** presumably meaning God the Father and God the Son — and, by extension, whatever is more than two, for since **He is only one God,** anything more than one cannot be one.

Since all things belong to Him, including those very beings to whom divinity is ascribed, no one but He is entitled to **perpetual obedience**. And since God is in command and control of everything, why should anything other than He be feared?

"Praise Be to God, Who Has Not Taken a Son"

17:111

And say, [O Muhammad:] "Praise be to God, who has not taken a son and has no partner in dominion, nor is there any protector for Him from weakness. And extol Him with [great] extolling."

In this verse, the divine Author of the Book emphasizes, through the mouth of His Last Prophet (S), that He alone, the Lord of Majesty and Honor, is worthy of praise. Singular and unique in His divine nature, He has no partner or associate in dominion or sovereignty, for He is free of the imperfection inherent in takng a son for Himself as an extension of His being, and of needing a partner or spouse. Nor does He require a **protector from weakness**, since weakness does not apply to Him, the All-Powerful, to whom all praise, glory and exaltation are due.

REFERENCES: Ibn Kathir/*T*, 17:111; Asad/*Q*, 17:fns. 133-134.

"To Warn Those Who Say, 'God Has Taken a Son'"

18:1-5

Praise be to God, who has sent down the Book to His slave and has not placed therein any crookedness. (1) [He has made it] straight, to warn of a severe punishment from Him and to give good tidings to the believers who do righteous deeds that they will have a goodly recompense, (2) abiding therein forever, (3) and to warn those who say, "God has taken a son." (4) They have no knowledge of it, nor had their fathers. Grave is the word that proceeds from their mouths. They speak nothing but a lie! (5)

(1) These well-known verses from *Surah al-Kahf* (The Cave), which are mentioned in ***ahadith*** as a protection against the Dajjal or Anti-Christ,[100] open with God's proclamation that the Qur'an is the divinely-revealed scripture granted to His slave Muhammad (S), which is totally straight and free of all deviation, distortion, confusion and contradiction.

(2-4) The various purposes of the Qur'an are then mentioned. One of these is **to warn** unbelievers or evil-doers **of a severe punishment from Him**, of a non-specific, unqualified nature. The second is **to give good tidings to the believers who do righteous deeds that they will have a goodly recompense,** the Paradise of bliss, **in which they will abide forever.** And the third purpose is to warn a specific group of people: **those who say, "God has taken a son."**

(5) God Most High then declares that those who make this claim have **no knowledge of it, nor had their fathers.** Rather, they are claiming something for which He has revealed no authority.

The admonition then becomes stronger: **Grave is the word that proceeds from their mouths**, for it ascribes to God, the Praised and Glorious, that which is not suitable for His exalted, unique divine nature, pertaining instead to finite, limited created beings who require both spouses and offspring to make them complete.

The divine rebuke becomes stronger still: **They speak nothing but a lie**, for the claim that they make about Him, the Most High, is totally false and devoid of all substance and reality. Moreover, it constitutes such a grave slander and negation of the divine Essence and Majesty that it amounts to a tremendous falsehood.

REFERENCES: Asad/*Q*, 18:fn. 1; Ali/*Q*, fn. 2327.

"It Is Not for God to Take a Son"

19:34-37

Such was Jesus son of Mary — a declaration of the truth about which they are in dispute. (34) **It is not for God to take a son, may He be glorified! When He decrees a matter, He but says to it "Be!" and it is.** (35) **[Jesus said:] "And indeed, God is my Lord and your Lord, so worship Him. This is a straight**

---

[100]See Chapter 27, pages 465-466.

path." (36) **Then the factions from among them differed. Then woe to those who disbelieved from the scene of a tremendous Day!** (37)

(34) These verses conclude the lengthy passage in ***Surah Maryam*** (19:1-33) that we cited earlier in connection with Zechariah's prayer for a son, the advent of John, the annunciation to Mary and the birth of Jesus, God's peace and blessings be upon them all.

Here God attests, concerning the foregoing narrative, that **such was Jesus son of Mary**, meaning that he was as is described therein. This account is, moreover, **a declaration of the truth about which they are in dispute**, meaning that whatever was stated concerning Jesus (A) and his orgin earlier in this ***surah*** is the absolute truth from Him, negating all other accounts or claims. Says Ibn Kathir:

> This truth dispels all the arguments, questions and doubts of earlier and later peoples, including the Jews, who asserted that Jesus (A) was a false prophet, the product of a shameful, illicit relationship, and of those Christians who asserted that He was God incarnate and the second person of the Trinity. (Ibn Kathir/*T*, 19:34-37)

(35) God Most High then emphatically refutes His alleged "kinship" to Jesus, for **it is not for God to take a son, may He be glorified!** That is, such a thing is not suitable or fitting for Him because He, the Praised and Exalted, has no equal or similar or parent or offspring, nor any partner in His divinity, and is infiniteiy removed from the thing that has been falsely attributed to Him.

Again, He makes it clear that He is not in need of visible means and causes to create whatever He wills, for He is the Creator and Sustainer of all things in existence. When He decrees anything, He has but to order it by that divine command that brings all things into being, whereupon — by any means He wills, or none — it so becomes. And while He willed to create both Jesus and Adam (A) without the agency of two human parents, that in no way implies that He is their father or that they are His sons and therefore divine.

(36) God Most High further makes it clear that Jesus (A) himself never claimed to be the Son of God or divine. Rather, he proclaimed that he was a creature and a slave to his Lord, declaring repeatedly, **"And indeed, God is my Lord and your Lord, so worship Him** alone. **This** and nothing else **is a straight path."**

(37) God then refers to the divisions among the sects of Christianity, stating that **the factions from among them differed** concerning Jesus (A). And He reminds **those who disbelieved** of the awesomeness of the inevitable Day of Judgment, when they will have to face the consequences of the erroneousness of their beliefs, even though they had been given minds and intellect with which to discern the truth.

Commenting on this passage, Ibn Kathir comments:

> The Jews said, "He is a child of fornication," and they continued in their disbelief and enmity toward him. Some others said, "He is God," and still others said, "He is the Son of God," while the true believers said, "He is the slave of God and His messenger, the son of His handmaiden and His word which He bestowed upon Mary and a spirit from Him." These latter are the ones who will be helped by God and are on truth, and they will be victorious, while those who contradict them in regard to this description of him are unbelievers and straying and ignorant. God has warned them, saying, **Then woe be to those who disbelieved from the scene of a tremendous Day!** [19:37]. (Ibn Kathir/*T*, 19:34-37)

REFERENCES: Ibn Kathir/*T*, 19:34-37; Ayoub/*Q*, II:184-187; Asad/*Q*, 19:fn. 25.

"It Is Not Befitting for the Most Merciful That He Should Take a Son"

19:88-93

> **And they say, "The Most Merciful has taken a son."** (88) **You have certainly done an abominable thing!** (89) **The heavens almost rupture from it, and the earth splits open and the mountains fall down destroyed,** (90) **that they attribute a son to the Most Merciful,** (91) **while it is not befitting for the Most Merciful that He should take a son.** (92) **There is no one in the heavens and the earth but comes to the Most Merciful as a slave.** (93)

(88) Here, it is noteworthy that the pagans of Mecca, who ascribed divinity to numerous entities in addition to God Most High, nevertheless referred to Him, as He refers to Himself, as **the Most Merciful (*ar-Rahman*)**.[101] This again confirms the fact that although they associated with God all sorts of alleged deities that had no reality except in their own imaginations, it never occurred to them to deny His *existence*. What they denied was rather His being the sole deity — that is, the Originator, Guardian, Sovereign, Law-Giver, Provider, and Controller of all affairs to whom they were directly

---

[101]See 17:110, 21:26, 36:15, 43:20.

accountable, who guides and coordinates the interrelationships of all things in existence — a mindset that we might compare to a child's insisting that he has several fathers or mothers other than his true parents who are entitled to be recognized as such.

(89-93) There now follow what are perhaps the most emphatic and hard-hitting of the Qur'anic verses describing the extreme gravity of ascribing a son or offspring to the Creator of all things. God Most High directly addresses those who make this claim, declaring that attributing a son or a child to Him is nothing less than "***shayan iddan***" — such a grave, horrendous, abominable blasphemy against His divine majesty that the heavens and earth are virtually shattered to pieces from the enormity of it. For He is God Almighty, the One, the Unique, the Holy, the Praised, the Exalted and Glorious, to whom all things come in a state of ***'ubudiyat*** or servanthood, and consequently such notions as His having a partner in divinity or producing offspring like a created being are not only totally unbefitting and degrading, but simply do not apply

Says Ibn Kathir concerning this passage:

> At the beginning of this *surah* [*Maryam*], it was shown without any doubt that Jesus (A) is a slave of God, for God created him without a father in the womb of Mary (A). Here their ignorance is mentioned again in that they called him "the Son of God," whereas God is highly exalted above having a son. And God says, "This is a very weighty thing. Indeed, it is so awful that the heavens may tremble and be shattered or the earth may shake and split, because the earth and the heavens know the greatness and sublimity of God Most High. They know the Oneness of the Creator; they know that foolish and mindless human beings have made up a slander against God, who has none to share His Essence, nor any parents or children, nor any partner or like. All creation is a proof of His Oneness, every particle of the universe is a witness to His unique Being, and consequently the whole universe trembles when one of God's creatures ascribes partners to Him.
>
> No action, however good it may seem, is of any use with *shirk*, while it is entirely possible that with the affirmation of God's Oneness, God may forgive all sins. As stated in the *hadith*, "Instruct your dying [to say] '*La ilaha illa-Llah*, there is no deity except God' [*Muslim*, 1996, 1998], for if anyone says this while dying, Paradise becomes guaranteed for him."
>
> A Companion [of the Prophet] then asked, "O Messenger of God, what about someone who said this while alive?"
>
> He replied, "It is absolutely guaranteed for him, by God in whose hand is my soul! If everything in the heavens and the earth and whatever

is between them were placed on one side of the scale and the affirmation of '*La ilaha illa-Llah*' on the other side, that side would be heavier."[102] (Ibn Kathir/*T*, 19:88-93)

The critical importance of believing in and affirming the Unity of the Creator is also mentioned in the following *hadith*, in which the Messenger of God (S) said:

> On the Day of Resurrection, God Most High will single out a man from my *ummah* above the heads of people, and He will open ninety-nine registers [of his bad deeds] in front of him, each register spread out to the limit of his sight. Then He will say, "Do you object to anything in them? Have My recorders wronged you?"
>
> He will reply, "No, O my Lord."
>
> Then God will say, "Do you have any excuse?"
>
> He will reply, "No, O my Lord."
>
> Then God Most High will say, "Indeed, there is a good deed of yours with Us, and indeed, there shall be no injustice to you this day." So a paper will be brought forth on which is inscribed, "*Ash-shadu an la ilaha illa-Llah wa ashhadu anna Muhammadun 'abduhu wa rasulihu* [I testify that there is no deity except God and I testify that Muhammad is His slave and messenger]." Then He will say, "Come for your weighing."
>
> He will say, "O Lord, what is this paper against these registers?"
>
> God will say, "You will not be done injustice."
>
> Then the registers will be placed in one side of the scale and the paper in the other. Then those registers will become light and the paper heavy, for indeed, nothing can be weightier than God's name. (Tirmidhi, Ibn Majah, Ibn Hibban, Hakim, Bayhaqi)

REFERENCES: Ibn Kathir/*T*, 19:88-93; Asad/*Q*, 19:fn. 77; Ali/*Q*, 2529.

---

[102]Similar *ahadith* are mentioned on pages 185, footnote 184, and page 290.

"THEY SAY, 'THE MOST MERCIFUL HAS TAKEN A SON'"

21:26-29

And they say, "The Most Merciful has taken a son [or child]." Glorified is He! Rather, they are [but] honored slaves. (26) They do not precede Him in speech and they act by His command. (27) He knows what is before them and what is after them, and they cannot intercede except for one of whom He approves, and they are apprehensive out of fear of Him. (28) And whoever among them should say, "Indeed, I am a god besides Him," that one We would recompense with Hell. Thus do We recompense the wrongdoers! (29)

Like 19:88-93, this passage begins by referring to the son or child who is attributed to **the Most Merciful.** God the Exalted then declares that the beings to whom people ascribe divinity, whether Jesus (A), angels or any others, are merely **honored slaves,** who may neither speak nor act but **by His command**. His knowledge encompasses them from every direction, and they are not even allowed to intercede for anyone except as He approves and permits. And if any of those to whom He has granted the honor of prophethood or servanthood were to set himself up as an object of worship in place of or in addition to Him, his recompense would be Hell.

Ibn Kathir states concerning these verses that the unbelievers of Mecca believed the angels to be God's daughters. God Most High here refutes their claim, declaring that the angels are merely **honored slaves** who obey His commands, while His knowledge of them includes perfect awareness of whatever is before and after them, at their right and their left, and nothing whatsoever is hidden from Him. Nor do these noble angels dare to speak by recommending anyone except as God permits (Ibn Kathir/*T*, 21:26-29).

REFERENCES: Ibn Kathir/*T*, 21:26-29; Asad/*Q*, 21:fn. 34.

"GOD HAS NOT TAKEN ANY SON"

23:91-92

God has not taken any son, nor has there ever been any deity with Him. (91) [If there had been,] then each deity would have taken away what it created and some of them would have sought to overcome others. Glorified is God above what they attribute [to Him]! Knower of the Unseen and the Witnessed, high is He above what they associate with Him. (92)

In this passage, while reiterating that He **has not taken any son** and declaring that there has never **been any deity with Him**, God Most High introduces a new proof of His Oneness: that there can be only one commander and controller of creation, for if there were more than one, there would be rivalry and conflict among them, as is seen in the mythologies of various polytheistic peoples.[103]

Here, the **Knower of the Unseen and the Witnessed** — that is, the spiritual and material realms — once again proclaims that He is endlessly **exalted above what they attribute** to Him and **high above what they associate with Him.** No matter what anyone may associate with Him or set up as a partner to Him, He, the Knower of all things in every aspect and dimension of His creation, is infinitely, unimaginably exalted above them all.

REFERENCES: Maududi/*Q*, 21:fn. 22, 17:fn. 47; Asad/*Q*, 23:fn. 53.

"He Who Has Not Taken a Son and Has No Partner in Dominion"

25:1-3

Blessed is He who sent down the Criterion to His slave [Muhammad], that he might be a warner to the worlds (1) — **He to whom the dominion of the heavens and the earth belongs, and who has not taken a son and has no partner in dominion, and has created each thing and determined it with [precise] determination.** (2) **Yet they have taken, besides Him, gods that create nothing, while they are [themselves] created, nor do they have power of harm or benefit for themselves, nor do they have power over death or life or resurrection.** (3)

(1-2) These are the opening verses of the *surah* entitled *Al-Furqan* (The Criterion), referring to the Qur'an.

Here, God Most High proclaims that He revealed this criterion of truth and falsehood to Muhammad (S) in order **that he might be a warner to the** dual **worlds** of jinn and humans, up to the end of time.[104]

---

[103]This is also stated in a verse of related meaning: **If there had been deities besides God therein** — that is, in the heavens and the earth — **they would both have been ruined** (21:22).

[104]See also the commentary on 72:1-4, page 432-433.

To God alone belongs **the dominion of the heavens and the earth,** and He has neither a son nor any other partner to share in it. Not only is He the Creator of every atom in existence, but He has determined all things with such precise and perfect determination that

> **You do not see any inconsistency in the creation of the Most Merciful. Then return the glance again; do you see any rift? Then return the glance yet again. The glance will return to you diminished and weary.** (67:3-4)

(3) God then rebukes those who have taken, **besides Him, gods that create nothing, while they are** themselves **created**, and who are able to control nothing whatsoever, since they have neither power **of harm or benefit for themselves,** nor **do they have power** to cause or defer **death or life or resurrection.**

REFERENCE: Maududi/*Q*, 25:fns. 1-10.

"If God Had Desired to Take a Son ..."

39:4

> **If God had desired to take a son, He could have chosen whatever He willed from among what He creates. Glorified is He; He is God, the One, the Prevailing!**

In this verse, God Most High puts forth yet another argument to defeat the claims of those who assert that He has a son. Says Ibn Kathir:

> This condition [**"If God had desired to take a son"**] is not mentioned as actual or possible, but rather indicates its impossibility and emphasizes the ignorance of people who claim the possibility of a creature's being God's son or child.
>
> It is not that God actually desired, nor is it possible for Him, to take a son, as in the verses, **If We had intended to take a diversion, We could have taken it from what is with Us, if [indeed] We were to do so** [21:17], or, **If the Most Merciful had a son** . . . [43:81]; for all these verses mention a condition which is impossible rather than a condition which is possible or actual, meaning, "Since *this* is impossible, *that* would also be impossible," for if the first condition is impossible, the second statement is likewise impossible. (Ibn Kathir/*T*, 39:4)

That is, while all things are possible for God, a self-contradiction is by its very nature impossible, as in saying, "Can God die?" which is impossible because if He died He would not be God. Thus, while God the Exalted is *able* to do all things, He does not do that which contradicts or negates His divinity, such as begetting offspring or becoming incarnated as a human or any other created thing. His taking a son therefore belongs to the category of impossible occurrences, similar to that of His creating His equal, because a created being cannot be God or equal to God.

Nevertheless, replying to the false claims of those who assert that He has taken a son, God Most High here says that *if* He **had desired to take a son, He could have chosen whatever He willed from among what He creates,** meaning that that son (if there were to have been a son) could have been any kind of a being, both from among what we know and do not know, and not necessarily Jesus (A). At the same time, the very wording of the sentence, **If God had desired to take a son, He could have . . . ,** makes it clear that not only did God not take a son but that He never even desired to.

REFERENCES: Ibn Kathir/*T*, 39:4; Maududi/*Q*, 39:fns.8-9; Asad/*Q*, 39:fn. 4.

"He Was Nothing but a Slave upon Whom We Bestowed Favor"

43:57-60

And when the son of Mary was presented as an example, forthwith your people laughed loudly (57) **and said, "Are our gods better, or is he?" They did not present it to you but as an argument. No, but they are an argumentative people!** (58)

He [Jesus] was nothing but a slave upon whom We bestowed favor, and We made him an example for the Children of Israel. (59) **And if We willed, We could have appointed angels among you, succeeding [one another] upon the earth.** (60)

(57-58) The first verse of this passage refers to a comparison sarcastically made in Muhammad's presence by some of the pagan Quraysh between their false gods and Jesus (A). God Most High then informed His Prophet (S) that **they did not present it** — this comparison — **to you except as an argument**, adding, **No, but they are an argumentative people!** (43:57-58).

The verb **"*yasiddun*"** can mean either to laugh loudly, call or cry out, raise a clamor, or turn away. In the the present context, it may mean any or all of these, for we have certainly seen enough examples of unbelievers' reacting in all these ways to previous prophets and their messages; in fact, verse 47 in the same *surah* speaks of how Pharaoh and his establishment laughed at the signs Moses (A) brought. The question, **"Are our gods better, or is he?"**

suggests that when Jesus, the son of a human woman, was compared with the various gods of the Quraysh, Jesus was regarded as inferior.

(59-60) Then, disposing of the arguments of those who sought to entrap His honored messenger by their deceit, God Most High revealed to the Holy Prophet (S) that, far from being a 'god' like one of their imaginary deities, Jesus (A) **was nothing but a slave** upon whom He had **bestowed favor**, making **him an example to the Children of Israel** of His endless power, as evidenced by his miraculous conception and other miracles, beginning from earliest infancy. Thus, the meaning of **We could have appointed angels among you, succeeding** one another **upon the earth**, is that, as Jesus (A) was a finite being, so are the angels finite beings, who are likewise utterly remote from the divinity ascribed to them by the Qurayshite idolaters.

REFERENCE: Ibn Kathir/*T*:43:57-62.

"If the Most Merciful Had a Son, Then I Would Be the First of the Worshippers"

43:81-82

Say, [O Muhammad:] "If the Most Merciful had a son, then I would be the first of the worshippers." (81) **Exalted is the Lord of the heavens and the earth, Lord of the Throne, above what they attribute [to Him]!** (82)

Arguing against the false logic of those who ascribe partners or offspring to Him, here again God Most High refutes the impossible supposition that He, the unique, partnerless Creator, could or would have a son. Again, as in 39:4, the wording, **If . . . then**, negates its possibility. In keeping with this argument, God instructs Muhammad (S) to say to the unbelievers that if (as is impossible) God were to have a son, he himself would be **the first of the worshippers** of that son.

God then defeats the untenable assertions of those who associate others, including His honored prophet Jesus (A) with His divinity by proclaiming that He, **the Lord of the heavens and the earth, Lord of the Throne** (a metaphorical expression for God's dominion and sovereignty), is highly **exalted . . . above what they attribute** to Him — namely, the begetting of offspring in the manner of the beings He has created.

REFERENCES: Ibn Kathir/*T*, 43:81-82; Maududi/*Q*, 43:fn. 64; Asad/*Q*, 9:fn. 171.

"He Has Taken Neither a Spouse nor a Son" 72:1-4

Say, [O Muhammad:] "It has been revealed to me that a group of jinn listened and said, 'Indeed, we have heard an amazing recitation [*qur'an*]. (1) **It guides to the right path, so we believe in it, and never will we associate anyone with our Lord.** (2) **And [it teaches] that He, exalted is our Lord's majesty, has taken neither a spouse nor a son,** (3) **and that our foolish one has been speaking excess about God."** (4)

Although this passage concerns jinn, we have included it here in order to show that the confusion and controversy concerning the divinity of Jesus (A) is not confined solely to human beings.

As mentioned in the story of Adam, jinn are another species of creatures who, like human beings and angels, have been endowed with both intelligence and free will. Like humans, they are created for God's service and worship, according to His words,

I did not create jinn and humankind except to worship Me. (51:57)

Hence, they are accountable to God and, like humans, will undergo judgment on the Last Day. Among jinn, too, there are both believers and unbelievers.[105] The fact that Muhammad (S) was sent as the prophet of the dual worlds of humankind and jinn is stated in 25:1, which we discussed on pages 428-429.

At the beginning of this passage, God Most High commands His Prophet (S) to make known that a group of jinn listened to the recitation of the Qur'an, recognized its truth and believed in its message. The story behind these verses is as follows:

Once, while the Prophet (S) was praying *'Isha'*, the night prayer at Nakhla, seven jinn from a place called Nasibin came and listened to his recitation. Grasping the divine origin and truth of what they had heard, these jinn returned to their community and reported what they had experienced. This event, but without the mention of Jesus (A), is also described in 46:29-32.

---

[105]See Volume One, page 18, for background material concerning jinn. Hasan al-Basri stated that, as humans are the children of Adam, jinn are the children of Iblis. Both humans and jinn share in God's reward and punishment, and among both species are believing, saintly individuals as well as unbelieving devils (Ibn Kathir/*T*, 34:12-13).

As the news of this occurrence spread among them, many delegations of jinn started coming and listening to the Qur'an and the teachings of Islam. Says Ibn Kathir:

> When they heard this recitation, these jinn at once recognized that the Book of God **guides to the right path**. They accepted it, believed in it, and rejected belief in all other objects of worship besides the Creator of all things. They declared that they would never **associate anyone with** their **Lord**, recognizing that **He, exalted is Our Lord's majesty, has taken neither a spouse nor a son**, and that all these false notions were merely the empty lies and deceit of their **foolish one,** Iblis [or, according to a variant reading, the **foolish ones** among them], **speaking excess** and misguidance about God Most High. (Ibn Kathir/*T*, 72:1-7)

The message of these verses is that, although they were members of same species as Iblis or Satan, the believers among the jinn understood without any difficulty that this confusion was the work of one or more of their own kind, in an attempt to divert both jinn and humans from recognizing the truth and seduce them from the pure worship of God, the One without a partner.

REFERENCES: Ibn Kathir/*T*, 72:1-7; Maududi/*Q*, 72:fns. 1-5; Asad/*Q*, 46:fn. 36, 72:fn. 3; Appen. III, On the Term and Concept of *Jinn*; Saheeh/*Q*, fn. 1638.

"He Does Not Father, Nor Is He Fathered"

112:1-4

> **Say, [O Muhammad:] "He is Allah, One [*ahad*];**[106] (1) **Allah, the Self-Sufficient [*as-Samad*].** (2) **He does not father [anyone] nor is He fathered,** (3) **and it is not for Him to have any equal."** (4)

The verses above constitute the third-from-last *surah* of the Qur'an, *Al-Ikhlas* (Sincerity), a *surah* that, after the opening *surah*, *Al-Fatehah*, is certainly recited by Muslims more often than any other.

The message of this very brief, concise *surah* is regarded as so important that, as mentioned in numerous *ahadith* reported by al-Bukhari, Muslim and others, the Prophet (S) declared it to be equivalent to one-third of the Qur'an, saying,

---

[106]For an explanation of the change from "God" to "Allah" in this and other passages, please refer to "Moses," page 38, footnote 38.

By Him in whose hand is my soul, indeed it is reckoned as one-third of the Qur'an. (*Bukhari*, 6:533; *Muwatta*, 15.6.17)

Indeed, God divided the Qur'an into three parts and He made **'Say: "He is Allah, One"'** one part among the [three] parts of the Qur'an. (*Muslim*, 1770)

Once the Prophet (S) asked some of his Companions, "Is any of you capable of reciting one-third of the Qur'an by night?" The Companions asked, "How could one recite one-third of the Qur'an [in a single night]?" He then said, **"'Say: "He is Allah, One"'** is equal to one-third of the Qur'an" (*Muslim*, 1769; *Bukhari*, 6:534).

On another occasion, the Prophet (S) came out to his Companions and said, "I am going to recite to you one-third of the Qur'an," and he recited, **"Say: 'He is Allah, One; Allah, the Self-Sufficient,'"** to the end of the *surah* (*Muslim*, 1772, also 1771).

Once the Prophet (S) sent on an expedition a man who used to recite to his companions during their *salat*, ending with **"Say: 'He is Allah, One.'"** Upon returning, they mentioned that to the Messenger of God (S), and he said, "Ask him for what reason he does this." So they asked him and he said, "Indeed, it is an attribute of the Most Merciful, so I love to recite it." Then the Messenger of God (S) said, "Tell him that God loves him" (*Muslim*, 1773).

The basic, most important concerns of the Qur'an are the knowledge of God Most High, knowledge of the future life, and knowledge of the straight path — that is, the rules and practices of the Islamic *Shari'ah* — says Imam al-Ghazali. Therefore, because this *surah* concerns the first kind of knowledge, conveying the "knowledge of God, His unity and His purification from partnership in genus and species," it is equivalent to one-third of the Qur'an (Quasem, *The Jewels of the Qur'an*, pp. 79-80).

In this *surah*, God Most High proclaims, first, that He is *the* Deity, whose proper name is **Allah** throughout the heavens and the earth. Next, He declares that He is but one [***ahad***], both in His person and in being the sole Planner, Willer, Creator and Director of all things in existence, possessor of absolute control and sovereignty. He then states that He is ***as-Samad***, meaning self-sufficient and independent of all things, lacking in nothing and needing none to complete and complement Him, the One besought by all, the Absolute, the Eternal. As such, He neither begets nor fathers anyone [***lam yalid***], nor is He begotten nor fathered [***wa lam yulad***]. Then, lastly, He states that nothing whatsoever is similar, equal or comparable to Him [***wa lam yakun lahu kufuan ahad***], the Unique and Partnerless Creator of all things in existence.

In a divinely inspired ***hadith*** (***hadith qudsi***), the blessed Prophet (S) said:

> God said, "The son of Adam lies about me, while it is not for him to do that, and he insults Me, while it is not for him to do that As for his lying about Me, it is his saying, 'He will not restore me as He originated me,' while the first creation was not easier for Me than his restoration. And as for his abusing Me, it is his saying, 'God Has taken a son,' while I am the One, the Self-Sufficient. I do not father nor was I fathered, and there is nothing comparable to Me." (*Bukhari*, 6:498; also 6:9)

The Prophet (S) also said,

> No one or nothing is more patient than God concerning hurtful things He hears. They ascribe a son to Him but yet He grants them health and provision. (*Bukhari*, 8:121)

Concerning the occasion of the revelation of this *surah*, a number of reports state that it was revealed when groups of polytheists, Jews and Christians came to the Prophet (S) on various occasions and asked him to tell them about God's ancestry and attributes. Among them, Ibn 'Abbas (R) reports that a deputation of Christians from Najran, together with seven priests, visited him and said, "O Muhammad, tell us what your Lord is like and what substance He is made of."

"My Lord is not made of any substance," the Prophet (S) replied. "He is unique and exalted above all things," whereupon God Most High revealed this *surah* (Maududi, *Q*/Intro. to *Surah* 112).

As for the variations among these reports, it may either be that *Surah al-Ikhlas* was revealed to the Prophet (S) on several different occasions, or that whenever such questions were asked of him after its first revelation, he responded by reciting this *surah*.

We may recall that the Prophet, God's peace and blessings be upon him, called people to belief in the Oneness of God in a milieu of deities who were believed to be descended from one another, who had spouses and offspring, and who were in need of food, drink and sacrifices from their worshippers. And although the Jews and Christians affirmed their faith in God Most High, their understanding of Him was also tainted by anthropomorphic notions. Against such a background, it is little wonder that the people whom the Prophet (S) called to their Lord required an explanation both of who He is and who He is not, such as that revealed in the few concise yet all-inclusive phrases of this brief *surah*.

These verses, then, constitute the declaration of the Lord of the universes and all they contain that He, the Creator, is One Indivisible, Eternal, partnerless, parentless, childless Being, who is absolutely Unique in His Nature and Essence. They constitute the decisive, incontrovertible proclamation of God's dissociation from any of the entities to whom humans beings have ascribed divinity, whether sons, daughters or associate gods, as well as from likeness to any created being.

REFERENCES: Ibn Kathir/*T*, "Mention of the Birth of the Slave and Messenger, Jesus, son of Mary, the Virgin"; al-Ghazali, *The Jewels of the Qur'an*, pp. 79-80; Maududi/*Q*, Intro. to Surah 112, 112: fns. 3-4; Asad/*Q*, 112:fns. 1-2.

PART FIVE: THE HOLY PROPHET SAID . . .

21. *AHADITH* CONCERNING JESUS

Such was Jesus son of Mary — a declaration of the truth about which they are in dispute. (19:34)

The Holy Prophet (S) often spoke about Jesus' prophetic rank, confirming his importance and honor among the messengers, as mentioned in the following ***ahadith***:

1. Earlier we mentioned the saying of God's Messenger, peace and blessings be upon him,

> Whoever testifies that there is no deity except God, One, having no partner, and that Muhammad is His slave and His messenger, and that Jesus is God's slave and His messenger and His word which He bestowed upon Mary and a spirit from Him, and that the Paradise is real and Hellfire is real, God will admit him into Paradise, no matter what deeds he may have done. (*Bukhari*, 4.644)

The Prophet (S) also said:

> If a person believes in Jesus and believes in me, he will have a double reward. (*Bukhari*, 4:655)

> [Among three kinds of people who will have a double reward is] a person from among the People of the Scripture who believes in his prophet and then believes in Ahmad [i.e., Muhammad]. (*Bukhari*, 1:97A)

2. We also related that once, when some of the Prophet's Companions were speaking together, one of them said that God had taken Abraham as a friend; another said that He had spoken directly to Moses; another said that Jesus was God's word and spirit; and another said that God had chosen Adam. The Prophet (S) then came out to them and said,

> I have heard what you said, and you are wondering that Abraham was God's friend, as indeed he was; that Moses was God's confidant, as indeed he was; that Jesus was His spirit and word, as indeed he was; and that Adam was chosen by God, as indeed he was. (*Mishkat*, 5762)

3. Speaking of the closeness between himself and Jesus (A), the Holy Prophet (S) said to some Companions,

"Of all people, I have more claim on Jesus son of Mary in this world and the Hereafter." They said, "How so, O Messenger of God?" Then he said, "The prophets are step-brothers,[107] and their mothers are different but their religion is one. And there is no prophet between [the two of] us" (*Muslim*, 5836, also 5834-5835; *Bukhari*, 4:651-4.652).

4. Regarding the words of God, the Exalted and Glorious, **And when your Lord took from the children of Adam, from their loins, their descendants** (7:172),[108] the following is transmitted by the Prophet's Companion, Ubayy bin K'ab (R):

He [God Most High] gathered them and paired them, then fashioned them and made them able to speak, whereupon they spoke. Then He took an agreement and covenant with them, and He made them testify concerning themselves, [asking,] **"Am I not your Lord?"**

They said, **"Yes, we bear witness** [to it]" [7:172].

He said, "Then indeed, I call the seven heavens and seven earths to witness concerning you, and I call your father Adam to witness concerning you, **lest you should say on the Day of Resurrection, 'Indeed, we were unaware of this'** [7:172]. Know that there is no God but Me and there is no Lord but Me, and do not associate anything with Me. Indeed, I willl send My messengers to you, reminding you of My agreement and My covenant, and I will send down to you My scriptures."

They said, "We bear witness that You are our Lord and our God. We have no Lord but You and we have no God but You," and they agreed to that.

Then Adam, peace be upon him, was raised above them, seeing them, and he saw the rich and the poor, and those of goodly form and otherwise, and he said, "My Lord, why have you not dealt equally among Your servants?"

He said, "Indeed, I like that I should be thanked."

And he saw the prophets. Among them were some like lamps having light upon them, distinguished by another covenant concerning messengership and prophethood — that is, the saying of the Blessed and Most High, **And when We took from the prophets their covenant,**

---

[107]This is understood as referring not to blood relationship but rather to the fact that that the prophets all brought one single faith, whose basic message and tenets are universal.

[108]This again refers to what is known as the Day of Promises, mentioned in Volume One, pages 80-81.

> **and from you [Muhammad], and from Noah and Abraham and Moses and Jesus son of Mary** [33:7]. He [Jesus] was among those spirits and He sent him to Mary (A). And Ubayy narrated that he entered by her mouth. (*Mishkat*, 122)

5. In the *ahadith* cited earlier which speak of the awesome suffering of people on the Day of Resurrection and their asking the greatest of the prophets to intercede for them, Jesus (A) is mentioned as one of those whom they will approach with this request.

After asking Adam, Noah and Abraham, who will decline due to mistakes they committed during this life, the people will go to Moses, who will likewise decline for the same reason and send them to Jesus.

> They will then will go to Jesus and say, "O Jesus, you are God's messenger and His word that He bestowed upon Mary and a spirit from Him, and you spoke to people while a child in the cradle. Intercede for us! Do you not see what state we are in?" Then Jesus will say, "Indeed, this day my Lord is angry with such anger as has never been before and will never be afterwards," and he will not mention any sin [of his, but will say,] "Myself! Myself! Myself! Go to someone else. Go to Muhammad, God's peace and blessings be upon him!"[109]

They will then go to Muhammad (S), and he will be told, "O Muhammad, lift your head. Ask; it will be given to you! Intercede; it will be accepted!" Then he will plead for his *ummah* and his intercession will be accepted[110] (*Bukhari*, 6:236; *Muslim* 373, 377-378).

In another version, Moses will say to those who ask for his intercession, "Go to Jesus, God's slave and His messenger and His word and His spirit." Then they will go to Jesus, but he will say, "That is not for me, but go to Muhammad, God's peace and blessings be upon him, the slave who has been forgiven his earlier and later sins." So they will go to Muhammad (S), the chief of the prophets and messengers, who will accept their plea. He will then

---

[109]While Adam, Noah, Abraham and Moses will decline to intercede because of mistakes they committed, Jesus will likewise decline, not because of any mistake of his but out of a sense that no one can be adequate to intercede at this most critical time except one — the beloved of God and most illustrious among His creation, whose intercession is certain to be accepted.

[110]A number of *ahadith* report that each messenger was given a prayer with which he supplicated for his *ummah*. And the Prophet (S) said, "I have reserved my supplication to intercede for my *ummah* on the Day of Resurrection, and it will be granted, God willing, for anyone among my *ummah* who dies without ascribing any partner with God (*Muslim*, 389-390, 392, 396, also 385-386, 388, 391; *Bukhari*, 8:317; *Muwatta*, 15.8.26).

intercede fervently with his Lord for his *ummah* and will be permitted to take great numbers of people out of Hell (*Bukhari*, 9.532C, 9:507). And the Prophet (S) said,

> My intercession will be for those who have committed major sins from among my *ummah*. (Abu Dawud, 4721)
>
> I was given a choice between having half of my *ummah* enter Paradise or being granted intercession. I chose intercession because it is more inclusive. Do you think that it is for those who fear God? It is for those who err and do wrong deeds. (Ibn Majah)

6. In a number of *ahadith*, the Prophet (S) spoke of meeting Moses, Jesus (A) and other prophets during his Night Journey and Ascension to the Divine Presence (*al-Isra' wal-Me'raj*). As mentioned previously, his meeting with Moses (A) in the spiritual world is commemorated in the words,

> **And We certainly gave Moses the scripture, so do not be in doubt concerning his meeting [with him]. (32:23)**

The fact that the Holy Prophet (S) could meet spiritually with individuals who had passed away thousands of years earlier is related to the Islamic belief that the souls of those who have left this life are alive in the intermediate existence between death and the Resurrrection known as *barzakh*. Concerning the life of the prophets in *barzakh*, the Prophet (S) said:

> The prophets are alive in their graves, occupied with *salat*. (Abu Ya'la, al-Haythami, al-Bayhaqi)
>
> Prophets are not left in their graves beyond forty nights but that they stand before God in *salat* until the Trumpet [of the Last Day] is blown. (Al-Hakim, al-Bayhaqi, Tabarani)

The Prophet's Companion Abu al-Darda' (R), reported the Prophet (S) as saying, "Invoke many blessings upon me on Friday, for that day is witnessed by the angels. Indeed, no one invokes blessings upon me but that his invocation is shown to me until he finishes it." Abu al-Darda' (R) then asked, "Even after death?" to which the Prophet (S) replied, "Even after death. Indeed, God has prohibited the earth from consuming the bodies of the prophets, so God's Prophet is alive and provided for" (*Mishkat*, 1366; Abu Dawud, 1042, and others). He also said, "No one greets me but that God returns my soul to me so that I may return his greeting" (Abu Dawud, al-Bayhaqi, Ahmad and others).

In light of this, the Holy Prophet's saying concerning his Night Journey, "I met Jesus," whom he described as being "of medium height and ruddy, as if he had come out of the bath" (*Bukhari*, 4:647; *Muslim*, 322), becomes readily understandable, as do his other descriptions of prophets, such as the following:

> I saw Jesus and Moses and Abraham. As for Jesus, he was ruddy, curly-haired, broad-chested. And as for Moses, he was brown, large and straight-haired, as if he were a man of al-Zutt. (*Bukhari*, 4:648; *Muslim*, 313, 316-317, 321-322).
>
> There was Moses, standing in *salat*, a large man with curly hair, as if he was tribesman of Shanu'a. There was Jesus son of Mary, peace be upon him, standing in *salat*; the closest in resemblance to him among people is 'Urwa ibn Mas'ud al-Thaqafi. There was Abraham, peace be upon him, standing in *salat*; the one most resembling him among people is your companion [meaning himself]. Then the time of *salat* came and I led them. (*Muslim*, 328)

The Prophet (S) also described Jesus (A) as having the most beautiful skin and hair ever seen, and water was trickling down from his hair. He had placed his hands on the shoulders of two men and was making *tawaf* of the [Sacred] House (*Muslim*, 323-325, 327).[111]

7. The Holy Prophet (S) said, through divine inspiration, that God, the Blessed and Exalted, said to Jesus (A),

> "After your time, O Jesus, I will send a people who will praise God when that which they like happens to them, and seek their reward from God and show endurance when that which they dislike afflicts them, although they do not possess forbearance and intelligence." He [Jesus] asked, "My Lord, how can this be, when they do not possess forbearance or intelligence?" God replied, "I will grant them something of My forbearance and My knowledge." (Tirmidhi, 1761)

8. The Prophet (S) said, "God loves the strangers most." When he was asked, "Who are the strangers?" he replied, "Those who escape with their faith to protect it. On the Day of Judgment, God Almighty will resurrect them in the company of Jesus son of Mary" (Akili/*Beauty*, p. 28, #39).

---

[111]This report, which also contains the Prophet's descriptions of the Dajjal or Anti-Christ, about whom we will speak shortly, is repeated with many variations in a number of other *ahadith*, such as *Bukhari*, 4:649-650, and *Muslim*, 324-325, 327.

[illegible]

[illegible]

[illegible]

[illegible]

[illegible]

[illegible]

[illegible]

[illegible]

PART SIX: THE SECOND COMING OF JESUS

22. THE QUR'ANIC VERSES RELATED TO JESUS' RETURN

And indeed, he is [a sign] of the knowledge of the Hour, so do not be in doubt about it and follow Me. This is a straight path. (43:61)

As mentioned earlier, a corollary to the belief that Jesus (A) was raised to God alive is the understanding that he will return to this world during its final period to complete the remainder of his appointed mission and die, as all human beings must, for **Each soul will taste death** (3:185, 21:35, 29:57).

While the return of Jesus (A) is not mentioned directly in the Qur'an, it is nonetheless suggested in 43:61 above, and the majority of classical commentators, including Ibn 'Abbas, Mujahid, 'Ikrimah, Qatadah, al-Suddi and Ibn Kathir, connect this verse with Jesus' second coming. And since this tangible sign of the Last Hour is promised and *must* therefore materialize, God instructs mankind in this verse **not be in doubt about it** but to follow Him, through obedience to His revealed guidance, on the **straight path** ordained by Him.

Also related to this theme are the following verses, cited earlier in connection with the crucifixion, in which God Most High declares, in such a manner as to leave no room for doubt, that Jesus (A) was not crucified nor killed, but was raised alive to Him:

> **They did not kill him nor crucify him, but it was made to appear so to them. . . . And of a certainty they did not kill him. Rather, God raised him to Himself, and God is Almighty and Wise. And there is no one among the People of the Scripture but will surely believe in him before his death, and on the Day of Resurrection he will be a witness against them.** (4:157-159)

The interpretation of the words, **"his death,"** in the last verse is of special interest in this context. Some commentators understand them to mean that at the time of death, each individual clearly grasps the reality of Jesus' prophethood. In keeping with this understanding, Ibn 'Abbas (R) and Mujahid (R) stated that not a single Jew dies without believing in Jesus (A) as a prophet. Indeed, Ibn 'Abbas (R) went so far as to say that if the head of one of the People of the Scripture were to be cut off by a sword, his soul would not leave his body until he believed in Jesus (A) and said to himself that he is God's slave and messenger. And when Ibn 'Abbas (R) was asked about the case of one who fell off a wall, he replied that even during his fall he would believe (Ibn Kathir/*T*, 4:156-159).

Another interpretation, which is also attributed to Ibn 'Abbas (R) among others, is that **"his death"** refers the death of Jesus (A) himself at the end of his second coming or descent (*nuzul*), which the Last Prophet (S) associated with the final period of this world, when, according to several *ahadith*, all the People of the Scripture will believe in Jesus' prophethood. Ibn 'Abbas (R) particularly noted that at that time not a single person professing Judaism will remain, for all will believe in Jesus (A) as a prophet. Similarly, Hasan al-Basri said, "By God, Jesus is alive in Heaven, and when he comes down to the earth, there will not be a single person among the People of the Scripture who will not believe in him [as God's messenger]." Qatadah (R) and other commentators concur with this understanding, and al-Tabari and Ibn Kathir also affirm that this is the correct interpretation of the verse, contradicting all claims to the contrary (Ibn Kathir/*T*, 4:156-159). At the same time, it may be that both interpretations of the verse are correct, for one interpretation does not in any way invalidate the other.

As for of the statement that **on the Day of Resurrection he will be a witness against them,** it is understood as meaning that since on the Last Day **God will assemble the messengers and say, "What was the response you received?"** (5:109/112), Jesus (A) will testify against those who ascribed divinity to him or rejected his prophethood and message.[112]

REFERENCES: Qur'an: 3:54-55, 4:157-159, 5:117/120, 43:61-62. Commentaries: Ibn Kathir/*T*, 4:155-159, 43:57-65; Ibn Kathir/*Signs*, p. 74; Maududi/*Q*, 4:fns. 196-197, 43:fns. 52-53, 55; Asad/*Q*, 4:fn. 173, 43:fns. 45-47; Ali/*Q*, fns. 560, 665-666, 4662; Saheeh/*Q*, fn. 204.

---

[112]Cf., Jesus' saying, **And I was a witness over them as long as I was among them** (5:117/120).

23. The Importance of Believing in Jesus as a Prophet

The Messiah, Jesus son of Mary, was but a messenger of God and His word which He bestowed upon Mary and a spirit from Him. So believe in God and His messengers. (4:171)

Now, it may logically be asked, Why should it be so critically important for everyone to believe in the prophethood of Jesus (A)?

The answer is simple: Because he *was* a prophet, one of the greatest, and belief in God's messengers and prophets, all of them, is essential for correct faith. That is, since all the prophets and messengers were equally chosen and appointed by God, all are to be equally accepted and believed in. This is emphasized in the following verses:

> **The Messenger believes in what was revealed to him by his Lord, and [so do] the believers. All of them believe in God and His angels and His scriptures and His messengers, [saying,] "We make no distinction between any of His messengers." And they say, "We hear and we obey. Your forgiveness, our Lord, and to You is the destination."** (2:285)

> **Say, [O Muhammad:] "We believe in God and in what was revealed to us and what was revealed to Abraham and Ishmael and Isaac and Jacob and the descendants [of Israel], and what was given to Moses and Jesus and [all] the prophets by their Lord. We make no distinction between any of them, and we surrender to Him [in Islam]. And whoever desires a religion other than Islam, never will it be accepted from him, and in the Hereafter he will be among the losers."** (3:84-85; also 2:136)

Belief in *all* the prophets must therefore be understood as obligatory, not optional. One claiming to be a believer does not have the choice of rejecting anyone whom his Lord has appointed as His messenger, nor of exercising his personal opinion or "veto" concerning him, for sound religion is not a matter of anyone's opinions or desires but of the ordaining of the Lord of creation. This is made clear in the following passage:

> **Indeed, those who disbelieve in God and His messengers and wish to discriminate between God and His messengers, and say, "We believe in some and disbelieve in others," and wish to adopt a way in between — those are the unbelievers, truly, and We have prepared a humiliating punishment for the unbelievers. But they who believe in God and His messengers and do not discriminate**

> **between any of them — to those God will grant their rewards. And God is ever Forgiving and Merciful.** (4:150-152)

To put it another way, sound belief means surrender to God Most High, and surrender means, above all, to accept without reservations the faith ordained by Him. And there can be no true faith without wholehearted acceptance of the holy messengers whom He saw fit to make His representatives to mankind — *all of them, without exception* — for **God chooses as His messengers whomever He wills.** So, we are commanded, **believe in God and His messengers** (3.179). Perhaps this is all the more important with respect to Jesus, God's peace and blessings be upon him, for when he returns to this world, it will be incumbent upon all believers to recognize him and follow his leadership, according to the Prophet's saying,

> There will be no prophet between me and him, and he will descend [to the earth]. Therefore, recognize him when you see him. (Abu Dawud, 4310)

24. The Holy Prophet's Knowledge of the Unseen

God is Knower of the Unseen, and He does not disclose His Unseen to anyone except one whom He has approved among messengers. (72:26-27)

As is obvious, ultimate knowledge of all things in both the material and the spiritual realms belongs only to One — the All-Knowing and All-Aware. But at the same time, as the above verse states, God Most High grants such knowledge of the Unseen as He wills to those with whom He is pleased among His messengers.

Now, the prophets and messengers were mortals like any others. But they were most definitely not ordinary men. Rather, they were divinely-empowered individuals who were granted evidences, signs and spiritual knowledge by the light of which they lived and carried out their appointed missions.

We have seen, in the preceding stories, repeated instances of unveilings and openings to the spiritual realm: the foreknowledge of Noah, Hud, Saleh, Shu'ayb and Jonah (A) of the punishment awaiting their sinful people; the divine instructions given to Noah (A) concerning the building of the Ark; Abraham's being shown **the realm of the heavens and the earth** (6:75), his foreknowledge of the birth of Ishmael and the vision concerning his sacrifice, his being informed by angels of the birth of Isaac and the punishment of Lot's people, and his knowledge of the future of Mecca and its inhabitants; and Hagar's encounter with the angel. We have seen similar unveilings in Joseph's childhood vision and his knowledge of the interpretation of dreams and events; the divine reassurances conveyed to the hearts of Jacob (A) and Umm Musa; the angels' intervention in the case of Lot (A); Moses' miracles and meetings with his Lord; the inner, secret knowledge conveyed to the heart of Sayyidina Khidr (A); Solomon's special powers; the miracles of Zechariah and Mary (A); and Jesus' numerous miracles, including his conception and extraordinary rescue from death. And while these are the spiritual openings that are mentioned in the Qur'an, no doubt each prophet and messenger was strongly in contact with the unseen realm and experienced successive or perhaps even continuous unveilings.

Given all this, it should not surprise us that the beloved of God, Muhammad (S), who reached the ultimate point of nearness to his Lord among all created beings, surpassing even that of the angel Gabriel (A), should have been granted by God the ultimate degree of knowledge and experience of the Unseen among His creatures. Indeed, a reading of his life-story and *ahadith* makes it clear that he dwelt simultaneously in the spiritual and material realms, moving seamlessly between the two in his everyday life, and having equal familiarity with beings and occurrences in both. Thus, he is the perfected one, the master of all spiritual masters, the most spiritually-powerful being among all creation up to the end of this world.[113]

Out of this ocean of spiritual knowledge and personal, direct experience, the Holy Prophet (S) often spoke to his Companions, the first Muslims, of his Lord's divine nature and attributes, the mysteries of the spiritual world and its inhabitants, angels and jinn, of the secrets of creation, the destinies of human beings, the Divine Decree, and death and resurrection. He also spoke, from his direct experience, of Paradise and Hell and their inhabitants, as mentioned in a number of *ahadith.*[114] The inspired Messenger of God (S) also spoke frequently about meetings with his fellow prophets, in whose company he had been during his Night Journey and Ascension — and, as is evident from what follows, on other occasions as well.[115]

He also spoke repeatedly about what was to come upon humanity in the future, reporting it as if it were taking place in front of his eyes — as most certainly, in his spiritual vision, it was.

---

[113]Vast amounts of material in the collections of *hadith* relate to the Prophet's interface with the spiritual world. Volumes have also been written about it by the classical commentators and scholars. See, for example, Chapter Four, Section 24, in Qadi Iyad's classic, *Ash-Shifa*, entitled "The Prophet's knowledge of the unseen and future events," pages 186-193.

[114]See *Bukhari*, 1:184, 1:716, 2:161, 4:462, 8:373, 8:737, 9:171, 9:397; *Muslim*, 142, 857, 1968, 1976.

[115]Mentioned in *Bukhari*, 4:647-4:650; *Muslim*, 313-314, 316-317, 321-325, 327-328.

25. THE SIGNS OF THE END-TIME

That is of the tidings of the Unseen which We reveal to you [Muhammad]. You did not know it, neither you nor your people, before this. Therefore, be patient. Indeed, the [best] outcome is for the righteous. (11:49)

"God the Exalted rolled up the earth for me, to the extent that I beheld its eastern and west extremeties" (Abu Dawud, 4239), the Messenger of God (S) said, revealing the depth of his knowledge of the Unseen. And from the spiritual vision of his illuminated heart, he informed his Companions about what was soon to happen to neighboring kingdoms; the victories that would be granted to Muslims; the spread of Islam; the divisions and conflicts, disasters and afflictions that would come upon his *ummah*; and the fate that awaited members of his family and a number of his eminent Companions, such as 'Uthman, Zubayr and his son 'Abdullah, 'Ali, Ammar and many others, may God be pleased with them all.

The Holy Prophet (S) also spoke repeatedly about what would take place during the end-time of this world. So immense was his knowledge of this matter that the Companion Hudhayfah (R), the transmitter of many *ahadith* concerning the events of the End-Time, reported that once the Prophet (S) stood up among the Muslims, and he did not omit the mention of anything that would happen, in its place, up to the coming of the Last Hour (*Muslim*, 6909, Abu Dawud, 4228). Hudhayfah (R) also reported that the Prophet (S) did not omit mention of the instigator of a single disaster that would occur up to the end of the world, more than three hundred in number, naming each of them with his own name and the name of his father and his tribe (Abu Dawud, 4231).

The numerous *ahadith* concerning this subject are contained in the sections entitled "*Fitan*" (plural of "*fitnah*," meaning trials, afflictions or tribulations) in the various collections of *ahadith*. Drawing upon the immense reservoir of the Prophet's inspired knowledge of the Unseen, the following signs of the Hour are among those mentioned in the *hadith* collection of al-Bukhari alone:

Two large groups will fight, among whom there will be heavy casualties, although their claim or demand will be but one. Approximately thirty lying deceivers (*dajjalun*) will appear, each of them claiming to be God's messenger. Knowledge [of the divine guidance] will be be contracted or pass away, while ignorance will be established and gain the upper hand. Earthquakes will become numerous. Time will be shortened or contracted. Afflictions will appear. There will be a great deal of killing [*harj*]. "Wealth will increase among you and will be so plentiful that the owner of wealth will be concerned about who will accept his charity," the Prophet (S) said, "to the extent that, when he offers it, he to whom it is offered will say, 'I have no need of it.'" People will compete in constructing tall buildings. A man passing by a grave will say, "Oh, if only I were in his place." The sun will rise from the West, and when it so rises and people see it, they will all believe, but that will be the time when **no soul will benefit from its faith if it had not previously believed or earned [anything] good through its faith** [6:158] (*Bukhari*, 9:237).[116]

Good deeds will decrease and miserliness will be cast into people's hearts (8:63, 9:183). A slave woman will give birth to her mistress, and the barefoot and naked will become the chiefs of the people[117] (6:300). Illicit sexual relations and the consumption of alcohol will increase (1:80-81, 7:158). The number of men will decrease, while that of women will increase until fifty women are under the charge of one man (1:81, 7:158).

Numerous Prophetic sayings concerning the state of mankind during the End-Time are reported in other collections of *ahadith*, as well. From among them, we mention the following:

Before the coming of the Hour, there will be a special greeting for people of distinction. Trade will become so widespread that a woman will assist her husband in business. Family ties will be severed. The giving of false witness will be common, while truthful witness will be rare. Writing [i.e., literacy] will be widespread (Ahmad). There will be years of deceit during which a truthful person will be disbelieved, a liar will be believed, and the insignificant will have a say (Ahmad).

Swearing by God who sent him with the truth, the Prophet (S) said that this earth would not pass away until people are afflicted by landslides, pelted by stones, and transformed into beasts. When asked when that would occur, he replied, "When you see women riding in the saddle, when singers are common, when bearing false witness becomes widespread, and when men lie with men and women with women" (Al-Haythami). Moreover, he said, the

[116]Also *Bukhari*, 1:80-81, 1:84-85, 2:146, 7:158, 8:63, 9:183-187, 9:231.

[117]These two signs are mentioned in *Bukhari*, 1:47, 6:300, and *Muslim*, 1, 4, 6, together with the prophecy that the shepherds of black camels will compete in the construction of buildings. The slave woman giving birth to her mistress ("master" in some versions) is understood as referring to the disrespect and disobedience that will be shown by children to their parents in the End-Time.

earth would not pass away until the one who enjoys it most is the depraved son of the depraved (Ahmad). Nor would the Hour come until time passes so quickly that a year is like a month, a month like a week, a week like a day, a day like an hour, and an hour like the time it takes a palm leaf to burn (Ahmad).

As for the condition of the Muslim *ummah* during this period, the *ahadith* dealing with this subject are very numerous, for the Holy Prophet (S) saw with his clear spiritual vision the calamities and tribulations that would befall his community, reflecting the general deterioration of society.

"No time will come upon you without that which follows it being worse than it until you meet your Lord" (*Bukhari*, 9:188), he said. And when he was asked, "Shall we be destroyed while there are righteous people among us?" he replied, "Yes, if wickedness increases" (*Bukhari*, 9:181).

The Prophet (S) therefore warned as well as prophesyed what Muslims might expect if they deviated from the divine guidance, saying,

> When booty is taken by turn, a trust is [regarded as a means of] profit and *zakat* as a fine; learning is for other than the faith; a man obeys his wife and is undutiful to his mother, and draws near his friend and is far from his father; voices are raised in the mosques; the head of a tribe is their most sinful one, the leader of the people is the most depraved of them, and a man is honored out of fear of his evil; female singers and stringed instruments become prevalent; alcohol is drunk; and the last of this *ummah* curses the first — then at that time look for a red wind[118] and an earthquake and a sinking [of the earth] and a raining of stones, and signs following one another as bits of a necklace follow one other when its string is cut. (*Mishkat*, 5450)

Addressing the Muslim emigrees from Mecca to Medina (*muhajirin*), the Prophet (S) warned them that they might be afflicted by five things that God forbid they should live to see. And he mentioned these five with all their consequences:

If illicit sexual relations become widespread, this has never occurred without new diseases befalling people that their predecessors never suffered. If people begin to cheat in weighing out goods, this has never occurred without drought and famine befalling them, and their rulers oppressing them. If people withhold payment of the obligatory *zakat*, this has never occurred without rain being stopped from falling, and if it were not for the sake of the animals it

[118]Understood in our time as referring to communism.

would never rain again. If Muslims break their covenant with God and His Messenger, this has never occurred without God's sending an enemy against them to take some of their possessions by force. If the leaders do not govern according to the Book of God, this has never occurred without God's making them into factions and causing them to fight one another (Ibn Majah).

On another occasion, in response to a questioner who asked about the Hour of Judgment, the Prophet (S) said that it would come when the leaders are oppressors, when people believe in the stars [i.e., astrology] and reject belief in the Divine Decree,[119] when a trust becomes a means of making a profit, when people give charity unwillingly, and when illicit sexual relations become wide spread. "When this occurs," he warned, "then your people will perish" (Al-Haythami).

During the last days, he said, there will be people who will be brothers in public but enemies in secret. When he was asked how that would come about, he replied, "Because they will have ulterior motives in their mutual dealings, and at the same time they will fear one another" (*Mishkat*, 5330)

'Abdullah bin 'Amr bin al-'As (R), reported that once when a group of Muslims were gathered around the Prophet (S), he mentioned that the period of trials [*fitan*] would occur "when you see that people's covenants have been impaired, [the fulfilling of] guarantees becomes rare, and they become thus," and here he interwined his fingers. 'Abdullah then got up and asked him, "What should I do at that time, may God make me a ransom for you?" The Prophet (S) replied, "Keep to your house, control your tongue, accept what you approve, abandon what you disapprove, attend to your own affairs, and leave alone the affairs of the generality" (Abu Dawud, 4329, 4328; *Mishkat*, 5398).

The Companion Abi Tha'labah (R) once asked the Prophet (S) about the verse, **O you who believe, [responsibility for] yourselves is upon yourselves. Those who have gone astray will not harm you when you have been guided** [5:105/108], wanting to understand whether this meant that, if one is responsible only for oneself, he should therefore cease to enjoin what is right and forbid what is wrong.[120] To this the Prophet (S) replied,

> "No, enjoin what is right and forbid what is wrong until you see miserliness adopted, passion followed, the world preferred, everyone enamoured of his own opinion, and you see matters from which you cannot escape. Then [responsibility for] yourself will be upon yourself; so leave

[119]For the meaning of the Divine Decree, please see Volume One, pages 50-52.

[120]Referring to what is mentioned in footnote 90.

the affairs of the generality, for indeed ahead of you will be days of endurance, and whoever shows endurance during them will be holding onto a live coal. Those active [in goodness] during them will have the reward of fifty men who act as he does." When the listeners asked, "O Messenger of God, the reward of fifty of *them*?" he replied, "The reward of fifty of *you*" (*Mishkat*, 5144; Abu Dawud, 4327).

The Holy Prophet, God's peace and blessings be upon him, also said:

This people of mine is one to which mercy is shown. It will have no punishment in the next world, but its punishment in this world will be trials, earthquakes and being killed. (Abu Dawud, 4265)

I fear for my people only the leaders who lead men astray, for when the sword is used among my people it will not be withdrawn from them until the Day of Resurrection. (Abu Dawud, Tirmidhi)

There will be turmoil [*fitnah*] which will render people deaf, dumb and blind regarding what is right. Those who contemplate it will be drawn by it, and giving rein to the tongue during it will be like striking with the sword. (Abu Dawud, 4251)

There will be a calamity such that one who sits during it will be better than one who stands, one who stands during it will be better than one who walks, and one who walks during it will be better than one who runs. Whoever comes upon it, it will control him, so whoever finds a shelter or refuge during it should take shelter therein. (*Bukhari*, 9:202)

Indeed, there was no prophet before me but that it was obligatory on him to guide his ***ummah*** to what he knew was good for them and to warn them against what he knew was bad for them. And indeed, this ***ummah*** of yours will have safety at the beginning, but calamities will afflict the last of it and things that you will hate. And trials will come one after another, each making the previous one seem lighter than the next. And a trial will come and the believer will say, "This is destruction of me!" Then it will ease, and the [next] trial will come and the believer will say, "This is it! This is it!" Therefore, whoever wishes to be saved from the Fire and enter Paradise, let him come to his death while believing in God and the Last Day, and let him do to people that which he would like them to do to him. (*Muslim*, 4546)

Before the Hour, there will be turmoil like pieces of a dark night, in which a man will be a believer in the morning and an unbeliever in the evening, or a believer in the evening and unbeliever in the morning. He who sits during it will be better than he who gets up, and he who walks during it will be better than he who runs. So break your bows, cut your bowstrings, and strike your swords on stones. If the people then come in to one of you, let him be like the better of Adam's two sons.[121] (Abu Dawud, 4246)

Woe to the Arabs from the great evil which is nearly approaching them! It will be like pieces of the dark night. A man will wake up as a believer and be an unbeliever by nightfall. People will sell their religion for a small amount of worldly goods. The one who clings to his religion that day will be like one who is grasping an ember or thorns. (Ahmad)

Worshipping during the [period of] killing will be like emigration to me. (*Muslim*, 7042)

The destruction of my *ummah* will be at the hands of the young men of the Quraysh. (*Bukhari*, 9:180)

One of the signs of the approach of the Hour will be the destruction of the Arabs. (*Mishkat*, 5991)

A lengthy *hadith* containing the Prophet's instructions as to how Muslims should conduct themselves during these trials has come down to us through Hudhayfah (R), who said:

People used to ask the Messenger of God, God's peace and blessings be upon him, about the good, but I used to ask him about the evil, fearing that it might come upon me. And I said, "O Messenger of God, indeed, we were in a state of ignorance and evil. Then God brought us this good [Islam]. Then will there be any evil after this good?"

He said, "Yes."

I said, "And will there be any good after this evil?"

He said, "Yes, but there will be murkiness in it."

I said, "And what murkiness?"

He said, "People guiding by other than my guidance, some of which you will approve and [some] reject."

I said, "Then will there be any evil after that good?"

---

[121]Regarding this allusion to Abel, please see Volume One, page 91. As for this *hadith*, there are a number of variations on it, such as Abu Dawud, 4243, in which the Prophet (S) advised that whoever possessed camels, sheep or land should remain with them, while if he had none of these, he should escape if he could. Abu Dawud, 4249, is similar to Abu Dawud, 4246, up to ". . . he who runs"; then when the Prophet (S) was asked, "Then what do you order us to do?" he replied, "Keep to your houses." *Muslim*, 213, reads: "Hasten to [good] deeds [before there overtakes you] a turmoil like pieces of a dark night. A man will be a believer in the morning and an unbeliever in the evening, or he will be a believer in the evening and an unbeliever in the morning, and he will sell his faith for worldly goods"

He said, "Yes. Callers at the gates of Hell; whoever responds to them will be cast into it."

I said, "O Messenger of God, make them clear to us."

He said, "They will be from our own people and will speak in our language."

I said, "Then what do you order me [to do] if that should come upon me?"

He said, "Keep to the community of Muslims and their *imam* [leader]."

I said, "And if there should not be a community of them nor an *imam*?"

He said, "Then separate from all those factions, even if you have to cling to the root of a tree until death overtakes you while you are thus." (*Bukhari*, 9:206; also Abu Dawud, 4230, 4232, 4284-4235)

What all the characteristics and behaviors mentioned in the foregoing *ahadith* indicate is that in the End-Time values will be distorted, the understanding of right and wrong will be turned upside-down, goodness will be rare, evil will flourish, and keeping to one's faith will be tremendously difficult. "Indeed," the Prophet (S) said, "Islam began as something strange and it will revert, as it began, to being strange. So blessedness to the strangers!" (*Muslim*, 270). For during that darkest period of man's history on this planet — and God knows whether it may not perhaps be the very period in which we are now — mankind, individually and collectively, will have forgotten that they are servants of the Lord of creation and under His divine command. Instead, regarding themselves as independent, self-sufficient masters of the universe, they will engage in every imaginable form of wrong-doing, causing corruption upon the earth and shedding blood, just as the angels predicted they would.[122] Therefore, whatever happens during this period will be nothing but the cumulative effect of mankind's own dark actions; as God says,

> **Corruption has appeared upon the land and sea because of what the hands of people have earned, that He may let them taste something of [the consequences of] what they have done, that perhaps they may turn back [to Him].** (30:41)

This state of affairs will continue up to the limit decreed for it by the Knower of all things. Numerous *ahadith* speak of what will happen at the

---

[122]See Volume One, page 21.

conclusion of this period, and the classical commentators have also written much concerning it. Among them, Ibn Kathir said:

> After the lesser signs of the Hour appear and increase, mankind will have reached a stage of great suffering. Then the awaited Mahdi will appear; he is the first of the greater, and clear, signs of the Hour. There will be no doubt about his existence, but this will only be clear to the knowledgeable people. (Ibn Kathir/*Signs*, p. 18)

The Mahdi (A), the leader of the Muslims who will be from among themselves, will rule until the False Messiah, known as the Dajjal, appears. The Dajjal will spread oppression, corruption and a false religion throughout the planet, and only those who have deep knowledge and faith will realize who he is and avoid his evil.

The Dajjal will remain for such time as God permits, bringing the greatest affliction the earth and mankind have ever known. Then the Messiah, Jesus, God's peace and blessings be upon him, will descend, dispensing divine justice. In due course he will kill the Dajjal, after which there will be years of blessedness and peace.

These three individuals, then — the Mahdi, meaning "the Guided One," the False Messiah or Antichrist known as the Dajjal, and Jesus Christ (A) — were named by the Holy Prophet (S) as the chief actors in the intense drama of the End-Time, through whom God's all-embracing divine plan for mankind will reach fulfillment. The various aspects of this End-Time tableau are detailed in numerous *ahadith*, by means of which we now present a brief picture of what will happen during that most troubled period of man's life on earth.

REFERENCES: Ibn Kathir/*Signs*, pp. 10, 12, 14, 16-18, 25-27, 29-31, 85, 90-94; Qadi 'Iyad/*Ash-Shifa*, pp. 186-187.

26. THE MAHDI (A)

Rejoice and rejoice again! My people are like rain, it not being known whether the last or the first of it is better; or like a garden from which a troop can be fed for a year, then another troop can be fed for a year, and perhaps the last troop which comes may be the broadest, deepest and finest. How can a people perish of which I am the first, the Mahdi the middle, and the Messiah [Jesus] the last? But in the course of that, there will be a crooked party which does not belong to me and to which I do not belong. (*Mishkat*, 6278)

While there is no mention in the Qur'an of the Mahdi (A), the divinely-empowered, holy *imam* who will lead the Muslims prior to the return of Jesus (S),[123] the Holy Prophet (S) spoke of him often.

Concerning the Mahdi's lineage, he said:

The Mahdi will be of my family, of the descendants of Fatimah [and 'Ali]. (Abu Dawud, 4271)

The world will not pass away before the Arabs are ruled by a man of my family whose name will be the same as mine. (Abu Dawud, 4269)

If only one day of this world remained, God would lengthen that day until He had raised up therein a man who belongs to me or to my family, whose father's name is the same as my father's, and who will fill the earth with equity and justice as it had [previously] been filled with oppression and tyranny. (Abu Dawud, 4269, also 4270)

The Mahdi will be of my stock, and he will have a broad forehead and a prominent nose. He will fill the earth with equity and justice as it had [previously] been filled with oppression and tyranny, and he will rule for seven years [in other versions, nine years]. (Abu Dawud, 4272)

The Mahdi is one of us, from among the people of my household. In one night, God will inspire him and prepare him to carry out his task successfully. (Ahmad, Ibn Majah)

---

[123]Over the past fourteen hundred years, a number of people have claimed to be the Mahdi. Among them were the tenth century Abbaside caliph, al-Mahdi, and the nineteenth century Sudanese revivalist bearing the same title. According to Shi'ah doctrine, the Twelfth or Hidden *Imam* (b. 256H/868CE), a descendant of the Prophet (S), disappeared from the world and is in occultation until he returns as the Mahdi of the End-Time. This belief, however, is not shared by Sunni Muslims, who believe that the Mahdi has not yet appeared.

The Prophet's son-in-law, 'Ali (R), once looked at his son Hasan (R) and said, "This son of mine is a *sayyid* [chief], as named by the Prophet (S), and from his loins will come forth a man who will be called by the name of your Prophet (S), who will resemble him in conduct but not in appearance." He then mentioned his filling the earth with justice (Abu Dawud, 4276).

Describing God's unprecedented favors and bounties to his *ummah* during the Mahdi's time, the Prophet (S) said:

> There will be the Mahdi among my *ummah*. My *ummah* will then enjoy prosperity such as they have never enjoyed. The earth will bring forth its fruit for them and will not hoard anything away from them. (Abu Sa'id al-Khudri)
>
> He [the Mahdi] will divide the wealth of the Muslims among them and will manage it in accordance with the *sunnah* of their Prophet. And Islam will encounter two seas on the earth, which will continue for seven years. (Ibn Hibban)
>
> A man will come to the Mahdi and say, "Give me, give me, O Mahdi!" and he will pour into his garment as much as he is able to carry. (*Mishkat*, 5455)

The Prophet (S) also said, "At the last of my *ummah*, there will be a caliph who will dispense money widely without count." This was understood as referring to the Mahdi. (*Muslim*, 6961)

The role of the Mahdi (A) among the Muslim *ummah* is summarized briefly in the Prophet's saying,

> "I give you glad tidings of the Mahdi, [who] will be sent in the midst of disagreements among people and earthquakes, and he will fill the earth with equity and justice as it had [previously] been filled with inequity and injustice, so the inhabitant of Heaven and the inhabitant of the earth will be pleased. He will divide the treasury *sihahan*." It was asked, "What is *sihahan*?" He said, "Equally among people. He will fill the hearts of the *ummah* of Muhammad, and his justice will extend to them to the extent that he will order a crier to call, 'Who is in need of anything?' No one will respond except one man. Thus will he [the Mahdi] be for seven years." (Ahmad)

And stressing the critical importance of being with the Mahdi (A) in his time, he said,

> . . . Then the earth will be filled with justice as it had been filled with injustice. If any of you live to see this, you should go to him, even if you have to crawl over ice. (Ibn Majah)

> . . . If you see him, go to him and give him your allegiance, even if you have to crawl over ice, because he is God's caliph, the Mahdi. (Ibn Majah)

The Mahdi (A) is thus awaited by Muslims as the forerunner of the return of Jesus (A), as well as of the enemy of God, the Dajjal, who will be killed by Jesus (A) and his armies of the righteous.

When Jesus (A) appears, however, he will defer to the Mahdi as the divinely-appointed leader of the Muslims, for the Prophet (S) said,

> How will it be with you when the son of Mary descends among you, and your *imam* [the Mahdi] will be from among yourselves? (*Bukhari*, 4:658; *Muslim*, 290)
>
> A section of my people will not cease fighting for the truth and will be victorious up to the Day of Resurrection. Jesus son of Mary will then descend. The leader of the Muslims [the Mahdi] will say to him, "Come, lead the *salat* for us," but he will say, "No, you yourselves are leaders over one another. God has honored this *ummah*." (*Muslim*, 293)
>
> Their *imam* will be a righeous man. And while their *imam* is going forward to lead them in the morning *salat*, Jesus son of Mary will descend upon them. Then the *imam* will move backward quickly in order that Jesus may go forward and lead the people in *salat*. Jesus, God's peace and blessings be upon him, will put his hand on his shoulders and say to him, "Go forward and pray, and it was established for you [to lead them]." Their *imam* will then lead them in *salat*. When he leaves, Jesus, God's peace and blessings be upon him, will say, "Open the door," and it will be opened and the Dajjal will be behind it. (Abu Dawud)

REFERENCES: Ibn Kathir/*Signs*, pp. 20-24; Ayoub/*Q*, II:175; Hendi/*Jesus*, pp. 5, 32-33, 35-37, 69-74, 85; Glasse/*Encyclopedia*, pp. 246-247.

27. THE DAJJAL

Between the creation of Adam to the establishment of the Hour. there is no creature more formidible than the Dajjal. (*Muslim*, 7037)

During the period prior to the return of Jesus (A), the Dajjal will have begun his work of spreading delusion, confusion and corruption upon the earth, by which a great portion of humanity will be deceived and destroyed.

The word "*dajjal*" means cheat, imposter, swindler or charlatan. The arch-deceiver to whom this term is applied is known in Arabic as *al-Masih al-Dajjal*, the False Messiah. He is also referred to as *al-Masikh al-Dajjal*, meaning the Disfigured Deceiver. Ibn Hajar al-'Asqalani says that he is called the Dajjal "because he will be able to cover the whole earth by traveling and because he will cover truth with falsehood," while according to al-Qurtubi, he is so named "because of his ability to deceive people with his evil and because he will try to make falsehood seem right and beautiful" (Hendi/*Jesus*, p. 63).

The Dajjal is not mentioned in the Qur'an. However, it is believed that he is indirectly referred to in the verse,

> **The day that some of the signs of your Lord come, no soul will benefit from its faith if it had not believed previously or earned any good through his faith (6:158),**

for the Holy Prophet said,

> [There are] three things [such that] when they come forth, **no soul will benefit from its faith if it had not believed previously or earned any good through his faith** [6:158]: the rising of the sun in its place of setting, the Dajjal, and the beast of the earth.[124] (*Muslim*, 296)

---

[124]An unknown creature or beast that is one of the signs of the Last Hour, mentioned in the verse,

> **And when the word [i.e., God's decree] comes to pass upon them, We will bring forth for them a beast of the earth, speaking to them, [saying] that the people were not certain of Our signs. (27:82)**

"Whichever of the two" — the rising of the sun from the West and the appearance of the beast in the forenoon of the same day — "occurs before its companion, the other will follow soon thereafter" (*Muslim*, 7025), the Prophet (S) said. According to the saying Ibn 'Umar, possibly going back to the Prophet (S) himself, the beast will make its appearance when there remains no one on earth who enjoins on people to do good and forbids them to do evil.

The Prophet (S) often spoke about the Dajjal, referring to him as "the worst of what is expected but has not yet come" (*Mishkat*, 5175), and warning mankind against him in the strongest terms.

The appearance of the False Messiah of the End-Time will have been preceded by a number of lesser ***dajjalun*** or deceivers, mentioned in the Prophet's saying, "The Last Hour will not come until . . . there appear about thirty lying ***dajjalun***, each claiming to be a messenger of God" (*Bukhari*, 9:237; Abu Dawud, 4319). In another version it is, ". . . [Each] lying about God and His Messenger" (Abu Dawud, 4320).[125]

REFERENCES: Ibn Kathir/*Signs*, pp. 41-42, 62-63; Ayoub/*Q*, II:132; Hendi/*Jesus*, pp. 63-64; Glasse/*Encyclopedia*, p. 91.

SIGNS AND CHARACTERISTICS OF THE DAJJAL

The Messenger of God (S) repeatedly mentioned the signs by which the Dajjal might be recognized, for having seen him clearly during his Ascension (*Me'raj*) "among the signs which God showed me" (*Bukhari*, 4:462, 4:608), and possibly at other times as well, he was thoroughly familiar with the personal characteristics of the Arch-Deceiver.

Perhaps the Dajjal's most prominent identifying mark is that one or both of his eyes are defective. This is mentioned in numerous ***ahadith***.[126] The word which the Prophet (S) consistently used to describe the Dajjal's ruined eye is "'***awar***," meaning blind in one eye, or one-eyed due to the lack of an eye or its drying up in its socket, while the same or the other eye is described as resembling "'***anaba taafiya***, a floating grape," as mentioned in the ***hadith***,

> Indeed, God is not blind in one eye, but the False Messiah is blind in the right eye;[127] his eye is like a floating grape. (*Bukhari*, 4:649)

Concerning this, Ibn Kathir says:

> One of his eyes will be be blind, protruding and repulsive; this is the meaning of the ***hadith***: ". . . as if it were a grape floating on the surface

---

[125]In Ibn Kathir's book, *The Signs Before the Day of Judgement*, eight ***ahadith*** are cited in which thirty ***dajjalun*** are mentioned; in two others, it is "many liars" (pages 41-42). These liars and deceivers include those who have deluded people by pretending to be prophets or by spreading falsehood about God and His Messenger.

[126]***Bukhari***, 4:553-4:554, 4:649-4:650, 8:194, 9:241, 9:245, 9:504, 9:505; ***Muslim***, 323-325, 327, 7005-7010, 7014-7015; Abu Dawud, 4302, 4306, 4739; ***Muwatta***, 49.2.2

[127]Meaning that the Dajjal's blindness belies his claim to be God, who is obviously not blind.

of water." Other reports say that it is "dull, with no light in it," or "like white spittle on a wall," i.e., it will look ugly. (Ibn Kathir/*Signs*, p. 62)

In some *ahadith*, the right eye is said to be blind,[128] while in others it is the left. Ibn Kathir comments:

> He could be partly blind in both eyes, or there could be a fault in both eyes. This interpretation could be supported by the *hadith* narrated by al-Tabarani, in which which he reports that Ibn 'Abbas said, "The Prophet (S) said, 'The Dajjal is curly-haired and white-skinned. His head is like the branch of a tree; his left eye is blind, and his other eye looks like a floating grape.'" (ibid., p. 62)

Another major sign by which the Dajjal will be recognizable will be by the inscription of the word "*Kafir*" ("Unbeliever") on his forehead. The Holy Prophet (S) said:

> No prophet was sent without warning his *ummah* against the blind liar. Indeed, he is blind in one eye but your Lord is not blind in one eye, and between his eyes is written "*Kafir*". (*Bukhari*, 9:245, 9:505; *Muslim*, 7007, also 7005, 7008-7009; Abu Dawud, 4302)

Among several, similar reports in which the Holy Prophet (S) spoke of the Dajjal from his direct spiritual vision, we cite the following:

> In a dream by night at the K'abah, I saw a man whose skin was brown and as beautiful as can be seen among brown-skinned men. His hair was so long that it fell between his shoulders, and it was half-smooth, half-curled, and water was dripping from his head. He was putting his hands on the shoulders of two men while making *tawaf* of the [Sacred] House. Then I asked, "Who is this?" They said, "This is the Messiah, son of Mary." Then I saw behind him a man with short, curly hair, blind in the right eye, resembling, among those I have seen, Ibn Qatan, putting his hands on the shoulder of a man while making *tawaf* of the K'abah. Then I asked, "Who is this?" They said, "This is the False Messiah." (*Bukhari*, 4:649, 4:650; also *Muslim*, 323-325, 327; *Muwatta*, 49.2.2)

REFERENCES: Ibn Kathir/*Signs*, pp. 45-46; 53, 62, 76; Hendi/*Jesus*, pp. 63-65.

---

[128]In *Bukhari*, 4:649-4:650, 9:504, and *Muslim*, 323, 327, the right eye is described both as being blind and like a floating or bulging grape, while in *Bukhari*, 9:505, and *Muslim*, 324-325, it is merely said to be blind.

AFFLICTIONS BROUGHT BY THE DAJJAL

The Prophet's warnings about the Dajjal's mischief have come down to us in numerous *ahadith*, such as the following:

> Indeed, I warn you against him, and there was no prophet but warned his people, and certainly Noah warned his people. But I tell you about him that which no prophet told his people: know that indeed he is blind and that indeed God is not blind. (*Bukhari*, 4:553; also 8:194, 9:241; Abu Dawud, 4739)

> Shall I not tell you about the Dajjal what no prophet told his people? Indeed, he is one-eyed and he will bring with him the like of Paradise and Hell. Then that about which he says, "Indeed, it is Paradise," it will be Hell.[129] And I surely warn you about him as Noah warned his people. (*Muslim*, 7014, 7010; also *Bukhari*, 4:554)

Concerning the emergence of the Dajjal and his trial, the Prophet (S) said:

> Then Dajjal will come forth, accompanied by a river and fire. He who falls into his fire will certainly receive his reward and have his burden removed from him, but he who falls into his river will have his burden retained and his reward removed from him. (Abu Dawud, 4232)

> Indeed, there will be water and fire with the Dajjal when he comes forth. Then as for what people see as being fire, it will be cold water, and as for what people see as cold water, it will be burning fire. Therefore, he who reaches [that time] among you should throw himself into that which he sees as fire, for it will be sweet and cool. (*Bukhari*, 4:659, 9:244; *Muslim*, 7011-7013; also Abu Dawud, 4301)

> Let him who hears of the Dajjal go far from him, for I swear by God that a man will come to him thinking he is a believer and then follow him because of the confused ideas aroused in himself by him. (Abu Dawud, 4305)

> I have given descriptions about him which no one has ever given before. He is a man whose left eye is ruined. He will be able to cure the sick. He will say, "I am your Lord." Whoever says, "My Lord is God," no calamity will touch him, and whoever says, "You [the Dajjal] are my

---

[129]Perhaps this is related to the narrative of *Muslim*, 7019, in which the Prophet (S) spoke about a Muslim who would be repeatedly tortured, killed in the most gruesome manner, and then brought back to life by the Dajjal for unhesitatingly testifying that he is the False Messiah against whom mankind was warned. The onlookers will suppose that this witness to the truth has been thrown into Hell, whereas he will actually have been thrown into Paradise.

> Lord," will have fallen into calamity. He will stay among you as long as God wills. Then Jesus son of Mary will descend, confirming what I have brought, and a guided *imam* [the Mahdi] will be at the head of my *ummah.* (Ibn Hajar; Ahmad)

The only cities which the Dajjal and his trial will not reach will be Mecca and Medina, said the Holy Prophet (S), for each entrance to them will be guarded by angels arrayed in ranks, protecting them (*Bukhari,* 3:105, 9:240, 9:247-248; *Muslim,* 3:103-105; also *Muwatta,* 45.4.16). The Prophet (S) said further:

> There are angels at the entrances of Medina. Neither the plague nor the Dajjal will enter it. (*Bukhari,* 3:104)
>
> The terror of the False Messiah will not enter Medina, for during that time it will have seven gates and two angels will be at each gate. (*Bukhari,* 3:103)
>
> No one plots against the people of Medina without melting as salt melts in water. (*Bukhari,* 3:101; *Muslim,* 3194-3199)
>
> The Dajjal will arrive, and he will be forbidden to enter the mountain passes of Medina. Then he will settle at some salt marshes which are beyond Medina. There will then go out to him that day a man who is the best of mankind or among the best of mankind, and he will say, "I testify that you are the Dajjal about whom the Messenger of God, God's peace and blessings be upon him, told us." The Dajjal will then say, "What would you think if I killed this one and then brought him back to life — would you be in doubt about the matter?" They will say "No," and he will kill him and then revive him. Then when he revives him, he [the good man] will say, "By God, I have not had a clearer understanding of you than now!" Then the Dajjal will want to kill him [again] but he will not have power over him.[130] (*Bukhari,* 9:246; *Muslim,* 7017, also 7019)

REFERENCES: Ibn Kathir/*Signs,* pp. 39, 56, 68-69.

SEEKING PROTECTION FROM THE DAJJAL'S EVIL

The Holy Prophet (S) repeatedly prayed for protection from the mischief of the Dajjal. His wife 'A'ishah (R) said:

[130]At the end of the narrative of *Muslim,* 7017, Abu Ishaq reports, "It is said that indeed that man was Khidr, peace be upon him." This is also said to have been the view of Ibn 'Abbas and others (Al-Barazanji).

> I heard the Messenger of God, God's peace and blessings be upon him, seeking refuge in his *salat* from the trial of the Dajjal. (*Bukhari*, 9:241)

He would say, in varying order,

> O God, indeed I seek refuge with You from the punishment of the grave, from the punishment of Hell, from the trial of life and death, and from the trial of the False Messiah. (*Bukhari*, 2:459, also 1:795, 9:243; *Muslim*, 6859; Abu Dawud, 1537; *Muwatta*, 15.8.33)

And he would instruct his Companions to do likewise, saying,

> When one of you utters the *tashahhud*,[131] let him seek refuge with God from four things, saying, "O God, indeed I seek refuge with you from the punishment of Hell, from the punishment of the grave, from the trial of life and death, and from the evil of the trial of the Dajjal." (*Muslim*, 1217, also 1216, 1218-1225)

The Messenger of God (S) also advised memorizing the beginning of the eighteenth *surah*, *Al-Kahf*, as a protection against the trial of the Dajjal,[132] saying,

> Whoever memorizes ten verses from the beginning of *Surah al-Kahf* will be protected from the Dajjal. (*Muslim*, 1766; Abu Dawud, 4309)

> Those of you who live up to his time should recite over him the opening verses of *Surah al-Kahf*, for they are your protection from his trial. (Abu Dawud, 4307; also *Muslim*, 7015)

> Whoever recites three verses at the beginning of *al-Kahf* will be protected from the trial of the Dajjal. (Tirmidhi, 2146)

And in part of a lengthy *hadith* concerning the False Messiah, the Prophet (S) said:

> He will start by saying that he is a prophet, but there will be no prophet after me. Then he will say, "I am your Lord," but you will never see your Lord until you die. The Dajjal is one-eyed but your Lord, glorified is He, is not one-eyed. On his forehead will be written the word "*Kafir*," which every Muslim, literate or illiterate, will be able to read. Among the tribulations he will bring will be the Paradise and Hell he will offer, but that which he calls Hell will be Paradise and that which he calls Paradise will be Hell. Whoever enters his Hell, let him seek refuge with

---

[131] *Tashahhud* refers to what is recited during the sitting portion of *salat* after the second and the final *rak'ats*.

[132] The closing verses of this *surah* have also been mentioned in this context (*Muslim*, 1767; Abu Dawud, 4310), indicating the importance of its last as well as its first verses.

> God and recite the opening verses of *Surah al-Kahf*, and it will become cool and peaceful for him, as the fire became cool and peaceful for Abraham. (Ibn Majah)

May the merciful Guardian and Protector of mankind save us all from the mischief of this most dangerous and terrible enemy!

REFERENCES: Ibn Kathir/*Signs*, pp. 41, 62, 68, 76; Hendi/*Jesus*, pp. 63-68, 70; Glasse/*Encyclopedia*, p. 91.

28. The Descent of Jesus and the End of the Dajjal

Then Jesus will descend and kill the Dajjal. After this, Jesus will stay on the earth for forty years as a just leader and an equitable ruler. (Ahmad)

In a lengthy statement concerning the Dajjal and the return of Jesus (A), the Holy Prophet, God's peace and blessings be upon him, said to the Muslims around him,

> "Indeed, he will come forth between Syria and Iraq, and will cause afflictions right and left. O slave of God, remain firm!"
>
> His listeners then asked, "O Messenger of God, how long will he stay on earth?"
>
> He said, "For forty days, one day like a year and one day like a month and one day like a week, and its remaining days like your days."
>
> Then they asked, "O Messenger of God, and that day that is like a year — will one day's *salat* be sufficient for us in it?"
>
> He said, "No. Make an estimate [of the interval between prayers] for it."
>
> Then they asked, "O Messenger of God, and what will his journey be upon the earth?"
>
> He said, "Like rain blown by the wind — thus will he come to people and call them, and they will believe in him and respond to him.
>
> "He will command the sky and it will rain, and the earth and it will produce crops. After grazing on these crops, their livestock will come in the evening with their humps high, their udders full, and their flanks distended.
>
> "Then he will come to another people and call them, but they will turn his words back upon him. He will depart from them and they will experience drought, having nothing of wealth in their hands. Then he will pass through the ruins and say, 'Bring forth your treasures,' and the treasures will follow him like swarms of bees.
>
> "He will then call a man brimming with youth. Then he will strike him with the sword and cut him into two pieces [and then place them] at a shooting distance. Then he will call him and the young man will come, beaming with joy and laughing." (*Muslim*, 7015; also Abu Dawud, 4307)

From all this, it is clear that the Dajjal will use every possible form of deception and delusion to confuse and destroy people's faith and understanding.

Because he will control the sources of food and water, they will believe in him and flock to him, while those who reject him will suffer drought, famine and other calamities as the price of keeping to their faith, to the extent that the earth will cease to produce food and all the animals will die. The seemingly miraculous feats he will perform, such as killing and reviving the young man mentioned above, will convince great numbers of people that he is a prophet or a divine being, and they will become his partisans and helpers, although in reality whatever God permits him to manifest is but a trial.

> Then while it is thus, [the above *hadith* continues,] God will send the Messiah, son of Mary, and he will descend at the white minaret in eastern Damascus[133] wearing two garments dyed with saffron, placing his hands on the wings of two angels. When he bends his head, drops will trickle down, and when he raises it, beads like pearls will flow from it. Then it will not be permitted for any unbeliever whom the air of his breath encounters but to die, and his breath will end at the point where his sight ends. He [Jesus] will then pursue him [the Dajjal] until he overtakes him at the gate of Lod [Lydda] and then he will kill him. (*Muslim*, 7015; also Abu Dawud, 4307)

Jesus (A) will be assisted in his task by an army of the righteous, mentioned in a number of *ahadith*, such as the following:

> A group of people from among my *ummah* will continue to triumph on the right path. Whoever deserts them will not harm them, until God's command [that is, the Last Hour] comes while they are thus. (*Muslim*, 4715, also 4716, 4718-4719, 4721)
>
> For whomever God desires good, He grants him understanding of the faith. And a group of Muslims will continue to fight for truth, being victorious over whomever opposes them, until the Day of Resurrection. (*Muslim*, 4720; also 4715-4716, 4718-4719)
>
> A section of my community will continue to fight for the right and will overcome their opponents until the last of them fights with the Dajjal. (Abu Dawud, 2478)
>
> The people of the West [*ahl al-gharb*] will continue to be victorious on the truth until the establishment of the Hour.[134] (*Muslim*, 4722)

---

[133]Originally a watchtower of the Church of St. John, which was later turned into a mosque, "the white minaret" is that of the Omayyad Mosque in Damascus, where John the Baptist is buried.

[134]Although the meaning of "*ahl al-gharb*" has been the subject of widely differing interpretions, perhaps it may leave room to hope that some people of Western origin may be among these righteous ones. And God knows best.

Concerning the end of the Dajjal, the Holy Prophet (S) said:

The [False] Messiah will come from the East, his intention being [to take] Medina, until he camps behind Uhud.[135] Then the angels will turn his face toward Syria and he will perish there. (*Muslim*, 3187)

When the enemy of God [the Dajjal] sees him [Jesus], he will melt as salt melts in water, for [even] if he [Jesus] left him, he would melt until he perished. But God will have him killed at his hand, and he will show them his blood on his spear. (*Muslim*, 6924)

REFERENCES: Ibn Kathir/*Signs*, pp. 42, 51, 53-54, 56-61, 66, 69, 71-73; Hendi/*Jesus*, pp. 4, 80.

[135]The mountain of Medina.

29. THE ROLE AND MISSION OF JESUS DURING HIS SECOND COMING

Indeed, there will be neither a prophet nor a messenger between me and Jesus son of Mary. Indeed, he will be my caliph among my ***ummah*** after me.
(Ibn 'Asakir)

The killing of the Dajjal will mark the end of the era of evil and herald a period of righteousness and justice which will continue until the death of Jesus, God's peace and blessings be upon him.

What, then, will the role of Jesus (A) be during this period? Will he continue his previously unfinished prophetic mission, or will he be granted a new revelation, containing a new divine law (***shari'ah***) for governing mankind, replacing that of Muhammad (S)?

The answers to these questions rest on the understanding of the most eminent classical scholars of the Muslim ***ummah.*** Basing their interpretations on the Qur'anic text and ***ahadith,*** they considered these matters from every possible point of view. We summarize their conclusions below.

"INDEED, THERE WILL BE NO PROPHET AFTER ME"

A fundamental article of Islamic faith is the belief that Muhammad (S) is God's last prophet and messenger, the final link and culmination of the prophetic line that began with Adam (A). Indeed, this is such a basic tenet of faith for Muslims that denial of it is considered unbelief. Hence, it is the unvarying criterion by all other claimants to prophethood after Muhammad's time are judged.

The proof and evidence for this belief rests, firstly, on God's unequivocal statement,

> **Muhammad is not the father of any of your men, but he is the Messenger of God and Seal of the Prophets [*khatam al-nabiyyin*] (33:40),**

"***khatam***" meaning a seal or stamp, the end or last. This verse alone is considered "an unequivocally decisive primary text establishing that there will be no prophet after him" (Keller/*Reliance*, w4.2, p. 847). And as mentioned in the following verses, among others, Muhammad (S) is the prophet for all mankind up to the Last Day, and his Message is a universal message for all the children of Adam:

We have not sent you except to all mankind without exception as a bringer of good tidings and a warner. But most people do not know. (34:28)

Say, [O Muhammad:] "O mankind, indeed, I am the messenger of God to you all, of Him to whom the dominion of the heavens and the earth belongs. There is no deity except Him; He gives life and causes death." So believe in God and His messenger, the Unlettered Prophet, who believes in God and His words, and follow him, that you may be guided. (7:158)

And We have not sent you [Muhammad] except as a mercy for mankind. (21:107)

Blessed is He who sent down the Criterion to His slave [Muhammad], that he might be a warner to the worlds. (25:1)

The finality of Muhammad's prophethood is also proclaimed in numerous *ahadith,* such as the following:

Each prophet was sent to his specific people but I have been sent to mankind generally. (*Bukhari*, 1:331[5])

O people! Indeed, there will be no prophet after me, nor any *ummah* [faith community] after you. (The sermon of the Prophet's farewell pilgrimage)

Each prophet was sent to his specific people, but I have been sent to every white and black one [i.e., all humanity]. (*Muslim*, 1058)

I have been sent to the totality of mankind, and the [line of] prophets ended with me. (*Muslim*, 1062)

Indeed, there will be no prophet after me, but there will be caliphs and they will increase [in number]. (*Bukhari*, 4:661, 5:700)

The Prophet, God's peace and blessings be upon him, also repeatedly referred to himself as the Seal of the Prophets, saying,

I am the leader [*qa'id*] of the messengers, and this is no boast; I am the Seal of the Prophets, and this is no boast; and I shall be the first to make intercession and the first whose intercession is accepted, and this is no boast. (*Mishkat*, 5764)

There will be thirty liars among my *ummah.* Each one will claim that he is a prophet, but I am the Seal of the Prophets and there will be no prophet after me. (Abu Dawud, 4239; Ahmad)

My likeness in relation to the other prophets preceding me is like that of a man who has built a building and made it good and beautiful, except for placing one brick in a corner. Then the people go around it and marvel at it, and they say, "If only this brick were put in its place!"

So I am that brick and I am the Seal of the Prophets. (*Bukhari*, 4:735, also 4:734)

The Prophet (S) also referred to himself as ***al-Muqaffi***, meaning the last in succession (*Muslim*, 5813), and as ***al-'Aqib***, the last[136] (*Bukhari*, 4:732; *Muslim*, 5810-5811; *Muwatta*, 61.1.1).

As for the Last Testament revealed to Muhammad (S), it remains among us in its original, pristine form. Recognized by many Arabic-speakers as a book whose content, language and style are unique and unparalleled in world literature, it is considered the Prophet's greatest miracle. A comparison of the the earliest written Qur'an, compiled during the time of the third caliph, 'Uthman (R), with the Qur'ans of later times up to the present, attests to the fact that it remains unchanged, just as it was transmitted to Muhammad (S) by the angel Gabriel (A) from his Lord more than fourteen hundred years ago. This means that, amazingly and wonderfully, the eternal words of the Creator of the universes remain in our hands in pure, unaltered form, conveying His final guidance to humanity, the only revealed scripture on earth unchanged by time or the hands of men. And God Himself has promised to guard it from alteration and distortion until the end of the world, declaring,

Indeed, it is We who sent down the Message [the Qur'an] and indeed We will be its guardian. (15:9)

REFERENCES: Ibn Kathir/*Signs*, pp. 74-76; Qadi 'Iyad/*Ash-Shifa*, p. 114; Keller/*Reliance*, w4.0-4.2, pp. 846-848; Ayoub/*Q*, II170-171, 174-175; Hendi/*Jesus*, pp. 19, 31, 86.

"He Will Be My Caliph Among My *Ummah*"

God's declaration that Muhammad (S) is the Seal of the Prophets and the foregoing ***ahadith*** are understood as conclusive evidence that when Jesus (A) returns to this world, he will not come as a prophet in his own right, representing himself, nor will he be granted a new law (***shari'ah***) or dispensation for the guidance of mankind.

Rather, Jesus' role will be that of the final caliph or successor of Last Prophet (S). In this capacity, he will rule according to the ***Shari'ah*** of Islam and the ***sunnah*** of Muhammad (S), as is clear from the Prophet's saying,

---

136 The full texts of these ***ahadith*** are quoted on page 482. Note also the ***hadith*** cited in "Moses," footnote 115, reporting that when the Prophet (S) made 'Ali his deputy in Medina during the campaign of Tabuk, he said to him, "Are you not pleased to be to me in the rank of Aaron to Moses — except that there will be no prophet after me?" (*Bukhari*, 5:700).

> Indeed, there will be neither a prophet nor a messenger between me and Jesus son of Mary. Indeed, he will be my caliph among my ***ummah*** after me. (Ibn 'Asakir)

This understanding of the role of Jesus (A) is further confirmed by a ***hadith*** in which the Prophet (S) asked some Companions, "How will it be with you when the son of Mary descends among you and leads you as one among yourselves?" These words are explained by one of the narrators of the ***hadith*** as meaning, "He will lead you according to the Book of your Lord, Blessed and Exalted, and the ***sunnah*** of your Prophet, God's peace and blessings be upon him" (*Muslim*, 292).

Al-Qurtubi mentions a similar ***hadith*** in which the Prophet (S) stated that Jesus (A) would not bring a new ***shari'ah*** abrogating the *Shari'ah* of Islam. "Rather," the Prophet (S) said, "he will come to renew that which has been effaced of it. He will be one of its followers" (Ayoub/*Q*, II:174-175). This is clarified by the eminient classical scholar, al-Suyuti, who states that while this does not negate Jesus' prophethood during his second coming nor the possibility of his receiving revelations through Gabriel (A) during it in the manner of the prophets who preceded him, it does mean that no ***new*** prophet will come after the Last Prophet (S) and that no one will bring a law abrogating Muhammad's law (Hendi/*Jesus*, p. 30-31). The well-known classical scholar, al-Nawawi, put the matter thus:

> The descent (***nuzul***) of Jesus is not intended to bring a law to abrogate our Law [*Shari'ah*]. There is nothing in the ***ahadith*** about this. In fact, authentic ***ahadith*** have stated that he [Jesus] will descend as a just ruler, ruling by our Law, and that he will revive matters in our Law that people have abandoned. (Nawawi, *Sharh Muslim*)

As the Holy Prophet's caliph and follower, Jesus (A) will scrupulously fulfill all the requirements of the Islamic *Shari'ah*. Thus, he will pray in the prescribed manner, either behind the Mahdi (A) while he is leading the *salat*, as mentioned in the ***ahadith*** cited on page 459, or leading the *salat* himself, as mentioned in the Prophet's saying,

> Jesus son of Mary will descend and will lead them [the Muslims] in *salat* . . . and when he finishes his bowing [***ruku'***], he will say, "God hears those who praise him [one of the integral phrases of *salat*]. May God kill the Dajjal and grant victory to the believers!'" (Ibn Hibban)

Jesus (A) will likewise perform the pilgrimages, major or minor, for the Prophet (S) said:

> The son of Mary will certainly pronounce ***talbiyah*** for *Hajj* or *'Umrah* or both in the valley of al-Rauha. (*Muslim*, 2877)

Indeed, the son of Mary will descend as an equitable judge and a fair ruler. And he will travel the way of *Hajj* or *'Umrah*, and he will come to my grave [in Medina] to greet me and I will answer him." (Al-Hakim)

Another indication that Jesus (A) will not return as a prophet in his own right but rather as the caliph of the Last Prophet (S) is related to the previously-mentioned belief that the prophets are alive in their graves. Consequently, they are not veiled from the spiritual vision of other prophets, as is confirmed by the fact of Muhammad's meeting the earlier prophets, including Jesus (A), during his Night Journey.

Because the Prophet (S) dwelt simultaneously in the physical and the spiritual plane, he also met Jesus (A) in a waking state, as mentioned in the *hadith* of al-Hakim cited above. The following *ahadith*, quoted in al-Suyuti's work, *The Descent of Jesus Son of Mary at the End of Time*, also provide evidence that the Holy Prophet (S) met Jesus at various times other than during his Night Journey (*al-Isra'*).[137]

Anas bin Malik (R) said, "[Once] while we were with the Messenger of God, God's peace and blessings be upon him, we saw a garment and a hand, so we said, 'O Messenger of God, what is this garment and hand we saw?' He said, 'Did you see him?' We said, 'Yes.' He said, 'That was Jesus son of Mary. He greeted me.'" (Ibn 'Adi, *Al-Kamil*)

Anas (R) said, "As I was making *tawaf* with the Messenger of God, God's peace and blessings be upon him, around the K'abah, I saw him shaking something that we did not see. We said, 'O Messenger of God, we saw that you shook something that we did not see.' He said, 'That was my brother, Jesus son of Mary. I waited for him until he finished his *tawaf* and then I greeted him.'" (Ibn 'Asakir)

Hence, says al-Suyuti, when Jesus (A) returns to the earth, he will meet the earlier prophets in the spiritual plane. Among them will be Muhammad (S), and Jesus (A) will take from him spiritually whatever he needs of the laws of his *Shari'ah* (Hendi/*Jesus*, pp. 18, 21).

---

[137]Because of the Prophet's spiritual meetings with Jesus, some classical scholars maintained that Jesus is among the Companions of the Prophet — that is, one who believed in the Prophet (S) and had been in his company. Based on this understanding, al-Dhahabi states,

> Jesus son of Mary, peace be upon him, is a prophet and a Companion of the Prophet, for indeed he saw the Prophet [as mentioned in the *ahadith* of Ibn 'Adi and Ibn 'Asakir above], God's peace and blessings be upon him, and greeted him. Therefore, he will be the last Companion to die. (Al-Dhahabi, *Tajrid as-Sahabah*)

REFERENCES: Ayoub/*Q*, II:171, 174-175, 238-239; Hendi/*Jesus*, 3-5, 18-21, 23, 30-31.

THE COMPLETION OF JESUS' MISSION

In light of the above understanding, it may logically be asked, If Jesus (A) does not return as a new prophet with a new *shari'ah*, what will his mission be?

This question is addressed in a number of *ahadith*, among which we cite the following:

> There will be no prophet between me and him [Jesus], and he will descend [to the earth]. Therefore, recognize him when you see him. He will be a man of medium height, of ruddy and fair complexion; he will be dressed in two yellow garments; the hair of his head will appear as though water was trickling down from it, whereas it will not be wet. He will fight people in the cause of Islam, and will break the cross, kill the pigs and abolish *jizyah*,[138] and God will put an end to all [religious] communities in his time except Islam, and he will kill the Dajjal and will stay on earth for forty years. (Abu Dawud, 4310)

> The son of Mary will descend as a just leader. He will break the cross and kill the pigs. Peace will prevail and people will use their swords as sickles. Every harmful beast will be made harmless; the sky will send down rain in abundance and the earth will bring forth its blessings. A child will play with a fox and not come to any harm; a wolf will graze with sheep and a lion with cattle without harming them. (Ahmad, *Musnad*)

> By the One in whose hand is Abu-l-Qasim's soul, Jesus son of Mary will descend as a just and wise ruler. He will destroy the cross, kill the pigs, eradicate discord and grudges, and money will be offered to him but he will not accept it. Then he will stand at my graveside and say, "O Muhammad!" and I will answer him. (Abu Ya'ala, *Musnad*)

Now, what is the meaning of these repeated references to Jesus' breaking of the cross and killing of pigs?

The answer to these questions is simple and indeed obvious, for at the time of Jesus' bodily return to the earth, the truth of God's decisive declara-

---

[138]The abolishing of *jizyah* (see footnote 80) by Jesus during this period is also mentioned in *Bukhari*, 4:657, and *Muslim*, 289. This is understood as meaning that, contrary to the practice of earlier times, the followers of other religions will not be permitted to pay *jizyah* while adhering to their previous faiths, for Jesus will abolish all faiths except the original faith ordained by the Creator for mankind, the faith of Jesus himself in both his earlier and later life, Islam.

tion that they **they did not kill him nor crucify him, but it was made to appear so to them. . . . And of a certainty they did not kill him. Rather, God raised him to Himself** (4:157-158), will be self-evident. His breaking of the cross therefore symbolizes his denial of his alleged crucifixion and his repudiation of the faith that was founded on the basis of this myth, together with the doctrines that support it.

As for Jesus' killing of pigs mentioned in these *ahadith*, it symbolizes both the divine disapproval and the end of the eating of unclean, prohibited flesh, revealed through both Moses and Muhammad (S), and likewise observed by Jesus (A), who confirmed, upheld and practiced the divine legislation revealed to the prophets preceding him.

At the same time, Jesus' prophethood, as well as that of Muhammad (S), whose caliph he will be, will also be self-evident to those who previously denied it or who believed in his divinity, for **there is no one among the People of the Scripture but will surely believe in him** as God's prophet **before his death** (4:159). This understanding is clarified in a ***hadith*** narrated by Abu Hurayrah (R), who reported the Prophet (S) as saying,

> "By Him in whose hand is my soul, the son of Mary will soon descend among you as a just ruler. Then he will break the cross and kill the pigs and put an end to war, and money will be so abundant that no one will accept it, so that a single prostration [to God] will be better than the world and whatever is in it." Abu Hurayrah (R) then added: "Then read, if you will, **'And there is no one among the People of the Scripture but will surely believe in him before his death, and on the Day of Resurrection he will be a witness against them.'"** [4:159]. (*Bukhari*, 4:657; also *Muslim*, 287)

Earlier, in the context of this verse, we mentioned Ibn 'Abbas' statement that at the time of Jesus' death not a single person professing Judaism will remain, for all will believe in Jesus' prophethood, as well as the saying of Hasan al-Basri, "By God, Jesus is alive in Heaven, and when he comes down to the earth, there will not be a single person among the People of the Scripture who will not believe in him [as God's messenger] (Ibn Kathir/*T*, 4:156-159). This understanding is confirmed by other commentators such as Qatadah (R), al-Tabari and Ibn Kathir himself.

Taken all together, these *ahadith* and commentaries make it clear that the culmination of Jesus' mission will be to confirm and establish the faith ordained for mankind by the Creator, and finalized and completed by the Last Prophet (S), the continuation and completion of the divine Message proclaimed by all the righteous prophets and their communities before his time, who, by virtue of their pure belief and surrendered hearts, constituted the *muslims* of the pre-Muhammadan era.[138]

In summary, then, the preceding constitutes conclusive evidence that the role of Jesus (A) in his second coming will not be that of a new prophet, bringing a new law. Rather, he will be a reviver of the true religion (*mujad-did*) of his predecessors in prophethood and a just ruler, governing by the laws of the faith appointed by God Most High for mankind, which embodies and sanctifies all the true, sacred, revered teachings of the earlier revealed paths, according to His words,

> **Indeed, this your religion is one religion and I am your Lord, so be mindful of Me.** (23:52; also 21:92)
>
> **And we believe in that which has been revealed to us and revealed to you. And our God and your God is one, and we are Muslims [surrendering] to Him** (29:46)
>
> **He has ordained for you [mankind], as the religion, what He enjoined upon Noah and that which We have revealed to you [Muhammad], and what We enjoined upon Abraham and Moses and Jesus: to establish the religion and not be divided concerning it.** (42:13)

REFERENCES: Ibn Kathir/*Signs*, pp. 74-75; Ayoub/*Q*, II:170-171, 174-175; Hendi/*Jesus*, ix-x, 3-5, 18-23, 29-30, 85-86.

---

[138] Please see footnote 183, page 181, for a citation of verses related to this point.

30. JESUS' DEATH AND BURIAL

We did not make them [the prophets] bodies not eating food, nor were they immortal. (21:8)

During the rule of Jesus, God's peace and blessings be upon him,

> Mutual enmity and hatred will disappear. Every harmful animal will be made harmless. . . . The earth will be filled with peace as a container is filled with water. People will be in complete agreement, and only God will be worshipped. Wars will cease. (Ibn Majah, *Kitab al Fitan*, 4077)

At that time, the most valuable commodity will be the worship and glorification of God, the Praised and Exalted.

> Peace and security will prevail on earth, so that lions will graze with camels, tigers with cattle, and woves with sheep; children will be able to play with snakes without coming to any harm. Jesus will remain for forty years, then die, and the Muslims will pray [the funeral prayer] over him. (Ahmad; also Abu Dawud, 4310)

Jesus' soul will be taken in Medina and he will be buried there beside the Messenger of God (S), according to the Prophet's saying, "No prophet was ever buried except in the place where he died" (*Muwatta*, 16.10.27), and "God takes [the soul of] a prophet only in the place where he wishes to be buried" (*Mishkat*, 5963).

The Holy Prophet (S) also said:

> Jesus son of Mary will descend to the earth and will marry and have children and will remain forty-five years, after which he will die and be buried together with me in my grave. Then Jesus son of Mary and I will arise from one grave [on the Day of Resurrection] between Abu Bakr and 'Umar.[139] (*Mishkat*; also Ibn al-Jauzi)

This is confirmed by the statement of 'Abdullah ibn Salam (R), the well-known Companion who had been a Jewish rabbi prior to his acceptance of Islam: "The description of Muhammad is written in the Torah, and also that Jesus son of Mary will be buried along with him." It is said that a place for another grave has remained [for Jesus] beside the Prophet's grave (*Mishkat*, 5772).

---

[139]The two beloved Companions of the Prophet, his first two caliphs or successors, who are buried beside him in the Prophet's Mosque in Medina.

Due to their awareness of these matters, Muslims, like Christians, are awaiting the return of Jesus, God's peace and highest blessings be upon him, not as the Son of God coming in glory, but as the final caliph or successor to the Last Prophet of God Most High. Fortunate indeed will be those who live to see the time of his return! May we be among them.

After Jesus' passing, there will be seven years of righteousness and tranquility before the events of the End-Time advance to their next stage, as mentioned in the following ***ahadith***:

> The Dajjal will go forth among my ***ummah*** and will stay for forty [days, one day like a year and one day like a month and one day like a week, and its remaining days like your days (***Muslim***, 7015; Abu Dawud, 4307)]. God will then send Jesus son of Mary, who will be like Urwah ibn Mas'ud, and he will pursue him [the Dajjal] and annihilate him. Then people will remain [thus] for seven years, [during which] there will be no enmity between any two people. Then God will send a cool wind from the direction of Syria, and it will not leave a single person on the face of the earth in whose heart there is an iota of faith or goodness but that it will take him away, so that even if one of you went into the interior of a mountain, it would certainly take possession of him until it caused him to die. (***Muslim***, 7023)
>
> God will send a wind like the scent of musk, whose touch will be the touch of silk. Then there will not be left a soul in whose heart is the weight of a grain of faith but that it will take him away. There will then be left the most evil of people. The Hour will come upon them. (***Muslim***, 4721, also 212)

REFERENCES: Ibn Kathir/Signs, pp. 55, 73, 75; Keller/*Reliance*, w47.1, p. 952, w4.0-4.2, pp. 846-848; Ayoub/*Q*, II:170-171, 174-175; Hendi/*Jesus*, x, 3-5, 18-23, 29-30, 85-86.

PART SEVEN: PROPHECIES CONCERNING THE LAST PROPHET

31. "A MESSENGER WHOSE NAME IS AHMAD"

And [mention, O Muhammad,] when Jesus son of Mary said, "O Children of Israel, indeed I am the messenger of God to you, confirming what preceded me of the *Taurat* and bringing good tidings of a messenger to come after me, whose name is Ahmad." But when he [Jesus] came to them with clear proofs, they said, "This is obvious magic." (61:6)

Given the fact that the prophets formed a single community, a chain of inspired messengers appointed by their Lord, it is only natural that they should have been aware of one another — both those who succeeded as well as those who preceded themselves. This is suggested by the following verse:

> **And [recall, O People of the Scripture,] when God took a covenant from the prophets, [saying,] "Whatever I give you of scripture and wisdom, and then there comes to you a messenger confirming what is with you, you will believe in him and support him." He [God] said, "Have you acknowledged and accepted My burden concerning that?" They said, "We have acknowledged it." He said, "Then bear witness, and I am with you among the witnesses."** (3:81)

The meaning of this covenant — made, according to some interpretations, by the prophets on behalf of their entire communities — is that, in exchange for the scripture and wisdom they had been granted, they would accept and support any prophet who came after them, especially the Last Prophet (S). Hence, this passage is understood as referring both to the prophets in general and to Muhammad (S) in particular, signifying, in the words of al-Suyuti, that "Muhammad's message and prophethood are for [all] the other prophets as well as humankind in general" (Hendi/*Jesus*, pp. 85-86).

Two other passages suggest that the earlier prophets were aware and informed of the culmination of their line in the Seal of the Prophets, God's peace and blessings be upon him and upon them all. One of these is Abraham's prayer that God would send among his descendants **"a messenger from among themselves who will recite to them Your verses, and teach them the scripture and wisdom and purify them"** (2:129).

The second passage is God's declaration to Moses (A) that a very special and important prophet — **the Messenger, the Unlettered Prophet whom they find inscribed in what they have of the *Taurat* and the *Injil*** (7:156) — would follow him in due course of time, as mentioned on pages 123-124.

In view of Muhammad's unparalleled importance in the divine scheme of things, it would indeed be surprising if Jesus (A) too had not been keenly aware of the prophet who would succeed him, and whose caliph he would in turn become. Informed by divine revelation, he conveyed to his people the **"good tidings of a messenger to come after me, whose name is Ahmad"** (61:6), thereby having the honor of giving mankind the direct news of God's beloved, Muhammad (S), the last in the long, unbroken chain of prophets who, according to a ***hadith***, numbered 124,000 in all (*Mishkat*, 664w).

Now, what is the connection between the names "Muhammad" and "Ahmad"?[140] A very integral connection indeed, for both are derived from the same three-letter Arabic root, ***h-m-d***, "Muhammad" meaning one who is praised, praiseworthy or commendable, and "Ahmad" one who is more or most praised, praiseworthy or commendable. Concerning these names, the Holy Prophet (S) said,

> I have five names. I am Muhammad and Ahmad. I am ***al-Mahi*** [the obliterator] through whom God will obliterate unbelief. And I am ***al-Hashir*** [the gatherer] in whose footsteps people will be gathered, and I am ***al-'Aqib*** [the last (of the prophets)]. (*Bukhari*, 4:732; *Muslim*, 5810-5811; *Muwatta*, 61.1.1)
>
> I am Muhammad and Ahmad and ***al-Muqaffi*** [the successor (of the prophets)] and ***al-Hashir*** and ***nabi al-taubah*** [the prophet of repentance] and ***nabi al-rahmah*** [the prophet of mercy]. (*Muslim*, 5813)

In light of all this, it may naturally be asked, If Jesus (A) indeed prophesied the coming of Muhammad (S), **whom they find inscribed in what they have of the *Taurat* and the *Injil*** (7:156), how and why was this prophecy not preserved and recorded in scripture?

Perhaps a clue to the reason is contained in God's saying, at the end of the verse cited at the beginning of this chapter, **But when he came to them with clear proofs, they said, "This is obvious magic"** (61:6).

---

[140]The name Ahmad had not been given to anyone in Arabia before Muhammad (S). However, since his time innumerable males have borne the names Muhammad, Ahmad and other derivatives of the ***h-m-d*** root such as Mahmoud, Hamid, Hameed, Hamdi, Hamudi, and their adaptations in the various languages of Muslim peoples.

Although it is quite possible that this prophecy was inadvertently lost, distorted or changed with the passing of time, these words suggest another possibility: that Jesus' prophecy concerning Muhammad (S) was deliberately denied and suppressed, together with information about his prophethood and true message, perhaps as a result of his enemies' atempts to discredit him and his mission, or by the early church fathers because it conflicted with the teachings that they wished to propagate concerning him.

REFERENCES: Ibn Kathir/*T*, 7:156-158; Ibn Kathir/*Q*, "Musa"; Qadi 'Iyad, *Ash-Shifa*, pp. 114-119; Hendi/*Jesus*, pp. 85-86.

32. THE BIBLICAL PROPHECIES CONCERNING MUHAMMAD (S)

The Lord your God will raise up for you a prophet like me [Moses] from among your own brothers. You must listen to him. (Deut. 18:15)

Despite the loss or suppression of Jesus' prophecy concerning Muhammad (S), the Jews and Christians of Arabia up to the Prophet's time were eagerly awaiting the coming of another prophet — the Jews their promised Messiah, whom they did not doubt would be from among the descendants of Isaac (A), and the Christians the prophet who would succeed Jesus (A). The Prophet's biographer, Ibn Ishaq, states:

> Jewish rabbis, Christian monks, and Arab soothsayers had spoken about the apostle of God before his mission when his time drew near. As to the rabbis and monks, it was about his description and the description of his time which they found in their scriptures and what their prophets had enjoined upon them [that they spoke]. (Ibn Ishaq/*Muhammad*, p. 90).

The signs and indications of this prophet-to-come and his time were familiar to many the Jews and Christians of Muhammad's time, as is stated by the eminent classical scholar Qadi 'Iyad:

> The proofs of his prophethood and the signs of his messengership include mutually complementary traditions from the monks, rabbis and scholars of the People of the Book regarding his description, his community, his names and his signs.[141] (*Ash-Shifa*, pp. 202-203)

THE OLD TESTAMENT PROPHECIES

Now, what is this description of this awaited prophet and his time that the Jewish and Christian men of religion are said to have found in their scriptures?

It is possible to identify with absolute certainty only that which is reported in the Qur'an — namely, Jesus' giving **"good tidings of a messenger to come after me, whose name is Ahmad"** (61:6). However, Muslim scholars have pointed out at least three Biblical prophecies that are believed to relate to Muhammad (S).

[141]For more details, see Section 28 in *Ash-Shifa'*, entitled "Reports about his attributes and the signs of his messengership," pages 202-204.

The first of these is contained in the following passage, attributed to Moses (A):

> The Lord your God will raise up for you a prophet like me from among your own brothers. You must listen to him.
>
> . . . [God said:] "I will raise up for them a prophet like you from among their brothers; I will put my words in his mouth, and he will tell them everything I command him. If anyone does not listen to my words that the prophet speaks in my name, I myself will call him to account. But a prophet who presumes to speak in my name anything I have not commanded him to say, or a prophet who speaks in the name of other gods, must be put to death." (Deut. 18:15, 18-20)

In the view of Muslim commentators, the prophet mentioned here could not be other than Muhammad (S). Which other prophet can be said to be from the "brothers" of the Jews — that is, the Arabs, who like the Jews, were descended from Abraham (A)? And about which other prophet can it be said with certainty that God "put in his mouth" the words by which he conveyed to people everything his Lord commanded him? As God says:

> **Your companion has not strayed nor has he erred, nor does he speak from fancy. It [the Qur'an] is nothing but a revelation revealed, taught to him by one mighty in power [Gabriel], endowed with strength** (53:2-5).

As for God's saying that He would hold accountable anyone who did not listen to the words that this prophet would speak in His name, they may indicate that in His sight, denial of Muhammad's prophethood and Message constitutes rebellion, defiance, disobedience and indeed unbelief.

Concerning the possibility of this prophet's presuming to speak in God's name anything that he had not been commanded to say, God Himself repeatedly proclaimed in the strongest language the terrible punishment that would have come upon Muhammad (S) if he falsified anything of the Message with which he had been entrusted, saying,

> **And indeed, they [the Meccan idolaters] were about to tempt you away from that which We revealed to you, that you might fabricate something other than it against Us, and then they would have taken you as a friend. And if We had not made you firm, you would nearly have inclined to them a little. In that case, We would have made you taste double [the punishment] in life and double in death. Then you would not have found for yourself any helper against Us!** (17:73-75)
>
> **Indeed, it [the Qur'an] is the word of a noble messenger [Muhammad], and it is not the word of a poet — little do you**

> **believe, nor the word of a soothsayer — little do you remember. [Rather, it is] a revelation from the Lord of the worlds. And if he [Muhammad] had made up some false sayings about Us, We would have seized him by the right hand; then We would certainly have cut off the aorta from him, and there is not one of you who could have restrained [Us] from him.** (69:40-47)

The second Old Testament prophecy believed to relate to Muhammad (S) is attributed to the prophet Isaiah:

> [God said,] Here is my servant, whom I uphold, my chosen one in whom I delight; I will put my spirit on him and he will bring justice to the nations. He will not shout or cry out, or raise his voice in the streets. A bruised reed he will not break, and a smoldering wick he will not snuff out. In faithfulness he will bring forth justice; he will not falter or be discouraged till he establishes justice on earth. In his law the islands will put their hope. (Isa. 42:1-4)

Quite naturally, Christians believe this passage to refer to Jesus (A). However, the description seems to correspond much more closely with the life and mission of Muhammad (S), who did not raise his voice harshly and dealt mercifully and kindly with people, and who pressed ahead with the establishment of God's religion until, by the implementation of the guidance revealed through him, justice was established among the nations, extending even to the farthest islands.

This interpretation is borne out by the following incident, reported by the Prophet's Companion, 'Ata' bin Yasar (R), who said,

> I met 'Abdullah bin 'Amr bin al-'As (R) and said, "Tell me about the attributes of the Messenger of God, God's peace and blessings be upon him, [mentioned] in the Torah." He said, "By all means! By God, indeed, he is certainly described in the Torah by some of the attributes mentioned in the Qur'an: **'O Prophet, indeed, We have sent you as a witness and a bringer of good tidings and a warner** [33:45], and a refuge for the unlettered. You are My slave and My messenger. I have named you *al-Mutawakkil* [the one who relies upon God]. You are not coarse nor harsh nor loud in the marketplaces, and you do not repel evil with evil but pardon and forgive.' And God will not let him die until He straightens the deviant community through him by making them say '*La ilaha illa-Llah*,' and thereby opens the blind eyes and hearing of the deaf and covered hearts." (*Bukhari*, 3:335)

Further confirmation of this understanding is found in the reply to a question asked of the Companion, K'ab al-Ahbar (R), a learned Jewish convert to Islam, by Ibn 'Abbas (R), "What description of the Messenger of God (S) do you find in the Torah?" Ka'b (R) replied:

> "We find him [named] Muhammad son of 'Abdullah. His birthplace is in Mecca, his place of migration is Taybah [Medina], and his kingdom is Sham [Palestine/Syria]. He is not coarse of speech nor loud in the marketplaces, and does not repay wrong with wrong but forgives and pardons." [In another version,] Ka'b added: "His *ummah* are the praisers [*al-hammadun*]. They praise God in every happy and sad occasion, and glorify God on every height. They wash their limbs, wear the waist-wrap, and line up for their prayers just as they do for battle. The sound they make in their places of worship is like that of bees. Their callers [to prayer] can be heard in the air of Heaven." (Al-Darimi, *Sunan*)

When 'Abdullah ibn Salam (R), a scholar and rabbi of Medina in the Prophet's time, accepted Islam, he said to the Medinite Jews, "O assembly of Jews, fear God, for by God other than whom there is no deity, you know well that he is the messenger of God and that he has come with truth" (*Bukhari*, 5:250, also 6:7). According to the account of Ibn Ishaq, he also said, "You will find him described in your Torah and even named"[143] (Ibn Ishaq/*Muhammad*, p. 241). And, as mentioned previously, Ibn Salam (R) also stated,

> The description of Muhammad is written in the Torah, and also that Jesus son of Mary will be buried together with him. (*Mishkat*, 5772).

REFERENCES: Ibn Ishaq/*Muhammad*, p. 241; Maududi/*Q*, 61:fn. 7(3), 8(1).

THE NEW TESTAMENT PROPHECIES

The third prophecy that Muslims believe to refer to Muhammad (S) is contained in the following passage from the Gospel of John:

> Now this was John's testimony when the Jews of Jerusalem sent priests and Levites to ask him who he was. He did not fail to confess, but confessed freely, "I am not the Christ."

---

[143]The truthfulness of 'Abdullah ibn Salam is attested to by the Companion Sa'd bin Abi Waqqas, who said, "I [myself] never heard the Prophet (S) say about anyone walking on earth that he was of the people of Paradise except about 'Abdullah ibn Salam." Sa'd added: "And this verse was sent down concerning him: **And a witness from among the Children of Israel testifies to the like of it"** [46:10] — that is, that the Qur'an is from God (*Bukhari*, 5:157). According to another report, the Prophet (S) stated that 'Abdullah ibn Salam would be the tenth to enter Paradise [among the ten who were promised it] (*Mishkat*, 6231).

They asked him, "Then who are you? Are you Elijah?"

He said, "I am not."

"Are you the Prophet?"

He answered, "No."

Finally they said, "Who are you? Give us an answer to take back to those who sent us. What do you say about yourself?"

John replied in the words of Isaiah the prophet, "I am the voice of one calling in the desert, 'Make straight the way for the Lord.'"

Now some Pharisees who had been sent questioned him, "Why then do you baptize if you are not the Christ, nor Elijah, nor the Prophet?" (John 1:19-24)

This passage makes clear beyond the shadow of a doubt that another prophet was expected by the Jews of Jesus' time — a prophet who was neither Elijah (who had been taken up alive to Heaven), nor John himself, nor Christ (that is, the awaited Messiah). Maulana Maududi comments that

> These words [of John's] expressly show that the Israelites were awaiting another Prophet besides the Prophet Christ and the Prophet Elias [Elijah], and he was not the Prophet John. The belief about the coming of that Prophet was so well known and well established among the Israelites that a mere reference to him as "that prophet" was enough to call attention to him without any need to add: "The one who has been foretold in the Torah." Furthermore, it also shows that the advent of the prophet to whom they were referring was absolutely confirmed, for when these questions were asked of the Prophet John, he did not say that no other prophet was to come and therefore the questions were irrelevant. (Maududi/*Q*, 61:fn. 8[2])

The following passages in the Gospel of John referring to the *Parakletos* (generally translated as "the Comforter" or, in the New International Version translation used in this text, as "the Counselor") who was to come after Jesus, have also been interpreted as referring to Muhammad (S):

> And I will ask the Father, and he will give you another Counselor [*Parakletos*/Comforter] to be with you forever — the Spirit of truth. . . . But the Counselor, the Holy Spirit, whom the Father will send in my name, will teach you all things and will remind you of everything I have said to you. . . . I will not speak with you much longer, for the prince of this world is coming. (14:16, 26, 30)
>
> When the Counselor comes, whom I will send to you from the Father, the Spirit of truth who goes out from the Father, he will testify about me. (15:26)

> It is for your good that I am going away. Unless I go away, the Counselor will not come to you; but if I go, I will send him to you. When he comes, he will convict the world of guilt in regard to sin and righteousness and judgment: in regard to sin, because men do not believe in me; in regard to righteousness, because I am going to the Father, where you can see me no longer; and in regard to judgment, because the prince of this world now stands condemned. I have much more to say to you, more than you can now bear. But when he, the Spirit of truth, comes, he will guide you into all truth. He will not speak on his own; he will speak only what he hears, and he will tell you what is yet to come. He will bring glory to me by taking from what is mine and making it known to you. All that belongs to the Father is mine. That is why I said the Spirit will take from what is mine and make it known to you. In a little while you will see me no more, and then after a little while you will see me. (16:7-16)

In an attempt to sort out the meaning of the term *Parakletos* from these ambiguous passages, Muhammad Asad writes that the designation "Comforter"/"Counselor"

> is almost certainly a corruption of *Periklytos* ("the Much-Praised"), an exact Greek translation of the Aramaic term or name *Mawhamana*. (It is to be borne in mind that Aramaic was the language used in Palestine at the time of, and for some centuries after, Jesus, and was thus undoubtedly the language in which the original — now lost — texts of the Gospels were composed.) In view of the phonetic closeness of *Periklytos* and *Parakletos* it is easy to understand how the translator — or, more probably, a later scribe — confused these two expressions. It is significant that both the Aramaic *Mawhamana* and the Greek *Periklytos* have the same meanings as the two names of the Last Prophet, *Muhammad* and *Ahmad*, both of which are derived from the verb *hamida* ("he praised") and the noun *hamd* ("praise"). An even more unequivocal prediction of the advent of the Prophet Muhammad — mentioned by name, in its Arabic form — is said to be forthcoming from the so-called Gospel of St. Barnabas,[144] which, though now regarded as apocryphal, was accepted as authentic and was read in the churches until the year 496 of the Christian era, when it was banned as "heretical" by a decree of Pope Gelasius.

---

[144]The Gospel of Barnabas is also discussed in the commentaries of Maulana Maududi, 61, footnote 8(9-12), and Yusuf Ali, footnote 416. In this Gospel, Jesus speaks extensively about the coming of Muhammad (S). Hence, it is, understandably, the subject of much controversy. Now well-circulated in print, it can be obtained from sellers of Islamic literature, such as the publisher of this work.

However, since the original text of that Gospel is not available (having come down to us only in an Italian translation dating from the late sixteenth century), its authenticity cannot be established with certainty. (Asad/*Q*, 61:fn. 6)

Yusuf Ali elaborates on this theme:

"*Ahmad*", or "*Muhammad*", the Praised One, is almost a translation of the Greek word *Periclytos.* In the present Gospel of John, xiv.16, xv. 26, and xvi. 7, the word "Comforter" ["Counselor"] in the English version is [used] for the Greek word "*Paracletos*", which means "Advocate", "one called to the help of another, a kind friend", rather than "Comforter". Our doctors [of Islamic knowledge] contend that Paracletos is a corrupt reading for Periclytos, and that in their original saying of Jesus there was a prophecy of our holy Prophet *Ahmad* by name. Even if we read Paraclete, it would apply to the holy Prophet, who is "a Mercy for all creatures" (xxi. 107) and "most kind and merciful to the believers" (ix. 128). (Ali/*Q*, fn. 5438).

REFERENCES: Maududi/*Q*, 61:fns. 7-9; Ali/*Q*, fns. 5438, 416; Asad/*Q*, 61:fn. 6.

33. THE ARABIAN PROPHECIES

Those to whom We gave the scripture know him [Muhammad] as they known their own sons. (2:146)

Indeed, among the People of the Scripture are those who believe in God and what was revealed to you [Muhammad] and what was revealed to them, humbly submissive to God. They do not barter God's verses for a small price. Those will have their reward with their Lord. Indeed, God is swift in reckoning. (3:199)

Thus it was that Muhammad, God's peace and blessings be upon him, came into the world in the sixth century after Christ in a climate of anticipation of a prophet-to-come because of what had been foretold concerning that prophet in earlier scriptures — possibly even from what had been retained from the tongue of Jesus (A) himself concerning **"the messenger to come after me, whose name is Ahmad,"** if that prophecy had not been completely lost by that time. Writes Emel Esin:

> In the second half of the sixth century A.D., religious unrest still prevailed in Arabia and the surrounding countries. The religions of the scriptures had large followings, but they had not yet succeeded in conquering paganism entirely. Many were still awaiting the coming of divinely inspired teachers: the Jews expected their Messiah; some of the multitudinous Christian sects hoped for the arrival of the Comforter who had been promised to them in St. John's Gospel. Members of dualist religions also, such as the Zoroastrians, sought a human manifestation of their principle of light. (*Mecca the Blessed, Madinah the Radiant*, p. 62)

Three incidents are reported in the collections of ***hadith*** and the biographies of the Prophet (S) which attest to the fact that Muhammad (S) was recognized and identified as the awaited prophet by certain devout Christians of his time.

The first such incident occurred during Muhammad's boyhood. While on a trading trip to Syria with his uncle Abu Talib and other Qurayshites, he was summoned and questioned by a reclusive monk named Bahira, who understood from certain signs that the future prophet was among the people of the caravan. Several years later, on another journey to Syria, the signs of his future prophethood were recognized again by another monk, Nestor. And immediately after the first revelation in Hira' cave, his prophethood was recognized and testified to yet again by a devout, aged Christian of Mecca, Waraqah bin Naufal (R).

We report this matter below, narrated by the Prophet's wife 'A'ishah (R), interspersed with some of the Prophet's own words, as given in *Bukhari,* 1:3 and 4:605. We have interspersed this narrative with material taken from Ibn Ishaq's biography of the Holy Prophet (S).

The Story of Waraqah (R)

'A'ishah's narrative begins as follows:

> The first of what was manifested to the Messenger of God, God's peace and blessings be upon him, of the Revelation was the good dream during sleep, and he used not to see a dream but that it came like the breaking of dawn.
>
> He was then made to love solitude, and he would seclude himself in Hira' cave and remain there in devotion. He would worship for a number of nights before yearning for his family and would take provisions for that; then he would return to Khadijah and take provisions for the like of it, until the truth came to him while he was in Hira' cave.[144]
>
> The angel came to him and said, **"*Iqra'a* — read!"**
>
> He said, "I cannot read." He [the Prophet] said, "Then he took hold of me and pressed me until I reached the limit of my endurance. Then he released me and said, **"Read!"**[145]
>
> I said, "I cannot read." Then he took hold of me and pressed me a second time until I reached the limit of my endurance. Then he released me and said, "Read!"
>
> I said, "I cannot read." Then he took me and pressed me a third time, and then he released me and said,
>
> > **"Read, in the name of your Lord, who created — created man from a clinging clot.[146] Read, and your Lord is the Most Bountiful!"** [96:1-3]. (*Bukhari,* 1:3)

---

[144]This night on which this occurred is known as *Lailat al-Qadr*, the Night of Power. According to a ***hadith***, it falls on one of the odd-numbered nights of the last ten nights of Ramadan (*Bukhari,* 1:777).

[145]The word ***"Iqra"*** means both "recite" and "read," and is given as both in various translations of the Qur'an. However, **"Read"** may be the more accurate meaning, since Muhammad (S) was asked read the inscription, and because the subsequent verses of what he was asked to read included mention of **"the Pen"**.

Now, Muhammad's purity and refinement of character were such that, in his own words, "None of God's creatures was more hateful to me than an [ecstatic] poet or a man possessed; I could not even look at them." Overwhelmed with despair at the possibility that he might somehow have become one of them, he thought, "Woe be to me, whether poet or possessed! Never shall the Quraysh say such a thing about me! I will go to the top of the mountain and throw myself down so that I may kill myself and find rest."

With this intention, he left the cave. But when he was midway on the mountain, he heard a voice from the sky, saying, "O Muhammad, you are the Messenger of God and I am Gabriel!" And looking toward the sky, he saw the angel in the form of a man with his feet astride the horizon, saying, "O Muhammad, you are the Messenger of God and I am Gabriel!"

Forgetting his intention, Muhammad (S) stood gazing at him, motionless. When he turned his face away from him, no matter what part of the sky he looked at, he saw him, as before. He continued to stand there without moving, while the messengers whom Khadijah (R) had sent in search of him returned to her without finding him. Then the angel left him.

> Then the Messenger of God, God's peace and blessings be upon him, returned with it [the words of the revelation transmitted to him by the angel], and his heart was shaken. And he came to Khadijah daughter of Khuwaylid, may God be pleased with her. (*Bukhari*, 1:3)

"O Abul-Qasim," Khadijah said when he reached her, "where have you been? By God, I sent my messengers in search of you, and they reached the high ground above Mecca and returned to me."

"Woe be to me, whether poet or possessed!" Muhammad (S) exclaimed in the anguish of his soul.

> "Wrap me up, wrap me up!" [he said,] so they wrapped him up until the alarm had left him. And he said to Khadijah, telling her about the matter, "Truly, I fear for myself!"
>
> She said, "By no means! By God, God would never disgrace you. Indeed, you preserve the ties of relationship [with kindred], bear [people's] burdens, help the destitute, treat guests hospitably, and help the unfortunate to secure their rights."

---

[146]The word here is "'*alaq*," which refers to the early clot-like, clinging stage of the embryo in the womb. This may be understood as a subtle reminder to us of our humble and insignificant origins, and the greatness of the Creator, who fabricates, out of such materials, a human organism, with its immortal soul, genetic makeup, personal characteristics, faculties and organs.

Khadijah then went with him to Waraqah son of Naufal son of Asad son of 'Abd al-Uzza, the son of Khadijah's uncle, who had become a Christian during [the period of pre-Islamic] Ignorance, and he used to write books in Hebrew and wrote whatever God willed he write of the *Injil* in Hebrew. And he was an old man who was blind.

Khadijah said to him, "O son of my uncle, listen to the son of your brother!"

Waraqah said to him, "O son of my brother, what have you seen?" and so the Messenger of God, God's peace and blessings be upon him, told him what he had seen. Then Waraqah said to him, "That was the spirit [*namus*] whom God sent to Moses. Oh, if only I could be young during it, if only I could be alive when your people drive you out!"

Then the Messenger of God, God's peace and blessings be upon him said, "Then will they drive me out?"

He said, "Yes. Never has a man come with the like of what you have come with without [arousing] hostility . And if I should last to your day, I would assist you with strong support." But Waraqah did not delay in dying, and the Revelation paused. (*Bukhari*, 1:3, also 4:605)

Later, in confirmation of the Prophet's experience and refutation of the charges that he was insane, possessed or power-hungry that were being hurled at him by the people of his own tribe, God Most High was to reveal the following powerful passage:

By the star when it descends, your companion has not strayed nor has he erred, nor does he speak from whim. It [the Qur'an] is nothing but a revelation revealed, taught to him by one mighty in power, endowed with strength. And he [Gabriel] rose to [his] true form while he was in the higher horizon. Then he approached and descended, and was at a distance of two bow lengths or nearer, and He revealed to His slave [Muhammad] what He revealed. The heart did not falsify what it saw. Will you then dispute with him about what he saw? (53:1-12)

Two further incidents of this nature concern the Christian Negus of Abyssinia and the Christians of Najran, all of whom, as we have seen, readily perceived in Muhammad (S) the signs of a true prophet. Yet another incident, which has been preserved in vivid detail, concerns Heraclius, the powerful Christian emperor of the Byzantines, and the Prophet's cousin, Abu Sufyan (R).

REFERENCES: *Bukhari*, I:3, 4:605; Ibn Ishaq/*Muhammad*, pp. 79-82, 105-107; Lings /*Muhammad*, pp. 16-17, 29-30, 34-35, 43-45; Esin, *Mecca the Blessed, Madinah the Radiant*, pp. 62, 76, 79.

The Story of Abu Sufyan and Heraclius Caesar

In about the year 628 A.C., Muhammad (S), now dominant in Arabia, wrote letters to the rulers of neighboring countries, informing them of his prophethood and inviting them to accept God's religion. As we saw previously, one such letter was sent to the Abyssinian Negus. Another was dispatched to the Byzantine emperor, Heraclius Caesar, who was a Christian.

Ibn Ishaq informs us that at the time Heraclius received this letter, he had recently routed the Persians from Syria and Egypt, and was possibly contemplating a military campaign southward into Arabia. In fact, reports Ibn 'Abbas (R), the emperor had but lately walked from Homs in Syria to the holy city of Jerusalem as a sign of gratitude to God for the victory He had granted him over the Persians.

The Prophet's letter reached Heraclius in Jerusalem. After reading it, the emperor said, "Seek out for me any of his people and ask them about the Messenger of God."[148]

Now, Abu Sufyan bin Harb (R) was the Prophet's distant cousin, but he had been, up to that time, one of bitterest enemies of both Muhammad (S) and his faith. At the time of these events, he was in Syria (Sham) with some Qurayshite merchants who had gone there for trading during the period of the peace treaty between the Prophet (S) and the Quraysh.

---

[148]It is reported that Heraclius was an astrologer who studied the stars. One morning the nobles surrounding him noticed that he seemed sad. When they tried to cheer him up, he said, "During the night, when I looked at the stars, the king of the circumcised people appeared. So who practices circumcision among this nation?" They said, "There are no circumcised people except the Jews, so do not be uneasy about their affair but write to the rulers of the cities [under your command] to kill the Jews that are in them." While they were occupied with this matter, a man was brought to Heraclius who had been sent by the king of Ghassan, bringing tidings of the Messenger of God (S). When he heard the news, Heraclius said, "Go and see whether he is circumcised or not." Then they looked at the man and informed him that he was circumcised, so Heraclius asked him about the Arabs and he told him that they practiced circumcision. Heraclius said, "This is the dominance of this nation" (*Bukhari*, 1:3; Ibn Ishaq/*Muhammad*, p. 654).

Later, when God opened his heart to accept Islam, Abu Sufyan (R) was to recount the details of his encounter with the Byzantine emperor to Ibn 'Abbas (R). He said:

> Caesar's messenger found us somewhere in Syria. Then he proceeded with me and my companions until we arrived in Jerusalem, and so we went in to him. And he was seated among his royal assembly with the crown upon him, surrounded by the dignitaries of Byzantium.
>
> He then said to his translator, "Ask them which of them is closest in relationship to that man who claims that he is a prophet."
>
> I said, "I am the closest of them in relationship to him."
>
> He asked, "What is the relationship between you and him?"
>
> I said, "He is my cousin on my father's side," for that day there was no one in the caravan from among the Bani 'Abd al-Manaf [Muhammad's kinsfolk] except myself.
>
> Caesar then said, "Have him come close," and he ordered my companions to stand behind me at my shoulder. And he said to his translator, "Tell his companions that I am going to ask that man about the one who claims that he is a prophet. Then, if he lies, they are to contradict him."
>
> By God, [Abu Sufyan added,] that day, if I had not been ashamed that my companions would report a lie concerning me, I would have lied about him when he asked me about him, but as I was ashamed of having a lie reported concerning myself, I told the truth."[149] (*Bukhari*, 4:191)

Heraclius first asked Abu Sufyan about the Prophet's lineage among his people, and he replied, "He is a person of good lineage among us." Heraclius

---

[149]Ibn Ishaq reports that Abu Sufyan, in telling the story later, said, "By God, I have never seen a man whom I consider more shrewd than that uncircumcised man," for after ordering Abu Sufyan to approach and seating him in front of himself, with his companions behind him, Heraclius said, "I will interrogate him," while to his companions he said, "If he lies, contradict him." Thus, Abu Sufyan was cornered. He later said, "But, by God, if I were to have lied they would not have contradicted me," meaning that since they were his people, they would not have pointed out his lies to others. "But," he continued, "I am a man of high birth, too honorable to lie, and I knew it was only too easy for them, if I lied to him, to remember it against me and repeat it in my name. Consequently, I did not lie to him."

Heraclius then said to Abu Sufyan, "Tell me about this man who has appeared among you, making these claims." Abu Sufyan then began to belittle Muhammad (S) and speak disparagingly of his affair. "Do not let him cause you anxiety," he said to Heraclius. "His importance is less than you have heard." But ignoring his words, Heraclius said, "Tell me what I ask you about him," whereupon Abu Sufyan told Heraclius to ask whatever he liked (Ibn Ishaq/*Muhammad*, pp. 654-655).

then asked him if anyone among them had said such a thing before him, and Abu Sufyan replied in the negative. Next, Heraclius asked if anyone had ever accused him of lying before he said what he said — that is, concerning his prophethood — and Abu Sufyan, mindful of his listening companions, replied in the negative.

Heraclius then asked if anyone among his ancestors had been a king, to which Abu Sufyan replied in the negative. Was it the eminent people who followed him or the weak? Heraclius asked, and Abu Sufyan replied, "No, rather the weak among them." The emperor then asked if his followers were increasing or decreasing, and Abu Sufyan truthfully replied that they were increasing. Had anyone apostasized in displeasure from his religion after entering it? Heraclius asked, and Abu Sufyan, ever conscious of his listeners, replied in the negative.

Had he ever behaved treacherously? Heraclius asked next. "No," Abu Sufyan replied. "But now that we have a truce with him, we are afraid that he will act treacherously." However, the emperor paid no attention to his words. Later, in reporting the matter, Abu Sufyan added, "I could not insert any word that would denigrate him out of fear that something other than it would be reported concerning me," meaning that this was the only point at which he was able to slip in anything against Muhammad (S).

"Then have you fought with him and has he fought with you?" Heraclius asked, and Abu Sufyan replied in the affirmative. The emperor then asked about the nature of the war between them, to which Abu Sufyan replied that it was variable and alternating, turning to the Quraysh at one time and turning to Muhammad at another. Abu Sufyan's narrative continues:

> Heraclius then asked, "So what does he enjoin on you to do?"
>
> I said, "He enjoins on us that we worship God alone and that we not associate anything with Him, and he prohibits us from what our forefathers worshipped, and commands us to observe *salat* and give charity and be chaste, and to fulfill promises and keep trusts."
>
> When I had said that to him, he said to his translator, "Tell him, 'Indeed, I asked you about his family among you and you declared that he was of good family, and thus are the prophets sent among the good families of their people. And I asked you if anyone among you had said such a thing before him and you declared that they had not, and if you had said that someone among you had said such a thing before him, I would have said that that man was following what had been said before him. And I asked you if he had ever been accused of lying before he said what he said and you declared he had not, so I understood that one who does not lie about people does not lie about God. And I asked you if

there had been a king among his forefathers and you declared there had not, and if you had said that there had been a king among his forefathers, I would have said that he was re-claiming his forefather's kingdom.

"'And I asked you if the eminent people follow him or their weak, and you declared that their weak follow him, and those follow the prophets. And I asked you if they were increasing or decreasing and you declared that they were increasing, and thus is faith, so that it may be complete. And I asked you if anyone had apostasized in displeasure from his religion after entering it and you declared that they had not, and this is the sign of faith, which enters into the innermost part of the heart so that no one is displeased with it.

"'And I asked you if he had acted treacherously and you declared that he had not, and thus do the prophets not act treacherously. And I asked you if you had fought him and he had fought you, and you declared that it had happened, and that your war and his war varied in fortune, turning to yourselves at one time and turning to him at another, and thus are the prophets tried, but the final victory is theirs.

"'And I asked you what he enjoins on you, and you declared that he enjoins on you to worship God and not associate anything with Him, and that he prohibits you from what your fathers worshipped, and charges you with *salat* and charity and chastity, and fulfilling promises and keeping trusts, and these are the characteristics of the prophet whom I knew would appear, although I did not know that he would be from among you. And if what you say is true, he will soon occupy what is under my feet. And if I could hope to reach him, I would certainly undertake to meet him, and if I were with him I would wash his feet!'"

Then he called for the letter of the Messenger of God, God's peace and blessings be upon him, which had been dispatched by Dihya to the governor of Busra, who had given it to Heraclius. And he read it and it was as follows:

> In the name of God, the Beneficent, the Merciful. From Muhammad, the slave of God and His messenger, to Heraclius, ruler of Byzantium. Peace be on him who follows the guidance.
>
> To proceed: Indeed, I invite you with the invitation of Islam. Accept Islam and you will be safe, and if you accept Islam, God will grant your reward twice over. But if you turn away,

then the sin of the Arisiyin will be upon you.[149] And, **O People of the Scripture, come to a word common between us and you: that we will not worship anyone but God, nor associate anyone with Him, nor take one another as lords besides God. But if they turn away, then say, "Bear witness that we are Muslims** [3:64].

When he had finished [reading] his letter, the Byzantine noble surrounding him raised their voices, and their clamor was so great that I could not understand what they were saying, and he ordered us [out] and we left. Then when I came out with my companions and was alone with them, I said to them, 'The affair of Ibn Abi Kabashah [a disparaging nickname for the Prophet] has reached the point at which even this king of the Bani al-Asfar [Romans] is afraid of him.'"

By God, [Abu Sufyan concluded,] I remained in a state of dejection, convinced that his affair would be victorious, until God caused Islam to enter my heart, even though I detested it. (*Bukhari*, 1:6, 4:191)

Indeed, Heraclius' conviction of Muhammad's prophethood, although it was based on hearsay, was so clear and strong that the emperor then abandoned thoughts of a military campaign southward. Instead, he proposed that a treaty be made with the Prophet (S), giving him the province of Syria on the condition that he not advance beyond its northern frontier. However, this proposal met with such hostility from his generals that he was forced to abandon it.

It is reported that Heraclius, recognizing in Muhammad (S) the prophet whose description was found in Christian scripture, then professed his faith in him. According to some reports, he did so openly, but according to others, he kept his Islam a secret, fearing for his life at the hands of his Christian clergy and advisors. Ibn Ishaq reports two incidents in which Heraclius tested the waters to ascertain his people's reaction to his acceptance of Muhammad's prophethood. When he saw how strongly they opposed it, even going so far as to beat to death one of their bishops who had declared his faith in Islam, he did not press the matter further with them, but, knowing that his territory would soon be conquered by the army of the Messenger of God (S), withdrew in haste to Constantinople.

---

[149]The Arisiyin are said to have been fire-worshipping Persian peasants and other menials, employed by the Christians. The meaning of the last sentence is that if the ruler of these people refused to accept the true faith, the responsibility for their misguidance would rest on him.

REFERENCES: *Bukhari*, 1:6, 1:48, 4:191; Abu Dawud, 5117; Ibn Ishaq/*Muhammad*, pp. 654-657; Qadi Iyad/*Ash-Shifa*, pp. 202-203; Lings/*Muhammad*, pp. 260, 317; Ayoub/Q, II:203-204.

34. A Final Word

O mankind, the Messenger has come to you with the truth from your Lord, so believe in it; it is better for you. . . . O mankind, there has come to you a conclusive proof from your Lord, and We have sent down to you a clear light. (4:170, 174)

With this, we bring to a close the stories of the prophets of Islam from Adam through Jesus, God's peace and blessings be upon them all, based on the accounts revealed in the Noble Qur'an.

God Most High refers to His Last Testament to mankind as **"the Criterion"**[150] (2:185, 5:48/51, 25:1). This means, among other things, that the Qur'an is the divinely-revealed standard by which all accounts of the prophets are to be weighed, confirming those that agree with it, and challenging and correcting those that contradict it. And the Lord of the worlds addresses all mankind, saying,

> **There is certainly a lesson in their [the prophets'] stories for those of understanding. Never was it [the Qur'an] an invented narration, but rather a confirmation of what was before it and a detailed explanation of all things, and guidance and mercy for people who believe.** (12:111)

The lessons of these stories — the stories of completely real human beings who once lived and carried out their divinely-appointed missions upon our

---

[150]That is, the criterion of truth and falsehood, because it is from the Knower of all things, who says concerning it:

> **This is the Book about which there is no doubt, a guidance for those who are mindful of God.** (2:2)
>
> **He has sent down upon you [Muhammad] the Book with truth, confirming what was before it.** (3:3-4)
>
> **O mankind, the Messenger has come to you with the truth from your Lord, so believe; it is better for you.** (4:170)
>
> **And We have revealed to you [Muhammad] the Book in truth, confirming that which preceded it of the scripture and as a criterion over it.** (5:48/51)
>
> **[This is] the revelation of the Book about which there is no doubt from the Lord of the worlds. Or do they say, "He has fabricated it"? Rather, it is the truth from your Lord, that you may warn a people to whom no warner has come before you, that perhaps they might be guided.** (32:2-3)
>
> **Then, by the Lord of heaven and earth, indeed it is the truth just as [surely] as it is that you are speaking.** (51:23)

earth — are universal, understandable to people of all times and places, from the keenest thinkers and deepest mystics among mankind, with all the complexity of their intellects and profundity of their spiritual insights, down to the simplest village elders, telling these stories to wide-eyed children. There is something in them for all people, in varying levels of complexity and multiple layers of meaning.

However, these stories are meant not only to inspire but also to provide examples for living, for while we cannot be prophets, we can nevertheless try to emulate the characteristics of the best of God's servants. The prophets' attributes, words and actions form a fabric of sincerity and God-consciousness that provides a working model for people of varying levels and walks of life under all sorts of conditions and circumstances.

Perhaps at some time during the course of our lives we may have occasion to recall and take example from what we know of these chosen ones — for instance, the prolonged forbearance of Noah; the steadfast surrender of Abraham and Ishmael; the trust and patience of Jacob and Job; the attentiveness to the working of the divine Will of Joseph; the courage and forthrightness of Moses; the worshipfulness of David; the wisdom and thankfulness of Solomon; the purity and devoutness of Mary; and the holy commitment to the requirements of nearness to God of John and Jesus, God's peace and blessings be upon them all. For some of us, these may constitute frequently referred-to models of servanthood, submission and spirituality, as well as of action, while for others, perhaps such examples may be recalled, like the fragments of a long-forgotten melody, in moments of distress or need, as markers guiding the way.

Now, while the prophets whose stories we have presented in this volume are indeed the noblest and best among mankind, they are, at the same time, the precursors and forerunners of the last in their line — the most perfect of all created beings, the beloved of God, Muhammad (S), whose exalted stature and unparalleled rank He lauds in numerous verses of the Qur'an, such as the following:

> **We have not sent you [Muhammad] but as a mercy for all the worlds.** (21:107)
>
> **Indeed, yours is an uninterrupted reward, and indeed, you are of a magnificent character.** (68:3-4)
>
> **O Prophet, indeed, We have sent you as a witness and a bringer of good tidings and a warner and one who calls to God, by His permission, and a luminous lamp.** (33:45-46; also 48:810)

> **There is surely an excellent example for you in the Messenger of God for one whose hope is in God and the Last Day, and who remembers God much.** (33:21)
>
> **Whoever obeys the Messenger has obeyed God.** (4:80)
>
> **Say, [O Muhammad:] "If you love God, then follow me; God will love you and forgive you your sins. And God is Forgiving and Merciful."** (3:31)
>
> **And God has revealed to you [Muhammad] the Book and wisdom, and has taught you that which you did not know. And God's favor to you is immense.** (4:113)
>
> **Indeed, God and His angels bless the Prophet. O you who believe, bless him and greet him with a goodly greeting.** (23:56)

Perhaps these few verses, in addition to those cited throughout this text, may be sufficient to give a very faint hint of the magnificent nature and exalted rank of God's Last Messenger (S), which is documented in verse after verse of the Qur'an and numerous ***ahadith.*** Indeed, there have been many luminous souls throughout the course of man's history who were granted an especially intimate relationship with their Lord. But Muhammad (S), the crown jewel and pinnacle of creation, the greatest spiritual luminary among all beings, surpassed them all in nearness to his Lord, connecting within himself and dwelling simultaneously in both the earthly and heavenly realms.

And God the Praised and Glorious granted His beloved one unprecedented honors and divine favors, admitting him to the ultimate station of nearness to Himself among all created beings, so that he beheld the seven heavens and hells and their inhabitants, and saw and conversed intimately with the Lord of Honor and Majesty.[151] And He promised to raise Muhammad (S) to **a praiseworthy station** (17:79), granting him, the **mercy for the worlds** (21:107), the highest of privileges and blessings: the assurance of acceptance of his intercession for His servants, by means of which countless numbers would be taken out of Hell.[152]

---

[151]That is, during the Prophet's Ascension (*Me'raj*) to the divine Presence, which is memorialized in the verse,

> **Glory be to Him who took His slave by night from the Sacred Mosque [in Mecca] to the Farthest Mosque [*Masjid al-Aqsa*, at the site of Solomon's Temple in Jerusalem], whose surroundings We have blessed, to show him something of Our signs.** (17:1)

[152]'Abdullah ibn 'Umar said, "Indeed, the people will be on their knees on the Day of Resurrection. Each nation will go after its prophet, saying, "O such-and-such, intercede!" until the inter-

May God's boundless and grace, blessings, mercy and peace be upon the chief of the prophets and messengers, Muhammad, through whom these stories of the prophets were conveyed, and who guided mankind to the knowledge of Him and to His light and love.[154]

Dear reader, I am happy that you have remained with me up to these final words. I hope you have found these stories as inspiring and fascinating in reading as I did in writing them, and that the lessons they contain may prove to be of value and meaning to you in your personal journey.

With all my heart, I thank and praise God Most Gracious who made it possible, filling the years of this work with satisfaction and light, and I ask His acceptance of this very humble effort and pardon for any inadvertent errors it may contain. To Him belongs all praise and honor and glory throughout eternity, to the number of atoms of His creation, with every heartbeat and breath and movement, every thought and feeling. We surrender to Him and beseech His forgiveness and mercy.

May His eternal peace and blessings be upon all His honored, holy messengers, especially upon His beloved Muhammad, the Seal of the Prophets and the noblest of mankind, the pattern and example of God-consciousness and every lovely characteristic. And may He, the Most Merciful, bless and guide you, and grant you faith, understanding and light. And so I bid you farewell, until the Day when our Lord shall gather us in His glorious Divine Presence, all together, for the Eternal Life.

And peace be upon the messengers, and praise be to God,
Lord of the worlds! (37:181-182)

---

cession ends with Muhammad, God's peace and blessings be upon him, for that will be the day when God will raise him to **a praiseworthy station**" [17:79] (*Bukhari*, 6:242).

[154]For readers desiring further material about the Holy Prophet (S), the following works are suggested: (1) Martin Lings reverent, sensitive work, *Muhammad, his life based on the earliest sources*, published jointly in U.K. in 1983 by George Allen & Unwin, Ltd. and The Islamic Texts Society (ISBN 0-04-297042-3). (2) The classic, *Muhammad, Messenger of Allah (Ash-Shifa of Qadi 'Iyad)*, by Qadi 'Iyad ibn Musa al-Yahsubi, translated from the Arabic by Aisha Abdarrahman Bewley, published in 1991 by Madinah Press, Granada, Spain, in association with the Islamic Book Trust, Kuala Lumpur, Malaysia, as part of the Islamic Classical Library Edition. It has been said that this book, which dates back to the twelfth century C.E., is perhaps the most frequently used and commented-upon work describing the Prophet's life, qualities and miracles. Indeed, this book was so highly regarded in the Muslim world that it was said that if *Ash-Shifa* were found in a house, that house would not suffer any harm, and that if a sick person read it or heard its recitation, God would restore his health. Inquiries concerning both books may be addressed to the publisher of this work or other booksellers.

Qur'anic References — The Family of 'Imran and Related Matters

2:87

And We certainly gave Moses the scripture and followed him by a succession of [other] messengers. And We granted Jesus son of Mary clear proofs and supported him with the holy spirit [Gabriel].

2:116-117

And they say, "God has taken a son." May He be glorified! Rather, to Him belongs whatever is in the heavens and the earth. All are devoutly obedient to Him. (116) Originator of the heavens and the earth, when He decrees a matter, He but says to it "Be!" and it is. (117)

2:136

Say, [O Muhammad:] "We believe in God and what was revealed to us, and what was revealed to Abraham and Ishmael and Isaac and Jacob and the descendants [of Israel], and what was given to Moses and Jesus, and what was given to [all] the prophets by their Lord. We make no distinction between any of them, and we surrender to Him in Islam."

2:253

Those messengers — We favored some of them over others. Among them were those to whom God spoke, and He exalted some of them in rank. And We granted Jesus son of Mary clear proofs and supported him with the holy spirit [Gabriel]. If God had willed, those succeeding them would not have fought each other after the clear proofs came to them. But they differed, and some of them believed and some of them disbelieved. And if God had willed, they would not have fought each other, but God does whatever He intends.

3:33-64

Indeed, God chose Adam and Noah and the family of Abraham and the family of 'Imran above mankind, (33) descendants of one another. And God is Hearing and Knowing. (34)

[Mention, O Muhammad,] when the wife of 'Imran said, "My Lord, indeed, I pledge to You what is in my womb, consecrated [to You], so accept this from me. Indeed, You are the Hearing, the Knowing." (35)

But when she gave birth to her, she said, "My Lord, I have given birth to a female," whereas God was well-aware what she had given birth to. "And the male is not like the female. And I have named her Mary, and I seek refuge in You for her and her descendants from Satan the accursed." (36)

So her Lord accepted her with gracious acceptance and caused her to grow in a goodly manner and placed her in the care of Zechariah. Each time Zechariah went in to her in the sanctuary, he found provision with her. He said, "O Mary, whence does this come to you?"

She said, "It is from God. Indeed, God provides for whomever He wills without reckoning." (37)

Then Zechariah called upon his Lord, saying, "My Lord, grant me, from Yourself, a goodly offspring. Indeed, you are Hearer of supplication." (38)

Then the angels called him while he was standing in prayer in the sanctuary, [saying,] "Indeed, God gives you good tidings of John, confirming a word from God, and honorable and abstinent, and a prophet from among the righteous." (39)

He said, "My Lord, how will I have a son when I have reached old age and my wife is barren?"

He [the angel] said, "Such is God; He does what He wills." (40)

He said, "My Lord, appoint a sign for me."

He said, "Your sign is that you will not speak to people for three days except by gesture. And remember your Lord much, and glorify [Him] in the evening and the morning." (41)

And [mention] when the angels said, "O Mary, indeed, God has chosen you and purified you and preferred you above the women of mankind. (42) O Mary, be devoutly obedient to your Lord, and prostrate and bow with those who bow [to Him]." (43)

That is of the tidings of the Unseen which We reveal to you [Muhammad]. And you were not with them when they cast their pens as to which of them should be responsible for Mary, nor were you with them when they disputed [concerning it]. (44)

[And mention] when the angels said, "O Mary, indeed, God gives you good tidings of a word from Him, whose name will be the Messiah, Jesus son of Mary, distinguished in this world and the Hereafter, and among those brought near [to Him]. (45) He will speak to people in the cradle and in maturity, and will be among the righteous." (46)

She said, "My Lord, how will I have a child when no man has touched me?"

He said, "Such is God; He creates what He wills. When He decrees a matter, He but says to it 'Be!' and it is. (47) And He will teach him the book and wisdom, and the *Taurat* and the *Injil*, (48) and [make him] a messenger to the Children of Israel, [saying,] 'Indeed, I have come to you with a sign from your Lord, in that I mold for you from clay, as it were, the form of a bird; then I breathe into it and it becomes a bird by God's leave. And I cure the blind and the leper and revive the dead by God's leave. And I inform you about what you eat and what you store in your houses. Indeed, in that is a sign for you, if you are believers. (49) And [I have come] confirming what preceded me of the *Taurat* and to make permissible for you some of what was prohibited to you. And I have come to you with a sign from your Lord, so be mindful of God and obey me. (50) Indeed, God is my Lord and your Lord, so worship Him. This is a straight path.'" (51)

Then, when Jesus became aware of disbelief among them, he said, "Who will be my supporters for God?"

The apostles said, "We are supporters of God. We believe in God and bear witness that we are *muslims.* (52) Our Lord, we believe in what You have revealed and follow the messenger, so inscribe us among the witnesses." (53)

And they [the enemies of Jesus] schemed and God schemed, and God is the Best of Schemers. (54) [Mention] when God said, "O Jesus, indeed, I will take you and raise you to Myself, and purify you of those who disbelieve and make those who follow you superior to those who disbelieve until the Day of Resurrection. Then to Me is your return, and I will judge between you concerning that about which you used to differ. (55) Then, as for those who disbelieved, I will punish them with a severe punishment in the world and the Hereafter, and they will have no helpers." (56) And as for those who believed and did righteous deeds, He will give them their rewards in full, but God does not like the wrong-doers. (57)

This is what We recite to you [Muhammad] of the verses and the wise Reminder. (58) Indeed, the similie of Jesus with God is like that of Adam: He created him of dust, then He said to him "Be!" and he was. (59)

The truth is from your Lord, so do not be among the doubters. (60) Then whoever argues with you about it after the knowledge has come to you, say: "Come! Let us call our sons and your sons, and our women and your women, and ourselves and yourselves, and then earnestly supplicate and invoke God's curse upon the liars." (61) Indeed, this is the true narrative. And there is no deity except God, and indeed, God is the Almighty, the Wise. (62) But if they turn away, then God is surely Knowing of the corrupters. (63)

Say, [O Muhammad:] "O People of the Scripture, come to a word common between us and you: that we will not worship anyone but God, nor associate anyone with Him, nor take one another as lords besides God." But if they turn away, then say, "Bear witness that we are Muslims." (64)

3:79-85

It is not for a mortal that God should grant him scripture and judgment and prophethood, and then he should say to people, "Be worshippers of me instead of God," but rather, "Be pious people of the Lord because of what you have taught of the scripture and because of what you have studied." (79) Nor would he order you to take the angels and the prophets as lords. Would he order you to unbelief after you had been Muslims? (80)

And [recall, O People of the Scripture,] when God took a covenant from the prophets, [saying,] "Whatever I give you of scripture and wisdom, and then there comes to you a messenger confirming what is with you, you will believe in him and support him." He said, "Have you acknowledged and accepted My burden concerning that?"

They said, "We have acknowledged it."

He said, "Then bear witness, and I am with you among the witnesses." (81) Then whoever turns away after that, they are the transgressors. (82) Is it then other than the religion of God they desire, while whoever is in the heavens and the earth has submitted to Him, willingly or unwillingly, and they will be returned to Him? (83)

Say, [O Muhammad:] "We believe in God and what was revealed to us, and what was revealed to Abraham and Ishmael and Isaac and Jacob and the descendants [of Israel], and what was given to Moses and Jesus, and what was given to the prophets by their Lord. We make no distinction between any of them, and we surrender to Him [in Islam]." (84) And whoever desires a religion other than Islam, never will it be accepted from him, and in the Hereafter he will be among the losers. (85)

4:155-159

Then [punishment came upon the Israelites] because of their breaking of their covenant and their disbelief in God's signs, and their killing of the prophets without right and their saying, "Our hearts are wrapped" — no, rather, God has sealed them because of their unbelief, so they do not believe, except a few; (155) and [because of] their unbelief and their uttering a great slander against Mary, (156) and their saying, "Indeed, we killed the Messiah, Jesus son of Mary, God's messenger," while they did not kill him nor crucify him, but it was made to appear so to them. And indeed, those who differ concerning it are in doubt about it. They have no knowledge concerning it except the following of assumption, and of a certainty they did not kill him. (157) Rather, God raised him to Himself, and God is Almighty and Wise. (158) And there is no one among the People of the Scripture but will surely believe in him before his death, and on the Day of Resurrection he will be a witness against them. (159)

4:163

Indeed, We have revealed to you [Muhammad] as We revealed to Noah and the prophets after him; and We revealed to Abraham and Ishmael and Isaac and Jacob and the descendants [of Israel], and Jesus and Job and Jonah and Aaron and Solomon, and We granted David the *Zabur*.

4:170-172

O mankind, the Messenger has come to you with the truth from your Lord, so believe in it; it is better for you. But if you disbelieve, then indeed, to God belongs whatever is in the heavens and the earth. And God is ever Knowing and Wise. (170)

O People of the Scripture, do not exceed the limits in your religion or say about God except the truth. The Messiah, Jesus son of Mary, was but a messenger of God and His word which He bestowed upon Mary and a spirit from Him. So believe in God and His messengers. And do not say "Three"; refrain — it is better for you. Indeed, God is but one God. Exalted is He above having a son! To Him belongs whatever is in the heavens and whatever is on the earth. And God is sufficient as Disposer of affairs. (171) Never would the Messiah disdain to be a slave to God, nor the angels, near [to Him]. Whoever disdains His worship and is arrogant, He will gather them to Himself, all together. (172)

5:17/19

They who say, "God is the Messiah, son of Mary," have certainly disbelieved. Say, [O Muhammad:] "Then who could prevail against God if He intended to destroy the Messiah, son of Mary, or his mother or everyone on the earth?" And to God belongs the dominion of the heavens and the earth and whatever is between them. He creates whatever He wills, and God is Powerful over all things.

5:46/49

And We sent, following in their footsteps, Jesus son of Mary, confiming that which preceded him of the *Taurat*, and We granted him the *Injil*, wherein was guidance and light, and confirming that which preceded it of the *Taurat*, as guidance and instruction for the righteous.

5:72-79/75-82

They who say, "God is the Messiah, son of Mary," have certainly disbelieved, whereas the Messiah said, "O Children of Israel, worship God, my Lord and your Lord." Indeed, whoever ascribes partners to God, God has forbidden him Paradise and his abode is the Fire. And the wrong-doers will have no helpers. (72/75)

They who say, "God is a third of three," have certainly disbelieved, while there is no deity except one God. And if they do not desist from what they are saying, there will surely afflict the disbelievers among them a painful punishment. (73/76) Will they not then repent to God and seek His forgiveness? And God is Forgiving and Merciful. (74/77)

The Messiah, son of Mary, was nothing but a messenger; messengers had passed on before him. And his mother was a woman of truth. They both used to eat food. See how We make clear to them the signs; then see how they are deluded! (75/78)

Say, [O Muhammad:] "Do you worship, besides God, that which has no power of harm or benefit for you, while it is God who is the Hearing, the Knowing?" (76/79) Say: "O People of the Scripture, do not exceed the limits beyond the truth in your religion, nor follow the fancies of a people who had previously gone astray and misled many, and have strayed from the soundness of the way." (77/80)

Those who disbelieved among the Children of Israel were cursed by the tongue of David and Jesus son of Mary. That was because they disobeyed and transgressed. (78/81) They used not to prohibit one another from wrong-doing that they did. Wretched indeed was that which they used to do! (79/82)

5:109-118/112-121

[Be mindful of] the Day God will assemble the messengers and say, "What was the response you received?"

They will say, "We have no knowledge. Indeed, it is You who are Knower of the Unseen" (109/112) — [the Day] when God will say, "O Jesus son of Mary, recall My favor to you and to your mother when I supported you with the holy spirit [Gabriel,] and you spoke to people in the cradle and in maturity; and when I taught you the book and wisdom, and the *Taurat* and the *Injil*; and when you molded from clay, as it were, the form of a bird by My leave, then you breathed into it and it became a bird by My leave, and you cured the blind and the leper by My leave; and when you brought forth the dead by My leave; and when I restrained the Children of Israel from you when you came to them with clear proofs, and those who disbelieved among them said, 'This is nothing but obvious magic.'" (110/113)

And [recall] when I inspired to the apostles, "Believe in Me and in My messenger [Jesus]."

They said, "We believe, so bear witness that indeed we are *muslims*." (111/114)

And [recall] when the apostles said, "O Jesus son of Mary, could your Lord send down to us a table from Heaven?"

He said, "Fear God, if you are believers!" (112/115)

They said, "We desire to eat from it and let our hearts be reassured and know that you have been truthful to us and be among the witnesses of it." (113/116)

Jesus son of Mary said, "O God, our Lord, send down to us a table from Heaven, to be a festival for us, for the first of us and the last of us, and a sign from You. And provide for us, and You are the Best of Providers." (114/117)

God said, "Indeed, I will send it down to you. But whoever among you disbelieves afterwards, I will surely punish him with a punishment by which I have not punished anyone among mankind!" (115/118)

And [be mindful of the Day] when God will say, "O Jesus son of Mary, did you say to people, 'Take me and my mother as deities besides God'?"

He will say, "May You be glorified! It was not for me to say that to which I had no right. If I had said it, You would have known it. You know what is within my self but I do not know what is within Your Self; indeed, it is You who are Knower of the Unseen. (116/119) I did not say to them except what You commanded me: to worship God, my Lord and your Lord. And I was a witness over them as long as I was among them; but when You took me up, You were the Observer over them, and You are Witness over all things. (117/120) If you should punish them, indeed, they are Your slaves; but if You forgive them, indeed, it is You who are the Almighty, the Wise." (118/121)

6:84-85

And We granted him [Abraham] Isaac and Jacob; each [of them] We guided. And previously We guided Noah, and among his descendants, David and Solomon and Job and Joseph and Moses and Aaron. And thus do We reward the doers of good. (84) And Zechariah and John and Jesus and Elijah — all were among the righteous. (85)

6:100-102

But they have ascribed partners to God — the jinn, whereas He created them — and have falsely attributed to Him sons and daughters without knowledge. Exalted is He and high above what they attribute [to Him]! (100) Originator of the heavens and the earth — how could He have a son while He does not have a consort? And He created all things and He is Knowing of all things? (101) That is God, your Lord; there is no deity except Him, the Creator of all things, so worship Him [alone]. And He is Disposer of all things. (102)

9:30-31

The Jews say, "Ezra is God's Son," and the Christians say, "The Messiah is God's Son." That is their saying with their mouths; they [but] imitate the saying of those who disbelieved [before them]. God will destroy them; how deluded they are! (30) They have taken their scholars and monks as lords besides God, and the Messiah, son of Mary, while they were not commanded but to worship one God; there is no deity except Him. Far removed is He from what they associate with Him! (31)

10:68-69

They say, "God has taken a son." Glorified is He; He is the Self-Sufficient! To Him belongs whatever is in the heavens and whatever is on the earth. No authority do you have for this. Do you say about God that which you do not know? (68) Say, [O Muhammad:] "Indeed, those who fabricate falsehood about God will not prosper." (69)

16:51-52

And God said, "Do not take two deities. He is but one God; therefore, fear Me alone." (51) And to Him belongs whatever is in the heavens and the earth, and to Him is due perpetual obedience. Then is it other than God that you fear? (52)

17:111

And say, [O Muhammad:] "Praise be to God, who has not taken a son and has no partner in [His] dominion, nor is there any protector for Him from weakness. And extol him with [great] extolling."

18:1-5

Praise be to God, who has sent down the Book to His slave and has not placed therein any crookedness. (1) [He has made it] straight, to warn of a severe punishment from Him and to give good tidings to the believers who do righteous deeds that they will have a goodly recompense, (2) abiding therein forever, (3) and to warn those who say, "God has taken a son." (4) They have no knowledge of it, nor had their fathers. Grave is the word that issues from their mouths. They speak nothing but a lie! (5)

19:2-37

[This is] a mention of the mercy of your Lord to His slave Zechariah, (2) when he called to his Lord a secret call. (3)

He said, "My Lord, indeed, my bones have weakened and my head has turned white, but never have I been unblest in my supplication to You, my Lord. (4) And indeed, I fear the successors after me and my wife is barren, so grant me, from Yourself, an heir (5) who will inherit me and inherit from the family of Jacob. And make him, my Lord, well-pleasing." (6)

"O Zechariah, indeed, We give you good tidings of a boy whose name will be John. We have not appointed this for anyone previously." (7)

He said, "My Lord, how will I have a boy when my wife has been barren and I have reached extreme old age?" (8)

He [the angel] said, "Thus! Your Lord says, 'It is easy for Me, for I created you previously while you were nothing.'" (9)

He said, "My Lord, appoint a sign for me."

He said, "Your sign is that you will not speak to people for three nights, [although being] sound." (10) Then he came out to his people from the *mihrab* and signaled to them to glorify [God] morning and evening. (11)

[It was said,] "O John, adhere to the scripture with determination." And We granted him judgment as a boy, (12) and affection from Us and purity, and he was mindful of God (13) and dutiful to his parents, and was not arrogant or disobedient. (14) And peace be upon him the day he was born and the day he dies and the day he will be raised alive! (15)

And mention Mary in the Book, when she withdrew from her family to a place toward the East (16) and kept seclusion apart from them. Then We sent to her Our spirit, and he appeared to her as a well-proportioned man. (17) She said, "Indeed, I seek refuge in the Most Merciful from you, if you are God-fearing!" (18)

He said, "I am but the messenger of your Lord, to bestow upon you a pure boy." (19)

She said, "How can I have a boy while no man has touched me and I have not been unchaste?" (20)

He said, "Thus! Your Lord says, 'It is easy for Me, and that We may make him a sign for people and a mercy from Ourself. And it is a matter decreed.'" (21)

So she conceived him and withdrew with him to a remote place. (22) Then the pains of childbirth drove her to the trunk of a palm tree. She said, "Oh, if only I had died before this and had been forgotten, utterly forgotten!" (23)

But he called her from beneath her, "Do not grieve. Your Lord has provided a stream beneath you. (24) And shake the trunk of the palm tree toward you; it will drop ripe, fresh dates upon you. (25) So eat and drink and be consoled. And if you see any human being, say, 'Indeed, I have vowed a fast to the Most Merciful, so I will not speak to any mortal today.'" (26)

Then she brought him to her people, carrying him. They said, "O Mary, you have certainly done an unheard-of thing! (27) O sister of Aaron, your father was not an evil man, nor was your mother a loose woman!" (28)

Then she pointed to him. They said, "How can we speak to one who is a child in the cradle?" (29)

He said, "Indeed, I am the slave of God. He has granted me the scripture and made me a prophet, (30) and He has made me blest wherever I am, and has charged me with *salat* and *zakat* as long as I live, (31) and goodness to my mother, and has not made me harsh and difficult. (32) And peace be upon me the day I was born and the day I die and the day I shall be raised alive!" (33)

Such was Jesus son of Mary — a declaration of the truth about which they are in dispute. (34) It is not for God to take a son, may He be glorified! When He decrees a matter, He but says to it "Be!" and it is. (35) [Jesus said,] "And indeed, God is my Lord and your Lord, so worship Him. This is a straight path." (36) But the factions from among them differed. Then woe to those who disbelieved from the scene of a tremendous Day! (37)

19:88-93

And they say, "The Most Merciful has taken a son." (88) You have certainly done an abominable thing! (89) The heavens almost rupture from it, and the earth splits open and the mountains fall down destroyed, (90) that they attribute a son to the Most Merciful, (91) while it is not befitting for the Most Merciful that He should take a son. (92) There is no one in the heavens and the earth but comes to the Most Merciful as a slave. (93)

21:26-29

And they say, "The Most Merciful has taken a son." Glorified is He! Rather, they are [but] honored slaves. (26) They do not precede Him in speech and they act by His command. (27) He knows what is before them and what is after them, and they cannot intercede except for one whom He approves, and they are apprehensive out of fear of Him. (28) And whoever among them should say, "Indeed, I am a god besides Him," that one We would recompense with Hell. Thus do We recompense the wrongdoers! (29)

21:89-91

And [mention] Zechariah, when he called to his Lord, "My Lord do not leave me solitary, while You are the Best of Inheritors." (89) So We responded to him and granted to him John and rectified his wife for him. Indeed, they used to hasten to good deeds and supplicate Us in hope and fear, and they were humbly submissive to Us. (90)

And [mention] the one who preserved her chastity, and We breathed into her of Our Spirit, and made her and her son a sign for mankind. (91)

23:50

And We made the son of Mary and his mother a sign, and sheltered them on high ground, a place of repose and flowing springs.

23:91-92

God has not taken any son, nor has there ever been any deity with Him, for [if there had been,] each deity would have taken away whatever it created and some of them would have sought to overcome others. Glorified is God above what they attribute [to Him]! (91) Knower of the Unseen and the Witnessed, high is He above what they associate with Him. (92)

25:1-3

Blessed is He who sent down the Criterion to His slave [Muhammad], that he might be a warner to the worlds — (1) He to whom the dominion of the heavens and the earth belongs, and who has not taken a son and has no partner in dominion, and has created each thing and determined it with [precise] determination. (2) Yet they have taken, besides Him, gods that create nothing, while they are [themselves] created, nor do they have power of harm or benefit for themselves, nor do they have power over death or life or resurrection. (3)

33:7

And [mention, O Muhammad,] when We took from the prophets their covenant, and from you, and from Noah and Abraham and Moses and Jesus son of Mary — and We took from them a solemn covenant.

39:4

If God had desired to take a son, He could have chosen whatever He willed from among what He creates. Glorified is He; He is God, the One, the Prevailing!

42:13

He has ordained for you [mankind], as the religion, what He enjoined upon Noah and that which We have revealed to you [Muhammad], and what We enjoined upon Abraham and Moses and Jesus: to establish the religion and not be divided concerning it.

43:57-65

And when the son of Mary was presented as an example, forthwith your people laughed loudly (57) and said, "Are our gods better, or is he?" They did not present it to you but as an argument. No, but they are an argumentative people! (58)

He [Jesus] was nothing but a slave upon whom We bestowed favor, and We made him an example for the Children of Israel. (59) And if We willed, We could have appointed angels among you, succeeding [one another] upon the earth. (60) And indeed, he is [a sign] of the knowledge of the Hour, so do not be in doubt about it and follow Me. This is a straight path. (61) And do not let Satan avert you. Indeed, he is a clear enemy to you. (62)

And when Jesus came with clear proofs, he said, "I have come to you with wisdom and to make clear to you some of that wherein you differ, so be mindful of God and obey me. (63) Indeed, God — He is my Lord and your Lord, so worship Him. This is a straight path." (64) But the factions from among them differed. Then woe to those who have done wrong from the punishment of a painful Day! (65)

43:81-82

Say, [O Muhammad:] "If the Most Merciful had a son, then I would be the first of the worshippers." (81) Exalted is the Lord of the heavens and the earth, Lord of the Throne, above what they attribute [to Him]! (82)

57:26-27

And We certainly sent Noah and Abraham, and established prophethood and scripture among their descendants; and among them are the guided, but many of them are transgressors. (26) Then We sent, following in their footsteps, Our messengers, and We followed [them] with Jesus son of Mary and granted him the *Injil.* (27)

61:6

And [mention, O Muhammad,] when Jesus son of Mary said, "O Children of Israel, indeed I am the messenger of God to you, confirming what preceded me of the *Taurat* and bringing good tidings of a messenger to come after me, whose name is Ahmad." But when he came to them with clear proofs, they said, "This is obvious magic."

61:14

O you who believe, be supporters of God, even as Jesus son of Mary said to the apostles, "Who will be my supporters for God?"

The apostles said, "We are supporters of God." And a faction of the Children of Israel believed and a faction disbelieved. Then We strengthened those who believed against their enemy and they became dominant.

66:11-12

And God sets forth an example for those who believe: the wife of Pharaoh, when she said, "My Lord, build for me, with You, a house in Paradise, and save me from Pharaoh and his doings, and save me from the wrong-doing people." (11) And Mary daughter of 'Imran, who preserved her chastity, and We breathed into her of Our Spirit, and she believed in the words of her Lord and His scriptures, and was of the devoutly obedient. (12)

72:1-4

Say, [O Muhammad:] "It has been revealed to me that a group of jinn listened and said, 'Indeed, we have heard an amazing recitation. (1) It guides to the right path, so we believe in it, and never will we associate anyone with our Lord. (2) And [it teaches] that He, exalted is our Lord's majesty, has taken neither a spouse nor a son, (3) and that our foolish one has been speaking excess about God." (4)

112:1-4

Say, [O Muhammad:] "He is Allah, One; (1) Allah, the Self-Sufficient. (2) He does not father nor is He fathered, (3) and it is not for Him to have any equal." (4)

GLOSSARY OF TERMS

'Aad – the people of the prophet Hud, whose story is told in Volume One.

Abu-l-Qasim – Father of Qasim, a title by which the Prophet (S) was called, after the name of his son.

Adhan – the call to prayer.

Al-'Adhra – the Virgin, one of the titles given to Mary.

Ahadith – plural of *hadith.*

'Ahd – covenant, commitment, obligation, responsibility, pledge, vow, promise, oath, contract, compact, pact, treaty or agreement.

Ahmad – lit., "the most praised one," one of the Prophet's names, derived from the same root letters, *h-m-d*, as Muhammad.

Ansar – lit., "helper"; a Muslim citizen of Medina in the Prophet's time.

Al-'Aqib – the last; one of the Prophet's titles, meaning the last in succession in the prophetic line.

'Asr – time, era, epoch, period, afternoon; specifically, the third of the five daily prayers, observed in the latter part of the afternoon.

'Ashura – lit., "ten"; 'Ashura Day, the tenth day of Muharram, commemorates the delivery of the Israelites from Pharaoh.

Awliya' (sing., *wali*) – helper, supporter, benefactor, sponsor, patron, protector, friend; *awliya'-Allah*, the friends of God, refers to the holy people or saints of Islam.

Barzakh – a barrier, obstruction, isthmus, bridge or transitional point at which different but similar entities meet; specifically, the intermediate state between bodily death and resurrection.

Al-Batul – the Virgin, one of the titles given to Mary, denoting a woman who abstains from relations with men and from the world.

Al-Dajjal (pl., *dajjalin/dajjalun*) – cheat, imposter, swindler, deceiver, charlatan; specifically, the False Messiah who will appear at the end-time of this world, seducing and corrupting people by means of satanic delusions to a false perception of reality and a false religion.

Dhikr – remembrance, recollection or mention, often used to refer to the Qur'an; *dhikr-Allah* signifies the remembrance of God by the repetition of His holy Names or phrases of glorification.

Du'a' – personal prayer, supplication.

Fard – obligatory, required.

Fasiq (pl., *fasiqin/fasiqun*) – a transgressor; one who is defiantly disobedient, iniquitous, godless, sinful, licentious, wanton.

Fasl – section, division.

Fir'aun – pharaoh.

Fitan/futun (sing., *fitnah*) – trials, calamities, afflictions, tribulations, disturbances.

Hadith (pl., *ahadith*) – reports of sayings or actions of the Prophet (S), painstakingly collected and compiled in numerous collections during the first century *Hijrah.*

Al-Hadith al-Futun – The Account of the Trials [of Moses].

Hadith qudsi – a *hadith* in which the Holy Prophet (S) speaks about God Most High through divine inspiration; the words are the Prophet's but the meaning is from God Himself.

Halal – permissible, lawful.

Al-Haqq – the Truth or the Reality, one of God's Holy Names.

Haram – prohibited, either in the sense of prohibited things or actions, or a sanctuary such as the K'abah in which sins and transgressions are prohibited.

Al-Haram ash-Sharif – the Noble Sanctuary; that is, the Temple in Jerusalem.

Al-Hashir – the one who gathers.

Hasur – one who has no desire for or interest in women.

Hawari (pl., *hawariyun*) – disciple, apostle.

Hayy – living, live, alive.

Hijrah – emigration; specifically, the Holy Prophet's emigration from Mecca to Medina in the year 1 of the Islamic (*Hijri*) calendar, equivalent to 622 A.C.

Hyksos – a dynasty of Egyptian kings, related to the descendants of Abraham, who ruled during the time of the prophet Joseph.

Imam – leader, master; specifically, a religious leader or the leader of a congregational prayer (*salat*).

Injil – the sacred scripture revealed to Jesus by God.

Insha'Allah – God willing.

'Isha' – night; also the name of the fifth of the five daily prayers, observed at night.

Al-Isra' wal-Me'raj – the Holy Prophet's Night Journey and Ascension to the Divine Presence.

Jihad – striving, exertion, struggle, which may be of three kinds: the spiritual struggle within the self ("the greater *jihad*"), striving by means of the written or spoken word, and striving by force of arms.

Jizyah – the tax levied in lieu of military service on the adult males of the People of the Scripture living under Muslim rule.

K'abah – the sacred House of God in Mecca.

Kafir (pl., *kafirin/kafirun/kufar*) – one who disbelieves, covers truth with falsehood or denies God's favors.

Khalifah – caliph, deputy, vicegerent.

Kalim-Ullah – the Speaker-with-God, Moses.

Kalimat-Ullah – God's word, Jesus.

Khatam – stamp or seal; Muhammad (S) is *Khatam al-Nabiyyin*, the Seal of the Prophets.

Kufr – unbelief, covering truth with falsehood, denying God's favors.

Kun – the divine word of command, "Be!"

Labbayk – Here I am!

La ilaha illa Anta – There is no deity except You; *La ilaha illa-Lah* – There is no deity except God.

Al-Masih – the Messiah or Christ; *al-Masih al-Dajjal*, the False-Messiah, refers to the Dajjal or Anti-Christ.

Al-Masikh al-Dajjal – the Disfigured Messiah.

Me'raj – the Holy Prophet's ascension to the Divine Presence.

Mihrab – prayer room or niche; sanctuary.

Min ladunna – from Us; that is, from God's own Presence.

Mithaq – covenant, contract, pact, agreement, treaty or alliance.

Mubahalah – the mutual invoking of God's curse.

Muhajir (pl., *muhajirin*) – an emigrant; specifically, a Muslim who emigrated from Mecca to Medina during the Prophet's time.

Mujaddid – one who renews or revives.

Al-Muqaffi – the follower; in the context of the prophethood of Muhammad (S), the one who follows after all the other prophets.

Mursal hadith – a *hadith* whose chain of transmission does not go all the way back to the Prophet (S).

Mushrik (pl., *mushrikin/mushrikun*) – one who ascribes divinity or its attributes to anyone or anything other than God; a polytheist or idolater.

Al-nabiyy al-umiyy – the Unlettered Prophet, Muhammad (S).

Nafs – self or soul; also used in the sense of lower self or ego.

Nuzul – descent, coming-down, arrival.

Parakletos – comforter, counselor, advocate.

Periklytos – the much-praised one.

Qasas al-anbiya' – stories of the prophets.

Qiblah – direction; specifically, the direction of Mecca, which Muslims face during *salat*.

Quraysh – the Prophet's tribe, who dwelt in Mecca.

Rabwah – a high, fertile place with greenery and water.

Al-rajfah – a tremendous quaking, shaking, trembling, rocking or convulsion.

Rak'at – the cycle of movements and words which comprises one unit of *salat*.

Rijz – punishment, dirt, filth; the plague.

Ar-ruh – spirit or soul; also refers to the holy spirit (*al-ruh al-quddus*) or the trustworthy spirit (*al-ruh al-amin*), the angel Gabriel.

Sahih – sound, correct.

Al-sayhah – a sound, noise, shout, cry or clamor.

Al-sa'iqah – a strike or blast that stuns, causes unconsciousness or destroys.

Sakinah – the Ark of the Covenant, the Israelites' movable shrine containing relics of Moses and Aaron.

Salat – the prescribed Islamic prayer or worship.

Saleh (fem., *salehah*, pl., *salehin/salehat*) – a righteous person, holy one or saint.

Salwa – quail.

Sayyid – leader, chief, one who is honorable, forbearing, devoted to religion, worship and knowledge; also a title given to the descendants of the Prophet through Fatimah and 'Ali ibn Abi Talib.

Shaf'ah – intercession.

Shari'ah – lit., a way or path, a divinely-revealed law or code of life.

Shirk – associating partners with God or ascribing the attributes of divinity to other than God, polytheism.

Siddiq (fem., *siddiqah*, pl., *siddiqin/siddiqat*) – a testifier to the truth, a truthful, righteous person, holy one or saint.

Sunnah – practice or tradition; the *sunnah* of the Prophet (S) consists of that which he did, said or approved of in others.

Surah – chapter of the Qur'an.

Surah al-Bakarah (The Cow) – the second and longest *surah* of the Qur'an.

Surah al-Ikhlas (Sincerity) – the one hundred-and-twelfth *surah* of the Qur'an, which describes the attributes of God Most High.

Surah Ale 'Imran (The Family of 'Imran) – the third *surah* of the Qur'an, in which much of the story of Mary, Zechariah, John and Jesus is told.

Surah al-Furqan (The Criterion) – the twenty-fifth *surah* of the Qur'an, whose title refers to the Qur'an.

Surah al-Kahf (The Cave) – the eighteenth *surah*, containing verses mentioned by the Holy Prophet (S) as protection from the Dajjal

Surah al-Ma'idah (The Spread Table) – the fifth *surah*, in which much of Jesus' life-story is told. (There is a slight discrepancy in the numbering of the verses of this *surah* among Qur'anic translations. In this text, the number preceding the slash is that of all translations except Yusuf Ali's, while the second number is that of Yusuf Ali's translation.)

Surah Maryam (Mary) – the nineteenth *surah* of the Qur'an, in which much of the story of Zechariah, John, Mary and Jesus is told.

Surah al-Naml (The Ant) – the twenty-seventh *surah*, named for the ant referred to in the incident concerning Solomon (A); this *surah* contains the story of Solomon and the Queen of Sheba.

Surah Yunus (Jonah) – the tenth *surah*, in which it is mentioned that no people of any warner prophet believed except the people of Jonah (A).

Tafsir – commentary.

Taharah – cleanliness, purity; specifically, the state of cleanliness required for worship.

Talbiyah – the special call uttered by pilgrims during the *Hajj*.

Taurat/Taurah – the original scripture revealed to Moses by God.

Tawaf – circumambulation of the K'abah, part of the rites of *Hajj* and *'Umrah*.

Thamud – the people of the prophet Saleh, whose story is told in Volume One.

'Ubudiyat – servanthood.

'Ulu-l-'azm – possessors of determination; the five greatest prophets, Noah, Abraham, Moses, Jesus and Muhammad (S).

Ummah – nation, people, faith community.

Umm Musa – the mother of Moses.

'Umrah – the minor pilgrimage to Mecca, performed at any time of the year.

Wahm – imagination, fancy, belief, guess, conjecture, bias, prejudice, presupposition, self-delusion, illusion, suspicion, misgiving and related meanings.

Wali (fem., *waliyah*, pl., *awliya'*) – holy one, saint.

Wudu' – ablution for prayer.

Yaqtin – any species of creeping vegetable that has no erect stem, such as squash, pumpkin, melon, etc.

Zabur – lit., writing or book; specifically, the sacred scripture revealed to David.

Zakat – the obligatory charity ("poor-due") prescribed through all the prophets, which is one of the five obligatory acts of worship ("pillars") of Islam.

INDEX

A

D

H

I

K

Q

T